Developmental Psychology Today

THIRD EDITION

Developmental Psychology Today

THIRD EDITION

Robert E. Schell

Director, Research and Training
Center for Research, Education, Applied Training, and Evaluation,
San Diego

Lecturer
San Diego State University
University of California at San Diego

Elizabeth Hall

Editor-in-Chief
Human Nature

RANDOM HOUSE

Third Edition

98765432

Copyright © 1971, 1975, 1979 by Random House, Inc.

Library of Congress Cataloging in Publication Data
Schell, Robert E
   Developmental psychology today.

   First-2d ed. entered under title.
   Bibliography: p.
   Includes index.
   1. Developmental psychology.   I.   Hall, Elizabeth,
1929–   joint author.   II.   Title.
BF713.D48   1978   155   78-11797
ISBN 0-394-32027-1

Cover art from *The Psychology of Children's Art* by
Rhoda Kellogg with Scott O'Dell. Copyright © 1967 by
CRM, Inc.

Chapter opener photos: 1—Joel Gordon; 2—Hank
Morgan/Black Star; 3—Ken Heyman; 4—Roberts Rugh;
5—Paul Fusco/Magnum Photos; 6—Rogier Gregoire;
7—William MacDonald; 8—Harry Crosby; 9—Jeffrey
Foxx/Woodfin Camp & Assoc.; 10—Benn Mitchell/The
Image Bank; 11—Joel Gordon; 12—Ken Heyman;
13—Paul Fusco/Magnum Photos; 14—Rogier Gregoire;
15—Doug Wilson/Black Star; 16—Peter Hudson;
17—Joel Gordon; 18—Charles Moore/Black Star; 19—
Michael Alexander; 20—Bob Fitch/Black Star; 21—
Dana Kasarsky; 22—Wayne Miller/Magnum Photos;
23—Wayne Miller/Magnum Photos

Cover Design: Meryl Sussman Levavi

Manufactured in the United States of America

PREFACE

People change; development is a fact of life. From birth to death, changes occur in nearly every psychological realm—emotional, intellectual, behavioral, and even perceptual.

The field of developmental psychology covers broad changes in behavior from conception to the grave. It seeks to answer such questions as what happens developmentally to an animal or to a human being as it grows up, grows old, and eventually dies. In this search, developmental psychologists are particularly interested in discovering the processes and mechanisms that bring about change during development.

In recent years, the content and breadth of the field have changed radically. To a large extent, the changes we see today in developmental psychology were ushered in by results of research in other fields. These fields include all areas of psychology as well as ethology, sociology, anthropology, linguistics, and the various branches of the biological sciences. These contributions have significantly influenced not only what we know and what we think we know about developmental processes today, but how we go about finding out about them.

Because of the nature of the field, the accent of this book is on change. A guiding theme is that development involves an interdependent matrix of changes in various areas of behavior. The infant's anticipation of patterned visual information and his preference for novel and complex visual information, for example, result in his preferring a face to a striped pattern. This choice has implications for the development of the infant's attachment to caregivers. Attachment, in turn, plays a role in the development of the infant's social behavior. A secure attachment leads to a sense of independent self in the infant, which enables him to find out about interpersonal relations and further to explore the world in general. Increased exploratory behavior, in turn, supplies increased data for language development and for cognitive development. The development of increased cognitive competence plays a significant role in determining the child's sense of self-worth and contributes to the development of the child's emotional behavior. And so on.

A major aim in this edition of *Developmental Psychology Today,* as in the previous one, was to present an up-to-date and balanced overview of information, topics, viewpoints, and issues in developmental psychology. In keeping with this goal, we have dropped, rewritten, and added various sections and discussions throughout the book, and have provided increased coverage and integration of new material on self-concept development (Chapters 9, 13, and 15) and brain development (Chapters 6, 10, and 17); the integration of recent research testing Jean Piaget's theoretical views (Chapters 7, 11, and 14); the addition of new material on adolescent conformity and social influences (Chapter 19); the addition of new material on alternatives to marriage (Chapters 20, 21, and 22); and the addition of a completely new final chapter on the end of life. The graphic changes were designed to be not only attractive, contemporary, and relevant, but educational.

Because the book covers the life span, it continues to be appropriate for use in courses on either child development or psychology, child and adolescent development or psychology, or human development. Because the book is organized in an age-period, life-span manner but also has a topic/process organization as well, it can be read or used either way. A topic/process approach to cognitive development, for example, can be taken by assigning or reading the related sections and chapters on cognitive development from infancy through adulthood.

In each chapter, we tried to be as comprehensive and informative as the subject matter and space would allow. In doing this, however, we also have tried to make each chapter interesting and to help the reader understand the material being discussed. A potential drawback of any book has to do with the amount of material it covers. Topic selection and coverage seldom meet all the wishes of a particular instructor or reader. We took several steps, however, to minimize the inevitable drawback; we used the history of developmental psychology as a guide in topic coverage, we focused on key problems and issues, and we looked at different sides of an issue when possible. Such an approach allowed us to represent the rapidly changing field of developmental psychology in an even-handed manner.

As you go through the book we would like you to notice several other things. In keeping with current trends, we emphasized the cognitive underpinnings of language, personality, and social development. In addition, we have tried to integrate theory and research so that the coverage is not tied to a single theory or theorist. This approach allows instructors to present a broad look at the field and then, through supplementary lectures or other means, to emphasize particular theoretical positions. Finally, we hope that the use of research and practical examples throughout the book will stimulate students' interest and further their understanding. The examples are written so that students with different majors, course backgrounds, and levels of skill should find them readable and understandable.

In covering the development of the human species, we were confronted with the problem of conveying gracefully and grammatically the growth of both sexes. Faced with a demonstrably sexist language, we chose to sidestep the issue whenever possible, using plural subjects and specific children (Matt, Susan, David, and Lauren) as examples in order to avoid characterizing the entire species as "he." But at times only a singular subject will do. "It" is both incorrect and inhuman. The neuter pronoun, "one," falls heavily on the ear, and the use of a plural pronoun ("they") to refer to a singular subject ("the baby") offends both logic and esthetics. So you will find certain references to "he," "his," and "him" when we really mean the prototypical human being. Until the language changes further—as it will do if the structure of society becomes more egalitarian—we are stuck with it.

ACKNOWLEDGMENTS

We are indebted to the following colleagues for their professional contributions to this edition. Dr. Douglas Ramsay of the University of California at San Diego supplied material on brain development for the physical chapters. Drs. Helen Ross and Robert M. Kaplan of San Diego State University contributed new material for the personality chapters. Dr. Carol Offir of Mesa College helped revise the language chapters and checked the discussions of sex differences throughout the manuscript. Dr. Margaret Reedy of the University of Southern California contributed revisions of each of the adulthood chapters. In addition, she helped plan and provided the original draft of the final chapter on the end of life.

We would also like to thank each of the following individuals who reviewed part or all of the manuscript for this edition, and whose comments and suggestions were very helpful to us in making significant revisions:

Richard N. Aslin	Indiana University
Elizabeth Douvan	University of Michigan
Gordon E. Finley	Florida International University
DuWayne D. Furman	Western Illinois University
David Goldstein	Temple University
Marshall L. Hamilton	University of Guelph
R. Peter Johnson	University of Illinois
Michael E. Lamb	University of Michigan
Judith Langlois	University of Texas
Charlton R. Lee	Cypress College
Michael Maratsos	University of Minnesota
Howard Mickelson	University of Minnesota, Duluth
G. A. Milton	University of Victoria
Michael Newton	Northwestern University Medical School
Niles Newton	Northwestern University Medical School
Willis Overton	Temple University
Sidney Rosenblum	University of New Mexico
Marvin L. Simner	University of Western Ontario
Lenesa White	Brooklyn College of the City University of New York
Diane S. Woodruff	Temple University

Finally, special thanks go to Linda Dutton and Wendy Janda for their research and typing assistance, and to Katie and Scott for their support and good cheer during the long hours required to prepare the final manuscript.

Robert E. Schell
Elizabeth Hall

CONTENTS

Unit I
The Meaning of Development

1 THE CONCEPT OF DEVELOPMENT 5

HISTORICAL BACKGROUND 6
STUDYING DEVELOPMENTAL
   PSYCHOLOGY 10
EXPLAINING HUMAN
   DEVELOPMENT 13
THE NATURE OF DEVELOPMENT 16
USES OF DEVELOPMENTAL
   PSYCHOLOGY 19
SUMMARY 20

2 THEORIES OF DEVELOPMENT 23

PHILOSOPHICAL VIEWS OF HUMAN
   BEINGS 24
MATURATION THEORIES 24
BEHAVIOR-LEARNING THEORIES 26
ADAPTATION THEORIES 29
PSYCHODYNAMIC THEORIES 35
THE CONCEPT OF STAGES 41
OVERVIEW AND EVALUATION 42
SUMMARY 43

**3 DETERMINANTS OF
   DEVELOPMENT 45**

CLASSES OF DETERMINANTS 46
BIOLOGICAL DETERMINANTS 46
ENVIRONMENTAL
   DETERMINANTS 51
STUDYING DETERMINANTS 59
SUMMARY 64

Unit II
The Beginning of Life

4 PRENATAL DEVELOPMENT 69

HOW LIFE BEGINS 69
PRENATAL GROWTH 74
BRAIN DEVELOPMENT 78
PRENATAL BEHAVIOR 78
BIRTH 79
DEVELOPMENT AND BIRTH
    COMPLICATIONS 82
SUMMARY 87

5 THE WORLD OF THE NEWBORN 89

BIRTH: THE NEWBORN 90
BASIC FUNCTIONS AND
    RHYTHMS 91
REFLEXES AND SENSORY
    CAPABILITIES 95
PERCEPTION AND ATTENTION 99
ADAPTING TO THE WORLD 102
PERSONALITY AND SOCIAL
    RELATIONS 104
SUMMARY 107

Unit III
Infancy: The Dawn of Awareness

6 PHYSICAL GROWTH:
   FUNDAMENTALS 111

DIRECTIONS OF GROWTH 112
NORMS 114
USING NORMS 118
INDIVIDUAL VARIABILITY 118
BRAIN DEVELOPMENT 120
DEVELOPMENT OF MOTOR
    ABILITIES 123
PHYSICAL AND SOCIAL
    CHANGES 127
SUMMARY 129

7 COGNITION: FROM SENSING TO
   KNOWING 131

COGNITION 132
PERCEPTUAL FUNCTIONING 133
ATTENTION 138
CONCEPTS AND SYMBOLS 140
INFANT-ENVIRONMENT
    INTERACTION 145
SUMMARY 149

8 LANGUAGE: BEGINNINGS 151

HUMAN LANGUAGE 152
PRESPEECH DEVELOPMENT 153
FIRST WORDS 160
FIRST SENTENCES 165
FROM TWO WORDS TO
    GRAMMAR 167
SUMMARY 168

9 PERSONALITY: FROM ATTACHMENT
   TO SOCIABILITY 171

PERSONALITY DEVELOPMENT 172
EARLY EXPERIENCE 173
ATTACHMENT 175
PARENT RESPONSIVENESS 179
INFANT RESPONSIVENESS 182
THE DEVELOPMENT OF
    SOCIABILITY 186
SUMMARY 193

Unit IV
Early Childhood: The Formative Years

10 PHYSICAL CHANGE: GROWTH AND SKILLS 197

GROWTH CHARACTERISTICS 198
ENVIRONMENTAL INFLUENCES ON
   GROWTH 200
DEVELOPMENT OF MOTOR
   ABILITIES 202
GIRLS AND BOYS 208
PHYSICAL AND SOCIAL
   CHANGES 209
SUMMARY 212

11 COGNITION: CHANGES IN THINKING 215

PERCEPTUAL ADVANCES 216
EDUCATING ATTENTION 217
CHILDREN'S THINKING 219
REPRESENTATIONAL SKILLS 226
SOCIAL INTERACTION AND
   COGNITION 232
SUMMARY 233

12 LANGUAGE: UNDERSTANDING AND USING 235

PROPERTIES OF LANGUAGE 236
THE CHILD'S AWARENESS OF
   GRAMMAR 237
TESTING COMPREHENSION OF
   GRAMMAR 240
RULES AND PERFORMANCE
   LIMITATIONS 242
LANGUAGE AND COGNITIVE
   DEVELOPMENT 244
LANGUAGE FUNCTIONING AND
   ENVIRONMENT 248
SUMMARY 252

13 PERSONALITY: ESTABLISHING SOCIAL INTERACTIONS 255

THE PROCESS OF
   SOCIALIZATION 256
SEX-ROLE DEVELOPMENT 257
SELF-CONCEPT 263
PARENT-CHILD RELATIONS 266
PEER INFLUENCE 268
FUNCTIONS OF PLAY 273
SUBCULTURES AND
   PERSONALITY 275
SUMMARY 276

Unit V
Later Childhood: Growing Up

14 COGNITION: ADVANCES IN THINKING 281

SELECTIVE ATTENTION 282
ADVANCES IN CHILDREN'S
 THINKING 283
CHANGES IN REPRESENTATIONAL
 SKILLS 291
SOCIAL INTERACTION AND
 COGNITION 297
THE CONCEPT OF
 INTELLIGENCE 298
SUMMARY 300

15 PERSONALITY: EXPANDING SOCIAL INTERACTIONS 303

ACQUISITION OF ROLES 304
PERSONAL-SOCIAL
 DEVELOPMENT 307
SELF-CONCEPT 312
PARENT INFLUENCE 314
PEER INFLUENCE 315
FUNCTIONS OF PLAY 318
TODAY'S CHILD AND
 TOMORROW'S 320
SUMMARY 323

16 MORALITY: FROM RULES TO CONDUCT 323

THE COURSE OF MORAL
 DEVELOPMENT 324
INCONSISTENCY IN MORAL
 CONDUCT 324
MORAL REASONING 326
ROLE TAKING AND SOCIAL
 INTERACTION 330
GUILT AND SELF-
 REGULATION 332
MORAL CONDUCT AND
 MODELING 336
CONSISTENCY IN MORAL
 DEVELOPMENT 338
SUMMARY 340

Unit VI
Adolescence: Building an Identity

17 PHYSICAL AND SEXUAL MATURATION 347

GROWTH CHARACTERISTICS 348
PREDICTING PHYSICAL
 DEVELOPMENT 352
SIZE AND MATURATIONAL
 TRENDS 353
REACTIONS TO PHYSICAL
 CHANGE 355
PHYSICAL-SEXUAL AND SOCIAL
 CHANGE 358
SUMMARY 362

18 IDENTITY AND EXPERIENCE 365

IDENTITY: SELF AND SOCIETY 366
COGNITIVE CHANGE 369
MORAL REASONING 372
SEXUALITY AND INTIMACY 373
VOCATIONAL IDENTITY 377
SUMMARY 380

19 SOCIAL RELATIONS AND INFLUENCE 383

SOCIAL-CLASS DIFFERENCES 384
FAMILY RELATIONS AND
 INFLUENCE 385
PEER RELATIONS AND
 INFLUENCE 390
THE GENERATION GAP 395
MOVING INTO ADULTHOOD 397
SUMMARY 399

Unit VII
Adulthood:
Functioning in Society

20 EARLY ADULTHOOD: SELECTING THE OPTIONS 403

THE CONCEPT OF MATURITY 404
PHYSICAL CHARACTERISTICS 404
NEW DEVELOPMENTAL TASKS 405
IDENTITY AND INTERPERSONAL
  BEHAVIOR 408
MARRIAGE 413
ALTERNATIVES TO MARRIAGE 419
SOCIAL LIFE AND CHANGE 422
SUMMARY 423

21 MIDDLE ADULTHOOD: MAKING THE MOST OF IT 425

MATURITY IN MIDDLE
  ADULTHOOD 426
PHYSICAL CHANGES 427
NEW DEVELOPMENTAL TASKS 428
IDENTITY AND INTERPERSONAL
  BEHAVIOR 430
MARRIAGE AND FAMILY LIFE 434
ALTERNATIVES TO MARRIAGE 439
SOCIAL-LIFE CHANGES 440
SUMMARY 442

22 LATER ADULTHOOD: LIVING SUCCESSFULLY 445

MATURITY IN LATER
  ADULTHOOD 446
PHYSICAL CHANGES 447
NEW DEVELOPMENTAL TASKS 449
IDENTITY AND INTERPERSONAL
  BEHAVIOR 450
FAMILY LIFE 456
ALTERNATIVES TO MARRIAGE 460
SOCIAL-LIFE CHANGES 461
SUMMARY 463

23 THE END OF LIFE 465

LIFE EXPECTANCY 465
LONGEVITY 466
MEANING OF DEATH 471
THE PROCESS OF DYING 475
COPING WITH DEATH 480
SUMMARY 483

GLOSSARY 484
BIBLIOGRAPHY 490
INDEX 516

Developmental
Psychology Today
THIRD EDITION

Unit I The Meaning of Development

Babies grow into adult human beings, full of the qualities and imperfections typical of humanity. But the behavior of an adult man or woman is very different from the behavior of a relatively helpless infant. A person watching a young baby gazing intently at his fist would be unable to predict whether that baby would grow into an adult who was honest or dishonest, rash or careful, confident or insecure. Developmental psychologists attempt to describe how the baby develops into the adult he will become and to explain why he develops into one kind of adult and not another. Heredity, culture, and personal experience all play their parts in that development, and different psychologists have explained their influences in different ways. When you finish this unit, you will begin to see that no one approach can answer every question and that there is more than one path to an adequate description of human development.

CHAPTER 1
The Concept of Development

HISTORICAL BACKGROUND
Emergence of Childhood
Emergence of Adolescence
Emergence of Late Adulthood
Emergence of Developmental
Psychology

**STUDYING DEVELOPMENTAL
PSYCHOLOGY**
Use of Theory
Contributions of Other Disciplines

**EXPLAINING HUMAN
DEVELOPMENT**
Levels of Explanation
Types of Knowledge
Individual Variation

THE NATURE OF DEVELOPMENT
Sequences
Phases

**USES OF DEVELOPMENTAL
PSYCHOLOGY**

SUMMARY

The development of a human being may seem mysterious—even magical. Can we possibly explain how a one-cell fertilized egg develops into a fully human newborn, a linguistically accomplished kindergartner, a budding engineer, a competent parent, and an involved citizen? The human life cycle is the subject of developmental psychology. This branch of psychology explores the ways in which human physical growth and intellectual and social behavior change over time, and it seeks to find how growth and behavior relate to each other.

Developmental psychology has a perspective on human development. It sees human behavior as a changing system that includes both biological and cultural determinants, which work together to produce behavioral development. At no time is a person without an environment or without biological systems that affect behavior. Rather, a developing person is an integration of biological and environmental forces that act together in an organized way. That integration changes over time. A person's development poses some of the most fascinating questions that one can ask about the nature of humanity.

In this chapter we will see how the concept of childhood emerged as a separate stage of life, when the idea of adolescence was born, and how the social and economic structure of a society shapes the way its members view the life span. We will discover that developmental psychology draws on different disciplines, on different types of information, and on different levels of explanation to describe changes in behavior over the life span. We will find out that research leads to statements that are good for describing average development but that these statements fail to predict the behavior of many individuals. We will learn that development is an orderly, ever-increasing, and more complex change in a consistent direction. In addition, we will find that it is helpful to regard behavior as proceeding through phases of development. When you finish reading this chapter, and the rest of the book, you may find yourself looking at the behavior of yourself and others around you in a different way.

HISTORICAL BACKGROUND

The contemporary student of developmental psychology may believe that the life span, from conception to death, has always been seen as we now see it. In the twentieth century, we recognize distinctions among the prenatal period, infancy, childhood, adolescence, and adulthood. But the human life span has not always been divided into these periods, nor need it be.

Philippe Ariès (1962) has examined the concept of the life cycle as it has been seen from the Middle Ages to the present. He has concluded that in the Middle Ages even the concept of childhood as it is defined today was virtually unknown. There was a clearly admitted infancy, lasting until approximately the age of seven. But thereafter, people whom we would consider children were simply assimilated into the adult world. The art and social documents of the Middle Ages show children and adults mingling together in one unified community, wearing the same clothes, and performing the same functions. Society made no distinction among them on the basis of age or phase of psychological development. The vast majority of children—and adults—were, of course, totally unschooled. But even those who obtained the minimal schooling required to become priests or clerks learned in ungraded schools where children, adolescents, and adults intermingled.

Emergence of Childhood

It was only in the seventeenth and eighteenth centuries that the concern with childhood as a separate stage of life slowly began to appear. A new and sentimental view of childhood sprang up along with new theories of education that were concerned with promoting children's moral and intellectual development, protecting them from the evils and corruptions of adult society, and preserving their real or imagined childhood virtues. At the same time, schools became increasingly graded by age, and both the average length of schooling and the number of children who received formal education increased.

From historical evidence it seems clear that childhood became a separate stage of life only

During the seventeenth century, when Velasquez painted this scene, childhood was just beginning to emerge as a separate period of life. Children still dressed and were treated like miniature adults. (Scala/EPA)

when large numbers of people entered the middle class, the amount of leisure time increased, and the rate of infant mortality decreased. As the middle class prospered, there was less need for their children to work in order to ensure the family's economic survival. The lowered rate of childhood mortality meant that more children would live to reach puberty; therefore, parents could devote themselves less cautiously to each child. And the new mercantile capitalism required that a larger portion of the citizenry be literate and fluent with numbers; thus, more children had to go to schools.

Ariès's analysis of the emerging concept of childhood has had far-reaching implications for understanding the relationship between historical change and psychological development. Ariès has spoken explicitly about concepts of childhood, but the experience of childhood changed as well, although perhaps less dramatically. In the Middle Ages, many children died before the age of six, and those who survived were apprenticed out or put to work. Both parents and masters often treated them with what we would consider a shocking lack of tenderness, protectiveness, attention, and care. Parents seem to have invested little emotional energy in their children; children were rarely spoken of as precious beings to be cherished and protected.

But as the concept of a stage of childhood began to emerge, a larger proportion of those between the ages of six and fourteen were deliberately segregated into schools. Such segregation increasingly sheltered them from the demands of adult work. Children found new freedom to play and to experiment and had systematic opportunities to develop new interpersonal and technical skills. In advanced Western societies, segregation of childhood is now virtually complete, but only in this century has it finally been extended to the working and lower classes. The mark of this full institutionalization of childhood is universal primary education. It has taken four centuries for us to move from an era in which childhood was unrecognized to an era in which we take it completely for granted and protect it with an array of legal, social, and educational institutions.

Emergence of Adolescence

The concept of adolescence is of more recent origin. Only after childhood had been marked off from adulthood was adolescence interposed between them. Adolescence as we think of it today

Because we are accustomed to a long period of adolescence, when physically mature human beings do not participate in the functioning of society, it is difficult to realize that for centuries children worked as hard as adults. Not until the twentieth century were most children in the working and lower classes free from long hours of drudgery. (Lewis Hine/The George Eastman House)

emerged only in the nineteenth and twentieth centuries, and the extension of adolescence as a stage of psychological growth is far from complete even today. Puberty in the sense of biological maturation occurs, of course, in all societies, but in early Western societies, it seemed to go largely unmarked. When children are considered neither innocent nor importantly different from adults, the fact of puberty constitutes neither a fall from innocence nor a change in status, and it therefore has little special meaning.

When a postpubertal stage of life was first noted in the eighteenth and nineteenth centuries, concepts of adolescence centered on two images: the cherubino (the androgynous youth) or the recruit (the young soldier in training). Only in our century did the modern concept of adolescence appear. And even today, images of adolescence are fluid and changing. Media still alternate between portrayals of the adolescent as awkward, acned, and anguished or deviant, wild, and uncontrolled, as an idealistic and accurate critic of society or as a person interested only in professional and personal gain (Dragastin and Elder, 1975).

Because social and economic changes have freed
young people past the age of puberty from the demands
of farm and factory labor, the period of adolescence
has emerged in Western societies. (© Paul Fusco/
Magnum Photos)

The recent emergence of the concept of adolescence does not mean that adolescence did not exist before society formulated the concept. Clearly, the potential for this experience is part of our endowment as human beings, and in previous centuries many men and women passed through what would now be recognized as an adolescent experience. But three things have changed in the last century. First, adolescence as a stage of life has been socially recognized and acknowledged. Second, society has begun to sanction and support adolescence, increasingly buttressing it with educational, familial, institutional, and economic resources. Third, these new resources, coupled with other changes in society, have given an ever-larger proportion of young people the possibility of continuing psychological growth during the years from thirteen to eighteen. This opportunity arose when society granted them protection from adult responsibilities, created educational institutions to fill their duty-free time, and developed a positive image of a postchildhood, preadulthood stage of life: adolescence.

As with the recognition of childhood, the emergence of adolescence is closely related to social, economic, and historical changes. Increasing industrialization has freed most young people past the age of puberty from the requirements of farm and factory labor. Indeed, the rising standards of economic productivity today make the adolescent, especially the uneducated adolescent, almost impossible to employ. The new attitudes toward adolescence are expressed in laws that make full-time employment before the age of sixteen or eighteen illegal. Growing affluence provides most families and the larger society with the wealth needed to support these economically unproductive adolescents in school. And all these changes have happened, on a mass scale, almost within living memory; even our child labor laws were passed only in the twentieth century. However, one must always remember that descriptions of the general society necessarily ignore pockets of poverty. Among migratory farm laborers, for example, financial considerations force children and adolescents to work in defiance of the law. In the inner city, the absence of jobs for adolescents whose families lack the resources to keep them in school has led to a large pool of young people with no income, nothing to fill their time, and limited prospects for the future.

Emergence of Late Adulthood

The period of late adulthood is also a recent phenomenon because until this century most people died before they reached the age of seventy or seventy-five. Today more adults are living until their physical capacities and economic self-sufficiency are threatened. In some societies older adults are venerated as wise, experienced advisers. Unfortunately, in the United States many younger adults view older people as irrelevant. Because older adults acquired their experiences during an era that no longer exists, the young regard them as passé and perhaps as uncomfortable reminders of their own fates. Like children and adolescents, older adults are often segregated into special institutions that keep them out of view and out of the

More and more Americans are living into later adulthood, a period of life when people are generally more capable than younger members of society realize. (Ken Heyman)

minds of younger people. This experience creates many problems for older adults.

Today we take the periods of childhood, adolescence, and late adulthood for granted, and divide development into phases that are marked by *social* events, such as the beginning of meaningful speech (the end of infancy and the start of childhood, at about the age of two) or the achievement of adult roles in employment, marriage, and reproduction (the end of adolescence and the start of adulthood, in the early twenties for many people). Other markers we attach to the life span are *biological:* birth (the end of the prenatal period and the start of infancy) and reproductive maturity at puberty (the end of childhood and the start of adolescence). We are not consistent in choosing markers for periods in the life span, and our markers are by no means universal. Other contemporary societies divide life into three periods—such as infancy, childhood, and adulthood—or even only two—infancy and adulthood (Mead, 1968).

The way in which people in a society view the life span depends largely on its social and economic system. If the preparation for adult roles is gradual and continuous from early childhood and if the necessary technology can be acquired by apprenticeship, then adulthood is likely to begin shortly after a person reaches reproductive maturity. On the other hand, if full participation in the economic system depends on years of technical education, a period of adolescence is likely to be recognized. Toward the end of the life span, when participation in the economic system becomes less active, older adults may be forced to retire from their jobs, creating a period that some call "old age." Older adults are, of course, still adults, but the loss of social and economic roles can drastically change the experience of later adulthood.

Emergence of Developmental Psychology

Developmental psychology has only recently emerged as a separate branch of general psychology. Like the science of psychology itself, it can be said to have had a long history but a short past. General psychology was founded in Germany in the last quarter of the nineteenth century and then introduced in the United States. The purpose of general psychology was to study normal behavior—primarily that of adults—and to discover what mental processes accompanied or led to behavior.

During the first several decades of this century, psychology broadened its goals, its methods, and its technology. As psychologists began to investigate other aspects of human and animal behavior, the range and amount of information increased rapidly, as did the development of new research methods. Specialization became inevitable, and the field eventually divided into different branches. Some of the first branches to split away were physiological, clinical, experimental, social, and child psychology. Other branches, like community, environmental, and mathematical psychology, have been around for only a decade or so.

Developmental psychology has grown out of the field of child psychology, although it includes material from all the other branches. Its emergence in this country has been greatly influenced by social and political change. For example, interest in developmental questions increased sharply when child-guidance and psychological clinics began to be founded around the turn of the century (Sears, 1975). Such clinics represented popular acceptance of the idea that children should be helped with their emotional and intellectual problems in order to enable them to lead constructive lives.

Other historical events have also shaped the course and content of developmental psychology. During the 1920s and 1930s, for example, a number of child-development research centers were established at major universities across the country. These institutes were set up to carry out research, to teach, and to disseminate information on child development. They investigated all aspects of children's development and welfare, and their shared goal was to acquire a comprehensive understanding of development that could be used to help children and those who care for them. Many of these institutes are still active, and much of the progress in developmental psychology rests on their findings.

As life-cycle research added information on the development of young adults, other researchers became interested in the latter years of the life span. The realization that development does not stop at age eighteen or twenty-one, together with the fact that an increasing percentage of the population would be over sixty-five, led to the establishment of centers to study the effects of aging and the developmental tasks faced by older people. At the University of Chicago, for example, Bernice Neugarten has supervised a study of middle-aged and aging adults, following more than 2,000 adults

since the late 1950s. Her research has helped destroy the stereotype of the unhappy old person who spends his or her time sitting in a rocking chair.

Developmental psychology today is much like the field of general psychology just before it split into various branches. The field covers perceptual, motivational, intellectual, and neuropsychological issues and problems, and uses various methods to study them. Until recently, the developmental psychologist was a generalist who had acquired knowledge in a large number of areas. Today the field covers an even broader range of topics and attempts to integrate them across the human life span. Many developmental psychologists find that, while they are generalists, they must also specialize in some aspect of the field. The amount of information on human development is now too great for any individual to master.

New content areas have continued to emerge, giving developmental psychology a different look and broadening its base. In the past twenty years there has been a decided shift in the emphasis of developmental psychologists. They have moved from stressing what people do at specific periods in life to emphasizing how circumstances affect what they do at different periods and what kind of sequence takes place in development. Along with this shift has come an increased interest in the intellectual aspects of development and a greater appreciation of differences among individuals.

STUDYING DEVELOPMENTAL PSYCHOLOGY

The concerns of developmental psychology cut across content areas to *describe* and to *explain* changes in human behavior across the years of the life span. The first step toward such an understanding of behavioral development must be an accurate and detailed description of those changes. The second step, or series of steps, concerns explanations for the observed changes.

A **behavior** is an observable act that can be described or measured reliably. **Reliability** means that two or more scientists can agree on the measurement. Behaviors can be measured in many ways, some simply by watching and others by using instruments of various kinds, such as recordings of heart rates, questionnaires, and films of children's interactions. Developmental psychologists do not pick any behavior at random to mea-

Developmental psychologists have moved from studying infants and children to examining the entire lifespan
of human beings. Studies of older people have dis-
proved many stereotypical ideas of aging. (Scala/EPA)

sure and describe; nor do they attempt to study all
possible behavior of human beings. To describe
every possible behavior and every individual variant of it is an impossible task. Instead, psychologists select for detailed study behavior that is
theoretically or practically important.

Use of Theory

To explain how and why behavior develops, psychologists have constructed sets of logically related
statements about the nature of development called
theories. A theoretical statement is usually abstract and does not refer directly to what is observed. For example, Erik Erikson's (1963) theory
of psychosocial development says that young children around the ages of two to four need to develop **autonomy,** a feeling of self-control and
self-determination. One cannot observe autonomy

directly, but if Erikson is correct about the young
child's need to direct his or her own behavior, we
should see behavioral evidence, such as the two-
year-old's emphatic "No" to parental requests, the
verbal response "Me do it" to proffered help, the
temper tantrums that sometimes occur when a
child's goals are thwarted, and so forth. Erikson's
theoretical statement about autonomy *predicts*
these diverse behaviors.

Theories should lead to testable hypotheses or
predictions about observable behavior. If the statements of a theory successfully predict a great deal
of human behavior, then we say that the theory is a
useful explanation of human development. Thus
far, no theory has satisfactorily covered all aspects
of human development. Rather, as Chapter 2
shows, theories tend to be restricted to some part of
development, such as social behavior or intellectual development or language acquisition.

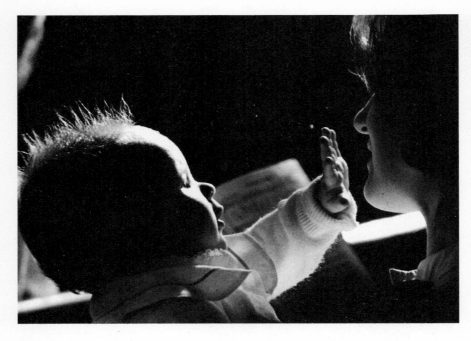

Babies develop rapidly, making it easy to note developmental change, and mothers are the major influence on early development. Studies of mother-baby interaction have, therefore, become an important focus of study. (© Roger Malloch/ Magnum Photos)

Like the rest of psychology, developmental psychology uses scientific methods and procedures to study human behavior. Researchers emphasize the testing of hypotheses derived from theories, using methods that can be described so that other investigators can apply them. If the studies are useful, they must lead to results that others can repeat and confirm. However appealing children and adolescents are, no anecdotal description of their actions adequately explains their behavior.

The prediction and explanation of behavior are two important goals of psychology. Another is *control.* For example, the control of behavior through rewards and punishments is of theoretical importance to psychologists and of practical importance to parents, teachers, and other adults who have responsibility for rearing children.

Because developmental psychologists are interested in development across the life span, information on behavioral changes in all periods is important. However, researchers have collected relatively more information on school-aged children and newborn babies than on older infants and adults. This situation has come about because it is extremely difficult to set up properly controlled experiments when people are scattered about and living in widely varied circumstances. Because maternity hospitals and schools gather people of similar ages together, they provide ex-cellent opportunities for psychologists to investigate human development. But other reasons are equally important. For example, during the early years, development is rapid, and changes can be measured in a shorter period of time. During adulthood, change is slow and often difficult to measure. Social problems may also play a part in directing research, since funds are more likely to be available when a problem becomes pressing. Compensatory education programs, such as "Head Start," which during the 1960s gave researchers a chance to work with preschool children, provide a good example of this. Theories also tend to guide research, and many developmental theories focus on what happens to a person from infancy through adolescence, paying scant attention to the adult phases of the life cycle.

Contributions of Other Disciplines

Several other scientific fields are also concerned with human development: biology, sociology, and anthropology. Developmental psychologists depend on information on the individual's biological history and maturation, on social organization, and on cultural influences, which comes from these other disciplines. They need such information to explain behavior because psychologists see the developing person as a changing system that integrates biological factors and experience. The kinds of experiences we have in growing up depend largely on what kind of family and society we live in (for example, how many brothers and sisters we have, how punitive our parents are, how our society divides people by age, what kinds of institutions exist) and on cultural values that distinguish right from wrong, good from bad. What we learn in the sociocultural context depends on both our readiness to learn and the availability of materials and ideas for us to acquire. In the case of children, maturational level has a profound influence on what they select from the world around them; a child's environment determines what is available for him or her to learn.

Take language, for example. The ability to learn a language is one of humankind's evolved characteristics. All normal members of the species learn to speak. But developmentalists know that children are not able to talk until they have attained a certain level of neurological development (Lenneberg, 1967). No six-month-old speaks in sentences. At the same time, a child living in a relatively unstimulating, unresponsive environment begins to speak later than a child reared in a more stimulating home. In the first case, the child is not biologically ready to speak; in the second, the child's world does not offer adequate speech models to learn from. The time and rate at which language develops in a particular child are the result of both his level of maturity and his previous experience in vocalizing, in listening to language, and in being rewarded for the use of language. The language the child learns to speak fluently is that of his cultural group.

Evolutionary biologists have given insightful accounts of humanity's evolutionary history, which have set the stage for understanding individual development. After all, children develop into human adults, not into chimpanzees. All children have more in common with one another than any one of them has with any other species. Despite our individual differences, as human beings we share much in common.

Developmental biologists have provided detailed descriptions of embryological development that can serve as a model of understanding all development. The complex integration of genetic and environmental influences across the life span, and from the level of the single cell to that of the whole organism, has made psychologists aware of the need to consider both classes of influences on human behavioral development.

Sociologists and cultural anthropologists have emphasized the importance of understanding development within a sociocultural context. A child is always a member of a human group: a family, a neighborhood group, a school class, and so forth. Much of children's behavior is influenced by this setting, both their immediate circumstances and their longer-range memberships in various groups. As shown in the historical perspective on childhood and adolescence, the ways in which a culture interprets the life span can have profound influences on the expectations that others have for a person's behavior at different times in life.

EXPLAINING HUMAN DEVELOPMENT

Developmental psychology adds to basic psychological principles information drawn from other fields. The explanation of any human behavior often includes elements from these various fields. But one must be very careful to adopt a level of explanation that is appropriate for that behavior.

Levels of Explanation

One frequent criticism of behavioral studies that emphasize biological variables, such as those explaining behavioral differences between males and females in terms of hormone levels, is that their explanations are **reductionist.** That is, they reduce the causes of a complex behavior to a simple explanation. For example, the level of male hormones may contribute (greatly or little) to sex differences in behavior, but it is not a sufficient explanation for most observed differences. As later chapters show, many factors that do not involve hormones—such as different parental responses to boys and girls, rewards for appropriate sex-role behavior, and so forth—may also play important roles in shaping sex differences in behavior. To explain the differences we observe, we must consider the effects of hormones along with other prenatal and postnatal differences in environment. In this example, hormones are only one component in the behavioral system; how important they are can be determined by research that varies hormone and rearing conditions separately (Money and Ehrhardt, 1972).

Psychological phenomena are not adequately explained by sociological or anthropological principles either. Most statements in these fields apply to average tendencies among groups of people, not to individuals. For example, a sociological study of

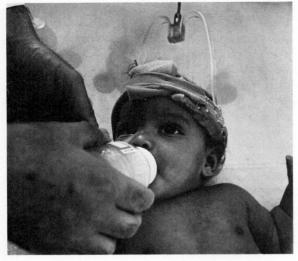

The sucking patterns of newborns show the four types of information used by developmental psychologists to explain behavior: the description of a specific behavior; its changes with age; its changes in response to the environment; and individual differences in its development. (Jason Lauré)

reproduction among subgroups in a society may lead to statements about the relative fertility of married versus unmarried persons, Catholics versus Protestants, younger versus older couples, and so forth. The sociological explanation of fertility does not describe individual people's behavior or their motives for having or not having children. To explain why certain people in a subgroup (for example, married persons) reproduce whereas others do not usually requires a psychological explanation. On the other hand, a psychological explanation of why some people want children and others do not does not adequately explain the declining birth rate in the United States; that requires a socioeconomic-cultural set of factors that psychology cannot provide.

In short, if we expect to explain behavior, we need to draw on findings from other fields, but we must be careful to integrate this information into our picture of human development at the level at which behavior is influenced.

Types of Knowledge

Most developmental psychologists gather information on (1) behavior at different ages; (2) behavioral changes as people grow older; (3) environ-mental events that influence behavior; and (4) variations among individuals in their development. These four kinds of information make up most of the knowledge in developmental psychology.

One must first gather descriptions of behavior before one can evaluate explanations and theories. The sucking patterns of newborns (Type 1 information), for example, have been extensively described by Lewis Lipsitt (1967a) and Arnold Sameroff (1968). All normal newborns show the components of sucking, which they combine in a rhythmic alternation of bursts and rests. Additional descriptions of later sucking behavior in one-month-olds allow us to evaluate the changes that occur with increasing maturity and experience (Type 2 information). Intensive investigations of the effects of rewards on rates of sucking have demonstrated that newborns will alter their sucking patterns to get sweetened water (Type 3 information). Finally, other studies show that individual babies have distinctive patterns of sucking, which, when recorded, identify them at least as well as their footprints. The individual baby's sucking pattern is a kind of "signature" (Type 4 information). Whereas all normal babies suck in bursts interrupted by rests, individual babies have different numbers of sucks per burst and shorter or longer rests between. The four types of knowledge are complementary and valuable, each in its own way. No explanation of behavior could be complete unless it took all of them into account.

Two additional kinds of information play a role in the field of developmental psychology: case histories of individuals and research on other species. Case histories of unusual patterns of development can sometimes give us insights about normal development. For example, Dorothy Baruch's (1964) case history of a boy who developed extreme fears illustrates how early parent-child relations affect later development. Around the turn of the century, a number of ardent parents kept diaries that described every change in their infants' behavior over the early years. Psychologists found these baby biographies useful in describing sequences and individual differences in development. Although the diaries were not objective, scientific descriptions, they provided a basis for further scientific study. Case histories by scientific observers, such as Jean Piaget's (1926) observations of his own three children, have provided a rich source of ideas for further investigation.

Research on nonhuman species has a long history in psychology. Although the albino rat has played a much smaller role in developmental than in some other areas of psychology, primates such as chimpanzees and rhesus monkeys have provided valuable information. For ethical reasons, some theoretically interesting ideas about development cannot easily be tested with human beings. No psychologist would isolate a human baby in a laboratory to observe the effects of deprivation. But Harry Harlow and his associates (Harlow and Harlow, 1966; Harlow and Zimmermann, 1959) have conducted just such research with rhesus and other monkeys. Their results, which are discussed in Chapters 9 and 13, demonstrate the importance of contact comfort for the normal social development of monkeys. Because monkey and human babies have similar periods of close infant-mother relationships, we can infer that human babies who are deprived of close contact with a caregiver will also show distorted social development. These inferences from research on other primates are supported by studying what has happened to babies reared in large impersonal institutions and by occasional case histories of babies who have been isolated by neglectful mothers (L. Yarrow, 1961).

Individual Variation

Most research in developmental psychology leads to conclusions that are general statements about the behavior or developmental change under investigation. The general statements summarize what was found to be true for the largest number of subjects or for the "average" subject in an experiment. But the behavior or development of some subjects may have been different from that of the majority. For example, William Rohwer's (1971) study of children's learning showed that categorically organized materials are easier to remember than randomly ordered lists. That is, the

Human beings are similar in many ways, but each is also unique, and the closer one looks the more differences one finds. These variations mean that research findings that apply to most people rarely describe everyone. (© Charles Gatewood)

list "car, boat, plane; chair, table, bed" is easier to remember than the list "car, bed, table; plane, chair, boat." Most elementary-school children will look at the first list and think "three things to ride in, three furnitures," which helps them recall the individual items. Some children, however, do not use categories to help them remember and thus recall as few items from the first list as from the second.

Developmental psychologists acknowledge that the results shown for most people do not apply to all individuals. Thus, one can say that elementary-school children are likely to use categories to help them remember lists of items, even if all children do not use that strategy. Or a developmental psychologist may say that young adolescents generally become self-conscious about their appearances without being proved wrong by the example of your best friend, who remained slovenly and paid no attention to his appearance until he was eighteen.

It is often important to study individual variation in behavior for clues about the many possible ways of behaving in the same situation. Children who learn to read successfully in the first grade seem to do so in a variety of ways. Choosing a single method to teach reading to less successful readers has been nearly impossible because no one method has been successful with all children who have reading problems. Studies indicate that some children learn more quickly with a phonic approach, whereas others learn best using a sight, or look-say, method (Chall, 1967). Individual differences in aptitudes for reading are only one example of normal variation.

The fact of individual differences in almost all behavior does not keep developmental psychologists from testing general hypotheses about development or from making general statements about their results. One must be aware, however, that whereas individual exceptions exist, general statements are often useful in practical as well as theoretical ways. We know, for example, that good day care does not harm most children (Fein and Clarke-Stewart, 1973). The development of young children in day care is as normal on the average as the development of children at home with their mothers. That statement has obvious practical implications. However, we must always realize that some day-care placements are not good and that some children are more upset than others about leaving their mothers. But on the average, day care

has no effects different from those of home care.

On the other hand, researchers might study a day-care center that by chance alone had a large number of unhappy children. It would be incorrect to conclude, on the basis of one study, that day-care centers and unhappy children go together.

The best safeguard against accepting such a chance finding as typical is to have other investigators study other children in other day-care centers in the same way to see if they find the same thing. This is called a **replication** study. Because so many factors can influence a study of behavior—including the investigator's own bias (R. Rosenthal, 1968)—it is important that others who do not have exactly the same ideas can repeat the results.

THE NATURE OF DEVELOPMENT

All normal infants grow first into children and then into adults, which is no surprise. This progression implies several characteristics about development, however: (1) development is orderly change; (2) it is directional; (3) it is cumulative to a large extent; and (4) it is characterized by increasing differentiation and complex organization.

Sequences

The notion of sequences of development pervades developmental psychology. Most theorists have acknowledged that behavioral development proceeds in an orderly fashion, and many have pointed to the increasing differentiation and complex organization of behavior at later ages. But before one can explain the development of any behavior, whether cognition, language, perception, social interaction, or personality, it is necessary to specify the exact nature of its sequence.

Anyone who has watched children develop knows that changes in their behavior occur more frequently and more rapidly during infancy than later. The changes in behavior over the life span are neither accidental nor random. There is an orderly sequence to behavioral development, whether we talk about language acquisition, social play, or moral judgment. Each kind of behavior can be described in a series of developmental steps. When children first use words, around eleven to fourteen months of age, they typically use one word at a time. Later, at about twenty-one to twenty-four months, they begin to put two or three words together. By three to three and one-half

years, most children use complex sentences and can tell brief stories. But no child begins by speaking in sentences and then develops to a one-word phase. The orderly sequence of language acquisition is directional and predictable.

The same sort of predictable development occurs in social play. Nine-month-olds hardly notice each other, whereas preschool children generally play together and enjoy each other's actions. By the early school years, most children interact in games that have specific rules and that require each child to play a role. The sequence is the same for all children.

These sequences of development often proceed from simpler, more global behaviors to increasingly differentiated but integrated sets of behavior. As children mature and incorporate more of the social world around them, they increasingly organize separate behavior into such complex sets. For example, moral judgments of young children are often based on global concepts of "right" and "wrong." Their ideas of rightness and wrongness depend more on the outcome of an act than on the intentions of the actor. A child of four or five may feel that a boy who breaks the cookie jar in the act of stealing a cookie is not worse than another who breaks the jar while reaching for a cookie his mother told him to get. In both cases the boy broke the cookie jar. But most older children and adults would separate the two cases and base their moral judgments on the boys' intentions. Older children can also differentiate shades of wrongdoing. Many adolescents and adults base specific moral judgments on complex ideals that they have abstracted from experience in concrete situations. The development of moral judgment closely parallels changes in children's thinking, which becomes more hypothetical from childhood to maturity.

Phases

This book uses the concept of phases to describe periods of the life span. As we have already noted, there is no one right way to divide up the life span. The ways in which periods of life have been conceived of in the past and in other cultures differ

The growth of a plant from seedling to maturity illustrates the gradual, orderly, and continuous process of development. The development from infancy to adulthood progresses in a similar manner. (Jerome Wexler/ Photo Researchers)

There are as many ways to divide the human lifespan as there are theorists. This popular nineteenth-century division of woman's life "from the cradle to the grave" rests on both social and biological markers. (*The Life and Age of Woman,* lithograph by N. Currier, 1850. Museum of the City of New York)

considerably. In talking about development, however, it is convenient to use five chronological periods or phases that roughly correspond to our cultural usage.

The *prenatal* phase begins at conception and ends at birth. This phase is the least arbitrary and the easiest to define because its beginning and end are clearly marked and observers can agree on them. *Infancy* begins at birth and continues until approximately age two. By the end of the second year, most children have begun to acquire language and symbolic thought. In addition, most adults think of two-year-olds as children rather than as infants, which corresponds to the developmental shift from nonlinguistic to linguistic communication. Of course, other important changes occur in social and emotional behavior from infancy to childhood.

The third phase, *childhood,* begins an early pe-

riod around age two and continues through late childhood at around age twelve. Puberty is usually accepted as the end of childhood and the beginning of adolescence. *Adolescence,* the fourth phase, is a less definite period because its end is not defined as well as the end of other phases of development. Adolescents are generally accepted as adults when they acquire adult economic and social roles. *Adulthood,* the fifth phase, generally begins in the late teens or early twenties and continues until death. This is clearly the longest phase, spanning early adulthood, the middle years, and late adulthood. There are many social and biological changes in adulthood, although the rate of development is much slower than in the earlier years.

Although dividing development into phases makes it easier to discuss behavioral changes that accompany one another, it is important to remember that development is continuous. Despite peri-

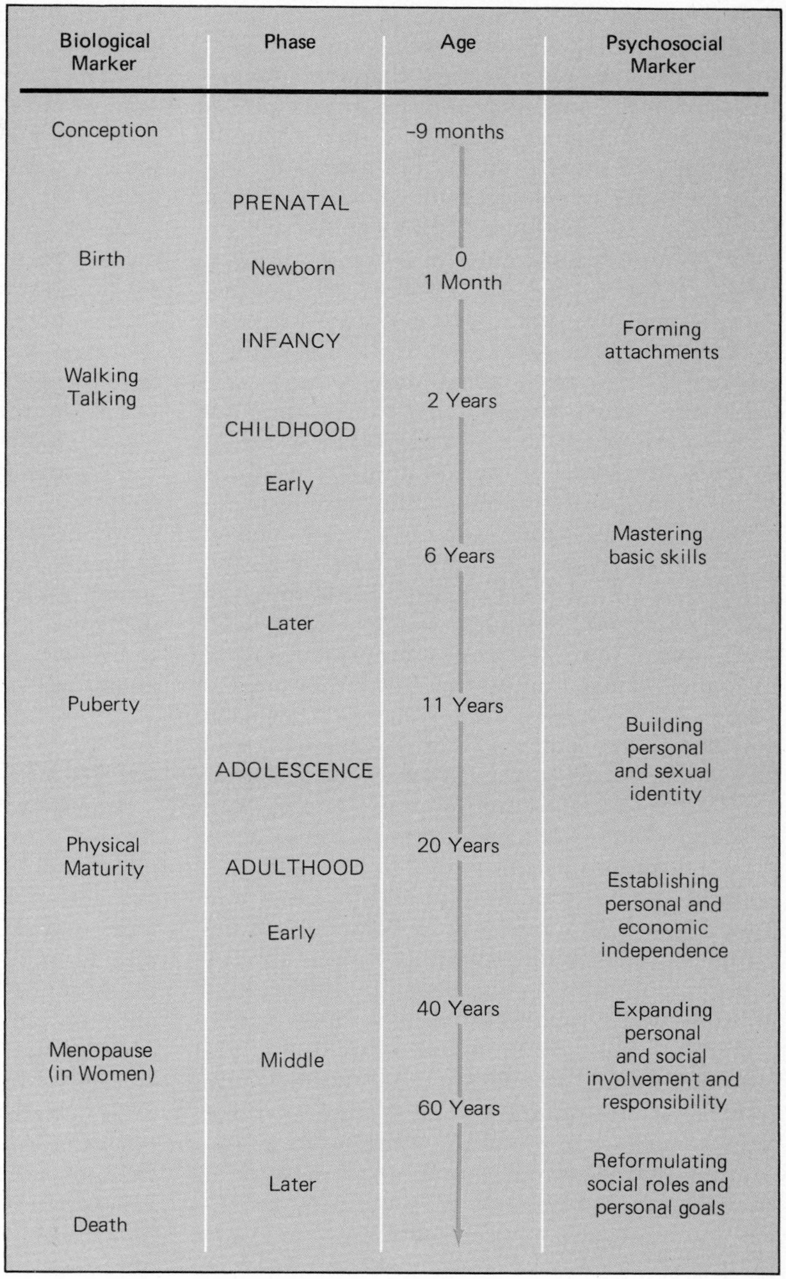

Figure 1.1   The five phases of development reflect chronological divisions based on cultural usage. This drawing shows examples of biological and psychosocial markers, subperiods of development, and approximate age ranges that are characteristic of each phase.

Biological Marker	Phase	Age	Psychosocial Marker
Conception		−9 months	
	PRENATAL		
Birth	Newborn	0 1 Month	
	INFANCY		Forming attachments
Walking Talking		2 Years	
	CHILDHOOD		
	Early		
		6 Years	Mastering basic skills
	Later		
Puberty		11 Years	
	ADOLESCENCE		Building personal and sexual identity
Physical Maturity	ADULTHOOD	20 Years	
	Early		Establishing personal and economic independence
		40 Years	Expanding personal and social involvement and responsibility
Menopause (in Women)	Middle		
		60 Years	
	Later		Reformulating social roles and personal goals
Death			

ods of relatively rapid or slow development, each person's life shows a continuity from conception to death.

USES OF DEVELOPMENTAL PSYCHOLOGY

When students enroll in a course on developmental psychology, they may first want to know *how* people develop. They may want a description of how children and adults behave at different ages. Typically they think of developmental psychology as a source of data about average development: When should children know their colors? When does the adolescent growth spurt begin? What differences are there in the IQ scores of people from different ethnic and socioeconomic backgrounds? Does intelligence really decline as people age? These students are partially right; developmental psychology does answer many questions about how development occurs. But more interesting than descriptive questions are questions that ask *why* development occurs as it does. Why do most children know primary-color names by kindergarten? (Why not earlier or later?) Why does the adolescent growth spurt begin and end so regularly? Why do people differ in IQ scores? And so forth.

Questions about the hows and whys of development have given us a sound basis for describing and explaining much about development. This book relies heavily on the results of scientific studies of development, and it interprets these results in terms of various theoretical positions. But it is neither a long narrative of the changes in behavior that occur across the life span nor an exposition on how to rear children or how to lead "the good life." As scientists, psychologists learned long ago that their primary mission is to provide sound and useful sets of information for consumers to evaluate rather than an arbitrary set of rules for them to follow. True, psychologists are always interested in and alert to the applications of psychological data and theories. Even so, they are more likely, for example, to discuss the effects of praise on a person's behavior than to tell employers that they must compliment their employees.

Studying developmental psychology may well provide you with a new way of looking at the development of human behavior. It is easy to view lower organisms with detachment, for their behavior is removed from anything you have experienced. It is more difficult, at first, to look at the behavior of a human being in a similarly objective fashion. But a major message of psychology is that human behavior has its antecedents and its consequences, that there is a regularity and a degree of lawfulness in development. With appropriate analysis and objective study you should be able to discover why certain types of behavior occur and how conditions may influence later behavior. After reading this book you should no longer be content, for example, to ascribe aggressive behavior to meanness, but you should demand (and should be able to begin to formulate) a more penetrating analysis of why a person so often fights with others.

The consumers of information from developmental psychology are students, parents, teachers, pediatricians, social workers, government planners, and others who need to understand how people's development can be enhanced or improved by life circumstances, how best to plan programs for the citizenry, young and old, and how to improve everyone's chances for optimum development. Parents face problems in the management and rearing of their own children. Teachers are confronted with difficulties in instructing their students. Pediatricians are more aware today of the relationship of behavior to physical problems in their young patients. Social workers must make decisions that affect the future successes of people in their charge. Government planners need to know what kinds of programs will best serve young children in day care, teen-agers in work-study programs, older adults in nursing care, and so forth.

Some questions about human development cannot be answered at present, but there is enough sound information and incisive theory for developmental psychology to offer exciting possibilities to anyone interested in understanding and influencing the development of human behavior.

SUMMARY

1. In the twentieth century, we generally divide the life span into the prenatal period, infancy, childhood, adolescence, and adulthood. But societies with different social and economic systems have viewed the life span differently. The concept of a separate childhood emerged with the rise of the middle class; adolescence, with rising industrialization; and late adulthood, with increased life expectancy.

2. The field of developmental psychology attempts to describe, to understand, and to explain changes in human behavior across the life span. Developmental psychologists construct theories of human behavior, using information from psychology as well as from biology, sociology, and anthropology.

3. Developmental psychologists are careful to use an appropriate level of explanation to explain a given behavior. They search for explanations by studying behavior at different ages, behavioral changes as people grow older, environmental events that influence behavior, and variations among individuals, as well as by conducting research on nonhuman species and studying case

histories of individuals. Replication studies are the best safeguard against accepting a chance finding as typical.

4. Development from infancy to adulthood involves orderly change that is directional, is largely cumulative, and involves increasing complexity and organization. Several concepts have been used to explain the relationship among developmental changes in behavior: sequences indicate that some behaviors precede others in a meaningfully related way; phases indicate that development is continuous across the life span and that the divisions are culturally determined.

5. Developmental psychologists' questions about the hows and whys of human development have led to much useful information about its regularity and lawfulness. Although some questions about human development cannot yet be answered, what is known offers insight into and understanding of many facets of human development.

CHAPTER 2
Theories of Development

PHILOSOPHICAL VIEWS OF HUMAN BEINGS

MATURATION THEORIES

BEHAVIOR-LEARNING THEORIES
Types of Conditioning
Social Learning

ADAPTATION THEORIES
Organismic Development
Piaget's Theory
The New Ethologists

PSYCHODYNAMIC THEORIES
Freud's Theory
Erikson's Psychosocial Theory
Ego Psychology

THE CONCEPT OF STAGES

OVERVIEW AND EVALUATION

SUMMARY

A couple is waiting in line to buy tickets to a concert when two adolescents push in front of them. "I'd like to talk to the parents of those kids," says the man, "and tell them how to raise children"; "What can their parents do?" the woman responds, "Boys are like that."

Each of us has a personal theory of how and why people behave as they do. Unfortunately, we rarely agree in our explanations of human behavior, and there is no easy way to decide which of us (if any) is correct. Private theories of development are derived from our personal experiences (which may be radically different from the experiences of others), the books and magazines we read, the motion pictures and television programs we watch, and the common assumptions of our culture, which may be contradictory in themselves and different from the assumptions of other cultures. Furthermore, what passes for explanation in casual conversation would not usually satisfy the scientific requirements for an explanation.

Our private, naive "theories" of development are not really theories in a formal sense. They are often internally inconsistent, and they are seldom specified clearly enough to generate testable predictions. The statement "Boys are just like that" does not readily suggest any way to test the validity of the statement or to find out whether the personal "theory" is correct.

In this chapter we will discuss the various views of human beings that have influenced theories of human development. We will explore four major types of developmental theories and learn the common assumptions that theories within each type share. We will investigate theories that regard maturation as dominant, theories that assume that the environment is all-powerful, theories that consider the evolutionary history of the human species to be the reigning force, and theories that spring from Sigmund Freud's insights into human motivations. Finally, we will consider the idea of stages in development, and conclude that, although no one group of theories can explain the development of all human behavior, each can make a useful contribution.

PHILOSOPHICAL VIEWS OF HUMAN BEINGS

All of us, whether or not we are scientific observers or theorists, make assumptions, often unstated, about the nature of human development. In developmental psychology, these assumptions frequently focus on the existence of inborn differences among people, on how much human behavior can change in response to the environment, on the role of humans in their own development, on the natural goodness or evil in humanity, and on the relationship of child to adult behavior.

As long ago as the third century B.C., Plato stressed that there were innate differences in aptitude among human beings and that these individual differences should be recognized and used in childrearing and education. His pupil Aristotle, in turn, proposed that although people were the same at birth (because the human mind was a *tabula rasa*, or blank slate), there also were individual differences in natural inclinations and talents, and that education and training should be designed to fit these differences.

During medieval times, as we noted previously, there was basically no distinction between children and adults, and human beings were considered to be sinful and corrupt by nature. Harsh, primitive training designed to correct people's depraved nature was common.

By the seventeenth century, a different view had emerged. Human beings were viewed as being born innocent and primitive and then corrupted by society. Childhood became distinct from adulthood, and moral education was stressed as the way to train children to be trustworthy, disciplined, and rational human beings.

In the latter part of the seventeenth century, John Locke, a British philosopher, proposed a different view. He (1690) stressed that all human beings are born equal in terms of inborn or native propensities. At birth, however, the human mind is a blank slate (as Aristotle had proposed), and ideas, concepts, and other human qualities are instilled only as a result of training or experience.

Almost a century later, Jean Jacques Rousseau (1762), a French philosopher, partly in reaction to a revival of the idea that human beings are inherently wicked, repopularized the view that human beings are born peaceful and compassionate, only to be turned from their good nature by an evil society. Their inborn propensities needed only to be allowed expression and given minimal guidance in order to bring about healthy and acceptable development.

Many of the issues in developmental psychology arise from these different views of humanity as they are applied to an understanding of psychological development. One of the most controversial problems is the issue of nature-nurture—whether one's heredity (nature) or one's environment (nurture) is primarily responsible for one's behavior and accomplishments. A person's position on this issue depends in part on how much he believes human beings can be changed and whether he regards children as inferior adults. Most developmental psychologists believe that heredity and environment interact in complex ways to determine all aspects of development, but some continue to stress one kind of influence at the expense of the other. The nature-nurture issue crops up in interpretations of practically every aspect of development.

Theories of development combine assumptions about human nature in various ways to explain different aspects of development. They fall into four broad categories, which we will call maturation theories, behavior-learning theories, adaptation theories, and psychodynamic theories. Each set of theories is based on different assumptions about human beings, and each generates testable hypotheses about the development of behavior. They have managed to exist simultaneously largely by avoiding one another.

MATURATION THEORIES

Theories of maturation are based on the idea that all aspects of development reflect the unfolding of an individual's genetic inheritance. Behavior appears when the organs and neural connections that make it possible have matured. Such ideas are heavily influenced by Charles Darwin's theory of evolution (1859), which influenced psychology as it did other areas of science. Darwin believed that as the human baby developed, it followed the pattern of the evolution of the species.

Darwin's ideas were elaborated and used to explain differences in intelligence by his cousin, Sir Francis Galton. Galton (1869) made a number of studies of the inheritance of traits, cross-breeding, and individual differences; he is best known for his view that genius has a genetic basis. His methods, to collect information on human characteristics across the life span and to analyze the information by statistical techniques, became widely adopted by American psychologists.

In the United States, a strong interest arose in how individuals differ in levels and patterns of behavior, and how these levels and patterns change with age. This interest led to the testing movement and to the development of numerous tests, questionnaires, rating scales, and methods of observation. Emphasis was placed on precise, objective measurement. One goal was to discover and describe the way behavior changes as a person grows; another was to establish standards of individual performance at different ages. Research in both these areas was expected to clarify the basis of human development at a theoretical level.

G. Stanley Hall, who is acknowledged as the founder of child and adolescent development as fields of study, helped foster this movement. His approach was to make broad generalizations about human development and functioning and to support these generalizations by collecting information through questionnaires. Because he viewed development as being determined primarily by genetic and biological factors until adolescence, he suggested that efforts to influence the natural unruliness of children would be ineffectual until they were about twelve (Hall, 1904). By then, the child would have matured and his character could be changed by training.

Two of Hall's students had a lasting influence on the maturational approach to human development. The first, Arnold Gesell (1928), was fascinated by the way the human embryo develops, so it is not surprising that he saw the stages he described as the result of maturation. He stressed that human behavior became progressively organized as a child grew and that this growth was determined by a fixed timetable of maturation. Although Gesell admitted that learning and practice played a role in development, he believed they were of minor importance compared with the natural unfolding of development during early childhood.

Gesell was a careful and precise researcher, and his observations of children were systematically planned and carried out, and always recorded in detailed form. The developmental standards he constructed for motor, visual, language, and personal-social behavior at different ages are still used to describe sequences of development.

Lewis Terman, the second of Hall's students,

pioneered mental testing in this country. His work was based on two assumptions about intelligence: older children, because they are smarter, should perform better on a test than younger children; and smarter children, regardless of age, should perform better than less bright children. In the tradition of Galton, Terman began a study of gifted children in 1921. The people in his study have been followed for over 50 years (Sears, 1977; Terman and Odem, 1959), and his information on the social development, personality, education, and achievement of these gifted individuals has become a lasting part of psychology.

With respect to intelligence, Terman took the side of heredity on the nature-nurture question. He assumed that mental growth was like other forms of growth and that it gradually unfolded, increasing until adolescence. Thus, as a child grew older he should do progressively better on an intelligence test, but in terms of his chronological age, his performance should remain relatively constant. Individual differences among people of the same age, and differences among groups of people of varied family and ethnic backgrounds, were supposed to reflect hereditary differences in native intelligence. According to this theory, if education or experience made any difference in intelligence, it was only to reduce or increase inborn variations in intelligence.

The testing movement and work of Gesell, Terman, and others reached its high point in the late 1940s. By that time there had been an outpouring of descriptive information on child development, but many psychologists had become disenchanted with collecting information on individual differences and had moved to testing maturational theories by controlling environmental experiences. Their work caused the relative roles of maturation and experience to be seen in a different light. Developmental psychologists came to see that maturational theories placed too little emphasis on motivation and experience. The issue shifted from determining whether maturation or experience was most important to the ways in which they interacted.

Today explanations that center on heredity and maturation are still used to describe some aspects of development, such as brain and body changes, and differences in temperament or intelligence. But both heredity-maturation and environment-experience are important, and both set limits on the course and rate of development.

BEHAVIOR-LEARNING THEORIES

Learning theories see the human being as an organism that has learned to behave in uniquely human ways. The newborn baby is regarded as a malleable recipient of environmental stimulation, prepared to react to stimulation from the environment but with few organizing properties of his own. Most of what he becomes is a matter of what he has experienced or learned, and his learning begins even before he leaves the uterus. Although the idea that human beings learn or acquire much that characterizes them has been advanced by thinkers as diverse as Aristotle and Locke, formal theories of learning had their beginnings after the turn of this century. At that time, psychology was dominated by the view that its proper focus of study was the mind and that the way to know the content of the mind was through trained introspection.

Not until the 1920s was the subjective-mentalistic view of psychology effectively challenged by behaviorism. John B. Watson (1913; 1924), who led the attack, argued that psychologists should study the relationship between stimuli in the environment and behavior, not mental events. The way to do this, he said, was not by asking people what they thought, but by watching what they did. With Rosalie Rayner (1920), he conducted a classic study in which a young boy, Albert, learned to fear a white rat after he heard a loud noise each time he played with the animal. Albert not only learned to fear the rat but became afraid of other white, furry objects as well. In a later experiment, Mary Cover Jones (1924), aided by Watson, worked with a three-year-old boy named Peter who was afraid of a white rabbit, but whose fear was eliminated when he began to associate the rabbit with pleasant experiences.

Although Watson became less certain about claims he made early in his career, when he offered to take a group of infants and produce any kind of adult his critics specified, his work left an indelible mark on American psychology. It was interpreted to mean that human behavior could be molded in almost limitless ways, and that human beings could be improved in any desired direction.

Watson's views on the control of behavior did not please everyone. Critics pointed out that, assuming such control was possible, there was no guarantee that it would be used for desirable ends. Aldous Huxley's novel *Brave New World* (1932) was an imaginative warning that extreme behavioral control could dehumanize people and turn them into robots.

Types of Conditioning

Over the years, adherents to learning theories have come to agree that at least two major types of processes are important in understanding how people learn. One process is called classical conditioning, and it is the one Watson stressed. The other process is called operant conditioning, and it was first described by B. F. Skinner (1938).

Classical Conditioning   Studies of classical, or respondent, conditioning grew out of the work of Ivan Pavlov (1927) in Russia. Pavlov demonstrated that certain behaviors, which he called **reflexes,** were responses to external stimuli. There are two kinds of reflexes: unconditioned reflexes and conditioned reflexes. **Unconditioned reflexes** are responses that—before any learning takes place—a person naturally pairs with a specific stimulus, such as blinking one's eye when a puff of air strikes the eyeball or salivating when food is placed in one's mouth. **Conditioned reflexes** are established when one associates a neutral stimulus, such as a bell or light, with the unconditioned stimulus. If the conditioned stimulus occurs repeatedly just before the unconditioned stimulus, a person comes to respond to the conditioned stimulus much as he originally did only to the unconditioned stimulus.

Emotions are particularly subject to classical conditioning, as Watson's work demonstrated. Parents have noticed the same process at work in their children, and commonly observe that, by the time their baby is a year old, he begins to cry when he sees a pediatrician who has previously been paired with painful injections. A child who has been bitten by a dog may come to fear the house or the whole city block in which the attack occurred. Furthermore, the child, like Albert, may generalize his fear. The infant who has been given injections by the pediatrician may come to fear all people in white coats or all rooms that look like a doctor's office. The child bitten by a dog may come to fear all four-legged creatures.

Operant Conditioning   The learning process that describes the effects of rewards and punishment is called operant conditioning, or instrumental conditioning. In this basic kind of learning, which is associated with B. F. Skinner, the frequency of a response changes as a result of **reinforcement.** For example, when a child receives a reward like candy or social approval immediately after he responds in a certain way, he is likely to repeat that response. The candy or praise acts as reinforcement.

If the child gets no reward, or if he is punished, he will not repeat the response so often. Responses that are not reinforced decrease in frequency or may even be eliminated **(extinguished).** Responses that are punished appear to be extinguished, but they are only suppressed; once the punishing stimuli are gone, the response may reappear.

For example, a father who wants his daughter to quit chewing her nails can use operant-conditioning techniques. He might decrease the frequency of nail-biting by offering praise when the child goes without biting her nails for ten minutes. Gradually, as she regularly goes for longer periods without chewing her nails, the father might offer praise at longer intervals. He must also ignore any nail-biting that he sees in order to allow the objectionable behavior to become extinguished. He should not punish the child for nail-biting, because she may only suppress her biting in her parent's presence and continue it when he is out of sight.

The application of operant principles has been remarkably successful in changing many kinds of behavior, such as overeating or disrupting the classroom, and in teaching students to read. Developmental psychologists who wish to use this technique search for the relationships that exist between responses and stimuli (including reinforcers). They also concentrate on how various ways of providing reinforcement change the frequency of observed responses.

These timetables for reinforcing behavior are called **schedules of reinforcement.** A child at first may be reinforced for each correct response, but once a behavior is established, such a schedule is not necessary. Numerous studies have shown that one can maintain responses just as effectively by reinforcing a person for his first response after a specified time has passed, or by reinforcing him only after he has responded a certain number of times. These schedules of reinforcement have real-life examples: Some children must do their chores, but they get an allowance only once each week, whereas other children get paid after they have completed a certain number of chores.

Another important procedure in operant learning concerns the development of new behavior. Some responses are infrequently given. However, by rewarding **successive approximations,** or behavior that resembles more and more closely the final desired response, it is possible to shape behavior. Using this technique some experimenters have taught pigeons to play ping-pong and to guide missiles (Skinner, 1960), and others have taught various cognitive, social, and language skills to children and adults (Semb, 1972).

Social Learning

Social-learning theory grew out of earlier behavior-learning views. Its proponents considered earlier views too narrow and inflexible. They believed that operant and classical conditioning accounted for only part of behavior and development and stressed that many kinds of behavior are not learned in a gradual way through shaping and reinforcement. Instead, people can learn simply by observation.

Thus, the concept of **imitation** has played a key role in most social-learning accounts of human development. Many studies have demonstrated the increasing resemblance of the child's social behavior to that of adult models. Some researchers have discovered that if a child is rewarded for imitating a model, the child will tend to imitate the model even when the child is not rewarded (Bandura, 1969b). If the child sees that the model is rewarded for his or her actions, the child will tend to copy the behavior.

Over the years there have been several different but supplementary social-learning interpretations regarding the role and importance of imitation. Some time ago Neal Miller and John Dollard (1941) proposed that nurturance from parents becomes the motivating force for a child's imitations. That is, as parents satisfy the child's needs for food, warmth, and affection, they become associated with the satisfaction of those needs and take on reinforcing properties themselves. Because the parents' behaviors are reinforcing, the child imitates them to reward himself. Jerome Kagan (1958) and John Whiting (1960) pointed out somewhat later that parents also have more power and control more possessions than the child does and that the child envies their status and therefore copies his parents in the hope that his imitations will enable him to acquire their influence and status. More recently, Albert Bandura and Richard Walters (1963) have stressed that children can learn new responses from merely

Albert Bandura (1925–   )

Courtesy Dr. Albert Bandura

Albert Bandura received his doctorate in clinical psychology from Iowa State University in 1952; after completing a postdoctoral internship, he accepted a position at Stanford University, where he is professor of psychology. His research and writing on personality and social development reflect his background in clinical psychology and his strong interest in child development. Over the past few years, his theories have had a major influence on the thought of developmental psychologists.

Early in his career, Bandura became dissatisfied with the gaps that existed between the concepts of clinical psychology and those of general psychology. He also believed that behavior-learning views, including social learning, were too narrow to account for socialization and the development of behavior.

To overcome the deficiencies, Bandura developed a broad, integrated sociobehavioral approach to human behavior. According to his view, direct experience is not the only teacher; human beings learn from infancy by simply observing what other people do and noticing what happens to them. Other symbolic models are provided by way of television, books, or magazines, and such models may teach unacceptable as well as acceptable behavior. Bandura emphasizes the importance of distinguishing between learning and performance. He stresses that although people learn to do many things, they are most likely to do the things that they or others consider acceptable or rewarding.

Bandura's work stresses the links between cognitive processes, learning, and performance. Thus, cognitive skills, information, and rules strongly affect what an individual does. And because people can think about what happened to them or what may happen to them, their behavior cannot be manipulated simply by reinforcement. Bandura sees people as freer to choose and to make changes in their lives than did the original behavior-learning theorists.

---

watching a model and that a child also is likely to imitate any behavior that he sees rewarded.

In the past few years, the gradual but radical shift in social-learning theory has continued. The work of Bandura and his colleagues is representative of this shift, and Bandura (1977) has restated many aspects of human learning and motivation in terms of cognitive processes. According to Bandura, an individual's cognitive processes take a central role in regulating learning. They regulate what a child attends to, how he describes or thinks about what he sees, and whether he repeats it to himself and lodges it in his memory. Short-lived daily experiences can leave lasting effects, because they are retained in memory in symbolic form. According to Bandura, learning from a model is

not simply a matter of imitation. As children and adults watch others, they form concepts about possible behavior that will later guide their own actions. As they then observe their actions and the consequences, they can change their concepts and act in different ways. Suppose a small boy watches his older brother fighting, and the brother knocks his opponent down. Because the boy admires his brother, he is likely to consider fighting a possible way of behaving. But suppose when the boy gets into a fight, he is thoroughly beaten. Now the boy may decide that fighting is not a good idea, or that fighting makes sense only when you are sure you will win, or that his defeat was an accident and he will win the next time. His behavior will depend upon the concepts he forms as a result of watching his brother win and himself lose, on whether his brother often fights and wins, and on what happens to him if he gets into another fight himself.

In this new view, the idea of stimuli as purely external physical events that control behavior has been replaced with the view that stimuli serve as signals that help people decide what to do. The person's conception of a stimulus, not the stimulus itself, regulates his behavior.

Cognitive social-learning theorists stress that people process and synthesize information from their experiences over long periods of time, which means that they are not bound by what takes place in the immediate situation. Based on their past experiences, they decide what behavior may be effective. As human beings develop, they construct and reconstruct expectations about future events. They estimate possible positive and negative consequences of various actions. In doing this, people set their own standards, which they use to evaluate their performance, to reward their actions, and to provide their motivation.

The new social-learning theorists have moved a long way from other behavior-learning viewpoints. They give human thought and knowledge central importance in explaining the development of human behavior, and see the individual as approaching, exploring, and dealing with things that he perceives are within his ability. He tends to avoid things that seem stressful or beyond his capabilities. Other people play a primary role in development. What they do and say, and the way they behave, become sources of information that developing human beings use in making judgments and creating expectations about themselves and their world.

ADAPTATION THEORIES

The group of theories loosely classified under the label "adaptation" view human development from an evolutionary perspective. In this respect, like maturation theories, they have been influenced by the evolutionary theory of Charles Darwin. Man, as a primate (a class shared with chimpanzees and other apes), has evolved to behave in uniquely human ways. Just as the internal organs and the external limbs have evolved to certain forms, so human behavior has characteristic patterns.

Adaptation theorists all stress the necessary *interactions* that must occur between the developing person and his environment. The present state of his development always depends on his internal structures (which result from past maturation and experience) and on what is available to him in his environment. Behavior at each phase of development is uniquely organized; development is not a smoothly continuous process from conception to death but is marked by shifts from one way of functioning and behaving to another.

Organismic Development

The two theorists discussed in this section, as well as some of those covered in the section on psychodynamic theories, demonstrate the European approach to development. Heinz Werner (1948, 1957) and Jean Piaget (1952b, 1970b) were reared and educated in Europe, and each proposed a comprehensive theory based on deductive reasoning. Neither of these theorists hesitated to speculate about development nor to use concepts that might be ambiguous and impossible to test. Consequently, their theoretical views were slow to be appreciated by American psychologists.

Werner and Piaget shared common influences: they were familiar with each other's work and were trained in the biological and natural sciences. Their developmental views were also heavily influenced by Gestalt psychology. Like Gestalt psychologists, they believed American psychologists were too concerned with reducing human development and learning to bits of behavior, specific stimuli, and their associations. They agreed that there are natural patterns (Gestalts) to behavior and events, and that these Gestalts cannot be fragmented to explain development or behavior.

Their training and interest in biology led both to emphasize the adaptive functions of behavior in maintaining an equilibrium between the individual and the environment. Each emphasized that genetic maturation and experience together determine development: as the two interact, they produce and regulate changes in behavior and functioning.

Werner and Piaget viewed cognition as a biological system. The function and characteristics of thought were like those of digestion or respiration—taking in, modifying, and using whatever elements were needed.

Both stressed that human behavior could not develop if people were not born with a set of specifically human functional systems (sensory-motor systems) that allowed them to interact with the environment and to incorporate experience and stim-

Heinz Werner (1890–1964)

Courtesy International
Universities Press

Heinz Werner was interested in formulating a comprehensive theory of cognitive development. He adopted principles and concepts from embryology, biology, and other natural sciences and applied them to mental development. Werner considered learning views of development wrong, because he believed development was much more than a gradual and continuous process of acquiring bits of behavior.

Because he was interested in explaining mental life, his approach was broad, eclectic, and comparative. He wanted his theory to explain the course of cognitive development over the life span and to account for differences in thought among species, among cultures, and among abnormal groups.

He stressed that the development of human beings shows both change and stability. People go through an ordered sequence of stages, which are characterized by different organizations of cognitive structure and functioning. Each stage involves both adaptive change and organizational stability. Adaptive change means that with maturation there is a progressive development of specific, separate ways of doing and seeing things, and that these more advanced ways take precedence over early, simple forms. Organizational stability means that, even though changes occur, a person retains an essential and basic organization.

Werner showed that even as infants, human beings are organized and have some degree of competence, and this inborn organization is the basis for adaptive behavior and learning. Although movement, vision, thinking, and so on, are always organized, they undergo progressive changes in a patterned order.

ulation. From birth, human beings actively engage and use their environment, and they construct their own understanding of the world.

Werner and Piaget also stressed the developing child's shift from egocentrism to perspectivism. At first, an infant makes no distinction between himself and the external world, or among feeling, thought, and the external world, so that feeling and thinking are fused. Thus, when a young child explains his idea of time as being "play time, sleep time, and eating time," his answer reflects an inability to separate emotional and behavioral experiences (Werner, 1948). As he develops, an individual gradually acquires a sense of himself as a person separate from the world, and develops objectively based concepts about the world that he shares with others.

Werner and Piaget were concerned with studying development at an everyday level; they generally intervened in an everyday situation and studied the effects of their experimental manipula-

tions on a child's behavior. This approach was consistent with their opposition to fragmenting natural patterns of behavior.

Piaget's Theory

Piaget's theory has had more influence in recent years than other organismic theories. It gives meaningful continuity to the development of human understanding, and it has strongly influenced research in the field of perceptual and intellectual development. Piaget calls his approach **genetic epistemology.** Epistemology is the study of knowledge—how we know what we know. The term "genetic" here means developmental. Piaget's theory covers the development of intelligence (ways of knowing) over the life span.

For Piaget, all knowledge comes from action. For example, the baby acts on objects around him—feels, turns, bangs, mouths them—and grows in his knowledge of those objects through structuring his experience. The baby's knowledge grows neither from the objects themselves nor from the baby himself but from the interaction of the two and the consequent links between actions and objects.

Schemes   Piaget sees the child's understanding of his world (as opposed to the mere recording of it) as arising from the coordination of actions and the interrelationships of objects: He is a **constructionist.** Both relationships—of actions and of objects—are the baby's constructions of reality, not something given by the actions or the objects alone. For example, an infant can throw a ball and roll it; he can apply those same actions to an orange. He learns that both objects roll (are round) but that, when thrown, the ball bounces and the orange goes "thud." From his apparently ordinary

and simple actions on objects, an infant comes to know some effects of his actions and some properties of objects. He also learns to coordinate his actions—he cannot throw and roll the same object simultaneously, but he can finger it first and then throw or roll it. Action patterns, which Piaget calls **schemes,** are built up and coordinated throughout development. In the infant, they are like concepts without words.

Older children and adults have more internalized action schemes, which they use to gain and structure their knowledge. Later schemes can be mental actions. Although the actions of thinking are internal, they derive from earlier concrete experiments that the infant performs on the world. Mental arithmetic replaces the physical act of counting; logical sequences of thought like "If

Jean Piaget (1896–   )

Yves de Braine/Black Star

Jean Piaget was born and reared in Switzerland. As a boy he was a keen observer of animal behavior, and when he was only fifteen, published a paper on shells in a scientific journal. He came by his interest in knowledge and knowing (epistemology) as a result of studying philosophy and logic. Whereas most American psychologists have been influenced by the evolutionary theories of Charles Darwin, Piaget was influenced by the creative evolution of Henri Bergson, who saw a divine agency instead of chance as the force behind evolution.

After receiving his doctorate in biological science at the University of Lausanne in 1918, he became interested in psychology. In order to pursue his interest in abnormal psychology, he went to Paris and, while studying at the Sorbonne, secured a position in Alfred Binet's laboratory. During his work there, he began to pay more attention to children's wrong answers than to their right ones, realizing that the wrong answers provided invaluable clues to the nature of their thinking.

Piaget's interests in children's mental processes shifted and deepened when, in 1929, he began observing his own children. As he kept detailed records of their behavior, he worked at tracing the origins of children's thought to their behavior as babies. Later, he became interested in the thought of adolescents. Piaget's primary method is to present problems in a standardized way to children of different ages. He then asks each child to explain his answers and probes these explanations with a series of carefully phrased questions.

Soon after completing his work in Paris, Piaget accepted an appointment as director of research at the Jean Jacques Rousseau Institute in Geneva. He has lived in Geneva ever since, conducting research and writing on cognitive development as professor of experimental psychology and genetic epistemology at the University of Geneva.

. . . then" statements replace the younger child's concrete manipulations of cause-effect relations. An older person need no longer literally try out the solution to every problem.

For example, most adults have come to understand the principle of gravity: When released from an elevated position, objects fall. But a ten-month-old baby explores gravity by dropping bits of dinner from the highchair tray and watching intently as the green bean hits the floor. (He also discovers that cups fall, spoons fall, cookies fall.) Fortunately, a baby's scheme of dropping objects in space soon becomes coordinated with many objects, so that he no longer creates the same mess over and over again. Furthermore, dropping food is antithetical to eating it, so that a hungry baby comes to recognize that eating and dropping the same object are not compatible schemes.

Assimilation and Accommodation In Piaget's theory, children's thinking develops through two processes: assimilation and accommodation. **Assimilation** refers to the incorporation of new knowledge through the use of existing schemes. For example, a child can bang a large variety of objects and assimilate to his existing scheme whether or not "banging" is a primary attribute of each object. Some objects make loud noises, others, soft; some break, others squeak; and so forth. **Accommodation** refers to the modification of the child's

existing schemes to incorporate new knowledge that does not fit them.

The processes of assimilation and accommodation always work together in complementary fashion. To assimilate is to use what one already knows how to do; to accommodate is to acquire a new way of doing something. Both processes continue to function throughout the life span. For example, in the United States we are being asked to convert our thinking to the metric system. In essence, we are being asked to restructure our existing schemes (accommodation). After we have learned the metric units of weight, volume, and linear measure, we will have to assimilate much of what we knew under the old scheme to the new one. Does one wear a sweater outdoors at 30°C? (No.) Is 80 kilometers per hour too fast a speed to drive on a freeway? (Probably not.) Is $3.50 per kilogram too much to pay for pork chops? (No.) In other words, any new way of acquiring knowledge will have to be applied to what we have already learned in a different way under other schemes.

At any given time, the developing person can change his or her cognitive structures only to a limited extent. There must always be some continuity. The balance, or equilibrium, between assimilation and accommodation changes over the life span in the direction of greater balance. **Equilibration** is the most general developmental principle in Piaget's theory; it states that the organism always

In Piaget's view, to obtain the toy this baby first tries a familiar grasping scheme (assimilation) and then alters it with new knowledge (accommodation) to get the toy through the bars. (George S. Zimbel/Monkmeyer Press)

tends toward biological and psychological balance and that development is a progressive approximation to an ideal state of equilibrium that it never fully achieves. A child's equilibrium at any one stage may be upset by external events such as new information he cannot readily assimilate or by internal processes that bring him to a new "readiness" to accommodate. In both cases, the child's previous temporary equilibrium is upset, and development advances to a new, higher level of organization.

Stages According to Piaget, intellectual development goes through a series of stages, and the organization of behavior is qualitatively different at each stage. The two conditions that Piaget sets for his stage theory are: (1) stages must be defined to guarantee a constant order of succession, and (2) the definition must allow for the progressive development of mental structures without relying totally on either heredity or environment.

Piaget proposes three major stages of intellectual development: a **sensory-motor** period, a period of **representational** thought (subdivided into **pre-operational** and **concrete-operational** periods), and a **formal-operational,** or propositional, period. The sensory-motor period, which is discussed in Chapter 7, begins at birth and extends through the first two years of life. The period of representational thought begins around the age of two with the preoperational stage, when children start to record experiences symbolically. This period is discussed in Chapter 11. Beginning at about seven or eight, children enter the concrete-operational period, discussed in Chapter 14, when they begin to understand new kinds of logical operations involving reversible transformations. By eleven or twelve, young adolescents begin to develop a formal logic that consists of propositions ("If . . . then" statements); at this time they enter the formal-operational period, which is covered in both Chapter 14 and Chapter 18.

The New Ethologists

In the past few years, a small group of dedicated naturalists who have sought to observe development in its real-life settings have become an emerging force in developmental psychology. The new ethologists translate biological evolutionary concepts into behavioral terms to study human development. The trend toward ethological-genetic thinking is increasing at a rapid rate. As we will see at various points throughout this book, observational techniques, so rigorously developed by ethologists, are gaining favor in all areas of developmental psychology.

These new ethologists are primarily interested in the role that behavior plays in survival and reproductive success. The human species (and every other species) has evolved in environmental contexts that are as important to understand as the nature of man himself. The necessity for human beings to be in harmony with their environment leads ethologists of human behavior to look at development as adaptation. They see social behavior as related to group cohesion, to the competition for mates, to survival of the young, and so forth. Intelligence is a prime mechanism for adaptation; those individuals who can solve problems in their world are more likely to leave offspring for the next generation.

One of the most useful ethological notions is that of **releasing stimuli,** those events that regularly evoke certain behavior in all members of a species, which can explain regularities in mating patterns, aggression, appeasement, and some other typical behavior. For example, observers have noted that children's play groups have "dominance hierarchies" much like troops of baboons or chimpanzees. Usually, the children in the group agree on who is "toughest," who is "smartest," and so forth. By the time children are six or seven, their groups are often structured with well-established roles of leader and follower. The followers seldom challenge the leaders, but when they do there are ritualized ways to settle the issue, short of physical combat. These descriptions also apply to baboon troops in the wild. The new ethologists have noted the remarkable similarities in the social behaviors of man and his nearest primate relatives (N. Blurton-Jones, 1972).

Courtship and greeting behaviors also show apparently universal ritualized aspects. Irenäus Eibl-Eibesfeldt (1970) has studied such behavior extensively in groups around the world. He has discovered amazing similarities in human facial expressions; for example, in flirtatious greetings by females, the eyebrows go up, the head tilts, the gaze lowers, and the eyelids drop. No matter which cultural tradition a woman comes from, she seems to display this form of greeting to the opposite sex. Both sexes usually employ the eyes and eyebrows in greeting other people, no matter where they live.

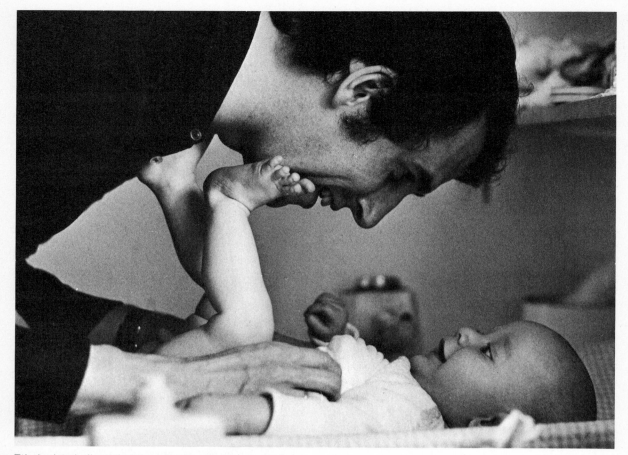

Ethologists believe that the affectionate response of adults to the cuteness of babies has evolved because it increases the chances of infant survival. (Thomas Höpker/Woodfin Camp & Assoc.)

And no matter where they live, most human beings respond to cuteness in babies and baby animals by wanting to pick them up and cuddle them. What makes baby forms of a species "cute"? Young animals are cute because they have relatively large heads, particularly foreheads, and foreshortened facial features. The toy industry takes advantage of this to make cute dolls with very small features embedded in large heads and small bodies. In other species, the baby forms elicit caregiving from adults, whereas adult forms do not. In human beings, the usual adult response to babies is also affectionate. Perhaps cuteness is a releasing stimulus for human caregiving as well, and perhaps human beings have evolved the response to cuteness because it improves the chances of adequate infant care and survival (Lorenz, 1943).

Jerome Bruner (1972) has speculated on the uses of the long period of immaturity in human development. Human educability is a prime species characteristic. The baby and child are easily taught many skills, and they yearn to explore and to learn. Play is an important way in which the young practice skills without suffering adult consequences, as when they play house or doctor or soldier or any adult role. Evolution has guaranteed that during the years between birth and adulthood, children will want to learn the many skills required of adults who will survive and leave offspring. According to Bruner, language, playfulness, curiosity, and the need to master one's environment appear to be evolved characteristics that make human development what it is.

In general, then, adaptation theories suggest that behavior grows out of biological development.

Human behavior is the product of man's evolutionary history, but the organismic theorists and the new ethologists focus on different aspects of that belief. Both groups believe that the structure of behavior is inherent in genetic-biological development and that behavior develops in interaction with the environment.

PSYCHODYNAMIC THEORIES

Most psychodynamic theories discuss and analyze human development in terms of various confrontations between the growing individual and the demands of his social world. They stress how the individual must accommodate to society while obtaining gratification for his basic drives. Most also emphasize that the child gradually develops a sense of self, an identity against which to judge his own behavior.

As a group, psychodynamic theorists have centered their attention on personality development. Their concern has been to understand and explain the development of both rational and irrational feelings and behavior. To some extent, all psychodynamic theories have tried to account for human development by looking for early experiences, usually emotional, that may influence later behavior.

Psychodynamic theories are generally concerned with inner development and view man as motivated by various internal and external forces. These forces in turn are considered to be determining factors in human behavior. Some psychodynamic theories view the internal forces as benign or positive growth forces that can be either impeded or facilitated by environmental events. In other psychodynamic theories, the internal forces are irrational or nongrowth forces, which must be controlled by various socialization practices and cultural standards.

The idea that there is a "me" or a "self" intuitively makes sense to most people. In most psychodynamic theories, the concept of a self is a major construct. It manages to capture each person's feeling of realness and uniqueness as well as to bring together, and seemingly to explain, a number of observations about a person that might otherwise appear meaningless.

Because there are many major psychodynamic theories, this section will discuss only those of Sigmund Freud and Erik Erikson in detail. In later chapters on personality, we will return to their work and to the work of others.

Freud's Theory

Sigmund Freud (1905) is the father of psychodynamic theories and the founder of psychoanalysis. Whether or not one accepts his theory of man's development, his influence on psychology, the arts, and literature has been enormous. In a prim Victorian Age, he put forth a theory of unconscious motivation, human sexuality, and instinctual aggression.

As Freud saw it, from earliest infancy man is motivated by his irrational urges toward pleasure. Rational behavior develops out of conflict between social demands and the young child's instincts, which are **sublimated** (altered in socially acceptable ways) in the course of the child's adaptation to his environment. Intelligence or adaptation is secondary to a sensuality that has become socialized.

Freud proposed three conflicting aspects of human personality: the id, the ego, and the superego. In the **id** reside all of the **unconscious** impulses (the person is unaware of these forces). The **superego** is his conscience, which develops in early childhood as he internalizes parental values and standards of conduct. The **ego** guides a person's realistic coping behavior and mediates the eternal conflicts between what he wants to do (the province of his id) and what he must or must not do (the province of his superego).

Freud's view of man's development is in part an evolutionary one. Man's biological urges are part of his evolved animal nature. His development proceeds through interaction with external reality, which transforms him, and with further maturation he continues to interact with reality, which again transforms him, and so forth. Almost inevitably, the cost of man's coming to terms with rational behavior is a loss of contact with his basic impulses and a denial of their direct gratification. As a consequence, most civilized men are anxious. In contrast, infants are not anxious until they begin to differentiate themselves from their caretaking environments and begin to cope with the demands of reality.

Freud believed that development is an unfolding of genetic stages in which instinctual impulses become attached to various pleasure centers of the body. He described the life cycle of man in sexual terms, tying psychological development to the res-

Sigmund Freud (1856–1939)

(Photo by Edmund Engelman, from *Berggasse 19*)

Sigmund Freud's theories reflect his training in the biological sciences and his clinical experience. He specialized in physiology, received his M.D. degree in Vienna in 1881, and began lecturing and doing research in neuropathology. A grant enabled him to go to Paris and study under the famous neurologist Jean Martin Charcot, who was using hypnosis to treat hysteria.

Later, as Freud treated his patients, he developed the therapeutic methods of free association and dream interpretation. He found that his adult neurotic patients had repressed their memories of early childhood emotional experiences, which generally involved sex, aggression, or jealousy. Because these experiences were unpleasant, Freud proposed that they became lost to awareness because they were pushed into an unreachable area of the mind, the unconscious.

In his theory of psychosexual development, he interpreted what he learned from treating his patients in the light of embryology and physics. He proposed that the emergence of psychosexual stages was primarily determined by maturation and that mental life followed the law of conservation of energy, which states that energy cannot be created or destroyed, only transformed. People's mental and emotional lives, he believed, show a comparable transformation of psychic energy (libido) from one stage to the next. This energy motivates people's thinking, their perceptions, and their memories, and it remains constant even though it becomes associated with different regions of the body during development.

olution of the conflicts that characterize each stage of life. Current psychodynamic theories are elaborations and modifications of Freud's thought or reactions to it. Once Freud's theories found their way into academic and popular thinking, the field of human development was changed.

Erikson's Psychosocial Theory

Erik Erikson (1963), one modifier of Freud's psychoanalytic theory, has developed an elaborate stage theory. Erikson describes emotional development across the life span, which makes his theory particularly important.

In Erikson's psychosocial theory, personality develops according to steps predetermined by the human organism's readiness to be driven toward, to be aware of, and to interact with a widening social world, a world that begins with a dim image of mother and ends with an image of humankind. Erikson saw development as consisting of the progressive resolution of conflicts between the child's needs and social demands. At each of eight stages, conflicts must be resolved, at least partially,

before progress can be made on the next set of problems. The failure to resolve problems at any stage can result in psychological disorders that affect the rest of the life span.

From Trust to Industry   A baby needs to develop a relationship in which he can get what he requires from a person who is ready and able to provide it—almost always a mother. He needs to develop feelings of comfort with his mother and needs to know that a consistent caregiver will be there when he needs her. Constant, reliable care promotes the baby's sense of *trust*. This consistency in care enables a baby to learn to tolerate frustrations and to delay immediate gratifications, because he knows that adults around him care and can be trusted to meet his needs. If a baby's needs are not consistently met, he can develop a sense of mistrust and will react to frustration with anxiety and upset.

After the infant begins to walk and to exercise some self-direction, he runs into social restraints. During this second stage, he increasingly demands to determine his own behavior ("Me do it!"), but

In Erik Erikson's psychosocial theory, the baby's first task in emotional development is to develop a sense of trust. (© Mark Haven/Magnum Photos)

Olive R. Pierce / Black Star

Erik Erikson (1902–   )

Erik Erikson was born in Germany of Danish parents. He was graduated from art school and went to Florence, Italy, intending to become an art teacher. In Vienna, where he had gone to teach children of American families, he met Freud and other analysts, and soon entered psychoanalytic training.

When Hitler came to power in Germany, Erikson emigrated to America. He held a series of positions in child-guidance clinics and major universities while maintaining a private practice. During an appointment at Harvard University, Erikson developed an interest in anthropology and studied the Sioux and Yurok Indians. During a subsequent appointment at the University of California, Berkeley, he studied adolescents, using a technique in which the way young people played with dolls revealed their unconscious thoughts and feelings.

Erikson is one of the few theorists to describe emotional development across the life span. In his theory, personality develops through eight stages, from infancy to the final stage of life. As a person interacts with a widening social world, he or she moves from a universe of self and mother to an image of humankind. Each stage has its own conflict to be resolved, and the failure to resolve any of these conflicts can lead to psychological disorders. Erikson's psychodynamic theory is important because, unlike Freud, he believes neuroses can develop at any stage during life, and that they are not necessarily the result of problems in infancy or early childhood.

During Erikson's second stage of emotional development, the toddler must gain a secure sense of autonomy. (Michael Hardy/Woodfin Camp & Assoc.)

because he has little judgment about his actual capabilities, he needs to be gently protected from excesses while granted *autonomy* in those matters that he can handle. It is particularly important at this stage, Erikson suggests, that parents not shame a child into feeling that he is incompetent. Shame can be a devastating experience for anyone, and it is particularly difficult for young children who are struggling for autonomy and who are not yet sure that they can develop competent self-regulation.

After the child has gained a relatively secure sense of autonomy, he enters the third stage of development and is ready to take the initiative in planning his own activities. As Erikson sees it, *initiative* adds to autonomy the quality of undertaking, planning, and attacking a task for the sake of being active and on the move. In the preceding stage, self-will often inspired acts of defiance. In the third stage, the child is ready for positive, constructive activities under his own initiative. The potential problem at this period is guilt; the child may come to feel that his intrusiveness and activity have evil consequences. This is the period of sexual attraction to the opposite-sex parent: of seductive behavior by little girls toward their fathers and of assertive, manly behavior of little boys toward

their mothers. As a child resolves these hopeless attractions, he identifies with the same-sex parent and develops a conscience. Harsh parental responses to a child's sexual overtures and other initiatives, however, can lead to an overdeveloped, harsh conscience that may always plague the person with guilt.

Erikson theorizes that, when the child has come to terms with his family by identifying with the same-sex parent, he enters the fourth stage and is ready to move into the larger world. About this time, in our culture, he goes to school. Before the child can become an adult in any society, he must become a worker; he learns that he will gain recognition by producing things (*industry*). The child, therefore, wants to learn the technical skills that characterize adults—be they literacy or hunting or herding. The potential problem in this period lies in a sense of inadequacy and inferiority, which can develop if a child is not praised for his accomplishments. In Erikson's theory, this is a decisive stage, for the child must prepare for effective adult roles.

From Identity to Ego Integrity   In the fifth stage, the adolescent questions all of his previous resolutions to problems of trust, autonomy, initiative, and industry. Rapid body growth and genital maturity create a "physiological revolution" within him at the time that he faces adult life. According to Erikson, the adolescent searches for continuity and sameness within himself—a sense of *identity*—and in his search he has to refight the battles of earlier years, usually casting his parents in the role of adversaries. He tries and discards roles and ways of behaving, then reformulates them and tries them again. The potential problem at this period is that the adolescent's identity will fail to become consistent and that he will have a sense of personal diffusion. Some adolescents cannot seem to develop a sense of who they are as people, as sexual beings, as adult workers, as potential parents. If a sense of role diffusion lasts into adulthood, the person may never be able to make consistent decisions about who he is and where he is going in life.

The young adult, emerging from the search for identity, is eager and willing to fuse his identity with that of others. In terms of Erikson's sixth stage, he is ready for *intimacy,* for relationships with others in which he is strong enough to make sacrifices for another's welfare without losing himself in another's identity. It is at this point that true sexual love can emerge. The young adult has the job of putting work and love together. The potential problem at this period is isolation from others, a failure to commit oneself to loving relationships because of competition or fear.

Generativity characterizes the seventh stage and refers to the adult's concern with establishing and guiding the next generation. According to Erikson, productivity in work and creativity in one's life are important concepts in this period. Having a sense of accomplishment in adult life depends on giving loving care to others and regarding one's own contributions to society as valuable. Merely producing

About the time this child entered school, she was on the threshold of Erikson's fourth stage and faced the task of developing a sense of industry. (Constantine Manos/Magnum Photos)

children does not give a person a sense of generativity; one must see one's role in rearing them as a contribution to humankind and the larger society. The possible dangers of this period are self-absorption and a sense of stagnation, a sense of going nowhere, doing nothing important.

In Erikson's theory, the final stage of the life cycle should result in a sense of wholeness, of purposes accomplished and a life well lived. If one "had it to do over again," he would change little about the choices he has made, about the way he has lived. In such a final consolidation of life's stages, death loses its sting. The potential problem in the final stage is regret and despair over wasted chances and unfortunate choices. A person in this stage who feels despair fears death in an ironic way that those with *ego integrity* do not. Although the despairing person expresses disgust over his life, he yearns for another chance. The person with integrity accepts death as the end of a meaningful trip.

Ego Psychology

Compared with Freud's theory, Erikson's psychosocial theory places greater emphasis on the development of adaptive behavior. A few contemporary psychodynamic theorists have been even more concerned than Erikson with ego functions and adaptive intelligence, and a number of ego psychologists disagree with Freud's position that throughout life man is motivated only by his basic instincts.

Abraham Maslow (1954) believed that theories of motivation and personality should stress healthy development. He proposed a hierarchy of needs to describe a person's developmental progression from physiological-instinctive motives to more rational, intellectual ones. Figure 2.2 shows the hierarchy. Maslow believed that human beings are **self-actualizing**—that they tend toward becoming all that they can be. He proposed that realizing one's potential in work and love is a basic human need. Before a person can become self-actualized, however, his more fundamental needs for food, security, esteem from others, and self-esteem must be met. If a person is chronically hungry or if his life is constantly threatened, he cannot be self-actualizing. His energies are tied up with survival. The final need in Maslow's hierarchy is to know and to understand in a cosmic sense, to feel oneself part of the larger order of the universe. Only a

Figure 2.1   Erikson's proposed sequence of psychosocial stages of development and the types of possible outcomes often associated with each stage. Beginning with the oral/sensory stage, Erikson's first four stages are, respectively, extensions of Freud's oral, anal, phallic, and latency stages. In the remaining four stages, Erikson has elaborated on Freud's approach by adding dimensions of interpersonal relationships. (Adapted from E. H. Erikson, *Childhood and Society*, 2nd rev. ed., copyright © 1963 by W. W. Norton & Company, Inc.)

Erikson's Stages of Development								
Stage	1	2	3	4	5	6	7	8
Maturity								Ego Integrity vs. Despair
Adulthood							Generativity vs. Stagnation	
Young Adulthood						Intimacy vs. Isolation		
Puberty and Adolescence					Identity vs. Diffusion			
Latency				Industry vs. Inferiority				
Locomotor/ Genital			Initiative vs. Guilt					
Muscular/ Anal		Autonomy vs. Shame						
Oral/ Sensory	Trust vs. Mistrust							

person who has accomplished his own actualization can strive for such understanding.

All the psychodynamic theorists mentioned and others whose work will appear in later discussions of personality and identity make important statements about the developmental course of human drives to become a complete person. Complete human beings not only have fulfilled their needs, but they cope, resolve conflicts, give support to others, and contribute to their societies as well. It is this sense of wholeness in ego functions that all these theorists have stressed.

THE CONCEPT OF STAGES

Stage theories make assumptions about the nature and course of development that stem in part from biology, but that apply to cognition as well as to other psychological aspects of development. The concept of stages is basic to the theories of Werner, Piaget, Freud, and Erikson.

When a person successfully masters Erikson's eighth and last stage, he has developed ego integrity, the sense of a life well-lived. (© Jill Freedman/ Magnum Photos)

Figure 2.2   Maslow's proposed hierarchy of human needs. The relative strength of the five main classes of needs changes progressively, as the graph shows: the peak of an earlier class of needs must be passed (needs satisfied) before the next higher need can begin to assume a dominant role. (Adapted from Maslow, 1954)

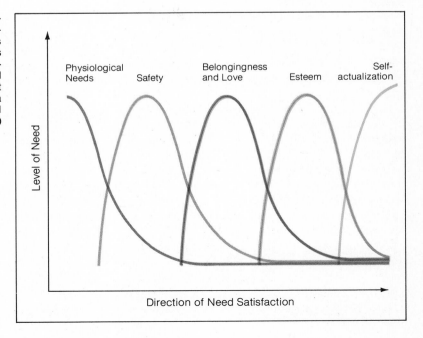

In stage theories, development and change always take place in a given sequence. As development proceeds, new forms of functioning emerge that are not a combination of earlier forms, but represent a new organization. Although people may make a partial return to earlier forms of functioning, as when a woman learns to play a piano or when a man who long ago gave up his childhood belief that objects have feelings angrily kicks a car that refuses to start on a winter morning, their development makes it impossible for them to return completely to an earlier stage.

Stage theorists believe that both continuity and discontinuity characterize human development. A stage theorist would agree with a proponent of behavior-learning theory that a change in amount, frequency, strength, or duration of a behavior shows continuity. But when ways of behaving that have an inherently new organization emerge, the stage theorist would point to discontinuity in development. This discontinuity indicates qualitative changes in behavior and functioning and in their underlying processes.

Although Werner and Piaget, whose theories were primarily cognitive, believed that emphasis on either the continuous or discontinuous aspects of behavior would lead to a distorted view of development, the idea that discontinuity is one characteristic of cognitive development gives rise to the concept of a succession of stages.

As an individual develops, he or she goes through the stages in a fixed order, without skipping any. Movement from one stage to another is gradual, and individual differences in development appear because people move through the stages at different rates and because some may stop developing before they reach the most advanced stage.

Few psychologists have had a theory of stage development more firmly based on biological development than Freud. Biological changes and discontinuities play a much larger part in Freud's theory of development than in that of any of the other theorists discussed. Erikson's stages are less tied to biology; instead they grow out of conflicts between the developing person's needs and social demands—and their resolutions.

Although stage concepts and theories have been useful, they have also come under criticism. For example, in a strict stage theory, a stage must represent qualitative changes in behavior from that of earlier periods. Quantitative changes, or changes in amounts, occur throughout the life span and give no evidence for stages.

The evidence for qualitative changes in behavior is mixed. Often a closer look at an earlier "stage" will reveal antecedents of behavior that seemed to pop up, full-blown. In number concepts, for example, Rochel Gelman (1972) has shown that three- and four-year-olds possess many parts of later skills. Indeed, when small numbers are used, they can count accurately, and they are not fooled by changes in the length of an array of three to five chips. Although most children do not easily manipulate large numbers until they are in the early school grades, preschool children already have many of the component skills. What appears to be a dramatic qualitative shift to a new "stage" of logical reasoning probably involves some important quantitative changes as well.

Another criticism of stage concepts is that behavior characteristic of the new stage is supposed to reach its maximum likelihood of occurrence immediately after the stage begins. This requirement is probably never met. There are always quantitative changes in a person's ability to use new behavior. For example, the preschool children studied by Gelman (1972) displayed advanced number concepts when only small numbers were involved. With some difficulty they could recall the strategies and apply them effectively to arrays of three to five items. They could not handle the concepts, however, when larger quantities were involved. Although they possessed the strategies for some problems, they did not possess them for similar but more complex problems. Gelman's research indicates that such skills do not reach their maximum likelihood of occurrence immediately after they first appear in the child's behavior.

OVERVIEW AND EVALUATION

Although the four groups of theories presented in this chapter may appear to have nothing in common, they are largely complementary. All believe that human growth and development is regular, and all agree that behavior is at least potentially predictable. But, as hinted earlier, they have usually avoided each other's company in two senses: They often attend to different behavior (even if they give it the same label, like "learning"), and they often explain different aspects of the developmental process.

On the other hand, various viewpoints appear

to be converging and may one day approach a common theoretical framework. All groups have a common concern with identifying the processes involved in human growth and development. They share the goal of synthesizing observations and experimental findings to explain how and why behavior originates and develops. They are concerned with looking at human development over the entire life span. In recent years, as we have seen, many theorists have begun to modify the early, narrow positions and to use insights from other viewpoints to expand their explanations of human behavior and development.

As you read this book, you will notice that different sections stress different theories. Work that implements cognitive theories will be discussed most heavily in chapters on language and intellectual development; psychodynamic theories will appear most often in the discussions of personality. Because behavior-learning theories regard all behavior as learned and because their techniques of study are used by psychologists of all persuasions, their work or their methods will appear throughout the book. Theories developed by the new ethologists, whose evolutionary approach is exciting, if unfulfilled, will appear wherever they seem to contribute to an explanation of human development.

SUMMARY

1. Theories of human development are based on different assumptions about human nature. These assumptions focus on inborn differences among people, environmental influences, the role of humans in their own development, the natural goodness or evil of humanity, and the relationship of child to adult behavior.

2. Maturation theories see human behavior as reflecting an unfolding of genetic inheritance. Early maturation theories stressed individual differences and led to the testing movement and the construction of developmental standards.

3. Behavior-learning theories view human behavior as primarily the result of experience. There are two major types of learning: classical conditioning

and operant conditioning. Social learning, in its recent development, has expanded behavior learning to include the role of human thought and knowledge in human development.

4. Adaptation theories see human behavior from an evolutionary perspective, stressing the interaction between the person and the environment; they see the development of behavior as progressing by stages. Piaget's theory, one example of such a view, sees the child as constructing an understanding of the world, and suggests the notion of schemes with which the child assimilates and accommodates new knowledge, thus maintaining equilibrium between his internal schemes and the outside world. Intellectually, the child progresses through the sensory-motor, the representational, and the formal operational stages. Ethological theories, another example of this view, take their methods from behavioral biology and their ideas from Darwin.

5. Psychodynamic theories see human behavior as motivated by various internal and external forces. For Freud, the unconscious forces of the id are tempered and sublimated by the ego and the superego. For Erikson, personality develops according to steps predetermined by the organism's readiness to interact with the external world. In general, psychodynamic theories stress that the development of how one feels about oneself is of great importance and that the individual follows a developmental course toward becoming an active, complete person.

6. Stages are central to the developmental theories of Werner, Piaget, Erikson, and Freud. In stage theories, developmental change takes place in a given sequence, with each new stage representing a higher form of functioning. Stage theories have been criticized for failing to meet certain proposed scientific requirements.

7. Although they focus on different aspects of the developmental process, the four groups of theories are largely complementary, and all can be useful in different ways.

CHAPTER 3
Determinants of Development

CLASSES OF DETERMINANTS

BIOLOGICAL DETERMINANTS
Genetic Factors
Heritability

ENVIRONMENTAL DETERMINANTS
Physical Factors
Social Determinants

STUDYING DETERMINANTS
Naturalistic Observation
Clinical Study
Field Study
Experimentation
Longitudinal and Cross-Sectional Designs
Ethical Considerations

SUMMARY

If a child in the second grade has difficulty learning to read, her teacher may say that she has poor eyesight, or that her parents tried to teach her reading too early, or that she is lazy, or that she is of low intelligence. The teacher seldom considers that all four factors could have been involved and that each one could have contributed to the child's reading disability. Human beings, including those of us who pride ourselves on our ability to understand the complexities and nuances of life, often search for a single answer when it comes to explaining behavior. In fact, however, few facets of behavior and development can be fully understood by looking at the relationship between a single developmental effect and a single cause.

In this chapter, we will explore some of the different causes of human behavior and the ways that developmental psychologists set about studying them. We will see that heredity and environment always work together to shape behavior and that maturation plays an important part in the process. We will discover that genetic research with animals can help us to understand heredity in human beings, and we will discuss some of the ways that researchers go about exploring genetic influences on individual differences. We will look at environments and observe how they influence the developing person. We will note that developmental psychologists use different kinds of studies and that each type gives them a different amount of control over the investigation of various biological or environmental determinants. We will find that no one type of study can supply all the necessary information about development and that all kinds are needed for a full account.

CLASSES OF DETERMINANTS

If a single cause rarely explains behavior, then any understanding of human development must involve the exploration and documentation of multiple, interacting causes. Yet before one can consider the way that causes interact, it is necessary to separate them and talk about different *classes* of causes. Thus, it is convenient to speak of hereditary influences (genetic and biological) on behavior, even though heredity cannot operate without the collaboration of the environment. The physical environment, such as the mother's uterus in the prenatal period, is another class of developmental determinant. And there are social influences on a child's behavior, even though the same environmental influences may work differently on persons of different body types, different skin colors, different ages, and even different generations.

Developmental psychologists are especially aware that behavior depends on both the person and the environment. Whereas other psychologists have been content to study behavior at one particular time, developmentalists study changes across time. As we noted in Chapter 1, most developmentalists appeal to both biological and environmental determinants to explain the changes that occur in the developing person. Both **nature** and **nurture** play necessary roles in development, although some theorists, such as those discussed in Chapter 2, stress one or the other.

Researchers ask two questions about the roles of genetic-biological and environmental aspects of development: "How?" and "How much?" The question "How?" refers to the ways in which heredity and environment combine to produce development. For example, how do **genes,** the microscopic elements that carry the blueprints of heredity, combine with environmental factors, such as nutrition, to produce growth? Answers to the question "How?" come from studies of people in general. The question "How much?" refers to the sources of differences among individuals. How much of the differences in height among people in your developmental psychology class is due to nutritional differences while the students were growing up (environmental effects) and how much to each student's different heredity (genetic effects)? Answers to the question "How much?" come from studies of the ways that individuals differ in their development. "How?" and "How much?" are both important questions.

BIOLOGICAL DETERMINANTS

Our heredity is of two kinds: the general inheritance of our species that makes us into that peculiar primate, *Homo sapiens,* and our specific inheritance from our parents and grandparents and great-grandparents that makes each of us visibly and temperamentally different from other members of our species. Both inheritances are biological determinants, and they begin working on us at the moment of conception and continue their work until we die. Your heredity determined your gender, the color of your eyes, the fact that you have two of them and that they perceive various wavelengths of light, your growth from an infant to an adult, and your susceptibility to various diseases, such as diabetes.

Genetic Factors

Answers to questions about genetic influence on behavior and development are difficult to obtain. Researchers cannot experimentally manipulate a human being's genetic structure. Nor can they select two people, ask them to mate and produce a child, and subject their offspring to one environment or another in order to determine the kinds of behavior that might be attributed to genetic differences or to experience. How, then, do we know about the contributions of genetics to human behavior?

Genetic Studies with Animals   One way to study human genetics is to derive a set of general principles from research on lower animals, in which nearly ideal genetic research can be performed. One type of experiment involves breeding genetically related animals until pure strains are produced. A variant of this technique involves breeding animals for a selected trait. For example, one might test a group of rats on their ability to learn the path through a maze and interbreed those rats that learn quickly. If one repeats this process with the offspring, generation after generation, a group of rats will at last be born that are almost "purebreds" for superior performance in mazes. Studies applying these breeding techniques to mice and rats have shown that genetic differences can affect aggressiveness, maze-learning ability, hoarding, exploratory behavior, sex drive, alcohol preference, and a variety of other traits (McClearn, 1970).

This kind of experimentation indicates that different strains of animals do not always respond to the same life experience with the same kind of behavior. Therefore, it is impossible to predict the outcome of a particular learning experience unless one also specifies the genetic make-up of the organism.

For example, Daniel Freedman (1958) was interested in the effects that indulging or disciplining a puppy during its early weeks of life would produce on its self-control. He selected dogs from each of four different breeds: Basenji, Shetland sheepdog, wirehaired fox terrier, and beagle. The caretakers indulged some of the dogs from each breed between the third and eighth weeks of their lives by encouraging them to play, to be aggressive, and to engage in rough-and-tumble activities. In contrast, the caretakers disciplined other dogs from each breed by restraining them, teaching them to sit, stay, come on command, and so forth. After this training, each dog was tested; when it was hungry, its caretaker took it into a room containing a bowl of meat. For three minutes the caretaker prevented the animal from eating by hitting it on the rump with a rolled newspaper and shouting "No" every time the dog approached the food. Then the handler left the room, and an experimenter recorded the length of time that elapsed before the dog began to eat the meat.

Some theories of development might lead to the conclusion that an overindulged dog will not be able to inhibit its impulse to eat in such a test. But the results of eight days of testing indicate that such a prediction is not valid for dogs. In two breeds, the terriers and the beagles, the indulged animals waited longer before approaching the food than their disciplined companions. Neither the indulged nor the disciplined Shetlands ever ate the food, and all the Basenjis dug right into the meal. Although this experiment tells us nothing about human beings, except to be cautious about sweeping predictions, it is clear that one cannot predict the effect of early indulgence versus discipline on a dog unless one first specifies its genetic make-up or breed.

Just as both the genetic make-up of an organism and its environmental circumstances affect the development of a given behavior, momentary environmental circumstances also affect the way that behavior is expressed or whether it appears at all. In many cases, organisms have hereditary behavior patterns, but they display these actions only in the presence of a releasing stimulus, as discussed in Chapter 2.

For example, Niko Tinbergen (1951) has observed that the male stickleback fish will attack a strange male stickleback only if the intruder is ready to mate, a condition revealed by a red belly. The fight that ensues looks natural and flexible, but the fish protecting its territory merely imitates the fighting characteristics of the intruder. If the intruder bites, the defender bites back; if it threatens, the defender threatens, and so on. The intruder's red belly releases the defender's attack, and each fighting thrust of the intruder releases a response that is identical to the stimulus. The result is an adaptive, natural, and flexible behavioral pattern, but its components are fixed patterns released by the specific stimuli of the intruder. Thus, genetic behavior requires the appropriate environmental stimuli in order for it to appear.

Human Genetics   How do we know about genetic effects in human beings, whose breeding cannot be manipulated? With our present knowledge, we cannot answer questions that ask *how* genes affect the development of behavior. No one has yet shown any behavior for which a single gene accounts for even a considerable amount of the differences among people (Freedman, 1974). Many genes contribute to the development of most behavioral characteristics. For example, at least 150 genes affect brain development. This estimate is on the low side and is based on the knowledge that 150 independent genes can cause different forms of mental retardation. We know that several hundred more genes are probably required to develop a normal brain, because the causes of many forms of retardation have not yet been identified. But we do not know the ways in which these hundreds of genes act together to produce a normal brain or normal intelligence.

Genes exert their influences throughout the life span. The timing of growth and aging and the sequence of development are related to gene action. Genes are "turned on" at some but not other points in development. The "turned on" genes are active in producing substances within the body that create new structures, regulate their functions, or maintain their state. Genes are carried on the **chromosomes,** which will be discussed in Chapter 4. The appearance of enlarged segments of chromosomes, called puffs, is related to genetic activity. Puffs appear on different segments of different chromosomes throughout life, suggesting that genetic activity continues to help determine how development proceeds. Lissy Jarvik and Donna Cohen (1973) have shown that breaks in chromo-

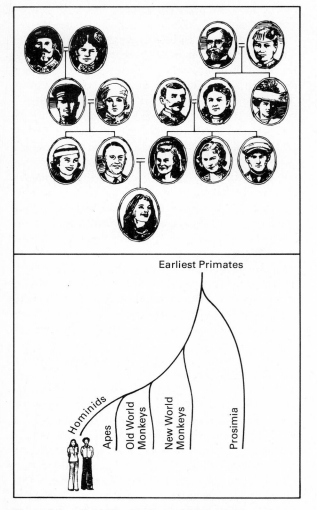

Figure 3.1   (top) The family tree of one human being. This tree traces the ancestry of a single individual and covers a time span of a little more than a hundred years. Inheritance on this scale accounts for the biological determination of certain characteristics that distinguish one individual from another.

(bottom) The evolution of *Homo sapiens*. This tree traces the ancestry of an entire species and covers a time span of tens of millions of years. Inheritance on this scale accounts for the biological determination of characteristics that all human beings have in common. (After Washburn and Moore, 1974)

somes and unusual numbers of chromosomes are increasingly found in people's cells as they grow older. As will be indicated in Chapter 23, aging may somehow be related to, among other things, gradual deteriorations in the genetic code.

Questions that ask *how much* genetic differences affect the development of individual differences are easier to answer. Still, we have

conclusive answers only for some abnormal physical traits that are caused by single genes, and in Chapter 4 you will see how such single-gene traits are transmitted from parent to child. In the case of normal traits, such as height, we get some idea of whether genetic factors are involved by comparing the trait among both related and unrelated people. The more closely these people are related and the more similar the trait, the more likely it is that genetic factors have influenced the trait. For example, appearance is obviously influenced by genetic differences, because genetically related people resemble each other more than unrelated people do, whether they grow up together or not. For example, taller parents tend to have taller children than shorter parents do.

Parents who make high IQ scores tend to have children who score higher than the children of lower-scoring parents. This tendency shows clearly in Table 3.1, which presents the correlations between the IQ scores of pairs of individuals who bear different degrees of genetic similarity to one another.

To understand this table one must know something about **correlation coefficients.** A correlation is a numerical expression of how closely two sets of measurements correspond. A correlation of .00 represents no direct relationship at all. For example, in Table 3.1 the correlation between the IQ scores of two children who are unrelated and reared apart is −.01, essentially .00. This number implies that knowing the IQ score of one child tells you nothing about the IQ score of the unrelated child. If a correlation coefficient were +1.00, then the correspondence between pairs of individuals would be perfect. In this case, knowing that one child had the highest IQ score in his group would indicate that the other child also had the highest IQ score in his group (but not necessarily the *same* IQ score). If the correlation were −1.00, then if one person had the highest score in his group, the other had the lowest score in his group. In psychological research, correlations are rarely exactly .00 or +1.00 or −1.00. Rather, they fall at various places in between. The larger the coefficient, the more closely two measures correspond and the closer the standing of pair members within their respective groups.

As the relatedness between two people increases, the correlation between their IQ scores also increases. Notice that in Table 3.1 the correlations for siblings (brothers or sisters) are not very

Table 3.1 Correlations of Intelligence Test Scores

CORRELATIONS BETWEEN	MEDIAN VALUE
Unrelated persons	
Children reared apart	−.01
Children reared together	+.20
Collaterals*	
Second cousins	+.16
First cousins	+.28
Uncle (or aunt) and nephew (or niece)	+.34
Siblings, reared apart	+.46
Siblings, reared together	+.52
Fraternal twins, different sex	+.49
Fraternal twins, same sex	+.56
Identical twins, reared apart	+.75
Identical twins, reared together	+.87
Direct line	
Grandparent and grandchild	+.30
Parent (as adult) and child	+.50
Parent (as child) and child	+.56

*Descended from the same stock, but different lines.
Source: Based on estimates reported in John C. Loehlin, Gardner Lindzey, and J. N. Spuhler, *Race Differences in Intelligence,* San Francisco: W. H. Freeman, 1975; and in Arthur Jensen, "How Much Can We Boost IQ and Scholastic Achievement?" *Harvard Educational Review,* 39 (1969), 49.

different from the correlations for fraternal twins (twins developed from two separate egg cells). This is to be expected, because on the average both siblings and fraternal twins share half their genes. But identical twins (twins developed from a split single female egg cell) have identical genetic make-ups, and their IQs show much higher correlations. Both the mother and the father also share half their genes with their children, so that the correlation for parents and children is about the same as for siblings and fraternal twins. Therefore, IQ scores appear to be directly related to the degree of genetic relatedness.

However, such evidence does not allow us to say that genetic make-up is the primary determinant of a person's intellectual ability. As relatedness between individuals increases, so does the similarity of the environment in which they live. Unrelated children reared apart share no common environment, and the correlation of their IQ scores is essentially .00. Brothers and sisters share some of their environment, but because they are born at different times and because each is subjected to some unique life experiences, their environments are not identical. In addition, because identical twins look alike, parents are more likely to treat them alike than if they were fraternal. As a result, it is possible to interpret the evidence presented in Table 3.1 as simply indicating that the IQ scores of

two people are similar when their environments are similar.

Another way of trying to discover how much genetic differences affect intellectual ability is to compare the IQ scores of related individuals, some of whom live in the same environment and the rest of whom live in different environments. For example, one could look at adopted children and compare their IQ scores with the IQ scores of both their biological parents and the parents who reared them. Researchers who have studied this problem (Honzik, 1957; Scarr-Salapatek, 1975; Skodak and Skeels, 1949) have discovered that correlation coefficients between the IQ scores of adopted children and their biological parents are greater (approximately +.35) than between those same adopted children and their rearing parents (near .00). In fact, there is little difference between the correlations for adopted children and their biological parents and the correlations for children reared by their own parents (Figure 3.2). This result presumably argues for a genetic component in intelligence.

However, when one looks at the *average* IQ score of these children, it appears that this score is closer to the average IQ score of their upper-middle-class foster mothers than to the average IQ score of their impoverished biological mothers. In one study the average IQ score of the biological mothers was 86, but the average IQ score for the children was 106, a score near the estimated IQ of the parents who reared them. This evidence argues for an environmental component of intellectual ability and suggests that the absolute value of an IQ score can be improved if the person is placed in a rich environment.

More recently, Sandra Scarr and Richard Weinberg (1976) tested the idea that an enriched environment can raise IQ test scores by studying more than one hundred black children who were adopted by middle-class white families, in which most of the parents were college graduates. They found that when black children are adopted early in life into such white families, their average IQ score is above the national average of both black and white children, indicating that environment has a profound effect on IQ scores.

Results like these illustrate a crucial concept for understanding genetic influences: the **reaction range.** The genetic make-up of each person has a unique range of possible responses to the environments that he may encounter. In other words,

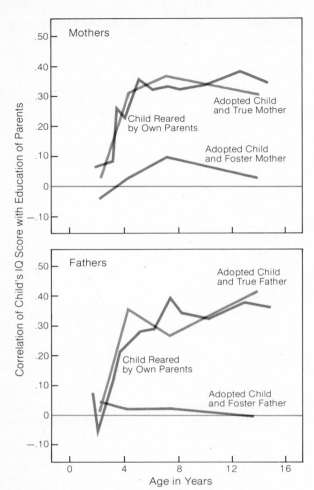

Figure 3.2 Correlations between children's IQ scores and estimated IQ scores of parents. Reddish lines are based on Skodak and Skeels's research, and the other lines are based on research by Honzik. Note that in this research parents' educational level was used as a rough estimate of their IQ score because it was not possible to administer a test to each parent. The two top lines in each graph show that as children get older, their scores correlate more closely with their true parents' scores. The bottom line in each graph shows that there is little or no change with age in the low correlation between adopted children's scores and those of their foster parents. (Adapted from Skodak and Skeels, 1949; after Honzik, 1957)

there are some limits on how each of us can respond to good and poor environmental conditions. In the case of height, good nutrition will make all of us taller than poor nutrition will, but in both kinds of environments some of us will be taller than others. Genes do not specify a particular height for anyone. They do specify a pattern of

growth that varies depending on nutrition and other environmental factors. The final height we achieve depends on both genetic and environmental factors.

The development of intellectual skills that are sampled by IQ tests also has a reaction range. No matter how stimulating the environment, few people become Albert Einsteins or Leonardo da Vincis. And in other than very deprived circumstances, most people do not become mentally retarded. Each person has a range of perhaps twenty to twenty-five IQ points in which his IQ score will tend to fall, depending on his rearing conditions (Scarr-Salapatek, 1975).

Heritability

A common misunderstanding of the way researchers describe genetic influence on a given trait has also fueled the nature-nurture controversy over IQ scores. Suppose one hundred people take an IQ test. Their scores will differ, and the difference between their individual scores is called **variability.** We know that the individuals in the group have different genetic compositions as well as different life experiences. But how much of the variability in IQ test scores is associated with differences in their genetic make-up rather than differences in life experience? The relative contribution of genetics to IQ test performance is the **heritability** of IQ in this group.

But heritability is only an estimate based on a small number of cases, which may or may not represent the general population. Suppose it were possible to find a group of people with identical genetic make-up. If these individuals were randomly placed in various environments and then given an IQ test, none of the differences in their IQ scores could be attributed to differences in their genetic composition. The heritability would be .00. On the other hand, if it were possible to rear a group of individuals with totally different genetic dispositions in the same environment, then all the differences in their IQ test scores would be associated with differences in their genetic make-up. Heritability would be 1.00.

These examples demonstrate that the size of the heritability coefficient depends on the specific research sample. Many estimates of the heritability of IQ came from research with white, upper-middle-class groups, and such families probably do not represent the full range of genetic make-up or environments among the population of a country—or a race or a social group (Loehlin, Lindzey, and Spuhler, 1975).

Because heritability depends on the specific characteristics of the sample, heritabilities for a given trait may change from one year to the next, especially if the factors that produce the trait change. Years ago, for example, the heritability for tuberculosis was quite high. At that time the bacillus for TB was widespread and nearly every individual came into contact with it. Therefore, whether one actually developed the disease depended primarily on one's inborn biochemical susceptibility to that bacillus. In contrast, the TB bacillus is now present only in the most unsanitary circumstances. Today, therefore, the major determinant of whether one succumbs to TB is exposure to the bacillus, because many people who have a biochemical susceptibility to TB never come in contact with the bacillus. Consequently, the heritability for TB is now quite low.

The cause of TB is the same today as it always was: the invasion of the TB bacillus in an individual with a biochemical susceptibility to that bacillus. But the heritability for TB has changed because whether one gets the disease is now more closely associated with where one lives than with biochemistry. Therefore, the fact that a trait has high heritability does not mean that genes cause it, nor does low heritability mean that environmental circumstances cause a trait to appear.

There is an old expression that genes set limits on development while environments determine what actually develops. This is *not* true. Environments are equally implicated in setting limits on development by providing only certain opportunities and stimuli for a person to develop a particular characteristic or behavior, whereas genes are equally responsible for determining the level of development by responding to given environments in unique ways. Individual differences among people, then, are caused by genetic differences in their reaction ranges *and* by specific differences in their environments.

ENVIRONMENTAL DETERMINANTS

Environmental determinants play a powerful role in the development of the growing child. Even the most radical of the biologically oriented theorists discussed in Chapter 2 would agree. But the term "environment" is too broad to have much scientific usefulness. One must always specify which features of any environment affect the behavior in question. For example, to explain why a number of children achieve low scores on IQ tests, some environmentalists merely point to the obvious disparities between advantaged and disadvantaged homes, schools, and neighborhoods, claiming that (somehow) all of the noticeable differences determine differences in IQ scores. However, as this section will make clear, there are various ways of defining the environment and of explaining how experience influences development. None of these ways is right in all cases; none is always wrong. All can be useful, depending on the behavior that one tries to explain. At the same time, it should be understood that, when two people say that environment determines a particular behavior, they may be speaking of different kinds of influence.

Physical Factors

Physical environments include those essential but mundane features that make life possible; more interesting physical influences, such as the mother's uterus in the prenatal period; and situations, such as growing up in a high-rise apartment or in a house. It is obvious that all organisms must have sufficient air, water, food, and light to maintain life. Without these there is biological deterioration and even death. What is not so obvious is the extent to which other features of the physical environment affect the course of development. For example, the environment of the mother's uterus is critical to the survival and development of the fetus, which requires an efficient exchange of oxygen and nutrients and the elimination of wastes. If the maternal environment is deficient in nutrients such as calcium or protein, the infant's development will be stunted. Other maternal environments are crowded: short mothers have small and premature babies more often than tall mothers do, and twins are often so crowded that they are born prematurely. As Chapter 4 will explain, the maternal physical environment also has other important effects on fetal development.

Physical environments at later ages encapsulate people metaphorically rather than literally, as the uterus does. Each of us develops in a physical context that has limiting and determining effects on our development. For example, life in a nomad's tent and life in an apartment have different influences on a growing child. Urie Bronfenbrenner (1973) has recently highlighted an **ecological** approach to development, one that

A rooftop serves as a playground for these children in New York City. The physical environment in which children grow up has a profound influence on their development. (Burk Uzzle/Magnum Photos)

takes into account a child's physical as well as social setting. Earlier, Roger Barker and Herbert Wright (1951) described the interplay between one boy and his Kansas town where he could dig, jump, run, explore fields, and engage in a variety of activities in a physical environment that was very different from the concrete and asphalt surroundings of an inner-city child in Detroit.

Think of a young boy who wants to dig. His parent must take him down fifteen floors in the elevator, then walk him four blocks through automobile traffic, crowds of pedestrians, noise, and a whirring visual kaleidoscope to a park. In contrast, the suburban child merely walks out into the backyard and digs by himself. Urban children, like suburban children, develop in a physical context that offers some kinds of experiences and limits others. Their social environments are equally different.

Just how potent the physical context can be is illustrated in the results of a study by Sheldon Cohen, David Glass, and Jerome E. Singer (1973). They wondered how long-term exposure to loud noise might affect the development of children's hearing and related abilities. To find out, they studied children who lived in a thirty-two-story apartment building located over a noisy expressway in Manhattan. As one went from the lower to the higher floors of the building, the noise level dropped. Cohen and his associates found that children who had lived at least four years on the lower, noisier floors were less able to tell the difference between subtle but contrastive speech sounds, such as "gear–beer" or "cope–coke," than children who lived on the higher, quieter floors. They also found that children who lived on the lower floors read less well than those on the higher floors. Both auditory discrimination and reading ability correlated highly with the noise levels in the apartments and the length of time the children had lived there. Although other factors may have been involved in the children's ability to hear or read well, the study seems to show that the physical environment can affect physical and mental abilities in a multitude of ways.

The type of play equipment that is at hand can also have an impact on social behavior, at least among preschool children. In a recent study, for example, Peter K. Smith (1974) found that when little equipment was available, children shared their toys and apparatus and tended to form large play groups. On the other hand, when many toys and equipment were available, children tended to keep the toys to themselves, playing either in small groups or alone. Even the kind of equipment affected the children's behavior. Some were given only apparatus, such as chairs, tables, and a ladder, to play with, while others were given only toys, such as puzzles, dress-up clothes, tea sets, and blocks. The children who had only apparatus to play with increased their verbal and physical contacts, played more in cooperative groups, smiled and laughed more, and devised new and creative uses for the apparatus. It seems that when the environment has few resources, people can cooperate and invent creative ways to use the available material.

Social Determinants

The social environment includes all those effects that people have on one another in families, in peer groups, and in neighborhoods. It also encompasses the influences of social institutions such as schools; cultural and subcultural values, attitudes, and beliefs; and media such as newspapers and television.

Family Most children grow up in the context of a family—father, mother, perhaps brothers and sisters. The family has been shown to influence many aspects of behavioral development: sex roles, self-concepts, and interpersonal and intellectual skills. Fathers have been shown to be important in the early years of a boy's life if he is to develop a traditional masculine sex role. This influence showed clearly when E. Mavis Hetherington and Jan Deur (1972) studied young adolescent boys who had lost their fathers. Boys who had lost their fathers before they were five years old were less traditionally masculine in behavior such as competitive and rough-and-tumble play. Boys who had lost their fathers later in life were no different from boys who had grown up with fathers present. But as the boys reached adolescence, the effects of a fatherless boyhood tended to decrease. On the other hand, another study (Hetherington, 1972) indicated that the early loss of a father had no apparent effects on girls until they reached puberty. Then the adolescent girls behaved inappropriately around males. This research, although limited to lower-class and lower-middle-class girls, indicates that girls may acquire from their fathers the social skills needed to interact with the opposite sex.

The age and sex of one's siblings also help determine sex-role development. Boys with older sisters show a weaker preference for the traditional masculine sex role than boys with older brothers or boys who lack older siblings (H. Koch, 1966; Sutton-Smith and Rosenberg, 1970). Girls with older brothers behave in more traditionally masculine ways than do girls with older sisters or no older

When the influence of the family on the growing child is mentioned, one assumes that the reference is to the nuclear family, made up of father, mother, and one or more children. (Hubbell/Woodfin Camp & Assoc.)

Not all children live in the traditional nuclear family. The single-parent family, generally with a mother at the head, has become increasingly common. (Tim Eagan/Woodfin Camp & Assoc.)

siblings. Because older siblings tend to act like parents toward younger children in the family, especially if there is a large age difference, it is not surprising to find that older siblings appear to affect the sex-role development of younger children.

Families also provide a context for intellectual development. The opportunities that are available to children and the way that the parents respond to their curiosity affect what they learn and how rapidly they learn it. If there are many children in the family, their intellectual skills tend to be less well developed than those of children in smaller families. Birth order also has an effect: first-born children and those early in birth rank tend to have higher IQ scores than children born later. The effects of family size and birth order seem to come about because parents pay less attention to any

one child when there are many and to later-born children in general (Belmont and Marolla, 1973). The dilution of parental attention may also be responsible for the lower IQ scores of twins as compared to those of single children. When there are twins to care for, the amount or quality of attention that parents can give seems to diminish.

Peers   Peers affect the behavioral development of people from early school age throughout the life span. When children go to nursery school, kindergarten, or first grade, they move partly out of the family world into the environment of the peer group. The peer group usually has its own values and rules of behavior, which may differ radically from those of the family.

The environment of the group affects even small children, as Lawrence Sherman (1975) found when he investigated how young children become involved socially and how sociability is maintained. He wanted to discover the factors that seem to trigger and maintain an atmosphere of glee among children. Sherman defined glee as a raucous, happy event that consists of laughter, yelling, and animated physical expression. By studying many videotapes of preschool groups, he found that gleeful episodes were more likely to occur when lessons included props and movement (e.g., drums and dancing) as compared to lessons requiring individual activity (e.g., simple construction). In more than 70 percent of the episodes, the children's glee began as a reaction to some triggering event, such as a call for volunteers. Once it started, the glee of one child stimulated glee in another, until the laughter and animated activity had spread through the group.

In middle childhood and adolescence, the peer group is almost as strong as the family in providing a testing ground for becoming a person. Because one cannot go through life being "Mama's boy" or "Daddy's girl," one has to establish other identifications and goals. Adolescent peers are decidedly important in the development of a sense of identity (Erikson, 1968). Because peers share the problems of establishing independence and identity, they provide positive support in the often painful process of becoming an adult.

In later years peers continue to influence behavior. They are friends, consultants on problems, people to compete with and emulate. Although little research has been done on the effects of peer groups in adulthood, young parents often consult

The rules and values of the peer group may be radically different from those of the family and provide children with a testing ground where they can establish their identities. (*top:* Constantine Manos/Magnum Photos; *bottom:* Bob Adelman/ Magnum Photos)

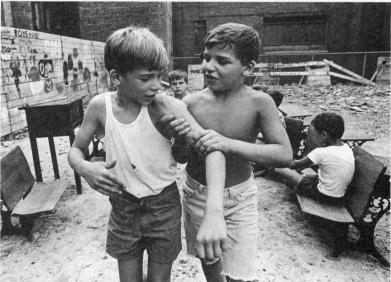

other young parents on questions about child rearing. Older adults share common experiences and gain support from peers in their increasingly difficult problems of adjustment to adult children, retirement, and changing physical status.

Neighborhoods   Over the years it has been found that many features of a neighborhood will influence its structure and function, thereby affecting the development and behavior of the people who live there. For example, in close-knit, active neighborhoods, children use the sidewalks to get acquainted, to meet their friends, and to play. They provide a setting that encourages contacts.

Many urban housing projects, which place families in an institutional environment, have become unsafe and unhealthy neighborhoods. (EPA/Documerica)

But if street traffic is dense and rapid, the sidewalks cannot be used as social areas and the neighborhood is less likely to be friendly. Similarly, unless the space near or around buildings is open to view and hence "defensible" (capable of supervision), people will not use it for play, recreation, or socializing.

Some neighborhoods provide playgrounds for children, and the type of equipment available appears to affect their use. Ordinary equipment, such as swings, slides, and wading pools, gets much heavier use than unconventional equipment, such as concrete mazes or pyramids.

In many cases, neighborhoods have a negative effect on families. For example, when low-income families move into high-rise apartments with an institutional type of environment, they feel isolated and regimented. They fail to develop the community identification that is generally found in city neighborhoods composed of smaller buildings. As Oscar Newman (1973) has pointed out, many of these buildings are designed so that the corridors and entries cannot be supervised, thereby encouraging crime and vandalism. Many such housing projects have become unsafe and unhealthy places to live.

Although neighborhoods tend to shape the development and activity of residents, residents also tend to shape the activity of neighborhoods. If, for example, a major change occurs in the ethnic background, age, interests, or life-style of neigh-

borhood residents, major changes in neighborhood events or projects and in friendship patterns are likely to follow. "Old-time" residents often resent and fight such changes, but gradually the reshaping of the neighborhood by its newer residents results in a different but stable pattern of developmental influences and experiences for both children and adults.

Schools   Schools socialize children in many of the same ways that families and peer groups do. The staff sets standards of conduct and values that may or may not be the same as those of the children's families and friends. Notable problems have arisen when the school represents an alien middle-class white world in the middle of a culturally different neighborhood. Some chicanos and blacks have recently demanded more control over what their children are taught in school, because they believe that the established curriculum (and perhaps the staff) is irrelevant. Most parents believe that schools have profound effects on their children's future success. They believe that getting along with teachers, earning good grades, and scoring well on standardized tests are related to opportunities for further education and to entrance into prestigious occupations.

Indeed, studies of nations where education is not available to all children suggest that schools do affect the intellectual achievements of children. At the very least, schoolchildren learn new ways to

Television can have both good and bad effects on children. But in families where a flickering parade of cartoons, commercials, and game shows substitutes for maternal care, its value is questionable. (Ken Heyman)

apply their cognitive skills to problems that the society says are important (and therefore puts in the school curriculum). The effects of schools are not limited to the intellectual realm. Schools also influence social skills, psychological growth, and children's feelings about the rules and regulations of society.

Media Television and other media affect behavior, for good and for bad. Many years ago a famous radio program, "The War of the Worlds," created panic in New Jersey. Many listeners believed that Martians had landed, and they either fled or prepared to defend themselves against the aliens.

Today, it is virtually impossible for a child to grow up without being exposed to heavy doses of television. Surveys indicate that 99 percent of all families with children own television sets, and most children spend from one-fifth to one-third of their waking hours before the flickering screen (Lyle, 1972). When children spend a good deal of their free time watching television, they go to bed later than other children and spend less time reading.

Recently, the effects of showing aggression on television have been hotly debated, and Chapter 15 will explore research that applies to the controversy. In general, watching violence on television does not seem to trigger aggressive behavior in most children, but some violence-prone youngsters appear to be influenced toward more aggression by watching aggressive models (Bandura, 1973).

Educational television programs like "Sesame Street" and "The Electric Company" have been designed to teach specific number and letter skills and reading to children who would usually have difficulty acquiring these skills at school. Both programs have demonstrated success in teaching specific skills to the children who watch them: the more often the children watch, the greater the improvement in their skills (Lesser, 1974). But middle-class children also watch these programs, and they seem to benefit as much as or more than the disadvantaged children for whom the programs were designed. This means that widespread watching of educational television maintains the greater literacy of advantaged children over disadvantaged children.

Culture It is easy to forget that what seems true or natural to us may seem false or unnatural to people in other cultures. If you had been raised in Budapest or Botswana or Bolivia, for example, you would be a much different person, and the influence of your culture would have begun the moment you were born. Culture shapes much of our behavior, from the way we dress and relate to others to the way we think and solve problems and the things we believe and value. Even appropriate male and female behavior varies widely among cultures.

Each culture has its own ideas, practices, technologies, institutions, and so on, that influence each of its members. There are, for example, cultures in which mothers or fathers have little to do with the rearing of their children; cultural practices and beliefs are passed on by others, such as brothers or sisters, older unrelated children or adults, who have been given the child-rearing function. For this reason, much reported research may show not what is typical of human development but what is typical of American or Japanese or Swiss or English development.

Within cultures there are also subcultural variations that are related to ethnic background, social class, and economic influences, each of which has a profound influence on how a person develops. We will discuss some of these distinctions in later chapters, but we can note one or two here. In the United States, for example, ethnic and social-class differences in wealth, education, and IQ test scores have developed in such a way that the three often go together (Hess, 1970). Because of the effects this sort of status has on individual opportunity, children in middle- or upper-class families are more likely to feel that they have the chance and ability to shape their own futures. On the other hand, lower-class children and adolescents may be wiser than middle- or upper-class children in other respects and better able to survive, should they suddenly be cast on their own resources.

It is obvious that the social environment has strong influences on the development of behavior. As has been noted, however, if one is to show what part of the environment affects some behavior, one must specify the determining aspects of the environment and describe how they affect development.

Each culture provides a different kind of environment for children. This small boy, growing up in an extended family in Germany, probably will be reared as much by grandparents as by parents. (Thomas Hopker/Woodfin Camp & Assoc.)

Social class may have a profound influence on the developing child; these children, crowded into an urban apartment, will never have many advantages taken for granted among the middle class. (Bruce Davidson/Magnum Photos)

STUDYING DETERMINANTS

How does a developmental psychologist who wants to discover the determinants of a particular behavior go about identifying them? Before the psychologist can gather the information that might explain that behavior, he or she must first design a study. Distinctions among methods for collecting information on human development depend on how much **control** the investigator has. He may or may not have control over (1) the selection of subjects for study, (2) the experience they have in the study, and (3) the possible responses they can give to that experience. At one extreme of control is the simple, **naturalistic observation** of behavior without any interference from the investigator. At the other extreme is **experimentation,** where the experimenter can control all three aspects of the study. Between the two extremes are **clinical studies** and numerous types of **field studies,** where some but not other types of control are possible.

No one study ever proves all that it proposes. A soundly designed and executed study can, at best, change our subjective judgment that a conclusion is correct. When the research design of an investigation conforms to acceptable scientific standards, we have more confidence in its results.

In psychology, there has probably never been a truly crucial study that provided a clear basis for choosing between two opposed theories. Such investigations are rare in any science. As noted in Chapter 1, the final test is replication. A scientific finding becomes established when it has been found in several investigations (and the more, the better) conducted by different researchers in different places but using the same basic methods.

Naturalistic Observation

Certain aspects of human behavior, particularly behavior in natural settings, are most appropriately studied through observational methods. Even naturalistic observations have rules for categorizing and recording what the observer sees. The major advantage of such observational studies is their closeness to what actually happens in everyday life. Because the observer is recording natural behavior, there are few problems in generalizing the results to "real-life" situations. The major problem is to determine which of many factors, or **variables,** that are uncontrolled in the study have important effects on the results.

For example, psychologists may wish to study the effects of racial integration on social behavior in a neighborhood. To conduct this study, they must observe the people's behavior before and after the groups have been integrated or contrast the behavior of people in integrated neighborhoods with that of people in segregated neighborhoods. These observations could be made in numerous ways. The psychologists could observe residents at predetermined intervals and count the number of people engaged in like-race and unlike-race social interaction. They could count the incidence of aggressive, dependent, and dominant types of behavior. Before any of this could be done, however, the observers must have clear definitions of the variables they are concerned with. Will they consider physical nearness to be an example of social interaction? How will they define aggression? Can two observers watching a scene at the same time get comparable results?

The critical aspect of naturalistic observation is having explicit rules for categorizing and recording what the observer sees. If such a study is conducted well, valuable information can be gained about the everyday effects of a potentially important environmental variable, such as racial integration, on human behavior. This information can be acquired only through the observational method.

Clinical Study

Clinical study often consists of in-depth interviews and observation. It may be controlled: the same methods can be applied in a standardized way to each subject, or the psychologist can vary the approach with each subject. When clinical study is designed with appropriate controls, it qualifies as a method of science and can yield interesting and important data. For example, Hetherington's studies of father loss used in-depth interviews and observation of adolescent girls and their mothers. The procedures for a controlled study must be clearly and precisely defined; the investigator can improvise only in such matters as introducing the subject to the clinical situation or maintaining the subject's cooperation, and even these actions may cause bias unless explicitly stated and controlled.

The studies of Jean Piaget (1952b) are another example of the clinical method. In his earlier studies, Piaget talked freely with a child, asking whatever questions seemed necessary to reveal the child's concepts and thinking processes. However, Piaget realized that differences in presenting the questions could affect his results. Because he was also critical of standardized tests, he chose an intermediate method. In his recent studies, he has used a more standardized procedure. By presenting the same questions to all children, Piaget has gained a stronger base for suggesting that the differences in children's responses at different ages are the result of actual changes in their cognitive activity.

Field Study

Field studies are studies of naturally occurring behavior in which the researcher controls some aspects of the situation. Such studies are often more closely controlled than simple observation or clinical studies. Because for ethical or practical reasons many developmental determinants cannot be brought under experimental control, an investigator may choose to use a field study. For example, a researcher who wishes to study the effects of prematurity on infant development or the effects of confinement to a mental hospital cannot randomly assign subjects to those experimental conditions. Nevertheless, a psychologist may want to study the effects of such events. This could be done by comparing premature infants with full-term babies and hospitalized persons with nonhospitalized persons.

Problems of sampling always arise in field studies, because random assignment is not possible. Premature infants, for example, may differ from full-term babies in more than their length of gestation. They are more likely to have younger, more disadvantaged mothers; they may receive less adequate maternal care. It is important, therefore, for the investigator to be aware of the ways in which the comparison groups differ. Because the researcher can never prove that all the differences between the groups have been found, the results of field studies are often less certain than those of true experiments.

In field studies the investigator may not have complete control over the experience the subject receives or over the possible responses the subject can give. Compromises are often necessary. In the study of prematurity, for example, the investigator might provide the mothers of both premature infants and full-termers with instructions for an infant-stimulation program. The investigator could visit the homes regularly to educate the mothers and to observe the babies; he or she could supply the same educational toys and give the same tests of development to both groups at the end of the study. In these ways, the researcher could gain partial control over the experiences of the two groups and could obtain the same samples of behavior at the end. In a study where standard tests are not possible, it also might be impossible to have good control over the behavior observed.

Ethologists often use field studies to ascertain the evolutionary significance of a behavior. For example, after a long period of natural observation of black-headed gulls, Niko Tinbergen (1972) wondered why black-headed gulls always removed eggshells from their nests as soon as the young gulls had emerged. To carry away the pieces of shell meant that the parent bird had to leave the nest when the young gulls needed warmth and protection from possible predators. After a series

of studies in which nests were set out in varying conditions and the researchers concealed themselves to watch the results, Tinbergen discovered that the white inside of the broken eggshell attracted predators to the remaining whole eggs or to the young birds that were in the nest. The gulls' quick removal of eggshells had definite survival value for the species.

Field studies are justified by the importance of the developmental events they investigate. Often the most important phenomena are those that researchers cannot legitimately control.

Experimentation

An experiment involves the investigation of the effects of particular variables on behavior. All the precautions of objectivity, clarity, reliability, and replicability required of controlled clinical and observational study are necessary in the experimental method. However, it is often much easier to attain these goals through an experiment, primarily because the investigator is better able to control and manipulate the variables under study.

Studying behavior through the experimental method is not as unnatural as some might think, and the method has been used successfully in thousands of psychological studies. In a typical experiment, Arthur Jensen and William Rohwer (1965) designed a study to show developmental changes in children's learning. Their subjects were children from kindergarten through the twelfth grade. Jensen and Rohwer showed the children pairs of pictures of common objects. Half of the children at each age level were asked to name each picture, and the other half were asked to construct a sentence that related each pair of pictures. Afterward, all the children were shown the pairs of pictures and were asked to learn the members of each pair well enough so that when one picture was shown, they could recall the other. From the second grade, children who made sentences learned the material much faster. This experiment, therefore, illustrates the powerful effects of requiring a child to relate objects in a meaningful manner through the construction of sentences and thus adds to psychologists' knowledge of learning in children. It is doubtful that this information could have been obtained so efficiently or so convincingly had the researchers relied on naturalistic observation or clinical or field studies.

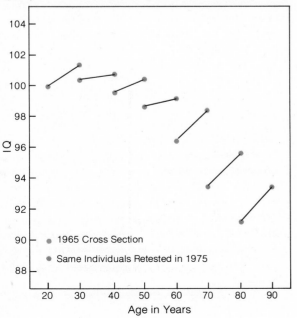

Figure 3.3 Hypothetical example illustrating apparent changes with age in IQ scores. The dots representing average scores of people at different ages tested in a cross-sectional study show a downward trend in IQ score with age. The dots representing average scores of these same samples of people tested again ten years later as part of a longitudinal study show a similar downward trend in IQ score with age, but each age group also shows an increase in the average score. (Adapted from Nesselroade, Schaie, and Baltes, 1972)

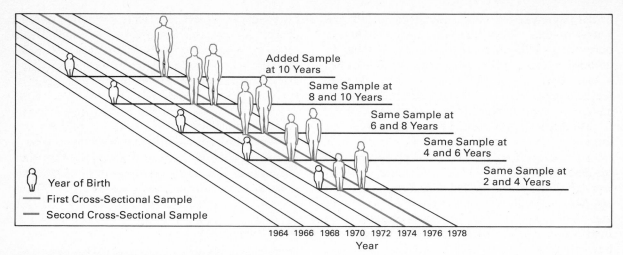

1964 1966 1968 1970 1972 1974 1976 1978
Year

Figure 3.4   A research design that combines cross-sectional and longitudinal research. First, samples of children at each of four ages (two, four, six, and eight) are selected and studied. Two years later the same samples of children are studied again, and another sample of ten-year-olds is included. Using both methods on the same group of children offsets the weaknesses inherent in each type of study.

Longitudinal and Cross-Sectional Designs

Much of the information we have concerning development comes from studies that compare different age groups, called **cross-sectional studies.** Most often the researcher assumes that the differences among such groups are the result of developmental changes. If the samples of people at various ages are not selected carefully, the cross-sectional design has two major flaws: different age groups may be affected by experiences peculiar to their **cohorts** (age-group members), and age-group changes may not represent the pattern of growth for individuals. For example, a cross-sectional study of the decline of IQ scores with age might show a curve like that in Figure 3.3. IQ scores appear to decline with increasing age. Remember, however, that people studied at age eighty in 1975 were born in 1895, whereas those studied at age twenty in 1975 were born in 1955. Much has happened to our cultural and social environment in the time between those two groups of cohorts, and

sociocultural influences affect the development and maintenance of intellectual skills. In fact, there is good evidence that, as a nation, each new generation scores higher on IQ tests, presumably because longer education and mass communications expose more people to the information required to score well on such tests (Baltes and Schaie, 1974). Younger cohorts score higher on IQ tests than older cohorts did at the same age. Thus, what appears to be a dramatic decline in IQ scores over age is in part an effect of the lower scores for older groups throughout their lives. Cross-sectional studies cannot detect cohort changes.

However, not all cross-sectional studies are flawed by cohort effects. If differences appear between closer age groups, such as three- and four-year-olds or even six- and ten-year-olds, it is improbable that cohort effects are responsible. The sociocultural environment changes too slowly to produce such effects in four years. With close age groups, it is more likely that differences are due to development.

Cross-sectional groups also may not show the

actual pattern of individual change, especially for a developmental shift that occurs rapidly. At puberty the growth of any one individual accelerates and decelerates rapidly, but because different individuals begin and end their growth at different times, graphs of group averages will show a smooth curve of growth for the entire cohort. Cross-sectional data alone would not reveal the pubescent growth spurt.

Studies that follow the same subjects over time, **longitudinal studies,** may seem to answer all problems in developmental studies. The same people can be compared with themselves at ages twenty and eighty. But there are problems here, too. The fact that the same people have been studied repeatedly over many years may have affected their development, and the long-term changes that appear in their behavior may be a response to sociocultural shifts as well as evidence of developmental changes. Life-span shifts in the sociocultural environment are obvious. Most people have lived through Sputnik, the assassinations of President John F. Kennedy and Martin Luther King, the Civil Rights Movement, moon landings, the resignation of a President, and so forth. These shifts in our environment may have had profound effects on some aspects of our development.

Neither cross-sectional nor longitudinal studies alone can provide the basic data for developmental studies. Because of this, K. Warner Schaie (1965) has proposed that the two designs be combined to provide controls over the biases in each design. He suggests that researchers sample subjects cross-sectionally and then follow them longitudinally until the samples overlap in age. For example, initial samples drawn at ages two, four, six, and eight can be followed for two years until the two-year-olds are four, the four-year-olds are six, and so forth. A final cross-sectional sample can be drawn at age ten to compare to the longitudinal eight-year-olds, who would then be ten. The effects of repeated testing, if any, will appear as differences between the starting scores for four-year-olds and the ending scores for the two-year-olds at age four. If the whole design is repeated some years later to detect shifts in the sociocultural environment, cohort effects will appear. If important environmental shifts had occurred, the scores at all ages would be higher or lower than the scores in the first study.

Fraternal twins at ages ten and fifteen. One way to understand the relative effects of genes and the environment on growth, IQ, and behavior is to study twins, using both longitudinal and cross-sectional designs for the experiments. (*top:* William MacDonald; *bottom:* Chris Engholm)

The desirability of using both cross-sectional and longitudinal designs becomes clear if we consider linear growth. Height measurements of a cross-sectional sample would indicate that people grow until middle adolescence and then begin to shrink. The "shrinkage" would be due to cohort effects. People born a number of years ago are shorter on the average than people born more recently, and they were always shorter. A longitudinal study of people now in their seventies would show that they grew until late adolescence and then maintained their heights until late adulthood, when they may actually have shrunk a bit. A longitudinal study of a younger cohort would find them reaching maximum growth at an earlier age; because of better nutrition, they are both taller and earlier maturing. In the case of height, it is necessary to separate the truth about development from long-term changes in the sociocultural environment. In the case of other factors, it is important to separate developmental change from the effects of repeated measurements.

Ethical Considerations

In the past few years there has been increased awareness that human research can lead to invasion of privacy and many kinds of social, physical, and psychological risks. As a result, most major scientific and professional organizations have formulated sets of standards and regulations to protect the people who serve as subjects.

Today, any proposed study must pass a number of tests. According to the ethical standards formulated by the American Psychological Association (1972), for example, it is the responsibility of researchers to obtain the informed consent of individuals who serve as subjects. People must be free to participate or not, as they see fit. And all must be protected from harmful psychological or physical stress. Should the procedures used in a study lead to undesirable consequences for any participants, the researcher is expected to detect and correct such consequences, including long-term ones.

Openness and honesty are an essential part of the relationship between a researcher and the people he or she studies. The investigator is expected to tell the participants about all aspects of the research that might affect their readiness to take part and to answer all their questions so they can understand the consequences of their participation. When the study is complete, the investigator is required to tell the participants about the purpose and uses of the research and to clarify any misconceptions that may have come up. All information about participants must remain confidential and anonymous, and the researcher must assume responsibility for all aspects of the research.

Adherence to high ethical standards is especially important in the case of children, adolescents, the infirm, the indigent, and the elderly. They are generally less likely to be fully informed about their civil and human rights and less able to take action to protect them. In research with babies, for example, the parent must give full consent, and when children are studied, informed consent must be obtained from both child and parent. When necessary, the informed consent of those who serve in a parentlike role (e.g., teacher, principal) must be obtained.

Given the subtleties involved in ethical decisions, no guidelines can cover every possible case. Therefore, most schools, hospitals, agencies, and foundations that engage in or sponsor research have established ethics advisory committees to evaluate proposed research, and to monitor studies once they are under way. The job of such a committee is to make sure that the rights of each participant are safeguarded. Although human research is intended to produce new knowledge about human beings, unethical practices do occur, and ethical research sometimes has unforeseen consequences. Ignorance, faulty thinking, or mixed motives can distress or harm the people who participate in studies. By establishing standards, researchers hope to protect participants while ensuring the discovery of knowledge that will help future generations.

SUMMARY

1. Human development is the result of multiple interacting causes operating through heredity—the person's nature—and through environment—the person's nurture. Questions arise over "how" and "how much" each contributes to development.

2. In studying the role of heredity, researchers frequently have studied animal genetics. Such studies help establish general principles and provide important information on the effects of genetic and genetic-environmental interactions. However, they cannot provide specific details about the way these interactions affect human development. The study of individuals of various degrees of relatedness has provided some insight into the way that genetic differences affect the development of human beings. An important concept in understanding research on the effects of genetic factors on human beings is the concept of reaction range, which refers to the limits set by genetic conditions on an individual's possible behavior.

3. The term heritability refers to the relative contribution of genetics to a trait or behavior. As an estimate it varies with who is studied and when. Heritability does not indicate that either genes or environment "cause" the trait or behavior. Instead, the appearance of a trait is a function of both genetic and environmental determinants.

4. Environmental determinants of human development include physical and social factors. Physical factors include those ecological features that maintain life—air, water, food, and light—and those features—life in a tent or apartment—that create different responses.

5. Social determinants include all those effects that cultures have on people and people have on one another in families, peer groups, social institutions, and the media. From birth to death, these influences direct, limit, and enhance the development of the individual.

6. In studying the determinants of human development, different methods have different advantages and disadvantages in terms of their reliability, efficiency, and representativeness. Most of these advantages and disadvantages are associated with a method's degree of control over who is studied, the setting or circumstances, and the behavior that can occur. At one extreme is naturalistic observation and at the other is experimentation, with many types of field and clinical studies in between. Longitudinal and cross-sectional studies, in which the same or different individuals are studied at various ages, provide some of the information needed to investigate different developmental determinants. Ethical considerations are basic to any research design.

Unit II The Beginning of Life

A newborn baby is both an end and a new beginning. The forty weeks of growth within the mother's body suddenly end with birth. No other developmental period will ever end so dramatically in so short a time. Birth represents both separation and deprivation, independence and the necessity for self-reliance. No longer will the baby be able to rely on the resources of the mother's body; he must rely on his own. Much that will distinguish the child for the rest of his life has already happened. The baby's heredity, fully determined at conception, has already had its initial expression in his physical form. An active, inquiring, responsive infant enters the world equipped with a growing body and rapidly expanding motor, sensory, and mental capacities. This unit describes the baby's development within the womb and traces his first four weeks of independent life.

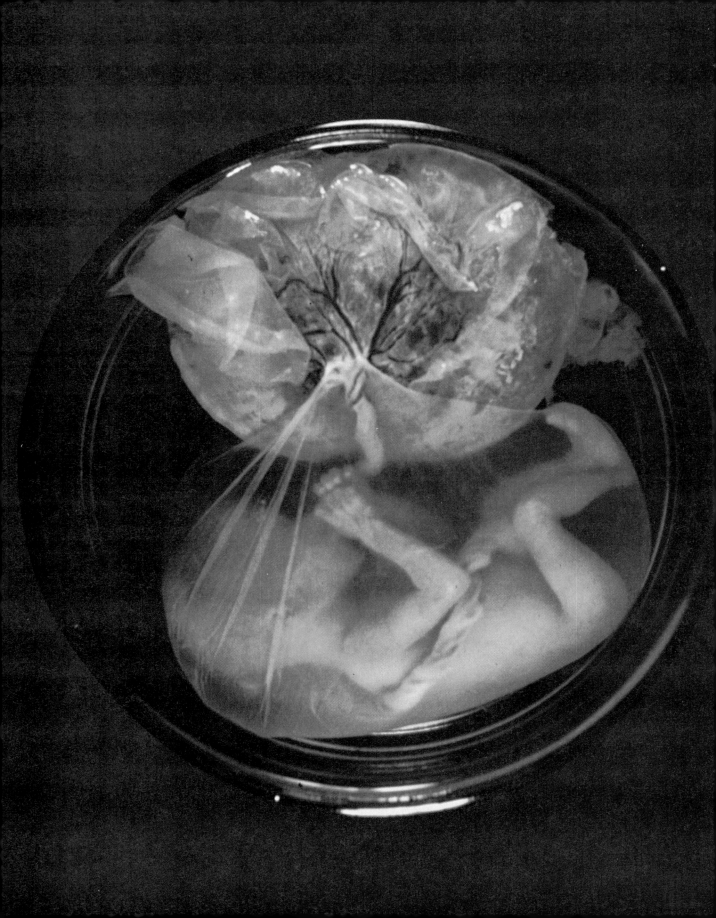

CHAPTER 4
Prenatal Development

HOW LIFE BEGINS
Conception
Chromosomes and Genes
The Production of Sex Cells
Genetic Transmission

PRENATAL GROWTH
The Germinal Period
The Embryonic Period
The Fetal Period

BRAIN DEVELOPMENT

PRENATAL BEHAVIOR

BIRTH
Labor and Delivery
Methods of Childbirth

DEVELOPMENT AND BIRTH COMPLICATIONS
Chromosomal Abnormalities
Amniocentesis
Prematurity
Maternal Health

SUMMARY

Life begins when two cells unite in the mother's body. At that instant, the inheritance of the new individual is established, giving him a unique physical appearance and disposing him toward certain personality characteristics and mental abilities. But this genetic composition is expressed only in an environmental context, and the two together determine how a person looks and behaves. Perhaps the oldest debate in psychology is how much influence inheritance or environment has in producing any given trait. Further, when a characteristic is "inherited," what does that fact tell us about how the trait will develop and about the possibility of changing that characteristic through life experiences?

When one considers that thirty-eight weeks after two tiny cells come together a viable and behaving human being emerges, it is clear that more growth and development take place during the prenatal period than during any comparable segment of life history. The structures and functions that emerge during this time form the basis of the new individual's body and behavior for the rest of his life.

In this chapter we will follow the development of the fertilized egg into a healthy, normal baby who is ready for independent life outside his mother's womb. We will study the transmission of specific traits from parent to child, a subject that was introduced in Chapter 3. The behavior and capabilities of the growing fetus will become apparent, and the problems that can arise in the course of development will be spelled out. We will look at the link between the mother and her unborn child and will discover the importance of maternal health, diet, habits, and emotions.

HOW LIFE BEGINS

During the course of history, people have held a variety of beliefs and superstitions about the beginnings of a human life. Until the

middle of the eighteenth century, it was commonly
believed that life began with a completely formed
and functioning miniature human being. During
the prenatal period this miniature person simply
became larger.

A major debate of this period raged over the
source of this preformed fetus (Needham, 1959).
Some biologists held that it was somehow contained in the mother's egg and that the father's
sperm merely stimulated the growth of the al-
ready-formed baby. Other scientists claimed that
the preformed infant existed in the head of the father's sperm and that the mother's womb served as
an incubator in which the preformed individual
grew. Anton van Leeuwenhoek, the inventor of the
compound microscope, observed semen with his
new instrument and in 1677 claimed that he saw in
the sperm little animals of both sexes who copu-
lated and produced new animals. Other scientists
reported being able to tell the difference between
the semen of donkeys and horses because the animals in the sperm of donkeys had longer ears.

In 1759 Kaspar Wolff asserted that both parents contributed equally to the beginning of life
and that an embryo began as a cluster of globules.
This assertion had major implications. Because it
contended that the very young organism lacked
the organ systems and structures that it must possess at birth, prenatal development had to consist
of the appearance and growth of new cells, structures, and functions, not simply an enlargement of
a preformed individual. More than fifty years
later, Karl von Baer (1827) substantiated this theory when he discovered the mammalian egg cell
under his microscope, and the science of embryology began.

Conception

The life of each person begins at the moment of
conception, when the sperm cell, or **spermatozoon,**
from the father unites with the egg, or **ovum,** of the
mother. The ovum is the largest cell in the human
body, and it can sometimes be seen without a microscope. The eggs mature in the female's ovaries,

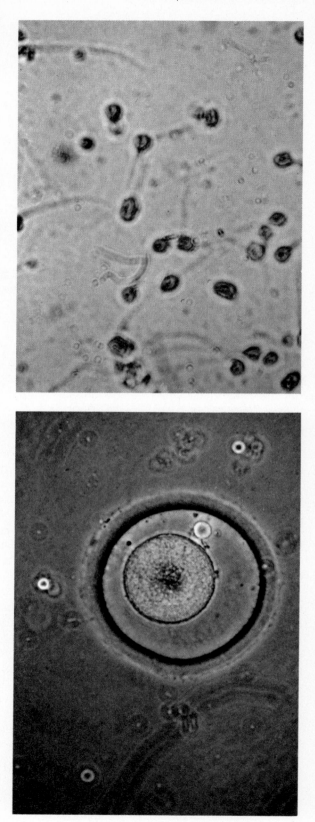

(*Top*) Living, active human spermatazoa, highly magnified. The waving tail propels the sperm toward the
ovum, and the head contains the nucleus, which carries the chromosomes. (*Bottom*) A living human ovum,
magnified. The human egg is smaller than one of the
periods on this page. Unlike many other vertebrate ova,
the human egg lacks large amounts of yolk, and the
fetus must get its nourishment through the placenta.
(From Rugh and Shettles, 1971)

and one egg is released approximately every twenty-eight days during the woman's fertile years. The freed egg, which probably can be fertilized for less than twenty-four hours, travels down the **Fallopian tube** toward the uterus (see Figure 4.2).

Whereas all the eggs that a woman will produce are present in immature form in the ovaries at the beginning of her fertile years, a man continually produces new spermatozoa. During normal intercourse, the male releases approximately 400 million spermatozoa, which may survive in the female genital tract for as long as seven days, although they probably are capable of fertilizing the egg for no more than forty-eight hours.

From one standpoint, it is a wonder that sperm and egg ever get together. First, the egg can be fertilized for only three of the twenty-eight days in a **menstrual cycle.** Second, only a small percentage of the sperm manage to pass through the cervical canal, the small opening in the **cervix,** or lower part of the uterus. Third, the sperm must be able to reach the Fallopian tube by their own motions and/or with the aid of the muscular action of the uterus. Fourth, the egg must be able to enter the Fallopian tube. Fifth, the egg must travel down the Fallopian tube fast enough to meet the sperm while both cells are alive. Such a variety of circumstances must be met before conception can take place that, some physicians estimate, one couple in ten is unable to conceive. On the other hand, it takes only one of those 400 million spermatozoa to fertilize an ovum, and some couples achieve conception after one act of sexual intercourse.

Chromosomes and Genes

The traits and dispositions that parents transmit to their offspring are coded in twenty-three pairs of chromosomes, which are present in every cell of the body. The chromosomes are composed of beadlike strings of genes, microscopic entities containing the codes that produce inherited physical traits and behavioral dispositions. These genetic codes are apparently embodied in a complex chemical called **deoxyribonucleic acid,** or DNA. Whatever one passes on to one's offspring is contained in approximately 10,000 to 50,000 genes composed principally of DNA molecules, which somehow contain a chemical code that guides the development of bones and eyes, brain and fingernails, as well as disposes the offspring toward certain behavioral patterns. All that information is contained in a fertilized cell smaller than the period on this page.

The Production of Sex Cells

Most cells of the human body contain twenty-three pairs of chromosomes, direct copies of the original twenty-three pairs with which each person begins life. There is one major exception, however, and that occurs in the production of the ova and spermatozoa, or **gametes.** At puberty the gametes begin to form by a special kind of cell division called **meiosis.** During meiosis, a normal cell containing twenty-three pairs of chromosomes divides and divides again to produce four cells that con-

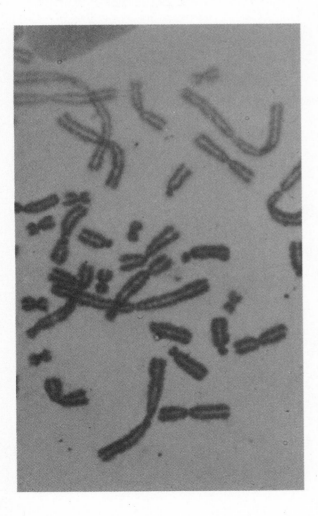

Part of the set of forty-six human chromosomes, magnified and stained. The chromosomes assume this form as they prepare to divide. (Courtesy Leonard Hayflick. Copyright © the President and Fellows of Harvard College)

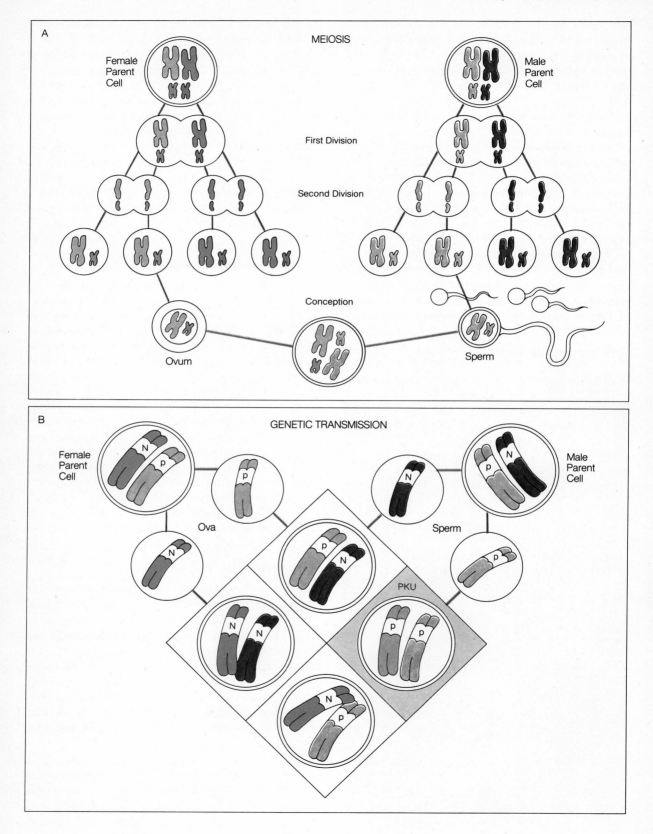

tain one of each type of chromosome. The process begins when chromosomes of the same type start to pair up within the nucleus of a cell. The members of each chromosomal pair divide and gravitate to opposite ends of the cell, which then splits into two cells each containing twenty-three *single* chromosomes rather than twenty-three *pairs.* These cells then reproduce themselves, producing four cells each having a set of twenty-three *single* chromosomes. At conception, when a sperm unites with an egg, the result is a single cell having twenty-three pairs of chromosomes. Figure 4.1A illustrates meiosis in two pairs of chromosomes.

Genetic Transmission

Children sometimes resemble their parents in certain physical characteristics and sometimes do not. For example, a mother and father may both have brown hair, but one of their three children may be blond. How are physical characteristics passed on from parent to child?

Although hair color is a common and easily observed characteristic, its transmission is complicated. It is simpler to explain genetic transmission by examining a characteristic that depends on a single pair of genes. Consider **phenylketonuria,** or PKU, an inherited inability to metabolize phenylalanine, a component of some foods. If this metabolic abnormality is left untreated, the afflicted child will have fair skin and hair, a small head in proportion to body size, eczema, agitated and rest-

less behavior, a stiff gait, and moderate to severe mental retardation.

In order to understand how PKU occurs, let N symbolize the gene corresponding to normal metabolic ability and p represent the gene for PKU. The related genes, N and $p,$ are called **alleles.** Now look at Figure 4.1B, which illustrates the alleles in only one pair of chromosomes. The parent cells in the figure contain the alleles of interest, labeled N and $p.$ In this example, the mother's and father's cells have a gene for both N and $p.$ When the parent cells divide to form gametes, half of the father's sperm cells and half of the mother's ova will contain a gene for PKU (p) and half will contain a gene for the normal metabolic condition $(N).$ During conception, one of four possible combinations of these gametes will result. Depending on which male gamete unites with which female gamete, the new baby will have a genetic inheritance of $NN,$ Np (which is the same as $pN),$ or $pp;$ these are shown in Figure 4.1B. If the selection process were perfectly random, one-fourth of the offspring of these parents would have the combination $NN,$ one-fourth would have $pp,$ and one-half would have $Np.$

But which of these offspring will be normal children, and which will show symptoms of PKU? In this example, the NN baby will be normal, and the pp baby will have PKU. These offspring are **homozygous,** which means that their cells have matching genes for this characteristic. But an Np baby is **heterozygous,** meaning that his cells have different genes for the same trait. Are these Np babies normal, or do they have PKU?

The answer depends on which gene is **dominant** and which is **recessive.** A dominant gene is one whose corresponding trait appears in the individual even when that gene is paired with a different gene for the trait. The paired gene whose corresponding trait fails to appear is recessive. In the case of PKU, the normal gene is dominant over the recessive PKU gene, and therefore Np individuals will be normal.

Notice that there is not a perfect one-to-one correspondence between the genes a person carries and the traits that appear. This lack of correspondence illustrates the difference between **genotype** and **phenotype.** The genotype is the specific combination of alleles that characterize one's genetic make-up, whereas the phenotype is the nature of the trait as it appears in the individual. The genes that produce PKU can combine to form three gen-

Figure 4.1   (*A*) The production of sex cells. Certain cells in the ovaries of the mother and in the testes of the father divide twice in a special pattern of cell division called meiosis to produce gametes—ova and sperm—that have only half the number of chromosomes of the parent cells. The chromosomes occur in the parent cells in pairs, and each chromosome is itself a double strand. For simplicity, only two of the twenty-three pairs of human chromosomes are shown here. In meiosis, first the members of each pair split up (*First Division*), and then the chromosomes themselves split in half (*Second Division*). They regenerate their missing halves in a subsequent step (*next line*). The union of the gametes in conception results in a zygote that has the full number of chromosomes, half from the mother and half from the father.

(*B*) Transmission of alleles in the inheritance of PKU. In this diagram only a single pair of chromosomes is represented. These chromosomes bear the alleles *N* and *p.* Both parents have both forms of the gene, and therefore they produce gametes with chromosomes bearing either the *N* or the *p* gene in equal numbers. Depending on which gametes happen to unite in conception, the new cell may have the alleles *NN, Np, pN,* or *pp.* Because *p* is a recessive gene, only babies with *pp* will have PKU.

otypes: *NN, Np, pp.* But there are only two pheno-types: normal and PKU. The genotypes *NN* and *Np* both produce the normal phenotype because *N* is dominant over *p.* Therefore, there are some differences between one's genetic make-up (genotype) and what one actually looks like and how one behaves (phenotype).

For a variety of reasons, genetic transmission is rarely as simple as it is in the case of PKU. First, dominance is not always all-or-none. That is, there appear to be gradations of dominance, so that one allele for a trait is not totally dominant. The result may be somewhat of an "average" of two extremes. Second, one allele may not express itself unless an allele of quite a different characteristic is also present. Consequently, it is possible to carry a "dominant" gene that does not affect one's phenotype. Third, most traits, especially behavioral ones, are **polygenic,** which means that several genes have an equal and cumulative effect in producing the trait. In other cases, some genes in the combination have more influence than others on the phenotype.

The more scientists study the process of human genetic transmission, the more complex it seems. One simply cannot point to a single gene that is responsible for a given behavioral trait. Later in this chapter we will discuss some of the issues and complexities of genetic transmission.

PRENATAL GROWTH

As soon as a sperm and an egg unite, development begins and progresses at a rapid rate. In approximately thirty-eight weeks, the organism goes from one tiny cell to a living, functioning, and behaving newborn baby.

The course of prenatal development falls into roughly three periods. During the first two weeks after conception, called the **germinal period,** the fertilized egg is primarily engaged in cell division. In the next six weeks, the **embryonic period,** the organism begins to take shape, and its various organ systems begin to form. Thereafter, from approximately eight weeks after conception to birth, the developing organism is called a **fetus.** The total **gestation period** usually lasts about 280 days (forty weeks or nine calendar months) calculating from the beginning of the mother's last normal menstruation (or thirty-eight weeks from conception). The **menstrual age** is the age of the fetus, when calculated in this way.

The Germinal Period

Almost immediately after fertilization, the egg begins the process of cell division that will eventually produce a human body made up of many billions of cells. Although the cells of an adult are highly differentiated according to their location and function in the body (for example, nerve cells are quite different in form and function from muscle cells), the cells at this point in development are all identical.

It is estimated that the fertilized ovum takes approximately three days to progress through the Fallopian tube to the uterus, where it floats freely for another four or five days before becoming **implanted** in the uterine wall. By the end of the first two weeks, the cells have multiplied greatly in number and have begun to differentiate themselves. An outer membrane **(chorion)** and an inner membrane **(amnion)** form a sac that surrounds and protects the developing organism. In addition, the microscope can distinguish the **placenta,** which transmits nourishment and wastes between the mother and the fetus, and three primary layers of cells. These layers are the **ectoderm,** which is the source of future cells composing the skin, sense organs, and nervous system; the **mesoderm,** from which the muscular, circulatory, and skeletal systems will develop; and the **endoderm,** which will give rise to the lining of the intestinal tract and to related organs such as the liver, pancreas, and thyroid.

One phenomenon that needs explanation is how cells become differentiated into nerve, muscle, fat, and blood. Some scientists have speculated that newly produced cells are essentially neutral, or undifferentiated. Somehow, these neutral cells are attracted to locations that need them, and then by some means, probably chemical, they are differentiated to serve the purpose required at that location.

For example, suppose that you cut your hand. Neutral cells are sent to the wound, where they are transformed into specialized skin cells by chemicals apparently released by layers of tissue immediately below the skin. If the wound is not too

Figure 4.2   The early development of the human embryo. Fertilization occurs at the upper end of the Fallopian tube. By the time the fertilized ovum reaches the uterus, it has already divided many times. Within seven or eight days, it is securely implanted in the uterine wall, where the process of prenatal development continues.

deep, the cell differentiation is almost perfect, and there is no scar. However, if the cut is deep enough to destroy the layers that produce the differentiating chemicals, the body's repair job is incomplete, and a scar forms. It is possible that the fetus develops by similarly transforming neutral cells.

By the end of the germinal period, the two-week-old organism is already anchored to the lining of the uterus, which maternal hormones have prepared for the developing egg. With both the organism and its host ready for development, life is on its way.

The Embryonic Period

Within four weeks after conception, the organism is already about one-fifth of an inch long, 10,000 times larger than the original fertilized egg. In addition, its heart is beating to pump blood through microscopic veins and arteries, and there are the beginnings of a brain, kidneys, liver, and digestive

tract and discernible indentations that will eventually become jaws, eyes, and ears.

Organs along the central axis of the body develop first; the extremities develop later. Thus, in the early weeks the organism is literally all head and heart. Later, the lower part of the body begins to enlarge and to assume its newborn proportion and size.

By the end of the embryonic period, the organism is almost an inch long, and it is clearly human. What look like gill slits of a fish are really rudimentary forms of structures in the neck and lower face. What seems to be a primitive tail eventually becomes the tip of the adult spine; the tail reaches its maximum length at about six weeks and then slowly recedes. The head is clearly distinct from the rounded, skin-covered body and accounts for about half the embryo's total size. The eyes have come forward from the sides of the head, and eyelids have begun to form. The face clearly

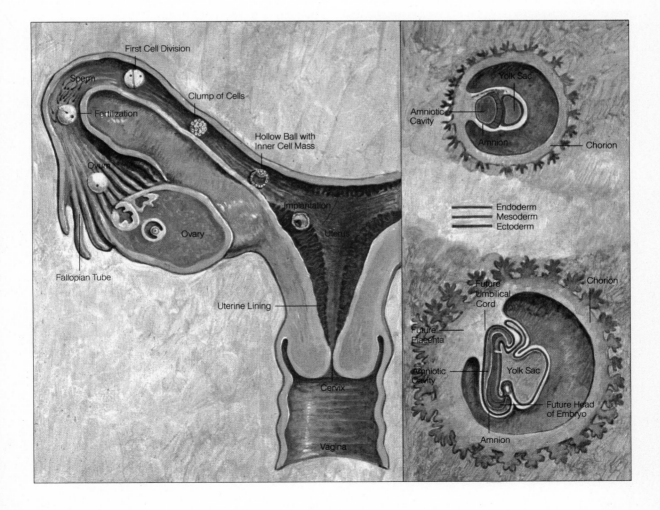

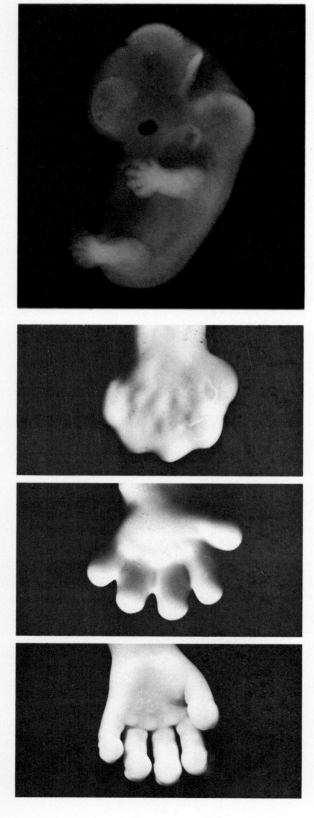

contains ears, nose, lips, tongue, and even the buds of teeth. The knobs that will be arms and legs grow, and in a matter of weeks, they differentiate into hands and feet and then into fingers and toes.

In this early period, the brain sends out impulses that coordinate the functioning of other organ systems. The heart beats sturdily, the stomach produces minute quantities of some digestive juices, the liver manufactures blood cells, and the kidneys purify the blood. One can distinguish testes or ovaries, and the endocrine system has begun to produce hormones. However, all these organ systems are in a primitive form, and it will be several months before they can be considered fully functional (Pritchard and MacDonald, 1976).

The Fetal Period

Approximately eight weeks past conception, when bone cells begin to develop, the developing organism is known as a fetus. Within twelve weeks it has begun to stretch out a little from its C-like posture, and the head is more erect. The limbs are nicely molded, and folds for fingernails and toenails are present. An external inspection could readily determine the sex of the fetus. The lips become separate from the jaws, rudimentary beginnings of teeth are apparent, the nasal passages of the nose have formed, the lungs have acquired their definitive shape, the brain has attained its general structure, the eye is organized, and the retina is becoming layered. The pancreas secretes bile, and the bone marrow has begun to produce blood. At this time the fetus weighs about an ounce and is approximately three inches long.

By sixteen weeks the fetus is approximately six to seven inches long and weighs about four ounces. Until now, its head has been enormous in relation to the rest of its body, but by sixteen weeks the lower part of the body has grown until the head is only about one-fourth of the total body size. The sixteen-week-old fetus looks like a miniature baby. Its face looks "human," hair may appear on the head, bones can be distinguished throughout the body, and the sense organs approximate their final

(Top) Normal embryo at forty days. Note the rudimentary brain, eye, ear, fingers, and toes. (From Rugh and Shettles, 1971)

(Bottom) In the fifth week, hands are a "molding plate" with finger ridges. In the sixth week, finger buds form. In the seventh and eighth weeks, the fingers, thumbs, and fingerprints form, and the touch pads are prominent. (Courtesy Carnegie Institution of Washington)

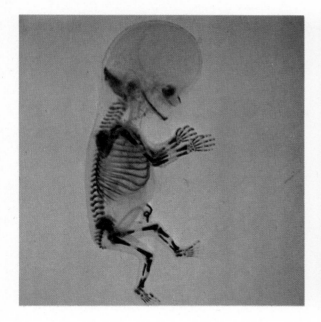

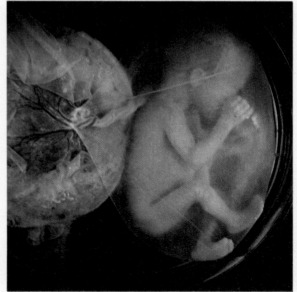

(*Left*) An x-ray of an eight-week-old fetus. The skeleton has developed and the advanced bone formations appear as darkened regions. (*Right*) Human fetus at twelve weeks, with the placenta attached. The placenta provides for the exchange of gases, nutrients, and metabolic wastes between the developing fetus and the mother. (From Rugh and Shettles, 1971)

appearance. All major internal organs have attained their typical shape and plan. Although the fetus could not survive if it were delivered at this point, its development has progressed so far that almost all basic systems and physical characteristics are present, down to hair on the head and sweat glands.

Although most basic systems are present in rudimentary form by sixteen weeks, certain functions necessary for survival outside the uterus are not yet fully developed. One of these functions is the ability to breathe. A necessary component in this process is the liquid **surfactin,** which coats the air sacs of the lungs and permits them to transmit oxygen from the air to the blood. Around the age of twenty-three weeks, the fetus develops a way to produce and maintain surfactin, but if it is born at this time, it often cannot maintain the necessary surfactin levels and may develop **respiratory distress syndrome** (formally called hyaline membrane disease of the lungs) and die. However, by about thirty-five weeks (sometimes earlier), the fetus develops a new system for maintaining surfactin, and this new method will allow it to live outside the uterus (Gluck and Kulovich, 1973).

Generally speaking, 180 days (twenty-six weeks or approximately six months) is regarded as the minimum possible age at which a fetus may survive. Babies have been born and survived from as early as 180 to as late as 334 days after conception, although the normal term of pregnancy is 266

days from conception (280 days or forty weeks from the onset of the last menstrual period). If born much before term, the fetus must be placed in an incubator, which helps regulate the baby's body temperature, facilitate breathing, maintain the acidity-alkalinity balance of the blood, and so forth. Fetuses born after 252 days of gestation (thirty-six weeks) are considered to be of normal term, although unusual circumstances may still make special care necessary for the first few days or weeks of life.

During the final period of prenatal development, at a time when the fetus could survive on its own, its organs step up their activity, and its heart rate becomes quite rapid. Fat forms over its entire body, smoothing out the wrinkled skin and rounding out contours. The fetus usually gains about one-half pound a week during the last eight or nine weeks in the uterus. At birth the average full-term baby is about twenty inches long and weighs a little more than seven pounds, although weight may vary from less than five to more than twelve pounds and length may vary from less than seventeen to more than twenty-two inches.

BRAIN DEVELOPMENT

The development of the central nervous system (brain and spinal cord) is both intricate and extremely fast. It starts out as a cluster of cells. As these cells continue to differentiate and multiply, they form a tubelike structure, which bends over at one end as it develops. This end eventually becomes the brain. By the end of the first four weeks of life, the embryo has a spinal cord and a recognizable brain with two lobes; by the sixteenth week the brain's major structures and shape resemble those of an adult. By the sixteenth week, too, the cortex—a mantle of neural cells covering the cerebral hemispheres—has grown back over the lower parts of the brain.

Although the lower parts of the brain are primarily responsible for sustaining life, the coordination of reflexes, and other primitive behavior, their development is not sufficient to maintain life outside the womb much before twenty-eight weeks. By thirty-two to thirty-six weeks, the cortical areas for motor and sensory behaviors are reasonably mature, as are parts of the primary audition areas. But at birth the remaining and larger mass of the cortex is still very immature.

During the prenatal period, two major events mark cell growth in the brain (Dobbing and Smart, 1974). The first is the development of all the neural cells, or **neurons,** that make up the adult brain. Neurobiologists estimate that the average adult brain has 10 billion neurons. Research indicates that these cells begin to develop when the fetus is about ten weeks old and that all 10 billion are developed by about sixteen to twenty weeks. The second major event involves the continuing growth of these neurons and the growth of other supporting and connecting cells in the brain. The other cells, called **glial cells,** seem to play an essential role in the nourishment of the neurons and in the development around each neuron of a sheath of **myelin,** a fatty substance that keeps nerve impulses channeled along the neural fibers and reduces the random spread of impulses from one fiber to another. This development begins at about twenty weeks and accelerates until the fetus is about twenty-eight to thirty-two weeks old. The glial cells continue to multiply until about the second year after birth, and myelination appears to continue until about the fourth year after birth.

The fetal brain remains immature in other respects. For one thing, the adult cortex is composed of nine types of neurons arranged in six different layers. Not all these cells reach a mature form in the fetal cortex, nor are the cells distributed in the neat, layered arrangement of the mature cortex. Further, according to best estimates, each of the 10 billion neurons in the adult brain has an average of 10 thousand connections with other cells. Connections among cells in the fetal brain are sparse, and the fibers that extend from the neurons are either short and stumpy or entirely absent. Although, as we will see in the next chapter, the newborn infant has many capabilities, it will take time for the almost unbelievably massive and rich interconnection to develop among the neurons. As the nerve circuits form, it is likely to be in a precise order and according to a rigid timetable (Hirsch and Jacobson, 1975).

PRENATAL BEHAVIOR

How early in its life can the fetus respond to stimuli, what kinds of responses does it make, and what kinds of spontaneous behavior does it show? The major behavior that characterizes the fetus is movement. Mothers sometimes report feeling such movement when the fetus is approximately sixteen weeks old, although the muscles of the fetus are capable of movement at about eight weeks.

It is difficult to study prenatal behavior, but some years ago Davenport Hooker (1952) studied embryos and fetuses delivered by Caesarean section but which were too immature to survive. His research shows that by twelve weeks the fetus can kick its legs, turn its feet, close its fingers, bend its wrists, turn its head, squint, frown, open and close its mouth, and respond to touch.

By twenty-three weeks the fetus shows much spontaneous activity, as many pregnant women report. It sleeps and wakes as a newborn does, but it also undergoes sluggish periods not found in the newborn. The fetus even has a favorite position for its naps. By twenty-four weeks it can cry, open and close its eyes, and look up, down, and sideways. By this time it has also developed a grasp reflex and will soon be strong enough to support its weight with one hand. It may hiccup. During the final eight or nine weeks, the fetus is quite active, although its actions become limited by the increasingly snug fit of the uterus.

Behavioral development in the prenatal organism corresponds to the development of its nervous system and of the muscles of its body. The earliest responses found in embryos appear at about seven and one-half weeks. When one strokes the area of the mouth with a fine hair, the fetus responds in a general manner, moving its upper trunk and neck. By nine weeks, the fetus will bend its fingers when the palm of its hand is touched and either curl or straighten its toes in response to a touch on the sole of the foot. By eleven weeks, the fetus can swallow. As the organism develops, more and more of its body becomes sensitive to stimulation, and the response eventually narrows to the area stimulated. Thus, when one touches the mouth, only reflexes about the mouth appear. Within the last few months before birth, the fetus behaves essentially as it does at birth, with grasping, sucking, kicking, and other typical infant reflexes.

Can a fetus learn? The answer is probably yes, depending on what you want to teach it. Lester Sontag sounded a loud noise near a pregnant woman's abdomen. At first the sound produced a large change in fetal heart rate, but after Sontag repeatedly made the noise near the woman's abdomen on successive days, the fetus no longer responded. Apparently, it had adapted to the sound—it had "learned" it in a sense (Sontag and Newbery, 1940). David Spelt (1948) showed that a fetus twenty-eight weeks old or more who responds to very loud noises can also learn to respond to the neutral stimulus of a vibrator applied to the maternal abdomen. Neither of these observations has ever been repeated, although both seem to suggest that a fetus is capable of a rudimentary kind of learning.

BIRTH

Near the end of a pregnancy, the fetus normally lies head down in the uterus, which resembles a large sack with its opening into the vagina constricted by the cervix. The exact mechanisms that begin labor are not well understood. They may involve changes in hormone levels in both mother and fetus. On the mother's side, her pituitary gland releases the hormone, *oxytocin,* her uterus stretches, the relationship of other hormones within her uterus changes, and her body releases a substance that causes the uterus to contract. When the fetus is ready to be born, its adrenal gland produces cortisol and its pituitary produces oxytocin. Although some researchers believe that the production of fetal oxytocin is the signal that begins birth, they have yet to establish the direct transfer

of the hormone through the placenta (Kumaresan et al., 1975).

Labor and Delivery

When the birth process begins, the upper portion of the uterus contracts at regular and progressively shorter intervals while the lower part of the uterus thins out and the cervix dilates to permit the fetus to pass through the birth canal. Later the mother's abdominal muscles also contract in a bearing-down motion. Unless drugs deaden sensations, she usually pushes hard to get the baby out. This process is called labor. For first-born infants, labor often lasts thirteen to fifteen hours, although its actual length varies greatly from mother to mother and is markedly less for later-born children.

Figure 4.3   Models indicating the position of the fetus during passage through the birth canal. (Reproduced, with permission, from the *Birth Atlas*, published by Maternity Center Association, New York)

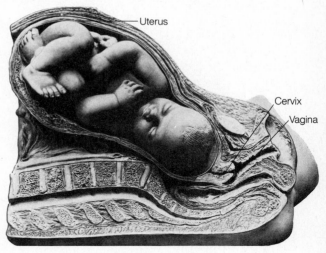

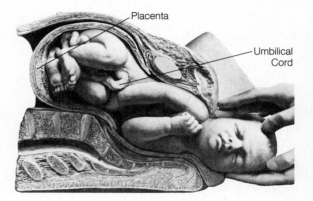

The first stage of labor lasts until the cervix is completely dilated. It usually begins with faint contractions that grow stronger and more frequent. In the second stage of labor, the fetus passes head first through the birth canal and is born, a process that lasts approximately eighty minutes. After birth the physician cleans the baby's nose and mouth with a suction apparatus to make breathing easier and to prevent substances from entering the lungs. Then the umbilical cord is tied and cut. In the final stage of labor, uterine contractions expel the **afterbirth**—the placenta, its membranes, and the rest of the umbilical cord. This process lasts approximately five to twenty minutes, and the afterbirth is immediately examined by the physician to determine whether it is complete and normal.

Not all deliveries proceed in this normal fashion. In a breech delivery, the baby's buttocks appear first, then the legs, and finally the head. Such deliveries can be dangerous because the baby may suffocate before the head emerges. Some babies must be delivered surgically, by Caesarean section, because the mother's pelvis is too small to permit her baby to pass through.

The newborn baby is assessed for appearance (color), heart rate, reflex irritability, activity, muscle tone, and respiratory effort to determine

Many young mothers, convinced that a hospital atmosphere is impersonal and unnatural, are having their babies at home. A trained midwife delivers this baby, a custom that is common in the Netherlands, where about half of all babies are born at home. (© Joel Gordon)

In this home birth, the newborn infant is placed in the mother's arms before the umbilical cord is cut. (Suzanne Arms/Jeroboam)

In the Lamaze method of childbirth, women learn exercises meant to help them have a more natural and less painful delivery. (Lilo Raymond/Woodfin Camp & Assoc.)

whether further medical help is needed. A much-used and practical scoring system for assessing these attributes is known as the **Apgar score** (Apgar and James, 1962). Each of the characteristics is rated 0, 1, or 2 (2 being best), and these scores are added to constitute the baby's Apgar score, which may vary from 0 to 10.

Methods of Childbirth

For a good many years, American obstetrical practices were generally accepted by women and physicians alike as the best possible care for both mothers and babies. But within the past few years, a growing number of parents and medical personnel have seriously questioned the procedures in many American hospitals, in which labors were regarded as difficult and painful, drugs were routinely given, and episiotomies (surgical incisions to enlarge the vaginal orifice) and forceps were used to speed the birth process.

Anthropologists reported that childbirth varied dramatically around the world and that in cultures that regarded birth as fearful and hidden, women often had prolonged and difficult labors. On the other hand, in cultures that regarded birth as an open, easy process, women generally had short, uncomplicated labors (Mead and Newton, 1967).

Grantly Dick-Read (1944), a British physician who had noticed that some of his patients found childbirth a relatively peaceful, painless experience, believed fear generated a tension that produced pain among most women. His urging of what he called "natural childbirth" met with some success, and his techniques, combined with the more recently introduced Lamaze method, have brought about changes in the way many obstetricians handle childbirth. In the Lamaze method, women learn to substitute new responses for learned responses of pain, and by concentrating on breathing, try to inhibit painful sensations (Chabon, 1966).

The rising popularity of the Lamaze method has gradually led many American hospitals to change their procedures. In most cities, a husband may accompany his wife into the delivery room, where he can offer her emotional support and can participate in the birth process. Further, some of the routine hospital customs, from automatic medication to episiotomy, that tend to make birth an abnormal and unpleasant procedure, have been eliminated for normal deliveries in a number of hospitals.

Frederick Leboyer (1975), a French obstetrician, has taken the psychological approach to childbirth a step further. He focuses on the emotions and sensations of the baby, urging peace and quiet, dim lights, delay in severing the umbilical cord, body contact for newborns, and an immediate bath in warm water that approximates the conditions within the womb. Leboyer contrasts the traditional picture of a screaming newborn held upside down by its ankles with the smiling, bright-eyed, contented infants delivered by his method.

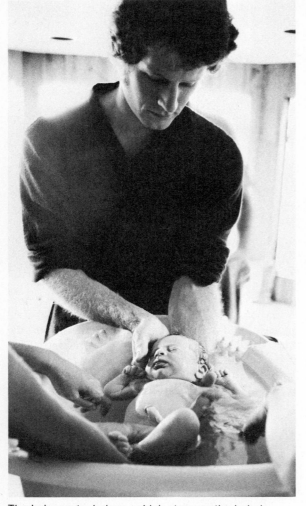

The Leboyer technique, which stresses the baby's emotional wellbeing, calls for an immediate bath in warm water, which is like the amniotic fluid of the uterine environment. (Suzanne Arms/Jeroboam)

DEVELOPMENT AND BIRTH COMPLICATIONS

Whereas most pregnancies follow a normal course of development and most babies are normal and healthy, a genetic abnormality or an environmental factor will occasionally affect the developing fetus. Some of the resulting defects are minor, some respond to medical or surgical intervention, and others are so serious that they threaten the life of the baby.

Chromosomal Abnormalities

When a cell divides to form a gamete, the process may go wrong. During meiosis, a pair of chromosomes may fail to separate, so that one of the gametes has one chromosome too many and the other lacks a chromosome. If the missing chromosome is a sex chromosome, the fertilized egg may live to develop into a baby that suffers from **Turner's syndrome.** Such children tend to have short stature, a webbing or shortening of the neck, a broad-bridged nose, low-set ears, and short, chubby fingers. They generally lack secondary sex characteristics and have mild to moderate mental retardation.

The cell with an extra chromosome may produce a person with an abnormal number of chromosomes in all his cells. Each of the twenty-three pairs of chromosomes has been numbered by researchers. If the fertilized egg has an extra Chromosome 21 (three instead of two), the egg will develop into a baby who suffers from **Down's syndrome** (formerly called mongolism). These children tend to be short and stocky and to have a broad nose bridge, a large, protruding tongue, an open mouth, square-shaped ears, a broad, short neck with extra, loose skin over the nape, and large folds of skin above the eyes that give the child an "oriental" appearance. These children frequently have congenital heart disease and other problems and often do not live past the teens. They have moderate to severe mental retardation, although the extent of retardation varies considerably from case to case.

Down's syndrome is caused in one of two ways. In one case, it arises when extra material from Chromosome 21 becomes attached to another chromosome. This process is much rarer than the other, but the tendency is inherited and is not related to the mother's age. The other cause of Down's syndrome arises when an error in cell division produces an offspring with an extra chromosome, a genetic make-up unlike that of either parent. This tendency is not inherited. The likelihood of producing children with Down's syndrome through this process increases markedly as the mother ages. For some reason, Chromosome 21 is more likely to fail to separate during meiosis in older women. Some studies show that the risk of producing a child with Down's syndrome is only about 1 in 2,500 for mothers less than twenty years old, 1 in 1,900 for mothers twenty-five to twenty-nine years old, and 1 in 1,000 for mothers thirty to thirty-four years of age, but the ratio rises to about 1 in 100 for mothers forty to forty-four years old and 1 in 50 for forty-five-year-old mothers (Frias, 1975). Other abnormalities also occur more frequently in children born to older mothers, which is the reason most geneticists encourage parents to have their children before the mother reaches forty.

Amniocentesis

Down's and Turner's syndromes are only two of many possible chromosomal abnormalities. In addition, as we will see in a later section, a fetus can suffer from a variety of life-threatening diseases. Obviously, it would be helpful to be able to detect a chromosomal abnormality or potentially fatal disease early in the course of pregnancy.

Fortunately, it is possible for a physician to insert a hollow needle through the maternal abdomen and draw out a sample of amniotic fluid. This process is called **amniocentesis.** It should be done sometime between the fourteenth and sixteenth week after conception.

The fetus sheds cells into this fluid, and if the fetal cells in the sample of amniotic fluid are grown in a culture, technicians can perform chromosomal analyses that will detect abnormalities such as Down's syndrome, Turner's syndrome, and others. In addition, the chemical composition of the amniotic fluid frequently provides clues to other diseases and reveals whether the fetus can produce enough surfactin to avoid respiratory distress when it is born. In addition, tests can detect the blood group and sex of the fetus. However, the process carries a slight risk for the fetus and is not used routinely.

Prematurity

A historical problem in dealing with the subject of the premature baby is the definition of that term. Years ago, "premature" simply referred to the baby that was born before **term, a gestational age** of 266 days from conception. This definition proved to be inadequate, because some early babies were of normal weight and health. Moreover, some babies born late had serious weight deficiencies and reduced abilities to survive. As a result, the definition of prematurity came to be made in terms of birth weight, and newborn babies were considered premature if they weighed less than 2,500 grams (about 5½ pounds) at birth, regardless of their gestational age. This criterion has also proved to be inadequate, because some newborns who weigh less than 5½ pounds may be less than full term but may otherwise be perfectly normal.

The potential problem baby is the one who is underweight for his gestational age, a condition referred to as **small-for-dates.** Under such circumstances, it is likely that some aspect of development has gone awry and has inhibited fetal growth.

Some babies are simply born small. For example, a baby may weigh only two pounds; if this baby was born substantially before term, his young gestational age explains his small size. If he gets proper premature-infant care, he may show an accelerated "catch-up growth" once he reaches approximately five pounds. (Catch-up growth is discussed in more detail in Chapter 6.) By three years of age, he may be of average height and weight. In contrast, the small-for-dates infant of two pounds who spent the full 266 days in the womb is likely to have physical problems. Whatever circumstance kept him from gaining weight also seems to inhibit his catch-up growth. Thus, a small-for-dates infant is likely to remain somewhat shorter and lighter in weight than one would expect (Cruise, 1973).

Maternal Health

Although the environment within the uterus is usually stable, it is not immune to influences that can alter or kill the developing organism. When the mother is exposed to excessive x-rays or other radiation, especially in the first few months of pregnancy, the fetus may be in danger of malformation. Deficient secretion of certain hormones from the mother's endocrine glands may affect fetal development, and the incompatibility of an inherited blood substance (the Rh factor) between mother and child can, if not detected, result in premature labor, mental retardation, or heart defects. Medication taken by the mother and nutrition can also affect the fetus.

Because most of the basic organ systems develop in the first third, or **trimester,** of pregnancy, problems in maternal health are likely to have a greater impact on the fetus at this time than later. Timing is apparently the crucial factor in determining whether an environmental influence will produce an abnormality in the developing fetus. If some destructive agent is introduced at the time an organ is forming, that organ may never develop fully. However, the agent may have less serious effects on organs already formed or those that are not ready to make their appearance.

Disease   If a pregnant woman contracts rubella (German measles) during the first trimester, the disease may cause such abnormalities in the developing fetus as blindness, deafness, brain damage, and heart disease. Fortunately, not all babies born to mothers who have suffered from rubella are abnormal, but the earlier the mother catches the disease, the more likely it is that her baby will be affected. A study by Richard Michaels and Gilbert Mellin (1960) indicates that 47 percent of the babies born to mothers who had rubella during the first month of pregnancy were abnormal, whereas 22 percent of babies whose mothers had the disease in the second month and 7 percent of those whose mothers contracted it in the third month were seriously affected.

Other diseases in the mother can also have unfortunate consequences for the fetus. Two that are approaching epidemic proportions in the American adult population are **syphilis** and **gonorrhea.** Although the placenta manages to screen a good many of the organisms that cause syphilis, some make their way from the mother's blood through the placenta, transmitting the disease to the fetus. Therefore, if a pregnant woman is in only the first or second stage of syphilis, with symptoms of canker sore, rash, or fever, and if she receives treatment, her baby is likely to be born without ill effects. But if she remains untreated or if she is in a more severe stage of the disease, the baby may be born with congenital syphilis. If the mother has a mild case of the disease, her baby may have a rash, anemia, jaundice, or other mild problems, but if the mother is seriously infected, her baby may suffer a wide variety of debilitating and severe abnormalities.

As the fetus moves down the birth canal, it can come into contact with the **gonococcus,** the bacterium that produces gonorrhea. A number of years ago, many babies became blind when their eyes were infected during the birth process. Because many women have gonorrhea without showing any symptoms, it has become common practice to place drops of silver nitrate or penicillin in the eyes of all newborn babies. The practice has almost wiped out this kind of blindness.

Maternal Sensitization   Human blood comes in many types. Most are not compatible, which is why a doctor who administers a transfusion always makes sure that a person receives blood that matches his or her own. Generally, no serious incompatibility exists between a mother and her baby, because blood types are transmitted according to the genetic principles discussed earlier. However, in about 1 in 200 births, there will be a crucial difference in the Rh factor of the blood of the mother and her baby.

This occurs when the mother is Rh negative and the father is Rh positive, and their child is born with the dominant Rh-positive factor. Unless the mother has previously received a transfusion of Rh-positive blood, there will usually be no problem when their first baby is born. The mother's and baby's blood circulations are kept separate by the placental barrier, so that only slight mixing occurs during pregnancy. This mingling of blood is increased at birth, when the membranes of the placenta are ruptured. However, if this couple has another baby and that baby is also Rh positive, it may suffer serious complications. In less than 10 percent of such cases, the fetus develops what is called **erythroblastosis.** In these pregnancies, the mother's immune system produces substances that cross the placenta, enter the baby's circulatory system, and begin destroying its developing red blood cells, causing it to become anemic and lack oxygen and nutritional supplies. Sometimes the baby is stillborn. If it survives, such a baby may become mentally retarded or have cerebral palsy.

At one time, it was necessary to monitor the Rh-negative mother's blood throughout pregnancy and, if she began to show signs of incompatibility, be prepared to exchange completely the newborn baby's blood by means of massive transfusions. Fortunately, there is now a relatively simple treatment for Rh incompatibility. The Rh-negative mother is given an injection soon after the delivery of each Rh-positive child, stopping the formation of immune substances in her blood and making her body safe for the development of her next Rh-positive baby (Freda et al., 1975).

Should the injection be omitted, the presence of erythroblastosis can be detected by amniocentesis. In such cases, blood compatible with that of the mother can be transfused into the umbilical vein of the fetus, which generally results in the delivery of a living but probably very sick baby.

Nutrition   Almost all vitamins, minerals, and nutrients are transported to the fetus through the placenta. The fetus stores none of these necessary substances against the time of its independent existence except iron. Consequently, the nutritional state of the mother, especially during the first trimester, appears to be important for normal development.

Severely deficient maternal diets are associated with increased rates of abnormality (Robinson and Robinson, 1965). Diets deficient in calcium, phosphorus, and vitamins B, C, and D are associated with higher frequencies of malformed fetuses. During the German occupation of the Netherlands in the 1940s, when food became extremely scarce, the rate of stillbirths and premature births increased among Dutch women, and birth weight and birth length of their babies decreased. After the war, when food again became plentiful, these rates returned to normal (C. Smith, 1947). Additional data supporting the importance of adequate prenatal nutrition for fetal development come from depressed areas of the United States and from other countries where individuals customarily exist on relatively poor diets. In these regions, dietary supplements (both protein and calories) have led to improved maternal health, higher infant birth weight, and reduced levels of disease and death among infants (Pitkin, 1976).

A review of the findings on maternal nutrition clearly shows that a poor maternal diet can be dangerous to normal prenatal development, but it is less clear how serious and widespread the effects of minor deficiencies in the mother's diet are on the developing fetus. However, there are many indications that maternal and fetal well-being may be affected by less than adequate nutrition.

Drugs and Smoking   A golden rule of obstetric practice has been to advise women to take as little medication during pregnancy as possible. The thalidomide tragedies of the 1960s, when many mothers who took the sedative thalidomide during the early weeks of pregnancy produced babies with grossly deformed arms and legs, vividly illustrated the terrible consequences of certain drugs.

Of more recent concern are the possible effects on the developing fetus of marijuana, amphetamines, and heroin and of hallucinogenic drugs such as LSD, psilocybin, mescaline, and DMT (Fort, 1970). Initial research reports suggested that these drugs may be **mutagenic;** that is, they may

Many fathers are taking an active role in the births of their children. This woman, who is in the early stage of labor, will receive encouragement and emotional support from her husband throughout labor and delivery. (Mariette Pathy Allen)

alter the genetic structure of the sex cells. In contrast to maternal diet and disease, mutagenic drugs may affect fetal development even though the mother stops using them before she becomes pregnant. More recent articles have questioned whether the use of these drugs is indeed associated with genetic abnormalities (Dishotsky et al., 1971). However, if the mother takes certain drugs during pregnancy, fetal malformations may be more likely than if she does not. Sometimes the newborn infant of a heroin user must go through withdrawal, because heroin can pass through the placental barrier.

Several years ago a small group of pediatricians in the United States and Europe noticed that babies born to alcoholic mothers often suffered from what has become known as *fetal alcohol syndrome*. This observation led Kenneth Jones (1975) at the University of California at San Diego and others to follow the pregnancies of alcoholic women. These first studies showed that a baby born to an alcoholic mother may be small-for-dates, may have an odd, conical-shaped head, and may be mentally retarded. These initial findings sparked the establishment of research programs at several places in the United States and France. The programs are designed to discover just when, how, and why maternal alcohol consumption causes such detrimental effects.

Animal research suggests that it is not just the alcoholic mother who risks malformation of her unborn infant, but that even moderate dosages of alcohol may cause malformations (Chernoff, 1977). At present it is not known whether small amounts of alcohol are likely to harm a developing human fetus, but some experts urge pregnant women to abstain from drinking during the course of their pregnancy.

Even cigarette smoking can influence the fetus. Cigarette smoking by pregnant women who normally do not smoke produces an increase in fetal heart rate. It is possible that heavy smokers do not eat properly, and the resulting dietary deficiency may have a greater impact on the fetus than the inhalation of nicotine and tar. Recent studies have shown that mothers who smoke during pregnancy give birth to babies who are, on the average, lighter and smaller (Butler and Goldstein, 1973).

Emotional Condition   It is not far-fetched to suspect that a woman who is pregnant and under considerable emotional stress is likely to produce a newborn baby that is in some way changed because of her emotional situation. The effect of maternal emotions has been a frequent subject of folklore.

Some scientific investigations have suggested that the mother's emotional state can indeed influence her offspring. A number of researchers have demonstrated that stressful experiences in human and rat mothers during pregnancy affect the activity level, birth weight, heart rate, motor development, and emotionality of their offspring (Joffe, 1965; Thompson, 1957). When mothers are under intense, brief emotional stress, their babies' move-

ments increase for only a short time, but when mothers undergo long-standing emotional stress, their babies' activity is greatly prolonged and may reach ten times the normal level (Sontag, 1966).

Abortion   Sometimes pregnancies are terminated, and the developing organism is expelled or removed from the uterus. If this happens spontaneously and without deliberate interference on the part of the mother or a physician, it is called a **miscarriage** or **spontaneous abortion** when the fetus is less than twenty weeks old and a **premature delivery** if the fetus is older. Years ago, it was popularly thought that miscarriages and spontaneous abortions were nature's way of eliminating an abnormal fetus and that such an event, although sad, should be viewed as a blessing. Today, science provides support for this notion; examinations of spontaneously aborted fetuses indicate a much higher rate of abnormalities than are found among normal, live births.

There is some evidence that male fetuses are spontaneously aborted more often than female fetuses. Although it is difficult to make such estimates, it is believed that approximately 130 to 150 males are conceived for every 100 females, but only about 106 males are born for every 100 females (Beatty and Gluecksohn-Waelsch, 1972). Consequently, it would appear that the prenatal death rate is higher for males than for females, a proposition that squares with the fact that following birth, females resist infection better, survive the infancy period more often, and live longer than males do (Fryer and Ashford, 1972).

Since the United States Supreme Court upheld the right of abortion, legal **induced abortions** have been more frequent. Physicians prefer to abort a fetus before it is twelve weeks old, because it is then a relatively simple procedure involving the use of suction to remove the embryo or fetus, together with the uterine lining that sloughs off during a normal menstrual period. From twelve to twenty weeks, an abortion usually requires injecting a substance into the amniotic fluid surrounding the fetus so as to make the uterus contract. This is a more difficult procedure and carries a greater risk to the mother. After twenty weeks, induced abortion is not advisable because there is a chance of delivering a baby who has a remote possibility of surviving.

The decision to have an abortion, especially when the life or health of the mother is in no danger, often presents complicated legal, psychological, social, and moral problems. From society's point of view, one important legal question is whether a fetus has a right to be born, and if so, at what point in his development does this right begin? Another important question is whether a woman has the right to determine how many children she will bear and when she will bear them. These issues become the focus of passionate debate and personal conflict.

In spite of all the possible complications of the prenatal period set forth in this chapter, most babies come into the world as normal individuals. As each baby emerges from the dark of the uterus, he ends his most intimate human relationship. Within the womb, he was completely dependent on his mother for the automatic satisfaction of all his needs. At birth he starts his life as a separate individual. In the next chapter, we will look at the beginnings of independent life—the world of the newborn child.

SUMMARY

1. The life of each person begins at the moment of conception, when the father's sperm cell, or spermatozoon, unites with the mother's egg, or ovum. These gametes each have twenty-three single chromosomes made up of genes, which make possible the genetic transmission of traits and predispositions from parents to their offspring.

2. The complex processes of genetic combination determine the offspring's genotype, the unique combination of genes that he carries. The phenotype, or physical expression of those genes, is often different from the genotype because some genes are dominant and some are recessive. The inherited metabolic abnormality called PKU appears when two recessive genes for the trait are paired. The dominant normal gene masks the gene for PKU.

3. During a 266-day gestation period, the organism rapidly progresses from a fertilized egg engaged in cell division (germinal period) to an embryo with organ systems beginning to take shape (embryonic period) to a fetus that increasingly resembles a human being (fetal period).

4. The central nervous system starts as a cluster of cells, develops rapidly, and by twenty weeks all the neurons that make up the adult brain have formed. Behavioral development corresponds to development of the fetal nervous system and muscles. At eight weeks, the fetus is capable of movement, and by twenty-eight weeks, a rudimentary kind of learning. Twenty-six weeks is the minimum possible age at which a fetus may survive outside the womb.

5. Birth begins with labor, in which strong uterine contractions push the infant and the afterbirth through the birth canal. The physician then evaluates the baby's appearance and functioning. The experience of childbirth varies dramatically around the world; the popularity of natural methods of childbirth has led to changes in the way American hospitals manage birth.

6. Complications occasionally occur in prenatal development and birth. Chromosomal abnormalities that occur during meiosis (detectable by a process involving amniocentesis) can result in a missing or extra chromosome, which often creates physical abnormalities. In prematurity, the small-for-dates baby, who at birth is underweight for his gestational age, is the potential problem baby.

7. Maternal health, including diseases, nutrition, use of drugs, and emotional stress, can also complicate prenatal development, depending on timing and other factors. Pregnancies are sometimes terminated through the natural processes of miscarriage and spontaneous abortion, or a legal induced abortion, a focus of heated debate.

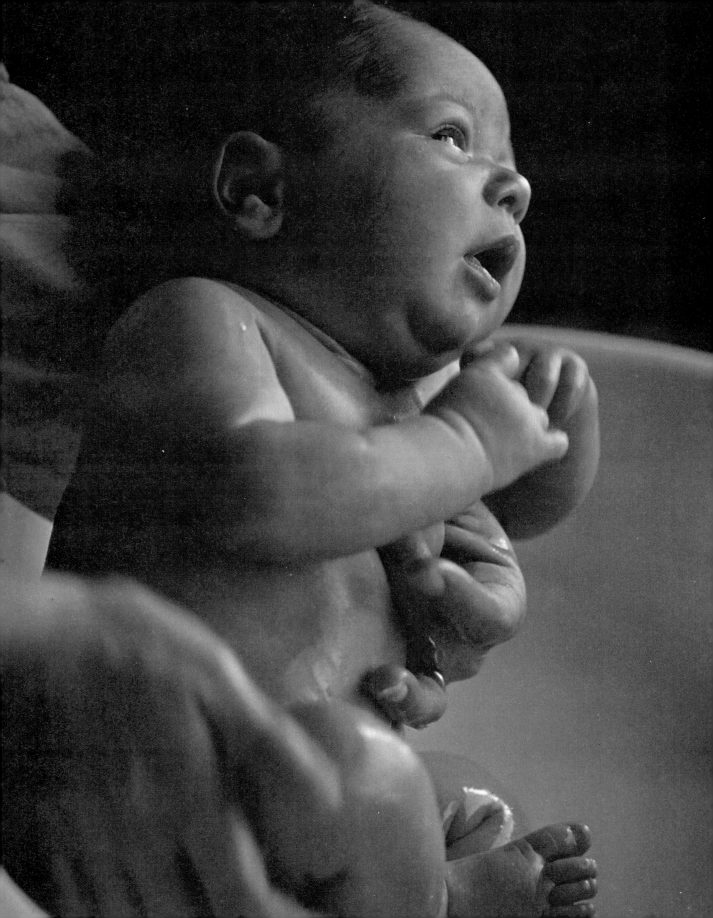

CHAPTER 5
The World of the Newborn

BIRTH: THE NEWBORN

BASIC FUNCTIONS AND RHYTHMS
Temperature
Sleep
Feeding
Elimination
Sucking

REFLEXES AND SENSORY CAPABILITIES
Reflexes
Sensory Capabilities

PERCEPTION AND ATTENTION
Visual Attention
Auditory Attention

ADAPTING TO THE WORLD
Memory and Perceptual Analysis
Conditions for Learning

PERSONALITY AND SOCIAL RELATIONS
Activity, Irritability, Responsiveness
Social Relations

SUMMARY

A newborn baby is a curious mixture of competence and incapacity. All his vital organs are formed and functional. Unlike the newborn kitten or puppy, his eyes are open. He can see and hear and smell; he can cry and feed and move his limbs. The evolution of his species, the genetic mixture presented him by his parents, and his experiences in the womb have already begun to shape his development and behavior.

Yet until recently, other ideas have dominated thought about the human newborn. One was championed by John Locke (1690), who proposed that a newborn baby comes into the world nearly devoid of behavioral dispositions and that the child accumulates all mental abilities and personality through learning and experience. Many years later, the American psychologist William James (1890) supposed that the world must appear terribly chaotic to such a naive baby, "assailed by eyes, ears, nose, skin, and entrails at once, [who] feels it all as one great blooming, buzzing confusion. . . ." These scholars emphasized the helplessness of the human newborn, who possessed almost no structure or functions to deal with his new environment and who waited passively for the environment to fill his unmarked psychological notebook with the marks of social and mental experiences.

In the last decade there has been considerable scientific interest in the psychological world of the human newborn. Recent studies suggest that Locke and James were wrong. In this chapter we will see two babies, Matt and Lauren, enter the world, each possessing a variety of functions and skills to cope with their environment and sample its character. As we follow them through the first few weeks, it will become plain that neither Lauren nor Matt is a passive sponge that soaks up the events taking place before them; instead, they are both active, searching, dynamic forces who create much of their own experience.

We will discover that although newborn babies spend most of their time asleep, their bodies are remarkably prepared for life outside the womb. We will find that many of Matt's and Lauren's basic body functions, such as sleeping and waking, hunger and thirst, sucking, elimination, and body temperature, are kept in balance according to rhythmic biological schedules. Various studies will demonstrate their possession of a set of reflexes, many of which they will lose in a few weeks, that help them accomplish the tasks of feeding and coping with this strange environment. We will look at Matt's and Lauren's sense organs and find that most of them are functional, or soon will be, and that they use them in an active and selective search of their environment. As we will discover, Matt and Lauren are capable of learning, and each possesses the rudiments of a unique personality and temperament. Finally, we will see how the way they look and listen or the way they quiet when upset may provide the roots for their different social developments, which begin with their parents.

The technical term for a newborn baby is **neonate,** a word derived from Greek and Latin terms. Although some would limit the neonatal period to the first week of life and others would limit it to the first two weeks, most researchers agree that we can refer to a baby as a neonate until the end of his or her first month of independent life (Pratt, 1954).

BIRTH: THE NEWBORN

To most of us, the thought of a little baby brings to mind images of a warm, roly-poly, cuddly, cooing bundle of softness and joy. Although this characterization will be apt in a few weeks, the sight of the newborn baby sometimes disappoints, if not shocks, parents. Although most parents regard their own babies as beautiful, outsiders often disagree. One of America's earliest child psychologists, G. Stanley Hall (1891), described the neonate as arriving with its "monotonous and dismal cry, with its red, shriveled, parboiled skin . . . , squinting, cross eyed, pot bellied, and bow legged. . . ." Others have likened the physical appearance of newborns like Matt to that of a defeated prize fighter—swollen eyelids, puffy bluish-red skin, a broad, flat nose, ears matted back at weird angles, and so forth. Of course, if one considers the wet, cramped quarters of the uterus and the violent thrusting necessary for his delivery, his ragged appearance is not surprising.

At the moment of birth, the newborn emerges blotched with his mother's blood and covered with a white greasy material called **vernix,** which has lubricated him for passage through the birth canal. His puffy, wrinkled appearance derives in part from the presence of fluid and small pads of fat under his skin. Some newborns have fine hair, called **lanugo,** over parts of their body. When the baby emerges, the lanugo appears pasted to his skin by the greasy vernix, but after he is cleaned and dried, he may look quite furry for a few weeks until the lanugo disappears.

A newborn baby often looks somewhat battered. For example, his head may be oddly shaped or even peaked, a condition made possible by the fact that the "bones" of his skull are not yet hard and consist of overlapping pieces of cartilage. This condition allows his head to compress so that he can emerge through his mother's pelvis. As a result, his head may be lumpy: hard in some places and soft in others. In fact, the soft areas at the crown of his head that lack cartilage frequently

A normal premature baby, showing lanugo hair on the face and illustrating the shape and proportion of facial features characteristic of most newborns. (A. K. Tunstill)

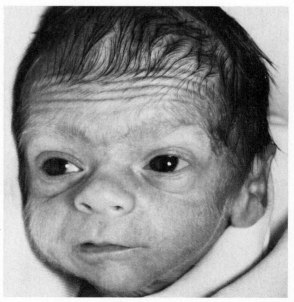

pulsate up and down as his blood supply is pumped about his brain. At the other end of his body, his legs are often bowed, and his feet may be pigeon-toed or even cocked at strange angles because his legs were tucked around him in the cramped quarters of the uterus.

The newborn baby looks odd, and he may sound strange as well. In the womb, he was suspended in liquid, and he arrives with his nasal and oral passage filled with *amniotic fluid* and mucus. In Western hospitals, the physician cleans these passages with a suction bulb as soon as the baby's head has emerged from the uterus so that the newborn does not inhale this liquid into his lungs with his first gasping breath. However, sometimes a little remains, and bursts of rapid gasps, chokes, gags, coughs, and pauses can sound like a badly operating steam engine.

After the umbilical cord is tied and cut, a nurse washes the vernix from the newborn's body with a medicated soap, drops silver nitrate or penicillin into his eyes to prevent infection, makes simple tests for certain diseases (such as PKU), and then swaddles him and allows him to sleep.

Although a newborn will occasionally jerk or cough up mucus, his first sleep is usually quite deep. He is difficult to arouse, and even a loud sound may fail to elicit any obvious response. During this sleep, his body is preparing to function on its own. In the womb the placenta linked his circulatory, digestive, temperature regulation, and excretory systems with those of his mother, but now his own physiological equipment must take over these necessary functions. While these systems are being balanced and tuned, a baby frequently does not eat. His stores of fats and fluids tide him over until his first nourishment, which may take place within several hours of birth or may not occur for several days. As a result of this delay in feeding, most newborns lose weight during the first few days of life.

BASIC FUNCTIONS AND RHYTHMS

Fortunately, the newborn is not thrust into the world without some mechanisms to keep his body systems in balance. A certain pattern or rhythm characterizes many of these basic body functions.

Temperature

The human being is a warm-blooded animal, which means that his body takes steps to keep its temperature within a certain range. In the newborn, temperature regulation is important because the functions performed by most cells and organs are governed by enzymes that can act only within a narrow range of temperature. If the baby's temperature is much lower than the optimum, several of his body functions might slow to dangerous levels. For example, his metabolic rate might decline so much that he dies. If his temperature is too high, his physiological activity might be too rapid, triggering a mechanism that tends to shut down enzyme activity. Moreover, when a newborn is too hot, he tends to breathe more rapidly, his blood becomes too acid, and several other biochemical and physiological systems are thrown out of balance. Consequently, the baby must maintain a relatively constant temperature.

When adults become overheated, their metabolism slows, their blood vessels dilate so that more blood can go to the body surface where heat is dissipated into the air, they sweat and lose heat through evaporation, and they pant and release heat by exhalation. Conversely, when adults are too cold, they conserve heat by shunting blood away from the surface of the body, where it would cool, and they may move around or shiver, thus generating heat. In adults these are surprisingly efficient systems; few people ever have difficulty regulating their body temperature.

The newborn baby, in contrast, has a problem. In proportion to body weight, the newborn has more surface area exposed to cool air and less insulating fat than an adult. Together these factors mean that a newborn loses heat almost four times as fast as an adult does (Brück, 1961). The newborn rapidly develops mechanisms to deal with this problem. Within fifteen minutes of birth, premature and full-term babies will respond to cold by constricting surface blood vessels and increasing their heat production. Two or three hours later, the newborn baby's metabolic response to cold is nearly as good as that of the adult, relative to the baby's body weight if not to his body surface area. The problem is not that the newborn lacks the equipment to regulate body temperature but that his task is so great.

The efficiency of the newborn's temperature control is quickly put to the test in its first encounters in the hospital environment. Whereas the uterus generally remains at a constant 98.6°F., the gaseous environment that greets the newborn is invariably colder: rarely over 80°F. and sometimes as low as 60°. Because babies are born wet and then bathed, they lose considerable heat through evaporation and exposure of their skin to cool air. In fact, the drop in temperature may be so steep and rapid that the baby would have to produce twice as much heat energy per unit of body weight as the adult does in order to offset these conditions (Adamsons, 1966). Although many hospitals try to minimize this shock, life in the uterus remains considerably warmer than life in the delivery room or hospital nursery, and newborns need to be able to regulate their temperature to handle the transition. This is one reason that very small neonates often require a stay in the incubator.

Sleep

Newborn infants sleep a lot—approximately sixteen out of each twenty-four hours, which amounts to two-thirds of the day. Unfortunately for parents, the newborn packages this sleep into seven or eight naps per day, with his longest single sleep averaging about four and one-half hours. Consequently, the newborn is roughly on a four-hour sleep/wake cycle, sleeping a little less than three hours in each four. However, by six weeks, his naps have become longer, and he takes only two to four of them each day. Even the newborn sleep a little more at night than during the day (about 60 percent of the newborn's sleep takes place during the dark hours), and by approximately twenty-eight weeks most children sleep through the night without waking even once.

In addition to differences in the amount and phases of sleep, the quality of the newborn's sleep is also different from that of the adult. Recently scientists have studied certain body activities that occur during sleep in both adults and babies.

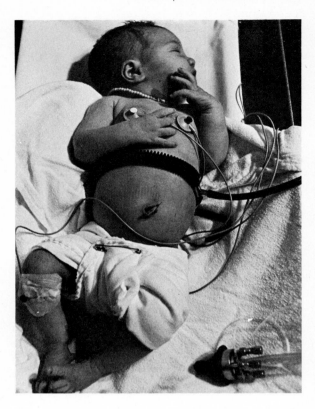

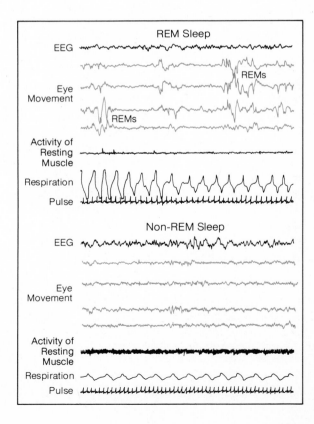

Figure 5.1 *(top)* This baby is in a stabilimeter crib, which measures his muscular activity. The belt around his abdomen measures respiration, and the electrodes on his chest produce electrocardiographic records. When electroencephalographic recordings are made, electrodes are placed at the outer corners of the eyes. Although cumbersome, the apparatus is not uncomfortable for the baby. *(bottom)* Recordings showing the differences between thirty seconds of REM sleep and non-REM sleep in a newborn. Besides the heightened eye activity during REM sleep, note the absence of muscle activity, the rapid respiratory rate, and changing respiratory amplitude. (Photograph by Jason Lauré; chart after Roffwarg, Dement, and Fisher, 1967)

There are two general kinds of sleep, distinguished principally by whether **rapid eye movement** (REM) occurs. During REM sleep, eye movements are accompanied by more rapid and changeable respiration, less muscular activity, and a more even pattern of brain waves. In Figure 5.1, the tube around the baby's stomach expands and contracts with his breathing, the electrodes on his chest detect his heart rate, and the stabilimeter that he lies on detects his body movements. In addition, electrodes placed near his eyes detect his eye movements, and other electrodes placed on his head record his brain waves on an electroencephalograph (EEG). The minute electrical changes that accompany muscular movements are amplified and written by a polygraph on a continuously flowing sheet of paper.

Figure 5.2 shows that the newborn spends almost half of his sixteen hours of sleep in REM sleep. Not until he is almost five years old does this proportion drop to approximately 20 percent, which is the adult average. The amount of non-REM sleep changes little over the childhood years, indicating that much of the newborn's extra sleep is composed of REM sleep.

What do the rapid eye movements of REM sleep signify? Adults awakened during REM sleep often report that they have been dreaming. Consequently, some people have supposed that newborn babies (and perhaps one's pet dog) dream during REM sleep. Physiologically, the REM sleep of neonates is nearly identical to that of dreaming adults, but it is unlikely that a newborn baby experiences anything like the integrated series of clear images that most adults do, especially when one considers the limited visual capability and experience of the newborn. But one cannot say that the neurological activity of REM sleep serves no purpose or is even irrelevant to dreaming. Most adults whose REM sleep is interrupted become nervous, anxious, and have trouble concentrating (Dement, 1960), and they make up for the loss of REM sleep by showing a higher percentage of it in subsequent sleep periods. Some scientists have suggested that the brain requires periodic neural activity, either from external or internal sources, and that REM sleep signifies self-generated activity in the absence of any external stimulus. Because newborns sleep so much and have less opportunity to re-

Figure 5.2 Proportion of REM/non-REM sleep over the life span. The proportion of REM sleep tends to decrease until about the age of five and then remain relatively constant. The proportion of non-REM sleep tends to increase during the first two years of life and then gradually decrease, in part because of the ongoing steady increase in waking time. The age scale used here is not proportionately true, and derived, approximate values are used for the age intervals. (After Roffwarg, Muzio, and Dement, 1966)

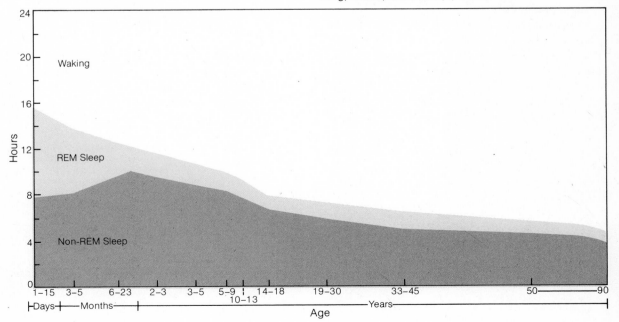

spond to events in the world around them, they require more of this neurological self-stimulation. Premature babies show even higher percentages of REM sleep than full-term infants do. It is possible that such activity is necessary before birth if neurological development is to occur. Therefore, the first function of REM sleep may be as an internal stimulus to neurological development; later it will carry the visual patterns and integrated experiences that constitute the dreams of older children and adults (Roffwarg, Muzio, and Dement, 1966).

Feeding

The newborn's sleep/wake cycle is closely tied to the need for nourishment. The typical neonate sleeps, wakes up hungry, eats, remains quietly alert for a short time, becomes drowsy, and then falls back to sleep. If fed every time he or she appears hungry, a baby may demand as many as ten to fourteen feedings each day (Trainham and Montgomery, 1946).

Books advising parents often suggest a four-hour feeding schedule. The four-hour schedule may have emerged from a study in 1900 of three newborns who were fed a barium-milk solution and were x-rayed periodically after they swallowed it. The study showed that within four hours the stomach had emptied (Frank, 1966). Some years ago it was common practice to feed young babies on a strict schedule regardless of whether

they appeared to be hungry. Parents even waked sleeping babies to feed them. Figure 5.3 shows what kind of schedule a baby might choose if left to decide, a regimen called **self-demand feeding.** C. Anderson Aldrich and Edith Hewitt (1947) studied one hundred babies who were allowed to establish their own feeding schedules during the first twelve months of life. At every age different babies demanded different numbers of meals. For example, during the first month of life, 60 percent of the babies ate every three hours, 26 percent ate every four hours, and approximately 10 percent demanded a feeding every two hours. Most newborns begin by putting themselves on a three-hour schedule and reach three meals a day by the time they are ten months old. Consequently, although all babies show some rhythm in their feeding patterns and all progressively require fewer daily feedings as they grow older, there are marked differences among babies with respect to the frequency of feeding. Because of studies like this, parents are now encouraged to feed their babies whenever they are hungry while working toward fewer and fewer feedings as their babies grow.

Elimination

As one might expect, because the neonate eats frequently, he also eliminates waste frequently. He may urinate up to eighteen times in a day and have four to seven bowel movements every twenty-four

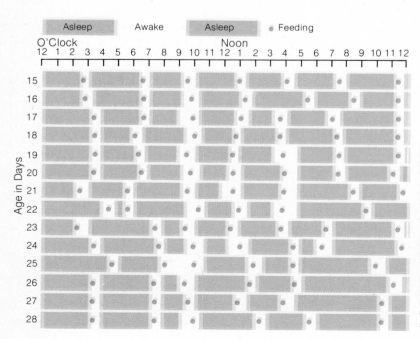

Figure 5.3   One baby's self-demand feeding schedule during her third and fourth weeks of life. Her feeding and sleeping periods during these two weeks occur fairly regularly. Note that during the third week she takes seven feedings and that she starts to stay awake longer at the late-morning and midafternoon feeding periods. During the fourth week, she begins to take six feedings, she tends to stay awake longer at feeding periods, and she sleeps longer before her early-morning and early-afternoon feedings. (After Gesell and Ilg, 1937)

hours. However, by the time he is eight weeks old, he eliminates less often and may have only two bowel movements each day, one when he wakes up in the morning and one during or shortly after a feeding. The newborn's tendency to eliminate is quite involuntary and cannot be trained. The infant's voluntary control over the neuromuscular mechanisms that control urination and defecation begins to emerge during the second year of life.

Sucking

A basic rhythmical behavior that has been studied in great detail is the newborn's sucking. Being able to suck effectively is the foundation of feeding and therefore of survival. Consequently, it is one behavior that the newborn must perform competently and precisely.

The young baby sucks rhythmically, in bursts separated by pauses. On the average, a baby will put together approximately five to twenty-four sucks in a single burst, sucking at a rate of approximately one to two and one-half times each second, and then take a brief rest. Although a baby's hunger, age, health, and level of arousal influence the pattern of sucking, individual babies also have their own characteristic patterns of sucking (Kessen, Haith, and Salapatek, 1970).

Although the neonate's feeding performance may be a little ragged during the first few days of life, he quickly develops a fairly smooth coordination between sucking, swallowing, and breathing. The fact that he can swallow almost three times faster than an adult and that he is able to suck at the same time he takes in air aids the baby in this feat. Adults who sucked in a liquid and breathed at the same time would probably choke. The baby can manage simultaneous sucking and breathing because he or she extracts milk from the nipple by pressing the nipple against the roof of the mouth instead of by inhalation.

REFLEXES AND SENSORY CAPABILITIES

Some years ago, many people believed that the newborn baby could not sense the physical energies in the environment. It was held that the baby could not see clearly, smell, or taste and could feel only pain, cold, and hunger. However, research has established that the neonate's senses, although not as precise as those of the adult, do inform him about the world. On the other hand, the reflexes of the newborn attracted the attention of neurophys-

iologists and pediatricians much earlier, and their studies have provided us with an extensive catalog of reflexive behavior.

Reflexes

The newborn comes equipped with a set of reflexive behaviors that are elicited by specific stimuli. Some of these reflexes are adaptive and may help the new baby feed or avoid danger. Others appear to be vestiges of the past, left over from man's nonhuman ancestors. Still others are simple manifestations of neurological circuitry in the baby that will later come under voluntary control or will be integrated in more useful patterns of behavior. Most of these reflexes disappear within a few weeks or months, primarily as the result of neurological development, especially in the cortex of the brain (Minkowski, 1967). There are a number of reflexes whose survival role is relatively obvious. Babies close their eyes to bright light and twist their bodies or move their limbs away from sources of pain. A hungry baby whose palms are pressed will respond by sucking.

The Rooting Reflex   The rooting reflex is the baby's tendency to turn his head and mouth in the direction of any object that gently stimulates the corner of his mouth. A baby is most likely to show this at about a week or two of age when he is quietly awake with his eyes open, especially if he is somewhat hungry. If one strokes the corner of the baby's mouth with an index finger, moving sideways from the mouth toward his cheek, the newborn may move his tongue, mouth, or even his whole head toward the stimulated side. At first this reflex appears even when one strokes the cheek a long way from the mouth. As the baby gets older, the reflex appears only when the stimulation is at the mouth, and only the baby's mouth will respond. This reflex has obvious adaptive significance because it helps the baby place the nipple in his mouth. Babies sometimes learn to suck their thumbs while rooting.

Grasping and the Moro Reflex   A baby in the first few weeks of life has a strong grasping reflex. If one places a one-week-old baby on his back and inserts a finger into his hand, the baby is likely to grasp it sturdily. Sometimes a grasping newborn can literally hang by one hand.

Ernst Moro (1918) first described the **Moro reflex,** which consists of a thrusting out of the arms

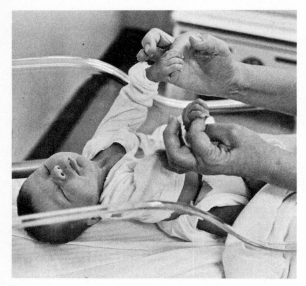

The grasping reflex. (William MacDonald)

Walking Movements A one- or two-week-old baby may show behavior that resembles the movements required in walking. One of these is a **stepping** motion that can be elicited by holding a baby under his arms while gently lowering him to a surface until his feet touch and his knees bend. If one slowly bounces the baby lightly up and down, he may straighten his legs out at the knees and hip as if to stand. Then if he is moved forward, he may make stepping movements as if he were walking, although he can neither support his weight nor maintain his balance.

The second walking motion, a **placing** response, is simply the baby's propensity to lift his feet onto a surface. If held up and moved toward a surface until the top part of his foot touches the edge, he is likely to lift up his foot and place it on the table.

in an embracelike movement when the baby suddenly loses support for his neck and head. It is easily seen after the first week when the baby is alert and his eyes are open or barely closed. It can be elicited by holding a baby with one hand under his head and the other in the small of his back and then rapidly lowering one's hands, especially the hand holding his head, to an abrupt halt. A second way to obtain the Moro reflex is to lay the baby on his back with his head looking straight up and then slap the mattress behind his head with enough force to jerk his head and neck slightly. Typically, his arms shoot out and upward and his hands curl slightly as if preparing to grab something. In fact, if your finger is in a baby's hand when somebody else provides the stimulus for the Moro, you can feel the baby suddenly tighten his grip on your finger. The Moro reflex decreases as the baby gets older; it is difficult to elicit after the baby is three months old, and it is almost always gone by five or six months.

The meaning and purpose of the grasping and Moro reflexes are not clear. It has been suggested that this behavior is an inheritance from our animal ancestors. Because monkeys carry their young on their backs or stomachs, a loss of support is less likely to produce a fall if the youngster reaches out and grasps its mother's fur or skin (Prechtl, 1965).

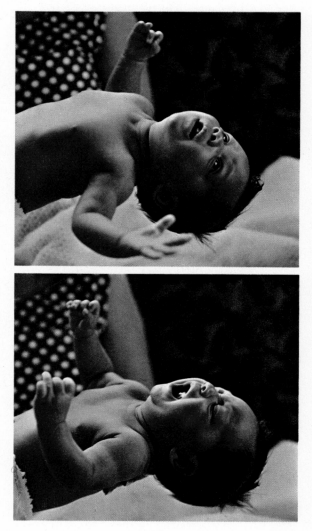

The Moro reflex. (William MacDonald)

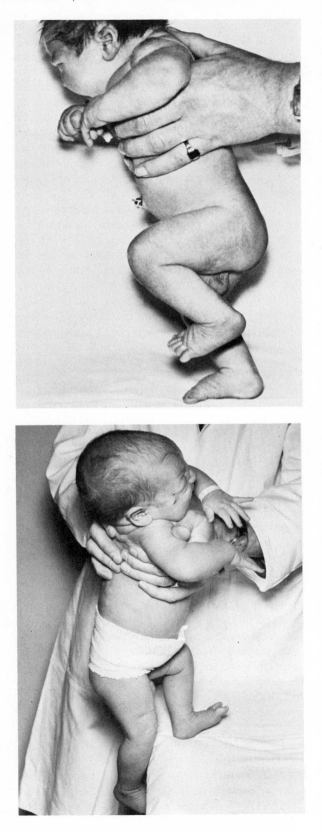

These behaviors have relatively little practical utility in themselves, because the one- or two-week-old baby possesses neither the strength nor balance either to walk or to step. However, the two reflexes appear to indicate a certain inborn neurological organization that forms the basis for later standing and walking. These reflexes tend to disappear between the third and fourth month, probably because the baby's cortex has developed to a point where it inhibits them. When stepping movements next appear, they will be voluntary acts from a baby who is getting ready to rise up and walk.

The appearance, disappearance, and reappearance of certain behavioral skills, such as those involved in walking, may have a broader significance than was previously thought. Recently Thomas Bower (1976) has proposed that skills such as reaching out and touching an object follow a similar developmental sequence. At about three weeks, the baby can reach out and touch an object, but this skill seemingly disappears in around four or five weeks, only to reappear in a more precise and coordinated form at about twenty weeks. This pattern suggests that the development of some complex abilities is not simply an accumulation of skills but the replacement of a primitive way of doing something with a precise and intricate way of doing it. We will return to this idea later in our discussions of the infant's physical development.

Sensory Capabilities

The human being's capacity to detect various stimuli provides the basis for subsequent development. The ability to think, to learn, and to become a social being depends upon one's perceptions of the world. Consequently, it is important to know about the person's sensory capabilities at birth. If we know what Matt and Lauren can see, hear, smell, and taste, we can discover which events in the environment might influence them.

Vision   If you hold one finger a few inches from your nose and another at arm's length, you can quickly alternate your focus from one to the other, an ability called **visual accommodation.** The newborn does not possess this capability but is instead like a fixed-focus camera: only objects that are about nine inches from his eyes will be in focus.

The stepping reflex (*top*). The placing reflex (*bottom*). (A. K. Tunstill)

Focal distance varies from baby to baby, ranging from seven to fifteen inches. By the age of six weeks, the baby's ability to accommodate appears to improve markedly, but he will not be as skilled as an adult until he is approximately four months of age (Haynes, White, and Held, 1965). You can begin to appreciate the staggering limits this places on the young baby's visual experience by focusing on your finger, held about nine inches from your nose, and then attempting to concentrate on other objects in the room. This limited focus is one mechanism that minimizes the baby's "blooming, buzzing confusion"; it sharply reduces the amount of distinctive visual stimulation that gets through. The newborn's peripheral vision is also quite limited. An adult's field of vision covers 180 degrees, whereas the newborn's is only 60 degrees, shutting out two-thirds of the available stimulation and further minimizing possible confusion.

When an adult looks at an object, he focuses both eyes on it. Each eye sees a slightly different image, and by a mechanism called **convergence,** the two images come together until only a single object appears. If you hold your finger at arm's length, focus on it, and then move it toward the tip of your nose, you can feel the muscles of your eyes perform this function. The newborn does not possess this ability until the age of about seven or eight weeks. If, therefore, one holds two objects nine inches in front of the baby's face, it is possible that his right eye will literally look at the right object and his left eye will look at the left one (Wickelgren, 1967).

Because the normal newborn's eyes are not usually aligned toward the same point, the baby often looks walleyed (*strabismus*) for the first month or so. Given their limited muscular ability, newborns are lucky if they move both eyes in the same direction half the time, let alone keep both of them trained on the same object. Even without convergence, however, newborns have some sense of depth perception (Yonas and Pick, 1975). Using only one eye, a newborn can tell whether an object appears to have moved nearer or farther by relying on the cues of changing size and clarity. Thus, when a relatively small and blurred image that is projected on his eye becomes larger and clearer, the baby detects and responds to the implied difference in depth.

Visual **acuity** refers to the ability to see objects clearly and to resolve detail. If a newborn could see equally well at all distances, then the week-old baby would have approximately 20/200 vision. In terms of adult standards, this means that at a distance of twenty feet from an object, the newborn sees it about as well as you would at a distance of 200 feet. Translated into experimental terms, 20/200 vision means that the baby can discriminate a 1/8-inch stripe from a gray background at a distance of nine inches. However, vision improves so rapidly that by the time he is three months old the baby can see 1/64-inch stripes at a distance of fifteen inches. By six months, he can see as clearly as the average adult (Dayton et al., 1964).

For almost a century, scientists have been trying to determine whether newborn babies can see color. Babies easily tell the difference between objects that differ in brightness, but no one has yet been able to separate brightness and hue in such a way as to test newborns for color vision (Maurer, 1975). Based on physiological evidence, it appears that the color-sensitive cells in the eyes of newborns are few in number and barely developed in structure. This suggests that for at least the first several weeks of life the newborn is likely to be color-blind. By the age of two months, the baby can make some color discriminations (Peeples and Teller, 1975), and other experiments show that by four months, the color vision of infants is similar to that of adults.

Audition   There is no question that newborn babies hear. Their ears operate four months before they are born, the basic neurology that enables them to discriminate between different tones and intensities is probably ready two months before birth, and approximately one month before birth they are prepared to direct their attention toward a sound. At first, the sounds reaching a neonate may be somewhat dampened, because for the first few days of life the middle-ear passages are filled with amniotic fluid. However, all normal newborns can hear, and some can hear very well. In fact, one study suggests that the faintest sound that a baby can detect is about as soft as the faintest sound heard by the average adult (Eisenberg, 1970). Although the newborn can hear a sound as opposed to no sound, babies have difficulty in discriminating between one sound and another. For example, the average newborn can only detect the difference between tones of 200 and 1,000 cycles per second, which is roughly comparable to the difference between a foghorn and a clarinet (Leventhal and Lipsitt, 1964). On the other hand, some exceptional infants have responded to tones that differ as little as 60 cycles per second, which is roughly equivalent to one step on a musical scale (Bridger, 1961).

Taste and Smell Unfortunately, scientists still know little about the newborn's ability to taste. It is likely that a baby has little taste sensitivity at birth. The newborn may not be able to detect much difference between salt, sugar, lemon juice, bitter quinine, and tasteless distilled water, although he or she may prefer milk or sweet-tasting glucose to a salty brine. Recent evidence indicates that within several days after birth a baby's taste sensitivity becomes more developed (Johnson and Salisbury, 1975). For example, when fed solutions of salt water, sterile water, artificial milk, or breast milk, a baby is likely to show a distinctly different pattern of sucking, swallowing, and breathing for each solution. Charles Crook and Lewis Lipsitt (1976) have been studying the newborn's sensitivity to solutions varying in their degree of sweetness. They found that a baby sucks more slowly and his or her heart rate increases with sweeter solutions. These results appear contradictory, because one might expect a baby to suck more vigorously when given a solution that tastes good. In addition, if the baby is sucking slowly, then he is exerting less effort, and it seems as if his heart rate should slow down. In an attempt to resolve this paradox, Crook and Lipsitt suggest that because the baby savors the taste of the sweeter solutions, he slows down to enjoy them and that pleasurable excitement causes his heart to speed up.

Newborns definitely react to strong odors. They will turn away from the smell of ammonia or vinegar and can distinguish between some complex odors (Engen and Lipsitt, 1965). Within two or three days, the newborn also recognizes for a time a strong odor he has smelled before. When first presented with the odor of anise oil, for example, a baby's activity increases and his heart rate and breathing pattern change. If the odor continues, the baby gradually stops responding to it. At this point, if a new odor, such as phenyl alcohol, reaches his nose, the baby again becomes more active, and his heart rate and breathing pattern change.

The keenness of the newborn's sense of smell may be further illustrated by the research of Aidan Macfarlane (1977) at Oxford University. He had noticed that when placed next to his mother's breast, a typical newborn turns his face toward it before seeing it or touching the nipple. Macfarlane wondered if this was because the baby could smell the milk beginning to drip from the nipple. To test this notion, he performed two simple and ingenious experiments. First, he collected breast pads that mothers had used to absorb the small amount of milk that leaks between feedings. For the first experiment, he simply placed the mother's breast pad on one side of a baby's head and a clean pad on the other side next to the cheek. Because many babies prefer one side or the other, usually the right, care was taken to alternate the pads' placement. Babies spent more time with their heads turned toward their own mothers' milk-scented pads than toward the clean pads. But the babies' noses were sharper than Macfarlane expected. In the second experiment, he substituted a milk-scented pad from another mother for the clean pad and compared the baby's reaction. He found that babies turned their heads toward both pads for about the same amount of time during the first two days, but that by the time they were six to ten days old, they turned most of the time toward their own mothers' pads.

PERCEPTION AND ATTENTION

If Matt were simply a passive recipient of anything that the environment presented him, he would not attend to or respond to some stimuli and ignore others. However, this is just what he does. He looks at some things and not at others, which indicates that he is actively selecting and filtering those aspects of his world that he will notice and learn about.

Visual Attention

As we will see in Chapter 7, the two-month-old baby notices brightness, movement, and pattern. But does the neonate respond to these aspects of the world? As far as brightness goes, objects that are too bright or too dim will not capture his gaze. Maurice Hershenson (1964) found that a baby who is two or three days old will look longer at objects of moderate brightness than at those that are too bright or not bright enough. This research confirms the experience of parents, who often report that their newborn shuts his eyes and turns away from bright lights, especially from sunlight.

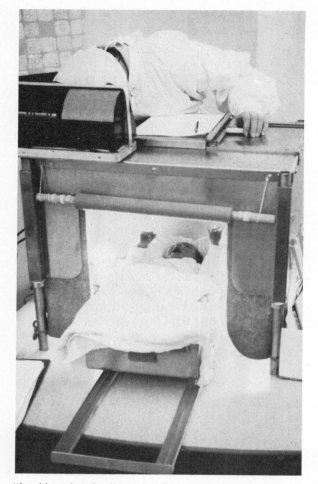

"Looking chamber" used in Fantz's studies of perceptual development in babies. The baby lies on his back looking up at two panels. Contrasting visual stimuli—for example, an outline of a human face and a half-white, half-black oval figure—are placed on the panels, and the baby's eye movements are observed and recorded to determine which of the two panels he looks at more often and for a longer period of time. (Courtesy Dr. Robert L. Fantz)

A great deal of research has been devoted to a baby's attention to pattern. As early as 1944, Fritz Stirnimann found that babies only one day old would look longer at a patterned surface than at a plain one. Robert Fantz (1965) performed some of the first modern experiments on the baby's attention to different forms. He used a "looking chamber" to study babies between two days and six months old. Fantz placed the baby in a drawerlike carriage and slid the carriage into the looking chamber, where stimuli were placed directly above the baby. When Fantz used this procedure, he also found that newborns attend more to patterns than to homogeneous gray stimuli. As the babies reached two or three months, they preferred more complex, three-dimensional stimuli and bull's-eye patterns. We will return to this experiment in Chapter 7.

Contrast   When babies look at a visual pattern, what aspect of it attracts their attention? In order to find out, William Kessen, Marshall Haith, and Philip Salapatek developed a device that records a baby's eye movements. The shifting gaze of six different babies can be seen in Figure 5.4. Notice that the newborn tended to look at the edges of a triangle, especially at the vertex, where black-white contrast is highest. These newborns did not systematically scan the entire shape; instead, they concentrated their attention on a corner and perhaps on the sides forming that corner (Salapatek and Kessen, 1966).

The conclusion seems to be that newborn babies do not look in a random fashion; instead, their attention is attracted to and maintained by points of high contrast. Moreover, once neonates find such a point of contrast, they are not likely to search the figure for another. That development must wait until they are a few weeks older.

Search Strategy   The newborn does not scan an object in detail but does possess some simpler visual strategies. Suppose Lauren wakes up in a to-

Babies respond early to movement. A five-day-old newborn who is sucking on a pacifier will stop this rhythmical sucking if a light moves across his visual field (Haith, 1966). Despite the fact that his right eye and his left eye do not always look at the same thing, the newborn can pursue a moving object with his eyes if it does not move too rapidly (Dayton et al., 1964). However, not until a baby is about three to six weeks old will his visual pursuit become coordinated and smooth. This suggests that if the movement is not too rapid, even newborns will be more attracted to a moving object than to a stationary one.

Figure 5.4   In this perception experiment, newborn babies were shown a large black triangle on a white field. (*left*) Infrared marker lights were placed behind the triangle and reflected in the baby's pupil, permitting the baby's eye movements to be traced and photographed. (*right*) Besides showing that the infants looked more toward the corners of the triangle, the six tracings illustrate the wide variation in patterns of scanning that occurs among babies. (Photograph courtesy Dr. William Kessen; data from Salapatek and Kessen, 1966)

tally dark room. She is more likely to open her eyes and scan the environment in a horizontal direction than in a vertical one. In addition, there is a certain rhythm to her scanning (approximately two scans per second) roughly the same as her sucking rate. In short, the rule appears to be: If there is no light, search systematically with a predominantly horizontal, rhythmical eye movement (Haith, 1966).

If there is light available, the baby first adopts the same strategy of horizontal, rhythmic search. But instead of searching for the light, Lauren searches for edges or points of high black-white contrast in her visual field. Because her scanning strategy is mostly horizontal, she is more likely to encounter a vertical line or a black-white edge than a horizontal one (Kessen, Haith, and Salapatek, 1970). Moreover, some research suggests that the brighter the contrast between the light and the dark areas of the object, the more likely the baby is to look at it. As Chapter 7 shows, the scanning strategies of the older baby are much more sophisticated.

Auditory Attention

Is the neonate a selective listener to sounds as well as a selective viewer of sights? The answer to questions of auditory attention are difficult to obtain for two reasons. First, it is relatively easy for scientists to determine when a baby looks at something or what part of an object he focuses on by observing where the baby's eyes are turned. It is much harder to tell whether an infant listens and even more problematical to tell what aspect of an auditory stimulus he listens to. Some information has been gained by monitoring the heart rates, respiration rates, and sucking patterns of babies when they are exposed to various sounds.

Babies do respond differently to sounds of contrasting frequencies or pitch. Low tones tend to

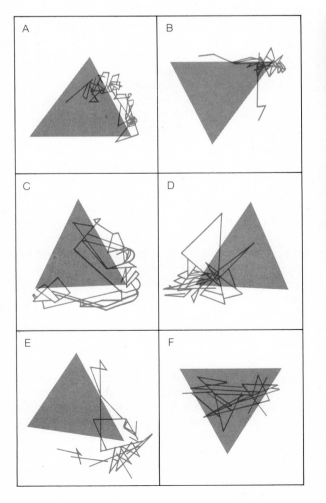

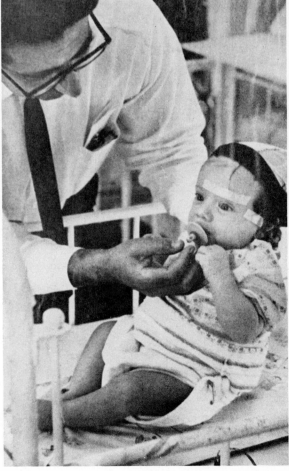

quiet a baby who is upset, whereas high frequencies are likely to distress him and may even produce a kind of freezing reaction (Eisenberg et al., 1964). Some scientists have called attention to the parallel between the newborn's response to these sounds and the tendency among adults to use sounds of different frequencies to convey feelings of distress or calm. For example, the acoustical properties of musical instruments, alarm systems, and even some words used to describe our reactions to certain events use high frequencies to alert and convey excitement or disturbance and low frequencies to communicate relative calm (Eisenberg, 1970).

There is also some indication that the newborn responds more to sounds in the frequency of the human voice (200 to 500 cycles per second) and to sounds of moderate length, approximately five to fifteen seconds in duration (Eisenberg, 1970). Chapter 8 describes how this response to the human voice plays a role in the development of language.

It should be clear from these examples of visual and auditory attention that the newborn's perceptual world is somewhat less confusing than psychologists once thought. Although the newborn's sensory systems do function, the ability to detect stimuli or to discriminate among them is seriously limited, and a considerable amount of the visual environment is simply not accessible. Although some babies are quite good at discriminating between one kind of sound and another, the average newborn perceives many sounds as the same that adults would detect as different. Finally, newborn babies are selective about what stimuli will attract their attention or increase their responses: they tune some things in and tune other things out. As a result, the newborn neither detects nor pays attention to much of what adults perceive. The newborn's perceptual world is probably simpler and more orderly than we might guess.

ADAPTING TO THE WORLD

Given that babies have many ways of sensing events in the outside world and certain coordinated patterns of behavior for meeting situations that might arise, what are the mechanisms by which they adapt to the environment? How does the newborn come to know more about the world?

The neonate can learn—at least some things under some circumstances. For example, like all newborns, Lauren learns to integrate sucking and breathing into an efficient feeding process, and she can learn to modify this behavior to fit the circumstances at hand. In addition, she is able to form crude memories of certain stimuli, to remember those stimuli for five to ten seconds, and then to detect whether a subsequent stimulus is different from that memory.

Memory and Perceptual Analysis

The newborn baby spends most of the time either asleep, fussing and crying because of hunger, or feeding. In fact, the average newborn probably is quietly alert only about thirty minutes in every four hours. Many parents are fond of putting mobiles and other objects in the crib with their newborn. Is it possible that a young baby, who is alert for such short periods, can become familiar with such objects—that is, can form a memory of them, retain that memory, and recognize an old mobile as familiar or detect a new one as strange?

Steven Friedman explored this possibility with babies from one to four days old (Friedman, 1972; Friedman, Bruno, and Vietze, 1974). One of the checkerboards pictured in Figure 5.5 was shown to a baby for sixty seconds at a time. Friedman presented the stimulus again and again until on two successive occasions the baby looked a total of eight seconds less than he had looked the first two times that he had seen the object. When this happened, the infant had **habituated.** The process of habituation is roughly analogous to becoming bored with a stimulus, which implies that the baby has learned and remembered something about it. Such a decline in looking after repeated exposure may signify that the baby has formed a memory of that stimulus. On the other hand, the baby may simply be tired or fussy; perhaps he does not remember the stimulus at all. To find out whether the baby was showing memory or fatigue, Friedman changed the stimulus on a later test. If the baby looked longer at the new stimulus than the last time he saw the familiar one, the baby must have had a memory for the familiar one that signaled that the new stimulus was different from the old. Figure 5.5 shows one neonate's pattern of looking at the repeated sight of a given stimulus and at the introduction of a new one. Notice that during the familiarization phase this neonate looked for about the same length of time again and again until suddenly the looking time dropped sharply on two successive occasions. When Friedman introduced a new stimulus, the baby looked a long time (almost the entire sixty seconds), indicating that he detected the new stimulus as being different from his earlier memory.

Given the stimuli used in this study, it was also possible to ask whether a newborn looked longer at a new stimulus that was radically different from the familiar stimulus than at one that was only slightly different. The results suggest that the length of time the babies looked at the novel stimulus depended on how different it was from the familiar one. It appears that newborns perform a crude perceptual analysis of the difference between the new stimulus and their memory of the familiar one.

On the basis of this and other research, we can conclude that newborns can form a memory of a stimulus, retain that memory for five to ten seconds, retrieve it, and make some kind of analysis of the relationship between the memory and the new stimulus.

Conditions for Learning

It is clear that human newborns can learn. However, just how much they actually do learn in their natural environment is another question. We have seen that newborns work under certain handicaps and that their environment may not satisfy the stringent requirements necessary before they can sense, perceive, attend, and perhaps learn.

One requirement of the learning situation appears to be *timing*. There can be almost no delay of reward for the newborn; the baby who does not receive reinforcement within one second is unlikely to learn (Millar, 1972). Another requirement is *repetition;* a stimulus must be presented over and over again with only short delays between each presentation in order for the young baby to form a memory of it (Lewis, 1969). However, as a baby grows older, learning proceeds even when there are greater delays between his response and the reward or between the presentation of one stimulus and another.

Although the scientist can construct a situation that satisfies the newborn's requirement for close timing, the baby's natural environment does not always meet that rigid standard. The delay between the baby's actions and their effects on the people and objects nearby will often be longer than a second, making learning unlikely. Even when the condition of timing is met, the condition of repetition may not be. For example, a bat of the baby's hand may immediately remove a blanket that has fallen across his face, but he may not have the opportunity to push away another blanket. In a sense, then, there may be a period of "natural deprivation" (J. S. Watson, 1966) in which the baby is capable of learning but in which environmental conditions provide no opportunity to learn.

Other studies have discovered additional limits

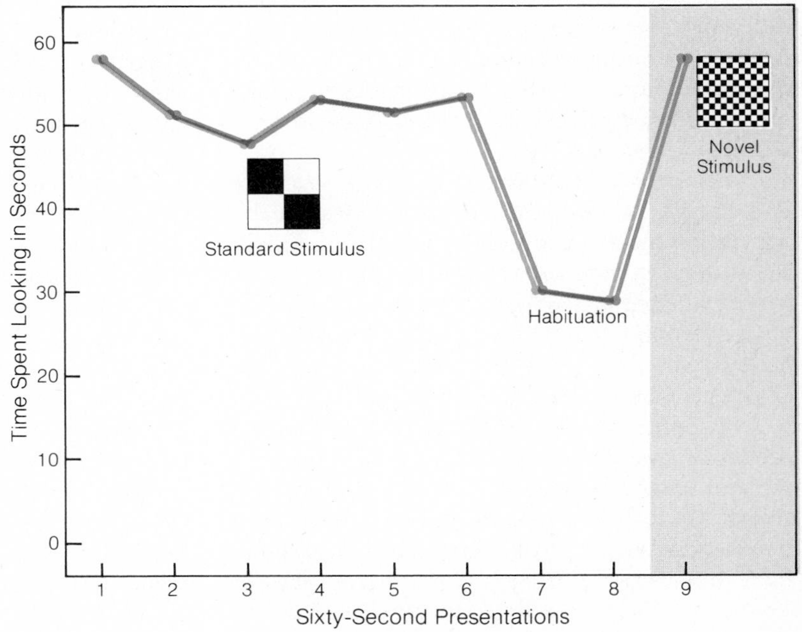

Figure 5.5 One newborn's response to familiar and unfamiliar checkerboard stimuli. After seven sixty-second exposures to the standard (familiar) stimulus, the baby became habituated. When the baby was then exposed to a novel (unfamiliar) stimulus on the ninth presentation, however, he immediately looked at it for an extended time. (After Friedman, 1972)

on the young baby's ability to learn (Fitzgerald and Brackbill, 1976). For example, even among very young babies, there are individual differences in the ability to learn. Some newborns can learn tasks that are difficult or impossible for other babies of the same age. It also matters whether the response to be learned is a voluntary or an involuntary one. An involuntary response, such as the blink of an eye at the sound of a buzzer, may be extremely difficult for a neonate to learn, whereas a voluntary response, such as learning to turn toward the buzzer, may be relatively easy.

PERSONALITY AND SOCIAL RELATIONS

It is difficult to talk about the personality of a newborn like Matt. Adults think of personality in terms of verbal, cognitive, and emotional behavior displayed in a social context. It is difficult for Matt to express a personality in this way. However, newborn babies do differ in their motor activity, irritability, and responsiveness, and they do engage in primitive social relations.

Activity, Irritability, Responsiveness

Some newborns are simply more *active* than others. Some frequently thrash about with their legs and arms or later bang toys and shake rattles with considerable gusto; other babies are more placid, moving more slowly and with less exaggeration. Mothers are sometimes aware of this kind of difference even before their babies are born: some fetuses kick and move about more than others, and there is some relationship between such fetal kicking and differences in behavior among children for at least two years (C. E. Walters, 1965).

Newborns also differ in general *irritability*. Some cry a lot, but others do not. Certain babies are restless sleepers and tend to have fits of irritability during sleep or wakefulness. There is also some evidence that irritable or fitful sleepers may have different personalities as young children from babies who do not show such restless sleep (Thomas, Chess, and Birch, 1970).

Newborn babies also differ in *responsiveness*. Some babies are cuddlers. They are soft and snuggly and seem to enjoy being cuddled, kissed, and rolled about in one's arms. In contrast, other babies resist such affectionate play by stiffening their bodies when they are handled (Schaffer, 1971). It is easy to understand how such a rudimentary social response might have a substantial impact on parents who had been looking forward to the opportunity to hug and kiss their newborn and who find themselves parents to a noncuddler. They may falsely infer that their baby dislikes them or that they are inadequate parents, forming negative attitudes that could color the way they subsequently interact with their child.

Many studies have documented these early personality differences among babies. An important early study by Margaret Fries (1954), in which she carefully observed the amount and vigor of neonate activity, led her to classify newborns into three activity types: the active, the moderately active, and the quiet. Joy Osofsky and Barbara Danzger (1974) went one step further; they observed the relationship between characteristics of newborn babies and their interactions with their mothers. They found that newborns they had rated as highly responsive to sound had mothers who often talked and cooed and sang to them. They also found that newborns they had rated as highly responsive to touch had attentive mothers with highly expressive faces who touched them a lot. Although the correlation between the babies' responsiveness and the mothers' reactions to them may have had a hereditary component, it is likely that the mothers quickly learned to give their babies the kind of stimulation that the babies seemed to respond to.

Other newborn predispositions that may be important to a child's personality have been identified and described by Alexander Thomas and his colleagues (1963). These researchers decided that the intimate knowledge mothers gain in the constant care of their babies would be a source of meaningful data. Using carefully formulated interviews, they conducted an extensive study that disclosed four major behavioral characteristics that seem important for personality: activity level; approach-withdrawal behavior, as seen in the baby's characteristic first reaction to any new stimulus; threshold of responsiveness, or the amount of stimulation required to evoke a visible or audible response from him; and general quality of mood, such as friendly, unfriendly, joyful, or angry.

Of course, child and adult personality are much more complex than these simple categories would imply. A child's personality is a developing and evolving set of tendencies to behave in various ways. Nevertheless, it is easy to see how the general tone of social interaction within the family could be influenced by the baby's characteristic activity, irritability, and social responsiveness.

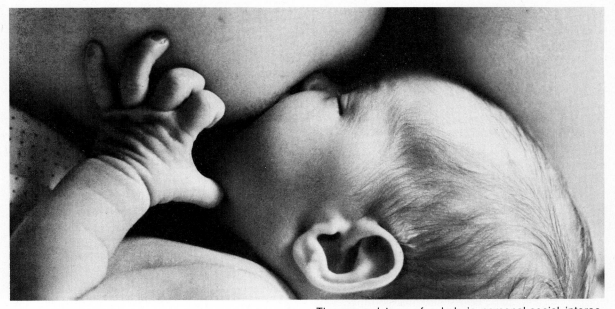

The general tone of a baby's personal-social interactions is often reflected in the complex and intimate interplay of his own and his mother's characteristics. (Ken Heyman)

Social Relations

Social relations in the newborn are primitive by adult standards, yet they exist. Whenever there is communication between individuals, there is a social relation, and newborns and their parents certainly carry on a rudimentary sort of nonverbal communication.

Historically, the way in which a newborn was fed was thought to have major consequences for both the child's developing social relations and personality. Such ideas stemmed from Freudian theory, which placed great emphasis on the possible impact of events early in the child's life. Because the newborn spends most of his or her waking hours feeding, it made good sense to assume that social relations began in the feeding situation. The design of the human body insures that nursing neonate and mother are placed in a situation that facilitates communication. When Matt's mother first breast-fed her newborn son, he was cradled in her arm with his face about nine inches from hers—the distance at which his eyes could most easily focus.

What appears to be a remarkable type of nonverbal communication between newborn and parent has to do with imitation. Using refined technical analysis, Andrew Meltzov (Meltzov and Moore, 1977) and other researchers have recently demonstrated that a one- to two-week-old baby will imitate an adult who is widening his eyes, clenching his hand, opening his mouth, or sticking out his tongue. Equally remarkable, this social ability soon disappears and does not seem to reappear until the end of the first year (Bower, 1976).

Perhaps the most obvious method that the newborn uses to communicate with the social environment is crying. Generally speaking, a baby cries as if to say "Help me," and even quite young babies display different cries depending on whether the crying is stimulated by hunger, pain, or anger. Each cry can be distinguished by the pattern of pauses between bursts of crying, by the duration of the cry, and by its tonal characteristics. The baby's crying appears to be a wired-in, autonomous activity. If earphones are placed on the crying newborn's head and sounds are played, the crying pattern shows no interruption, even though such competing stimulation would disrupt the speech of an adult (P. Wolff, 1967).

One wonders if the differences in crying are detectable by parents or only by scientists armed with complex technical instruments. Complex instruments are superfluous. If a mother hears tape recordings of the cries of her own baby and the cries of four other babies all responding to a slight pinprick on the foot, the mother readily picks out the cry of her own baby even when her infant is only a few weeks old (Lind, 1971). When a mother responds to the hunger cry of her baby, it may be with more than a simple verbal statement that her child is hungry. In fact, mothers respond physiologically and prepare to breast-feed; the increased flow of blood and milk raise the surface heat of her breasts (Lind, 1971). Many a lactating mother can relate occasions when her baby has given a hunger cry and she has discovered milk gushing from her breasts in response.

But social communication is necessarily a two-way street, and Judith Bernal (1972) discovered that whether or not a mother picked up and fed her crying newborn depended primarily on the context of the cry. Among the English mothers she studied, unless three hours had passed since the last feeding, most left their babies to cry, perhaps limiting communication to the news that crying had little effect.

It appears that almost from the moment of birth, the neonate detects some social dimension to crying and responds emotionally. Marvin Simner (1971) found, for example, that two- to three-day-old babies start to cry much more frequently when they hear another newborn crying than when they hear nonhuman sounds of equal range and volume. People working in hospital nurseries have made similar observations, noting that when one baby starts to cry, other babies in the nursery soon join in. Abraham Sagi and Martin Hoffman (1976) at the University of Michigan have confirmed this finding and suggest that it may be an inborn, early precursor to later forms of human empathy.

Communication also occurs when a parent responds to a crying baby. There are several ways to quiet a crying baby besides feeding him. One is to stabilize the baby's temperature and keep something in contact with his skin. Perhaps it is for this reason that babies have been swaddled for centuries.

Movement also quiets a crying baby, but certain types of movement are better than others. One psychologist developed a rocking machine to determine how rapidly and how much rocking would quiet a baby best. The result: one rock per second, approximately 2-3/4 inches in depth, will calm a

In response to her baby's hunger cry, a mother physiologically prepares to breast-feed, as shown by thermographs of changes in the surface heat of her breasts, generated by the increased flow of blood and milk. (Steve McCarroll; Professor John Lind)

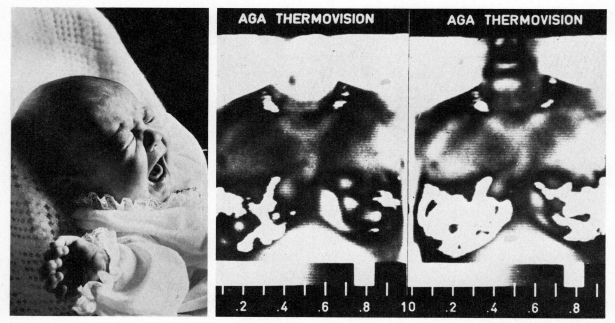

baby within fifteen seconds. Further, the baby will remain quiet even after the rocking stops (A. Ambrose, 1969).

Auditory stimulation, especially pulsating sounds, also appears to quiet an infant. In an early experiment, babies who listened to sounds roughly comparable to human heartbeats for four days cried less and gained more weight than babies who did not hear the sounds. This result prompted the researchers to conclude that the baby was conditioned while in the womb to the mother's heartbeat and that heartbeats therefore have special importance throughout human life (Salk, 1962). However, subsequent research has indicated that heartbeat sounds, the beats of a metronome, and even a lullaby are equally effective in quieting a newborn infant, and any of these is better than no sound at all. In fact, even continuous sounds, sights, or pitching and rocking movements have calming effects on one-month-old babies, and the more of these different stimuli that one applies at a time, the more effectively the infant's distress is reduced (Brackbill, 1971). Consequently, almost any stimulus, but especially moderately varied stimuli, will quiet a baby.

As noted earlier, a baby is especially responsive to the human voice. Recent studies indicate that babies as young as twelve hours move their bodies in apparent rhythm with human speech (Condon and Sander, 1974). Babies responded to live or recorded speech, in either English or Chinese, but failed to respond to disconnected vowel sounds or to tapping. The investigators suggest that from the first day of life the newborn may be preparing for later speech.

SUMMARY

1. Newly arrived from complete dependence on the uterine environment, the newborn, or neonate, undergoes a period of remarkable development.

2. The newborn quickly begins to function with patterns or rhythms: body temperature becomes regulated soon after birth; sleep, composed of both REM and non-REM patterns, evolves into a four-hour sleep/wake cycle for many newborns; feeding, left to the newborn's self-demand, occurs every three to four hours for many newborns; and elimination patterns develop in accordance with feeding.

3. From birth, the newborn is equipped with a set of reflexive behaviors that may be elicited by specific stimuli. These include the rooting reflex, the grasping reflex, the Moro reflex, and stepping and placing responses.

4. The sensory capabilities of newborns keep them in touch with their environment. Although they may be color-blind for the first several weeks, they become capable of accommodation, or focus; of convergence, or seeing one image with both eyes; and of acuity, or seeing detail. Their auditory sense allows newborns to discriminate loudness and pitch, and their senses of taste and smell become increasingly acute.

5. Newborns actively select and filter the visual and auditory stimuli around them. They direct their visual attention to objects according to brightness, movement, pattern, and contrast, and according to certain search strategies. Auditory attention is similarly selective.

6. In adapting to the world, the neonate forms short-term memories of certain stimuli and then compares new stimuli to them. This learning appears to depend on the timing of reward and the repetition of the stimulus.

7. Newborn babies differ in their motor activity, general irritability, and responsiveness to affection; these predispositions influence the tone of the baby's social relationships and thus may influence the evolving set of tendencies later defined as the child's personality. Feeding and responses to their crying offer newborns their first chances for social interaction.

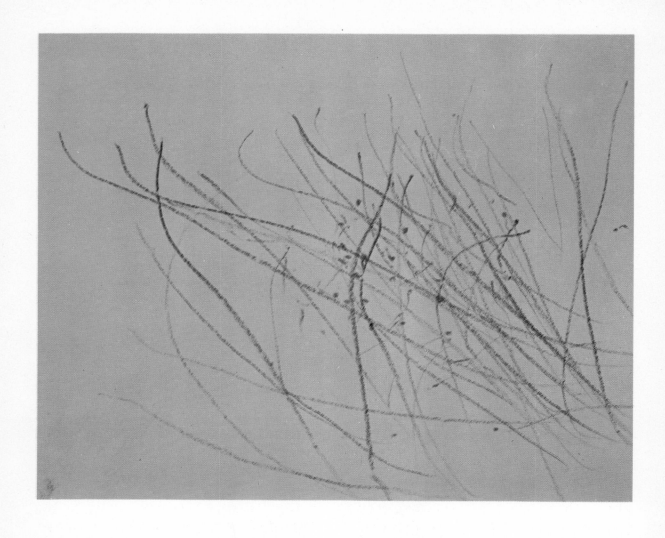

Unit III Infancy: The Dawn of Awareness

In the course of the first two years of life, a normal infant develops the ability to communicate with his parents and other people and to understand what they say to him. He gains some twenty pounds in weight and a foot or two in height. He changes from a sensory being that may only partially understand his world to a thinker who not only perceives the world in detail and acts effectively on it but also remembers his past and plots his future actions. By the time a child is two, the hand that held a rattle clutches a fat crayon and produces scribbles that appear to bring him pleasure. With the beginning of language, the child's social capabilities expand far beyond the smile and coo that he brought into the world. His early attachment to his mother expands, and the independent toddler makes friends with other children. This unit is about how and why these developmental changes take place.

CHAPTER 6
Physical Growth: Fundamentals

DIRECTIONS OF GROWTH
Cephalocaudal Development
Proximodistal Development
Differentiation and Integration

NORMS

USING NORMS

INDIVIDUAL VARIABILITY
Individual Time Patterns
The Role of Nutrition

BRAIN DEVELOPMENT
Brain Growth
Cortical Control

DEVELOPMENT OF MOTOR ABILITIES
Handedness
Coordination of Movement
Maturation and Experience

PHYSICAL AND SOCIAL CHANGES

SUMMARY

Lauren, who is eleven months old, has just learned to stand up. Each time her mother places her on the floor, she creeps to the nearest piece of furniture and pulls herself to her feet. Then she wails loudly for help because she cannot walk and she is afraid to let go. She has learned to keep her knees stiff and support her weight, but she cannot keep her balance. As soon as her mother sets her back down on the floor, Lauren creeps to another part of the room and repeats the scene. It will be several weeks before she learns to slide back to a sitting position or to let go and simply sit down.

Lauren's physical development follows the norm, but some babies her age have been walking for several months and others will not stand for another three or four months. Although it is possible to generalize about the physical development of babies, the first thing one notices about a group of infants is how different each appears. Marked structural differences have existed among them since soon after conception. Newborn infants differ in such physical variables as height (length), weight, muscularity, hairiness, dental development, and a host of other measurable characteristics. As the child grows, these physical differences persist. Some, such as height and weight, may become more pronounced; others, such as hairiness, less pronounced.

The process of growth can be described as a series of interactions between the growing organism and its environment. As a by-product of this process, a baby becomes larger, the structure and function of his body become increasingly complex, and he approaches ever more closely his adult size, organic structure, and body build. He will never again grow as fast; the rate of physical change is greater at infancy than at any other time after birth.

One of the major reasons psychologists study physical changes is to gain insight into the relationships between inherited factors and factors in the child's environment. If they can establish such relationships, they can begin to identify the conditions that lower a child's efficiency or hinder normal development. Once such interactions are understood, there is some possibility of controlling unwanted deviations from normal patterns of growth.

In Chapter 4 we traced the development of the fetus from the moment of conception to the time of birth. In Chapter 5 we considered the first few weeks of the baby's life outside the mother's womb. In this chapter we will follow the baby's physical development until the age of two. Basing our discussion on some of the basic principles that govern all physical growth, we will outline some of the ways in which psychologists have tried to summarize growth, the measures they have used, and the descriptions they have developed of the average infant. We will develop a general picture of the growth that takes place and the motor abilities that appear in the first two years of life. Because each baby's combined environment and heredity are unique, we will consider the ways in which physical development may differ from one child to the next. We will see how such differences can affect a child's personality and social behavior and how the motor changes of infancy influence the baby's intellectual and perceptual growth, broadening his world in many ways.

DIRECTIONS OF GROWTH

The systematic study of any phenomenon, whether it is growth or gravity, usually begins with a description of the way that phenomenon ordinarily occurs. Thus, the systematic study of physical development requires the observation of large numbers of infants over a considerable period of time. From such observations, scientists have learned how growth appears to operate most of the time, and they have formulated some basic principles of growth and outlined the general development of the average infant.

At the most general level of description, three basic principles underlie the growth and development of all body systems. These are cephalocaudal development, proximodistal development, and differentiation and hierarchic integration.

Cephalocaudal Development

The word "cephalocaudal" comes from the Greek word for "head" and the Latin word for "tail," and cephalocaudal growth in infancy refers to the direction of the body's physical growth. It is re-

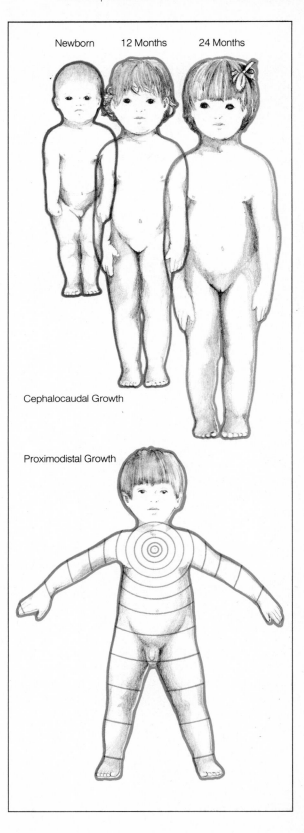

Newborn   12 Months   24 Months

Cephalocaudal Growth

Proximodistal Growth

flected in the order in which parts of the body become larger and in the order in which functions and structures become more complex. Cephalocaudal growth progresses from head to foot; a baby's head develops and grows before his torso, arms, and legs. This pattern of growing seems to reflect the fact that the most rapid embryological development occurs in or near those cells destined to be parts of the brain and nervous system (Debakan, 1959).

At birth a baby's head is nearer to its adult size than any other portion of his body. From birth to adulthood, a person's head doubles in size, and the trunk trebles. His arms and hands quadruple in length, and his legs and feet grow fivefold. Much of the increase in height that takes place in childhood is an increase in the length of the lower limbs. As a child grows, his head contributes proportionately less to total body length, shrinking from one-quarter of the total at birth to one-twelfth at maturity (Bayley, 1956). These changes in body proportions are shown in Figure 6.1.

The movement and motor ability of a baby also become more controlled and complex in progression from head to toe. The baby first gains control over the muscles of his head and neck, then his arms and abdomen, and finally his legs. A baby learns to hold up his head before he learns to sit; he learns to sit before he can walk. He uses his hand as a unit before he can control the finer movements of his fingers. Long before he can walk or run steadily, a baby can make complicated, controlled movements of his arms and fingers, picking up even tiny specks of lint.

Proximodistal Development

Physical growth and motor development also proceed in a proximodistal direction. That is, growth progresses from the center of the body toward the periphery. A baby learns to control the movements of his shoulders before he can direct his arms or fingers. In general, control over movement seems to travel down a baby's arm as he becomes increasingly accurate and sophisticated in his attempts to reach for and grasp an object. In the same manner, a baby gains control over his upper leg before he can manage his lower leg or his foot.

Figure 6.1   (*opposite*) Physical growth and motor abilities develop in two directions simultaneously: from top to bottom (cephalocaudal) and from center to periphery (proximodistal).

Drinking from a cup requires the integration of specific skills and actions. This year-old infant uses and adjusts her grasping and sucking skills as she learns to drink from a cup. (Tom Suzuki)

Differentiation and Integration

A third trend of growth and development has been labeled in a number of ways. We will call it differentiation and integration. Differentiation means that an infant's abilities become increasingly distinct and specific. He gains mastery of movement after movement. For example, a baby may react to a shoe that is too tight with his whole body, wiggling, thrashing, crying, and generally creating a ruckus. As the baby grows older, his movements become more specific, so that his response to a tight shoe is to thrash about only the offending foot. Eventually he learns to make very specific responses; for example, he may ultimately say, "Foot hurt." Sensory stimulation from the foot travels to the brain, where it is interpreted. The interpretation influences the form of the infant's language, which is a complex behavior.

Complex responses require the infant to combine and integrate many more specific, distinct, and differentiated skills. *Hierarchic* integration is the term Heinz Werner (1948) used to describe this trend toward combining simple, differentiated skills into more complex skills. For example, after the baby has mastered the use of his arms as levers, the muscles of his abdomen as lifters of the upper body, and his neck muscles to control his head, he develops hierarchic patterns of movements that bring each separate motor capability into the service of the others in a highly organized way. At last, after each of these various simpler movements has been developed, the baby puts them all together and soon can sit up.

Consider another example, the combination and integration of simple skills involved in learning to drink from a cup without help. Little Lauren must first be able to sit up and to fixate her eyes on an object. She must then be able to use her visual information to reach out, find the object, grasp it, and hold it upright. She then must combine visual information with kinesthetic information about the position of her own head and mouth, arms and hands, in order to bring the cup to her mouth, tilt it at the correct angle, stop tilting it before it spills, and swallow. Of course, the information described here is just a fraction of the information Lauren

uses in drinking from a cup, but she combines and integrates it all so smoothly that one seldom considers the number of simple abilities that may be involved.

NORMS

The principles we have just discussed describe growth and development at a general level. Psychologists interested in normative development have compiled detailed, specific outlines of individual events in the infant's growth process. A number of investigators (Bayley, 1956; Cattell, 1940; Gesell, 1925; Griffiths, 1954; Lenneberg, 1967) have analyzed the developmental sequence in which various physical characteristics and various motor, language, and social skills emerge. Investigations like these have produced outlines that describe the development of important attributes and skills and the approximate ages at which they appear in the average child. Such descriptive outlines are called **norms.**

Drawing on these norms, we can summarize the patterns of infant growth and development and present a profile of the growing infant's first two years. During the first year of life, the baby shows extensive growth changes. His body length increases more than one-third, and his weight almost triples. Matt, who was twenty inches long and weighed seven and one-half pounds at birth, will probably be twenty-eight or twenty-nine inches long and will weigh approximately twenty-two pounds by the time he is one year old. During these first two years, his head will grow more

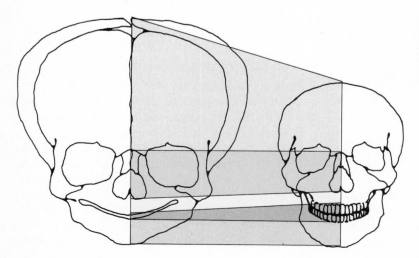

Figure 6.2   Changes in skull and facial proportions with growth. The skull outlined at the left is that of a newborn, whereas the skull at the right is that of a mature adult. (Adapted from Jackson, 1923)

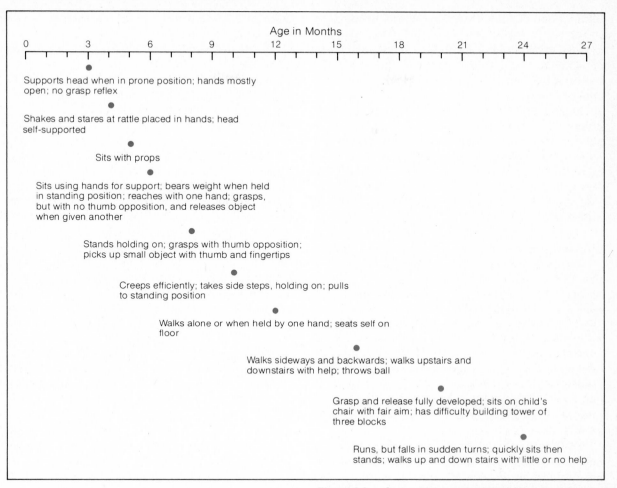

Figure 6.3   Some of the major milestones in motor development that occur over the first two years of life. Each dot indicates the approximate average age of occurrence. Individual infants may demonstrate these skills somewhat earlier or later than the average indicated. (After Lenneberg, 1967, and Bayley, 1969)

slowly than his trunk and limbs, so that his proportions become more adultlike. In addition, his facial skeleton will become relatively larger, so that his cranium is no longer so out of proportion with his face (see Figure 6.2).

In the first two years of life, the difference between boys and girls in growth rate and body proportion is so slight as to be of no practical significance. Even so early, however, the composition of male and female bodies differs. Baby girls have proportionately more fat and both less muscle and less water than boys (Falkner, 1966).

By carefully observing many children, scientists have described and charted literally hundreds of small but important motor developments that occur in the first two years of life. Figure 6.3 presents a simplified look at some of these norms for motor development. You should note that each of

the motor milestones in the figure emerges in small steps over a period of weeks or months and that it is possible to outline a number of further steps in the development of a single ability such as grasping or walking. Drawing on these detailed descriptions, we can develop portraits of the infant at different periods in the first two years of life.

In the first three months of life, an infant spends a great deal of time sleeping, eating, and crying. During these weeks, the parents see the small but steady changes in their baby's behavior and come to believe that the infant is beginning to see and hear and notice his new world. Although the amount of time an infant spends sleeping or crying varies greatly from one child to the next, the average infant shows a noticeable decrease in these activities at about twelve weeks. By this time, he has usually given up at least one feeding. Now parents can get some sleep.

During this period, vocalizations other than crying also increase. This development comes about partly because when a baby cries less, he has more time to make other sounds. He also pays more attention to things that go on around him. His crying may increase again during a later period; if it does, however, the causes will be different.

About the third month, the infant begins to show even more visual involvement in the world around him. He begins to respond more to repetition and to show more signs of boredom (or habituation) when the same scene or object is presented over and over again. At this time the baby's first appreciation of a three-dimensional world also appears. Once a baby like Matt can raise his head over the edge of his crib or bassinet, he can begin to explore and interact with his environment. This physical development allows him to acquire more information about his world, and as we will see in Chapter 7, an increase in mobility is followed by an increase in knowledge.

During the period from four to seven months, many developmental changes occur. Perhaps the most important of these is improved eye-hand coordination, which allows the baby to reach for and grasp objects accurately. Although the newborn infant could reach for an object, his eye-hand coordination disappeared by the end of the first month. Not until he is about five months old does he again make eye-guided, purposeful reaches for objects (Bower, 1976). Now that he can control his hands, most of the things the infant does reach will end up in his mouth, regardless of their size, shape, or sanitary condition.

By the time he is six months old, the infant usually can roll over completely, both from back to stomach and from stomach to back. At this age he also often discovers his own feet and becomes quite fascinated by them, especially since he still has little muscular control over his feet and legs. It may seem to the infant that his feet pass quite unexpectedly in and out of his visual field. In most respects, he now seems to be a more human creature, responding warmly to people and events with the smiling, cooing, and wiggling that foreshadow

those social and emotional developments that we will discuss in Chapter 9.

At about seven months a baby may begin to sit up without help, and "drop and fetch" becomes a favorite game. The baby does the dropping; adults do the fetching. Because he seems capable of endless repetition, his parents tire of the game long before he does.

At about eight or nine months, the baby may begin to crawl. Crawling differs from creeping, which occurs about a month later. Crawling is done on the belly, often with the feet dragging along behind. Creeping is done on the hands and knees. Babies crawl in a wide variety of ways. Some scoot along either sideways or frontward on their bottoms. Some push themselves with their legs, using a leg motion rather like that used when swimming the breaststroke. Some propel themselves with their arms or with just one arm. Many infants learn to move backward first. Some babies do not creep or crawl at all, but one day they simply get up on their feet and walk.

During the first half of the second year of life, the majority of infants, but by no means all, take their first steps (Falkner, 1966). The consequences of this development for the life of a child and his parents are incalculable. The increased opportunity that walking gives to a child and the increased danger that it can place him in only begin to suggest the importance of adultlike mobility. Fortunately for parents, a child at this stage usually begins to respond well to simple commands, and he also may be able to express some of his own desires in simple one- or two-word utterances. When his parents react positively to his simple requests, the baby often becomes fascinated with naming objects. The fact that nature provides for the nearly simultaneous development of extreme mobility, adequate comprehension, and at least the rudiments of expressive language may play some role in the survival of the human species.

By eighteen months an infant can run, if somewhat clumsily, and can drag or push a toy along as he propels himself through the environment. During the next six months, there is also likely to be a dramatic increase in the child's vocabulary (Lenneberg, 1967). In fact, some children speak and move so well by the middle or end of the second year that they hardly qualify as infants. Selected norms for motor development during the infant's second year, shown in Figure 6.3, indicate that his range of physical capabilities also continues to ex-

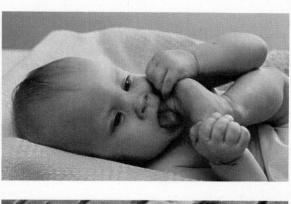

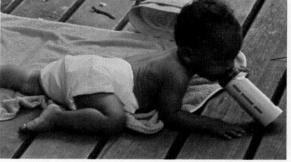

The baby begins to explore his environment with his eyes. As his eye-hand coordination develops, he can grasp and manipulate objects. At eight or nine months, the baby's improved coordination allows him to crawl. Walking means new opportunities and new dangers. (*Clockwise from left:* Charles Harbutt/Magnum Photos; Suzanne Szasz; Bill Stanton/Magnum Photos; Frostie/Woodfin Camp & Assoc.; Kryn Taconis/Magnum Photos)

pand during the period from eighteen months to two years.

By the time the infant is two, he will be able to walk well and to run reasonably well, if incautiously. He may be able to use 200 different words, point to the parts of his body, and play alone for short periods of time. His parents will probably stop referring to him as "the baby." The child at this point has emerged from the infant.

USING NORMS

It is important to understand the significance of norms, what they can and cannot do. Norms are based on simple mathematical calculations that reflect the average growth tendencies for a large number of children. Norms do not tell us what is abnormal or unacceptable. They do not explain growth or development; they merely describe it. Norms do not tell us what is ideal; they merely indicate what is most likely to appear in the development of children at various ages.

Norms can be useful in describing how most infants develop. For example, they can provide guidelines for assessing the effects of environmental change on behavior, such as the effect of separating a child from his mother, or they can be useful in studying cross-cultural and subcultural variations. They have also been used to examine the effects of institutionalization, of sex, and of birth order on a child's development. They have been helpful in studies of prematurity and of early pathology (Kessen, Haith, and Salapatek, 1970). However, except for cases of large, obvious deviation, the value of norms as a predictor or diagnostic tool for an individual child is usually limited.

Two problems arise when one attempts to use norms as diagnostic tools. First, the wide range of variability among normal children limits the usefulness of norms in making statements about one particular child. Second, developmental tests in infancy do not correlate with childhood measures of intelligence. This is an important point, because many parents expect norms of, say, motor-skill development to tell them something about their child's intellectual capacities. However, several authors, including Nancy Bayley (1949) and Psyche Cattell (1940), have shown that the relationship between such developmental measures in the first eighteen months of life and intelligence-test scores

between five and eighteen years is, for all practical purposes, zero.

It is equally important to recognize that there is great specificity in skills. That is, Lauren's ability to catch a ball cannot be used to predict her ability at the high jump or the hundred-yard dash. After early infancy, practice also plays a large part in the level of a child's motor skills.

INDIVIDUAL VARIABILITY

As we have seen, the most common way of looking at growth is to compare a child at successive ages with the average of a large group of normal children of the same ages. The resulting individual curve of growth shows the child's growth scores relative to the average child and his relative position in a representative group of children. Despite the nearly universal sequences of growth that are described by some norms, there is great variability among children. If a rule must be established, it would emphasize deviation from the norm. Newborn infants, for example, show great individual differences in the relative proportions of various parts of their bodies. These differing proportions lend some infants a long and thin look, some a short and round one, and others every conceivable aspect in between. Also, there is greater variation in growth among boys than among girls, and individual growth patterns are more stable for girls (Tanner, 1970). A study by Howard Meredith (1963) illustrates the amazing range of individual differences in physical growth. In his study of Iowa males, the lightest boy at the age of eighteen weighed no more than the heaviest boy had weighed when he was eight. The boy who was lightest at age eight weighed about the same as the heaviest boy had at age two.

There is, of course, also great variability in the age at which perfectly normal children master motor skills. We have noted that some normal children never crawl or creep at all but go directly from sitting to standing and taking their first steps. The normal range for the onset of walking is itself large, perhaps from as early as eight months to as late as twenty.

Individual Time Patterns

There also are great differences in *patterns* of growth. Some normal children mature much slower or faster than the mythical average infant described by pediatricians' and psychologists' charts. Researchers have found, for example, that rates of maturation seem to be related to certain types of body build. The child who is broadly built, large, and strong is likely to be a fast grower, whereas a slender, long-legged but small, lightly muscled child is likely to grow more slowly (Bayley, 1956).

It may well be that in some areas, individual development that does not match the norm even has some distinct advantages. Paul Mussen and Mary Cover Jones (1957) have found, for example, that male children who develop earlier than their age-mates may experience some psychological and social benefits. In a number of ways, early-maturing boys appear to be better adjusted than late-maturing boys.

One possible solution to the problems created by great differences in growth among infants is to look at an individual's growth only in relation to his own time pattern. Data on the same child over long periods of time allow one to make statements about that child's growth relative to himself. This means that one takes the child's own status at a particular time (for example, height, weight, the closure of the bones in his hand) and uses it as the standard against which to compare his status at other times. Such time patterns for individual children can be compared to relevant norms in order to find any indications of relative precocity or slowness in patterns of growth.

Individual time patterns are more or less stable measures of growth. However, there is some evidence that severe dietary deficiencies and stress can affect these patterns, resulting in a temporary slowing of growth. When the condition responsible for the retarded growth is eliminated, a child often goes through a period of "catch-up" growth. J. M. Tanner (1970) calls this temporary deviation from the child's normal growth curve and the subsequent return to it the **canalization** of growth. He argues that the growth curves of individual children are genetically determined and self-stabilizing. Illness or malnutrition may temporarily deflect a child's growth from this natural curve, as a stream can be temporarily deflected from its normal course by an obstruction, but the child later catches up if his environment becomes normal.

Newborn babies also show catch-up growth in both weight and height. From birth to six months or so, smaller babies gain more weight than larger ones (Tanner, 1970). This explains the fact that small women often bear babies who become large adults. Such newborn catch-up growth is usually completed by the end of the third year. Because most babies have caught up by that time, if one knows the height and weight of a three-year-old, the chances of predicting the child's approximate weight and height as an adult are quite good.

The Role of Nutrition

Dietary deficiencies are a common cause of abnormal growth patterns during infancy. In Chapter 4 we saw the effect of extreme dietary deficiency on the developing fetus. The importance of diet in growth and development continues after the baby is born. If, for example, one of two groups of average babies has a protein-deficient diet while the other eats protein-rich food, the deficient babies will grow to be shorter and less muscular, on the average, than the well-fed babies will. If the two groups are compared to the norms of growth, it becomes clear that it is the deficient babies who are behind in development, while the well-fed babies are growing according to the average.

Figure 6.4   An illness in which food intake was greatly reduced for approximately one year affected the growth of a young child. When the illness ended and food intake was restored to normal levels, the child caught up with his own time pattern in approximately two years, providing an example of canalization. (Adapted from Prader, Tanner, and von Harnack, 1963)

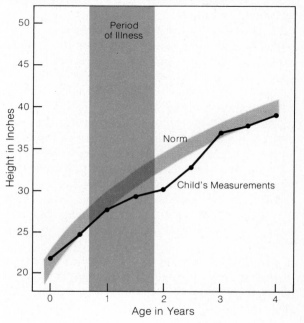

Severe, prolonged protein deficiency can lead to **kwashiorkor,** a severe, often fatal disease found among infants in developing countries whose diets consist largely of breast milk after they are a year old (Scrimshaw, 1969; Waterlow, 1973). The symptoms of this disease include scaly skin, profound apathy, diarrhea, swollen limbs and abdomen, and liver degeneration. According to studies reported by Heinz Eichenwald and Peggy Crooke Fry (1969), when infants who are suffering from kwashiorkor eat adequate protein, they begin to grow rapidly but never catch up with normal children of their own age. This finding underlines the importance of diet as a central environmental determinant of normal physical growth.

The importance of nutrition for human growth is also reflected in growth records of infants who have been exposed to wartime famine. These children show delayed growth during such periods of malnutrition (Tanner, 1970). If the episode of malnutrition is neither too severe nor too long, children can usually overcome effects of acute malnourishment (catch-up growth). However, a child who is chronically undernourished will suffer permanent effects. Such children generally grow to be smaller adults than they would have been had they eaten an adequate diet. Nevin Scrimshaw and John Gordon (1968) have discussed the probable effects of severe malnutrition on the human nervous system. They point out that, although head circumference shows no relationship to intelligence among normal children, it is a reasonably good indicator of brain size. They then cite the reports of researchers in Mexico, Guatemala, Peru, Uganda, and other developing countries, which show that children who have had severely deficient diets from birth show smaller head circumference than children of the same ethnic group who have always been well-fed.

Severe malnutrition in laboratory animals, especially when the animals are very young, also stunts brain growth. John Dobbing (1968) and others have shown that young pigs that suffer severe malnutrition during their first year of life never catch up with normal animals. Even after two and one-half years of normal feeding, such animals show structural changes in their nervous systems.

Although this combined evidence provides a picture of the effects of general malnutrition on physical growth, it is also known that specific deficiencies can have specific effects. For example,

calcium is an essential element in the diet of infants because it is crucial to the replacement of cartilage in the skeleton with bone. A deficiency of calcium during infancy and childhood can lead to a condition known as **rickets,** which is characterized by softening and malformation of the bones.

Nutrition, then, plays an important role in a baby's development, both while he is in the womb and after he is thrust into the world. When dealing with middle-class infants in developed countries, it is easy to forget nutrition's part in establishing the internal environment of the child. But when looking at babies who have never received adequate diets, one finds it hard to overestimate the importance of proper food.

BRAIN DEVELOPMENT

As motor abilities develop and become coordinated, a baby undergoes correlated physiological growth. In early infancy, for example, when changes are most rapid, a baby's ability to perform motor functions correlates highly with his muscular development. The repeated observation of correlations between physical growth and motor development has led some researchers to look for internal growth that may be related to both, as in growth of the brain.

Brain Growth

At birth the baby's brain has already reached about 25 percent of its adult weight and size. Within two years, it will reach about 75 to 80 percent of that size. This increased growth is due in part to increases in the sizes and shapes of supporting glial cells (Bullock, Orkand, and Grinnell, 1977). Another part of it is due to growth within the neurons; certain substances increase, indicating that protein is being synthesized, and small, fibrous structures appear. Myelin that continues to form around the neural fibers, and the increased number and complexity of connections among neurons, also add to brain growth.

The course of this growth is genetically fixed, and it proceeds in an orderly and patterned way. The major pathways that connect parts of the nervous system and brain and are responsible for the sustenance of life are fully functional at birth. As other neural circuits develop, the cells show a great variety in shape and size, and their conducting fibers are relatively small and short. In keeping with nature's blueprint, each region of the brain eventually becomes characterized by specific types of cells arranged in specific patterns. As the connecting fibers spread, the distance between the cells of the infant's cortex increases, and the enlarged surface of the cortex continues to fold and become increasingly wrinkled (Rose, 1973).

Perhaps because of its extensive, rapid growth during infancy, the baby's central nervous system is more plastic than it will be later in life. It has been found that if an infant is born with a maldeveloped major brain tract, his nervous system may be capable of correcting for it, possibly by developing the same function in a different area. In addition, when an infant suffers brain damage, he is likely to recover quickly and to show no apparent aftereffects (Searleman, 1977). If, for example, the part of his brain that controls language function should be injured, the baby is still likely to develop normal language abilities.

As you will recall from Chapter 5, at the time a baby is born, the electrical activity of his brain shows characteristic wave patterns when he is awake or sleeping. When he is two or three months old, he begins each sleep period with quiet sleep instead of going immediately into REM sleep, as he did at birth. Other regular changes in the electrical activity of his brain, including a typical pattern that occurs during the transition from wakefulness to sleep, appear during the last half of the first year. Although Robert Emde and his colleagues (1976) have been trying to establish a connection between the development of infant wave forms and the appearance of certain emotional expressions, their data show no close relationships. Other investigators, however, have found that when a baby sees something new or hears a sound, he responds with increasingly complex patterns of wave forms in various areas of his brain (Cobb and Mozocutti, 1967). The size and speed of these wave forms may continue to undergo maturational changes until he is six years old.

Cortical Control

Jesse Le Roy Conel's pioneer studies (1939–1963) of the postnatal development of the human cerebral cortex are among those that demonstrate a possible basis in the central nervous system for the orderly development of an infant's motor and sensory functions. This and other work show that certain areas of the brain control particular sensory and motor functions and that these areas develop at different rates. As soon as the specific area in the

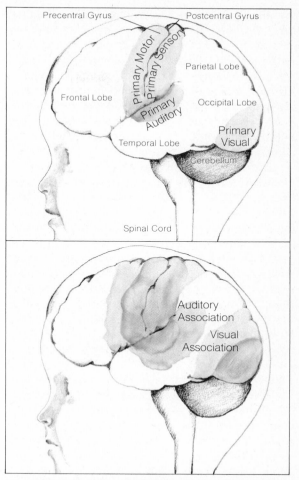

Figure 6.5   (*top*) Drawing of the human brain, showing some of its major structures and their location and indicating the location of those primary sensory and motor areas of the cerebral cortex discussed in the text. (*bottom*) Similar drawing, showing location of later-developing association areas of the cerebral cortex, as discussed in the text.

cortex develops, the corresponding functions appear in the infant's behavior.

Postnatal development of the cortex can be followed in two directions. One is the sequence in which the functional areas of the brain develop; the second is the advancement of body functions within each of these areas (Minkowski, 1967). The early stages of development are characterized by an orderly sequence in which the primary areas of the cortex begin to function efficiently. First, the primary motor area in the precentral gyrus develops, then the primary sensory area in the postcentral gyrus (see Figure 6.5). Next, the primary visual area, at the back of the head in the occipital lobe, develops, followed by the primary auditory area at the side of the head in the temporal lobe. At first, these primary areas function at a simple level. For example, the baby can control some of his basic body movements, and he can hear and see. However, the cortical association areas, which must develop before the baby can integrate and interpret the stimuli he encounters, lag behind the corresponding primary areas.

The cortical control of behavior develops sequentially. Whereas most of the cerebral cortex thickens during the baby's first three months, the primary motor area develops more rapidly. Again, the cephalocaudal and proximodistal developmental patterns hold true; cortical control of the head, upper trunk, and arms appears before that of the legs, and cortical control of arm movements appears before the baby can use his hands skillfully. The other primary cortical areas develop in sequence, and the infant is capable of controlled movement and simple visual and auditory functions. At this time the cells of the motor and sensory areas rapidly develop a sheath of myelin, which speeds the transmission of nerve impulses.

When the baby reaches the age of six months, the primary motor and sensory areas are still the most advanced, but other areas of the cortex are beginning to catch up. There is marked growth in the cortical motor areas that control the hands, upper trunk, head, and legs. Between six and fifteen months, growth of these motor areas slows down. The infant can then control his hands and

arms, but control over his legs is not nearly so well developed. In fact, some children still do not walk at fifteen months. During the period from six to fifteen months, the visual association areas of the cortex are still more advanced than the auditory association areas. By the time the child is two, however, his primary motor and sensory cortical areas are well advanced and his cortical association areas have developed further. This continued cortical development enables the two-year-old to integrate the information he gets from his environment and his own movements into more complex patterns of behavior.

The relationship between growth of particular cortical areas and the development of motor functions is *correlational*. You will recall that correlations do not tell us what is cause and what is effect. Therefore, some authors have argued that the baby's use of his body and nervous system causes the growth of appropriate brain areas, instead of brain growth leading to increased physical and mental control. Steven Rose (1973) is among those who suggest that the barrage of sensory information that assails the newborn when he emerges from the shelter of the womb leads the cortex to grow and neural connections to develop. In support of this position, one can point to studies of animals that have shown that parts of the nervous system atrophy without stimulation (Rosenzweig, Bennett, and Diamond, 1972; Wiesel and Hubel, 1963). Yet studies of premature human babies show that they reach various motor milestones at what would be the same age, calculated from the

The baby gains control over his hands, arms, and upper trunk well before he can control his legs. (Jan Lukas/Photo Researchers, Inc.)

moment of their conception rather than from the time of birth, as those born at full-term, despite the fact that premature babies receive an extra month or two of external stimulation as a result of their early birth (Douglas, 1956).

DEVELOPMENT OF MOTOR ABILITIES

Almost every sequence of motor development has been studied. Some appear to develop in simple, orderly fashion, whereas others are complex and show little consistency in their development. Even some simple sequences depend on an intricate interplay between maturational changes and experience.

Handedness

A puzzle in the field of motor development is handedness. Only 5 to 10 percent of the world's adult population is left-handed, although a full 15 percent of preschoolers are "lefties." The frequency of left-handedness in both identical and fraternal twins is significantly higher than it is among single births (Hicks and Kinsbourne, 1976). But there is no known genetic or constitutional basis for handedness (Hardyck and Petrinovich, 1977), and it is certain from the variety of clever and capable southpaws in the world that they are at no real disadvantage in a world designed for the convenience of the right-handed. The facts suggest a partially experiential basis for handedness. Rhesus monkeys, who do not encounter human society, split half and half in left- and right-handedness.

It is not at all clear why such a small percentage of the human species start out left-handed, although one possible explanation has to do with **cerebral dominance.** That is, the left side of the brain controls the voluntary muscles of the right side of the body, and the right side of the brain controls the voluntary muscles of the left side of the body. In most people, the left hemisphere becomes dominant. But whether most of us are right-handed because we are left-brained or left-brained because we are right-handed is uncertain (Hécaen and Ajuriaguerra, 1964).

Handedness begins to become evident in the latter part of the first year. Almost as soon as the infant can use his two hands independently, he prefers the right. Several findings suggest that this preference develops according to a timetable. In the first few months of life, when babies turn their heads, they will extend an arm in the direction their head is turned. This asymmetrical posture,

called the tonic neck reflex, predicts which hand they will prefer later, because the arm they extend reflexively is likely to be that of the dominant side. By about three months, most infants tend to hold a toy longer when it is placed in their right hand than when it is placed in their left. By about six to nine months, most babies also prefer to use their right hands when they reach for an object that is directly in front of them.

Because in nearly all adult right-handers and some left-handers the left side of the brain is primarily responsible for the production and comprehension of language, several investigators have suggested that both the onset of handedness and the beginnings of speech may be due to the establishment of the left hemisphere's dominance in the control of motor functions. One piece of evidence that supports this idea is that from about twelve to fifteen months, most infants begin to use their hands in coordination, adopting a consistent right- and left-hand strategy when faced with a task that requires both hands (Ramsay, 1977). In exploring toys with movable parts, right-handed babies are likely to hold the base of the toy in their left hands and manipulate its movable parts with their right. The baby's first words and this coordination both occur at around twelve to fifteen months; the development of left-brain dominance may play a role in their appearance.

Differences in the way the brain processes linguistic and nonlinguistic auditory stimulation also appear to develop very early in life (Molfese, Freeman, and Palermo, 1975). When infants hear consonant-vowel sounds or extended passages of speech, their brain-wave recordings show greater cortical activity over the left than over the right hemisphere. When they hear musical chords or passages of music, however, their right hemispheres show increased cortical activity compared with their left hemispheres.

Despite an early preference for the right hand, the establishment of hemisphere dominance is not complete by the time a child is two. As we will see in Chapter 10, the process may not be complete in some children when they enter school.

Coordination of Movement

Developments in the baby's coordination of motor activities parallel the growth of the appropriate cortical areas. The orderly development of the baby's ability to grasp provides a good illustration of this increasing coordination of movement (Gesell, 1929). During his first few weeks, when shown an object, a baby will reach for it but will not grasp it because he lacks control over the muscles of his hand and fingers. This reaching reflex disappears at about four weeks, but his visual attention continues to develop, and by sixteen weeks he fixes his eyes on the object for long periods and strains his body toward it, showing apparent attention and interest. By twenty weeks he makes crude approaches to the object with both hands. Four weeks later he uses only one hand to reach toward it and usually manages at least to scratch the object. After another four weeks, the baby flexes his whole hand while he reaches. Somewhat later he pokes at the object with his index finger. Finally, at about forty weeks mature grasping appears, and the baby opposes his thumb and forefinger when trying to grab a toy.

The development of walking and running also illustrates the increasing complexity of the infant's brain and abilities. A normal baby's first attempts at locomotion, for example, rely heavily on the use of the arms. Thus, Lauren may drag her rump along the floor while sitting or crawl on her belly, dragging her legs along behind. Next she learns to pull herself up, using her arms for support and balance. At this point she takes her first few wobbly steps, and then more complex developments appear in rapid succession. Between fourteen and twenty-four months, for example, the baby learns to walk sideways, backward, upstairs and downstairs, and to run (Bayley, 1969). In discussing cortical control, we pointed out that the primary motor and sensory areas are quite advanced by the age of two. The increasing sophistication and integration of a child's locomotion reflect this growth. Consider the sensory information and motor skill that a child must integrate if she wishes to walk up and down stairs. She must use both visual information and kinesthetic feedback to guide her steps, as well as posture changes, weight shifts, and further visual responses. When we consider walking from this perspective, it seems a minor miracle that most babies walk so easily and well at such an early age.

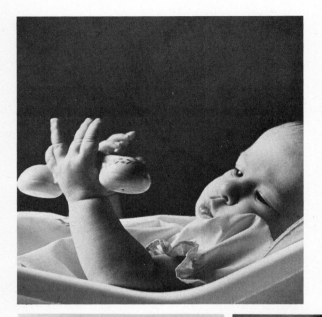

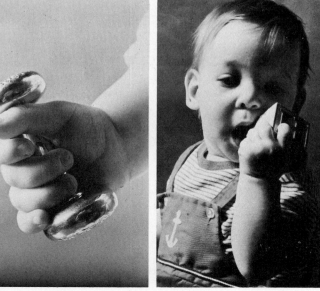

At twenty weeks, infants hold objects without firmly grasping them. By twenty-eight weeks, they can use their palms to close in on and pick up an object. By forty weeks, they use the thumb and forefinger in opposition, grasping much as an adult does. (Steve McCarroll)

Although Hopi infants spend much of their first year bound to cradle-boards, which limit motor activity and practice, they begin to walk at about the same time as most infants in other cultures. (Marcia Keegan)

Figure 6.6   Ages in months at which infants in several cities took their first steps. (Adapted from Hindley et al., 1966)

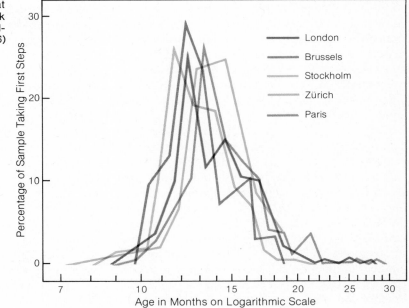

As we noted in Chapter 5, there also may be a developmental sequence to certain skills, in which early, more primitive coordinations disappear and then reappear later in more advanced forms. Although the causes of this sequence are not known, it is possible that they are connected with developmental changes in brain and nervous system organization. Depending on the skill involved, the changes appear to be influenced by stimulation. If, for example, babies are given practice in the stepping reflex for about ten minutes each day from two weeks until they are eight weeks old, they are likely to walk a bit earlier than the average baby (Zelazo, Zelazo, and Kolb, 1972). And if babies are given practice in reaching for an object during the first four weeks of life, the skill reappears earlier than it ordinarily would, and the babies are more proficient at seizing dangling objects than babies who have not had earlier practice (Bower, 1976). Such results illustrate how maturation and experience interact in the development of skills.

Maturation and Experience

The relative roles of maturation and experience in the development of various motor skills have been studied in a number of ways. One method is to observe the age at which infants in different cultures acquire these skills, because different cultures give babies different opportunities to practice them. For example, Hopi Indian infants spend their first year bound to cradleboards; nevertheless, they walk at about the same time as infants in other cultures who have had more practice in muscular coordination (Dennis and Dennis, 1940). Records from five of Europe's largest urban centers show that, even though child-rearing methods differ and, as a result, infants in some areas receive more encouragement to walk, most infants in the five cities take their first steps within a few months of one another (see Figure 6.6).

Another method of studying the relative contributions of maturation and experience is **co-twin control,** in which the experimenter gives one of a pair of twins some experiences believed to be important in learning a skill and withholds or delays those same experiences for the other twin. In Myrtle McGraw's (1935, 1939) classic co-twin control study, one twin received practice in crawling and standing and the other was kept from all opportunities. Despite the difference in their experience, both twins crawled and walked at the same age. Practice did make a difference, however, in the

way the twins developed individualistic skills, such as swimming and skating.

A third method that has been used to evaluate the relative roles of maturation and experience is to deliberately restrict a child's movement. For example, Wayne Dennis (1941) left a pair of female twins on their backs from birth to nine months, never allowing them to sit or to stand. Yet the sitting and standing of both twins emerged fully developed, with little or no practice. It should be noted, however, that except for the experimental restriction, both girls had a fairly normal environment.

A number of years later, the same investigator conducted a series of studies designed to examine the possible effects of a poor environment on the development of motor skills (Dennis, 1960; Dennis and Najarian, 1957; Dennis and Sayegh, 1965). The studies were conducted in institutions that were, by most standards, socially and environmentally impoverished. Children were neither attended to by adults nor surrounded by a stimulating environment. The children showed retarded motor development from the time they were two months old. In one study, Dennis and Yvonne Sayegh (1965) worked with infants in The Creche, a foundling home in Lebanon. In that institution infants spent most of their first year lying on their backs in cribs. Some of the infants in their study who were more than one year old could not sit up. The infants in the experimental group were propped into a sitting position and were allowed to play with such simple attractive objects as fresh flowers, pieces of colored sponge, and colored plastic disks strung on a chain for as little as an hour each day. Despite this seemingly small amount of stimulation, the babies' developmental age jumped dramatically.

In a related study, Burton White and Richard Held (1966) investigated the effect of enriched stimulation on the development of grasping. They concluded that appropriate extra stimulation could accelerate the baby's acquisition of grasping. However, more detailed studies have suggested (B. White, 1967, 1971) that stimulation must be appropriate to both the age of the baby and his abilities. Too much stimulation, for example, may be irritating or confusing to the baby, at least for a short time, and may fail to accelerate the development of his motor skills.

It seems clear from studies such as those of Dennis, White, and their colleagues that, even

In the usual institutional crib, there are few things to look at or touch. In a massively enriched environment, there are many things to look at or touch. But, as White and Held discovered, a slightly enriched environment, which gave an infant only one object to explore at a time, resulted in the fastest development of the baby's ability to grasp. (Courtesy Burton L. White)

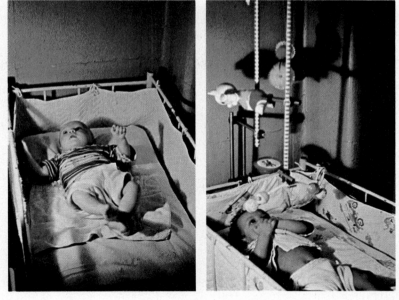

though a baby's motor development may not require any practice beyond normal freedom for spontaneous activity, some environments promote development, whereas others retard it. It is also obvious that a certain amount of stimulation is necessary for the growing infant.

PHYSICAL AND SOCIAL CHANGES

Each new development—sitting, crawling, or walking—vastly increases the infant's perceptual, social, and emotional world, as we will see in later chapters. When Matt becomes strong enough to lift his head over the edge of his crib, he infinitely expands his ability to initiate social contact or perpetuate it, to explore the environment with his eyes, and to learn to cope with it. An infant who can sit demonstrates some control over his abdominal muscles, but, what is perhaps even more important, sitting frees his hands for exploration. Now he can experience the world tactually by grasping, poking, turning, dropping, pouring, and throwing. He can initiate physical contact with other human beings by reaching out to be picked up, grabbing a hand, poking at a face, patting an arm.

Crawling and walking give Matt a full chance to satisfy his curiosity, to go and touch, to pull and push and drag and chase, and to initiate and sustain social interactions. At last he can find some-

one by himself, follow that person, tug on him, and walk hand in hand. It is easy to forget that infants discover the world by banging, chewing, touching, and dismantling. Curiosity and exploratory behavior are essential to learning, language development, concept formation, and social development. Each time a child's physical abilities increase and his perceptual world widens, his potential for learning more about his social world increases. He learns what people do, how they feel, and what they like and do not like. He learns that touching brings a smile, tugging gets attention, and hitting brings a reprimand. He learns whom to seek out and whom to avoid.

It has been emphasized that children differ in their growth and development. Some are large, some small, some fast, some slow. Richard Bell and Lawrence Harper (1977) remind us that, although parents affect their children, children also stimulate their parents to behave in certain ways. For example, David Levy (1958) studied mothers and their newborn infants before they left the hospital. He found that the infant's physical state (awake, asleep, crying, and so on), not the mother's "maternal attitude," appeared to account for the way each mother handled her baby. Michael Lewis (1971) found that, at least among middle-class mothers, a baby's gender also seemed to influence the way a mother treated her infant, and that women were more likely to decide to breast-feed a daughter than a son.

At each succeeding stage of development, the child becomes more able to discover and explore his world. The child who can walk leaves behind the status of babyhood. (© Joel Gordon)

It seems clear that a baby who responds to cuddling with obvious pleasure will not be treated in the same manner as a baby who stiffens when held close. In addition, the child who walks early, say at nine or ten months, but who learns to respond to commands at fourteen or fifteen months is likely to require much more parental patience and physical restraint, to provoke more irritation, and generally to get into more trouble than the child who learns to walk later. On the other hand, the child who walks late may be the focus of much parental anxiety and concern. His parents may devote much time to pulling him upright, encouraging, perhaps even dragging him. Or his parents may view his relative slowness as a reflection of their own failure and therefore ignore him.

As an infant develops, his increased skills and abilities are likely to have major effects on his parents' personal lives (Harper, 1975). As he becomes more mobile and inquisitive, for example, his par-

ents are likely to increase their protective supervision: admonishing the baby not to touch hot appliances, covering open wall sockets, removing and storing breakable or dangerous objects. If there are no playmates of the same age in the immediate vicinity, some parents may even feel compelled to move to a different neighborhood when their child is about two years old, in order to give him an opportunity to play with other children.

The mastery of a skill such as walking, as Erik Erikson (1963) points out, helps to make the child a part of his culture; the child becomes "one who can walk" and acquires a status different from that of "one who cannot walk." The consequences of this transition are hardly trivial; in Western, industrialized, child-centered America the consequences are profound. Cultural recognition, plus the physical mastery itself, contributes not only to the child's social relations and status but also to his necessary and budding self-esteem.

SUMMARY

1. From the systematic study of physical development, scientists have formulated three basic principles that underlie the growth and development of all body systems: cephalocaudal and proximodistal development describe directions of growth; differentiation and integration refer to increasing specificity and complexity of growth and skills.

2. Psychologists have also compiled descriptive outlines of important attributes and skills. These summary outlines are called norms and are based on simple mathematical calculations that indicate average tendencies for a large number of children. Although norms are used to describe how most infants grow and develop, they do not explain or indicate what is abnormal or ideal.

3. Despite nearly universal sequences of development described by some norms, there is great variability among children. Because a given child also shows variability, looking at his growth only in relation to his own pattern usually provides the most stable measure. Nutrition continues to play an important role, and malnutrition can result in diseases that temporarily or permanently affect a child's growth pattern.

4. Development of an infant's motor abilities follows the course of development in the brain and central nervous system. Different areas of the brain develop at different rates, and, as a certain area develops, corresponding sensory and motor abilities appear. Handedness is a puzzle in motor development and may be due to either genetic-constitutional or experiential influences. Coordination of movement also appears to follow nervous-system development.

5. Psychologists have used several methods to study the relative roles of maturation and experience: determining the age at which infants in different cultures acquire certain skills, giving only one of a pair of twins some experience considered necessary in learning a skill, and determining the effects of certain restrictions in a child's experience. In general, it appears that, although only minimal normal practice may be necessary, some environments promote effective development whereas others do not.

6. Changes in strength, coordination, and stature are likely to have a strong impact on the infant's personal and social development. Being able to sit, crawl, or walk permits the infant to explore the world and allows him to test and understand what he can do and who he is in relation to other people.

CHAPTER 7
Cognition: From Sensing to Knowing

COGNITION

PERCEPTUAL FUNCTIONING
Seeing
Hearing
Sensory and Sensory-Motor
Coordination

ATTENTION

CONCEPTS AND SYMBOLS
Object Identity
Object Permanence
Memory and Thought

INFANT-ENVIRONMENT
INTERACTION
Learning
Exploring
Adapting

SUMMARY

David, who is fifteen months old, discovered his mother's pen, which was left lying open on the coffee table. When his mother came to check on her quiet son, she found ink on his mouth, on his hands, and on his clothes. She took away the pen, put it on a high shelf and, when David protested, picked him up for a moment. As soon as she put him down, he toddled over to the shelf, stretched out his arm, opened and closed his fingers, and said "Day-boo"—his word for himself—to indicate he wanted the pen. Although he cannot see the pen, he knows that it is lying on the shelf. David has not always been so persistent. When he was eight months old, he forgot about forbidden playthings when his mother distracted him. But now that he is older, his memory has developed and he has a mental image of the forbidden toy.

David has taken the first steps on the long and challenging journey called cognitive development. In order to understand the demands of the journey, it is important to realize what is involved in the development of the human mind.

The adult mind is organized. Healthy adults clearly distinguish between what is within them—their thoughts, feelings, and dreams—and what is outside them—the physical world of objects and the social world of people. The things outside bear relationship to one another. Some are related by being members of the same category of things. The banana, potato, and pork chop are all foods. The hammer, knife, and saw are all tools. Some things are related in terms of action and its effects. The light switch on the wall is related to the physically dissimilar and spatially remote light on the ceiling. The pressing of a key on the typewriter is related to the letter that appears on the blank page.

Adults recognize that some things that appear to be dissimilar are in fact similar. The water that pours from the tap is the same substance that escapes as steam from the teakettle spout or that clinks as ice in a glass of lemonade. Adults accept such transformations as maintaining the identity of the object that has been transformed. They accept certain different things as equivalent to one another, such as A and a. Other transformations surprise people and demand explanation. If a friend covers something with a handkerchief and it has disappeared when he removes the handkerchief, you are puzzled. Your expectations about the behavior of the world are violated.

All these features of adults' orientation to the world seem so commonplace, so natural, that it is hard to believe that human beings do anything other than passively observe the way things are. It is hard to believe that this commonplace organization of things into categories and into cause-and-effect relationships is, in fact, the product of years of maturation and experience.

In Chapter 6 we watched the way that infants' motor skills develop as they mature and interact with the world. In this chapter we will follow the development of David's and Lauren's **cognition** during their first two years of life. The term "cognition" refers to the way in which each of us comes to know about our world and to what we know about our world. It includes several processes such as sensing, perceiving, using symbols, and reasoning, and we will learn how these processes develop in the growing infant. We will discover what infant studies allow us to infer about the developing mind, and we will see how biological maturation and cumulative experience produce cognitive progress during these two years. Finally, we will consider how babies' interactions with their environment affect their subsequent intellectual growth.

COGNITION

The lengthy story of cognitive development is the story of how David and Lauren progress from the limited and dissociated store of knowledge and intellectual skills they possess at birth, through childhood, to the concept-rich, well-ordered store of knowledge that most adults use so well.

By the time we complete our tale of the first two years, we will have seen babies as remarkably active organisms, curious about the world and themselves and eager to make sense of them both, constructing from their varied experiences new hypotheses about how its parts fit and mesh and about which of their actions are permissible and

which are forbidden. We will see them as architects of time, space, and objects and as designers and users of symbols. Cognition is the vehicle by which infants become so intellectually accomplished.

In 1949 Gilbert Ryle, an English philosopher, distinguished between at least two kinds of knowledge. The first he called *knowing that* or *knowing about* something, and the second, *knowing how* to do something. For example, after studying the grammar of a foreign language, you may be able to state quite precisely all the rules of conjugating its verbs. Yet when called on to speak the language, you may be unable to do so without many errors in your choice of verb form. You know *about* but not *how*. On the other hand, you may speak English fluently and without error, yet be unable to state the grammatical rules that describe the words you are uttering so effortlessly. You know *how* but not *about*.

As we look at the nature of the infant's knowledge, it is wise to keep in mind this distinction between knowing that such and such is the case and knowing how to do something. Because infants are incapable of using language to describe what they know about the world, we must infer what they know about it from what they do and from when and how frequently they do it. In making such inferences about the ideas and perceptions of infants, we must be careful not to assume that they perceive and conceptualize things and events the way that we do.

The environment makes its mark through the various sensory receptors that the infant possesses as a living organism. Infants are biologically constructed so as to be able to pick up certain aspects of the physical world; in other words they are capable of **sensation,** of receiving stimulation or information from the external world. It is important, however, to distinguish between sensitivity to a certain physical or chemical property of the universe and the act and experience of seeing, hearing, smelling, tasting, and touching.

A higher level of knowing about the world is reflected in the infant's **perceptions** of that world. Perceptions are built on sensation but go beyond it. What infants do with the sensations they receive at their sense receptors determines what those perceptions will be. And what they do is affected primarily by their previous experiences and also by the innate characteristics of their nervous systems.

Cognition, in turn, includes more than just

sensation and relatively immediate perception. We adults are much less bound in our thinking to concrete experience than young children and infants are. Most of our concepts and beliefs have been translated into symbols, such as words and pictures. This ability to represent our knowledge of the world with symbols and to use those symbols to assist us in imagining new combinations and transformations of reality that we have never experienced is one of the great cognitive achievements of the human species (Flavell, 1977).

In trying to understand perception and cognition in infants, it is particularly important to realize that infants may perceive or know certain things that they cannot easily convey to us because of inability, fatigue, lack of interest, or unwillingness to behave in a way that would reveal this knowledge. Indeed, a considerable amount of the methodological ingenuity of infant research derives from attempts to get around this problem. Consider a concrete example. If you show five-month-old Lauren a toy, she will reach out and pick it up. If, however, you drop a cloth over the toy before it has been picked up, she will sit quietly and will make no attempt to remove the cloth and get the toy. Lauren's failure to look for the hidden toy could be due to any of several reasons. Perhaps she does not try because out of sight means out of mind to the infant, so that the vanished object no longer exists for her. Or possibly, she simply lacks

the motor skills necessary to remove the cloth and get the toy. She may even have the motor skills but no longer be interested in the toy because some other interesting thing has captured her attention.

The difference among these three interpretations is not trivial. It is important that we be able to distinguish lack of conceptual skill from lack of motor skill and both from lack of interest. The extensive use in infancy research of autonomic responses such as changes in heart rate and in galvanic skin response and of simple-to-execute motor movements such as slight head turns, eye fixations, and eye movements is a way of getting at what the infant knows without requiring that she use any difficult motor skill to inform us. The concern with taking into account the physiological state of the infant, such as when she last ate or slept, is a way of minimizing "lack of interest" factors as reasons for her failure to respond to certain tasks or situations that test her knowledge (Kessen, Haith, and Salapatek, 1970).

PERCEPTUAL FUNCTIONING

Before they can investigate the baby's cognitive processes, researchers must know how well the baby's senses function. It is through his senses that the baby transforms the raw material of stimulation into information. David, for instance, relies on his eyes, ears, mouth, hands, nose, and skin to ex-

Figure 7.1 Experimental conditions used to test infants' perception of distance. Although the retinal size of the novel (test) and original stimuli were the same, infants responded less frequently to the test stimulus, indicating that they perceived the difference in distance between the two experimental conditions. (Adapted from T. G. R. Bower, "The Visual World of Infants," copyright © 1966 by Scientific American, Inc. All rights reserved)

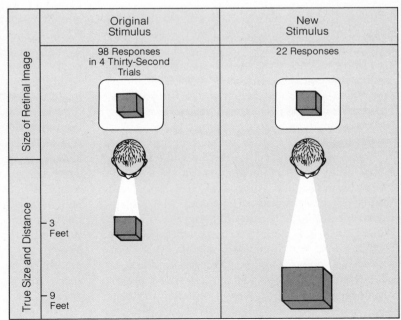

tract information about the pains and pressures, the sounds and sights, and the tastes and smells in his world.

Seeing

Before the end of his first year, the baby's visual system functions like that of an adult in many respects. By the time they are four months old, for example, babies perceive color as hues like red, blue, green, and yellow (Bornstein, 1975, 1976). These categories and their perceptions of them tend to correspond to the apparently universal and nonarbitrary psychological color categories used by older children and adults (e.g., Heider, 1972). What the sight means to them, of course, is very different from the meaning the same sight will convey several years later (Haber and Hershenson, 1973). Yet vision is probably the baby's most important source of information about the environment during the early months of life.

A study by Thomas G. R. Bower (1966) indicates that even a baby of six to eight weeks may be able to judge the distance of objects. Bower trained infants to turn their heads to the side whenever a twelve-inch cube was placed about three feet away from them. After the babies had learned to discriminate between the presence and absence of the cube, he showed them a thirty-six-inch cube at a distance of about nine feet. At that distance, the large cube produced the same size image on a baby's retina as the small cube had at three feet. The only basis for discrimination was the distance of the two objects, but the babies could tell them apart. Furthermore, they could do it even if they were allowed to use only one eye.

During the third month of life, other significant changes occur in the visual world of the infant (Kessen, Haith, and Salapatek, 1970). For one thing, as babies' ability to discriminate improves, they begin to watch strange objects in preference to familiar ones. For example, Joseph Fagan (1971) showed infants of five, seven, and ten weeks of age visual stimuli, some that were already familiar to the babies and others that were novel, and studied their responses. He found that seven-week-olds preferred the familiar stimulus, whereas the ten-week-olds preferred the novel one. Fagan, Robert Fantz, and Simon Miranda (1971) were interested in knowing whether biological maturation of the visual system played a role in these preference changes over time. They conducted the same familiar-versus-novel preference test using one group of infants born four weeks before they were due and another group born at full-term. When they compared the results, they found that eleven-week-old "preemies" did not behave like eleven-week-old full-termers. In fact, the preemies did not behave like eleven-week-old full-termers until they were fifteen weeks old. In other words, the preemies' four additional weeks of visual experience in the world did not affect their visual preference. Before they could respond to the familiar-novel dimension of visual information, their visual systems needed to reach a certain level of biological maturation.

It is one thing to perceive the quality of relative distance, which Bower demonstrated in small babies. It appears to be quite another to use these visual cues as "warnings" about possible dangers associated with depth, such as falling off tables or chairs. In a novel experiment, Eleanor Gibson and Richard Walk (1960) studied infants' use of depth information by placing the infants on what appeared to be the edge of a cliff. Their experiments showed that an infant who is old enough to crawl will not crawl over the deep side of a visual cliff, even to reach his mother. And when restricted to using only one eye, infants avoided the deep side of the cliff just as the infants with normal vision did, showing that binocular differences are not required to perceive the apparent danger. Because the infants in these experiments were between eight and twelve months old, it was difficult to say whether they had learned the behavior or whether it represented a maturation of vision. Subsequently, however, Sandra Scarr and Philip Salapatek (1970), using the visual-cliff apparatus designed by Gibson and Walk, found that infants begin to use depth cues to avoid edges shortly after they reach seven months of age, but only if they have begun crawling before that time. It seems, then, that some crawling experience is necessary before the infant can learn that visual cues of depth signify possible hazards. Without that experience, a baby may sense the difference yet show no fear. When two-month-old babies are placed on the deep side of the cliff, their hearts slow down, suggesting they make some sort of discrimination related to depth. When nine-month-olds are placed on the deep side, however, their hearts speed up, suggesting they are afraid (Campos, 1976).

Visual-cliff apparatus. An infant who can crawl (about six to seven months) may cross the glass surface over the ''shallow'' side (*top left*) to reach his mother, but he is likely to refuse to venture out over an edge that appears to be a sudden drop (*top right*) or to cross over to the surface on the ''deep'' side (*bottom*), even if his mother is on the other side urging him to join her. (Steve McCarroll)

Hearing

Another major source of environmental information for the developing infant is sound. Auditory perception is important in learning to understand and speak language and in determining the location of people or events. One way to discover a baby's sensitivity to various sounds is to show him a checkerboard pattern until he habituates (which, you will recall, refers to the decrease of responsiveness to a stimulus with prolonged or repeated exposure to it), then add some specific sound and see if his perception of the sound reawakens his interest in the checkerboard. Using this method, Frances Horowitz (1975) and her students have discovered that five-week-old babies who have stopped looking at a checkerboard seem to look again with interest when they hear music, and that eight-week-old babies increase their looking when they hear the recorded voice of a woman. By the time they are nine weeks old, they seem to discriminate between the voices of their mothers and the voice of a female stranger, as measured by the length of time they look at the checkerboard after hearing the voices. Although some babies as old as eleven weeks could not tell the difference between slides of their mother's faces and those of female strangers, when Horowitz accompanied the slides with the appropriate voices, the babies could distinguish between them.

In another study, Jerome Kagan and his colleagues (1971) tested the extent to which eight-month-old boys could recognize familiar sounds. They read four sentences to each baby in the study. Two of the sentences used such words as "smile" and "daddy" that are frequently part of parents' interactions with their babies, and the words were arranged in a meaningful way. The two other sentences were nonsensical. Kagan and his colleagues found that the babies responded in a different manner to these different combinations of sounds. The meaningful sentences with familiar words brought about a higher rate of babbling in the eight-month-old babies than did the nonsensical ones. This effect occurred even when the person who read the sentences was a male stranger, whose voice was unfamiliar.

Toward the end of his first year, the infant has progressed considerably beyond his auditory capacities of the first few months, which even then were quite impressive. At that time he was sensitive to such things as the frequency, duration, and intensity of sounds. By the end of the first year,

however, he is also sensitive to the differences between various combinations of sounds and recognizes certain words. As was the case with the development of his visual perception, the baby becomes increasingly sensitive to the meanings of the sounds he hears. He is now on the threshold of language acquisition, which will progress rapidly during his second year.

Sensory and Sensory-Motor Coordination

The senses of the healthy infant do not function independently of one another or of the infant's motor abilities (Gibson, 1969). Rather, they work as a team. Everything the child can reach enters his mouth, there to be explored with his tongue and lips. The baby is a tireless reacher, grasper, and handler of objects, which he studies not only with his eyes but also with his fingers. As Jean Piaget (1954) has shown, by the latter part of his first year, the infant will construct notions of objects in terms of their combined touchable, tastable, smellable, hearable, seeable, graspable, and reachable characteristics. Because most events or objects provide multiple kinds of stimulation, infants discover that one kind of sensation signals that sensations of other kinds are probably near them in space or in time. For example, if David hears a sound, he learns that it pays to look because he may see some interesting sight.

According to Morton Mendelson and Marshall Haith (1976), babies come into the world prepared to learn about relations between sights and sounds. Mendelson and Haith studied babies less than one week old, measuring the babies' glances by the position of reflected infrared lights on the pupils of their eyes. The researchers found that the sound of a male voice increased the amount of time the babies kept their eyes wide, increased their eye control, and caused them to look more at the center of their visual fields and to scan with smaller eye movements. The sound appeared to make the babies alert to possible visual stimulation. When the researchers played a repeating tape recording of a man reading an excerpt from a children's poem by A. A. Milne, they found that the babies looked in the direction of the voice when it began; but as the voice continued, their gaze gradually tended to wander away from the sound.

Very early during the first year, babies learn to expect certain kinds of auditory-visual correlations that we take for granted and notice only when our

Experimental set-up in Aronson and Rosenbloom's investigation of the effects of voice displacement on infants. The mother's voice can be displaced so that it is heard coming from one of the speakers at the side, although the infant sees her speaking in front of him. (Eric Aronson)

expectations are violated. For example, you may have watched a film in which the sound track was not precisely synchronized with the picture and noticed the discrepancy between the mouth movements of the actors and their voices. You may have been disturbed because you expected a temporal correlation between what you saw and what you heard. Other relationships between sights and sounds are spatial: they often come from the same location. At what age do infants expect a definite relationship between what they see and what they hear from people talking to them? Eric Aronson and Shelley Rosenbloom (1971) studied this expectation of a correlation between what is heard and what is seen in three-week-old infants. They used the spatial relationship between the sights and sounds of the mothers to detect the babies' expectations. Each infant sat facing his mother, who talked to him in any way she chose. (One mother recited the Gettysburg Address.) After some time, a mechanism displaced the mother's voice so that it sounded to the infant as if it came from a point three feet to the right or left of her mouth. The dislocation disturbed the infants, indicating that by three weeks a baby has already detected and expected an association between the location of his mother's mouth and the sounds she makes.

When does the baby search with his eyes for the source of a sound that is outside his field of vision? Nancy Bayley (1969) found that 50 percent of the normal two-month-old infants she observed moved their eyes in apparent search when an unseen bell or rattle sounded. However, they did not necessarily look for the source in the correct direction. The more precise ear, eye, and head coordination required to turn the head and look in the correct direction for the sound source developed somewhat later in the babies that Bayley studied. Half of all four-month-old babies did this, and almost all had reached that level of intersensory and sensory-motor cooperation by the time they were six months old.

Another important coordination that develops in the first half year is that between the eyes and the hands (described in Chapter 6). We adults take it for granted that our hands will reach out the proper distance to touch or grasp objects that appear in our line of sight. But it is not until they are four and one-half months old that half of all infants will be able to touch a cube that is placed in front of them on a table, and not until six months are virtually all infants that skilled.

The importance of this eye-hand coordination is reflected in the view of many students of infancy and early childhood that the origins of intelligence lie in the sensory-motor experiences and developments of infancy. For example, Piaget's books (1952b, 1954) on infancy are full of vivid descriptions and perceptive interpretations of age changes in infants' sensory-motor coordination and of

It takes six months for most babies to develop the co-ordination between eyes and hands that enables them to grasp and explore the objects before them. (Tom Myers/Taurus Photos)

their link to concepts of objects, space, time, and causality.

By the time they are eight months old, babies can transfer information from touch to sight. Peter Bryant (1972) and his colleagues devised a pair of semiround objects that were identical except for a small square notch in the end of one. When activated, either of the objects could make a "bleep." Both objects were shown to the baby while he sat in his mother's lap, then were taken away. Without the baby's being able to see the objects, one of them was placed in his hand and, while he held it, it was made to bleep. After the hidden object was removed, both objects were shown again to the infant. About two-thirds of the babies, who ranged in age from six to twelve months, reached without hesitation for the object they had just touched, indicating their ability to translate information from a tactual to a visual mode.

Some of the intersensory and sensory-motor coordinations that emerge during the first year of life clearly reflect the infant's experiences. For example, Lauren learns that she must fully extend her arm to reach a stuffed animal one foot away,

because in the past she has not been able to grab a toy at that distance without reaching for it. On the other hand, maturation of the visual and motor functions in the central nervous system also may contribute to the development of the four-month-old's visually directed grab for an object. All these coordinations improve during the second year of life, because the infant has greater opportunity to use them on the diversity of objects and events he encounters.

ATTENTION

People do not and cannot attend to all the stimuli in their environment. Selective attention begins almost at birth, and a number of factors determine why a baby attends to one thing rather than to another. For example, certain absolute features of stimuli may determine attention. Robert Fantz (1961) showed infants ranging in age from one to six months a set of six flat disks. Three of the disks were patterned; the other three had no patterns but were brightly colored. At all age levels, infants preferred to look longer at the patterns than at the brightly colored but unpatterned disks. Fantz hypothesized that the ability to recognize a pattern, particularly that of the human face, has played a more significant role in infant survival over the course of human evolution than color recognition has. If so, it suggests that human infants are constructed so that when patterns and colors are presented simultaneously, the patterns are more likely to attract their attention.

As infants get older, the relationship between a given stimulus and their previous experiences with related stimuli plays a greater role in determining what will attract their attention. They are said to build up an **expectancy** for certain stimuli, and violations of this expectancy make them attend. In general it has been found that stimuli that differ somewhat from those the baby has previously encountered will be particularly attractive (J. Kagan, 1972). For example, Charles Super and his colleagues (1972) exposed infants to mobiles at home every day for three weeks. These mobiles differed in varying degrees from a standard mobile. The researchers then showed the infants the standard mobile. They found that babies whose original mobile was of medium similarity to the standard one attended most to the standard mobile. But babies whose original mobile was closely similar to the standard and those whose mobile was extremely different showed less interest when presented with the standard.

A concept closely related to deviations from expectancy is **novelty**. A stimulus can be novel without being discrepant from some previous expectancy; therefore, novelty and discrepancy are not identical, although it is not always easy to separate the two. Hildy Ross, Harriet Rheingold, and Carol Eckerman (1972) studied the attractiveness of novel objects to one-year-old infants. They gave babies an opportunity to explore one of two rooms and to play with one of two toys that differed in their novelty. The infants chose to explore the

more novel of the rooms and to play with the more novel of the toys. Another study by Meyer Parry (1972) suggests that the strength of the attentional "pull" of novelty may be reduced if a baby encounters a novel situation or an object in an unfamiliar setting.

Other studies indicate that contour and movement are likely to catch two- to four-month-old infants' attention, but that by the time the babies are three or four months old, novelty or discrepancy have become just as powerful. As the baby's cognitive abilities develop, the informational properties (discrepancy, novelty, etc.) of an event become as important as the physical properties (contour, movement, number of elements, etc.) in recruiting and sustaining attention (e.g., Cohen, 1976; Cornell, 1975; Kagan, 1976).

Often an infant's selective attention is a result of the "payoff" he or she receives for attending to one aspect rather than to another. If, for example, Lauren, who initially prefers form to color, is rewarded with a smile, a tickle, or some other pleasant consequence for looking at color and gets no reward for looking at form, she may learn to shift her attention to color, the feature she originally preferred less. This is an example of learning to attend rather than of spontaneous attention, and as the child grows past infancy, learning to attend plays an increasingly important role in intellectual development. However, such learning can and does occur even in the baby's earliest weeks.

Another concept related to attention is that of habituation. Stimuli that attract the attention of infants come to bore them after a while, and babies will shift their attention to another stimulus or even fall asleep. Habituation and the response to novel stimuli are basic to the infant's ability to learn. Unless the infant can remember a stimulus, there can be no conditioning, no adaptation, no learning of any sort (McCall, 1971).

Infants habituate to some stimuli more rapidly than to others. Leslie Cohen (1972, 1976) has attempted to distinguish between the physical properties of stimuli that attract the attention of infants and those that sustain their attention once it has been attracted. Using a specially designed checkerboard pattern, he found that the overall size of the checkerboard played a more important role in catching the attention of the infants, as measured by the time it took them to turn toward the checkerboard, than did the number of squares in the design. On the other hand, once the checkerboard

Figure 7.2 In Fantz's experiment, disks were shown to infants in a looking chamber. Fixation-time percentages indicate that, whether the infants were younger or older than three months, they looked at pattern longer than at color or brightness. (Adapted from Robert L. Fantz, "The Origin of Form Perception," copyright © 1961 by Scientific American, Inc. All rights reserved)

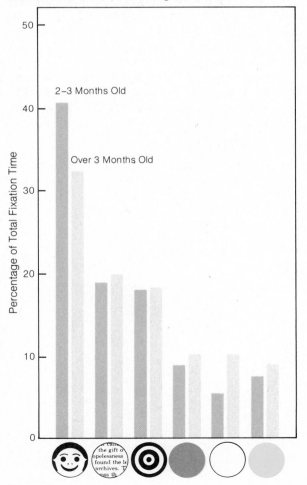

had grabbed their attention, the number of squares that the board contained was more important than its overall size in determining how long the infants looked at it.

Attention is important because of the intellectual processing that goes along with it. As we mentioned before, sensation underlies perception, which in turn underlies cognition. To investigate the cognitive aspects of attention, some researchers have studied the baby's response to a human face. Daphne Maurer and Philip Salapatek (1976), for example, had one- and two-month-old babies look at the faces of their mothers and of male and female strangers. They found that the month-old babies tended to look at the edges of a face, such as an ear, the chin, and so on, whereas the two-month-olds inspected internal features, such as an eye, the nose, or the mouth. Other researchers have found that by about two months, infants pay increased attention to the internal features of the face, especially the eyes (Hainline, 1978). In addition, whether the face is moving slightly from side to side or remaining still or talking, two-month-old infants concentrate their scanning around the eyes (Haith, Bergman, and Moore, 1977). Not even the extra mouth movements that accompany speech could attract attention from the eyes to the mouth.

It may be that babies are attracted from the periphery of the face to the eyes because, after about three weeks, babies come to see the face as a meaningful entity instead of simply as a collection of features. It is also possible that by this time the eyes have taken on social meaning and that babies have learned that when a face is accompanied by speech, fixing their attention on the eyes keeps the sound of the human voice going. Throughout the first year, the infant's perception of the face appears to rest on a gradual discovery of its invariant features and an integration of its parts into a meaningful configuration (Fagan, 1976; Haaf, 1977).

CONCEPTS AND SYMBOLS

You believe that objects remain the same, even though they may move from one place to another or undergo other transformations that do not affect their basic identity. On the other hand, if at the same time you see two objects with identical features, you assume that they are separate objects. And if you see an object on Tuesday and an object with identical features on Wednesday afternoon, you assume that you have either seen the same object twice or two separate objects at two different times. To make certain, you may try to find out what has happened to the object since you first saw it. Even if you find out that you have seen two separate objects, you usually believe that the first object still exists somewhere, even though it is now out of sight.

These interrelated ideas about the identity and permanence of objects and about their potentials for moving from one place to another or for disappearing from view and reappearing are not present at birth. Babies devote a good part of their first two years to building this intricate conceptual network of objects, movement, time, space, and causality. They acquire these ideas as a result of their sensory, perceptual, and motor interactions with the environment. Our understanding of the infant's gradual acquisition of beliefs about reality comes in part from Piaget's observations (1952b, 1954) of his own three children and from subsequent studies inspired by his reports.

Piaget noted that, if an object being watched by a baby of less than four months disappears from view, the baby will tend to act as if the object had never been there or perhaps will keep looking at the spot where he last saw it. Typically, he will not initiate an active search for it. It is as though the object exists only when it is being immediately perceived.

During the next four months or so, however, the baby often initiates a search for an object that he sees disappearing from view. For example, if David's cup falls from his high chair while he is looking at it, he may lean toward the floor to see where it went instead of just staring at the spot where it was. Even though the cup is out of sight, he now acts as though he expects it to be some-

where else. But this occurs only when he sees it starting to move away. If the cup were suddenly covered by a towel or a napkin, he would not try to pick up the covering to get it, even though he is physically quite able to do so. At this point in the development of his object concept, the object seems to exist for him only to the extent that he can continue an activity he was already performing on the object, such as looking at it.

Object Identity

Several experimenters have supplemented Piaget's early observations with more precise analyses of the responses of young infants to different types of movements, disappearances, and features of objects. For example, Alastair Mundy-Castle and Jeremy Anglin (1969) conducted an experiment in which an object appeared on the infant's right and rose vertically out of sight; then an identical object dropped down on the infant's left and subsequently fell vertically out of sight, while the one on the right rose into view again. After viewing a number of such cycles, infants of less than sixteen

Figure 7.3 Representation of an experiment, like that of Bower's investigating the development of object identity in young infants. When infants younger than about sixteen weeks see a moving object emerge from behind a screen and then come to a stop, they are likely to continue to track its path of movement. This suggests that they do not realize that the moving and stationary objects are one and the same.

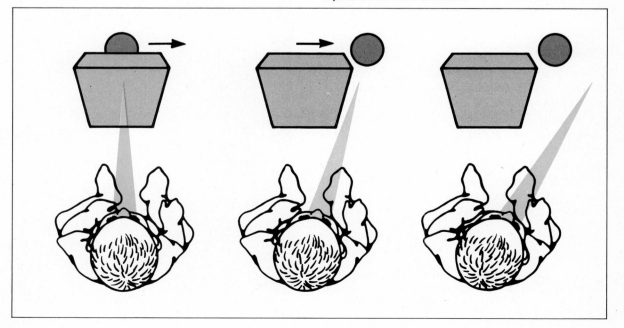

weeks simply looked from side to side in order to see the objects. However, sixteen-week-olds assumed that a single object was traveling on a circular trajectory; their eyes followed a circular path that corresponded to the possible trajectory of the object. Thus, after babies are four months old, the moving object continues to exist for them, even though it is temporarily out of view. Mundy-Castle and Anglin also found that, if the object that vanished on the right did not reappear on the left, sixteen- to eighteen-week-olds, unlike twelve- to fourteen-week-olds, looked back to the right. From such behavior we can infer that a four-month-old infant realizes that an object can change direction.

Undoubtedly the most important object for the infant is his mother. But for some time he does not seem to realize that the mother he sees at different times in different places is one and the same person. Using special optical devices, Bower (1971) showed four- and six-month-old infants simultaneous multiple images of their mothers. The younger infants responded to each of the images with delight. The older infants showed signs of distress. Bower inferred from these findings that the younger baby does not realize he has only one mother, so when he sees several figures, he experiences no incongruity. An older infant realizes he has only one mother, who, although she may be seen on many different occasions, is never seen more than once at a single time. Simultaneous multiple images violate his understanding, and he becomes upset.

Object Permanence

If the young infant does not assume that his mother exists when he is not looking at her, then her sudden disappearance without a trace should not surprise him. Because for the infant she no longer exists, the absence of any clue about her new location does not contradict any of his notions about her, and he should not wonder "Where did she go?" Using mirrors and special lighting to show a baby an image of his mother, Bower (1971) tested this deduction, making the image gradually

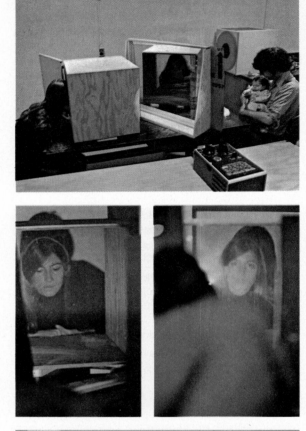

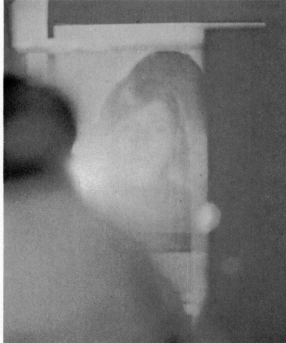

This experimental set-up shows how the mother actually disappears and how her disappearance probably appears to the baby. (Steve McCarroll)

dissolve into nothingness. Infants under twenty-four weeks watched their mothers fade away and disappear with no evidence of upset. However, infants older than twenty-four weeks reacted to the dissolution of their mothers with considerable upset and appeared to search for them. This behavior of the older baby indicates a conceptual advance, a belief that, regardless of what he has just seen, mother must exist somewhere.

The baby soon extends this belief in the permanence of his mother to other human beings and indeed to other objects. But the extension of the belief does not facilitate the search, which can only be expedited when the baby acquires specific knowledge about objects. One of the first things that the infant more than six months old learns is that some objects are self-mobile. People, for example, move of their own volition. Other objects are inanimate and must be moved. The inexplicable disappearance of an inanimate object is thus likely to upset the baby, whereas the similar disappearance of an animate object will produce searching. The baby's search is guided by growing knowledge of the characteristics and abilities of the object in question.

In observations of his own children, Piaget (1952b, 1954) found that, during the last four months of their first year, his children searched for objects that they saw him place behind a screen. Although this search represents a definite advance in children's understanding of what happens to objects that are removed from their view, their notion of object permanence is not yet like ours. Consider the following: Piaget moved a toy behind a screen while his child was observing. The child retrieved it. Piaget made his move in this game again, and the child again responded appropriately. This was repeated several more times. Then Piaget, with his child attending to his actions, modified the game by hiding the toy behind a screen located in a different place. As surprising as it may seem, the child insisted on searching for the toy in the original location. Piaget concluded that the baby's concept of space is based on his failure to dissociate the objects of the world from his own actions on them, and that he remembers a place solely in terms of the movement he made when first retrieving the toy.

Because this reaction by the baby is basic to understanding the development of the infant mind, researchers have tested Piaget's explanation in an attempt to discover the nature of the baby's error. They have found that babies continue to reach toward Point A even when the toy is not hidden but is plainly visible at Point B (Butterworth, 1977; Harris, 1974), and also when a toy different from the one hidden at A is hidden at B (Evans and Gratch, 1972). The error depends in part on memory, because babies rarely make it if they already are reaching for the toy as it is being

(top) This infant of about six months has not yet developed a concept of object permanence. (left) She looks intently at a toy elephant that is in front of her (right), but when the elephant is blocked from view, she gives no indication that she understands the toy is still there.

(bottom) This older infant realizes that the disappearance of an object does not necessarily mean that it is no longer there. (left) When the object he sees (middle) is shielded from his view by a towel, he searches for it (right), crawling under the towel to find the object. (George Zimbel/Monkmeyer Press)

hidden or if they are allowed to reach for it immediately after it has been hidden at B (Gratch et al., 1974).

J. G. Bremner and Peter Bryant (1977) designed an experiment to test whether the error was due to infants' simply making the same response that earlier brought them the toy from Point A or whether they remembered that the toy was first hidden there. After hiding the toy at Point B, Bremner and Bryant either moved the baby to the opposite side of the table or rotated the table halfway round. If the baby remembered the place, he would have to make a different movement to get the toy. Nine-month-old infants most often responded just as they had before the table was rotated, indicating they remembered the response and not the place.

Bremner and Bryant conclude that the results support Piaget's interpretation and that the baby's reliance on movement instead of place may develop because the first nine months of life are relatively nonmobile. Before a baby can move about freely on his own, objects remain static. The baby stays in the same place in relation to them, and once he locates an object visually, he does not need visual information to relocate it; he can get it simply by repeating his previous reach. Once the baby begins to crawl, however, his relations to an object in space vary as he moves so that he now must use visual information to guide his actions. Bremner and Bryant point out that a general **egocentrism,** or the infant's inability to differentiate the self from the world, can also explain the error: the child's frame of reference for spatial relations is himself, and he repeats his reach because that is the side where the toy was in relation to himself. But, they note, the explanation could be even simpler. Babies may know the toy is now at Point B, but lack the control that allows them to inhibit an established response.

When Piaget followed up his observations of his children during the first half of their second year, he found that they still reached for the toy at Point A unless they had watched him move the toy behind the screen to Point B. By the second half of the second year, Piaget's children were able to infer not only a single invisible displacement of objects, but several. When Piaget successively hid the object enclosed in his hand first at Point A, then at B, then C, and so forth, the children systematically searched his hand and all these locations. They inferred that the object had to be somewhere that Piaget had been, even though they did not actually see him move it. They had now developed an understanding about the permanence and existence of objects independent of their own activity with respect to them.

Piaget believes that all infants acquire their final concepts of the permanence of objects by going through the same sequence of stages that he observed in his own children, although various children will move through the stages at varying rates. Recent studies of larger samples of infants tend in general to corroborate Piaget's view (Gouin-Décarie, 1965; Uzigiris, 1976).

Most theorists agree that babies acquire their concepts of object identity and permanence and their knowledge of the distinctive features of objects by their active involvement in the world of objects. By looking at, listening to, smelling, tasting, grasping, sucking, throwing, and moving all kinds of things frequently and repeatedly, they learn which objects are small or large, rough or smooth, squeezable or hard, and bitter or sweet and which produce loud or soft noises when struck. As they get older, they notice specific features of objects, and their definition of objects becomes more differentiated. In a similar manner, infants derive their ideas about space, time, and physical causality from their observation and manipulation of people, things, and events.

Memory and Thought

How well does the infant remember the past? How adept are babies at using mental images and names to stand for things that are not present? Toward the end of their first year and throughout the second, infants begin to create and use symbols. Imitation, language, and imaginary play are particularly important ways in which infants can represent absent people or objects. These representational activities appear in rudimentary form in infancy and develop rapidly during the preschool years.

Although at first infants may imitate only behavior they have just watched in others, later they are able to defer their imitations for several hours. When Lauren is thirsty or hungry she will say "Milk, milk," and the word becomes a symbol for the thing. But the baby's concept precedes her acquisition of the word (R. Brown, 1977). When she realizes that some pictures or photographs correspond to people or objects, she begins to acquire the notion of graphic representation of objects.

Her inclination to search in several different places for objects that have been hidden also suggests a use of mental imagery.

These representational skills, which become increasingly important cognitive acquisitions and tools during children's second year of life, are related to their memory capacities. Unfortunately, we still have no clear picture of the development of memory in infancy. We can, however, divide memory itself into several component processes, such as the ability to code and store information and the ability to retrieve it by recognizing or recalling it.

Babies' ability to store information is important for their ability to recognize discrepancies. If they do not remember a previously seen pattern, they cannot realize that a later pattern is different. Fagan (1971), who studied visual preference in younger babies, also studied the recognition memory of older infants. He found that five-month-olds preferred novel stimuli to familiar ones when both were presented seven minutes after the babies first saw the familiar stimuli. This indicates that the five-month-old can recognize certain visual stimuli at least seven minutes after having seen them.

Memory is also an important factor in the acquisition of the concept of object permanence. We saw that when infants of two months are looking at an object that is covered by a screen, they seem to lose interest in it, suggesting that it no longer exists for them when out of sight. However, an experiment by Bower (1971) indicates that it may be necessary to qualify this statement. After covering an object with a screen, Bower surreptitiously removed the object. He then took away the screen, immediately with some two-month-old infants and after ten seconds with others. As we would expect from Piaget's observations, those infants for whom the objects had been out of sight for ten seconds showed no surprise at not seeing it again. If the object no longer existed, there was no reason why it should reappear when the screen was removed. However, those for whom it had been out of sight only momentarily were surprised that the object had disappeared. They seemed to have a fleeting belief in the existence of the disappearing object. But this belief was not sustained when the babies had to rely on their memory of the object for at least ten seconds.

Another limitation on infants' cognition that may result from their relatively short-term mem-

ory is illustrated by the effects of delayed reinforcement on learning. For example, a study by Craig Ramey and L. Lynn Ourth (1971) showed that, if a reward is to reinforce a baby's behavior, the reward must come immediately after the baby acts. When there is a delay of even three seconds, infants do not learn to connect the reward with their own behavior. This suggests that, by the time they get the reward, they have forgotten what they did—the behavior has slipped from their short-term memory, just as a telephone number might slip from their mother's memory if she were interrupted before she began to dial the phone.

This research seems to indicate that babies younger than eight months have great trouble both in retrieving recent experiences from their memory and in holding the recollections in their short-term memory for more than a few seconds. But the baby of less than eight months also shows excellent memory. When younger babies do recognize events after delays of days or even weeks, it is probably because the world supplies them with many cues to help them locate the representations in their long-term memory. Without a single cue, as in the case of babies whose view was blocked by a screen, they cannot remember (Kagan, 1978). By the time they are ten or twelve months old, babies can hold events longer in their short-term memory, need fewer cues to recall past events, and can compare present events with stored knowledge of the past.

INFANT-ENVIRONMENT INTERACTION

The perceptual and cognitive developments that we have examined are products of the child's interactions with his or her environment. Each influences the other, and these effects occur in several ways and may be studied from different perspectives.

Learning

The term "environmentally induced developmental change" corresponds roughly to what most psychologists call learning. Babies learn, and their behavior is modified by either classical or operant conditioning processes, which were described in Chapter 2.

One of the most important and powerful unconditioned reflexes is the baby's sucking reflex, which is elicited by the presence of the mother's nipple in the baby's mouth. Shortly after birth, the

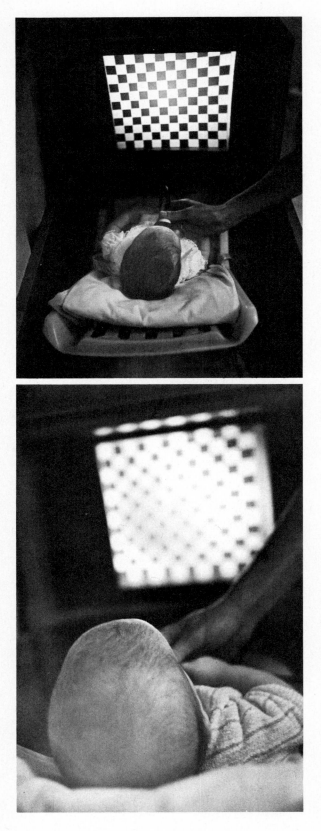

sight, smell, sound, and feel of mother as she prepares to nurse the baby will be enough to elicit sucking. These previously neutral stimuli become associated with the unconditioned stimulus "nipple-in-the-mouth," thereby acquiring the ability to influence the infant's sucking behavior. Researchers have classically conditioned numerous other reflexes of the infant and have conditioned them to a wide variety of previously neutral stimuli. But, as Hanuš Papoušek (1967) has shown, stable classical conditioning occurs more readily in older infants than in younger ones, and it appears that biological maturation is an important factor in the changing capacity of the infant to respond to classical conditioning.

As early as the first week of life, however, a baby's behavior is subject to operant conditioning, as the studies in Chapter 5 show. In one study by Harriet Rheingold, Jacob Gewirtz, and Helen Ross (1959), four-month-old infants who were tickled and smiled at when they babbled tended to increase their rate of babbling. Researchers have operantly conditioned sucking, smiling, crying, head turning, looking, and many other kinds of behavior by arranging for the baby to get some reward only if the behavior occurs. The rewards that have proved effective are quite varied; one of them is the privilege to see a sharply focused pattern. Einar Siqueland and Clement Delucia (1969) designed a special pacifier that controlled the focus of a pattern on a television screen. When the infant sucked the pacifier vigorously, the pattern remained in focus. But if his sucking slowed, the picture blurred. When this consequence was linked to his behavior, the baby tended to suck energetically.

By experimenting with the behavior they can perform, infants learn which of their actions are most effective in getting the world to do their bidding and in what circumstances the desired results are produced. John S. Watson (1971) has suggested that the responsiveness of the environment is of primary importance to the development of a

In Siqueland and Delucia's study of learning in young babies, the four-month-old infant is shown a pattern on a televisionlike screen. (*top*) He can keep the pattern in sharp focus by sucking on a pacifier connected to the projector. For a while he will suck with great energy and interest to keep the picture in sharp focus. (*bottom*) Like most babies, he eventually becomes bored, slows his sucking, and the picture fades. When a different picture appears before him, he will again suck vigorously. (Jason Lauré)

A baby's mouth and hands are important tools in his exploration of the world. As he mouths an object, he discovers its form, texture, solidity, and taste. (Linda Rogers/Woodfin Camp & Assoc.)

baby's behavior and perhaps plays a greater role than the amount of stimulation the child receives. He placed automated mobiles over the cribs of two-month-old infants for ten minutes a day over a period of two weeks. The babies who were able to control the mobile, switching it off and on with a turn of the head, benefited more from this experience, as measured by a learning test given six weeks later, than did babies who simply watched the moving mobile but could not control it.

Babies are highly adaptive and can overcome many deficiencies in their early experience. Nevertheless, because their perceptions and cognitions come from their experiences, it appears that the infant reared in a bland, restricted, and nonresponsive environment is less likely to be intellectually competent than one brought up in a diversified, responsive world. A child cannot know about places and things if he has not dealt with them, and the more varied and frequent his dealings with them, the more he comes to know. A concept of a ball based exclusively on having seen one is "poorer" than a concept of a ball derived from learning how it feels and what happens to it

when you bend or bite or roll it. And, as we will see in Chapter 9, the broader and more responsive the social environment, the more the infant will understand about how different people think, act, and feel.

Exploring

Although many of the sensations from which perceptions are formed impinge on infants no matter what they do, babies are far from docile organisms. As was pointed out in Chapter 6, from the earliest weeks of life, infants actively explore the world during their waking hours. They stare at and fixate segments of their visual field. They scan it with their eyes; they chase after moving light and moving objects. If all that their world offers is repetitive exposure to the same things, they become bored and search with their eyes for novel sources of stimulation.

Although his eyes are the most important sense organs for exploring the world, an infant investigates with other parts of his body as well. As you recall, the lips, tongue, and teeth, the hands and fingers, and the ears are all tools of the infant explorer. As a baby, David, for example, will grasp objects and try to suck them, not just for the pleasure of sucking but for the information about the form, texture, hardness, and taste of the object that he gets from the touch and taste receptors of his mouth and its parts. Or when David is not sucking objects, he may run his nimble fingers over the surfaces of objects and through their crevices. If objects are squeezable, they will be squeezed; if crushable, crushed; and if throwable, thrown. The baby will drop objects to produce bangs and thuds and other noises and will coo and cry and listen to his own improvisations in sound. All of these activities of the infant generate stimulation that never would have occurred if a baby were nothing more than a passive spectator observing the world that chances to go by.

Another aspect of the infant as explorer is demonstrated in a study by Hanuš Papoušek (1967), who found that even in the first months of life infants will master complex learning tasks purely for the joy of solving a problem. He reinforced babies when they turned their heads twice to the right, three times to the left, and once to the right again. The reinforcement was a seconds-long burst of white light. But the babies barely glanced at the light; they apparently used it only to prove to themselves that they had solved the problem. These six-month-old infants enjoyed the challenge of a puzzle.

Older infants often deliberately set difficult tasks for themselves. They work on these tasks for long periods, often showing signs of frustration yet persisting for days until they solve the problems. A clear example of this striving for competence in the environment arose in Bower's longitudinal study of the development of the concept of object permanence. In this laboratory experiment, the infants were often confronted with various hidden objects as in the object-permanence experiments described earlier. Later, according to their mothers, they spent hours at home hiding objects and retrieving them. At a later stage, when the problem in the laboratory was to find an object that had gone out of sight while moving on a complex trajectory (for example, ricocheting off the wall), the babies when at home would roll objects under tables, under beds, and off walls and would crawl after them until, at the end, they could readily retrieve a vanished object. The point is that these infants developed a concept of object permanence somewhat earlier than the average baby. This ac-

celeration was not the direct result of any intervention by the experimenters. In this case, the experimenters simply introduced the infants to a problem, and then the infants actively explored and developed their own cognitive understanding.

Adapting

Life is full of challenges for the infant. Lauren's knowledge about the world and her knowledge of how to deal with it that was effective yesterday may be less effective today as she encounters new objects, people, and events. She has been exclusively breast-fed for several months and she uses her mouth very competently to suck. Now she is given a cup or a spoonful of solid food. At first she tries to incorporate, or *assimilate,* the cup or food to her mouth-using skills by sucking at them just as she sucks the nipple. Because this is not successful, she has to modify, or *accommodate,* her mouth-using skills to these new elements of her environment. By the time she successfully adapts, Lauren has simultaneously assimilated new objects to her prior mouth-using skills and changed these skills so that they can be effective with the new elements. This explanation of the infant's adaptation is closely associated with Piaget's (1952b, 1954) theory of cognitive development.

Consider another example, young David, who uses his fingers and hand to hold and squeeze rubber balls or rattles. He knows that a certain pressure on these objects will produce an entertaining squeak. Now give him a luscious red tomato. Although the tomato feels somewhat different from a ball or rattle, he may try to squeeze it—he tries to assimilate or fit the new object into his squeezing skills. Unfortunately, its texture does not fit his hand-using skills, and tomato juice runs down his arm. Quickly he learns that tomatoes can indeed be held but only if they are held with less pressure than he applies to rubber balls; he modifies his hand-using skills. This adaptive response includes both assimilation and accommodation. Of course, some infants are not so perturbed by the effects of squeezing tomatoes as their mothers are. If this is the case, the infant's challenge becomes that of accommodating to his mother rather than to the tomato. As the infant grows, he will continue to use old responses on new objects and to modify his old responses, assimilating and accommodating his skills as he learns to adapt to his widening world.

SUMMARY

1. Human infants are active and curious about their world. During their first two years, they organize and reorganize their understanding of the world and the people, objects, and events that fill it. Their increasing cognitive understanding builds on their sensations and perceptions of the physical and social world, but their ability to think is not restricted to concrete experience alone.

2. By the end of the first year, infants can judge distance, discriminate familiar from unfamiliar objects, and use visual cues as warnings. Their hearing becomes sensitive to combinations of sounds, so that they recognize certain words and attach meanings to them. Most important, all the infants' senses working together, and combined with their motor skills, provide them with extensive knowledge of the environment.

3. Selective attention to certain stimuli continues from the moment of birth. Previous experience as well as certain physical features of objects appear to determine what infants usually will attend to. Stimuli that violate an expectancy or that are novel are often most likely to attract an infant's attention, and human faces may hold a unique fascination for infants, partly because of their growing cognitive competence.

4. Much of the first two years appear to be spent building a conceptual network of interrelated ideas about objects and events. Gradually, infants come to recognize that objects remain the same and are permanent even when certain changes may make it appear that this is not the case. Infants' play and their ability to imitate and to remember all contribute to their ideas about objects and events, and—from infancy—these cognitive skills aid their abilities to imagine, symbolize, and recall.

5. In general, infants' cognitive development can be seen as a complex product of their interactions with the environment, which involves learning, exploring, and adapting. They learn how to respond to the world and how it responds to them; they actively explore generating new stimulation and information; and they adapt to the world either by assimilating objects to fit their skills or by accommodating their skills to the demands of the situation.

CHAPTER 8
Language: Beginnings

HUMAN LANGUAGE

PRESPEECH DEVELOPMENT
Attention to Speech
Prespeech Sounds
Cognitive Precursors to First Words
Communicative Precursors to First Words

FIRST WORDS
Functions of First Words
Form of First Words
Meanings of First Words

FIRST SENTENCES
Meaning at the Two-Word Stage
Cataloging the Two-Year-Old Mind

FROM TWO WORDS TO GRAMMAR
Intonation
Word Order
Inflection

SUMMARY

Little Lauren is nearly a year old and her mother is playing with her, making various cooing noises. Among the noises comes something like "givemommyakisssweetie . . . givemommyakiss." At the same time, Mommy expectantly puts her cheek near Lauren's lips. Lauren does not know much about language, but she senses that she is supposed to do something. She also senses that this particular set of noises that her mother is making sounds somehow different from the cooing, and the specially accented noise "kiss" reverberates in her ears. Another time Daddy says "lookatthedoggy" when a small furry animal comes into sight. Lauren is ready to learn to talk. What does she have to do? What does she have to know?

If you had never learned to understand speech and to talk, it would have been difficult to live in your family and to grow up in this (or any) human society. You could learn only what you saw others do. There would be some things, of course, that you could learn or figure out by yourself; not all thinking is verbal. For example, musicians, engineers, and artists make use of aural and visual images and spatial relationships. But imagine trying to learn what you now know of history or of how our society works without being able to understand or speak a language.

The word "infant" comes from the Latin word for "without language," and if one does not possess a language until he has command of its *structure*, then the immature human being is an infant throughout most of his second year. For although a baby may communicate, until he begins to put words together, he is not truly dealing with the structure of his native language.

In this chapter we will discuss some of the early achievements of the child in deciphering his native language. We will examine some of the ways in which the very young baby responds to speech sounds, the first sounds that the baby makes himself, and the distinction between babbling and talking. We will set forth the level of cognitive development and the human attempts to communicate that must precede the baby's first words and the form those first words will take. We will learn how the infant overextends and then shrinks the meaning of these early words so that "bow-wow," for example, changes in meaning from "dog" to "animal" and back to "dog" again. We will discover the significance of the infant's progress from one- to two-word utterances and the way he masters the basic grammatical machinery of his language. In the first two years, the infant tunes up his cognitive and linguistic abilities until he becomes a speaking human being. This tuning is the result of a complex interplay of cognitive and linguistic development, paced by neurological maturation.

HUMAN LANGUAGE

How does the language of human beings differ from the language of animals? After all, a worker bee can dance on the floor of the hive to tell its fellow workers where to find nectar (Von Frisch, 1967). A father quail can warn its foraging family of approaching danger, and your dog can use a combination of whines, barks, and body movements to tell you when it wants its dinner, when it wants to play ball, and when it wants to go outside.

Roger Brown (1973) has suggested that human language, whether English, Russian, Chinese, or Urdu, possesses three important properties. First is **semanticity,** or meaningfulness. By semanticity, Brown means that the symbols of human language represent an enormous variety of people, objects, events, and ideas. A mynah bird may mimic human speech perfectly, but it does not use these sounds in any meaningful way, and so it does not possess language. Although animals such as the honey bee with its dance or chimpanzees with their calls and grunts can communicate limited meanings, the number of things that they can "talk" about is quite small.

Brown's second property of language is **productivity,** the ability to combine individual words into an unlimited number of sentences. As Noam Chomsky (1972) has pointed out, except for common clichés such as "How are you?" or "Have a nice day," almost every sentence we hear or speak is brand new. According to one estimate, if you were to utter all the possible twenty-word sentences in English, you would be talking for 10,000,-000,000,000 years (Farb, 1974).

The last essential property of language, according to Brown, is **displacement,** the ability to communicate information about objects in another place or another time, such as the book in the

Before the baby can speak, he communicates his feelings by crying or smiling. When he attends to the sounds of his parents' speech, he begins the long process of acquiring human language. (Suzanne Szasz)

next room or the pot roast you ate last Sunday. Displacement is the property that allows us to transmit information from one generation to another so that we do not have to rediscover all knowledge every thirty years or so.

At every linguistic stage, the child's cognitive understanding of the world about him lays the basis for the development of his own ability to understand and to speak a language. The development of language cannot begin until the baby can recognize objects and events in his world (see Chapter 7) and can relate his perceptions to each other in memory. Once maturation brings him to the point where he can form and store internal representations of objects and events, he is ready to hook the system that he uses to communicate his emotions into his cognitive understanding. The first words emerge and, with them, the fundamental basis of human verbal interaction. By two or two and one-half years, the rudiments of word combination and grammar are present and, with them, the roots of complex communication.

The infant's development of language depends on two important notions: *structure* and *figuring out*. Speech relates to meanings, or ideas, in precise ways.

The words "kiss" and "this" have different meanings in English simply because they begin with different sounds. "Mommy kisses baby" and "Baby kisses Mommy" have different meanings in English just because the order of the words is different in the two utterances. These are *structural principles* of English that the child must discover, because such principles differ from language to language. Linguists call these structural principles the **grammar** or **syntax** of a language.

Each language has its own collection of speech sounds, which are used to build words in that particular language. And each language has its own ways of combining words into sentences. For example, in Russian the equivalent of "Mommy kisses baby," with the three words in that order, could mean either that Mommy gets kissed or that baby gets kissed, depending on whether the word for "Mommy" or the word for "baby" has a particular sound on the end of it. "Mama tseluyet malyutkU" means "Mommy kisses baby," but "MamU tseluyet malyutka" means "Baby kisses Mommy." So, if you were a Russian one-year-old, you would have to learn to pay special attention to the sounds that come at the ends of words, but if you were an American one-year-old, you would

have to learn to pay special attention to the order of words.

In either case, the baby must be able to pay attention to the ways in which speech is structured or organized. If he is to communicate meanings and understand what people are saying, he must actively *figure out* the ways in which speech is organized in his native language. No baby knows, to begin with, what particular native language he is destined to acquire, yet all children manage to acquire their native language with amazing ease and rapidity. This leads us to believe that human beings are in some way endowed with specialized information-processing abilities that make it possible for them to figure out the structure of their own language, just as they are able to figure out the structures of the other sights and sounds and smells and feelings that are necessary in order to function as thinking and feeling human beings in society.

But the infant who is figuring out his own language cannot depend on isolated words; he must learn enough about meanings in the nonlinguistic world to discover how the two systems are related. He can and sometimes does learn about this relationship before he begins to speak. In fact, some children who cannot speak at all because of physical handicaps show that they completely understand the function of language and its intricacies. Eric Lenneberg (1962) studied one such child and tested him in several ways for language comprehension. The child, who was then eight, was told a short story and questioned in complex grammatical constructions about its contents. From his responses, there was no doubt that he had learned to understand his native language, English. Such experiments make it clear that having knowledge of a language is not identical with speaking. Because knowledge of a language may be established in people who lack the ability to speak, knowledge must be fundamental, and the ability to speak, accessory.

PRESPEECH DEVELOPMENT

Before a baby is ready to say "dada" or "mama" or "milk" or "bow-wow," he has a long road of development and learning to travel. He seems born prepared to attend to speech and takes his first steps along the language road in the very first months of life, almost before his parents are aware that he is interested in anything more than a full stomach and a dry bottom. As was noted in Chapter 5, William Condon (1975) has found that babies move in harmony with human speech as early as the day of birth, showing a synchrony that Condon believes indicates that newborn infants participate in communication from their first hours.

Earl Butterfield (1968) studied newborn babies in the hospital and found that they already attended to sound, which is a basic step in attending to and developing language. When the babies were only twenty-four hours old, he gave them a chance to hear music. By sucking a pacifier, the babies could turn on tape-recorded classical, popular, or vocal music. The babies clearly sucked to get the musical reinforcement. Although these babies were not learning a language, they were attending to the sounds in their environment and actively controlling them.

Attention to Speech

Long before he can actually speak, a baby pays special attention to the speech he hears around him. Within the first month of life, his response to the sound of the human voice will be different from his response to other sorts of auditory stimuli (Menyuk, 1971). He will stop crying when he hears a person talking, but not if he hears a bell or the sound of a rattle. At first, the sounds that an infant notices might be only those words that receive the heaviest emphasis and that often occur at the ends of utterances. By six or seven weeks, he can detect the difference between syllables pronounced with rising and falling inflections. Very soon, these differences in adult stress and intonation can influence a baby's emotional states and behavior. Long before he develops actual language comprehension, the baby can sense when an adult is playful or angry, attempting to initiate or terminate behavior, and so on, merely on the basis of cues such as the rate, volume, and melody of adult speech.

Adults make it as easy as they can for babies to pick up a language by exaggerating such cues. C. A. Ferguson (1964) observed babies and their mothers in six diverse cultures and found that, in all six languages, the mothers used simplified syntax, short utterances, and nonsense sounds, and transformed certain sounds into baby talk. Other investigators have noted that when mothers talk to babies who are only a few months old, they exaggerate the pitch, loudness, and intensity of their words. They also exaggerate their facial expres-

Researchers have found that mothers in various cultures use a special kind of language to their infants, simplifying their syntax and exaggerating their facial expressions. (Suzanne Szasz)

sions, hold vowels longer, and emphasize certain words (Stern, 1977).

More significant for language development than his response to general intonation is recent evidence that a tiny baby can make fine distinctions between speech sounds. Peter Eimas and his colleagues (1971) have shown that one-month-old babies can hear the difference between the sounds "ba" and "pa," a very subtle distinction. These investigators used an intriguing method to make their discovery. They knew that a baby will suck on a nipple at a constant rate as long as nothing new or startling strikes his senses but that a sudden change in stimulation will cause him to suck at a more rapid rate. By giving a baby a pacifier attached to electronic recording equipment, Eimas and his colleagues were able to monitor the baby's rate and intensity of sucking. They repeatedly presented the sound "ba" to the baby until his sucking reached a stable rate; that is, until he habituated to that stimulus. Then they switched to the sound "pa"; babies as young as one month immediately increased their rate of sucking, indicating their ability to distinguish between these two very closely related sounds. This study suggests that a baby comes into the world with the ability to make precisely those perceptual discriminations that are necessary if he is to acquire human language.

Babies obviously derive pleasure from sound input, too: even as young as nine months, they will listen to nursery rhymes, songs, or stories, although the words themselves are beyond their understanding. Even some adults find themselves lulled by sound and never think to seek the meaning of words in Mother Goose rhymes: What is the *tuffet* that little Miss Muffet sat on? And what exactly are *curds* and *whey?* For several years, in fact, it is the surface of sound, in both what children hear and what they say, that attracts them. When children begin to use words, they continue the playful use of language in combinations of nonsense words and in rhyming games. For them, language is a sensory-motor delight rather than the route to prosaic meaning that it often is for adults.

Prespeech Sounds

Despite the infant's sharp discrimination and enjoyment of certain speech stimuli, it usually takes at least a year before he is able to produce sounds that can be identified as words. It is much more difficult for him to acquire motor control over the various muscles and organs involved in producing speech than it is for him to perceive auditory distinctions (McCarthy, 1954). The progress from crying to babbling to speech usually follows the same sequence in most infants, but some, of course, pass through the various linguistic developments shown in Figure 8.1 earlier or later than the suggested ages.

The first sound a baby makes is a cry, and within days, if not hours, he is able to use his cries to communicate gross messages to his parents. When Peter Wolff (1969) studied infant vocalization, he found that even in the first weeks of life a baby has three patterns of crying, as mentioned in Chapter 5: the basic rhythmic pattern (often erroneously called the hunger cry); the anger cry; and the pain cry. By playing a tape recording of a baby's cries on different occasions when the mother was out of the room, Wolff discovered that a mother recognizes the differences in the cries of her own baby and responds dramatically. Whenever Wolff played the pain cry, for example, the baby's mother immediately rushed into the room with a worried expression on her face. Other investigators have found that parents of three- to five-month-old babies are unable to distinguish among the basic cries unless the context of the cry provides some sort of cue (Muller, Hollien, and

Figure 8.1   Highlights of language development during the first two years of life. Some infants may not show all the linguistic developments indicated. The average ages shown are approximations, and the length of the bars reflects the range in average ages that different researchers have reported for a particular linguistic development. (Adapted from Lenneberg, 1967; McCarthy, 1954; and Bayley, 1969)

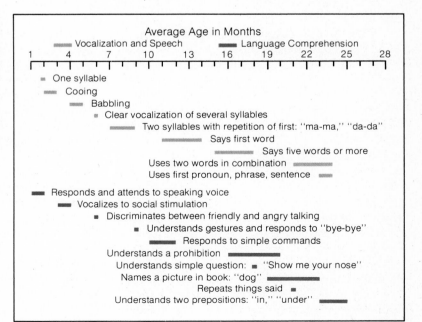

Parents' responses to the infant's sounds and gestures
encourage his attempts to communicate. (Linda
Rogers/Woodfin Camp & Assoc.)

Murry, 1974). By the time a baby is seven or eight
months, though, a parent has no trouble distinguishing its cries.

After three weeks of age, the baby's vocalizations gradually increase in frequency and variety.
Some sounds, of course, are physical and digestive
mouthings and gurglings, but by the second month
he invents new noises, from squeals to Bronx
cheers, and repeats them in a circular fashion (P.
Wolff, 1969). Sounds of joy, called cooing, also
may begin to occur at this time, usually when
babies appear to be happy: after eating, while
watching a smiling face, when listening to singing,
and while looking at or handling objects.

After three months adults can increase the frequency of the baby's sounds by responding to
them. From the very start, sounds and gestures develop as communicative acts because of the way
that others react. Crying and cooing and attempts
to make contact with other human beings prepare
the baby for the ability to speak. Infants in institutions with few adults around make fewer spontaneous noises and may not even cry much, because

crying is a part of the child's social interaction. If
no one comes to answer a cry, crying becomes a
useless vocalization. For example, in a series of
experiments, Harriet Rheingold, Jacob Gewirtz,
and Helen Ross (1959) used simultaneous smiles,
sounds, and light touches to the abdomen to condition institutionalized babies' vocal responses.
They did not reinforce coughs, whistles, squeaks,
snorts, fusses, or cries of protest. The reinforcement, which closely resembled a common variety
of adult-infant play, quickly doubled the babies'
vocalizations.

By the age of five or six months, the baby produces sequences of alternating vowels and consonants, such as "bababababa." Such sound sequences,
called **babbling,** give the impression that the baby
is uttering a string of syllables. The capacity to
keep saying the same sequences over and over
again, as in repeating syllables, indicates that the
baby has achieved a great extension of motor
control.

The primary function of babbling is probably
to develop motor control over the speech muscula-

ture and to coordinate the production of sounds with the perception of sounds. That is, when the baby feels certain patterns of motor activity involving the muscles of his throat, tongue, and lips, he associates those movements with the sounds that he hears himself making. Babbling may thus be a form of motor practice that facilitates later speech development.

But babbling may not be directly related to the acquisition of any particular native language (McNeill, 1970a). The speech sounds of children from different language communities cannot be distinguished from one another until near the end of the first year, when intonational variations begin to appear in the child's vocalizations. Babbling includes many sounds that adults do not make and that the baby may not be able to say a year later. Much babbling also appears to be sheer motor play, in which the baby produces many accidental sounds that have nothing to do with communication.

Even deaf babies babble, which suggests that at first this sort of vocalization is indeed motor play. Because the babbling of normal six-month-old babies shows a greater diversity of sound than the babbling of deaf infants, we can suppose that hearing speech sounds stimulates the baby. Soon after six months, deaf infants stop babbling, and hearing infants go on to greater diversity and experimentation in their speech play (Lenneberg, 1967).

Near the end of the first year, the infant's *intonation,* or the rising and falling pitch of his utterances, becomes more and more like adult speech. At this time the infant may produce long, complex sequences of meaningless sounds with the pitch contour of adult sentences. These charming sequences may appear when the child is pretending to read or to talk to a doll when no one else is present. By the time such sequences are present, a listener can distinguish the intonation differences among language communities. Once the infant begins to consistently use certain "words" that adults can recognize and interpret, he has entered the final prespeech stage.

Cognitive Precursors to First Words

As we pointed out in Chapter 7, a child cannot use words meaningfully until he has some notion that there is a world of enduring objects and people and that people can act on objects. These notions of object permanence, object identity, and causality are partly the result of the baby's sensory-motor development during his first year of life. By the time he celebrates his first birthday, the infant has begun to imitate events well after they have occurred, which is convincing evidence of his ability to *represent* objects and events to himself. Jean Piaget (1951) has described and analyzed various facets of the development of this important ability.

Piaget watched the development of his own three children closely and made detailed observa-

Young babies of different speech communities produce similar babbling sounds, but by the age of one year, they have already begun to learn the intonation patterns of their own language. (Susan Johns/ Rapho/Photo Researchers)

tions. He reports many instances of the one-year-old's ability to imitate what he has experienced. For example, when his daughter Jacqueline was sixteen months old, she was impressed by an eighteen-month-old boy's tantrum. As Piaget describes it:

He screamed as he tried to get out of a play-pen and pushed it backwards, stamping his feet. J. stood watching him in amazement, never having witnessed such a scene before. The next day, she herself screamed in her play-pen and tried to move it, stamping her foot lightly several times in succession. (page 63)

Piaget points out that, because Jacqueline did not imitate the boy's behavior until the following day, she must have been able to store some representation of the event in her mind, acting it out in imitation much later. This cognitive development is, of course, an essential prerequisite for language.

An infant at the same stage of development also tries to use his own motor acts and sounds to represent events to himself. For example, Piaget reports how a year-old infant tried to keep track of the demonstrated manipulation of a matchbox:

T. was looking at a box of matches which I was holding on its end and alternately opening and closing. Showing great delight, he watched with great attention, and imitated the box in three ways. (1) He opened and closed his right hand, keeping his eyes on the box. (2) He said *"tff, tff"* to reproduce the sound the box made. (3) He reacted . . . by opening and closing his mouth. (page 66)

The ability to talk about things rests on the ability to picture them to oneself. About the time that the infant is able to do this, he begins to imitate the words that he hears. Before he can use these words in his own speech, he must remember them along with his memories of what was happening at the time that he heard them. Just as the one-year-old is able to imitate events some time after he has experienced them, he is able to use words some time after he has heard them. So the abilities to imitate and to store internal images of sights and sounds are necessary prerequisites for the development of language.

By the time an infant like Lauren is one year old, she will begin to remember and imitate sound sequences such as "kiss" and "doggy." But this is not enough, because language is not only a collection of words: it is a collection that makes sense. Unless Lauren has begun to make sense of the world, she will have no way of relating words to

their meanings. So Lauren must notice that, when Mommy says "Give me a kiss," she waits for Lauren to touch Mommy's cheek with her lips, and when Daddy says "Look at the doggy," there is some recognizable thing in the perceptual world of sight and sound and touch that will come to be known as a "doggy." Parents try to make the connection between sound and meaning clear by talking mainly about the here and now, repeating important words, and pointing to objects as they name them.

However, words are only one means that the infant uses to symbolize his ideas. His first words emerge at the same time that he begins to use symbolic gestures and to engage in make-believe play. The little boy who opened and closed his hand and his mouth after watching Piaget open and close the matchbox was using a symbolic gesture. At another time, such an infant may push a little stone along the table, pretending that it is a car, or he may rub his hands saying "soap," pretending that he is washing. Spoken language emerges as one of a complex of symbolic behaviors that help the infant to remember and play with what he has experienced. Words, gestures, and make-believe play all reflect the level of an infant's understanding of the world. And as the infant engages in these symbolic behaviors, they assist him in refining and organizing his cognitions and feelings.

Communicative Precursors to First Words

At the same time that the baby is busily exploring the world of objects and events around him, he is also trying to communicate with other people in his world. Long before his first words appear, the baby communicates by the use of gesture and vocal sounds. As early as two months, he responds to human attention with rudimentary lip and tongue movements and a ritualized hand waving that is different from his early movements toward objects (Trevarthen, 1975). As he grows, his intentions become more obvious. He makes contact by smiling and babbling. He makes demands by reaching, grasping, calling, and crying. He gets the attention of adults and refers to objects in the environment by pointing. A baby's gestures require adults to respond with an action or an answer, just as his verbal assertions and requests will later demand a reply. Even when an infant is simply exploring objects, he indicates his involvement by vocalizing at the same time that he examines a toy

After the baby perceives the dog as a distinct, recognizable thing in his environment, he learns to attach the label "dog" after hearing his parents say the word. (Suzanne Szasz)

and emphasis can affect utterances profoundly, sometimes even reversing the meaning of a remark, this early learning of intonation plays an important part in the continuing development of language ability.

Even when a baby is not trying to communicate, he may be learning something about the nature of human conversation. Parents often respond to a baby's movements and sounds as if they were meaningful, and encourage infants to "take their turn" in a conversation. For example:

Infant: (smiles)
Mother: Oh, what a nice little smile! Yes, isn't that nice? There. That's a nice little smile.
Infant: (burps)
Mother: What a nice wind as well! Yes, that's better, isn't it? Yes. Yes.
Infant: (vocalizes)
Mother: Yes! There's a nice noise (C. E. Snow, 1977).

or tugs at the cat's tail. The baby's vocal sounds have characteristic intonation patterns that others can interpret as communicating such things as desires, frustration, satisfaction, or rejection. As you will remember, he could communicate his general condition when he was less than a week old.

R. V. Tonkova-Yampol'skaya (1973), a Soviet investigator, studied the development of intonation patterns in the prespeech vocalizations of Russian children. She found that such patterns stabilize before infants develop words and that babies in the first year of life are able to learn intonations signaling happiness as well as commands, requests, and questions. Infants' intonation patterns for several kinds of communication correspond closely to typical adult patterns, as Figure 8.2 shows. For example, babies at seven to ten months of age express commands with the same sharply rising then falling pitch that adults use. About the beginning of the second year, infants first use the intonation that signifies a question. This pattern is easily distinguished from others by the sharp rise in pitch at the end. Because pitch

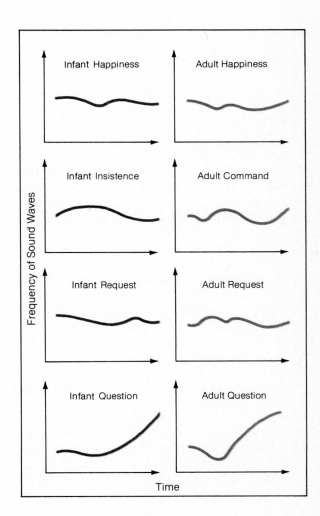

Figure 8.2 Comparison of several kinds of intonation patterns of infants and adults. The sample illustrations for infants are based on data for infants from seven to twenty-four months of age. Each graph represents a change in pitch of the voice (frequency) over time (seconds). (Adapted from Tonkova-Yampol'skaya, 1973)

As time goes on, the adult may require a more extensive response from the baby—first babbling, and then words.

FIRST WORDS

Although some babies begin to use a variety of single words toward the end of their first year, most will pass their first birthdays before their vocabulary has more than three words. Although most studies report no sex differences in language ability until about eighteen months, some have shown a clear but slight edge for girls, and others have found that, in newborns, girls vocalize more than boys (McCarthy, 1954).

Functions of First Words

It is natural that an infant's first words will carry on the patterns of behavior and intent that he has developed during the prespeech period. He has already been using speechlike sounds, intonation patterns, and gestures to express several basic functions of communication, and his first words will function in the same way. They will *refer* to objects and events, *express* mood states, and *command* adults to carry out actions that the infant desires. These functions show clearly in Table 8.1, which gives the first seven words of a child whose language development was studied in detail by her linguist father, Werner Leopold (1949). Some of her first words, such as "dididi," primarily express emotion, and Leopold believes that language begins to develop when a baby attaches some emotional meaning to one of her babbles. You can see that early words like "uh?" perform several functions at once for the little girl. For example, when she said "uh" and pointed to a toy that had fallen, she was simultaneously referring to the toy, expressing her concern that it had fallen, and requesting that it be given back to her. The single word thus functions to refer, express, and command in an undifferentiated utterance. As we will see, once the child is able to combine *several* words in one utterance, these functions will become differentiated in her speech. For example, the statement "Dollie fell," which refers to an event, is clearly different from the command "Give dollie." But all of the functions are already implicit at this early linguistic stage when the infant can say only "dollie," "fell," or "give."

The period in which the infant can utter only one word at a time often lasts until he is nearly

Table 8.1 The First Seven "Words" in One Child's Linguistic Development

UTTER-ANCE	AGE IN MONTHS	MEANINGS
uh?	8	An interjection. Also demonstrative, "addressed" to persons, distant objects, and "escaped toys."
dididi	9	Disapproval (loud). Comfort (soft).
mama	10	Refers vaguely to food. Also means "tastes good" and "hungry."
nenene	10	Scolding.
tt!	10	Used to call squirrels.
piti	10	Always used with a gesture, and always whispered. Seems to mean "interest(-ed), (-ing)."
deh	10	An interjection. Also demonstrative. Used with the same gesture as above.

Source: Adapted from David McNeill, *The Acquisition of Language: The Study of Developmental Psycholinguistics* (New York: Harper & Row, 1970), p. 22; based on material from Werner F. Leopold, *Grammar and General Problems in the First Two Years,* Speech Development of a Bilingual Child: A Linguist's Record, Vol. 3 (Evanston, Ill.: Northwestern University Press, 1949), p. 6.

two. As Paula Menyuk and Nancy Bernholtz (1969) have shown, during this period the infant often relies on intonation to communicate the intention of a single word. For example, in Figure 8.3 you see intonation patterns of the word "door" as spoken by an infant on three different occasions. Menyuk and Bernholtz tape-recorded these utterances and played them to listeners, who agreed when the child's use of "door" was a declaration, a question, or an emphatic statement. It was clear that the child was not simply using the word "door" to name an object. When the child used a falling pitch (frequency contour), listeners judged the utterance as having a naming, or referential, function. But when the same word was uttered with a rising intonation, listeners interpreted it as a question. And when the intonation rose sharply and then fell, it was heard as an emphatic assertion or demand. Thus the single word "door" could mean: "That's a door" or "Is that a door?" or "Are you going to open the door?" or "Open the door!" or "Close the door!" and so forth.

However, such simple utterances—early one-word utterances and later two- and three-word utterances—can be fully understood only in *context*. On hearing a recording of the word "door" spoken

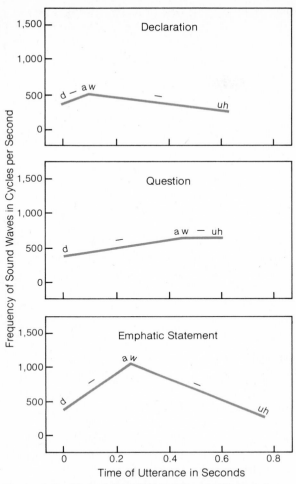

Figure 8.3   Three intonation patterns for the word "door" spoken by an infant at the one-word stage. (After Menyuk, 1971)

only 7 percent of the information we give to others comes from our words; the rest comes from our intonation, our gestures, our facial expressions, and the way we hold our bodies. Because the child's communicative needs are always embedded in an ongoing context of activity, it is generally possible for adults to figure out what he is trying to say. As his vocabulary and grammar develop, he will be able to talk about objects and people that are not present, about things he did yesterday or wants to do tomorrow. Context will no longer be so necessary; his language will have the property of displacement, and true conversation will become possible.

Form of First Words

Early words, unlike babbling, do not sample a wide range of sounds. Indeed, when a baby first

A toddler who says the single word "door" can be understood only in context. The word might mean "Open the door," "Close the door," or any of several other statements. (Sybil Shelton/Monkmeyer Press)

with an emphatic intonation, you may not be able to decide whether the child wanted the door opened or closed or merely wanted the listener to pay attention to the door. But if you are watching a toddler stand in front of a closed door and you know that on the other side of the door her father is repairing a light switch, you would know immediately that the emphatic utterance "door" means that you have been asked to open it. Communication succeeds at these early stages because adults are good at guessing the child's intentions. The child gives a partial clue to his intentions in his speech, intonation, and gesture. The importance of intonation and gesture will not decline as the child matures. Even adults rely on these cues when communicating with their peers. For example, Albert Mehrabian (1971) has estimated that

begins to speak, he may be unable to imitate sounds that he made earlier in playful babbling. His first words tend to be short, of one or two syllables, and each syllable generally consists of a consonant followed by a vowel. The first words will probably consist of a front consonant like "b" or "p" and a back vowel like "a." This is true no matter what language the infant is to speak. Roman Jakobson (1968) reports that an infant who is to learn English says "tut" before "cut"; one who will speak Japanese says "ta" before "ka"; and an infant growing up in Sweden says "tata" before "kata."

Suppose the baby's first word is something like "ba" for "ball." An observer with a tape recorder who is lucky enough to get many examples of a baby using this word will find that its pronunciation varies from "bee" to "bow" and that the consonant also varies: it is sometimes *pa, va, da,* or *tha.* It is because the listener expects to hear and thinks of the word "ball" that he believes the baby has a stable pronunciation of it. In fact, although the baby is able to perceive the differences among sounds in the adult speech that he hears, he devotes a great deal of effort to figuring out how to produce the whole complex of sounds that correspond to adult words.

Arlene Moskowitz (1970) believes that the first units the child organizes in his speech may be syllables rather than separate vowels or consonants. The first syllable may be produced when the infant simply releases his lips while vocalizing, producing a sound such as "ma" or "ba." The first distinction between consonants that an infant makes is often between a sound such as "ma," which he produces by releasing air through the nose with his lips together and then opening his mouth, and "ba," which he produces by suddenly letting the air out between his lips. Once he has reached this point, he may be able to say "mama" and "ba" as distinct words.

Because the infant has few consonants at his command during his second year, his store of syllables is small and he often repeats them. For example, David may say "pa-pa" or "bi-bi" or "car-car." He may also utter two different words with different meanings, and they will sound the same because his small collection of syllables offers few possibilities for different word forms. For example, David may say "ba" to imitate the words "ball," "bird," and "flower." The first time he says "ba," his mother or father will probably

say "ball" when a ball is nearby or "bird" when a bird flies by. Such auditory reinforcement helps the infant to shape his "ba" until at last he does say both "ball" and "bird" (McCarthy, 1954).

The child continues to work at differentiating among speech sounds and then at producing the appropriate ones, often well into his second and third years when he enters the stage of grammatical speech. By the time he is four, he has learned some amazingly complicated aspects of word construction, but he may still have motor difficulties in articulating one or two sounds. These difficulties do not stand in the way of his basic grand achievement, the understanding and production of sentences, which begins to develop about six months to a year after he first uses meaningful words. Many young children spontaneously outgrow any problems of articulation. If such speech difficulties persist into later childhood and cause a child to be socially stigmatized, however, they may play a significant role in his social and psychological development.

Meanings of First Words

By the time the infant can use single words, he has acquired the object permanence and object identity discussed in Chapter 7. Now that he is beginning to speak, his words make it possible to infer quite a bit about his development of concepts. Among the communicative functions performed by his first words, that of reference reveals the way that he perceives and arranges his world (Clark and Clark, 1977). An infant's first words are usually very different in their apparent range of meaning from the conventional meaning that adults attribute to the sounds. For example, one little girl used a single word to refer to a dress, a coat, a white hat, and the carriage she rode in and to ask to take a walk or to report that she had taken one. It is easy to see how the mother's use of a word while dressing the girl to go out may have led the girl to include in its meaning all the related events and experiences for which she had no separate names. In another case, a little boy used a single word to refer to breast, biscuit, a red button on a dress, a bare elbow, an eye in a portrait, and his mother's photograph. The perceptual basis for these generalizations is obvious.

Eve Clark (1973) has studied such **overextensions** of early word meanings in detail. She has examined many of the nineteenth- and twentieth-century diary studies kept in various languages by

When a mother "reads" a picture book to her baby, the ritual identification of pictures exemplifies informal parental language teaching. (Joel Gordon)

linguist and psychologist parents and has concluded that, when an infant extends a word to include a number of dissimilar objects or events, it is usually possible to find some perceived similarity among the objects or events. These overextensions of meaning give us a glimpse of the similarities that very young children notice. Clark gives six examples of major categories that various young children have used to sort out their worlds:

Movement. An infant first used "sh" to refer to the sound of a train and then extended "sh" to refer to all moving machines.

Shape. This is a common basis for overextensions. A category of small round objects appears in many of the studies. For example, one infant first used "mooi" to refer to the moon and then successively extended this word to cakes, round marks on a window, writing on windows and in books, round shapes in books, tooling

on leather book covers, round postmarks, and the letter O.

Size. "Fly" began, for one infant, as the name for a specific insect and then generalized to specks of dirt, dust, all small insects, the infant's own toes, crumbs of bread, and a toad.

Sound. "Koko," for one Yugoslav infant, first referred to the crowing of a cockerel. Subsequently the child used it to refer to tunes played on the violin, tunes played on the piano, tunes on an accordion, tunes on a phonograph, and finally to all music and even to a merry-go-round.

Taste. This category appears infrequently in the diary studies. One example is the word "candy," which an infant extended first to mean cherries and then to refer to anything sweet.

Texture. An infant extended the meaning of "bow-wow" from a real dog to a toy dog, then to a fur piece with an animal head, and finally to other fur pieces without heads.

As new words enter the child's vocabulary and as new experiences refine his concepts, he restructures and reorganizes these early word meanings. His new discriminations allow him to reverse the process, gradually refining his grand generalizations. This development becomes clear when it is charted for a single word (see Figure 8.4). Clark shows how an infant could first overextend and then restructure the meaning of "bow-wow" and how that restructuring relates to the child's acquisition of other animal names. At first, the infant might learn "bow-wow" from his mother, who uses it when they see a dog. Soon after, however, he uses the same word to refer to a variety of animals—dogs, cows, horses, sheep, and cats—presumably setting up a conceptual category on the basis of shape and movement. Then he learns the word "moo" for cows and is able to distinguish cows from other animals. At this step his animal vocabulary contains two words: "moo," referring to cows, and "bow-wow," referring to all other animals. As he learns more animal names, he keeps subdividing his initial general class, so that eventually he has separate names for dogs, cows, horses, sheep, and cats.

Clark points out that at each step the available animal names take on more precise meaning, based on those perceptual features that the infant uses to distinguish animals. For example, at Step

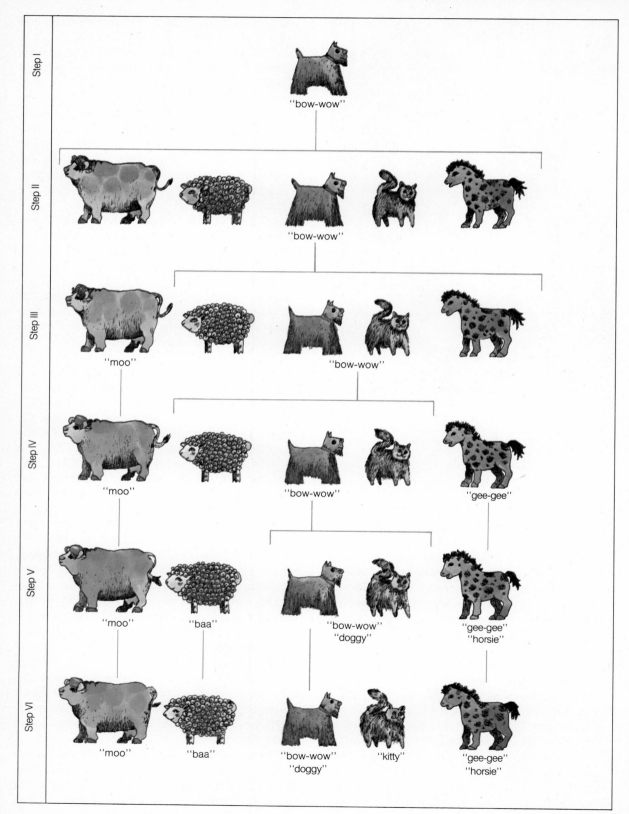

IV, the category "bow-wow" may include the feature of small size, because "bow-wow" refers only to fairly small animals like dogs, cats, and sheep, whereas the words for horse and cow may include among their features the meaning of large size. This demonstrates the process by which the global meanings of an infant's first words narrow as he learns new words and begins to attend to new features of objects and events. Each time the infant learns to notice and apply a new feature to his world, such as small, living, soft, and so forth, he may restructure the meaning of a number of words (McNeill, 1970a).

The earliest words of infants vary markedly among different families and even among children in the same family, according to the interests of a young child and of those around him. But the first words usually express the same basic notions (K. Nelson, 1973). Most commonly, babies begin by naming *movers,* that is, common objects that are able to move on their own, and to manipulate other things. These include people, vehicles, and animals. Babies also refer frequently to *movables,* objects that can be moved and manipulated but which cannot move independently. These include toys, food, articles of clothing, and household items. Less often, babies refer to places (objects where other objects are kept, or locations where certain events take place); recipients (people who act as places or who possess things); and instruments (objects like "spoon," which are used as tools to achieve certain goals). Once the infant has acquired these basic vocabulary tools, he is ready for the momentous step of combining words into longer utterances. But just as his first steps on his own two feet had to wait for a certain level of motor control, so the emergence of *grammar* must wait for a certain level of neurological maturation. And just as crawling prepared the infant to walk, one-word utterances prepare him to speak in a truly human way.

FIRST SENTENCES

An infant knows more than he can say. Even when he can speak only one word at a time, he appears to understand the longer utterances of his parents and his older brothers and sisters. He can also

Figure 8.4   A hypothetical example of how an infant overextends and restructures the meaning of the word "bow-wow," as discussed in the text. (Adapted from E. Clark, 1973)

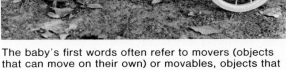

The baby's first words often refer to movers (objects that can move on their own) or movables, objects that can be moved or manipulated. (Suzanne Szasz)

mean more than he can say, as a number of researchers have pointed out (McNeill, 1970a).

Meaning at the Two-Word Stage

Toward the end of the one-word period, the infant makes sequences of separate one-word utterances that seem to relate to a larger meaning, even though he speaks each word separately, with its own falling intonation. For example, Lois Bloom (1973) has described a one-year-old girl who struggled to put a button into her pocket while she sat on the pocket. She said "button" and then "pocket," but she was not able to join the two words together into a single utterance. A month or two later the same girl was able to say "button pocket" with no long pause between the two words and with a falling intonation that spread over the whole utterance. The emergence of the two-word stage seems to be the result of some increase in neurological capacity that allows the young child to plan and to produce a two-word utterance before running out of immediate memory. Thus, the new development at this stage is an increase in the amount of information that the child can fit into one utterance. It is important to note, however, that the words and concepts that the young child expresses with two words were already present in his one-word utterances. Although the ability to speak a two-word sentence represents a clear advance in the young child's expressive capacity, it does not represent a new level in his thinking (Slobin, 1973). He can use his language only to express concepts and relationships that he already understands at least in part. The child continues to refer to the same things he did at the one-word stage. The two-word stage is significant because it represents a striking advance in the young child's ability to code his understanding in linguistic terms and to begin to project his ideas more fully into the world of human social and intellectual interaction.

The meanings expressed in two-word sentences reflect the level of understanding of a child of about two years of age. Early language development has now been studied in many different cultures, and everywhere the picture is the same. Somewhere around his second birthday, the child starts to put two words together to express the same universal range of basic concepts. These concepts form the core of all human language. Indeed, a large part of later language development is simply a matter of elaborating and refining the basic notions that are already present at this beginning stage.

Cataloging the Two-Year-Old Mind

A number of psycholinguists have been gathering child language data from around the world (R. Brown, 1973; Slobin, 1972, 1973). The following list of basic meanings expressed during the two-word stage comes from data collected among children who speak English, German, Russian, Finnish, Turkish, Samoan, and Luo (spoken in Kenya). But it would probably be possible to compile the entire list from two-year-old speakers of any single language. It is, essentially, a catalog of the two-year-old mind.

Identification. Such utterances as "See doggy" are extensions of the simple pointing responses that the baby makes during the prespeech period and the same responses, accompanied by the object's name, that he makes during the one-word stage.

Location. Along with pointing, the infant can signal the location of an object with such words as "here" and "there," as in "Book there." If he wishes to indicate the relationship of being in, on, or under something else, he uses a fixed juxtaposition of words with no preposition: "Baby chair," "Baby car," "Dollie down."

Recurrence. Presence, absence, and repetition seem to be aspects of things and actions that infants take into account very early. Such utterances as "More write," "Another bang," and "Book again" are among the first sentences that he speaks.

Nonexistence. An infant who observes the repetition of an experience also notices the disappearance of an object or the cessation of an activity. His early sentences express nonexistence in such forms as "All-gone ball" and "Milk all-done."

Negation. An infant uses a negative construction to *contradict* an adult utterance or to avoid a possible misunderstanding. For example, he may point to a picture of a dog and say "Not cat." He can use a similar form to *reject* the imposition of an adult desire, as when he says "No water" when offered a drink.

Possession. An infant at the one-word period who says only "Daddy" when he sees Daddy's coat or chair later may say "Daddy coat" or "Daddy chair."

Agent, action, and *object.* Although the infant obviously understands that agents act on objects, at the two-word stage he can express only two terms of this three-term relation in a single sentence. So he can say "Daddy throw" (agent-action), "Throw ball" (action-object), and "Daddy ball" (agent-object), though he cannot yet say "Daddy throw ball."

Action-location. The infant can talk about an action and at the same time specify where the action takes place, provided he does not want to say anything else about the situation. His utterances are ruled by the same two-word limit that left him unable to say "Daddy throw ball." Thus, if he wants his mother to sit in the rocking chair, he can say either "Sit chair" (action-location) or "Mama sit" or "Mama chair" but not "Mama sit chair" or "Mama sit on chair." When these longer utterances finally emerge, they will once again reflect understanding that the infant already possessed at the two-word stage.

Action-recipient. The infant can talk about who is to benefit from various actions, saying such things as "Give papa," meaning that something should be given to his father, or "Cookie me," leaving no doubt in the listener's mind that he is demanding a cookie, although the imperative verb that makes the command is unspoken.

Action-instrument. The infant who uses utterances such as "Cut knife," as distinguished from "Cut bread," indicates that he has some notion of the use of instruments to carry out actions.

Attribution. The infant begins to modify nouns with attributes, saying "Red truck" and "Big ball," slightly later than he learns to state other basic relationships. Sometimes the range of such alternatives available to him is very limited.

Questions. The infant can transform all the preceding sentence types into simple questions merely by saying them (in most languages) with a rising intonation. At this early period he generally also possesses several question words, especially "where," which he uses simply with nouns ("Where ball?") or verbs ("Where go?") in two-word combinations.

The universality and comprehensiveness of the list of meanings found at the two-word stage is impressive. The child is clearly communicating a wide range of ideas. In fact, it is hard to think of basic notions to add to the list in order to describe adult speech. What do these simple utterances lack besides length?

FROM TWO WORDS TO GRAMMAR

The crucial feature that develops in the next several years is what the linguists refer to as *grammar,* and it is a feature hinted at on the first pages of this chapter. Grammar does not mean the schoolbook rules of how to speak "properly" but rather the rules that all of us know implicitly and use to organize our words into sentences. You recall that most of the two-word utterances found among children who speak various languages are difficult to interpret outside of *context,* that is, outside the situations in which they were uttered. If David says "Baby chair," for example, does he mean "This is the baby's chair" or "The baby is in the chair" or "Put the baby in the chair" or "This is a little chair"? The list of possible interpretations

could go on and on, because there is not enough *grammatical* information in the simple two-word combination "Baby chair." It is grammar that makes it possible for you to understand all the possible interpretations in the previous sentence, although you are not now in an actual situation containing babies and chairs. For example, you understand the difference between "the baby's chair" and "baby in the chair" because you know the grammatical functions of the possessive *'s* and the locational "in the" as they are expressed in English. Knowledge of the role of inflections, prepositions, word order, and so on makes it possible for you to produce and understand sentences outside any immediate, relevant physical context. It is the development of this grammatical knowledge that will actively occupy the child's mind from two to five, and we will further explore this development in Chapter 12.

When linguists first began to analyze the speech of children at the two-word stage, they concentrated on the formal grammatical rules that govern the distribution of word classes, such as nouns and verbs, in the child's sentences. Lois Bloom (1970) argues that such an analysis is of little use because it treats a sentence like "Baby chair" the same no matter how it is used. And if David says "Baby chair" at lunchtime to mean "Baby Lauren is sitting in her highchair," he may say "Baby chair" to mean "That is Baby Lauren's highchair" when visiting Lauren's house. In both cases, David uses two nouns, but on one occasion he indicates Lauren's location, and on the other, her possession of the chair.

The rudiments of grammar appear in the child's speech toward the end of the two-word stage. These first grammatical devices are the basic formal tools of human language; they are intonation, word order, and inflection

Intonation

We have already discussed the important role that intonation plays in earlier periods of language development, when a baby can indicate a request with a rising tone or a demand with a loud, insistent tone. But toward the end of the two-word stage, another device, a contrastive stress, becomes available. In the example of "Baby chair," an English-speaking child may emphasize the first word, saying "BABY chair" to indicate possession ("That is baby's chair"), or emphasize the second word, saying "Baby CHAIR" to indicate location

("Baby is in chair") or destination ("Put baby in chair"). Of course, you recall that intonation may also be used to differentiate a statement from a question. For example, "Daddy book" spoken without a rising tone may mean "This is Daddy's book," whereas "Daddy book?" with the rising tone means "Is this Daddy's book?" or "Will Daddy read a book?"

Word Order

In English and in many other languages, the order in which the words are spoken partly determines the meaning of word combinations. English sentences typically follow a subject-verb-object sequence, and children learn the rules early. In the example presented earlier, "Daddy throw ball," children use some two-word combinations ("Daddy throw," "Daddy ball," "Throw ball") but not others ("ball Daddy," "ball throw," "throw Daddy"). As soon as a child has a sense of this basic word-order rule of English, he can distinguish between the meanings, for example, of "Tickle Daddy" and "Daddy tickle." In other words, as Roger Brown (1973) and other psycholinguists have pointed out, the child does not produce a random collection of words, using the two words that are his limit in any order. Instead, he uses his knowledge of word order grammatically to distinguish the meanings of the word combinations that he produces. And linguists, parents, and other children can use their own knowledge of word order to decipher the speech of a child in the two-word stage.

There are individual differences, however, in the way children initially combine two words to express meanings. Martin Braine (1976) argues that children discover different patterns of word order at the beginning of the two-word stage. One child may communicate the idea that an object is at a particular location by naming the object first and the place second ("baby chair"); another may first discover a pattern in which the place comes first ("here baby," "there book"). In general, some children seem to prefer at first to combine two content words, as in "play bed" and "doggie bark." Others begin by combining content words with pronouns in most of their utterances, as in "I finish" (Bloom, Lightbown, and Hood, 1975).

Inflection

Grammatical markers, such as the possessive 's and the past tense -ed, that are added to words to change their meanings are called inflections. English uses few inflections compared with some other languages, and the child learns such English inflections as the plural and the possessive quite early, making it possible to mark, for example, the possessive meaning of "Baby's chair" and the plural "Baby chairs." Some languages provide different word endings (inflections) to express a large number of contrasts in meaning, such as the Russian example of "Mommy kisses baby" that appeared earlier in this chapter. Children who learn highly inflected languages are quick to acquire the word endings that express those notions implicit in speech at the two-word stage, such as direct and indirect object and locations. The direct-object inflection (as in the Russian example) is one of the first endings that children pick up in learning such languages as Russian, Serbo-Croatian, Latvian, Hungarian, Finnish, and Turkish (Slobin, 1973).

From this discussion, it should be clear that by the time he reaches the end of the two-word stage, the young child has mastered much of the basic grammatical machinery that he needs in order to acquire his particular native language: words that can be combined in order and modified by intonation and inflection. These rules occur, in varying degrees, in all the languages of the world. As a result, all languages are about equally easy for children to learn, and all children are ready to master the grammatical subtleties of their particular native language by the time they are about two and one-half years old. In Chapter 12 we will discuss the further course of language development and will explore some of the possible reasons that all children master the complexity of grammar with such apparent ease and rapidity.

SUMMARY

1. Human language possesses three important properties: semanticity, productivity, and displacement. During his first two years, the infant becomes a speaking human being by discovering the structural principles of his language—its grammar—and by actively figuring out how speech is organized.

2. From the first month of life, the baby pays special attention to the speech that he hears around him. Despite his ability to discriminate between sounds, it usually takes at least a year for him to acquire sufficient motor control to be able to produce identifiable words. He acquires this muscular

control first through crying and later through babbling. Given the close interplay between the infant's increasing cognitive understanding and his linguistic development, his spoken language emerges as part of a complex set of symbolic behavior that helps him to remember and use what he has experienced. By the end of his first year, the infant's intonation patterns usually communicate commands, requests, and questions, as well as involvement.

3. The infant's first words usually function to refer, express, and command. Most often, such one- and two-syllable utterances can be understood only in context. First words are likely to be repeated syllables made up of a consonant and a vowel, which will eventually be shaped into actual words. These early words often have an overextended range of meanings based on perceived similarities such as movement or shape. These global meanings become more precise as the infant re-

structures them and makes sharper discriminations.

4. The infant often knows and means more than he can say. Thus, although two-word sentences may communicate more information, they do not represent a new level of thinking. By about two years of age, however, the infant can usually put several words together and can express and understand an impressive range of basic universal concepts involving objects, actions, and events.

5. A rudimentary grammar appears in the infant's language toward the end of the two-word stage and includes the basic tools of human language: intonation, word order, and inflection. With these first grammatical devices, the child is ready to master the further subtleties of his native language and to produce and understand sentences outside an immediate context.

CHAPTER 9

Personality: From Attachment to Sociability

PERSONALITY DEVELOPMENT

EARLY EXPERIENCE
Types of Effects
Limits on Effects

ATTACHMENT
Attachment in Monkeys
Attachment in Human Beings

PARENT RESPONSIVENESS
Parental Styles
Class and Cultural Differences

INFANT RESPONSIVENESS
Separation Distress
Wariness of Strangers
Multiple Caregiving

THE DEVELOPMENT OF SOCIABILITY
Interactions with Parents
Self-Concept
Interactions with Peers
The Significance of Play

SUMMARY

"She's not a playmate—she can't do nothin'," Matt said, regarding the new baby with disgust. The baby's eyes opened, seemed to wander uncoordinated, and then came to rest on the happy-face button that Matt was wearing. "Hey, she's looking at my button!" cried Matt, snatching it off his shirt and moving it back and forth in front of baby Susan's eyes. His sister briefly followed the button with slow, jerky movements of her eyes; she even turned her head to follow it to one side. A fleeting upturn of the corners of her mouth evoked a response from her brother: "She's smiling, look, she's smiling!" In his excitement, Matt slipped and fell heavily against the bassinet. The baby startled and reacted with her whole body: flailing arms and legs, screwed-up red face, and imperative screams. Matt ran to get his father. After his father rocked Susan and soothed her, he placed her back in the bassinet. Matt, who had been observing quietly, headed outdoors to play. As he walked out of the room, he looked back and said, "She's nothin' but a cryer and a wetter."

From these unpromising beginnings, Matt's new sister will develop into a complex, social, unique individual. Susan will pursue numerous goals in life; relate to people in a variety of ways; be angered, frightened, and elated; and have beliefs, attitudes, and values that in part reflect her upbringing and in part are unique to her.

This chapter traces the beginnings of that development. In it we will see how early experiences, which begin at the moment of birth, contribute to a baby's developing personality. We will find wide agreement with the supposition that these early experiences often affect later development but little agreement as to how and why these effects come about. We will look at a baby's first social bond with her primary caregivers and discover that this attachment plays an important role in the baby's developing trust in the world and in her growing sense of self. Even her early play will affect the development of her personality. By the end of the chapter, we will have examined the ways in which the important lessons of the infant's first two years of life lay the groundwork for the person that the baby will eventually become.

PERSONALITY DEVELOPMENT

It is easy to see that infants learn to walk, to eat with a spoon, or to say their names. However, people often think of personality as given, as something that one is born with. Although each baby comes into the world with certain temperamental predispositions that tend to shape the course of his or her personality development, most psychologists are convinced that what we think of as personality is largely the product of social learning. How people feel about themselves, whether they are assertive or demure, whether they are anxious in social situations, how they enact their roles as females or males are all learned patterns of behavior.

Personality development refers to the growth of the individual as a social being, a person who carries on the important activities of life in interaction with other people. For example, Susan's sense of herself as a separate being will be closely connected with her sense of other people as continuing, existing beings. The behavior of important people in her life will contribute to Susan's consistent definition of them. Thus, their attitudes and actions will powerfully affect her sense of personal identity, of the continuity and sameness of "me" over time and across situations. How other people respond to her will affect even the way that she incorporates such "facts" of her existence as sex and race into her sense of gender and ethnic identity. And the specifics of her self-concept, her thoughts and feelings about the kind of person she is, will first form when she adopts the attitudes toward herself held by important others in her life.

Another way of looking at the development of such enduring dispositions as self-concept is to say that various aspects of social interaction become internalized. At first Susan will be regulated by her parents, but later she will be able to regulate herself in their absence. She will eventually be able to criticize herself, pat herself on the back, and carry on private conversations with herself. A sense of separateness, a sense of the continuity of one's existence, a sense of one's qualities and value, and the continuing dynamics of one's relationship with oneself are all central aspects of personality functioning, and all are developmental achievements.

SIGMUND FREUD, the founder of psychoanalysis, emphasizes the sensual nature of the infant's early interactions with his world. In Freud's view, the infant's attachment to his parents is based on his desire for sensual gratification. He suggests that infants go through psychosexual phases of development—oral, anal, and phallic—during which they derive sensual pleasure from stimulation of the corresponding area of their bodies. Parents affect children's personality development by either gratifying or frustrating these desires.

ERIK ERIKSON is a psychodynamic theorist who proposes that the infant learns early to distinguish between himself and those who satisfy his biological needs. In his theory of psychosocial stages of development, the interactions between the infant and his parents give him an ego identity, or a self-concept; pleasant interactions create an attachment to his parents and a trust in them. In this view, if the infant learns to trust his parents because they meet his needs successfully, he will develop a coherent self-concept and a sense of self-esteem.

WALTER MISCHEL is a social-learning theorist who emphasizes the role of social experience in the infant's personality development. Mischel evaluates early experience in relation to what it teaches the infant and according to whether it aids or impedes his social development. In this view, the infant's attachment to his mother or parents is a behavior that develops when the baby learns to associate his parents with the gratification of his needs and the reduction of discomfort. Parents shape behavior and learning by the way they respond to the infant's actions in particular situations. The infant learns to exert control over his environment to reduce his discomfort and to satisfy his needs.

Figure 9.1 Summary descriptions of some major theoretical viewpoints on personality development during infancy.

Each of these aspects of "self" emerges out of social interaction, each has great import for feelings and emotions, and each has a basis in cognitive structure.

EARLY EXPERIENCE

The notion that early experience is of primary importance for later life was popularized by Sigmund Freud (1917). His idea that certain experiences during infancy are crucial for personality development has been adopted by developmental psychologists with very different theoretical outlooks.

Types of Effects

Much of the evidence demonstrating the effects of early experience comes from studies of nonhuman species. Severe restriction or deprivation of experience in early infancy causes a variety of striking behavior in animals, and much of this behavior seems to persist into adulthood. These deprived animals are often quite different from normal animals in both social and emotional development. For example, puppies who spent their first few months in isolation from other puppies and from human beings showed "bizarre postures and a tendency to be unresponsive to playthings, people, and other puppies" (J. Scott, 1967). A puppy less extremely deprived will behave more normally but may have an intense fear of strange people and strange situations. Chimpanzees reared in a restricted environment also are more timid, especially in novel situations (Menzel, Davenport, and Rogers, 1963).

If impoverishment of the early environment can have such strong effects, we might expect that enrichment of the early environment would also have a major impact on infant animals. A variety of evidence suggests that this is so. Although restriction often produces animals that are more fearful than normal, extra stimulation at an early age often produces less fearful animals (Denenberg, 1966), even when the extra stimulation consists of mild electric shocks. Animals raised in enriched early environments also tend to be bold and curious in new situations (Forgus, 1954). Such evidence seems to indicate that, at least for some species or strains of animals, early experiences have important and enduring effects on developing patterns of response to the world.

Limits on Effects

Although early learning can have pervasive and enduring effects on later development, other research suggests that such a formulation is too simplified. For one thing, there is good reason why dispositions cannot be stamped in at an early age. A brief look at some investigations of imprinting and of fear and laughter, for example, suggests that there are strong constraints on early experience.

Sensitive Periods Research with animals has led many investigators to conclude that only during a certain period of its life can an animal form a particular kind of strong, long-lasting social attachment. In certain species of birds, this attachment,

Imprinting. A few hours after they were hatched, these baby geese saw ethologist Konrad Lorenz instead of a mother goose. Thereafter the goslings followed Lorenz around as if he were their mother. (Thomas McAvoy/Time-Life Picture Agency, © Time, Inc.)

called **imprinting,** occurs when a baby bird, fresh from the shell, sees a certain type of moving object, which it then follows. In the normal course of events, the young bird becomes imprinted to its mother, but a human being, a rubber ball, or any other moving object may also produce imprinting. The bird will overcome substantial obstacles in order to continue to follow this moving object (or others like it) and will show great distress when the object is out of sight (E. Hess, 1964). A young bird will try to feed the object to which it is imprinted and may even use it as a model for a suitable mate (an effect that introduces complications into the lives of certain ethologists). Imprinting occurs *only* during a certain critical or sensitive period of an animal's infancy. Such an attachment can be highly resistant to change, but, with effort, a switch can be made. William Mason and M. D. Kenney (1974) managed to change a young monkey's attachment from another monkey to a dog.

Some theorists have suggested that, just as normal young birds or goats or sheep become imprinted to their animal mothers, so human babies become attached to their mothers. This concept oversimplifies the process in human beings, but it does not contradict the theories of Freud and other personality theorists. The imprinting phenomenon is important, for it suggests that a human being is open to certain types of experience during certain developmental periods. If the proper learning does not occur during these periods, it may not occur at all.

Other Constraints Although strong emotions may affect human learning, some learning is necessary for emotion to develop. Consider, for example, some of the complex relationships that are involved in the emotional aspect of personality development referred to as fear. When Matt stumbled against the bassinet and Susan responded with wails and other signs of distress, she was not truly afraid. Although sudden loud noises, unexpected events, and physical pain may produce crying, distress, and avoidance reactions in newborns and very young babies, their responses are not fear in the sense that adults mean when they say that someone is afraid.

True fear requires a rather sophisticated level of cognitive development, and several studies have demonstrated the cognitive underpinnings of the emotion. To be afraid, the baby must be able to hold the feared object or situation in his memory,

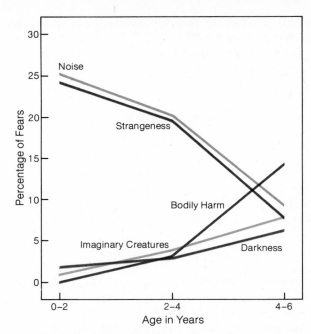

Figure 9.2 Developmental changes in the nature of children's fears as indicated by their responses to a few different objects and situations. (Adapted from Jersild and Holmes, 1935)

and the appearance of the object must call up the perceptual and emotional experiences that were connected with it in the past. Later, the mere mention of the object will be enough to evoke fear.

The changes in the nature of children's fears reported in early studies by Arthur Jersild and Frances Holmes (1935) clearly indicate the increasing importance of cognitive development (see Figure 9.2). For example, no children below the age of two years were afraid of bodily harm and few were afraid of the dark, being alone in the dark, or imaginary creatures, whereas a significant percentage of four- to six-year-olds feared these things. These fears, in contrast to "fear" of sudden loud noises, require imaginative constructions based on the generalization of past experience.

In a more recent study, Sandra Scarr and Philip Salapatek (1970) found similar developmental trends. They reported that, between the ages of five and eighteen months, there was an increase in infants' fear of strangers, of a grotesque mask, and of heights (as measured by the visual-cliff technique described in Chapter 7). These fears could develop only after the infants learned about the familiar and safe aspects of their environments. During the same period, there was no increase in infants' fear of loud noises or of a suddenly appearing jack-in-the-box.

Suppose that when Susan was six months old Matt suddenly thrust his head over the side of her crib and made a grotesque face. Would she scream with fear? She might laugh at Matt's face but scream at the same behavior in a stranger. Laughter and fear both seem to occur in response to a stimulus that is unfamiliar or incongruous in comparison with a familiar standard of reference.

For example, L. Alan Sroufe and Jane Wunsch (1972) studied the development of laughter from its appearance at around four months through the first year and found that babies laughed when confronted with a mask instead of becoming fearful, as the infants in the Scarr and Salapatek study did. There were important differences between the two studies: The mask that elicited laughter in the Sroufe and Wunsch study was human-looking and was worn by the baby's mother; the mask that elicited fear in the Scarr and Salapatek study was nonhuman and was worn by the experimenter. Sroufe and Wunsch speculated that an incongruous event arouses tension that, depending on the circumstances, will either lead to crying and avoidance or be released in laughter.

Findings such as these on fear and laughter suggest additional limitations to the notion that early learning experiences automatically establish enduring personality dispositions. They indicate, just as the imprinting data do, that an infant or a child is not always open to the same learning experiences. In addition, the same learning experience may produce opposite effects, depending on the maturational state of the infant, his cognitive growth, his past experiences, and his surroundings.

ATTACHMENT

A human baby arrives on the social scene prepared by millions of years of primate evolution to respond to the sights and sounds of people and to behave in ways that elicit responses from them. These built-in biases are the building blocks for complex systems of social behavior that begin in the family. In most cultures, the closest relationship of all is between mother and infant. They are involved for a time in a close symbiotic relationship in which the child is almost an extension of the mother's being.

In this light, it is no surprise that investigators have taken a keen interest in the development of the special bond between an infant and its caregiver called **attachment.** A look at attachment helps answer some questions already raised: How does early learning shape basic personality? How do parents and others influence children? How do predispositions help to determine personality development?

Some theorists call these systems of social behavior "instinctual," but that does not mean that the systems are rigidly determined. Instead, this social behavior, as it develops through the infant's interactions with others, serves functions that have always been related to survival in the evolutionary past. The final organization of such human ways of relating to others as smiling and crying is complex and flexible; such behavior is a predisposition that the long course of socialization in a particular human society shapes and elaborates.

Susan, for example, came into the world with the predispositions common to all human infants; she also possesses her own bundle of individual characteristics, such as her activity level and her general irritability. In the first two years of life, she will develop patterns of interactions with adults and children that are inseparably linked with the rest of her personality development. Through this social interaction, she will develop a sense of self, of a "me" who is distinct from parents and peers. In turn, this emerging sense of self will change the pattern of her social interaction.

The patterns of this social commerce coordinate with Susan's other developmental achievements. Her early social behavior reflects her cognitive development. For example, her level of cognitive understanding sets limits on the kinds of social behavior that can be expected at various stages of development. Before Susan can move out to interact with her peers, she must establish a primary social bond. The nature and function of that primary attachment is the focus of much psychological investigation.

Attachment in Monkeys

As with studies of early experience, research on attachment is heavily indebted to work with animals. Early views on attachment, both psychoanalytic and behavioral, assumed the importance of the feeding process. J. P. Scott has noted that this assumption can lead us to an unromantic conclusion: Infants love us only because we feed them. However, the work of Harry and Margaret Harlow and other researchers has demonstrated

SIGMUND FREUD bases his theory of attachment on instinctual drives and views attachment as a particular kind of object choice: the infant initially goes through a stage of complete self-preoccupation, called narcissism, but later recognizes people as instrumental in satisfying his drives and becomes attached to those who feed, care for, and protect him.

RENÉ SPITZ is a neoanalytic theorist who considers need-gratification essential in forming an attachment and who uses naturally occurring infant behavior to demarcate different stages. In Spitz's view, smiling at human faces identifies the beginning of a transition stage, whereas fear of strangers heralds the stage of true object relations. According to Spitz, fear of strangers is the earliest indication that the infant can discriminate the loved one from other people, a distinction necessary for a real love relationship.

JOHN BOWLBY is a British child psychiatrist in the neoanalytic tradition who proposes an ethological theory of attachment based on the interaction between certain predispositions in the infant and in the adult caregiver. Bowlby suggests that definite types of stimulation (a human face, a human voice, a strange object) elicit particular behavior in the infant (smiling, alertness and scanning, crying). The infant's behavior, in turn, elicits complementary behavior in the adult. Thus, an infant's smile may trigger a smile in the adult and perhaps a strong attraction to the infant as well. In addition, an infant's cry may cause the adult to soothe the infant, thus ending the crying.

MARY AINSWORTH is a developmental theorist with an ethological view of attachment who emphasizes how the constant feedback between the caretaker and the infant continually modifies the predispositions of each. In this view, each infant-adult pair evolves its own pattern of interaction. As an infant becomes more experienced, he fears fewer things, and he also develops more elaborate ways of communication. According to Ainsworth, these advances may cause a decline in both the frequency and the intensity of attachment behavior.

ROBERT SEARS is a developmental-learning theorist who views attachment, or dependence, as a secondary drive derived from other drives. In this view, the caregiver satisfies the baby's primary drives, such as hunger, thirst, pain, and discomfort. Consequently, caregivers become valuable to babies. Thus, a secondary drive for the caregiver's presence develops, resulting in each infant becoming attached to his or her caregiver.

JACOB GEWIRTZ is a behavioral-learning theorist who proposes that attachment develops through reinforcement. In this view, the interaction between an infant and his caregiver reinforces both parties. The adult and child exert some control over each other's behavior, and attachment develops.

LAWRENCE KOHLBERG is a cognitive-developmental theorist who believes that the infant's desire for competence in his relations with others underlies the formation of human attachments. Until the infant acquires the concept of object permanence at around nine months and with it a notion of "selves," such responses as smiling at familiar faces and showing distress when confronted with strange faces are not specifically social but merely reflect the child's general cognitive responses to the familiar and the unfamiliar. According to this view, a specific infant-caregiver attachment during the first year is not critical to later capacities for social attachment. If mutually stimulating interaction motivates true attachment, then interaction with a variety of persons, including peers, should promote attachment at any age.

Figure 9.3 Summary descriptions of some major theoretical viewpoints on the development of attachment during infancy.

convincingly that there is more to attachment than being fed, even for infant monkeys. In one ingenious series of studies by the Harlows (1966, 1969), infant monkeys were raised in cages with two surrogate mothers. One mother substitute was covered with soft terry cloth; the other was of hard wire mesh and was equipped with a feeding mechanism. If feeding were the only or the most important factor in attachment, the little monkeys would have spent more time expressing their attachment to the wire "mother," which fed them. But the monkeys spent much more time clinging to the cloth mother, which gave them no nourishment at all.

The monkeys seemed genuinely attached to the cloth mother; when these monkeys were given a choice of things to observe in the Harlows' "love machine," which allowed them visual access to various objects, they chose to look at the cloth mother much more often than they chose the wire mother. Infant monkeys raised under normal conditions showed no preference for either artificial mother and rarely chose to look at them. Monkeys raised under experimental conditions also used the cloth mother, but not the wire mother, as a security base when they were put in a strange place or when a fearful object was placed near them. In such a situation, the infant monkeys at first appeared to be terrified, but when they could cling to the cloth mother, they soon ceased showing signs of distress. Eventually, they began to use the cloth mother as a base for exploration, leaving to manipulate some of the novel objects but returning frequently to cling to their soft, snuggly mother, as monkeys raised with real mothers do. The wire mothers were never used in this way.

Clinging is a behavior that young monkeys normally display at birth; it seems to be as natural to them as scanning and vocalizing are to human infants. It should not be surprising, then, that clinging has proved to be so important to the monkey's development of attachment. The attachment also is lasting. A monkey raised with a terry cloth

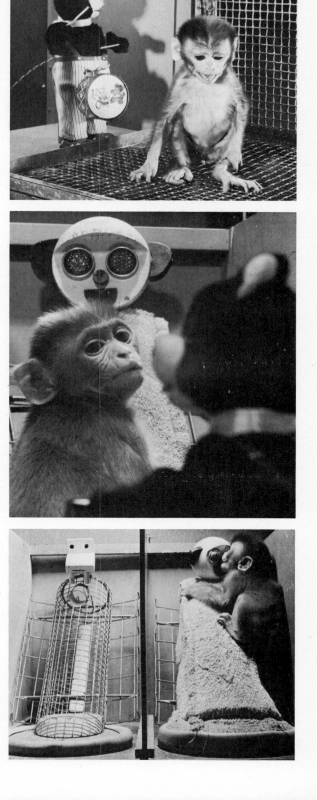

(*top*) When a large and frightening toy was placed near a baby monkey in the Harlow experiments (*middle*), it ran to the cloth-covered surrogate mother for comfort. Later it ventured out to explore the bear. Monkeys with only a wire mother (*bottom left*) to cling to remained afraid of the toy. (Harry F. Harlow, University of Wisconsin Primate Laboratory)

mother will, after a year's separation, run to embrace its soft form and cling to it passionately. But monkeys raised with wire mothers show no "love" at all after any appreciable separation, providing evidence that contact is important to the formation of attachment in monkeys.

Attachment in Human Beings

Unlike the immediate imprinting that occurs in lower animals, the development of attachment in human beings takes months to appear, requires a complex intermeshing of infant and caregiver behavior, and is subject to much variation. Although attachment in human beings and in monkeys follows a similar pattern, the response of the human baby to his mother develops more slowly than the monkey baby's attachment to its mother.

Attachment in human babies refers to the early love relationship between baby and caregiver (usually a parent), and developmental psychologists study it by examining the kinds of behavior associated with such a relationship. The signs of attachment include smiling and joyous greeting when the caregiver appears and crying when he or she leaves. One of the most important aspects of behavior that signifies attachment is that it is directed toward some people and not toward others.

A baby's earliest responses to people are rather indiscriminate and do not reflect true attachment.

Any person is likely to make an infant smile or vocalize in the early months of life. Some evidence indicates that both smiling and vocalizing develop whether or not a baby ever sees or hears other human beings. You will recall that deaf babies babble and coo during the first six months. Irenäus Eibl-Eibesfeldt (1970) has reported that blind children also begin to cry, smile, and laugh at the same time that sighted children do. Instead of smiling in response to a human face, these children smile in response to their parents' voices or to social play (Freedman, 1964). The early onset of smiling and vocalizing in all children, regardless of their perceptual abilities, suggests that their initial appearance is controlled primarily by maturation. Once they appear, the baby elaborates them into a system of attachment behavior that has had adaptive value over the centuries.

Babies first show discrimination in responding to specific people at about five months. They continue to smile at familiar faces as often as or even more frequently than they did earlier, but the smiling at strange faces that was so prevalent at about two or three months drops off or even disappears. Harriet Rheingold (1969) has suggested that the talking, smiling human face, with its changing expressions and movements, interests and attracts a young baby. Gradually, through a variety of experiences, the face of the principal caregiver comes both to elicit positive emotional and social re-

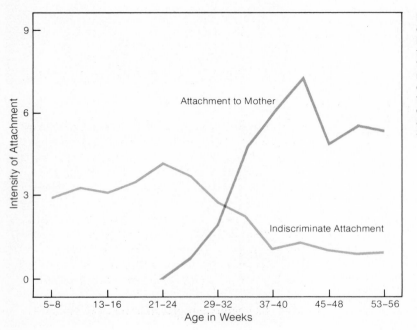

Figure 9.4 During the early weeks of life, most infants prefer not to be separated from the person they are with regardless of who that person is. Such "indiscriminate attachments" begin to decline at about the same time that the infant starts to show preferences for specific persons, such as his mother. (Adapted from Schaffer and Emerson, 1964)

sponses in the baby and to reinforce them. Although these learning experiences include situations in which the baby associates the parent or caregiver with the cuddling and food that satisfy his primary needs or drives, the interactions are not limited to such basic situations.

This change in social smiling is one of the earliest indications that the baby is differentiating the world into the familiar and the unfamiliar and is evidence of the baby's developing memory. Clearly, the baby must be able to recognize familiar faces in order to be able to give them his special smile. The attachments to specific people that he develops about this time increase in intensity until just before his first birthday and then seem to level off (see Figure 9.4).

It is likely that specific attachments are related to the baby's development of object permanence, which is discussed in Chapter 7. Silvia Bell (1970) has found that most babies are aware of their mothers as objects who continue to exist when out of sight slightly before they demonstrate such an awareness with physical objects. Although there is some question as to whether person permanence actually does develop before object permanence (Jackson, Campos, and Fischer, 1978), it may be that because the comings and goings of the human caregiver are related to the satisfaction of the baby's needs, the baby pays special attention to the location of this very important "object." Bell also found that babies who had developed secure and stable attachments to their mothers were aware of their mothers as permanent objects earlier than babies with less stable attachments. Furthermore, babies who acquired the concept of person permanence early also developed the concept of physical object permanence early, suggesting that understanding in the social realm has positive effects on understanding in the physical realm.

PARENT RESPONSIVENESS

Although the infant learns attachment to a caregiver, the emotions involved in the parent-child relationship run both ways. The love of the mother, father, or other caregiver for the baby and the baby's love for his parents each affect the development of the other's emotion and the fears or anxieties that may complicate it. One way to make this circular relationship clear is to look at it from each side.

Parental attitudes toward children differ; some simply feed, clean, and shelter their babies, others cuddle and play games with them. (Ken Heyman)

Parental Styles

Even in the same culture, no two sets of parents have precisely the same attitude toward their children, nor do they rear them in exactly the same way. Some parents limit their caregiving to the essentials of feeding, cleaning, and sheltering their babies; others interact extensively with cuddling and games. H. Rudolph Schaffer and Peggy Emerson (1964a) found that, whether the mother-infant interaction consists primarily of caregiving activity or of social play, the attachment that develops seems equally strong. It appears that the crucial factor in the relationship is the baby's development of a cognitive representation of his mother as a distinct person, a step facilitated by increased exposure to his mother. As noted in Chapter 7, this occurs at about the time (twenty-two to twenty-four weeks of age) that a baby begins to show surprise when he sees what appear to be several copies of his mother.

The notion that experience with the caregiver speeds the development of attachment finds support in the work of Mary Salter Ainsworth (1967). She has noted that Ugandan infants, whose mothers generally interact more extensively with them than Western mothers do, form specific attachments somewhat earlier than the Scottish babies studied by Schaffer and Emerson. Among the Ugandan babies, attached infants received more care from caregivers than nonattached infants did.

The behavior of parents also appears to affect a baby's social initiative and his ability to cope with frustration and stress. For example, Leon Yarrow (1963) found that the sensitivity of parents to their baby's signals (such as distressed crying or sociable cooing) and how appropriately, consistently, and flexibly they respond are more important than the amount of physical contact they give. Such flexibility requires that the parent adapt to the baby's individual characteristics and rhythms.

Fathers become as deeply attached to their infants as mothers do. As caregivers, they have been found to be nurturant and competent, and their involvement with their babies tends to complement that of the mothers. During the first few days in the hospital, for example, middle-class fathers and mothers tend to spend an equal amount of time with their newborn babies. Both fathers and mothers look and smile at their babies, talk to and kiss them, explore their bodies, and give them their bottles. Given the opportunity, lower-class fathers also appear to be nurturant and competent with their newborn babies (Parke and Sawin, 1976). When, for example, their baby shows distress during a feeding, both the father and mother show their sensitivity by stopping the feeding, and looking at the baby and patting him.

Fathers are not only likely to be attached to their infants and involved in their development during the first two years but also to interact with the babies in a different manner from the pattern shown by mothers (Lamb, 1977a). Fathers, for example, are more likely than mothers to engage in rough-and-tumble play with babies, regardless of an infant's sex.

Perhaps in response to the differences in the way fathers and mothers behave with babies, when infants from twelve to eighteen months are with both parents in a stressful situation, they will go to the mother (Lamb, 1977a). But when they are alone with either parent, they will go to that parent. When alone with either parent in a stress-free situation, a baby is likely to smile at him or her and vocalize more frequently than the baby does when both parents are in the room. In addition, in terms of overall interaction, when observed in their homes, infant boys generally show a preference for their fathers, whereas infant girls may prefer either parent (Lamb, 1977b).

Class and Cultural Differences

Because adults in different societies or in different socioeconomic classes in the same society react to infants in different ways, class and culture also affect personality development. Jerome Kagan and Steven Tulkin (1971) have studied the influence of social class on maternal attitudes and behavior. Their observations of ten-month-old babies showed that, whereas both middle- and lower-class mothers hold, tickle, kiss, and bounce their babies, a great deal of other maternal behavior often differs between these social classes. A middle-class mother was more likely than a lower-class mother to vocalize within two feet of her baby, imitate the baby's sounds, engage in prolonged "positive interaction," give verbal rewards, and encourage her baby to walk. About two-thirds of the lower-class mothers in the study used food to soothe their irritable babies, whereas less than one-third of the middle-class mothers solved problems with food.

When Kagan and Tulkin tested these babies in the laboratory, they found no class differences in the babies' levels of reactivity to meaningful and meaningless speech. However, middle-class babies quieted more dramatically to highly meaningful speech with a high degree of inflection than to other stimuli, and they were more likely to look at a stranger after hearing such speech than the lower-class children were. Middle-class infants also quieted more to their mothers' voices than to strangers' voices, and they vocalized more than lower-class infants did after listening to recordings of their mothers' voices.

Parent-infant relationships also vary across societies. Urie Bronfenbrenner (1970) has described some of the differences between the Soviet Union and the United States in the parent-infant relationship and the socialization of children. These differ-

Although most primary caregivers are mothers, fathers are nurturant and competent with their babies. Fathers and mothers generally interact in different ways with infants. (*top*: Susan Johns/Rapho/Photo Researchers; *bottom*: William Hubbell/Woodfin Camp & Assoc.)

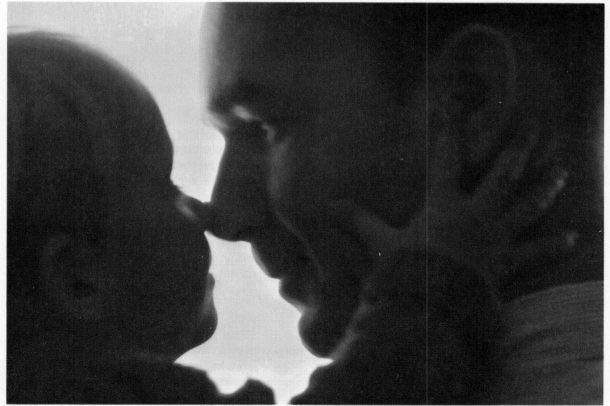

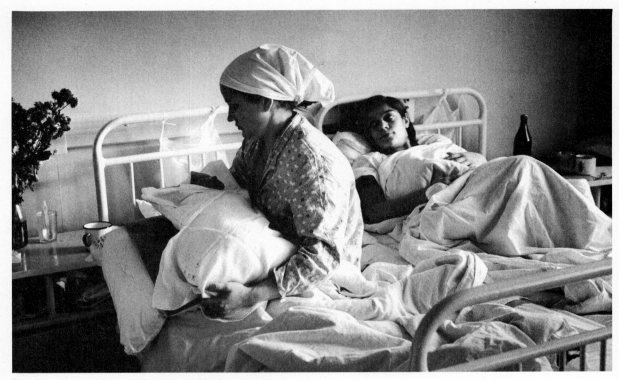

This Russian newborn will get more kissing, hugging, and cuddling than an American baby, but he also will be held more tightly and have less freedom of movement. (Martine Franck/VIVA/Woodfin Camp & Assoc.)

ences can be traced to the contrast between a family-centered and a collective-centered system of child rearing.

Russian babies receive significantly more physical handling than their American counterparts do. Breast feeding is virtually universal in Russia, and babies are held most of the time, even when not being fed. Russian babies get much more hugging, kissing, and cuddling than American babies do, but at the same time they are held much more tightly and are allowed little freedom of movement. Russian mothers are generally much more solicitous and protective, and their efforts to protect the baby from discomfort, illness, or injury curtail the baby's mobility and initiative. Such differences in childrearing across cultures can have subtle but deep effects on personality development.

INFANT RESPONSIVENESS

Although the effects of parents on infants have been heavily investigated, the effects of the infant's characteristics on caregivers have tended to be overlooked. To see the importance of the infant's reactions, contrast the satisfaction of the mother of a highly active, irritable, uncuddly baby with the satisfaction of the mother of a peaceful, snuggly infant. You will recall from Chapter 5 that research has established the presence among infants of various activity or temperament types that affect the emotional quality of the mother-infant interaction. A study by Schaffer and Emerson (1964b) indicates that babies who actively resist cuddling tend to develop attachments later than cuddlers do. "For some infants," say Schaffer and Emerson, "it appears, contact is not comforting." Cuddlers have a more intense attachment to their caregivers throughout the first year of life than noncuddlers do, but this difference seems to disappear during the second year, apparently as a result of the infant and mother adapting to each other's style. In Schaffer and Emerson's study, babies who actively resisted contact did not always prevent social interaction between themselves and their parents. Instead, each baby and his or her parents gradually evolved a system of social interaction that did not depend on physical contact. The intensity of these attachments bore no relation to feeding, weaning, or toilet-training practices. Once again, maternal responsiveness and the amount of mother-child interaction were related to attachment. Babies were more strongly attached to mothers who responded rapidly to their needs and who spent more time interacting with them.

Because the distress and comfort of infants and their parents are likely to be reciprocal, a fussy baby can be especially difficult for parents. Studies show that parents of babies who fuss frequently are likely to wait longer before responding to their fussing baby than do parents of babies who fuss infrequently (Dunn, 1977). This may be analogous to the tale of the boy who cried wolf; parents of fussy babies may interpret their signals of distress as being simply bids for attention, or, if the babies don't quiet easily, the parents may decide that since responding has little effect, they may as well ignore the babies' cries until they become too loud to disregard. Babies who quiet easily, on the other hand, are likely to reinforce their parents' attention and make them feel more secure as caregivers. In this connection, Susan Goldberg (1977) notes that because parents need to feel they can respond to their baby's signals and satisfy his needs, the baby whose signs are easy to read enhances his parents' feelings of competence. Thus the baby whose signals say clearly, "I'm hungry," "I'm bored," or "I'm wet," who sucks vigorously and who smiles freely is also the one who is most likely to make parents feel successful and important.

As the baby develops the primary attachment to his mother or other caregivers, other emotional responses occur. These responses include the positive features of trust and security, but they also include the baby's fear of strangers and of losing contact with his mother. Once a baby can appreciate the joys of trusting and feeling secure, he is also capable of fearing the loss of contact with his mother and of fearing strangers.

Separation Distress

A baby's distinctly negative reaction to being parted from an attachment figure is called separation distress. When a baby's mother leaves him in an unfamiliar place, he tends to cry and stop playing. He may reach out for her when she leaves and later may crawl or walk in pursuit of her.

Although the age when separation distress first appears varies in different cultures, it seems to be a universal phenomenon. When separated from their mothers, Ugandan babies begin to protest as early as six months (Ainsworth, 1967). Separation distress among Guatemalan babies, on the other hand, emerges a bit later and shows a developmental pattern similar to that of North American babies (Lester et al., 1974). Distress begins to appear at about eight or nine months, reaches a peak at around twelve months, then declines.

Separation distress seems to be based on a fear of unusual situations, a fear that the presence of an attachment figure appears to reduce. The attachment figure becomes a security base for the baby. For example, Ainsworth and Barbara Wittig (1969) have demonstrated that a baby, when placed in a strange situation, will first establish contact with a caregiver. Somewhat later he will venture out on short forays into the strange environment, exploring bits of it, but he always returns to his caregiver between expeditions.

This tendency can be observed when a mother brings her infant or toddler on a first visit to a friend's home; the young child clings to (indeed, hides behind) the parent. Only after he becomes accustomed to the new setting is the child likely to let go of his parent's leg. You may recall that both the Harlows' cloth-surrogate-reared and normally reared young monkeys showed a similar reaction in a strange environment.

When a baby's primary caregiver leaves him in a strange place, he is overcome by fear and often begins to cry, a response known as separation distress. (Courtesy L. Sroufe and Byron E. Geland. Photo by Laszlo Hege)

On the other hand, Rheingold and Carol Eckerman (1970) saw no distress in a similar separation-and-return pattern among infants placed in a novel situation. The infants they studied seemed to share their joy and excitement with attachment figures. It is undoubtedly true that babies use attachment figures both to reduce their fear and to share in the pleasures of life, and it seems that the same general pattern of behavior serves both purposes.

The quality of a baby's attachment may also affect the way he reacts to separation. Ainsworth and her colleagues (1978) have discerned three major kinds of attachment among babies. After a separation, "securely attached" infants actively seek out their mothers when they return, and the babies' contact with their mothers quickly ends the separation distress. Less securely attached infants fall into two major groups: "avoidant" infants, who shun contact with their mothers upon being reunited, and "ambivalent" infants, who alternate between seeking contact with their mothers and squirming to get away from them. Some babies seem less able to cope with strange situations, and that inability shows itself in different ways.

Wariness of Strangers

When this fear of the unusual is provoked by a person, it is called wariness of strangers. This wariness usually develops a month or two after specific attachments begin. A baby appears to go through four phases in his reaction to strangers. At first he does not discriminate between strange and familiar persons. Later he responds positively to strangers, although less positively than to familiar people. Then he goes through a period of reacting to strangers with fear if an attachment figure is present, looking back and forth between the stranger and his caregiver as though comparing the strange person with the familiar one. At this time, he merely becomes sober and stares at the stranger. It is not until he is around eight months old that he responds to strangers with fear and withdrawal, and this reaction is particularly intense when his attachment figure is absent (Ainsworth, 1967).

George Morgan and Henry Ricciuti (1969) investigated both the developmental timing of fear in the presence of strangers and the calming effect of a caregiver's presence. They found that at eight, ten, and especially at twelve months a baby responds more positively to the approach of a stranger if he is seated on his mother's lap than if he is four feet away from her. At four or six months, however, a separation of four feet makes little or no difference; the baby responds positively to the stranger in either case.

Fear of strangers, like separation distress, appears sharpest when the baby is in an unfamiliar setting. Babies are much less likely to show wariness in their own homes than when they are observed in a laboratory. Russel Tracy and his colleagues (1976) studied babies from the time they were three weeks old until they were more than a year old. The babies were observed in their own homes for four hours every three weeks. Tracy and his colleagues found that once babies began to crawl, they tended to follow their mothers from place to place and to play comfortably in the presence of strangers. Although no baby at any age ever followed a stranger, few cried or showed other distress at a stranger's approach. Babies also engage in more exploration and vocalize more freely at home than they do in the psychologist's laboratory.

Wariness at the appearance of strangers is less likely to develop if a baby develops a secure attachment to his caregiver. Ainsworth and Wittig (1969) found that a year-old infant with a secure attachment to his mother uses her as a base from which to explore a strange situation and that he is not distressed by the presence of strangers. Infants who appear to have developed insecure attachments are upset by the appearance of a stranger. Securely attached infants also spend much more time exploring at home, but insecurely attached babies tend to be inactive and fussy.

These studies are in harmony with Erik Erikson's (1963) theory of personality development. The child's first task is to solve the conflict between trust and mistrust in interpersonal situations. The baby who has developed secure attachments will show evidence of basic trust. Trust is usually assumed to be something that a person possesses, an inner attitude. Yet trust reflects a system of interaction with the social world. A rudimentary sense of personal identity emerges in the infant, which depends on his recognition that his memories and anticipated sensations and images are firmly linked with the familiar and predictable things and people of his world. This relatively comfortable, nonanxious certainty about the world and one's place in it allows a baby to venture into new realms of experience. These forays bring new challenges and anxieties.

Multiple Caregiving

Problems of separation raise the problem of the maternally deprived infant and the possibility that multiple caregivers may assume childrearing tasks. In today's world, multiple caregiving is a frequent form of infant care even among babies who are not in institutions. Does the lack of a central caregiver mean that a baby will suffer from discontinuous or inadequate interaction? Research by Michael Rutter (1971) indicates that when the main attachment figure shares caregiving with other people, as when mothers work or when the baby is part of an extended family, children will thrive as long as the other caregivers provide stable relationships.

Additional research indicates that children reared in Israeli kibbutzim show normal social and emotional development (for example, Gewirtz, 1965). In some of these kibbutzim, infants are reared communally in residential nurseries by several caregivers and see their parents only for a few hours a day or on weekends. In such arrangements, the kibbutz caregiver sees to the daily needs and training of the child, and the parents primarily provide emotional gratification (Beit-Hallahmi and Rabin, 1977). Again the conclusion emerges that parents may be absent for significant amounts of time without radically influencing attachment patterns, as long as someone who cares is present.

There is little evidence that infants reared by multiple caregivers will develop differently from those reared by a single caregiver. Although Zambian and !Kung San infants are reared by multiple caregivers, their development of attachment and stranger wariness follows a course similar to that of infants reared by a single caregiver. Studies of infants in day care have failed to find any evidence that their care interfered with the development of their attachment to their mothers or other primary caregivers. In one such study, Richard Kearsley and his associates (1975) followed twenty-four day-care and twenty-eight home-reared infants from the time they were three-and-a-half months until they were twenty-nine months old. The babies were from white and Chinese-American families, who were both working- and middle-class. The investigators found no differences in the amount of separation distress shown by the day-care and home-reared infants, and in both sets of babies, separation distress peaked at around nine and again around thirteen months.

A more serious challenge to an infant's well-being is a loss or lack of mothering. Rutter (1971) has reviewed the research on **maternal deprivation** and suggests that the concept is really a catchall term for a variety of early experiences. It is necessary to specify the nature of the caregiving arrangements and the kinds of stimulation that babies receive in order to investigate long-term emotional effects.

Thus, researchers have not shown that the primary caregiver is absolutely essential for normal development. Although early studies of children reared in institutions found devastating effects on their social and intellectual development, it is now clear that these unfortunate children suffered from a general lack of the stimulation necessary to social and cognitive growth as well as from the absence of a single stable caregiver. The babies in Lebanese institutions that you read about in Chapter 6 showed gains in cognitive growth as well as in physical development when interesting objects were introduced into their lives for only a few minutes each day.

Research with monkeys also suggests that development can follow a relatively normal course in the absence of a parental relationship. Monkeys raised without mothers or mother surrogates but with other baby monkeys for company were more normal in their adult social and sexual behavior than were monkeys raised with a surrogate mother but without peer contact. These findings support Lawrence Kohlberg's (1969) suggestion that it is the opportunity for pleasurable social interaction that is important to the infant's social-emotional development, not a specific tie to a caregiver.

Not all infants who suffer maternal deprivation are able to cope with their loss. An infant who finds his attachment to his primary caregiver ruptured may develop depression, or an extreme sadness. The British child psychiatrist John Bowlby (1953) has observed what he regards as depression in fifteen- to thirty-month-old healthy infants after they had been separated from their families and placed in a hospital or other resident institution. After an initial phase of active protest and crying, such an infant falls into a phase of despair. He becomes withdrawn and inactive, makes no demands of the environment, cries intermittently though without specific cause, and seems to feel increasing hopelessness and sadness. Later, the depressed infant gradually moves out of this phase into one of increased emotional distance. He begins to interact in a pleasant but shallow manner with his institutional caregivers, and when his parents visit him, he responds in an aloof and detached way.

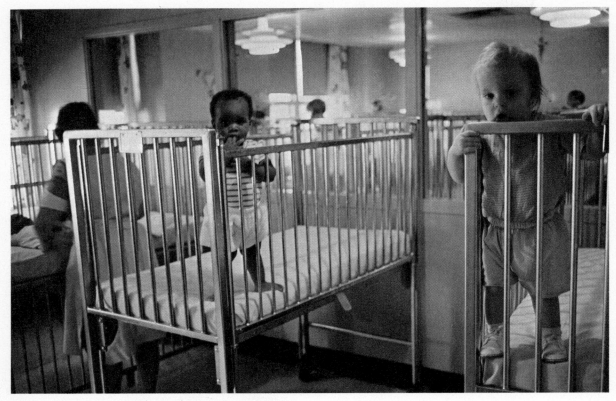

Children reared in institutions require stable relationships with caregivers and a stimulating environment if they are to thrive. (Elliott Erwitt/Magnum Photos)

THE DEVELOPMENT OF SOCIABILITY

Although attachment to parents is of primary significance in the life of the infant, the spectrum of significant relationships soon broadens. Susan will have to contend with Matt as a potential threat or aid to her well-being, just as she will have to contend with Matt's playmates, her playpen peers, and possibly her younger siblings. It is within the first two years of life that we find the rudimentary development of personality usually called sociability. As we have seen, the early experiences of infants and young children dispose them in varying degrees to regard and to approach other human beings with warmth, positive expectations, and trust.

Interactions with Parents

The baby's early sociability is largely a product of interactions with his parents. And, as emphasized before, the process of socialization is always a mu-

tual affair, affecting the behavior of participants on each side of the interaction.

As the baby begins to venture away from his mother, he can explore a wider and wider world. Eckerman and Rheingold (1974) investigated ten-month-old infants' exploratory responses to toys and people. They placed the babies in an unfamiliar environment and gave each the opportunity to approach and touch an unfamiliar person or toy. The babies promptly approached the toys and played with them. They rarely made physical contact with the strangers; instead they looked at the strangers and smiled. These results suggest that looking and smiling at people serves an exploratory function similar to touching and manipulating toys.

Some investigators have noticed sex differences among year-old infants in response to separation from their mothers. Susan Goldberg and Michael Lewis (1969) watched the behavior of mothers and

Sociability has its roots in the interactions of baby and parents, and these early experiences will either encourage or deter the baby's tendency to approach human beings. (Suzanne Szasz)

their infants and discovered that boys played more roughly with toys than girls did, that they manipulated light switches and doorknobs instead of playing only with toys, and that, when separated from their mothers by a picket fence, they tried to get around it. Girls played quietly with toys, stayed near their mothers, and, when separated from them by a fence, cried.

But Goldberg and Lewis believe that they failed to document any biological sex differences. They noted that mothers treated boy and girl infants differently. Mothers discouraged their sons from touching them and suggested that their sons play with toys that lay across the room. Mothers of girls, on the other hand, allowed their daughters to play near them and to touch them. It may be that mothers deliberately encourage boys to be independent from a very early age. Western society has long expected males to be more independent than females.

Studies by Rheingold and Eckerman (1970) also suggest that early behavior does not depend on gender. They recorded children's forays from their mothers, placing forty-eight children between one and five years old in an L-shaped yard behind a house, which allowed a child to leave his mother's field of vision. Age, not sex, was the critical factor in whether the child left his mother's sight. Although there were wide individual differences among children who were two or older, one could predict how far a boy or girl would travel from his or her mother if one knew only the age of the child.

Self-Concept

Detailed studies of the moment-to-moment interactions of babies with their mothers reveal that a baby is a social creature from birth (Sander, 1977; H. R. Schaffer, 1977). Although they may not be aware of their changing responses, most mothers quickly learn to read the cues sent by their babies and adjust their own behavior so that the baby takes the lead in their interactions. As he leads his mother and takes turns with her, the baby controls the rate, level, and nature of his experiences (Stern, 1977). From these experiences, and from others in which he cannot always control the actions of people and objects, an infant appears to develop a first crude sense of "me" and "not me."

During the latter part of the first year and throughout the second, the infant's own sense of self forms an increasingly noticeable and integral part of his sociability. As a result of continued cognitive development, he becomes conscious of himself as a separate and distinct person with certain characteristics. This blossoming self-awareness in turn influences his interest in others and how he relates to them.

The baby's developing sense of self has recently been explored in a series of experiments by Michael Lewis and Jeanne Brooks (Brooks and

Babies begin to develop a self-concept early, and by twenty-four months it is established; they recognize themselves and identify both themselves and other people. (James M. Wall)

Lewis, 1976; Lewis and Brooks, 1974, 1975). They studied infants ranging from less than one year to two years old. Their results suggest that by twenty to twenty-four months, babies have developed a self-concept. They readily recognize themselves; they think of and identify themselves and other people; and they react to other people in terms of their gender, age, familiarity, height, and facial features. In one experiment, Lewis and Brooks found that infants, some as young as seven months, stare intently with apparent surprise when they see a midget. Their eyes widen, their eyebrows arch, and their mouths round as if they expected a small body to have a child's face.

In an experiment designed to test an infant's recognition of himself, Lewis and Brooks placed babies before a mirror after first surreptitiously placing a small dab of rouge on their noses. Few babies under a year seemed to recognize that the smudged nose in the mirror belonged to them, but among babies from fifteen to eighteen months, 25 percent immediately touched their own noses, and by twenty-four months, 88 percent grabbed for their noses as soon as they looked in the mirror.

In other experiments, Lewis and Brooks studied reactions of infants as they looked at pictures of themselves and other people, or as they watched videotapes of themselves and other infants of the same age and of both sexes. They found that infants looked longer and smiled more at their own pictures and at those of other babies of the same sex than at any other pictures. In watching videotapes of themselves and other babies, infants reacted most to images of themselves and to other babies of the same sex. They vocalized and imitated themselves twice as much as they imitated strange babies, blinking, waving, and sticking out their tongues. These findings suggest that infants as young as nine months may recognize and react with pleasure to themselves, and that they are especially responsive to those who are most similar to themselves—most "like me."

Striving for Competence   As a baby's cognitive skills and his sense of self develop, he finds increasing satisfaction in acting on, exploring, and getting to know the social world. Rheingold and Eckerman (1970) point out that, although an infant shows distress at being left by his parents, he shows no distress when he leaves his attachment figure to explore. They suggest that a separate motivational system, which they have called **detach-**

ment, coexists with the attachment system and interacts with it. The infant's movement toward detachment in the second year of life is motivated by the desire to be competent, to know the social and object world: to touch, take apart, put together, figure out toys and other objects, and to evoke responses (smiling or attention) from new people. Novelty, complexity, and change—interesting new stimulation—draw infants away from the comfortable familiarity of attachment figures.

But detachment is not the opposite of attachment, nor does it signal the end of attachment. The desire to be close to familiar and loved people and the desire to try out new experiences and expand one's competence appear to coexist throughout the life of the individual. An infant who is secure in his attachments feels safe to explore and to develop his sense of self as an independent agent or a causer of effects in the world. From his explorations, an infant brings back new knowledge and abilities that he may incorporate into increasingly differentiated and interesting interactions with familiar and cherished others. The concepts dependence and independence have often been used to describe these two movements, but these concepts are usually thought of in either-or terms, without an awareness of their reciprocal relationship.

The development of a secure attachment may also enable a baby to grow into a competent child. When Leah Matas, R. Arend, and L. Alan Sroufe (1978) presented two-year-olds with problems to solve, such as using a stick to remove an attractive object from a tube, they found that babies who had been rated as "securely attached" at eighteen months were more enthusiastic, persistent, and effective at solving the problems than were babies who had earlier been rated as insecurely attached and either "ambivalent" or "avoidant." In addition, the securely attached two-year-olds cooperated more with their mothers in solving a problem that was clearly beyond their abilities (weighting down a lever to raise a piece of candy through a hole in a plastic box) than did the insecurely attached two-year-olds.

Autonomy   Toward the end of the second year, the infant enters a period of social development that parents everywhere have observed and decried: the two-year-old's "negativistic crisis." This apparent reluctance on the part of the infant to agree with anything his parents suggest and his consistent response to all questions or commands

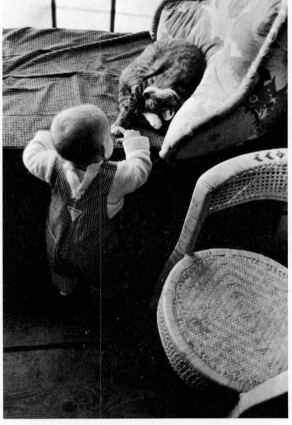

As the baby begins to detach himself from his mother, novelty, complexity, or change draws him away. He wants to touch, take apart, put together, and figure out everything in his world. (Linda Ferrer Rogers/ Woodfin Camp & Assoc.)

with "No" represent a push toward autonomy in its first concentrated form.

With the advent of language and the mental activity that accompanies it, the infant becomes aware of a distinction between self and other that is not only physical but mental, a distinction between his own will, or intentions, and the will of other people, most notably his parents. Prior to this time, the infant depends on parents and caregivers for the satisfaction of most of his needs. David Ausubel (1958) has called this an executive dependence: The parent acts as an executive arm, instrumental to the infant's needs. As an infant becomes even more aware of his competence and his effect on the world, he strives for executive independence, or autonomy: he wants to do things for himself. The negativistic infant is attempting to discover the substance and limits of the center of activity and initiative that he is constructing: the self. Parents frequently note that the clash of wills seems to be conflict for conflict's sake; the infant is concerned not with an issue but with a principle. In terms of the infant's developing awareness of self and others, that is a wise observation.

The child's developing sense of control, competence, and autonomy will be important throughout his life. It appears to underlie what will later become his sense of **locus of control.** People with an internal locus of control generally believe that they are in control of what they do and of what happens to them. People with an external locus of control generally believe that what they do makes little difference and that other forces, such as luck, fate, or powerful other people, determine what happens to them.

Interactions with Peers

Although most of Susan's social relationships during her first two years are with adults, she also has some social contact with her peers. The earliest data concerning the importance of infant peer re-

As an infant's competence increases, she becomes more aware of her intentions, needs, and desires—and expresses them. She also becomes less dependent on others for their fulfillment. (Suzanne Szasz)

lations come from some observations of institutionalized babies. Katharine Bauham Bridges (1933) reported that by the age of two months, institutionalized babies would orient toward the movements of a baby in an adjoining crib. She found that a baby rarely responded to the cries of other babies until the tenth month. From this time, there was a marked increase in peer interaction.

Another study describes peer interaction from six to twenty-five months. Maria Maudry and Maria Nekula (1939) used a "baby party" technique. They found that babies between the ages of six and eight months ignored about half the overtures of other babies. The interactions that took place were little more than exploratory looking and grasping, the same sort of interactions that they conducted with their toys. Fighting between babies, mainly over toys, peaked between nine and thirteen months and then decreased.

In the past, many investigators simply did not look for social interaction between infants, perhaps because of the general belief that young babies are too egocentric for such sociability. Ask any park-bench mother, however, and she will report that infants as young as nine months who meet regularly and explore the world together while their mothers talk, play give-and-take the toy, peek-a-boo, or simply crawl after each other in follow-the-leader fashion. When Jacqueline Becker (1977) observed pairs of nine-month-old babies in their homes with their mothers present, she found that babies who were with each other for a period of ten sessions paid more attention to each other than to toys or to their mothers. The magnitude of the infants' social interaction and play increased across the ten sessions. The babies reached toward and followed each other, passed toys, and looked at each other far more frequently than the infants who played together for only two sessions. In addition, when Becker subsequently placed each infant in a play situation with a baby who was unfamiliar to him or her, infants who had previously played together for ten sessions played more with the unfamiliar baby than did babies who had previously played together for only two sessions.

Toward the end of the first year, a baby begins to see peers as an even greater source of enjoyment. The one-year-old will often pass a toy to a peer and display obvious pleasure when the other child receives it. That same object can quickly become the target of a tug-of-war, however, and the

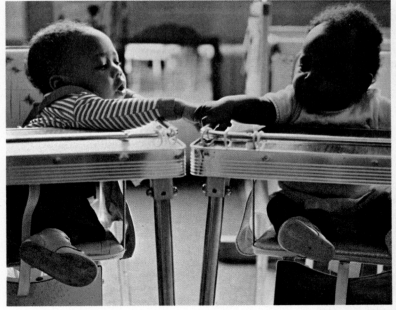

Peer interactions change considerably during the first two years of life. From minimal interactions during the first nine months, a baby goes through a period characterized by fighting for toys, then during the second year develops cooperative, satisfying, enjoyable patterns of social play. (*top left:* Rogier Gregoire; *top right and bottom:* William MacDonald)

loser in the battle will scream in distress. One-year-olds also stimulate each other to begin play sequences. For example, one infant starts banging on a table or taking toys out of the toy box, and the others join in. As each new treasure is pulled from the box, mutual smiles break out. Real enjoyment seems to come from this mutual play.

Both the Bridges study and that of Maudry and Nekula found that, toward the middle of the second year, infants attend positively to peers once they have resolved their conflicts over play materials. In other words, toys serve as vehicles for both positive and negative social contact. For the eighteen- to twenty-four-month-old, play objects and playmates are more successfully integrated, and social interactions begin to predominate. An infant of this age now modifies his behavior to adjust to his playmate's activity. Thus, Judith Rubenstein and Carollee Howes (1976) found that seventeen- to twenty-month-old playmates who met regularly with each other in their own homes not only played freely and made few demands on the adults present but also seldom squabbled over toys. Play between a pair of playmates was also more intricate and constructive than solitary play by either member of the pair or play by one of the babies with his mother.

Peer interaction is one example of the great social expansion that takes place in the second year

of life. During this year, almost all infants are mobile, and many become quite adept at speech. Peer interaction allows young children to try their skills and to explore their differentiating sense of self.

Children may begin to have truly reciprocal relationships, learn to take turns, and enjoy each other's actions. Some understanding of others' feelings can usually be seen at this time. Many children will start to form real attachments with specific peers and squeal with delight on spying them. An infant of one and one-half to two years may appear to comfort a peer in distress, or at least to observe him with concern.

The Significance of Play

Given the importance of peer play in the development of sociability, as well as the universality of early play, many investigators have been drawn into deeper study of play. The baby's developing cognitive structure, evolving emotions, and broadening view of self and others are all involved in play. It is through play that the baby finds out much about the world of people and things in relation to himself. Lest this statement make it sound as if games are all work and no play, it should be noted that, although play serves all these functions, the baby may play just for the fun of it. As Brian Sutton-Smith (1971) has pointed out, "The pleasure in play is the pleasure of mastery; the functional becomes fun."

The baby's fun begins as soon as he becomes familiar with his environment, can attend to events around him, and has control over the parts of his body used in the game. John S. Watson (1972) has analyzed early social games between the two- and three-month-old baby and another person as a special instance of the way that a baby can experience clear control over some part of his world. In social play, the response of the other person shows the baby his power. Each time the baby does something, such as make a sound, the other person responds by doing something, such as making another sound. Or perhaps the baby blinks, and the other person touches the baby's nose; or the baby squirms, and the other person blows on his tummy. Watson's research indicates that such play leads the baby to smile and coo, which delights the other person and makes the game likely to continue for some time. This entire sequence, in which the baby registers a connection between his action and its clear effect in the world and the intrinsic pleasure that it brings him, serves as a prototype for later, more complex forms of play.

The question arises, of course, as to the importance of parents or peers in such games. The development of sociability through games may simply be a by-product of the infant's basic desire for control or mastery of the environment. Consistent with this view, Watson found that a mobile turning above a crib in response to a baby's movements will release the same kind of smiling and cooing as play with another person. It may be the relationship between the baby's behavior and its clear effect in the world that is critical in early social play, not the interpersonal relationship with a person who produces the effect. According to Daniel Stern (1977), however, during social games the caregiver provides the baby with stimulation that more closely corresponds to the range of stimulation the baby is "preset to receive" than any other stimulation in a typical environment. The game allows excitement to build up and fluctuate within a range that generates positive emotional experiences for both mother and baby and, with no specific intention on the mother's part, instructs the baby about the nature of the social world.

These games are one of the first forms of communication between baby and mother, and the communication is a means of achieving a joint goal. As Jerome Bruner (1975) points out, the game is a form of dialogue in action. He traces the "give-and-take" game, which begins at about three months when the mother "gives" an object to her baby and he "takes" it by having it pushed into his hand. By the time he is six months old, the baby reaches actively for the toy when she proffers it. By a year, the baby is giving the toy as well as taking it, and gets real pleasure from the exchange itself. Over the months, the baby has gradually learned what the mother's signals mean, how to signal her, and—in playing the game—how to get things done with another person.

Almost from the start, infants seem to feel pleasure and satisfaction when they repeat behavior they already know. The infant "repeats his behavior not in any further effort to learn or to investigate, but for the mere joy of mastering it and of showing off to himself his own power of subduing reality" (Piaget, 1951). Thus the baby's first type of play is practice play. He bangs the side of the crib, shakes a rattle continuously, or swings his arms back and forth in front of his face. This kind of early practice play is thoughtless, devoid of any social reference, and intrinsically pleasing.

As the infant enters the second year of life, play comes to reflect his growing self and social conceptions. During this period there is likely to be a developmental progression in the way an infant plays with toys and objects. Larry Fenson and his associates (1976), for example, observed infants with an average age of seven, nine, thirteen, and twenty months as they played with a toy metal tea set. They found that at seven months most of the babies were content merely to mouth, chew, or bang a cup or spoon. At nine months, most of the babies spent much of their time using two pieces of the tea set together, perhaps tapping the teapot with a spoon. At thirteen months, all the infants used two pieces together in an appropriate social way, such as putting the lid on the pot or a spoon in a cup; about half of them engaged in at least one symbolic activity, such as pretending to drink, pour, or stir a cup of tea. By twenty months, all the infants were engaged in such symbolic social activities.

From these early beginnings, children's play will become increasingly imaginative and complex. As they interact, children will build on the play of early childhood, learning to share, take turns, and allow for the feelings of others.

SUMMARY

1. Most psychologists are convinced that personality—how people feel about themselves and how they respond to others—is largely a product of learning and that, from the moment of birth, learning affects the infant's developing personality.

2. Although early experience can have pervasive and enduring effects on later development, investigations of different kinds of early learning and behavior suggest that there are strong constraints on the effects of early experience. These constraints may involve sensitive periods in development as well as maturational state, cognitive growth, and previous experience.

3. In studying personality development, psychologists have paid special attention to the primary attachment bond between infant and caregiver. Studies of both monkey and human infants have illustrated the complex nature of this relationship. In human babies, this early love relationship takes months to develop, requires extensive meshing of infant and caregiver behavior, and is subject to much variation.

4. Differences in parent and infant styles of responding are shown in the mutual and reciprocal nature of the attachment. In general, differences in parental styles do not seem to affect the strength of attachment. However, parental sensitivity and flexibility of response to the baby's needs do seem to affect such personality characteristics as the baby's initiative and reactions to stress.

5. As the infant develops a primary attachment, separation distress and wariness of strangers may appear. These reactions seem to depend on the quality of the infant's attachment to the caregiver. In cases where caregiving is shared or temporarily absent, research suggests that its effects on the infant are likely to vary with the infant's reaction and the amount and kind of stimulation.

6. The baby is a social creature from birth, and his early personality and sociability are largely a product of interaction with his parents. As his sense of self develops and he becomes motivated by a desire for competence, the infant generally begins to show detachment from his parents and increased autonomy. Play and interaction with peers increasingly become sources of enjoyment and reflect the child's growing sense of self and social concepts.

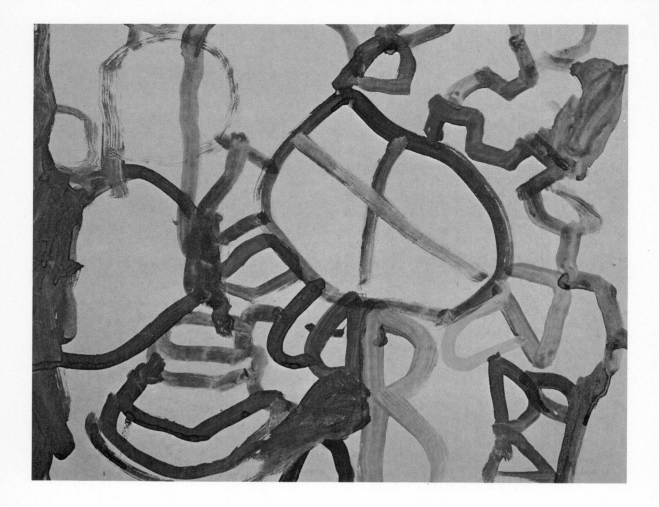

Unit IV Early Childhood: The Formative Years

Between the ages of two and six, the toddler becomes a child. His chubby body begins to slim, and his sometimes awkward attempts at the games of childhood become smooth and skilled. As he uses more sophisticated techniques to explore the environment, his increased experiences and rapidly developing understanding allow the young child to enter a wider world. Although his parents retain the strongest influence on his development, other children and adults begin to play an increasingly important role. Society further strengthens its influence on the growing child by transmitting cultural values and by holding him to what it considers appropriate behavior for one of his sex. When you finish this unit, you will see that there are many ways in which the continuous interaction of child and society affects development.

CHAPTER 10
Physical Change: Growth and Skills

GROWTH CHARACTERISTICS
Body Growth
Brain Growth

**ENVIRONMENTAL INFLUENCES
ON GROWTH**
Diet
Illness
Socioeconomic Status
**Maternal Care and Emotional
Stress**

**DEVELOPMENT OF MOTOR
ABILITIES**
Strength, Speed, and Coordination
Skills
Practice and Instruction
Cortical Control

GIRLS AND BOYS

**PHYSICAL AND SOCIAL
CHANGES**

SUMMARY

Although the facts of physical development are interesting in themselves, their major psychological impact lies in the fact that sheer changes in physical size radically change the fundamental aspects of the child's world. As Lauren gets bigger, she can do more with her increased physical and behavioral potential, and she can interact in different ways with her physical and human environment. Lauren as a baby could neither move nor reach effectively. As a toddler, she was limited to climbing on low furniture and pulling down whatever she could reach. Although she has discovered how to use tools—she can get the dishes off the table by pulling the tablecloth—as she grows taller, she can interact directly with the objects on the table. And as her body and muscles develop, she acquires the ability to do things more skillfully. There is also no question that parents and others treat a larger, older, more capable child differently. Lauren's increased abilities allow her to interact with others in a greater variety of ways.

As you recall, Chapter 6 described the physical growth and development of the infant and pointed out that, as infants begin to gain control over their bodies and their environment, their opportunities for exploration increase sharply. In tracing an infant through those first two years, we noticed the uses and limits of norms and the wide individual differences among infants.

In this chapter we will follow the young child until the age of six, looking at normative development during those years and again stressing individual differences. We will continue to examine the influence of the environment on the growing child and notice that diet, illness, socioeconomic status, and maternal care and emotional stress can affect physical growth. We will trace the continuing development of motor abilities, especially strength, speed, and coordination, seeing that the acquisition of individualized skills depends in part on appropriate practice and instruction. We will explore differences between boys and girls in motor and physical growth. Finally, we will consider some of the ways that physical changes during early childhood influence children's personal development and affect their behavior in social settings.

GROWTH CHARACTERISTICS

Growth in early childhood is not as dramatic as it was during infancy. The rate of growth, in both height and weight, decelerates markedly during infancy and, about the time a child is three or four, settles into a steady rate. Figure 10.1, which charts the average child's annual height increase, shows a velocity curve that flattens and remains about the same until just before the child enters puberty (Falkner, 1966). Growth, however, continues to be relatively rapid, and the average child grows two and one-half inches in height and gains five to seven pounds each year.

As this period of growth starts, there is often a sudden, marked change in appetite. The child eats less, and parents often become alarmed. This decrease in appetite is normal and comes from the smaller energy needs of a child in the steady period of growth.

Body Growth

There is little difference between the size of boys and of girls throughout the childhood years, although girls tend to be a little shorter and lighter. The size of a baby at birth and his or her adult size show little correlation. But by the age of three, a child has settled into an individual growth curve on the way to a destined adult size. Thus, as we noted in Chapter 6, stature during early childhood correlates highly (+.70) with adult size, making predictions of adult stature practical (Bayley, 1956).

Most body tissue, with a few exceptions, follows this general curve of growth. Fat, which increased rapidly during the baby's first nine months and then remained steady, begins to lessen. Most children undergo a true loss of body fat during early childhood. This is sometimes referred to as loss of "baby fat."

In addition to these increases in size and changes in body tissue, a child undergoes other physical changes. The head and upper body approach their adult proportions; the limbs grow rapidly and the trunk appreciably, so that by the age of five or six, a child's physical proportions are far

closer to those of an adult than to those of the large-headed, round-bodied infant.

A child's pelvis and shoulders do not broaden substantially during these years. The boy's body lacks the V-shape of the adult man, and the girl's lacks the curves of a woman. At this time body proportions of boys and girls are similar: straight and flat.

A five-year-old's heart rate is slower and more stable than that of an infant. The young child's respiration also steadily becomes slower and deeper, and blood pressure shows progressive increases. These maturational processes enhance the child's capacity for continuous and strenuous effort.

In discussing these general trends in growth, one should remember the importance of individual differences. Recall the studies of "normal" children in Chapter 6 in which the lightest eight-year-old boy was no heavier than the heaviest eight-year-old had been at the age of two. Figure 10.1 presents a few of the many possible growth curves that appear in a large sample of normal children.

Because genetic influence plays such a large part in determining growth patterns, it is always important to compare children with their parents and siblings before comparing them with a standard for a large population. This is especially necessary when the child may appear to diverge greatly from such standards. Growth standards based on mean parent size, now being developed, will be a great help to pediatricians and developmental psychologists.

Brain Growth

Another important exception to the growth curve is the skull, and of course skull size correlates highly with brain mass. There is such a rapid growth of skull and brain mass that, as we noted before, by the time the child is two or three, this mass has reached about 80 percent of its adult size. By this time the child has emerged from the sensitive period of brain growth, when adequate nutrition is essential to normal brain development (Dobbing, 1974). Although most of the myelination of fibers is complete around two years, some myelin sheaths continue to develop, and the number and size of nerve endings within and between cortical areas continue to grow at least until adolescence (Yakovlev and Lecours, 1967). When a child is about four, the fibers that connect the cerebellum to the cerebral cortex are mature. The cerebellum, as shown in Figure 10.2, is part of the

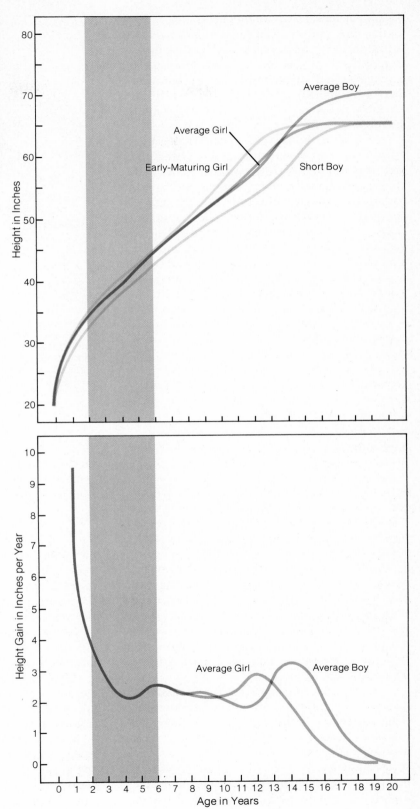

Figure 10.1   Sample growth curves for children two to six years of age (shaded area). (*top*) The growth curves of an early-maturing girl and a short boy are compared to similar curves depicting the rates of growth for an average boy and girl. (*bottom*) Averaged and smoothed curves for boys and girls show inches gained in height per year. After the initial growth spurt of infancy, the rate of growth (velocity) first declines and then remains relatively stable until puberty. (Adapted from Bayley, 1956)

brain stem, and the connecting fibers are necessary to the fine control of voluntary movement involved in such skills as writing. The reticular formation, tissue within the brain made up of both myelinated and unmyelinated fibers, continues to mature throughout childhood (Tanner, 1970). It is probably essential to the maintenance of arousal and attention.

As these maturational developments in neural connections and myelination go on, changes also take place in the brain's electrical activity. The alpha rhythm, for example, continues to change its pattern throughout childhood. There is also evidence that other wave forms follow a different course of onset and development. Robert Dustman and Edward Beck (1966) found, for example, that a marked increase occurs in the magnitude of the brain's electrical response to visual stimulation when a child is five to seven years old. In addition, a particular wave form that occurs when a person is waiting expectantly to do something first appears shortly after a child is six or seven and increases its stability as the child grows older (McCallum, 1969). Just what changes in neural organization underlie the emergence and development of these forms are unknown, but they suggest a complex pattern of maturation.

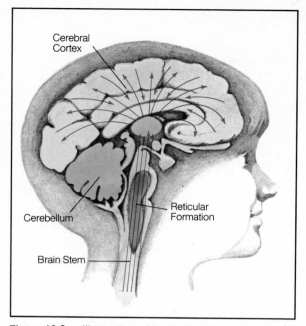

Figure 10.2   Illustration of brain development and activity of the reticular formation. Neural impulses traveling up from the spinal cord and down from various cortical areas pass through the reticular formation, causing it to send diffuse messages to the rest of the brain, arousing and activating it.

ENVIRONMENTAL INFLUENCES ON GROWTH

A variety of environmental factors can greatly affect a young child's growth. These factors, which include diet, general health, and other socioeconomic determinants, can either support or impede normal growth and development.

No one is entirely sure how or why environmental factors influence growth during early childhood. J. M. Tanner (1970) has discussed some of the possible hormonal and chemical factors that may be part of the internal mechanism that regulates growth. Nutrition, illness, and stress may affect the composition and production of these chemicals.

Socioeconomic background, illness, and stress may influence growth at least in part through their indirect effect on nutrition. Children who are ill or extremely upset may not eat as much or as well as healthy, contented children. Children from lower socioeconomic classes may have parents who cannot afford to provide proper nutrition and medical care or who do not understand how to provide suf-

ficient proteins, vitamins, and minerals on limited budgets by using inexpensive but unfamiliar high-protein food such as soybean flour.

Diet

As Chapter 6 made clear, children must have an adequate diet if they are to grow and develop normally. High-quality protein provides most of the material for growth, and carbohydrates provide the enormous amounts of energy that the two- to five-year-old expends. Finally, the proper amounts of fat, minerals, vitamins, and water allow the growing child to develop properly and to utilize other nutritional elements.

Students of childhood growth have made numerous studies of the effects of malnutrition on the young child. Georg Wolff's (1935) study of Berlin children during World War I demonstrated that malnutrition at age five retards the development of height and weight. However, once these children had a normal diet, they began to overcome the adverse effects and by adolescence had caught up with their well-fed contemporaries. (The phenomenon of catch-up growth was described in detail in Chapter 6.) Studies of war children in Russia, Spain, France, Belgium, and Japan have shown the same general results as those in Berlin (Acheson, 1960).

Ironically, dietary excesses can also upset normal growth patterns. I. P. Bronstein and his colleagues (1942), Hilde Bruch (1957), and other researchers have found that obesity in children most often results from overfeeding; malfunctioning glands are rarely responsible. In affluent Western nations such as the United States, the opportunities for excessive feeding are great, and an excess of even the healthiest of foods produces, instead of ever-larger, healthier children, children who may become unhappy and socially maladjusted. Some studies (Dwyer and Mayer, 1973) have suggested that overnutrition in infancy (often caused by a mother determined to have a large, healthy baby) may lead to a multiplication of

extra-large fat cells. Such a baby is susceptible to obesity and may easily become a fat child or adult. Parents may also produce obese children by forcing food on a two- or three-year-old whose growth rate has settled into the childhood plateau described earlier.

Illness

A child who escapes serious illness will have a more regular and satisfactory pattern of growth than one who is very ill for any length of time, because severe illness tends to slow certain growth patterns. Children from two to six years old catch the greatest number of communicable diseases. Some of these diseases involve the respiratory or intestinal tracts, but few, if any, have important effects on growth in most children. Although a child's growth rate may slow slightly during an extended bout with illness, catch-up growth normally compensates for such slowing. For example,

A child who grows up in a refugee camp and a child who grows up in a protected middle-class environment may show very different rates of growth, which can be the result of diet, illness, socioeconomic status, emotional stress, or the quality of maternal care.
(Robert Capa)

Roy Acheson (1960) found that one year of severe, confining illness resulted in a height loss of only about one-fourth inch.

In general, a child who is ill for a short period, as most children are, will have no difficulty overcoming the growth deficit arising out of the illness. But if a child has serious and protracted illnesses, permanent underdevelopment may result, not merely from the effects of the sickness but because the child has lost the periods of reasonably steady growth needed for adequate development.

Socioeconomic Status

The setbacks to growth caused by illness are most readily seen among children of the lower socioeconomic classes. As pointed out in Chapter 6, inadequate medical care and poor diet combine to make the children in developing nations and impoverished children in wealthy nations the most likely victims of growth abnormalities produced by insufficient diet and long illness.

Inadequate nutrition can have less dramatic but more insidious results than actual starvation. The low energy levels that come from malnutrition can produce a sluggish child whose interest is hard to arouse. Undernourished children are more vulnerable to all infections, but especially to disease of the eyes, skin, and respiratory and gastrointestinal tracts. Because these children are unlikely to have regular medical care, they may also suffer from nagging ailments, including badly decayed teeth.

In England, the 1958 National Child Health Survey demonstrated that the more skilled the father's occupation, the more rapidly the children grew. The differences between the children of highly skilled and less skilled fathers grew steadily larger among children between the ages of two and four and one-half. Studies conducted in Scotland support the results of the English survey (E. Scott, Illsby, and Thomson, 1956). Children of higher socioeconomic backgrounds tend to be larger at all ages. Part of the difference in stature among socioeconomic groups is probably a result of the fact that children of the wealthier classes grow and develop earlier. However, as the slowly developing children mature, they do not make up all the height difference, which means that there is a socioeconomic difference in adult height.

Differences in nutrition and availability of medical care are no doubt partially responsible for these socioeconomic differences. Children from poor homes suffer more illnesses, are more vulnerable to accidents and disaster, and undergo more physical trauma than middle-class children do (R. Hess, 1970). Some have suggested that class differences in habits of sleep, exercise, and general home life may also contribute to the effect.

Maternal Care and Emotional Stress

In another set of English studies (Acheson, 1960), maternal care was related to children's height. A group of social workers rated the "efficiency" of the mothers, a measure that included how organized the mother seemed to be at meeting her child's basic needs. The more efficient the mother, the taller the children. When inefficiency was combined with poor socioeconomic conditions, the effect on growth was even more striking.

In these same studies, birth order also appeared to correlate with height. First-born children tended to be taller. This height advantage could be, at least in part, a result of greater maternal efficiency. It may be that the more children in a family, the more difficult it is to provide organized, efficient care.

Some investigators also believe that severe psychological distress can retard growth. E. M. Widdowson (1951) found that children in an orphanage under the regime of a punitive and unfair house-sister grew more slowly than orphanage children whose diet had 20 percent fewer calories. An extreme form of physical retardation called "deprivation dwarfism" also seems to be associated with severe emotional distress in young children (G. Powell, Brasel, and Blizzard, 1967). If these children are removed from their disturbed environments, they show catch-up growth. But only very severe psychological or physical stress can affect a child's growth; the everyday stresses and illnesses of a child's life have little impact.

DEVELOPMENT OF MOTOR ABILITIES

Young children participate in a much more demanding and complex world than they encountered as infants. They steadily acquire new skills and abilities that allow them to take part in new activities, and their experiences at play and in nursery school elaborate and refine these abilities. Running, jumping, manipulating objects, competing with peers in games, and learning to dress themselves all contribute to this new efficiency. During these years, many of these new abilities develop through maturation. As they grow, children become stronger, faster, and more coordinated. However, individual skills that depend on instruction and practice also become important.

Strength, Speed, and Coordination

How each child responds to new physical demands depends on a number of physiological factors. The ability to exert force is limited by the strength of the body's muscles. The speed with which the child can move is influenced by the mass of that part of the body being moved. And the child's reactions depend on the type of stimuli, the nerves' transmission of the impulses, the relative complexity of the movement, and general physical and psychological condition. These motor abilities—strength, speed, and coordination—are components not only of childhood play but ultimately of all mature activity.

As size and weight, particularly of muscle tissue, increase, *strength* is enhanced. A child's strength doubles between the ages of three and eleven. Three- to six-year-old boys and girls exhibit similar degrees of strength, but after age six boys start to gain strength more quickly than girls do, although this difference is not great until adolescence is reached.

Speed is a sensory-motor function that starts to be important in the more demanding play of young children. A major factor in speed is **reaction time,** the interval of time that elapses between the instant a stimulus is presented and the individual's reaction to it. Speed also can be a measure of the absolute time it takes a child to perform a given task. During these years, children learn to use their speed in games that require fast reactions from their minds and bodies, as well as in simple tasks such as running across a playground.

Coordination refers to many aspects of motor performance, including accuracy of movement, poise, smoothness, rhythm, and ease. Coordination involves far more than strength or speed alone and is therefore a better index for determining which child is more able and agile. A child acquires coordination more slowly than strength and speed, because coordination requires the interplay of sensory and motor skills that often depend on the maturation of the small muscles and on practice. Children themselves are extremely conscious of their own and their playmates' degree of coordination. Thus, children's relative mastery of tasks re-

Young children steadily acquire new skills and abilities. Only a few years before, these children jumping on the trampoline had difficulty managing their first halting steps. (Suzanne Szasz)

quiring coordination can influence their self-sufficiency and self-confidence.

Many skills depend on increased coordination. For example, a child begins throwing a ball by jerking his arms from his sides, standing with feet planted firmly in one place and body facing the target. At the age of two, a child can manage to execute this pattern using a small ball such as a tennis ball. By the age of four, the child has developed a relatively smooth, easy pattern that includes throwing overhand, shifting his body weight, and rotating his body away from the target and then toward it as he throws the ball (Sinclair, 1973).

Skills

The expansion of a child's physical activity fascinates his parents; it is also important to his pattern of social development and maturation. There are, of course, large individual differences in the ages at which various children are able to do different things, as well as differences in the degree of their skill and coordination in each activity.

Although maturation of muscles and bones plays a large part in the emergence of such skills as running, jumping, and skipping, the opportunity to practice and the encouragement of others help to guarantee smooth, speedy, confident mastery and refinement of such abilities. While mastering a particular motor skill, a child must carry it through several stages of proficiency. M. V. Gutteridge (1939), after conducting research on more than 2,000 preschool children, produced a scale of motor-skill development. This scale is reproduced in Table 10.1; it can be employed to measure the specific skills of any child.

The Gutteridge scale is particularly useful because it provides four general phases of motor development; within each phase are varying degrees of skill. The first ten degrees of skill mark the progressive acquisition of the ability; the final four degrees (A–D) measure the child's elaboration and use of the ability after he has achieved competence.

The work of Gutteridge and others helps to outline the child's developing abilities between ages three and six. For example, Lauren, like most other three-year-olds, has mastered the basic human walk. She takes steps that are uniform in height, length, and width, alternates her feet when going upstairs, and can jump from the bottom stair with both feet. She also has tricycle riding down to an art.

Lauren also displays a fair amount of control over her arms and hands. She can catch even a small ball if it is well thrown, even though she keeps her arms straight out in front of her, and she can hold a crayon with her fingers and can copy a circle. Lauren is faster at everything than when she was two, and she is also stronger. She is just beginning to develop the balance so vital to many skills and sports. She can stand with both feet on a walking board that is elevated slightly above the floor, and she can alternate her feet part way down the board.

All these new skills are reflected in Lauren's personal and social development. She feeds herself proficiently, puts on her own shoes, and unbuttons almost anything. Her highchair has disappeared, and Lauren joins the family circle, functioning independently and even enlivening the conversation from time to time with a tale from nursery school or a searching question.

David, a typical four-year-old, is now a well-coordinated, versatile person, and he manages everything better than Lauren does. He walks downstairs, alternating feet, and climbs a ladder like an adult. His walk is easy, swinging, and graceful, sometimes revealing his own special swagger or grace. His running has so improved that he runs and kicks soccer-style with a consis-

Table 10.1   Gutteridge Scale of Motor Skills

PHASE	SCALE	DEGREE OF MOTOR SKILL
No attempt made	1	Withdraws or retreats when opportunity is given
	2	Makes no approach or attempt but does not withdraw
Skill in process of formation	3	Attempts activity but seeks help or support
	4	Tries even when not helped or supported but is inept
	5	Is progressing but still uses unnecessary movements
	6	Is practicing basic movements
	7	In process of refining movements
Basic movements achieved	8	Coordinates movements
	9	Performs easily with display of satisfaction
	10	Shows evidence of accuracy, poise, and grace
Skillful execution with variations in use	A	Tests skill by adding difficulties or taking chances
	B	Combines activity with other skill or skills
	C	Speeds, races, or competes with self or others
	D	Uses skill in larger projects such as dramatic play

Source: Adapted from M. V. Gutteridge, "A Study of Motor Achievements of Young Children," *Archives of Psychology* (1939) No. 244. Copyright © 1939 by the American Psychological Association and reproduced by permission.

The precision required to paint develops after the skills involved in walking and running. This child can now control her brush and create recognizable shapes. (©Joel Gordon)

tent, smooth apposition of his arms and legs. David's arm and hand control has become increasingly refined. He can draw a man that is unmistakably human, if somewhat oversimplified. He can also throw a ball overhand, shifting his weight and rotating his body from side to front in relation to a target.

David puts his new skills to use in the personal and social realms as well as on the playground. He is an independent person. He gets up by himself in the morning, can tell the front of his T-shirt and blue jeans from their back (an immense help if you dress yourself), and puts them on. He can wash his face and hands and brush his teeth without help, pour a bowl of cereal and douse it with milk, grab a spoon, turn on "Sesame Street," and pull up a chair. Because David lives in a relatively safe neighborhood with no busy streets to cross, he can run down to the corner and mail a letter by himself.

Matt, who is five, can do everything David can do with greater ease and grace and less intense study. He runs so well that he uses running as a tool in games. He has complete control over starting, stopping, and turning, can walk or run while he bounces a ball, and can even stand on one foot with his eyes closed. Matt can execute a beautiful somersault with his head tucked and his back rounded, and he criticizes his own performance.

Matt's new physical skills affect his personal and social development; they also make it possible

for him to enter the world of formal schooling. He can use a knife and fork like a professional, dress and undress himself, count up to ten objects, and print a few letters. He can draw a man complete with head, body, arms, and legs, and occasionally he even puts in teeth and eyebrows.

Practice and Instruction

The emergence of many of the skills just discussed is largely a matter of growth and maturation, but a child needs the opportunity, the place, and the encouragement to engage in them. Caroline Sinclair (1973) points out that instruction and coaching are not really necessary for simple movement patterns and suggests that a child needs only the time, space, equipment, and encouragement.

There are, however, more complicated motor skills that children learn only with formal instruction and equipment. These include such sports as swimming, skating, skiing, tennis, and so forth. Many children receive their first exposure to these skills during early childhood. Early exposure to and practice of these complicated skills appear to give children an advantage in their performance. For example, in Myrtle McGraw's (1935) co-twin study, discussed in Chapter 6, although one twin seemed to gain little from training in such skills as walking and stair climbing, early training in swimming had some advantages. Researchers began training one twin to swim at eight months, and, when he was seventeen months old, he could swim

Practice and encouragement are as necessary as maturation for the development of some skills, whether they require large or small muscle coordination. (*top:* Taurus Photo; Streshinsky/The Image Bank; *bottom:* Eiji Miyazawa/Black Star; Gary Gladstone/The Image Bank)

up to fifteen feet without help. McGraw also had success in teaching diving and skating. Other studies have demonstrated that observation and verbal instruction increase a child's skill at throwing and catching, and, of course, fine motor skills like writing and drawing improve with certain kinds of instruction.

Bryant Cratty (1967) has developed a set of guidelines for teaching skilled performance to children. He suggests that any skilled performance can be divided into three phases—pretask, task, and posttask—and that the best instruction varies with each phase. For example, pretask instructions should be kept to a minimum, describe the basic mechanical principles of the skill, and present information about the task's extent, intensity, duration, and difficulty. During the task, instructions should not interfere with the child's performance. At this time, a child finds visual demonstrations or minimal manual guidance helpful. Posttask instructions should give the child immediate and clear feedback about his success or failure.

Generally, directions should always emphasize what the child should do instead of what not to do, and, if speed is important, it should be emphasized early. Cratty believes that repeatedly slowing down a child's performance on a task that requires speed may ultimately be detrimental.

Cortical Control

Now that Matt is five, he always uses his right hand to throw a ball and kicks with his right foot. His friend David, who is four, kicks with his right foot but throws a ball with his left hand. Although most children behave like Matt, who clearly has a dominant left hemisphere, not all children—or adults—show such a clear, consistent hemisphere dominance.

A preference for the right or left hand is generally established in infancy, but children continue to make definite improvements in the adeptness and accuracy of their preferred hands. When Donna Piazza (1977) asked three-year-olds to tap out a given sequence with their fingers, most showed greater ability with their right than with their left hands. This superior right-handed performance reflects increased experience and practice with the preferred hand, but it also indicates an increase in the dominance of the brain's left hemisphere and specialization in the serial organization of motor skills.

Although right-handed children show agility with their preferred hands in a variety of skills, in certain skills they are likely to perform better with their left hands. Dianna Ingram (1975a) found, for example, that by the time children are three, they do better with their left than with their right hands when they try to imitate hand postures modeled by another person. Blind children scan Braille better with their left than with their right hands (Hermelin and O'Connor, 1971), but this left-hand superiority is what would be expected, since the brain's right hemisphere is superior at processing spatial information and the left hand is controlled by the right hemisphere.

In general, research on eye and ear dominance parallels that for handedness, showing that right-ear and right-eye dominance correlate with left-hemisphere activity. To establish which ear is dominant, researchers generally use a **dichotic** listening technique, in which two stimuli are presented at the same time, one to each ear. Because an individual is more likely to report hearing the stimulus in the dominant ear, and because what is heard in each ear is projected to the opposite hemisphere, the results of a dichotic listening test make it possible to tell which ear-hemisphere relation is dominant. Studies using this technique indicate that right-ear, left-hemisphere dominance becomes established quite early in a majority of people. It has been found, for example, that when children hear nouns such as "ball," "cup," and "dog," they already show right-ear preference by three years, the youngest age tested (Ingram, 1975b). Such results apparently reflect the left hemisphere's involvement as a major processor of linguistic information.

Research on left-handers has produced mixed findings, perhaps because only about 60 percent of the people who think they are left-handed are solely left-handed when tested. The brains of left- and right-handed people appear to be organized differently; about 60 percent of left-handers process language in the left hemisphere, as nearly all right-handers do. The rest use either the right hemisphere or both sides of the brain. This apparent difference in brain organization showed up in a study by J. Lomas and Doreen Kimura (1976), who found that when right-handers tap with the right hand it interferes with speech, but when they tap with the left hand, it does not. But when left-handers tap with either hand, it interferes with speech.

Developmental research on sighting dominance suggests that eye dominance may become established earlier than ear or hand dominance. Stanley Coren (1974), for example, studied sighting dominance by noting which eye (the dominant one) suddenly stops converging or diverges when a light that shines from directly between and in front of the eyes is gradually brought toward the face. He found that, when tested in this manner, sighting dominance was present among a majority of infants at about one year, and that the incidence of right-eye dominance did not change among older children. But not all right-handed adults are right-eyed; among adults, as among children, approximately 65 percent of the right-handed show right-eye dominance (Dziadosz and Schaller, 1977).

It is important to note that a large proportion of children and adults fail to show the expected associations among handedness, ear or eye preference, and cerebral dominance. Within a group of three- to five-year-old right-handed children, for example, Merrill Hiscock and Marcel Kinsbourne (1977) found that only 60 percent showed a right-ear dominance when listening to numbers. In another study of three- to five-year-old right-handers, Dianna Ingram (1974b) failed to find any relation between ear preference and the hand preferred for gesturing during speech. Because mixed patterns of dominance occur frequently among normal children and adults—and might even be associated with superior abilities in processing various types of information (Kershner, 1974)—it is clear that interaction between the two hemispheres and the rest of the brain is more complicated than it might at first seem.

GIRLS AND BOYS

As noted in the section on growth characteristics, until puberty the differences in appearance between girls and boys are slight. During early childhood, the developmental differences between the sexes are relatively minor, and discerning them requires fine measurement. For example, until adolescence, boys are about 80 percent as mature as girls of the same age on measures of skeletal maturity (Tanner, Whitehouse, and Healy, 1962). Although the average boy is slightly taller than the average girl, girls are usually ahead of boys in motor development.

Adolescent girls and women have greater amounts of subcutaneous fat than adolescent boys and men, and this sex difference is apparent from

birth. Young girls also lose their fatty infant tissue at a far slower rate than their male contemporaries do (Stolz and Stolz, 1951).

Although boys grow faster than girls during the first few months of life, girls outstrip boys from seven months until they are four years old. Between four and puberty, there are no apparent differences in the velocity of growth.

There is an old rule that states that children reach half their adult height by the end of their second year. However, differences discovered in the growth patterns of boys and girls make this old rule unreliable. Most girls grow up faster than most boys, and therefore girls reach the halfway mark sooner: between the ages of one and one-half and two. At the rate most boys grow, they reach the halfway point in height at about two and one-half (Acheson, 1966).

Until they are four, girls have a slight advantage in the development of motor skills. Around the age of three, boys become more proficient than girls at tasks that require strength, such as throwing (Sinclair, 1973). By age seven, girls demonstrate about 10 percent less muscular strength than boys. Louis Govatos (1959) tested ten-year-old children and found no sex differences on tasks as diverse as jumping, reaching, the standing broad-jump, the twenty-five yard dash, or throwing a ball for accuracy. Boys were more proficient than girls in tasks that require superior strength in the arms and legs, such as soccer-style kicking or throwing a ball for distance.

Physical sex differences occur in some involuntary functions as well (one such difference is shown in Figure 10.3). In a measure of **vital capacity** (lung capacity), girls, when asked to inhale as much air as they could and then to expel it, demonstrated 7 percent less vital capacity than boys (Sherman, 1973). Vital capacity can be an important factor in tasks that require sustained energy output. Females exhibit lower **basal metabolism** rates than males; that is, they require less energy while resting to maintain the same amount of body tissue. Boys develop larger hearts and lungs than girls. In addition, boys have a lower heart rate than girls (Hutt, 1972).

There are also indications that the brain develops differently in boys than in girls. Jesse Le Roy Conel (1963) found some evidence that, at about the age of four, neural tissue grows and matures earlier in the brain's left hemisphere for girls and in the right hemisphere for boys. Another study

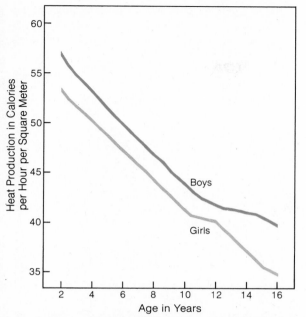

Figure 10.3   As this graph shows, the basal metabolic rate of boys is higher than that of girls, indicating that boys convert food and oxygen to various forms of energy faster than girls do. The difference is slight throughout childhood but increases somewhat during adolescence. (Adapted from Lewis, Duval, and Iliff, 1943)

(Taylor, 1969) suggests that the female brain matures more rapidly and that one hemisphere becomes dominant earlier than it does in the male brain.

Corinne Hutt (1972) is among those who have tried to show that the earlier dominance of the left hemisphere in girls can explain their superior verbal abilities. There is also speculation that boys demonstrate superior spatial abilities because the left hemisphere becomes more dominant later and less completely in males than in females. This speculation appears to be supported by recent research, which suggests a greater right-hemisphere specialization in boys than in girls for visual-spatial and other nonverbal skills. Sandra Witelson (1976), for example, had children explore by touch alone two differently shaped objects presented at the same time, one to each hand. The children then tried to identify the objects they had felt with each hand by selecting ones like them from a group of six variously shaped objects. Witelson found that by the time they were six, boys found it easier to identify shapes with their left hands, whereas girls identified shapes equally well with either hand. Peter Wolff and Irving Hurwitz (1976)

also found that, after children are about five years old, girls are more accurate with both hands than are boys when asked to reproduce a sequence of taps. Taken together, such results seem to indicate either that boys use their right hemispheres more than girls do in performing visual-spatial tasks or that girls use both hemispheres in such tasks.

It may be that reported differences in hemisphere dominance between the sexes are biologically based; if so, can these differences be modified by experience? Studies have found that on visual-spatial tasks, which are performed more efficiently by the right than by the left hemisphere, training improves performance among girls but not among boys (Connor, Serbin, and Schackman, 1977). This suggests that any biological sex differences in cerebral organization are likely to be influenced in a very complicated way by experience. It also suggests that although girls may not find that right-hemisphere tasks come as easily to them as they do to boys, girls may be as capable as boys of acquiring them.

During early childhood, motor abilities and physical growth play an important part in the developing self-image of both boys and girls, as the next section will demonstrate. When children are asked what they like and do not like about themselves, physical characteristics, appearance, and motor abilities play an important part in their answers (Jersild, 1952). However, boys are more likely than girls to make a direct social test of their physical abilities (Herron and Sutton-Smith, 1971). As later discussions of personality development will show, the "social hierarchies," or patterns of dominance and submission, for groups of boys more often seem to rest on who is bigger, faster, and tougher than girls' hierarchies do. Children's social hierarchies, of course, reflect their parents' values. Studies of sex-role behavior clearly show that adults value strength and athletic abilities more in males than in females (Sherman, 1973).

PHYSICAL AND SOCIAL CHANGES

Crawling and walking, as Chapter 6 stressed, widen the infant's social and emotional world. Physical growth and motor development continue to affect the young child's social and emotional behavior. A boy who is much smaller than his peers or one who is clumsy and throws a ball poorly will find his size or lack of skill an important factor in his relationships with his peers. Investigators have, therefore, addressed themselves to a number of childhood skills and physical development patterns in order to understand their relationship to social behavior.

During early childhood, children can begin to determine for themselves whether they are physically the equal of their classmates. Running, climbing, jumping, and tumbling have been the subjects of research because they are easy to measure and present almost limitless opportunities for young children to compete with one another. Boys, especially, seem to spend a good deal of time establishing social hierarchies on the basis of physical strength and skill. Questions like "Who is the toughest?" and "Who is the biggest?" and "Who can run the fastest, climb the highest, or jump the farthest?" seem to have great social significance for the young boy (Herron and Sutton-Smith, 1971). In Chapter 13, we will look again at the possible effects of skills and strengths on personality development.

As long as forty years ago, L. M. Jack (1934) established that the child who has achieved proficiency in some motor ability is more likely to be chosen as a leader in athletic and social activities. Children who fail to establish leadership become less sure of their talent and experience stress and unhappiness. In order to demonstrate how this kind of situation can be influenced, Jack taught certain skills to five nursery-school children. The children were all low in social interactions with their peers. When the children had mastered the special skills, they were paired with others in situations that would allow them to use the new abilities. In every case, the children showed significant changes in behavior. They asserted themselves, gave directions to the children who lacked their special ability, and in general showed social ascendancy. The change was not complete; it applied only to activities in which they could display their specific talents. But children who at first had been unable to lead or to assert themselves demonstrated that, with the appropriate experience, they could effectively take an assertive role.

Although physical prowess does not seem to play as important a part in the social hierarchies of girls, motor skills and outdoor play are still related to female social development. Their importance was shown clearly in the case of Polly, a three-year-old girl who demonstrated problems in both motor skills and social development. Joan Buell

Boys compete to decide who can run fastest, jump farthest, or climb highest. Such status has great social significance for them. (Charles Gatewood/Magnum Photos)

As children gain increasing control over their bodies, they appear more like adults, and society responds by expecting more mature behavior from them. (*top:* © Cary Herz; Elyse Lewin/The Image Bank; *bottom:* Jeffrey Foxx/Woodfin Camp & Assoc.)

and her colleagues (1968) instituted a program in which Polly was rewarded whenever she used outdoor play equipment. As long as Polly stayed on the equipment, a teacher remained close, smiling and talking to her. As a result, Polly's use of outdoor play equipment increased substantially, and so did other play and social behavior that the researchers had not directly rewarded. Polly began to touch and talk to other children more frequently, to use their names, and to engage more often in cooperative play. Buell and her colleagues concluded that outdoor play is intimately related to a child's social relationships. Children of both sexes who enjoy and participate in these activities experience increased social contact and develop advanced patterns of play and social interaction.

In addition to the effect that motor skills may have on a child's social behavior, physical shape itself (how tall, short, broad, or muscular a child becomes) can influence social and personality development. For thousands of years, people interested in human behavior have tried to classify patterns of physical growth into "body types." The early Greeks hoped to use body type to predict the diseases a person might develop. In more recent times, psychologists like William Sheldon and his colleagues (1954) have tried to predict behavior from body type. However, this approach remains inconclusive. About all that can be said at present is that, for example, a boy with a muscular body is likely to be better at motor skills and elicit admiration and approval from parents, teachers, and peers. In turn, he may be inclined to become more self-confident and ambitious in his athletic activities and social relationships.

Just how the physical characteristics of a child are perceived, and how well they fit into a family, can make a great deal of difference to a child's development. A frail, poorly coordinated five-year-old boy may be a delight to a scholarly father but a deep disappointment to an athletic one. A healthy, super-coordinated five-year-old girl who is outstanding in sports may be a delight to her sports-minded father but a disappointment to her mother.

The different aspects of physical development combine to contribute to the social integration and personal integrity of the child. They make children appear more adultlike, which enhances society's tendency to treat them as such. Erik Erikson's (1963) explanation of the relationship between

physical and social-emotional development, which was discussed in Chapter 6, builds on his idea of walking as the first step toward making the child a part of his culture. Children strive to imitate and to become adult, and their increasing physical resemblance to adults and increasing ability to act like them facilitate this goal. The little boy who has the strength and stamina to imitate Daddy in play automatically becomes more like Daddy both in his own eyes and in those of onlookers. As children become more like adults, their self-esteem is enhanced, and this process continues into later childhood. Cultural integration and acceptance play their role, as do the moment-to-moment approval and encouragement of parents. But probably the greatest boost to self-esteem comes from children's own internally generated satisfaction when they demonstrate their physical competence. Competence is a real, approved, and apparent indication that a child is growing up.

SUMMARY

1. The rate of growth in both height and weight decelerates markedly during infancy and settles into a steady rate by the time a child is three or four. However, growth continues to be relatively rapid. During early childhood, there is a loss of "baby fat"; in contrast, skull size and brain mass, including nerve endings and connections between brain areas, continue to grow and mature; and the child's body begins to approach adult proportions.

2. As at other times in development, a variety of environmental influences can either support or impede the child's physical growth. These influences include such features as diet, general health, and type and quality of maternal care. In general, proper nutrition and good health are likely to result in more rapid and fuller physical growth and development.

3. Increases in strength, speed, and coordination enable the young child to participate in more demanding and complex activities. He steadily acquires new physical skills and abilities such as those involved in jumping and dressing himself. Although maturation and practice are basic to the child's development of skills, encouragement and some formal instruction in more complicated skills are often required if the child is to acquire or become proficient in them.

4. During early childhood, physical growth and developmental differences between the sexes are relatively slight: the average boy is a little taller than the average girl, whereas girls are a little more advanced in some areas of motor development. Differences between the sexes have been found in vital capacity and metabolic rate, and some evidence suggests that differences in cerebral dominance of boys and girls may be associated with different kinds of abilities.

5. Motor skill and physical growth continue to affect the development of the young child's social and emotional behavior. Research suggests, for example, that a child's self-image and social status are likely to vary with how skilled he is in certain games and activities. In addition to his physical prowess, a child's personal and social acceptability may vary with the way that he, his family, and other children and adults evaluate his body appearance.

CHAPTER 11
Cognition: Changes in Thinking

PERCEPTUAL ADVANCES
Perceiving Distinctive Features
Sensory Coordination

EDUCATING ATTENTION
Attention Preferences
Focused Attention

CHILDREN'S THINKING
Conservation
Types of Concepts
Egocentrism

REPRESENTATIONAL SKILLS
Imitation
Language
Play
Memory
Using Graphic Symbols

SOCIAL INTERACTION AND
COGNITION

SUMMARY

David and his father were having a heart-to-heart talk. With all the seriousness of his four and one-half years, David began to speak about getting married when he grew up. "I'll move into a different house," he said, "then I won't be your son anymore." One of the attributes that defined David's concept of "son" was living in the same house as his father. He had heard the word "son" used in various situations and had even used it himself. Because in David's experience the father of the child referred to as "son" had either been present or clearly known to be living at home, David's understanding of the concept was not illogical. Although young sons usually do live in the same house with their fathers, such a definition does not correspond to the culturally accepted one, and David's definition will have to be modified to remove the notion that residence is a defining attribute of the concept "son." In order to communicate effectively, he must transform his early definition of "son" into a new one that more closely fits society's understanding.

Redefinition of concepts is one of the intellectual tasks that face the young child. In this chapter we will look at the cognitive changes that occur during early childhood and will find that they are considerable. We will discover that what the child's senses pick up and what he gives his attention to will determine his concepts of the world. We will see that the young child uses self-generated as well as culturally transmitted symbols, that he accumulates knowledge about the objective world, and that he continually refines his concepts in the direction of their adult use. We will examine the pervasive role of private and social play in the child's daily encounters with the world, and look at the way his burgeoning linguistic capabilities mesh with his intellectual skills. Throughout these early years, one characteristic remains fairly constant: the child's basic curiosity about his environment and his quest for meaning.

PERCEPTUAL ADVANCES

As the perceptual skills of young children develop, they isolate and abstract more of the distinctive features of their environment. One-year-olds have learned to discriminate the features of the human face; by the time they are six, many children are already adept readers, differentiating the features of the alphabet that distinguish one letter from the other letters.

Perceiving Distinctive Features

A two-year-old is aware of certain parts of the human body. As an infant David probably spent considerable time observing his own hands and fingers. He has seen numerous people from different angles and has watched them move their faces, torsos, and limbs in a variety of ways. However, there are many levels of awareness of objects. Knowing that the human hand has fingers on it is not as differentiated an awareness as knowing that it has five fingers, each a unique size and shape and each occupying a particular position with respect to the others and to the rest of the hand. As children get older and have more experience with objects and events, they tend to isolate more of the distinctive features and to relate these features in a comprehensive manner.

The child's changing perception of the human body during this period illustrates his continual differentiation of features and their integration into the whole. For example, David requested a paper and pencil and began drawing a picture of a man. Suddenly he stopped and asked, "Daddy, is the neck attached to the head?" Although the child had seen heads and necks on many people and on himself in the mirror, he was unsure of the precise spatial relationship and wanted another opinion before proceeding with his picture. This incident provides a glimpse at a perception in the midst of a shift.

In a more controlled situation, Beverly Celotta (1973) studied the development of children's ability to differentiate the parts of the human body and to perceive the spatial relationships between them. She devised a Mannikin Construction Test and used it with three-, five-, and seven-year-olds. Each child was given sixty pieces of felt representing legs, arms, neck, clothing, and so forth. In front of the child was a red felt board on which the investigator placed a part representing a human head. She instructed the child to complete the figure, using any of the sixty pieces spread out before

him that he wished. Celotta found that seven-year-olds did better than five-year-olds in building mannikins and that five-year-olds did better than three-year-olds, both in number of body parts used and in the appropriate placement of the parts. This improved performance with age shows how a sophisticated perception of the human body develops gradually during early childhood.

Sensory Coordination

How well do the young child's different senses communicate? There is considerable evidence that a youngster's ability at tasks of intersensory recognition improves dramatically between the ages of three and six (Abravanel, 1968; Blank and Bridger, 1964; Zaporozhets, 1965).

In one study V. P. Zinshensko and A. G. Ruzskaya (see Zaporozhets, 1965) presented children of three, four, five, and six with abstract forms that they were permitted to explore by touch but could not see. These researchers then tested the children to check their visual recognition of the objects that they had explored with their fingers. At about age five, there was a sharp improvement in performance. This improvement in intersensory coordination probably develops because the mental images of five- or six-year-olds become increasingly detailed and precise as a result of their exposure to objects and sophisticated methods of exploration.

Another kind of intersensory coordination, in this case the relationship between visual and auditory perception, has been investigated by Alice Vlietstra and John Wright (1971), who taught young children to discriminate between intensities of sounds. The researchers wondered if learning how to tell differences between intensities of sounds makes it easier for youngsters to tell diffferences between intensities of visual stimuli. If young children come to understand that the quality "stimulus intensity" can be perceived by any of their sense organs, then their experience with intensity in one sense, such as hearing, should transfer to a different sense, such as vision. However, if experience with intensity does not transfer from one sense to another, children would find their experience with sound of no help when they tried to discriminate between the intensity of two visual stimuli, such as two lights of varying brightness. When Vlietstra and Wright tested children who had learned to discriminate the intensity of sounds, they found that the skill indeed transferred

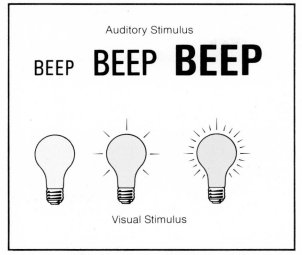

Auditory Stimulus

BEEP **BEEP** **BEEP**

Visual Stimulus

Figure 11.1 After learning to discriminate among different intensities of sound, young children found it easier to discriminate among comparable differences in intensities of light, indicating transfer of experience from one sense to another, as discussed in the text.

to another sense; the children found it easier to discriminate differences in visual intensity provided that the same general levels of intensity were considered correct in both tasks. Such transfer helps children coordinate the information they gather through their separate senses into increasingly complex perceptions of the world.

EDUCATING ATTENTION

Children's concepts of the world depend on which characteristics of it get their attention. During early childhood their thought processes become increasingly sophisticated, and their ability to shift their attention improves sharply, particularly in response to the verbal instructions of others.

Attention Preferences

In Chapter 7 we learned that the infant prefers to attend to some features of stimuli rather than to others. Such preferences are also found in the young child, and they play an important role in his learning to discriminate among objects and events. For example, most, though not all, children between the ages of four and six tend to pay greater attention to the form of objects than to their color, whereas those between two and three generally prefer color to form (Stevenson, 1972). If young children are required to sort objects of various

colors according to their shapes, those children who initially attend to shape will find this task easier, whereas those who first attend to color will find the task more difficult.

Joan Gusinow and Louis Price (1972) attempted to discover how resistant to change the color and form preferences of four- to six-year-olds are. The researchers first determined whether children preferred form to color by asking them to match blocks. Then the children were allowed to earn toys by matching the blocks on the basis of the unpreferred dimension. That is, children who matched blocks by shape had to match by color to get a toy and vice versa. When these children were later given another matching test, many of the children voluntarily switched preferences; many of those who had originally preferred color matched by shape, and many of those who had originally preferred shape matched by color. In addition, Gusinow and Price found that children who were

Two- and three-year-olds tend to sort objects by color; by the time they are four, most will pay more attention to the form of objects. (© Frostie/Woodfin Camp & Assoc.)

also required to name their unpreferred dimension (color or shape) to earn toys were more likely to switch their preferences on later tests than children who were not required to name the dimension. This study goes beyond demonstrating that four- to six-year-olds have dimensional preferences. It shows that not all young children prefer the same dimensions and that appropriate rewards can alter the child's preferences. Finally, it shows that the appropriate use of language is also effective in altering children's preferences.

Focused Attention

One may hear a frustrated parent or nursery-school teacher complain that a young child cannot concentrate on a task. There is both truth and falsehood in this assertion. Is the child who rapidly switches attention from one toy or activity to another "easily distractible" or "curious and exploratory"?

It is true, for example, that, when confronted with a problem that requires sustained attention to one or two properties or dimensions and deliberate ignoring of other, irrelevant information, the four- or six-year-old is usually less effective than the eight-year-old in solving the problem (Osler and

Kofsky, 1965). Younger children tend to respond to irrelevant cues, which of course hinders their performance. They also are not as proficient as eight-year-olds in classifying information into categories that are relevant to the task.

This developmental difference showed clearly in an experiment by Sheldon White (1966). Young children were compared with nine- and ten-year-olds on three discrimination-learning tasks. In each task White presented the child with pairs of bird pictures. When the child selected the correct picture, he was given a marble or a piece of candy; when he selected the incorrect picture, he got nothing. The correct, rewarded stimulus was the positive cue, and the incorrect stimulus, the negative cue. In White's first task, both the positive and the negative cues remained the same for all trials; the children saw the same pair of bird pictures on each trial, but the position of the birds changed. In his second task, the positive cue was always the same, and the negative one changed from trial to trial. In his third task, the negative cue remained the same throughout, but the positive cue was different on each trial. Eight- and nine-year-olds learned all three of these discriminations at the same speed. But young children were hampered by White's procedure of varying the cues on the second and third tasks. They learned which cue was correct much faster in the first discrimination problem. However, although younger children had

Figure 11.2 These pictures are similar to those used in White's experiment on the discrimination learning of younger and older children. (Adapted from S. White, 1965)

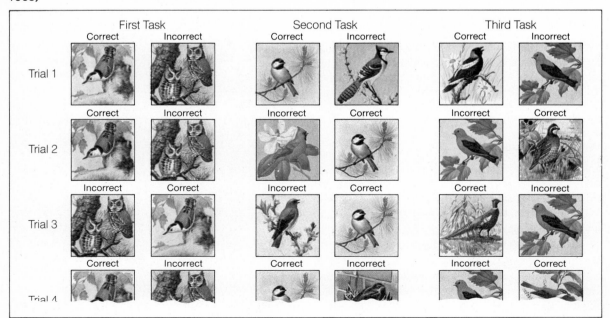

greater difficulty than older children did, they were still able to solve the problems.

The young child's less efficient attending does not mean that he has a "short attention span." Many youngsters spend long periods of time exploring objects that interest them. Their dedicated perseverance at a task may even bewilder their parents. For example, after the fourth or fifth reading of a picture book, Lauren may say, "Daddy, read it to me again," although by that time her father may be quite bored and inattentive to the simple plot with its limited vocabulary and sentence structure. Whose attention span is longer, the child's or the father's? Obviously, attention spans depend as much on the nature of the material being attended to as on the intellectual level of the person whose attention span is being measured.

John Wright and Alice Vlietstra (1975) believe that between the ages of three and six a major shift occurs in the features that control children's attention. Before children are three, their attention is motivated by curiosity and is caught by the prominence of a stimulus. As children grow older, this playful exploration gives way to a systematic, goal-oriented strategy based on the relevance and informativeness of stimuli rather than on their prominence. Exploration is playful and involves rapid, impulsive responding, whereas searching is focused, task-oriented, and slower. Exploration is controlled primarily by features in the environment, whereas searching is guided mostly by logic and need for information related to the task. Despite the impulsive nature of exploration, some tasks are more appropriately handled by its use. Wright and Vlietstra point out that tasks requiring imagination or novel solutions are best handled by curiosity and exploration, but tasks that have a logical solution require the collection of information that characterizes a searching strategy. A child's cognitive competence, they believe, depends to a large degree on his ability to bring his attentional processes under the control of internally maintained goals and purposes so that he is not continually distracted by objects and events in his environment.

CHILDREN'S THINKING

Young children's minds, like their bodies, are in perpetual motion. In Chapter 7 we saw how the processes of assimilation and accommodation op-erate in the intellectual life of the infant. It is possible to interpret many of young children's cognitive activities in a similar way. As they fit newly observed phenomena into their patterns of understanding, they constantly modify their concepts of the world. Sometimes this modification consists simply of adding new members to a category that they already know. For example, most five-year-olds know the difference between the concepts of color and shape. If you give them a red circle and a blue square and ask them to name the color of the items, most will say "Red and blue." Similarly, if you ask them to name the shape, they will say "Circle and square" (or some other words that they use to refer to shape, such as "wheel" or "tire" for a circle). However, because of limited experience, children may not be aware of the existence of such colors as beige, violet, or maroon or such shapes as diamonds or parallelograms. When they are exposed to these new instances, they modify their concepts by extending the range of items included in them. Sometimes, however, the modification requires a drastic revision instead of an extension.

Jean Piaget has studied the thought of young children extensively (Piaget and Inhelder, 1969). In his view there are certain general features that characterize early ways of thinking about many aspects of the physical and social world. One of the most characteristic of these is the young child's tendency to base many of his ideas about things on their most conspicuous perceptual features. He will defend these "incorrect" perceptually influenced ideas about objects, even though some transformation of their perceptual features would easily prove him wrong. Indeed, the four- or five-year-old sometimes does not imagine transformations at all. In other instances he does, but his immediate perceptual experience is more convincing to him than is his awareness that the objects' appearances would differ after some hypothetical transformation.

Conservation

This aspect of young children's thinking shows clearly in their ideas about the conservation of quantity. This particular concept has probably been the most extensively studied of the four- or five-year-old child's basic concepts relating to the nature of physical substances. In a simple experiment devised to explore the young child's grasp of the conservation of volume, the researcher fills two

A conservation experiment. The child is shown two
rows of seven checkers, evenly spaced, and asked
which has more checkers. Most children reply that they
are the same. When one row is rearranged so that the
checkers are bunched together, as shown, children
four or five years of age usually say that the original
row contains more checkers. (William MacDonald)

glasses of the same size and shape to an equal level
with colored water. A child is asked whether the
two glasses contain the same amount of water.
When the child asserts that the amounts are the
same, the researcher pours the water from one
glass into a shorter, broader glass, so that the levels
of colored water in the two glasses differ. A four-
year-old, when asked whether each glass now contains the same amount of water, usually will say,
"No! This one has more water in it because it is
higher." When the water is poured back into its
original glass, the child usually will again say that
the two glasses have the same amount of water in
them. When he is asked, "How do you know?" he
answers, "Because I can *see* that they do."

Other changes in the external appearance of
identical objects may also seem to convince the
young child that the total quantity of one has been
altered. For example, place in front of a four- or
five-year-old two rows of seven checkers each.
Then ask the child if one row has more, less, or the
same amount of checkers as the other. The child
may correctly answer that the two rows have the
same amount of checkers. Next bunch the checkers in Row 1 together. Ask the child if Row 2 has
more, less, or the same amount of checkers as Row
1. To the surprise and chagrin of many parents
who have tried to prove Piaget wrong by adminis-
tering this test to their own clever children, most
four- or five-year-olds respond quite emphatically

that there are more checkers in Row 2 than in Row 1. They may even retain this view despite their realization that, if the checkers in Row 1 are returned to their original position, the two rows will once again have the same number of checkers (Piaget, 1952a). These young children apparently believe that the number of checkers varies with the dominating perceptual feature of the row, in this case length or spread. However, by the time the child is seven, he responds to the posttransformation question with an emphatic "Of course they are the same, you didn't add any or take any away, you just put them closer together." He may even respond in a tone of surprise mixed with disdain at an experimenter who could ask such a silly question.

At one time, most developmental psychologists believed that the replies of five-year-olds in these two experiments clearly demonstrated that the children did not understand the conservation of quantity or number. But recently, researchers have begun to question this conclusion. For one thing, when children are allowed to pour the colored water themselves, more of them solve the problem correctly, replying that both glasses still hold the same amount of water. Margaret Donaldson (1978) has pointed out that the conditions of the experiment push children toward the wrong answer. When the experimenter pours the water or shifts the checkers, he generally says "Now watch what I do," indicating to the child that the change is important and will affect whatever follows.

Susan Rose and Marion Blank (1974) conducted a version of the conservation experiment in which they did not ask the child about the quality of the two items *before* they manipulated their appearance. They propose that asking the same question both before and after the manipulation suggests to the child that he should change his answer. When they tested six-year-olds with only the final question, they found that the children not only made fewer errors on the task at hand, but also scored much higher a week later when tested in the manner devised by Piaget.

Rochel Gelman (1977) notes that two-and-one-half-year-olds to five-years-olds who may not seem to understand conservation on traditional Piagetian tasks do not totally lack the concept. If they are shown three checkers, for example, and then a fourth is surreptitiously added or one of the three is surreptitiously removed, the children show surprise and point out that a checker was added or

subtracted. If the checkers are surreptitiously spread out, without changing the number, the children again notice the change but indicate that it is irrelevant, demonstrating their understanding of conservation.

Gelman does *not* claim that such results mean that the young child has exactly the same abilities as the older child who demonstrates his grasp of the principle on a Piagetian task. Younger children show conservation of number only when the task uses five items or less, and in judging whether two sets are equivalent, they first try to count the items in each set. In contrast, older children don't concern themselves with the exact number of items, but simply consider the effect of a transformation apart from the specific number of items involved. Before children can deal with transformations, says Gelman, they must know about correspondence—that is, they must know how to compare quantities—a position that is compatible with recent statements by Piaget (1975).

As this work demonstrates, one should be cautious about asserting that a child is unable to learn or to understand certain discriminations or concepts. Often, all that is really meant is that the child has greater difficulty than other children in mastering these concepts or that an appropriate method of teaching him has not yet been formulated. Of course, some concepts or tasks may indeed be beyond some children's ken regardless of the ingenuity of any parent, teacher, or psychologist. However, the literature on intellectual development provides many instances where what was once thought to be beyond a child's level of comprehension has been shown to be teachable by newly developed modes of instruction (for example, Schimmel, 1971; Brainerd, 1977; Zimmerman and T. Rosenthal, 1974).

Other general concepts of the physical world that Piaget and others have studied in children are weight, volume, and area and their relationships; time, movement, and speed and their interrelatedness; and spatial properties of two- and three-dimensional objects. The general picture emerging from these studies is that the young child's concepts differ from those of older children and adults in many respects. As we saw in Chapters 2 and 7, Piaget believes that each of these adult concepts is the final product of an orderly progression through several versions and revisions of earlier forms of the concept. He further believes that the order in which people acquire these various versions and revisions is unalterable and universal, although different children may progress through each sequence of concept development at different rates, and some people may never even attain the most advanced form of the concept.

Types of Concepts

Specific physical properties such as volume, weight, and so forth are not the only concepts children must learn if they are to function effectively in their environments. As we have just seen, on a relatively simple level children learn about visible properties of specific objects. They know, for example, that the trucks called fire engines are red and have long hoses and sirens and that animals known as elephants are massive and have long trunks and tusks.

Many concepts are defined by the conjunction, or combination, of several attributes or properties. In **conjunctive concepts** all the attributes of a category must be present in a specific object in order for the object to be included in the category. For example, among the defining attributes of "dog," at least at the level of the average person's usage, are four legs, furriness, and a bark. The three-year-old who sees a cat and hears it meow and yet calls it a dog probably has a concept of "dog" that includes four legs and furriness but not the attribute of having a bark rather than a meow. This type of error in concept acquisition is frequent and understandable in the preschooler (Saltz, 1971); it is similar to that overgeneralization demonstrated by the infant in Chapter 8 who called all four-legged animals "bow-wow." A child usually requires repeated exposure to learn which attributes define concepts and which do not.

A second type of concept that is even more difficult to learn is the **disjunctive concept.** In this type of "either/or" concept, a member of the category may possess some, but need not possess all, of several different attributes. For example, a citizen of the United States is someone who *either* was born in the United States *or* has been naturalized in this country (Saltz, 1971).

In many instances, attributes that relate to the use or *function* of an object define common concepts. These attributes are not apparent on inspection, and members of the same class may look very different. For example, if young Lauren's parents do not tell her explicitly that "food" refers to all edible things, she may err in using the term until she discovers for herself the common attribute of

fruits, vegetables, fish, meat, and poultry: edibility. Until Lauren has abstracted the property of edibility, she may refer to some nonfoods as food, and may fail to include in the category some of the things she eats that she has never heard others call food. Because adults tend to provide young children with fewer verbal definitions of concepts than they give to school-aged children, the younger child has to rely extensively on his or her own powers of discovery and abstraction in figuring out adult concepts. These powers may not always be equal to the challenge (Ausubel, 1968). In fact, one important function of formal schooling is to remove some of the guesswork in concept learning. Teachers and books supplement the child's self-discovery method with systematically presented verbal and nonverbal definitions or examples of concepts.

Many concepts are challenging to learn because they involve fairly complex *relations* between things and events. Jean Piaget (1952a) has also studied several of these complex concepts and believes that they are difficult for the average youngster to master. A four- or five-year-old child who happens to have eight lemon drops and five

Figure 11.3 A young child is likely to have difficulty reasoning about the relation of a part or parts to a whole, and, if shown a collection of lemon drops and licorice drops, he is likely to say that he has more lemon drops than candy.

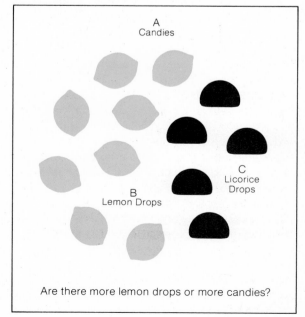

Are there more lemon drops or more candies?

licorice drops is likely to say that (1) lemon drops are candy and (2) licorice drops are also candy but still insist that (3) he has more lemon drops than candy. However, he knows that he has more lemon drops than licorice drops. He does not seem to realize that if A includes both B and C, as in Figure 11.2, then A *must* be greater than B alone or C alone. Piaget's explanation is that the young child cannot think of both an entire class and a subclass at the same time; therefore, he cannot compare them.

A variation on the lemon and licorice drops experiment, however, indicates that part of the problem may lie in language, not in concept. James McGarrigle (see Donaldson, 1978) tested forty-eight children, who were about six years old, with four toy cows. Three of the cows were black and one was white. McGarrigle placed all the cows on their sides and told the children they were sleeping. When he asked the standard Piagetian question "Are there more black cows or more cows?" only 25 percent of the children correctly answered "More cows." But when he asked "Are there more black cows or more sleeping cows?" 48 percent of the children correctly said "More sleeping cows." The inclusion of an adjective that encompassed the entire class enabled many more children to compare class with subclass.

Features of the test materials may also affect a child's answers on this kind of problem. Obvious examples of a class work better than obscure ones (Carson and Abrahamson, 1976). Dogs and horses, for example, are better examples of animals in the eyes of young children than are bees or butterflies. Thus, if young children are shown dogs and horses and are asked "Are there more dogs or animals?" they are more likely to give the correct answer than if they are shown dogs and butterflies or horses and bees.

It may be that young children try to answer class-inclusion questions by counting the elements, which keeps them from succeeding (Wilkinson, 1976). That is, when a child is asked "Are there more lemon drops or candy?" he may begin to count the lemon drops and may find himself stuck because he follows the rule that something can be counted once and once only. To answer the question correctly, he would have to return the lemon drops to the to-be-counted category of candy. Since he can't, he is likely to go ahead and count only the licorice drops for comparison.

Another relational concept that is self-evident

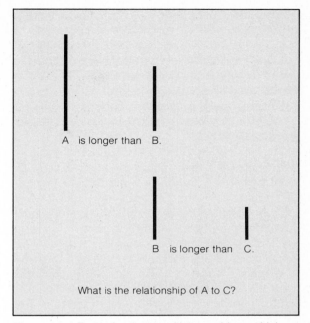

Figure 11.4 Example of a transitivity problem, which requires the joining together of two instances of the relational concept "longer than."

to adults is the concept of **transitivity**. If Matt is older than David and David is older than Susan, then obviously Matt is older than Susan. Yet many four-year-olds have difficulty making this deduction, which requires the joining together of two instances of the relational concept "older than." According to Piaget, this concept is vital for operational thought, and rarely found in children younger than seven. He tests children's grasp of the concept in the following manner:

> We present two sticks to a child, stick A being smaller than stick B. Then we hide stick A and show him stick B together with a larger stick C. Then we ask him how A and C compare. Pre-operation children will say that they do not know because they have not seen them together—they have not been able to compare them.

Peter Bryant (1974), Thomas Trabasso (1977), and a number of other psychologists disagree with Piaget's contention that children younger than seven cannot understand transitivity; they believe that children as young as four can grasp the concept. These researchers believe that investigators have used the wrong type of experiment to test children. Piaget's original test contained three separate steps: A was compared directly with B, then B was compared directly with C; then the child was asked to compare A *indirectly* with C. The contention is that young children fail to make the inference about the relationship between A and C because they have forgotten the information in the first two steps by the time they are asked the third. The success of older children might simply be due to their remembering their answer in the initial comparison between A and B and parroting it for the final comparison.

The only valid way to test children's grasp of transitivity, say some researchers, is to give the children enough training on the initial comparisons so that they can recall this information when they are asked to make the inference, and to increase the initial comparisons from three steps to five. With five quantities, the researcher can construct four one-step combinations (A and B, B and C, C and D, and D and E) in which three of the quantities occur as both the larger and the smaller. In this way, an inference based on B and D cannot be answered correctly by parroting "larger" or "smaller."

Bryant and Trabasso (1971) combined both practice and the five steps in a study with four-, five-, and six-year-old children. In the initial training stage, the children were taught that A is larger than B, B is larger than C, C is larger than D, and D is larger than E. Bryant and Trabasso made sure the children could recall these comparisons correctly and then tested the children's ability to combine these relations inferentially by asking them to compare B and D. All the children learned and remembered the initial four direct comparisons, although it took the four-year-olds more time to learn them than the five- and six-year-olds required. When asked to compare B and D, 78 percent of the four-year-olds, 88 percent of the five-year-olds, and 92 percent of the six-year-olds were able to make the correct inference, a result that is inconsistent with Piaget's belief that children cannot grasp the concept of transitivity until they are seven.

John Flavell (1977) agrees with Trabasso that experiments like this one show that children solve problems of transitivity earlier than has been commonly believed and by using a different cognitive process than had been supposed. Both children and adults may construct a mental image of the sticks and, when asked to compare lengths, as Flavell puts it, just "read off" the answer "as if the sticks were all lined up in an ordered row in front of their eyes." If they were trying to work out their answers using a step-by-step deductive process, widely separated pairs should take longer to compare. But they don't. Instead, questions about adjacent pairs in the middle of the series take longer to solve. The conclusion appears to be that these problems are solved essentially without the use of inference.

Egocentrism

According to Piaget, the baby first "defines" or knows objects in terms of his activity upon them and somewhat later differentiates himself from the objects of the world. This differentiation is not, however, complete in early childhood. Although at the sensory-motor and the perceptual level a very young child distinguishes himself from the rest of the world as an object in space and time, he may be egocentric in some ways. He sometimes thinks that other people see things the way he sees them and that they experience his own behavior, thought, and feelings about things.

Most evidence for the young child's egocentrism comes from tasks in which the child has to describe abstract forms or objects for a blindfolded person or in a way that someone in a different position might see them. It may be that children appear egocentric in such situations because their lack of information, their inadequate memory, or their still developing language skills are simply not up to describing the situation. When children are given tasks that fit their cognitive skills, their level of egocentrism appears to drop sharply. When Marilyn Shatz (1973) asked four- and five-year-olds to help her select presents for two-year-olds and for children their own age, the children selected toys appropriate to the recipients' ages. As one five-year-old put it, "I didn't pick this [a number-letter board] because he [the two-year-old] can't read."

In another study, Ellen Markman (1973) asked five-year-olds about their memory and motor skills and about those of two-year-olds and of teenagers, putting such questions to them as how many pictures they could remember or how far they could jump. The children's predictions showed they realized that two-year-olds cannot do as well as four-year-olds, but that teen-agers can do much better. In addition, the children indicated that although they thought that two-year-olds had a fair degree of motor skill, they doubted that two-year-olds could remember much, if anything. The five-year-olds were correct; the motor skills of two-year-olds are more advanced than their cognitive skills.

Robert Marvin, Mark Greenberg, and Daniel Mossler (1976) found that even children as young as four realize that a secret can be shared by those who see an event take place, but can't be shared by someone with closed eyes who could not have seen the event. These researchers (Mossler et al., 1976) also had two- to six-year-olds watch a videotaped story. A five-year-old child of the same sex as themselves sat at a table, stood up, walked over to his or her mother, and asked for a cookie. After each child watched the story, his or her mother entered the room and watched the tape with her child—but this time the sound was turned off. Afterward the child was asked if his or her mother knew the child in the story was sitting at a table and if she knew what the child wanted. The task seemed to be beyond the ability of the two- and three-year-olds, and only one of the three-year-olds answered both questions correctly. But 60 percent of the four-year-olds and 85 percent of the five-year-olds answered both questions correctly. They said their mothers knew the child was sitting at the table, but did not know what the child wanted. All the six-year-olds answered both questions correctly.

Another aspect of the young child's egocentrism is his apparent tendency to ascribe thoughts, feelings, and life itself to inanimate objects. This aspect of the child's thinking is reflected in many of his notions about the causes, purposes, and activities of such things as dreams, night and day, the sun, moon, and clouds, and mountains and rivers. Because the sun and moon appear to follow the young child around, he may believe that they do. And because he tends to think that other people see things the way he does, he may believe that others also perceive the sun and moon as following him around. The young child may also believe that the "purpose" of mountains and other worldly objects is their utility to him and to the world he knows. Thus, although the child is not egocentric when he recognizes the mountains as distinct physical objects, he seems to fall into egocentrism when it comes to ascribing meaning to objects in his world.

This level of thought affects the young child's view of reality. For example, Monique Laurendeau and Adrien Pinard (1962) used an interview procedure to investigate the ideas that four- to twelve-year-old children had about dreams.

Among the kinds of questions they asked children were:

> Where does a dream come from?
> Who makes the dreams come?
> While you are dreaming, where is your dream? Where does it go? In what place is it?
> What is a dream made of? Can you touch your dreams?
> Why not?
> Are dreams true?

These questions were meant to find out how well the children distinguished dreams from reality. Laurendeau and Pinard found a clear difference in the kinds of answers given by four- and five-year-olds on the one hand and seven-year-olds on the other. About half of the four-year-old children believed that dreams originate from a source external to the dreamer and that they take place in front of him, on the wall or on the pillow. Quite "logically," they often believed that their eyes were open while they dreamed, because one could not see a dream with one's eyes closed. But almost none of the seven-year-olds "reified," or made "real," their dreams. Their overwhelming response was that dreams both originate and occur inside the individual and cannot be seen by anyone else. Thus, in general, the four-year-olds failed to differentiate clearly separate levels of experience, the *truly* external and objective things that they see when awake from the *apparently* external but subjective visions they see in their dreams, whereas seven-year-olds easily made this distinction by substituting a new realistic understanding for an old belief. Some of the children, particularly six-year-olds, were in a transitional stage. Their explanations included both internal and external viewpoints about their dreams, even though at a strictly logical level the two explanations were contradictory.

This kind of reasoning is described as **precausal:** the child maintains that some events are either completely or partly caused by psychological, subjective factors. For example, he may believe that good dreams come to him because the dreams want to entertain him and that nightmares come because they want to punish him. But even three- and four-year-olds are probably more sensitive and aware of cause-and-effect relationships than they have been credited as being. They tend to associate two events on the basis of contiguity, so they may in some instances believe that causes follow effects.

Asking preschoolers about what causes the wind and rain, why rivers flow, how bicycles and other machines work is asking them to talk about things they have had little experience with (Gelman, 1978). Since they lack the knowledge, they make up animistic but plausible answers. When Michael Berzonsky (1971) questioned children about such remote events, asking "Why does the moon change shape?" they generally gave precausal answers. When asked about familiar events, such as tires going flat or flying kites, however, they usually gave a physical, mechanical answer.

Although most young children appear to take a relatively nonchalant attitude toward logical contradictions that arise when they hold conflicting explanations for an event, proper exploitation of these contradictions can spur their intellectual development. Several investigators have even hypothesized that logical inconsistencies are fundamental to cognitive growth. Presumably, contradictions involve cognitive conflict that motivates the child to seek new information and to reorganize the old, thereby clarifying his understanding of the world and reducing the tension.

REPRESENTATIONAL SKILLS

During the second year of life, the infant begins to use symbols, and this frees him somewhat from the constraints of the immediate world of experience. As noted in Chapter 7, among these symbols are language, imagery, imitation, and play. During the next few years, the young child uses symbols to represent an ever-widening range of objects and events. But imitation, language, play, and imagery are more than ways to represent previous experiences. They function as tools for the young child's understanding and intellectual mastery of his world, and become closely linked to his learning, reasoning, and acquisition of concepts.

Although symbol use develops extensively during this period, the young child continues to be an active explorer of the concrete, real world. His use of symbols to represent reality does not replace his natural curiosity about and exploration of the physical universe but supplements it. In fact, precisely because many of the concepts that young children acquire about people, events, and objects derive from their actual experiences, the concepts are often imperfect when measured by adult definitions.

Imitation

The infant's ability to imitate what he sees and hears advances markedly at the beginning of the second year. These imitations are symbols themselves, and provide evidence for the existence of other symbols, in picture or in sound, within the child's mind. These mental symbols, of course, cannot be observed, but adults can infer their presence from the child's actions.

When four-year-old David watches his father read a book and himself takes up a book, turns the pages, and pretends to read, his behavior stands for the actions of another. This kind of direct and immediate imitation of an action is a primitive symbol.

However, if David picks up a book the next day and imitates his father reading, then in addition to viewing his behavior as a symbol of reading at the level of action, we can infer that David has created a mental image of his father in the act of reading. This memory is a condensed, internal imitation, in thought rather than in action, and it allows the child to imitate some behavior long after the event. Deferred imitation is frequently observed among young children.

Drawing, which is discussed later in this chapter, is another form of imitation. In this case, the imitation is reduced to a graphic, schematic representation. The child depicts only certain features of a scene, and the drawing's resemblance to the original scene of father reading is less a "copy" than his physical imitation of the act was. In general, the symbolic nature of imitation makes it a milestone in intellectual development, because it forms the basis for human civilization: for language, mathematics, science, and the arts (Piaget, 1951).

Language

Language is the representational skill par excellence, and the relationship between language and thinking is close. If you had a tank with fifty octopuses and removed ten of them to give to a friend for her birthday, how many octopuses would remain in your tank? Correct—forty.

Notice that you solved the octopus problem in a second or two and without getting your hands wet. You use verbal symbols for things and actions to help you reason rapidly and efficiently. If you had a tank of octopuses and the time to move them, you could solve the problem by manipulating your octopuses, although the verbal solution

When children imitate the actions of others, their symbolic play both represents their previous experience and advances their understanding and intellectual mastery of the world. (*top:* © Sepp Seitz/Woodfin Camp & Assoc.; *bottom:* © Joel Gordon)

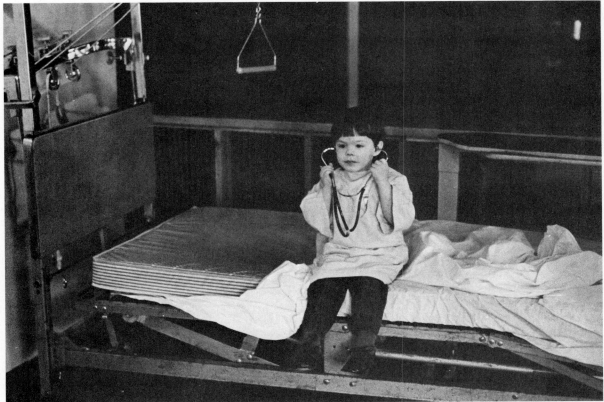

remains easier and quicker. We use language to refer not only to concrete entities and simple actions performed on them, but to complex events and intangible relationships as well. It is only because we possess well-developed symbol systems that we are able to consider and reason about things at complex and abstract levels. We can even reason about unicorns and time travel, about purely imaginary or hypothetical situations that never have occurred and probably never will.

Investigators have used a variety of approaches to look at the developmental relationship between language and thought in children. John Flavell, David Beach, and Jack Chinsky (1966) were interested in finding whether five-year-olds spontaneously use language to help them solve a simple memory problem. They showed children pictures of familiar objects, pointing to some of them, and later asked the children to point to the same pictures in the same order. The five-year-olds performed less well than the eight-year-olds. It appears that the children's difference in performance on this task related to differences in their use of language. A majority of the eight-year-old children repeated the names of the pictures that they had to remember. However, almost none of the five-year-olds spoke the names aloud. The younger children did not spontaneously use their knowledge of the words to help them remember the pictured objects. Thus, although the young child understands language and communicates with it, he does not automatically use it in all cases where it would be helpful.

Some investigators (Kendler, 1972) believe that language is critical to concept formation, and Marion Blank and Wagner Bridger (1964) have found at least one instance in which it is essential. They discovered that young children could not discriminate between one and two flashes of light unless they could attach verbal labels to them. When the experimenters told a child to "pick the one that goes like this," and pointed to the light flashing once, but "don't pick the one that goes like this," and pointed to the light flashing twice, a young child could not master the task. But a child of the same age who was told to pick the light that flashes one time but not the light that flashes two times easily learned to follow the experimenters' instructions.

Although a five-year-old may not use language on his own as an aid to memory, he does use it extensively to guide his behavior and to help him plan his actions. For example, young children often talk to themselves as they play. Indeed, a child may actually engage in a dialogue with himself as he draws a picture or builds a tower of blocks: "First I'll put this block over here and it will be the fence . . . no, put it there. OK . . . now this one goes here . . . and this one on top. Oh-oh, it's going to fall down . . . so put it next to the fence where it won't fall." In this case, the child's language is "thinking out loud."

The relationship between language and cognitive development has also been studied by Hans Furth, who has spent many years conducting research on the intellectual abilities of deaf children. Most children who are born deaf or who become deaf in infancy learn to speak their native language haltingly, if at all. However, intellectual development proceeds even among those who never learn a spoken language. According to Furth (1964, 1969), the thinking processes of deaf, linguistically deficient, elementary-school-aged children are generally similar to those of children who hear and are linguistically competent. On some types of cognitive tests, young deaf children do not perform as well as young hearing children, but Furth attributes this difference to the restricted experience and training of the very young deaf child, which becomes a less important factor when he enters school. Based on research with the deaf, Furth (1969) agrees with Piaget (1967) that intellectual development is considerably less dependent on linguistic ability than most people assume.

Although it may be possible to think, reason, and solve problems without a spoken language, some kind of symbol system is necessary for many activities. But language is only one of several symbol systems used by man. The deaf themselves frequently use sign language, and human beings also use visual imagery, pictorial representation, and written notational systems (such as the symbols of music or complex electronic circuits) to depict the world. People often think with these tools. However, some intelligent behavior can be acquired without any symbol system at all. Indeed, the infant himself acquires a substantial set of intelligent behaviors before he begins to use verbal symbols. It is probably safe to say, however, that language development and cognitive development go hand in hand, that they continually interact, and that both are primary tools for bringing order to the world.

No one formally tutors the young child in the

intricacies of either language or cognitive development. It is as if he gradually discovers their subtle features and comes to use them without being able to explain what he is doing. Many of his developmental tasks consist of acting upon the world to find out how it works and how it responds to his actions. Often, as we will see, this activity takes the form of play.

Play

Between the ages of two and seven, a substantial part of the child's waking hours are devoted to imaginative and other kinds of play (Herron and Sutton-Smith, 1971; Singer, 1973). In symbolic or make-believe play, a child engages in monologues or dialogues with imaginary playmates and plays games of pretense with them or with his flesh-and-blood friends. He uses his own internal imagery to create things that stand for something else. Children can become so involved in their world of make-believe that they may even react with fear to an imaginary character that has been assigned a threatening or terrifying role. One perceptive moralist stated that insensitively grabbing a toy boat from the young child who is its imaginary captain is an offense to the child comparable to depriving an adult admiral of the command of his ship.

Young children also play games with rules that specify constraints on permissible activity (for example, games of marbles). In addition, they also engage in mastery play, which focuses on dealing competently with challenging materials, such as in putting together the pieces of a puzzle or in riding a tricycle without losing one's balance (Singer, 1973).

The active play of young children appears closely related to their cognitive development, and children often use play to help them assimilate new information from the environment into their existing modes of understanding (Piaget, 1951;

Imaginative play, in which the child may talk to toys or invisible playmates, helps her assimilate new information into her framework of understanding. (© Linda Ferrer Rogers/Woodfin Camp & Assoc.)

Schachtel, 1959). In the world of make-believe, children can repeat and reflect upon statements or comments that they have heard adults make and that they do not initially understand. By repeating, reflecting, and transforming this information during make-believe, they integrate it into what they find to be a satisfying framework of understanding. For example, Jerome L. Singer (1973) tells of a three-and-one-half-year-old boy pretending to drive an ice-cream truck. He made the usual ding-a-ling noises and commented about the different kinds of ice cream he had for sale. When Singer asked him about this game, the boy replied, "I'm playing college." The boy, it seems, had heard his father tell about his work as an ice-cream truck driver while attending college. For this three-and-one-half-year-old, "father being in college" was a novel and incomprehensible piece of information. In his attempt to process it so that it would fit into his level of knowing, he put together his understandings of ice cream, driving, trucks, and selling and repeatedly played his game, which was somehow related to "being in college." After a while, he probably felt that he better understood "being in college."

Memory

The young child's memory—that is, his ability to code, store, and retrieve information—develops steadily from babyhood. At about four months, you will recall, the baby seems to realize that a moving object continues to exist when it is out of sight; at about six months, he seems to realize that he has only one mother; and at about eight months, he will search for an object that has been placed behind a screen. And, of course, his acquisition of language is even further proof of his growing memory.

Three- and four-year-old children frequently recognize and even recall events or objects after the lapse of several months or a year in which no reference to the event or object was made by others. Often the child recollects some aspect of the original scene, such as the color of a hat worn by a guest, that the parent hardly noticed. The young child's vocabulary also increases at a rapid pace, and remembering which words are associated with which objects demands considerable skill. In general, then, the young child remembers those things that he attends to, that he considers interesting or important, and that occur in the natural course of daily living.

There is evidence that the young child's memory for information also is enhanced when information is presented in a meaningful context. For example, Ann Brown (1976) showed three- and four-year-olds sets of four pictures. Some of the sets depicted a sequence of events; others showed unrelated pictures. Half of the sequences were presented in a scrambled order. The children easily remembered, either immediately or after a delay, the sequences that had been presented in order. They also had no difficulty remembering the scrambled sequences immediately, but did less well after a delay, suggesting that they couldn't store the scrambled sequences as well as the ordered ones. The kind of errors they made in recalling the scrambled sequences indicated that they found it difficult to ignore the inherent order that could be found in such sequences, for many of the children tended to recall scrambled items in an ordered sequence.

Young children are less likely to do well, or may fail, if they have to impose their own order on a sequence or retrieve a sequence they learned in a reversed order. If they are shown one picture at a time, instead of all four at once, they have a great deal of trouble recalling the sequence even if the pictures have been shown in the proper order. Other studies have shown that even when they can recognize or reconstruct the order of a story, they are likely to mix the events when they retell the story. And, even though they may be able to recall the path a lion took through a jungle, they find it difficult if not impossible to describe the path backward.

Using Graphic Symbols

During these early years, the young child also begins to use artistic media, representing objects, animals, and people with crayons, pencils, paints, and clay. Many investigators have noted a three-step sequence in young children's drawings of a person. At first the child tends to make a circular figure with few or no differentiating parts, such as the various organs and limbs. Somewhat later the drawings assume the shape of a tadpole: The head and limbs are attached directly, but the body has no trunk. Finally, the child draws a complete person with head, trunk, and attached limbs.

Claire Golomb (1973) attempted to discover whether a child's early imperfect drawings reflected limited cognitive competence or the explorations of a graphic medium by an inex-

When watching a child draw a crude human figure, it is easy to forget that all children's drawings are aspects of problem-solving. (© Jeffrey Foxx/Woodfin Camp & Assoc.)

Figure 11.5 Two examples of the scoring criteria used by Golomb to assess children's cognitive competence from the way they produce human figures using different media. (From Golomb, 1973)

The close interplay between language and cognitive development is shown in the coordination of thinking and talking aloud as a child plays. (from *Film Guide to Developmental Psychology Today Films*, © 1973 by CRM, Inc.)

perienced artist trying to create adequate symbols. Golomb reasoned that, if the child's early drawings reflect an imperfect analysis and synthesis of the human figure, this limited representation should appear uniformly across a wide variety of media, even when the child receives explicit instructions. On the other hand, if the youngster is experimenting with ways to represent a body that he perceives adequately, he will produce variations in the number and choice of parts and in the organization of the figure, according to the medium he is given. To test these opposing hypotheses, Golomb asked 105 children ranging in age from about three and one-half to seven and one-half years to represent the human body using a variety of media. Older children produced more differentiated and better-organized figures than younger children did, but the overall pattern of results showed that the media and the investigator's instructions had a definite effect on the nature of the figure that children constructed. Golomb interpreted these findings as supporting the view that the young child is an inventor of symbols rather than a confused and incompetent copier of what he sees, and she believes that the inferior performance of younger children may be due in part to the younger child's inexperience in using artistic media and his more playful attitude toward the symbols he creates.

The charm and playfulness of children's art may keep us from realizing that all features of children's drawing are aspects of problem solving. In fact, the course of cognitive development can be traced in the increasing complexity of their graphic symbols. As Jacqueline Goodnow (1977) points out, "graphic work is truly 'visible thinking.'"

SOCIAL INTERACTION AND COGNITION

One aspect of intelligent thinking is being able to consider an idea from more than one perspective. As young David interacts with his family and his friends, he is exposed to different outlooks, and these experiences affect his intellectual development. Often a child learns that he has misunderstood a concept when others correct him by refusing to accept his view. Young children often engage in vehement debates as each pits his understandings against those of his peers. Such debates spur reflection and, through cognitive conflict, ultimately modify a child's understanding.

For example, two five-year-olds argued over whether cave men are real. The young believer said, "My father's father's father's father's father was a cave man." The other remained skeptical. The believer retorted, "You go home and ask your mother if cave men are real. She will tell you to go ask your father, and he will tell you that they are real!" In view of the seriousness and vehemence attending the dispute, the skeptic probably asked his father and either modified or clarified his understanding. Were it not for the social interaction, the child may never have questioned his belief that cave men are imaginary. But his argument probably led to a more differentiated concept: Cave men were real long ago, but they are no longer real today.

Social interaction also appears to affect a young child's comprehension of the rules that govern children's games. Some time ago, Piaget (1932) found that young children tended to believe that the rules of a marble game were fixed and absolute rather than conventions for play that could be changed by mutual consent of the players. The children in this study lived in homes where the parent-child relationship was one-sided and authoritarian. Children were not asked for their views, nor did they receive explanations when they were told how to behave. As they got older, the children interacted more with peers and less with parents, and they played the game according to more flexible rules. As they interacted more with other children, they had greater opportunities to assert their own points of view, to have them challenged, and to hear diverse opinions. The younger children's rigid interpretation of rules may have been due, in part, to the limited and one-sided nature of their social interaction, whereas the more flexible and realistic rule comprehension of the older children may have been affected by the cooperative nature of their social interactions. Thus many kinds of social interactions have increasingly important effects on the child's developing cognition.

SUMMARY

1. As young children's perceptual skills develop, they isolate and relate more distinctive features of the objects and events in their world. Their ability to coordinate the information that they receive through their separate senses also improves dramatically as a result of greater experience, more sophisticated ways of exploring, and changes in cognitive understanding.

2. Children's concepts of the world continue to depend on which aspects of it get their attention. As in infancy, previous experience as well as certain physical features of objects and events are most likely to determine what a given child will attend to. Focusing and shifting attention are likely to vary with the complexity of a task, its rewards, and the effectiveness of instruction.

3. During early childhood, children continue to fit newly observed phenomena into their understanding and to modify their concepts of the world. They may have difficulty recognizing or imagining that certain perceptual changes do not actually alter given aspects of the physical world, as in a conservation task; but this apparent difficulty is sometimes due to specific features of the task. Children's thinking gradually changes as they add new examples of concepts that they already know, discover which attributes define a concept and which do not, learn that an example of a concept may possess some but not all of several attributes, and find that some concepts are based on different and complex kinds of relationships. The degree of egocentrism displayed by young children is likely to vary according to the requirements of a situation.

4. The cognitive skills involved in imitation, language, play, and memory continue to fulfill a major role in children's construction of conceptual networks of interrelated ideas about objects and events. Symbolizing and imagining supplement rather than replace their natural curiosity and exploration of the real world. Increasingly, advances in these skills become closely linked to advances in a child's ability to learn, reason, and acquire concepts.

5. During early childhood social interaction appears to have a strong effect on children's cognitive development. Through their interactions with family members and age-mates, children are exposed to different viewpoints that may change their own understanding.

CHAPTER 12
Language: Understanding and Using

PROPERTIES OF LANGUAGE

THE CHILD'S AWARENESS OF GRAMMAR
Observation
Overregularization

TESTING COMPREHENSION OF GRAMMAR

RULES AND PERFORMANCE LIMITATIONS

LANGUAGE AND COGNITIVE DEVELOPMENT
Learning and Parental Teaching
Semantics and Communication

LANGUAGE FUNCTIONING AND ENVIRONMENT
Social-Class Differences
Special Schooling
Dialects and Language Development

SUMMARY

On a beautiful spring day, six-year-old Lauren and her grandmother decide to walk back to Lauren's house after visiting a neighbor. After they have gone about a block, Lauren looks back over her shoulder and sees that her mother and father, who were also at the neighbor's house, have started the family car and have pulled out of the driveway. "Hurry, Grammy, hurry!" she calls. "They're gaining on us. They're gaining on us." Then she stops, looks up at her grandmother, and says, "What does 'gaining on us' mean?" Although a child may use a word in its proper context, one cannot always be certain that she knows its precise meaning. Once children learn the basic structure of their native language, they still have to master the intricacies of a vocabulary that is replete with idioms, metaphors, and assigns more than one meaning to words.

Between the ages of one and one-half and four years, normal children all over the world master the basic grammar of one or more of the world's thousands of different languages. This ability of a small child to learn the complex structure of a language is remarkable. Moreover, each child is exposed to a different sample of the language; that is, children like Lauren and Matt hear a personally unique set of sentences from the adults and children that they interact with in their early years. Yet all children exposed to one language or dialect of that language learn to understand other speakers of that language and end up using the same pronunciation, grammar, and vocabulary as the other members of their speech community. This means that each child in a speech community arrives at the same basic linguistic rules. As stated in Chapter 8, this process appears to be a result of the child's ability to figure out the underlying structure of human language.

When young children and their parents move to a country where a different language is spoken, the children learn to understand and speak the new language with an ease and rapidity that their parents cannot hope to equal. With time, the young immigrant or visitor to a foreign land will sound like a native speaker of the new language, but his parents rarely, if ever, achieve perfect mastery of the same new language. The saying "so simple a child can do it" is thus turned around. How does the child do it?

In Chapter 8 we brought the child to the threshold of grammatical development. We left him at the point where he could make simple two-word sentences, using the universal linguistic devices of intonation, inflection, and word order to convey basic meanings through combinations of words. In this chapter we will examine some of his information-processing abilities in greater detail and find that young children tend to impose regularities on language beyond those that exist. We will look at the methods that psycholinguists and developmental psychologists use to test a child's awareness of the rules of his language. The role of learning in language acquisition and the dependence of language on cognitive development will be discussed, and we will examine the influence of socioeconomic and ethnic differences on language development. When you finish this chapter, you should have a general understanding of how the child who could speak only in two-word utterances rapidly becomes a competent master of his complicated language.

PROPERTIES OF LANGUAGE

All languages have a large but finite vocabulary of words whose meanings must be learned. You will recall that semanticity, or meaningfulness, is an important property of language. In Chapter 8 we suggested that the child learns the features of meaning for each word in his vocabulary, gradually refining his meanings as his experiences broaden. One cannot ordinarily guess the meaning of a word from its sound, and even after the child adds a word to his vocabulary, its use cannot be divorced from context. Most words have more than one meaning: "meet" can be used in "The swimming meet has been postponed" and "We meet on Saturday"; "light," in "This is a light color" and "This suitcase is light when empty" and "Turn on the light." Some aspects of word formation are productive; for example, by using affixes, a person can compose new meanings from words he already knows: "sad," "sadness"; "begin," "beginning"; "operate," "operation."

It is the *syntax* of a language—the underlying rules that determine the form of sentences—that provides for the richest expression of creativity. As noted earlier, syntax makes it possible to combine individual words into an unlimited number of sentences. People do not understand sentences by recognizing the precise sequence of words. Rather, they understand sentences because they know the rules of combination that make up the syntax of a language. Because people cannot possibly memorize all possible sentences of their language (the number is potentially infinite), each must learn in childhood the basic rules for making and understanding sentences.

At first it may seem surprising that the number and variety of possible sentences in a language is unlimited. But consider, for a moment, the sentences in this book. Although they are not difficult to understand, probably only a few are exact repetitions of sentences you have seen or heard before. Each is a novel event. You will not find the last sentence "Each is a novel event" anywhere else in this book; and the same is true of almost every sentence you speak or hear.

This fact of linguistic creativity, or *productivity,* makes special demands on a psychological explanation of how language is learned (Chomsky, 1972). Most combinations of words do not work. If the last sentence had been written as "words most work of not combinations do," you would not have understood it. Although a child hears sentence after sentence, he ends up knowing not a list of sentences but the rules for making sentences, and these rules enable him to eliminate combinations that his language does not permit. Because these rules are not visible or audible in the speech he hears, he cannot imitate them or directly copy them. In fact, not even the most skillful linguist can state all the rules for the English language, and certainly no parent ever tries to teach his three-year-old the rules of English language production. Because linguistic structures cannot be given to the child from outside, he must construct them in his own head, applying his basic linguistic capacities to the sounds and sights and experiences of his world (Clark and Clark, 1977). Psychologists and psycholinguists are just beginning to understand how this complex cognitive feat is possible.

The third essential property of language set forth in Chapter 8, *displacement,* has been present in the child's language ever since he could ask for a cookie that was in the kitchen or for his father who was at the office (R. Brown, 1973). As the child matures, his language will include increasingly remote elements, and he will speak of events that occurred hundreds of years before and of such abstractions as the elements of formal logic.

THE CHILD'S AWARENESS OF GRAMMAR

Psychologists studying language development discover the facts of early language acquisition by observing the child's natural speech and by studying his attempts to systematize, or simplify, language.

Observation

When observing young children, psycholinguists use indirect evidence to infer a child's knowledge of rules. Children sometimes correct their own speech; for example, Lauren catching a glimpse of herself in a mirror might say, "I see me in the mirror . . . I see myself in the mirror" or, on another occasion, "I seed . . . saw it." Each time a child corrects his own language errors, he shows that he believes certain combinations of words are incorrect, thereby revealing that he has a formal system of grammar (W. Miller and Ervin, 1970). But such instances, though revealing, are relatively rare and give information on only a few scattered aspects of language. To discover children's knowledge of language regularities, one must examine the evidence from large samples of children's speech, noting the sets of well-formed utterances, the types of omissions and errors, and, most important, the sets of utterances children produce that they probably have not heard.

Roger Brown, Courtney Cazden, and Ursula Bellugi-Klima (1968) have studied the speech development of three children, whom they call Adam, Eve, and Sarah. At the start of their study, Adam and Sarah were twenty-seven months old, and Eve, eighteen months. Adam and Sarah were studied until they were five years old; Eve was studied for nine months (at which time she moved away). In those nine months, however, Eve had already passed far beyond the stage of development that Adam and Sarah had reached at the beginning of the study (see Figure 12.1), demonstrating that there is considerable difference among children in the ages at which they begin to combine words and in their rate of progress through the levels of linguistic development.

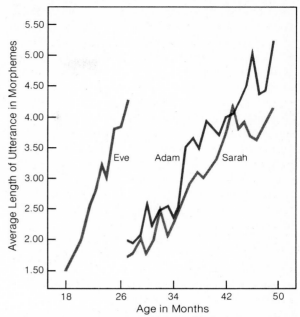

Figure 12.1 As Eve, Adam, and Sarah grew, the average length of their utterances increased. Morphemes are small linguistic units of speech that have definable meanings. (Adapted from Brown, 1973)

Brown and his colleagues selected these children because they were just beginning to combine words into two-word utterances and because their speech was clear and easy to understand. The researchers visited Adam and Eve at two- or three-week intervals, spending two hours each time; they visited Sarah every week for a half hour. During these visits, they recorded everything the children said and everything that was said to the children, and they kept notes on the objects and actions that accompanied speech. A full record of the contexts in which the children spoke was necessary because children often rely on the nonlinguistic context of their utterances to convey part of their messages.

Between visits, Brown and his co-workers met in a research seminar to discuss the state of the children's development and to suggest experiments. For example, at one point Adam would sometimes pluralize nouns and sometimes not. Someone suggested that he be tested to see whether he could distinguish a correct form from an incorrect form. On the next visit, a researcher asked, "Adam, which is right, 'two shoes' or 'two shoe'?" His answer, produced with enthusiasm, was "Pop go the weasel!" This response, which is known among psycholinguists as the "pop-goes-the-weasel-phenomenon," demonstrates that the young child is not a model experimental subject. Only special techniques can reveal the details of what he knows about his language.

But Brown's recordings over this crucial period in language acquisition produced valuable information, and the techniques of observation and analysis developed by Brown and other researchers have become the standard first phase of investigation in studies of languages other than English (Ferguson and Slobin, 1973). The following dialogue between Eve and her mother, when Eve was about two, gives some idea of what natural conversation can show about the nature of early childhood speech:

Eve: Have that?
Mother: No, you may not have it.
Eve: Mom, where my tapioca?
Mother: It's getting cool. You'll have it in just a minute.

. . .

Eve: You gonna watch me eat my lunch?
Mother: Yeah, I'm gonna watch you eat your lunch.
Eve: I eating it.
Mother: I know you are.
Eve: It time Sarah take a nap.
Mother: It's time for Sarah to have some milk, yeah. And then she's gonna take a nap and you're gonna take a nap.
Eve: And you?
Mother: And me too, yeah. (Bellugi, 1970, page 33)

Notice that both participants in the dialogue make statements, requests, and negative sentences and ask questions. However, interesting differences appear between the speech of the adult and the child. Certain elements that are characteristically and systematically missing from Eve's speech are present in her mother's sentences. Eve's mother uses auxiliary verbs (forms of *to be, to do,* and so forth) wherever English syntax requires them. These grammatical elements are not present in the child's speech. Eve, for example, says "It time," whereas her mother says "It's time." The child's speech, although understandable, lacks the required auxiliary verb.

Within three months, Eve's language showed a dramatic change. Compare her sentence structures in the previous dialogue with sentences in this dialogue:

Mother: Shut the door, we won't hear her then.
Eve: Then Fraser won't hear her too. Where he's going?

. . .

Eve: Could I get some other piece of paper?
Mother: You ask Fraser.
Eve: Could I use this one?
Mother: I suppose so.
Eve: Is Fraser goin' take his pencil home when he goes?
Mother: Yes, he is.
Eve: Then we don't see him.
Mother: Nope, probably not. He'll share the paper with you while he's here.

. . .

Eve: Now let me draw you a lady. I can't. I not know . . . make one.
Mother: You don't know how to make one? You look at Fraser's lady and see if you can make one.
Eve: I can't. I think I have tear one and I think I can write one. (pages 33–34)

Now Eve uses auxiliary verbs in negatives, questions, and statements. Her sentences are also longer and more complex. She can join simple sentences together with words like "when" and "and." She still makes errors, of course, and some of these errors reveal that she is beginning to figure out the rules of English. For example, she says, "Then Fraser won't hear her too," whereas an adult would say, "Then Fraser won't hear her either." There is an odd rule in English that changes "too" to "either" in negative sentences (it is correct to say "Fraser will hear her too"). Eve has not figured out this rule for negative statements, but her use of "too" indicates that she understands the general function carried out by both "too" and "either," even though she does not use "either" in negative statements.

Overregularization

Developmental psychologists and psycholinguists are especially interested in a child's speech errors, because grammatical errors reveal the extent to which a child has control of certain language rules. Many errors that children make can be looked on as their attempts to make the language more regular or systematic than it actually is. For example, Eve's use of "too" in both positive and negative utterances is a regularization of adult English, which requires one to use "too" in positive sentences and "either" in negative. You will recall that, as children build vocabulary, they gradually move from a generalization such as "bow-wow" for all animals to a separate word for each species. Their syntax also suffers from overgeneralization, because they force each utterance to follow the rules they have figured out. Children's errors in their use of the past tense of verbs and the plural forms of nouns most clearly reveal overregularization in English.

English verbs, in most cases, change form from present to simple past tense: "I *walk* to school; I *walked* to school." Although a few verbs do not change their form to express the past ("hit," "hit"), the regular way to form the past for English verbs is to add *-ed:* "walk," "walked"; "ask," "asked." However, many common verbs form their past tense in an irregular manner: "go," "went"; "come," "came"; "drive," "drove"; "break," "broke." Investigators in the field of child language have found that some children learn a number of these irregular past forms as separate words at an early age and produce correct sentences: "It broke"; "Daddy went out"; "I fell." Often they use these correct past tense forms for many months. After a while, however, children discover the rule for forming regular past tenses, and the irregular forms they had correctly produced may disappear from their speech, to be replaced by overregularized forms. The child now may say: "It breaked"; "Daddy goed out"; "I falled." Indeed, these overregularizations persist into the elementary-school years, and it is hard to believe that a six-year-old who persistently says "It breaked" said "It broke" when he was two.

What looks like regression is actually a sign of progress in the child's analysis of language. Clearly, children have not heard the overregularized forms from their parents, and such forms occur even in the speech of first-born children, who have no older siblings to learn the incorrect forms from. Children construct such overregularized verbs to conform with the regularities they have noticed in the speech of others. And so a change from "went" to "goed" is not evidence that Lauren is regressing; on the contrary, it indicates that she has, on her own, discovered a regular pattern in the language and is using it in her speech.

During these periods of overregularization, the child's speech sometimes seems remarkably impervious to gentle efforts at correction. The following conversation, reported by Jean Berko Gleason (1967), may serve as an example:

Child: My teacher holded the baby rabbits and we patted them.
Mother: Did you say your teacher held the baby rabbits?
Child: Yes.
Mother: What did you say she did?

Child: She holded the baby rabbits and we patted them.
Mother: Did you say she held them tightly?
Child: No, she holded them loosely.

Although his mother substitutes the correct verb form twice in this short dialogue, the child persists in repeating "held" as "holded," tenaciously clinging to his own linguistic structures. Apparently, regularity heavily outranks previous practice, reinforcement, and immediate imitation of adult forms in its influence on children. The child seeks regularity and is deaf to exceptions (Bellugi, 1970).

The formation of plurals is another area in which children tend to overregularize. For example, the English language has several ways to indicate whether a speaker is talking about one or more objects. If you pay close attention to the way that you pronounce the plural, you will find that there are three regular plural sounds in English: *s* (as in "roots," "books"), *z* (as in "barns," "bees"), and *ez* (as in "horses," "matches"). A child must learn the rules for using these three plural endings, depending on the final sound of each word. English also has some irregular plural forms, many of them common words: "foot," "feet"; "mouse," "mice"; "man," "men"; "child," "children." These irregular forms, like irregular verb past-tense forms, must be learned as separate vocabulary items.

The linguistic context in English does not always indicate whether the speaker is considering one object or more than one. If someone says "Point to the sheep," it would be as correct to point to one sheep as to many. Based on this fact, Jean Berko (1958) constructed a way to test the child's knowledge of the rules for forming plurals from several singular nouns.

For the test, an investigator shows a child some object for which there is no name. (Large stuffed toys of unfamiliar shape, like those used in one test, are shown in the accompanying photograph.) The investigator names these objects with possible but nonexistent English words. She presents the child with one object and says, for example, "Here is a wug." Then she puts down another, similar object next to it and says, "Now there is another wug. There are two _____?" The child obligingly fills in the nonexistent but regular item, "wugs," pronouncing it *wugz* if he knows the appropriate rule for forming plurals in English.

From these tests and from observations of free speech, researchers have found that the child who

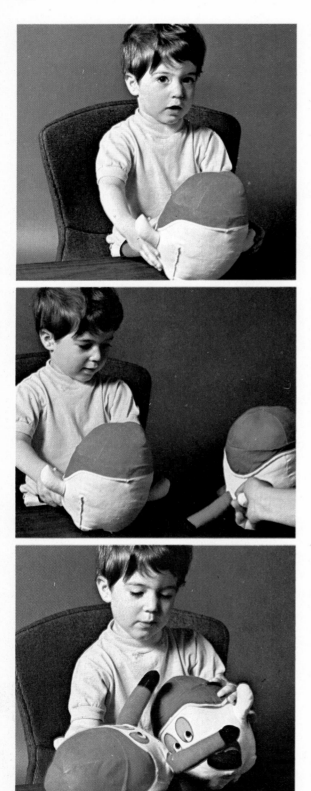

has been correctly using some irregular plural forms ("feet," "men," "mice") may, for a time, overgeneralize his newly discovered rules of formation and say "foots," "mans," "mouses," another example of the kind of overregularization that appears in the child's use of verbs. A child may even learn the irregular form but apply the plural rule anyway, saying "feets," "mens," "mices."

TESTING COMPREHENSION OF GRAMMAR

The ways in which a child comprehends speech give the psycholinguist additional evidence of the child's understanding of syntax. When a child responds correctly to a command or question, his parents often believe that he understands all or most of the language that they address to him. Susan's mother may say to her small child, who can speak only two or three words at a time, "Go over to that chair and bring me my knitting." When Susan does so, her mother may be impressed by Susan's apparent understanding of a lengthy command. However, Susan needs to understand only a word or two of the adult sentence ("knitting" and perhaps "chair") to be able to comply. In addition, it is likely that her mother looked in the direction of the chair on which the knitting was prominently displayed; she may have pointed to it and then held out her hand. The linguistic and environmental context of speech addressed to the child is usually rich with cues that aid in understanding, just as the contextual cues of one-word utterances permit adults to interpret the speech of toddlers.

To test adequately for a child's comprehension of some grammatical rule, it is necessary to eliminate all cues of intonation, gesture, or facial expression. In the preceding situation, for example, a tester, with hands folded in her lap, might look at Susan (not at the object she wants her to bring) and might ask her first, "Bring my knitting to me." Then, after returning the knitting to its original

In this singular-plural test, (*top*) the child is handed an object for which he has no name and is told, "Here is a wug." (*middle*) Then another is put down, and the child is asked to finish the sentence "Now there are two
_____. (*bottom*) If the child knows the rule for forming plurals, he responds with "wugs." (William MacDonald)

To test a young child's comprehension of active/passive sentences, (*top*) a car and truck are placed before her on a table. (*middle*) When told, "Show me the truck follows the car," she responds correctly to this active sentence. (*bottom*) After the vehicles are placed before her again, she is told, "Show me the car is followed by the truck." This time she responds incorrectly to the passive sentence. (William MacDonald)

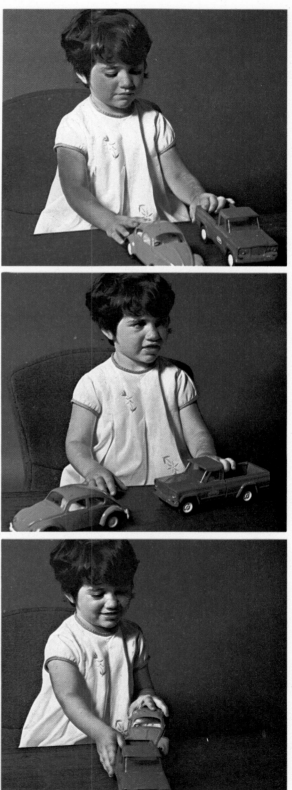

position, she would ask Susan, "Bring me to my knitting." Perhaps she would try other variations as well: "Me to knitting my bring" and just "Knitting, please." The point is to establish carefully controlled conditions that test the child's knowledge of grammatical rules.

Careful testing of this sort reveals that children often develop their own simple rules for figuring out the meanings of sentences, although these strategies sometimes lead the child into misinterpreting some kinds of sentences. A good example comes from studies of children's comprehension of *active* and *passive* sentences. Children hear many examples of simple declarative sentences, each containing an actor, an action, and the object of that action: "Mommy is eating soup"; "Jane feeds her doll"; "Alfred loves Suzette." In each of these sentences the relationship between the actor ("Alfred"), action ("loves"), and object of the action ("Suzette") is expressed by word order.

Colin Fraser, Ursula Bellugi, and Roger Brown (1963) have developed some tests that reveal a child's comprehension of grammar. In one of their tests, the child sees several pictures and must point to the one described by the sentence he hears. For example, he is given a pair of pictures, one in which a dog chases a cat and another in which a cat chases a dog. The child is asked to point to the picture that shows "The cat chases the dog" or "The dog chases the cat." Another technique, developed by Janellen Huttenlocher, Karen Eisenberg, and Susan Strauss (1968) and by Thomas Bever (1970), asks the child to act out sentences such as "The car follows the truck" when given a toy truck and a toy car to manipulate. Most children of about three perform well on these tests, and they also use the correct word order in their own speech. But tests of simple active sentences alone do not make clear what sort of sentence-interpretation rule the child follows.

Not all English sentences place the actor before the verb and the object of the action after the verb.

In *passive* sentences, for example, these relationships are reversed. Compare "The truck was broken by John" and "John broke the truck." The two sentences have the same meaning, but the order of major elements is different. In both sentences, it is clear that John is the actor and the truck the object, because toy trucks cannot break boys. But in sentences such as "The car follows the truck" and "The truck is followed by the car," you must know more than simple word order if you are to figure out what is doing the following and what is being followed.

When a four-year-old's understanding of passive sentences is tested by showing him pictures or by asking him to demonstrate, for example, "The truck is followed by the car," he is seldom correct. In fact, most four-year-olds point to the wrong picture or carry out the opposite action each time.

Thomas Bever (1970) has studied the development of children's interpretive strategies for such active and passive sentences and has shown that children go through several strategies before they arrive at the complex rules of adult English grammar. For example, he gave children between the ages of two and four a toy horse and a toy cow and asked them to act out sentences such as the following:

1. The *cow kisses* the horse.
2. It's the *cow* that *kisses* the horse.
3. It's the horse that the *cow kisses.*
4. The horse *is kissed by* the cow. (pages 303–308)

Surprisingly, two-year-olds act out the first three sentence types correctly, but their performance is random on the fourth (passive) sentence. They are as likely to have the horse kiss the cow as to have the cow kiss the horse.

Bever suggests that, if two-year-olds hear a noun and a verb in a row, they will assume that the noun is the actor. This noun-verb sequence is "a kind of primitive *gestalt*"—a perceptual unit that is heard as meaning "actor-action." But if another word or words interrupt this simple sequence, as in the passive Sentence 4, the strategy fails, and the children make a random choice of actor.

Four-year-olds, according to Bever, have developed a different strategy, in which they hear the first noun in a sentence as the actor and the noun following the verb as the object of action. This strategy leads them astray on sentences like "It's the horse that the cow kisses," and they tend to pick the horse as the actor. In addition, following

such an interpretation rule, they process a passive sentence as if it were an active sentence with some extra, uninterpretable parts. Thus they consistently reverse the interpretation of passives and act out Sentence 4 by having the horse kiss the cow.

Bever's demonstration of children's strategies for interpreting sentences indicates that children do not progress directly toward adult grammar but rather construct and discard a variety of provisional grammars as they go along. As a result of these changing strategies, sentences that are correctly interpreted at one age (for example, the two-year-olds' correct understanding of "It's the horse that the cow kisses") may be misinterpreted at a later age.

RULES AND PERFORMANCE LIMITATIONS

Children who are just beginning to speak seem to operate under severe performance limitations and can produce only one- or two-word utterances. Recall from Chapter 8 Lois Bloom's example of the one-year-old girl who, when trying to get a button out of her pocket, said "button" and "pocket" as two separate one-word utterances but could not put them together into a two-word utterance. And a child at the two-word stage could say "Daddy throw," "Throw ball," and "Daddy ball," yet could not say "Daddy throw ball" in a single utterance. At these very early phases of language development, the limitations on a child's performance seem to be simply a matter of the number of words. Later, however, the limitations seem to be a matter of the number of rules or grammatical operations that a child can carry out when producing a single sentence. Performance limitations at these stages can, therefore, give additional indirect evidence of the child's grasp of linguistic rules.

A study by Ursula Bellugi (1968) provides a good illustration of how a child's ability to form questions is limited by his facility with particular linguistic rules. In English, in order to ask a question that can be answered yes or no, the order of the subject of the sentence and the auxiliary verb is inverted. For example, you may say "He can swim" but ask "Can he swim?" If you want to ask a specific kind of question (for example, a question about place or time or manner or cause of swimming), you must insert a specific question word at the beginning of the sentence and then invert the order of subject and auxiliary. For example, you ask "Where can he swim?" "When can he swim?" and so forth.

Children, however, frequently ask questions such as "Where he can swim?" "What he can ride in?" "Why he's doing it?" and the like. In such questions, the child has correctly placed the question word at the beginning of the sentence but has failed to invert subject and auxiliary. However, the same child is able to invert subject and auxiliary in a simple yes-or-no question. For example, the child who asks "What he can ride in?" can also ask, correctly, "Can he ride in a truck?" Apparently a child can either insert the specific question word or invert subject and auxiliary, but cannot carry out both operations in the same sentence.

At the next level of development, the child can handle two operations simultaneously and will correctly produce questions such as "What can he ride in?" The performance limitation, however, still blocks the application of a third rule to sentence production. For example, if the question is negative, the child appropriately attaches the negative element to the auxiliary in simple yes-or-no questions, producing forms such as "Can't he go out?" He can also invert subject and auxiliary, asking questions such as "Why can he go out?"

But the child can handle only limited complex-

ity at this point. Combining negation, inversion, and a question-word in the same sentence appears to be too much for him to handle, as illustrated in the following example:

Adult: Adam, ask the Old Lady where she can find some toys.
Child: Old Lady, where can you find some toys?
Adult: Adam, ask the Old Lady why she can't run.
Child: Old Lady, why you can't run? (Bellugi, 1968, page 40)

Clearly then, the child regularly applies each of these three grammatical operations—insertion of the question word, inversion of the subject and auxiliary, and negation—to his speech production, but at a certain level of development he can apply no more than two of these operations in the same utterance.

By the time they are about four years old, normal children have mastered most of the grammar of their language, although they will continue to add to their knowledge of complex syntactical structures (Palermo and Molfese, 1972). This seems to be true regardless of the language they are learning and regardless of the setting in which they have been exposed to it (Slobin, 1975). They spend the school years in learning details, such as irregular endings, complex vocabulary items, and involved sentence constructions, as the rest of this chapter will show. But the basic rules of word

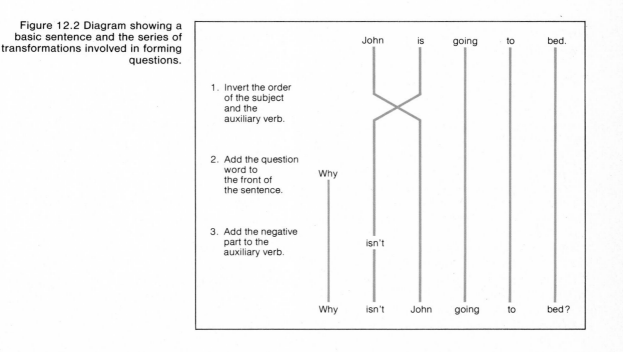

Figure 12.2 Diagram showing a basic sentence and the series of transformations involved in forming questions.

1. Invert the order of the subject and the auxiliary verb.

2. Add the question word to the front of the sentence.

3. Add the negative part to the auxiliary verb.

order and of forming proper endings are well sta-
bilized by kindergarten age, as are the rules for
question formation and for negation.

LANGUAGE AND COGNITIVE DEVELOPMENT

Asking whether language is the result of learning
or of neural maturation is like asking whether a
person's intelligence is the result of environment or
heredity. As noted in Chapter 3, both nature and
nurture are important. Donald Hebb, Wallace
Lambert, and G. R. Tucker (1971) have pointed
out that posing such a question is like wondering
whether the length or the width of a field contributes most to its area. Before a child can handle his
native language, he must have certain nearly universal human experiences, and he first must reach
the appropriate level of cognitive development.

Learning and Parental Teaching

Of course, an American child learns the rules of
English, a Russian child learns those of Russian,
and so on; a child can learn only the particular
language that he is exposed to. Although some
psychologists stress the role of imitation and reinforcement, by word and by deed, in the child's
learning of language rules (Staats, 1971), many
psycholinguists stress instead the creativity or productivity of syntax. They point out that the child
develops rules that allow him to produce and interpret an endless variety of novel sentences. A
child cannot imitate rules, they say, because he
hears only sentences.

A child's sentences are often different from
adult sentences. When a child like Matt says "All-
gone sticky" after washing his hands or asks
"What he can ride in?" or says "I seed two
mouses," he is not imitating precise forms that he
has heard others use. Instead he is generalizing,
applying his grammatical rules to his store of
words. Indeed, children seem unable to comprehend speech except in terms of their own level of
grammar. Recall the child who persisted in saying
"holded," even though the experimenter repeatedly said "held." David McNeill (1966) gives another example of a child's tendency to imitate only
in terms of his own grammatical rules:

Child: Nobody don't like me.
Mother: No, say "nobody likes me."
Child: Nobody don't like me.
[Eight repetitions of this dialogue follow.]

Mother: No, now listen carefully; say *"nobody likes
me."*
Child: Oh! Nobody don't like*s* me. (page 69)

Although the child picks up the elements of language from the speech he hears, he must reassem-
ble them each time he speaks.

A great deal of learning about the nature and
use of language occurs during its development,
and a young child may practice different combinations of words, actively testing the language. Ruth
Weir (1962) set up a tape recorder near her son's
bed and for several nights recorded the solitary
talk of her two-year-old at bedtime. The transcript
reveals the boy working at the language, trying out
different nouns, pronouns, adjectives, and verbs:

> On the blanket—Under the blanket. . . . Berries—
> Not berries. . . . Too hot—Not too hot:
>
>   .   .   .
>
> Can bite—Bite—Have a bite. . . . Broke the vac-
> uum—The broke—Get some broke—Alice broke
> the baby fruit. (page 19)

Some concepts can be learned only in terms of
other words. Neither a child's sensory-motor responses to the questions of others, such as touching
a pair of boots when someone asks "Why is the
boy wearing boots?" nor his own pointing and
gesturing will express concepts like "how" and
"why." As Marion Blank (1974) makes clear, it
may be that young children learn the meanings of
"why" and "how" only by producing the terms
before they understand them and by using the
words over and over in numerous situations. Once
children learn to ask "why" and "how" questions,
however, they have automatically forced adults
into the role of teachers.

Although in the nobody-likes-me dialogue a
mother is actively trying to correct her child's
speech, attempts at formal language teaching like
these are rare. Most of the time, parents are too
busy interacting with children to pay much attention to their grammar. If three-year-old Lauren
asks, "Why cause horses can't fly?" her parent will
answer the question instead of pointing out that
her grammar is faulty. Indeed, communication can
be carried on remarkably well regardless of the
child's grammar level, as the conversations in this
chapter have shown.

Roger Brown, Courtney Cazden, and Ursula
Bellugi-Klima (1968) examined a large body of
tape-recorded interactions between adults and
children and found no evidence that conscious

Although parents do not consciously instruct their children, the way they change their speech in speaking to young children makes them active teachers of language. (© Joel Gordon)

teaching on the part of parents plays any serious role in grammatical development. They noted that parents often corrected gross errors in a child's choice of words, and, once in a while, the parents corrected a pronunciation error. But most often it was the truth of an utterance that determined a parent's approval. When Eve wanted to say that her mother was a girl and produced "He a girl," her mother replied, "That's right." But when Sarah said, with perfect grammar, "There's the animal in the farmhouse," her mother corrected her, because the building was a lighthouse; and when Adam stated, "Walt Disney comes on on Tuesday," he met with disapproval, because the Disney television program appears on Sunday. Truth, not correct grammar, is more likely to evoke verbal reinforcement from parents. But words are not the only reinforcement that parents give. Whenever a child successfully communicates and his language gets him a cookie, an open door, a glass of water, or some other thing he wants, his verbal behavior is reinforced. The requirement for reinforcement, however, is still intelligibility, not grammatical precision.

Although parents do not consciously instruct their children in grammar, they are very active in helping them learn language. Recent studies have shown that when primary caregivers speak to young children, they become active teachers of language even if they are not aware of it. They speak more slowly and use simple sentences. To slow their speech, they insert pauses. Almost all utterances addressed to children of two are followed by pauses, compared with about 75 percent of ut-

terances addressed to children aged four to six, and about 25 percent of utterances addressed to adults (Broen, 1972). Parents also use very short sentences, replace difficult consonants with easy ones, substitute nouns for pronouns, and repeat words, phrases, or whole sentences.

Another feature of the speech adults use with small children is its expressiveness. Pitch and tone change, as the adult seems to be both conveying affection and capturing the child's attention for the task at hand. As Roger Brown (1977) puts it, the adult is trying "to keep two minds focused on the same topic."

Adults also talk to children primarily about the here and now. They comment on what they are doing, or what the child is doing or is about to do. They limit their vocabularies, using words that are easy for a child to pronounce and understand. And they select words that are most useful for the child, words that relate to what children usually want to talk about. The process of "teaching" involves dialogues, in which the parent pays close attention to the child's reactions, regulating the "lessons" according to the progress of the child. As Jerome Bruner (1978) has pointed out, in early dialogues the caregiver supplies both parts, asking and answering his or her own questions. But as the child grows and begins to acquire language, the parent demands more from him, and may repeat a question until the child supplies the answer. This dialogue form provides a forceful way to elicit the child's attention and to establish a mutual orientation.

Other evidence suggests that simple exposure

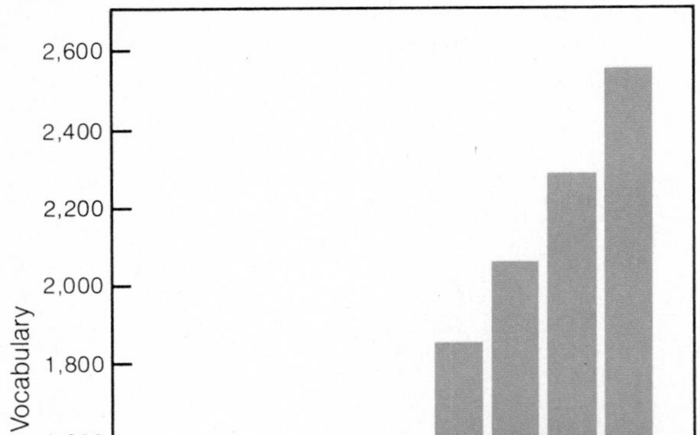

Figure 12.3 The increase with age in average size of vocabulary. Although the learning of new words does not necessarily indicate the learning of new concepts or meanings, they are likely to develop together. (Adapted from Lenneberg, 1967)

speech they hear is probably too rapid, it is not aimed at the child's immediate situation, and, of course, no attention is paid to the child's reactions.

Semantics and Communication

Although children appear to have mastered the major syntactical rules of their language by the time they are four or five, they still have a long way to go before they reach an adult level in semantic development and in the ability to adapt their language to the situation. Until recently, most psycholinguists have been more interested in syntax than in the meaning of a language, but an increasing number of studies (such as those discussed earlier that examine a child's mastery of the passive construction) indicate that form and meaning become closely intertwined (Clark and Clark, 1977).

The way young children first overgeneralize and then restructure the meanings of words was discussed in Chapter 8. Children also often attach meanings to words that are different from those that adults give them. Thus, words such as "bright," "hard," and "sweet" have both a physical ("The light is bright") and a psychological ("She is a bright child") meaning to adults. Solomon Asch and Harriet Nerlove (1960) showed that three- and four-year-olds first learn the physical meaning of these words and often deny that such concepts as "bright" or "sweet" can be applied to people. Seven- and eight-year-olds are aware of both meanings, but see no relationship between a bright light and a bright child. A few nine-year-olds relate the two meanings, but not until a child is eleven or twelve is he likely to have a firm grasp of the dual functions of words. Apparently a child learns the two meanings separately and only much later unifies them. David Palermo and Dennis Molfese's (1972) survey of semantic studies turned up many such examples of the child's gradual semantic development.

In the absence of other people, of course, none of us would need language. Our utterances are meant to communicate meanings to others, and we learn to use language socially in many different ways for many different purposes: to express emotions, to describe objects or events, to ask questions, to give commands, to tell stories, and to speculate.

John Flavell (1970) studied the way that children's ability to adapt their language to the audience and the situation develops. On one occasion,

to normal adult speech that is not intended for children does not enable a child to acquire language. J. S. Sachs and M. Johnson (1976), for example, studied the hearing child of deaf parents who used only sign language with him. Although the child heard a good deal of adult speech on television, when he was four his language lagged far behind that of other children. He had only a small vocabulary, probably learned from playmates and from television jingles. It has also been found that children who watch television programs in a language other than their own do not seem to acquire the second language (Snow *et al.,* 1976). The

for example, Flavell gave children the task of explaining to two adults how to play a game. One of the adults was blindfolded; the other was not. Older children gave the blindfolded adult much longer and more detailed instructions than they gave to the adult who could see the game. Younger children tended to give the same message to each, and some of the younger children even talked to the blindfolded person as if he could see, directing the adult to "This one" and "Over there." When Flavell set up a different situation, in which one listener was an adult and the other a child, older children again gave different instructions to each person, whereas younger children were less able to allow for differences between their listeners.

Subsequent research, however, has shown that whether children effectively communicate in such situations depends largely on what is required of them, and that even children as young as three or four adjust their speech to the situation if circumstances permit (for example, Maratsos, 1973; Sachs and Devin, 1976). That is, when young children do not seem to be able to communicate effectively or when they appear egocentric, it is often a matter of their unfamiliarity with the demands of the situation, their inability to understand the instructions

During the pre-school years, children learn the rules of conversation, discovering how to adjust their speech to the needs of others. (© Jeffrey Foxx / Woodfin Camp & Assoc.)

or to remember what they are supposed to do, or their preoccupation with figuring out the experimenter's wishes interfering with their ability to formulate an understandable message. When they are asked to do something they understand and are capable of doing, they seem to have little difficulty communicating in a relatively nonegocentric, effective way.

Thus Rochel Gelman and Marilyn Shatz (1977) found that when four-year-olds had to explain the workings of a toy (a dumping station with trucks and marbles) to two-year-olds, they tended to explain much as parents and other adults do. One four-year-old explained:

> I gave you it. You want to have something funny? Put the marbles in here. Put the marbles in here. I'll give you the marbles. Now pour them in here. Go up here. And pour them in here. Now we have to dump it. Dump it. No, not in here. Pour it in here. Pour it in here, OK? That's funny. No, not like that. I'll do it. See, Sara? (page 43)

The four-year-olds modified their messages to fit the limited capabilities of their young listeners. They used repetition and simple, short sentences, and adopted a "show and tell" approach in which they told about and demonstrated what the younger children were to pay attention to and do. In explaining the same toy to peers or adults, on the other hand, four-year-olds tended to use long sentences, talk more about their own thoughts, and ask the listener to provide information or clarification.

Other work also shows that young children are capable of coherent communication, whether at play or engaged in a task (Garvey, 1974). Between the ages of two and five, they increasingly learn how to adjust their speech to the needs of others. As Susan Ervin-Tripp (1976) points out, they learn to stay on the topic by using expressions like "and" or "because." They learn to soften their requests, adding "please." They learn more about how to take turns when talking with someone, timing their speech so it doesn't overlap or disrupt what their partners say. They learn how to keep their conversation focused on the matter at hand by thinking ahead and planning what to say next. Gradually, they also learn the convention that when they change the topic, they are supposed to indicate the shift in some way; by about eight or nine, they are likely to signal a change by saying, for example, "Oh yeah, that reminds me . . ."

LANGUAGE FUNCTIONING AND ENVIRONMENT

All children learn to handle their native languages, but the language young children hear from their parents helps shape the style of their developing speech. The attitudes of parents toward language, the richness of their vocabularies, their response to a child's attempts at speech, and the amount and kind of conversation that takes place in the home are likely to affect children's attitudes toward speech, vocabulary size, fluency, and language style, as well as to influence their success in formal education.

Social-Class Differences

One might expect to find differences in the way that children from different social classes use language. Studies that compare language use of children from different social backgrounds indicate that children from the more advantaged sections of society do score higher on tests of pronunciation, vocabulary, and sentence structure than children of families from lower socioeconomic groups do (R. Hess, 1970). However, there is no conclusive evidence to show that middle-class children use superior sentence structure or grammatical patterns.

Children from different social classes, on the other hand, do show differences in their expressive language. For example, Daniel Miller and Guy Swanson (1966) have pointed out that individuals in lower socioeconomic groups tend to express themselves with gestures, whereas those in higher socioeconomic groups tend to express themselves with words. A series of studies by Basil Bernstein (1962, 1966) also seems to indicate these kinds of language differences. Bernstein analyzed the speech of sixteen-year-old boys from the lower and middle classes who were matched for intelligence. He discovered that the middle-class boys used more elaborate descriptions of experience, showed a wider vocabulary, used more nouns, and spoke fluently, with short pauses in their utterances. The boys from the lower socioeconomic class made fewer distinctions, used more common words, tended to use more pronouns, and seemed to make longer pauses in their speech. As E. Tory Higgins (1976) notes, however, whether such differences hold true seems to vary with such factors as the topic the boys are asked to talk about, the setting, and the purpose.

Given the usual high correlation between the language of parents and that of their children in vocabulary, style, and choice of particular forms, socioeconomic differences in such aspects of child speech probably are to be expected. The linguistic environment of middle- and lower-class homes is likely to differ in many ways. Esther Milner (1951) and Suzanne Keller (1963), for example, found that middle-class families are likely to eat together, using the mealtime for whole-family conversations, whereas children from lower-class families tend to eat alone or with siblings, thereby missing such opportunities for verbal interaction with adults.

However, peers also influence speech. William Stewart (1964) observed that, among black families who have lived in Washington, D.C., for two or three generations, it is common for children to speak a variety of English much closer to the speech of newer immigrants from the South than to their parents' Standard English. It may be, therefore, that children from lower socioeconomic families lag behind on some measures of language development merely because they talk less with adults and talk more with their peers.

Special Schooling

In the last few years, several programs have been organized to develop language skills in disadvantaged, but otherwise normal, children. Some of these programs have used learning-based procedures, including instructions, adult modeling, social approval, and other rewards. The results of these efforts indicate that such programs can improve specific language skills. They can increase the rate of children's spontaneous speech and its correctness, teach them to time their conversation appropriately, and improve their storytelling skills and their descriptions of their own behavior. But note that these programs do not focus on the basic structure of a language.

Much of the thinking behind compensatory education programs for lower-class minority children in the United States supposes that "cultural deprivation," or poverty, results in various kinds of language deficits and that these various aspects of deficient language delay or block full cognitive development (Bereiter and Engelmann, 1966). Most studies, however, indicate that all children learn basic rules of language equally well, accord-ing to universal patterns of development. In this sense there is no such thing as a "language deficit" in child development. But there is a "language difference." Social environments certainly differ in regard to how well they match the school environment. Clearly, children who have acquired the motivations, habits, speech forms, and vocabulary and pronunciation skills demanded by the school system will perform better in that system than children whose social backgrounds have led them to acquire different motivations, habits, speech forms, and vocabulary and pronunciation skills. The mismatch between home environment and school that has been observed in various social groups in this country and others is not based on purely linguistic factors.

Attempts at compensatory education, such as this Project Head Start class, have been based on the idea that lower-class minority children have a "language deficit." Recent studies have shown that there is not so much a "deficit" as simply a difference. All children learn the basic rules of language equally well, but they learn the language of their social environment. (© Joel Gordon)

A recent study by Marida Hollos and Philip Cowan (1973) presents evidence that supports such a position. They studied in detail the cognitive development of children in several different social settings. Consider their description of one setting:

> Children spend most of their time in solitary play or in observation of others. Since there are few commercial toys and games, solitary play involves manipulation or observation of objects that occur naturally in the environment. . . . Most frequent interaction takes place with the mother; the father spends much of the day away from the house. . . . The amount of verbal interaction between mother and child is limited. Mothers do not prompt or encourage children to talk, ask questions, or suggest activities. There are no periods of storytelling or of discussions. . . . Interaction and communication between adult members of the family is limited to mealtimes and evenings. The major part of the evening is devoted to watching television. . . . (pages 632–633)

This sounds like the "culturally deprived" situation that has been described as typical of lower-class blacks in our city slums. It is, however, a description of life on an isolated Norwegian farm, a setting that has for many an aura of "wholesomeness" far removed from the atmosphere of the inner-city slum. Hollos and Cowan compared these isolated Norwegian farm children with children of families of similar size and educational background in a small village and in a medium-sized town in Norway. The village and town children spent much of their time playing with other children and encountering many adults in a variety of social settings; in the evenings they returned to more talkative family situations than the isolated farm children did. Yet basic language development was similar in all three groups, even though the village and town children had many more opportunities for verbal interaction.

What might we expect of the cognitive development of these children? A psychologist who stresses the role of verbal interaction and contact with the viewpoints of other people would predict more advanced cognitive development in the village and town children. A psychologist who minimizes the role of language in cognitive development would predict no important differences among the three groups. In fact, the actual results are more varied and more interesting than either of these simplified positions would lead one to believe.

The children took a number of different tests of cognitive ability. The first set of tasks tapped the child's ability to think logically about physical properties of objects and their relationships. Another collection of tasks dealt with the child's ability to take a viewpoint other than his own. Hollos and Cowan found that the isolated farm children were relatively advanced on the first set of cognitive tasks and that the village and town children were relatively more advanced on the second set.

This finding paints a complex picture of the roles played in early cognitive development by language and verbal interaction. Apparently, the manipulation of objects and close observation of physical changes helps a child acquire the ability to think logically about the physical properties of objects and their relationships. Verbal interaction with different persons helps a child develop the cognitive abilities necessary to take a point of view other than his own. Both abilities are important for schooling and necessary for development. And, indeed, all children eventually reach acceptable levels of development on both sets of abilities. Because the verbal environment affects only some aspects of cognitive development, the role of verbal training as a preparation for schooling must be looked at in a less simplistic manner (Hollos, 1974).

The problem of schooling, therefore, is neither one of teaching the child to think nor of teaching him to speak. Instead, after making the child feel at home in the school environment, psychologists and educators should find out which aspects of cognition need stimulation for a particular child or group of children and then devise the appropriate means (not necessarily verbal) to foster those facets of cognitive growth.

Dialects and Language Development

Much of the impetus in compensatory-education programs has been devoted to getting American black children to speak standard middle-class (non-Southern) American English (generally referred to by teachers as "correct English"). Although it is certainly the case that a person's chances of social and economic progress in our society are enhanced if he speaks the dominant dialect, there is no basis for relating a particular dialect to special success in normal mental development.

In linguistic terms, Black and Standard English are minor variants of the same English language;

in developmental terms, the acquisition of the two dialects follows similar patterns. For example, studies by Dan Slobin and Claudia Mitchell-Kernan (Slobin, 1975), of black children in the Oakland ghetto show no serious differences between the basic pattern of language development in ghetto children and in the middle-class Harvard children studied by Roger Brown. The Oakland children spend most of their time learning language from older siblings and playmates, who watch over them during much of the day. This situation, however, is common in cultures around the world and seems to have no effect on the basic rate of a child's acquisition of syntax. The two dialects are especially close at the preschool period, as shown in the examples in Table 12.1. They are roughly equivalent on functional and grammatical grounds, although their social consequences in the contemporary American social system are vastly different.

During later childhood, the dialects diverge. But even at the adult level, the difference is only superficial, as linguist William Labov (1973) has pointed out. For example, school teachers often criticize Black English because it apparently lacks the verb *to be*. Labov (1969) has shown, however, that the verb occurs in many places in Black English. Speakers of Standard English often contract *to be* to a simple *'s* in the present tense ("He's big" rather than "He is big"). Wherever Standard English can contract, Black English can, but does not always, omit the verb ("He big"). But omission in such instances is not an indication that Black English lacks an important part of English grammar. As you can see in Table 12.2, wherever it is impossible to contract *to be* in Standard English, it is impossible to delete *to be* in Black English. In order to emphasize a statement, Standard English puts heavy stress on the verb ("He IS big"). In this situation, "is" also appears in Black English, and the Black form is the same as the Standard.

Given differences as subtle and superficial as these, it is difficult to believe that the acquisition or

Although Black English is only superficially different from Standard English, its use outside the black community is likely to prove an obstacle to a child's social and economic advancement. (*top:* Barbara Young/Photo Researchers, Inc.; *bottom:* Ken Heyman)

Table 12.1   Dialect Differences in Negative Utterances of Preschool-Age Children

OAKLAND CHILDREN	HARVARD CHILDREN
That's not no bathroom.	It wasn't no chicken.
I'm not doing nothing.	I wasn't doing nothing.
I don't get no whipping.	I don't want no milk.
Nobody wasn't scared.	But nobody wasn't gonna know it.
Why bears can't talk	Why I can't put them on?
But Renée or nobody wouldn't peel me no kinda orange.	Nobody won't recognize me.
Why she won't sit up?	Why we didn't?
	Why it's not working?
Nobody wouldn't help me.	No one didn't took it.
I don't have no suitcase.	It don't have no wings.
Never I don't get no whipping.	I never won't get it.

Source: The Oakland examples are drawn from unpublished data of Claudia Mitchell-Kernan, and the Harvard examples from unpublished data of Roger Brown.

Table 12.2   Examples of *be* in Two Dialects of American English

BLACK ENGLISH	STANDARD ENGLISH
Deletion	*Contraction*
She the first one.	She's the first one.
But he wild.	But he's wild.
You out of the game.	You're out of the game.
We on tape.	We're on tape.
He always complainin'.	He's always complaining.
He gon' try to get up.	He's gonna try to get up.
Nondeletion	*Nondeletion*
I was small.	I was small.
You got to be good.	You've got to be good.
Be cool, brothers!	Be cool, brothers!
He *is* an expert.	He *is* an expert.
Is he dead?	Is he dead?
Are you down?	Are you down?
Is that a shock or is it not?	Is that a shock or is it not?
I don't care what you are.	I don't care what you are.
Do you see where that person is?	Do you see where that person is?

Source: Adapted from William Labov, "Contraction, Deletion, and Inherent Variability of the English Copula," *Language,* 45 (1969), 715–762. The Black English examples are drawn from Labov (with some abbreviation), and the Standard English equivalents have been supplied for the purposes of this comparative table.

use of Black English has major consequences for cognitive development. However, the vocabulary, pronunciation, and style of Black English label the child speaker in the eyes of the middle-class speaker of Standard English. Sometimes communication even breaks down. If a black child tells his teacher "Dey ain't like dat," the teacher assumes that the child has said "They aren't like that." Instead, the message that the child intended was "They didn't like that." When communication continues to break down, the teacher decides that, because the child's speech is unintelligible, he is unintelligent. A vicious circle is set up. Because the teacher expects the child to do poorly, the child fulfills her expectation and fails.

One way to break the circle is to instruct teachers in Black English so that they can understand their students. (This suggestion, of course, applies equally well to middle-class teachers of Chicano or Puerto Rican students or any students who speak a different language or dialect in their homes.) However, speaking Black English has major consequences on success in American society. Unless these children are helped to come to terms with the Standard dialect, they will lack a basic tool for social and economic advancement.

SUMMARY

1. As they grow, children become essentially competent in understanding and using their complicated language. They continue to learn and to refine the meaning of words (semanticity), to master basic rules for making and understanding sentences (productivity), and to extend their ability to talk about things that are not present (displacement).

2. By observing young children's natural speech and by examining their omissions, errors, and well-formed utterances, psycholinguists have found that a child attempts to simplify language by making it more systematic or regular than it actually is. In English, for example, this is shown when a child overregularizes the past tense of verbs ("breaked") and the plural forms of nouns ("foots").

3. The ways in which children comprehend speech also indicates an increased knowledge of grammatical rules. Thus, over time, children appear to construct and discard a variety of provisional

rules, and may correctly interpret a certain kind of sentence, such as a passive one, at one age but not at another.

4. Children's ability to use an increasing number of rules or grammatical operations gives additional evidence of their grasp of linguistic structure. For example, a child's ability to form questions in English appears to move from using only one operation to using two or more.

5. Although parents do not consciously instruct their children in grammar, they are very active in helping the children learn the language. Children actively test and expand their use and understanding of their native language. They structure and restructure the meanings of old and new words and continue to learn to use and adjust their language to express emotions, tell stories, describe objects or actions, ask questions, and so forth.

6. The developmental effects of variations in linguistic environments on language skills are indicated by research on social class, special schooling, and variations in American dialects. Although such studies reveal no major differences among children in their acquisition of the basic grammar of their native language, observed social-class and ethnic differences in pronunciation, vocabulary, fluency, and other kinds of skills have often been mistakenly interpreted as indicating language "deficits" rather than language differences.

CHAPTER 13
Personality: Establishing Social Interactions

THE PROCESS OF
SOCIALIZATION

SEX-ROLE DEVELOPMENT
Cultural Bases
Assertion and Aggression
Dependence and Independence

SELF-CONCEPT
Self-Appraisal
Self-Regulation

PARENT-CHILD RELATIONS

PEER INFLUENCE
Peer Influence in Monkeys
Peer Reinforcement
Peer Modeling

FUNCTIONS OF PLAY

SUBCULTURES AND
PERSONALITY

SUMMARY

When David was eighteen months old, his big sister used to amuse herself by dressing him like a girl. She would drape a cloth around him like a dress, put a woman's hat on his head, a pair of their mother's shoes on his feet, bedeck him with jewelry, and carefully paint his lips and rouge his cheeks. David thought it was fun, and would stagger through the house in high heels, showing himself off to friends and family. David is now four; the last time his eight-year-old sister tried to dress him in girls' clothes, he objected violently. "Boys don't dress like that!" he said indignantly. David has accomplished one of the social tasks of early childhood; he has established his identity as a male.

The years from two to six are the magic years of childhood. Probably at no other time do children experience so much that is new, exciting, and pleasurable. And at no other time in their lives do they confront so many challenges, conflicts, anxieties, and fears. During these formative years, children turn away from caregivers and expand their world to include other children, other adults, and an ever-widening environment. Like all children, as they grow up, David and Lauren become more and more like adults. By learning from their parents what is correct and valued, from imitating the acceptable behavior of their brothers and sisters, from observing other adults in person and on television, all children absorb a way of behaving that is similar to the behavior of those around them.

Because the people in one child's world are different from the people in the world of another, each child has a different way of behaving. Sometimes the differences are great, as exist between a child raised in a simple native culture in New Guinea and one raised in an urban American family. Sometimes the differences are relatively small, as between an American child raised by parents of French heritage and one raised by parents of English heritage in the same small town. But the differences can run deep and can extend to such modes of thinking as approaches to solving problems, the tendency to plan, and basic value systems.

In this chapter, as in Chapter 9, we will consider the development of personality as a function of socialization. We will see how children's contacts with their parents, their peers, and their culture affect their personalities. After discussing the general process of socialization, we will look at the process of identification, a major mechanism of socialization. We will examine the development of sex roles and of self-concept as significant aspects of personality. Finally, we will consider the various sources of socialization—parents, peers, play, and culture—paying special attention to sex-role development and to various methods of socialization: reinforcement, punishment, and modeling.

THE PROCESS OF SOCIALIZATION

The process of psychologically growing into a society is called socialization. Socialization pressures a person to become part of his society and to share in its culture. The individual learns to behave in culturally approved ways and to pay at least lip service to the dominant values, ideals, and motivations of the numerous groups that include him. The socialization process prescribes acceptable behavior for each role and discourages behavior that it deems undesirable. The outcome of socialization for any child depends on his cultural, familial, and physical environment.

Although what constitutes socialization differs across cultures, many psychologists believe that the same individual and social mechanisms operate in all children in all cultures. The four basic mechanisms are (1) the desire to obtain affection, regard, acceptance, and recognition; (2) the wish to avoid the unpleasant feelings that follow rejection or punishment; (3) the tendency to imitate the actions of others; and (4) the desire to be like specific people whom the child has grown to respect, admire, or love—a process called **identification.** By focusing on identification in the development of sex roles, the next section will demonstrate how each of the major mechanisms affects the growing child. Later in the chapter, discussions of parent, peer, and cultural influence will illustrate other aspects of childhood socialization.

Much of a child's socialization comes about when he takes on the characteristics and matches the behavior of the people he admires. Sigmund Freud (1917) called this process identification and saw it as particularly important, especially in the development of moral standards, sex roles, and social attitudes.

Although identification has a central role in social-learning and cognitive approaches to personality development as well as in Freudian theory, each group ascribes a different role and function to the process. Freud believed that identification evolves from the child's psychosexual conflict with, and attachment to, his parents. The child

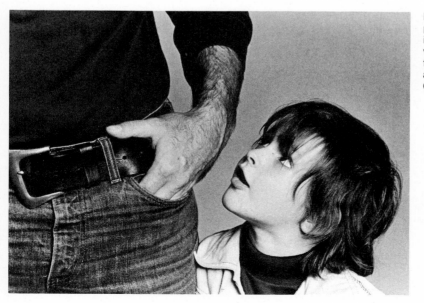

Identification with the same-sex parent is a crucial part of socialization; it enables this boy to develop the complex behavior of his father and to grow into the role of a male. (Tim Eagan/Woodfin Camp & Assoc.)

SIGMUND FREUD emphasizes the notion that early childhood is critical in the socialization of the individual. In his view of the psychosexual stages of development, during early childhood the child's sensual pleasure is focused on the genitals, and the child's fantasies about gratifying these desires results in sexual conflict with the parent of the opposite sex. According to Freud, the conflict is resolved when the child comes to identify with the parent of the same sex, and this identification forms the basis for appropriate sex-role development. Whether the opposite-sexed parent responds with warmth and affection to the child, thereby indirectly satisfying the child's desires, affects his personality development. The same-sexed parent, with whom the child learns to identify, becomes the model for the values that will be part of the child's adult personality.

WALTER MISCHEL sees the process of socialization as continuous from infancy through childhood. From his interactions with his environment, a child learns increasingly complex behavior as well as the consequences that accompany it. In Mischel's view, sex-role development involves learning appropriate behavior, which is modified by the consequences of performing it. Parents serve the child as models; they also, as peers will later do, shape the child's behavior by the way they respond to the child's actions.

ERIK ERIKSON concurs with the view that peer and parental responses are important factors in socialization during early childhood. Appropriate sex-role behavior develops when a child identifies with his same-sexed parent and assimilates his parent's behavior into his own personal identity. In Erikson's theory, peer-group and parental support and encouragement when the child first attempts to acquire appropriate sex-role behavior can help the child achieve a positive self-image and a strong personal identity.

LAWRENCE KOHLBERG emphasizes cognitive development as the most important factor in socialization. He takes the position that identification with the same-sexed parent develops once a child understands sex roles rather than the other way around. Thus, once girls or boys begin to think of themselves as girls or boys, they want to talk, think, and act as others of their sex do; in the process, they come to identify with them. In this view, although parents and others are important in socialization because they provide models and approval, children socialize themselves as they discover how to behave in competent and prescribed ways.

Figure 13.1   Summary descriptions of some major theoretical viewpoints on personality development during early childhood.

identifies with the parent of the same sex, thus undergoing structural changes in personality. The social-learning view presented by Walter Mischel (1968) sees identification as part of the general process of learning and, therefore, important if the child is to acquire complex behavior. Lawrence Kohlberg (1963), who along with Jean Piaget (1951) represents a cognitive-developmental perspective, presents identification as an aspect of a particular phase of cognitive development and considers it a way for the child to enhance his or her competence by sharing the skills of others.

Despite these differences in their views of the origin and functioning of identification, all three groups hold in common: (1) the central place of

identification in the socialization process; (2) the child's development of new, complex behavior by matching the behavior of parents; and (3) the particular significance of this mechanism in the development of sex roles.

SEX-ROLE DEVELOPMENT

Matt and Susan were not born male and female—psychologically. They became so. Sex-role development is a complex process of socialization, with far-reaching implications for personality functioning. The development of sex differences also highlights important questions about the interaction of biology and social experience in the determination of behavior.

Freud thought that, around the age of five, a child becomes psychologically feminine or masculine by incorporating, through identification, the traits of the same-sexed parent. Recent research indicates, however, that children include their gender in their basic self-concept as soon as they begin to acquire language—if not before—and that this self-labeling occurs before there is any real understanding of the various traits and behaviors associated with being male or female (Money and Ehrhardt, 1972). Parents and others, of course, communicate to the child in a variety of ways that he is a boy or she is a girl. Lois Gould (1972) writes satirically about the consternation caused by a set of parents who would reveal only that their child was an X. How, others fretted, was this X to be treated?

An important personality task in early and middle childhood consists of learning the behavior and qualities that society considers appropriate and desirable for a person of his or her gender. Cultures make many distinctions, both large and small, between the social roles of the sexes, and these **sex roles** encompass behavior that has little to do with the reproductive and erotic differences dictated by biological equipment (Tavris and Offir, 1977).

In their precise meanings, the terms *gender identity* and *sex role* are not synonymous. However, for the purposes of this text, they will be used more or less interchangeably. One distinction that developmental psychologists can make is that there is wide variation in the degree to which a person who clearly identifies with his or her gender manifests stereotypically masculine or feminine traits. For example, a child may identify with a

Learning "appropriate" sex-role behavior begins almost at birth. The ways others respond to children, the toys they are given, the models they see, and the rewards or punishments they receive for attempts at sex-role behavior contribute to this learning process. (Burk Uzzle/Magnum Photos)

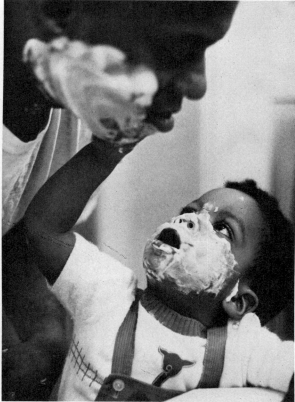

same-sexed parent who shows characteristics more traditionally associated with the other sex, such as a nurturant father or an achieving mother. Presumably, such a child still would have an unambivalent gender identity, but his or her sex-role behavior would be less conventional than usual.

Children whose behavior deviates widely from their socially defined sex roles may be rejected by adults and peers (Mussen, 1969). This problem more often arises with boys (who dread the epithet "sissy") than with girls (who usually regard "tomboy" as acceptable). Boys appear to have a greater need than girls to differentiate themselves from the opposite sex in order to gain a secure sense of gender identity, possibly because of their heavy contact with an important female (mother) during their formative years (Chodorow, 1971).

Sex-role behavior has typically received more attention than gender identity because of the importance society places on a child's behaving in socially appropriate ways, as defined by sex roles. Because cultural conceptions of what is masculine and what is feminine have important influences on the kind of person that a child will become, the next section will look more closely at the cultural bases of sex-role development.

Cultural Bases

Before a child even learns that there are two sexes, parents begin a training program (pink for girls, blue for boys) devoted to having her or him acquire the proper gender identity and learn the behavior, attitudes, and feelings that fit the social role of her or his sex. Every culture establishes acceptable and unacceptable patterns of behavior and psychological standards for the sexes, and these sex-role standards are imposed at an early age (Schell and Silber, 1968).

Sex roles are inevitably interwoven with the status that society attaches to each role. Male dominance was one of the earliest bases of discrimination among human beings, presumably because survival among hunting and gathering tribes depended on the ability to move about unencumbered by childbearing and nursing. The burden of advanced pregnancy or of carrying a small child would make it impossible for a woman to throw a spear accurately or to run after game (Friedl, 1978). Male children have always been valued, and many cultures regularly killed excess female babies at birth.

The superiority of the male sex role has been perpetuated by incorporating it into the customs, laws, and socialization practices of successive generations. A cross-cultural survey of tribal societies by Herbert Barry, Margaret Bacon, and Irvin Child (1957) disclosed that the more its economy requires physical strength, the more strongly a society emphasizes sex differences in socialization. In most societies, whether ancient, primitive, or modern, the prestige of the task determines whether it is assigned to males or to females. Women have generally been treated as if they were members of a minority group, and there are some parallels between traditional treatment of women and the treatment of blacks in American society.

Children learn these status differences early. While they are growing up, both sexes generally prefer the male role with its freedom, authority, and power (J. Kagan, 1964). Studies have shown that children in our society think men are very important and able to do whatever they like. Men are the bosses, they have the most money, they get the most comfortable chairs, and they get angry a lot. Children also describe men as being more fun than mothers and as having better ideas.

As we will see in the discussion of adolescence, as a boy grows, he discovers that society has defined his vocational role as primary and his role as spouse and parent as secondary; the reverse is true for a girl. To fulfill these social roles, boys are likely to be reared to achieve and girls are likely to be reared to nurture others. Thus, as soon as children enter early childhood, almost all societies foster achievement and self-reliance in boys and obedience, nurturance, and responsibility in girls. One boy, asked by Ruth Hartley (1960) what boys have to know and should be able to do, answered:

> They should know what girls don't know—how to climb, how to make a fire, how to carry things; they should have more ability than girls; they need to know how to stay out of trouble; they need to know arithmetic and spelling more than girls do.

The difference between male and female roles goes beyond actual sex-role behavior; it extends into **sex-role stereotypes**—simplified, fixed concepts about the behavior and traits typical of each sex. Learning their society's stereotypes is a major developmental step for young children. Lawrence Kohlberg (1966) has found that, by the time they are five or six, children have clearly sex-typed the virtues. A girl comes to perceive that feminine competence and status are based on being attractive and nice rather than on being powerful, ag-

Children learn early that prestigious occupations generally go to men. As this girl plays at the typewriter, she probably sees herself as a secretary. (Ken Heyman)

gressive, or fearless. In a similar way, Jerome Kagan (1964) has described the social stereotypes of males and females in contemporary American culture:

> In sum, females are supposed to inhibit aggression and open display of sexual urges, to be passive with men, to be nurturant to others, to cultivate attractiveness, and to maintain an affective, socially poised, and friendly posture with others. Males are urged to be aggressive in face of attack, independent in problem situations, sexually aggressive, in control of regressive urges, and suppressive of strong emotions, especially anxiety.

In studying these sex-role stereotypes, psychologists have taken a particular interest in the development of two sex-related traits—aggression and dependence.

Assertion and Aggression

Children around the world bicker, toss epithets, shove, kick, hit, fight, and break things. All cultures have rules for socializing aggressive behavior, for teaching youngsters the dos and don'ts of managing their feelings of hostility and anger. These feelings arise in situations that pose a personal threat by appearing either to jeopardize an individual's physical well-being or to interfere

with values and goals that he or she believes are important. The immediate emotional response is anger at the threatening person or object; the adaptive response involves taking effective action to avert the threat.

Unfortunately, the concepts of assertiveness and aggressiveness become tangled in our thinking. This is particularly true with respect to competition and strivings for success. A person tends to describe behavior in himself as assertive that he would label aggressive in anyone else. And because this culture values gentleness in women, an assertive girl is likely to be called aggressive; her behavior violates the female sex-role stereotype. One way to avoid this subjective dilemma is to define **assertiveness** as verbal or physical behavior that is appropriate to the occasion and that injures no one and **aggressiveness** as verbal or physical behavior that is inappropriate or harms someone. The confusion between the terms can have disastrous consequences. An environment that seeks to stamp out all aggressive behavior in children may also inhibit legitimate self-assertion. In the healthy socialization of aggression, the child learns effective ways to "stand up" for himself without injuring others.

As a child grows and becomes more independent, he is likely to find that his new assertive behavior meets increased parental demands and restrictions. This situation leads many developmental psychologists to agree that the development of assertiveness needs serious study. However, past research has been devoted to understanding aggression. This emphasis is in part the result of the social consequences of aggression and in part the result of Freud's early concern with it. The rest of this section will focus on male and female differences in aggression; nevertheless the importance of assertiveness should be kept firmly in mind.

There is a good deal of evidence that in this society it is difficult for females to be either assertive or aggressive. Studies (Cosentino and Heilbrun, 1964) have found more anxiety and conflict about aggression in females than in males. Women who feel angry tend to feel guilty about it and to cope with their anger in ineffectual ways, with indirect displays of hostility, with sudden hostile outbursts, or simply by avoiding the situation.

Data gathered by developmental psychologists consistently show that aggressive behavior has been stereotyped as appropriate only for boys

Only the circumstances can reveal whether these boys are assertive or aggressive. But in either case, society has made such behavior easier for boys than for girls. (*top:* © Jeffrey Foxx/Woodfin Camp & Assoc.; *bottom:* Dan Budnik/Woodfin Camp & Assoc.)

(Maccoby and Jacklin, 1974). In a study that followed eighty-nine children from early childhood to young adulthood, Jerome Kagan and Howard Moss (1962) found that the amount of aggressive behavior in males remained stable over the years but that aggressive behavior declined in females. Our society tolerates aggressive behavior in boys, so the aggression they show in early childhood is not likely to be the target of systematic efforts toward change.

Other investigators have found that boys as young as two are more physically aggressive and more negativistic than girls. Studies with nursery-school children show that by this age boys are quite selective in the targets of their physical assaults (Maccoby, 1976). Their victims are usually other boys, in particular those who give in; rarely is a girl the target of assault.

The consistency of the finding that males are, on the average, more physically aggressive than females suggests possible biological contributions to such behavior. By now, however, it should be clear that the developing child's behavior is a product of continuous interaction between constitutional factors and the child's own social environment. The question is whether any constitutional factors that are linked with sex might predispose boys toward physical aggressiveness. Seymour Feshbach (1970) has suggested that males may not be predisposed to aggressiveness but that their greater physical strength and more vigorous motor impulses may lead to different social experiences. For example, boys have greater success than girls in getting what they want by hitting. Also, parents more often frustrate a boy's impulsive acts, thereby stimulating his aggressive reactions.

Regardless of any predisposing constitutional factors, the social environment can overwhelmingly influence aggressiveness in one direction or the other. Whereas physical aggressiveness is the hallmark of masculinity in many cultures (for example, in the warrior), patterns of aggression for each sex vary widely from one culture to another (B. Whiting, 1963). The problem comes down to the relative ease with which children of each sex can learn whatever sex-role behavior their culture values and considers appropriate. Thus, facilitating or inhibiting aggression to the desired level, as well as channeling it into the desired forms, may require socializing agents that devote more effort to children of one sex than to the other.

As Feshbach (1970) and others have indicated, the form of aggression, which is influenced by society, is important in considering the differences in aggressive behavior between males and females. A variety of studies have demonstrated that, from nursery school on, boys are likely to express aggression in physical ways, whereas girls are likely to scold or argue or to use indirect forms of aggression, such as gossip, a concerted resistance to demands, and subtle forms of rejection. Girls who are overtly aggressive tend to be rejected by their peers and disliked by their teachers (Levitin and Chananie, 1972). Boys are just as likely as girls to meet disapproval for overt aggression, but, because they are stronger and more active, their aggressive attempts are more likely to be successful.

Although girls and boys may differ in the extent to which they find aggression a useful and accepted way to solve problems, girls are just as capable of aggression. When Ann Frodi, Jacqueline Macauly, and Pauline Thome (1977) reviewed numerous studies on sex differences in aggression, they found that in some circumstances women may be just as aggressive as men. In face-to-face encounters with another adult, women are less likely than men to engage in verbal or physical aggression. In situations where aggression is justified, however, or when they can remain anonymous, women tend to be as aggressive as men.

Dependence and Independence

As you will recall, Chapter 9 described the process of attachment in infancy, pointing out that infants attach themselves to one or more persons and that they attend to them, seek attention from them, derive pleasure from interacting with them, show distress when separated from them, and seek physical contact with them in strange or threatening situations. Such manifestations of attachment undergo drastic changes as young children venture into the world of playmates and other adults. By the time they are three or four, their attachment has evolved into the somewhat similar but less intense behavior that psychologists have described as **dependence.**

Most developmental psychologists distinguish between two kinds of dependence: emotional, referring to the child's relations with people; and instrumental, referring to the child's relations with the environment. In **emotional dependence,** children's aims are affection and support; they find contact with people rewarding and satisfying. In **instrumental dependence,** children seek help and comfort as a means to other ends, as when they ask adults to help them perform tasks or to aid them in conflicts with their playmates.

Several factors influence the type and degree of dependence shown by young children. When they find themselves in situations that evoke anxiety or stress, they are likely to show increased emotional dependence. And when children are deprived of social contact, particularly with adults, they are also likely to behave in ways that indicate increased emotional dependence (Hartup, 1964b). In early childhood, there is a high correlation between emotional and instrumental dependence, but as the child gets older they become less related. Thus, a four- or five-year-old who shows extreme instrumental dependence may show little emotional dependence (Emmerich, 1966).

By the time boys and girls are six or seven, they show relatively stable and well-defined differences in dependence (Mischel, 1970). During this period,

As children grow, attachment evolves into dependence. In emotional dependence (*left*), children seek affection and support; in instrumental dependence (*right*), they seek help to accomplish a task. (*left:* Suzanne Szasz; *right:* © Joel Gordon)

boys tend to check with their mothers less often and to become more independent, exploratory, and assertive. Girls, on the other hand, generally continue to check more frequently with their mothers, to be less assertive and more dependent, and to stay in secure surroundings. The stable pattern of dependence in girls generally continues into adulthood, probably because the cultural sex-role stereotype supports such behavior in women.

However, sex-role stereotypes are undergoing continued change in contemporary American society. Traditional conceptions of masculine and feminine behavior are becoming more fluid, and more and more husbands and wives share career, housekeeping, and child-care roles. Such parents

are less likely than conventional parents to exhibit rigid sex-role differences and are less likely to expect them from their children. They are likely to encourage their children to develop a combination of feminine and masculine attitudes and behavior that allows them to be flexible and match their behavior to the situation.

SELF-CONCEPT

Throughout early childhood, children increasingly come to perceive themselves and others in terms of categories that consist primarily of concrete attributes such as sex, age, physical appearance, and possessions. Although these aspects of a child's self may seem superficial to an adult, they have great meaning for the child and form a basic part of his or her sense of being. They are closely tied to experiences with other people and the environment children live in.

Because young children take such a strong present-oriented view of themselves, their self-concepts necessarily reflect this here-and-now quality. Asked to describe themselves, they reply in terms of those attributes: "I'm Lauren" (name), "I'm four" (age), "I have a brother" (kinship), "I'm pretty" (physical appearance), "I play dolls" (activities), "I like ice cream" (likes), "I'm little" (size), "I have a kitty" (possession).

Self-Appraisal

Although by the time they are two or three most children understand that certain people are called girls and women and others boys and men, and that some activities are strictly for boys and others for girls, they are only on the threshold of learning what it means to be female or male (Maccoby, 1976). Even when a child reaches the ripe old age of six, he or she still may not appreciate some of the implications of gender. More than a few six-year-olds, for example, don't realize they will always remain the same sex. So there are undoubtedly some six-year-old girls who think they can grow up to be fathers and some boys who think they can grow up to be mothers.

Although preschool children may not understand the implications of gender, research suggests that they do recognize that attractiveness is an asset and unattractiveness is a liability. Karen Dion (1973), for example, found that both young boys and girls prefer attractive peers as potential friends and expect them to be friendly and nice, but they reject unattractive peers and expect them to be unfriendly and mean. Judith Langlois and Cookie Stephan (1977) found that kindergarten children generally hold the same views. They found, for example, that black, Anglo, and Mexican-American children see attractive peers, regardless of their race, as being more likable, smarter, more friendly, and more willing to share than unattractive peers. Attractive Anglo children are particularly likely to benefit from shared social stereotypes since they are likely to be perceived by all children, regardless of their race, as being the smartest, kindest, and happiest, and as doing the best in school. The social advantage this gives to Anglo children may enable them to maintain or

Children strive to resemble others whom they respect and admire. The more the child believes he can be like the other person, the stronger his identification becomes. (© Alvis Upitis/The Image Bank)

develop a comparatively more positive self-concept than children from other groups.

Children want to be liked and loved by others, and in striving to be self-directing, competent, and autonomous they try to do so in ways that meet with the approval of others. It is largely out of discovering what their parents, siblings, other relatives, and peers expect of them and learning to match their behavior to these expectancies that children acquire many of their basic concepts about themselves. This is especially true of such aspects of self-concept as self-esteem. To the extent that children's social experiences communicate that they are competent, admirable, and acceptable, they are likely to develop positive self-concepts, regarding themselves with pride, satisfaction, and approval.

Children are generally attracted to and try to emulate those who have power over them, who help them, and who show them affection. They want to be like others whom they respect and admire and, in striving to do so, are said to identify with them. It is traditional to emphasize the importance of the child's identification with the same-sex parent, but it is clear that children also may identify with older siblings or with others whom they admire and respect. Many factors may influence whom the child identifies with and how strong the identification becomes. But basic to the identification is the child's sense of perceived similarity. That is, the more a child believes he is or can be like the other person, the more strongly he is likely to identify with him. In trying to be like the person he identifies with, the child comes to include in his self-concept the degree to which his personal attributes match those of the other person.

Self-Regulation

All societies expect young children to assume increasing responsibility for themselves as they get older. In our culture, for example, from the time children are toilet-trained, they are expected to show increasing self-control and self-reliance. By the time they are four or five, most children have learned to go to the bathroom by themselves, brush their teeth, feed themselves, dress themselves, tie their shoelaces, get ready for bed, and so on. In addition, most have learned to some degree how to tolerate delay when they must wait to do something they want.

Learning self-control obviously takes time. Most parents recognize this and adjust their standards to their children's changing abilities and interests. Although most young children want what they want immediately, research indicates that even three- or four-year-olds are quite capable of delaying gratification. Whether they do so, however, varies with such factors as their mood and what they do while waiting.

A study by Bert Moore, Andrea Clyburn, and Bill Underwood (1976) indicates how children's moods may affect their ability to delay gratification. Some three- to five-year-olds were asked to talk and think about things that made them sad, and others were asked to talk and think about things that made them happy. Afterward, each child was given a choice between a less-valued treat (a round pretzel), which he or she could eat immediately, or a more-valued treat (a small lolli-

pop) several hours later. Children who talked and thought about sad things more often chose the pretzel, but those who talked and thought about happy things more often chose the lollipop. This suggests that negative moods may increase children's tendency to be impulsive, whereas positive moods may increase their willingness to be patient.

Other research shows that what children do while they wait affects how long they can delay gratification. Children are more likely to be willing to wait and to wait longer if they distract themselves by doing or thinking about something else. It has been found that children who sing, whistle, talk to themselves, play games with their hands or feet, and so on, are able to wait longer for something they want than children who do not distract themselves. Walter Mischel and Nancy Baker (1975) have found that the way children think about objects they want but must wait for can also play a part in how long they will wait. Mischel and Baker gave children a choice of eating one pretzel or marshmallow immediately or getting two pretzels or marshmallows if they waited. Children who thought about the pretzel sticks in front of them as being "little brown logs" or "crayons" or who thought about marshmallows as being "cotton balls" or "clouds" managed to wait for a relatively long time—an average of fourteen minutes. But when they thought about the "crunchy, salty, toasty taste" of pretzels or the "chewy, sweet, soft taste" of marshmallows, they gave up and took their single pretzel or marshmallow after an average wait of less than five minutes.

Children's reactions to the world vary depending on what they perceive as the cause of their behavior (Lefcourt, 1976). If they believe they get along with their friends or play games well because of their own ability and effort, they are likely to take pride in those accomplishments. If they believe that such results are due to outside factors over which they have little control, they are likely to take little satisfaction in whatever they do.

Children with an internal locus of control are likely to have been encouraged to be self-reliant at an early age. Such children are likely to have stayed away from home overnight or been left alone to do things on their own by the time they are four years old. Children who have an external sense of control, on the other hand, generally get no such encouragement until they are older (V. Crandall, 1973; Wichern and Nowicki, 1976).

By the time they are in kindergarten, most

children have developed consistent explanations for the results of their efforts and social interactions. These explanations are likely to depend in part on their intelligence and socioeconomic level. Toni Falbo (1975) found, for example, that five-year-old middle-class children were more likely than working-class children to stress the causal relationship between a person's effort and success or failure at a task. Bright children generally explained success as being due to personal ability and failure as due to the difficulty of the task. Less bright children tended to explain success as being due to the ease of the task but used lack of personal ability to explain failure. Falbo points out that the bright children's explanations encourage them to perceive themselves as responsible for success ("I'm smart") and not responsible for failure ("It was too hard"). In contrast, less bright children's explanations encourage them to perceive themselves as responsible for failure ("I'm dumb") and as deserving no credit for their success ("It was just easy").

For many activities there are no precise measures of competence or success. Instead, children learn to compare what they are like now with what they were like in the past. But very early, children also learn to compare their own performances and characteristics with those of other children. Even three-year-olds, however, are likely to be selective, choosing others of similar age, sex, and competence as their standards of comparison.

By the time they are six, most have learned to become discriminating in their comparisons. Because they have increased their understanding of their own assets and liabilities, their evaluations are likely to vary depending on the situation and the activity. Lauren, for example, may regard herself as being high in physical attractiveness but average in physical skill, whereas Susan may regard herself as being high in physical skill, average in academic skill, and low in attractiveness.

PARENT-CHILD RELATIONS

Parents' goals, values, and manner of living have a great effect on growing children and can lead to admiration and imitation or alienation and rejection. As the earliest and most durable source of socialization, a child's parents are the first people with whom he or she identifies, and they remain the strongest influence in sex-role development. This overwhelming importance has led develop-

mental psychologists to take an intense interest in parent-child interactions.

Traditionally, parent-child interactions have been studied in terms of child-rearing practices. This has involved measuring certain aspects of parental behavior (such as permissiveness or hostility) and certain aspects of child behavior (such as aggression or dependence) and then seeing if any of those aspects of parent and child behavior are correlated. Some studies indicate that highly permissive parents have extremely independent children (Winder and Rau, 1962). Restrictive parents, on the other hand, tend to have highly dependent children.

Frequently, however, it appears that various aspects of child rearing interact in other ways. Parental permissiveness, for example, may lead to high levels of aggression in a hostile family situation but to low levels of aggression in a warm, nurturant home environment. The same kind of parental behavior also appears to have different effects on boys and girls. Thus, parental rejection or hostility appears to increase dependence in boys (H. Smith, 1958), but maternal hostility is associated with increased independence in girls (J. Kagan and Moss, 1962).

Over the years, and partly as a result of these mixed findings, most developmental psychologists have become increasingly skeptical about studying parent-child interactions through child-rearing practices. Among other difficulties, it is apparent that the particular results from a study of child-rearing practices depend on what group of families is studied, how the investigators define factors such as aggression or dependence, and how they measure them. In addition, other research indicates that the behavior of parents is likely to change over the years (J. Kagan and Moss, 1962). That is, a parent who is permissive with a three-year-old may be restrictive by the time the child begins school. And a parent who is aloof and cold to a young child may be warm and nurturant when that same child reaches adolescence.

Because developmental psychologists want to identify more precisely the ways that parents serve as influential agents in the growing child's socialization, detailed approaches to studying parent-child interactions have centered on such factors as the significant role of parents in reinforcing and punishing a child's behavior (Patterson, 1972). For example, if Matt is highly aggressive, an examination is made of the situations in which his aggression takes place (such as when playing with his sister Susan or at the dinner table) and what happens after he takes the aggressive action (such as getting to play his favorite game, or not having to eat spinach, or being sent to his room).

Based on the findings from studies of particular interactions between parents and children, and between adults and children in general, it is clear that the way an adult responds to a child's behavior can have a potent effect. Paul Brown and Rogers Elliott (1965) found, for example, that when nursery-school teachers ignored boys' physical and verbal aggression and at the same time paid attention to and praised their cooperative acts, the boys' aggression dramatically decreased. Then the teachers stopped reinforcing cooperative acts. Verbal aggression among the boys remained low, but physical aggression increased. As soon as the teachers went back to ignoring aggression and praising cooperation, physical aggression again decreased.

As might be expected, similar analyses of sex-role development indicate that boys and girls are likely to be reinforced or punished differently for the same kind of behavior. Parents are likely to encourage independence earlier in their sons than in their daughters. Beverly Fagot (1974) found that mothers discouraged their toddler sons from following them around the house. Their daughters, on the other hand, were encouraged to stay near them. Other studies show that boys are allowed to investigate wider areas of the community without parental permission (Saegert and Hart, 1976) and

that they are expected to run errands at an earlier age. When mothers of four-year-olds were asked at what age they thought children should be permitted to be independent, mothers of boys, compared with mothers of girls, listed younger ages for behavior such as crossing the street alone, using sharp tools, and going off to play without telling a parent their destination (Callard, 1964).

Early school experiences are likely to encourage the development of sex-related differences in independence. Lisa Serbin, K. Daniel O'Leary (1973) and their associates, for example, observed teachers in fifteen nursery-school classrooms and recorded how they behaved toward boys and toward girls. They found that teachers were helping to shape traditional sex roles, often unwittingly, by prompting and reinforcing independent, assertive behavior in boys and dependent, passive behavior in girls. In one classroom, for example, the children were making party baskets, a task that required them to staple a paper handle in place. The teachers provided instruction as the boys manipulated the staple gun and attached the handle. The teacher, however, was likely to take the basket from a girl, staple the handle to it, and hand it back. Serbin and O'Leary point out that most teachers don't realize that they demonstrate things and explain them more to boys than to girls and that they give boys more directions that require them to accomplish things on their own. From such findings, Serbin and O'Leary conclude that most girls learn to be submissive, to remain near

Children learn traditional sex roles early. By kindergarten, these children automatically enact the roles they have learned from their families and their past experience. (© Jeffrey Foxx/Woodfin Camp & Assoc.)

an adult, and to be rewarded with affectionate hugs, whereas most boys learn to be assertive and to receive praise for being independent problem solvers.

Most parents, teachers, and other people who work with children claim that they permit no more physical aggression by boys than by girls. What evidence there is, however, indicates that they react to physical aggression in selective ways that are consistent with traditional sex-role development. Teachers in nursery schools, for example, show that they expect boys to fight, pay strong attention to such aggression, and thereby inadvertently reinforce it. Fathers and mothers also expect more physical aggression from boys than from girls (Maccoby, 1976), and they are likely to praise or otherwise reinforce aggression when it is not directed at them. Most parents are also inclined to overlook instances of mild physical aggression by their sons and punish only extreme acts. By doing so, of course, they teach their sons that aggression is acceptable in some situations.

Although punishment will be discussed further in Chapter 16, the topic requires general comment here. The easiest and most common way of getting a child not to think or act in certain ways is to punish him (R. Parke, 1977). As most parents find, punishment works and is often effective in controlling a child's behavior. However, punishment also produces undesirable results, particularly when it is physical. When parents use physical punishment on a child, the child is likely to respond with fear or more anger, negative feelings that he or she may come to associate with parents or the situation. In addition, the parent who hits his child is serving as a model of physical aggression. He demonstrates to the child that, when one disapproves of another person's behavior, the appropriate way to react is to hit him.

PEER INFLUENCE

As Chapter 9 followed Susan through her first two years, it was pointed out that an infant interacts primarily with members of her own family. As Susan grows and can move about more easily, other people, especially other children, begin to enter her life. She begins to play outdoors more often, and she encounters other children in her neighborhood. She may go to a nursery school or a day-care center, where she meets children from other neighborhoods. All these trends change

Susan's world from one that is populated almost entirely by giants to one in which an ever greater number of people are near her own size and share her interests. During these early childhood years, the child first has a real peer group, and the importance of that group steadily increases.

Much of what young children learn about their world they learn from other children, and most of what they learn, from whatever source, they practice and rehearse within the peer group. Thus, the peer group is the place where children perfect the roles that they will play in later years. During early childhood, a child's dependence on adults often decreases while dependence on peers (such as in seeking approval or asking for help) increases. In fact, well-adjusted youngsters tend to have a comfortable reliance on their peers (Emmerich, 1966).

Peer Influence in Monkeys

The role of peers as agents of socialization is not uniquely human. Students of primate behavior are generally convinced, both from laboratory studies and from studies conducted in the wild, that early contact with peers is necessary for the normal development of most primates. In fact, it is almost impossible to conceive of socialization among rhesus monkeys or chimpanzees in the absence of peer interaction. Because of this similarity across species, primate social interaction can provide insights that help clarify the role of peers in the socialization of the human child.

In many primate species, young animals spend much of their time in a play group consisting of other infants and juveniles. Within this group, young primates practice the behavior they will later be expected to perform as adults. It is here that primates perfect the intricate patterns of facial gestures and social threat. And it is here, by approach and mounting during play, that young primates learn adult sexual behavior. Rough-and-tumble play within the peer group also develops the aggressiveness that primates use both to maintain status and to defend the group against predators.

Harry and Margaret Harlow (1969) reviewed a series of laboratory studies documenting the importance of peers as socialization forces in primates. As described in Chapter 9, the Harlows and their associates raised some infant monkeys with surrogate mothers; other infants were raised in total isolation from other members of their species. These young monkeys never learned to play the

When the Harlows took baby monkeys away from their mothers and raised them with only peers for company, some strange, but temporary, patterns of behavior developed, such as this "choo-choo train" clinging. (Harry F. Harlow, University of Wisconsin Primate Laboratory)

usual monkey games; they never had the opportunity to acquire the social roles that they would need in later life. After six to twelve months of such isolation, these monkeys found it almost impossible to fit within a group when, as adolescents, they were introduced to others of their kind. They tended to remain isolated from the rest of the group; they rarely engaged in social play; and when they did, it was with other isolates. Even individual play was infrequent among monkeys that had been isolated for twelve months.

Such isolated monkeys encountered great difficulties when they became sexually mature. Males did not know how to approach young females (or even that it was females that they should approach), and the females did not know how to entice and yield to the males. Both males and females showed episodes of abnormal aggression. For example, they attacked and bit young monkeys, which normally reared animals almost never do. They also launched attacks against the largest and most dominant adult males, an extraordinarily maladaptive action for an adolescent.

Clearly, these monkeys had severe social problems (Suomi and Harlow, 1975). To try to pinpoint the cause of these problems, researchers raised more monkeys, but each group was raised in a different manner. Some monkeys spent the first few months of their lives with their mothers but had no contact with any other monkeys. Another group of

monkeys spent the first few months of life with other monkey infants. The infants raised with only their mothers behaved in a far less abnormal manner than did the monkeys raised in isolation. They were, however, less affectionate with peers and more aggressive than monkeys raised in a normal manner. Furthermore, the longer the baby monkeys were isolated with their mothers, the more abnormal their behavior.

Researchers had suspected that the peer-raised animals would show severe social problems, and for the first several days it appeared that their suspicions were correct. The infants simply clung together in a "choo-choo" pattern, as shown in the photograph above. This pattern soon broke up, however, and the monkeys established normal play with strange monkeys. The later development of peer-raised monkeys seemed almost completely normal. They showed affection and played normally, and they demonstrated only normal aggression. There was a tendency for these monkeys to show closer ties with their early companions than with other monkeys, but even this difference was slight.

In view of the importance usually assigned to parents (see Chapter 9) in the rearing of monkey and human infants, these results are surprising. They seem to indicate that, at least among rhesus monkeys, parents may be less important in some respects than the peer group as a socializing agent.

Peer Reinforcement

One important way in which children influence each other is through actions that support or encourage behavior. That is, if one child supports another child's behavior, his or her approval will make it more likely that the first child's behavior will occur again. Approval, affection, and attention usually are encouraging social behavior. But such behavior does not always reinforce an action, and many other social acts also have reinforcing effects. In addition, the kinds of events that reinforce an activity such as aggression differ from those that reinforce an activity such as sharing. And because of differences in his past experience, one child may respond to behavior that has little or no effect on another child. Nevertheless, many actions, such as praise and affection, act as encouragement for nearly everyone in a wide variety of situations.

These social reinforcers seem to be strongly related to popularity within the peer group. Popular youngsters approach others in a friendly manner and are generous with praise and approval. Rosalind Charlesworth and Willard Hartup (1967) found, for example, that popular young children who frequently were supportive of other children tended to distribute their approval among nearly all their peers. This study also found a strong positive correlation between the amount of reinforcement a child gave and the amount he received.

On the other hand, in another study Hartup (1964a) found that young children performed better at simple tasks when they disliked a child who praised their performance than when they liked him. Hartup used a marble-dropping task to assess reinforcement among four- and five-year-old children. A child picked up marbles one at a time from a bin and dropped them through holes into a container. Periodically, either the child's best friend or another child that he disliked expressed approval. During the short session, a child dropped marbles faster when the disliked child approved his performance than when his friend approved.

The effectiveness of approval from a disliked child may have something to do with expectations. Joanne Floyd (1965) found that children who received unexpectedly large or small rewards in a sharing task changed their patterns of sharing more radically than children who got rewards they had more or less expected. Thus, it may be that children expect their friends to approve their actions, so that a friend's behavior merely meets the expectation. However, a child may expect disliked children to disapprove of his or her actions, so that approval from such children exceeds expectations and has a powerful influence on performance.

A child's playmates can also affect his aggressiveness. Gerald Patterson, Richard Littman, and William Bricker (1967) describe just how this process works in a nursery school. These investigators observed children and recorded their reactions to aggression. When attacked, 97 percent of the children either became passive, cried, assumed a defensive posture, told the teacher, retrieved their property, or retaliated with an aggressive act of their own. In other words, after nearly every instance of aggressive attack, a child reacted in a way that was either potentially reinforcing or punishing. When a physical attack was followed by passiveness, crying, or defensiveness, the young attacker soon tended to act aggressively against the original victim. Counteraggression, on the other hand, was often followed by changes in the attacker's behavior. He was likely either to act in a changed manner toward his former victim, to pick a different victim, or both.

Other studies of how children encourage one another's behavior have shown that direct manipulation can change the way that children interact in the schoolroom. For example, Robert Wahler (1967) observed a group of nursery-school children and selected five whose behavior was related in some way to encouragement from their peers. He then enlisted the aid of the children's friends. Wahler asked the friends of children whose behavior was tied closely to peer reinforcement to pay less attention to their friend when he acted in a certain way. He asked the friends of the children whose behavior was less closely linked to other children's support to increase their attention and approval. Within a few days, the selected behavior dropped among the first group of children and increased among the second group. When Wahler told the children's friends to resume their usual treatment, the five children went back to behaving just as they had before the experiment began. Studies such as this one indicate that, by remaining alert to established patterns of peer reinforcement, parents and teachers can often use the peer group to help solve its own problems.

Peer Modeling

Reinforcement is not the only way in which children influence one another's behavior; **modeling** is

Children encourage one another's behavior, and a child's peers can affect the amount of aggressiveness he shows. (Bob Adelman/Magnum Photos)

also powerful. Seeing another child behave in a certain way can affect a child's behavior for at least three different reasons (Bandura, 1977): First, the watching child may learn how to do something new that he previously either could not do (such as working a puzzle) or would not have thought of doing (such as riding a bicycle with "no hands"). Second, a child may learn what happens when one acts in a certain way—for example, that aggression gets other children into trouble or that disobeying does not always bring punishment. As a result of this knowledge, the child's own behavior may change. Third, a model may suggest how a child can behave in a strange situation. For example, a child may stand around nervously at a birthday party until another child begins throwing cake. Immediately, the child and others join in the new tribal ritual.

Experiments by Albert Bandura, Dorothea Ross, and Sheila Ross (1963) and by David Hicks (1965) provide a good illustration of modeling. In these experiments, they showed a group of young children a film in which a model struck a large rubber doll with a mallet, sat on the doll, and screamed at it. When the children who had seen the film were given the same kind of doll and a mallet, they proceeded to assault the doll, copying a number of the filmed model's actions.

A model can also establish a situation in which his peers are likely to behave in a certain way. For example, Thomas Wolf (1972) told young boys that they were not to play with a particularly at-

tractive toy in the experimental room. Later, some boys heard another boy say that he expected most children would obey and would not play with the toy. Other boys heard a peer say that most children would disobey. The children who heard the model say that he expected disobedience disobeyed more often. Apparently, the model's statement made the attractive option of playing with the toy seem the appropriate thing to do.

Additional research has shown that the pleasant or unpleasant consequences received by a model affect the watching child as if he had received those consequences himself. If the model is reinforced, the child is more likely to imitate his behavior, whereas when the model is punished, the child is less likely to imitate him. Suppose that one child sees another grab a third child's toy. If the aggressive child gets to keep his booty, the watching child is likely to grab another child's property. If, however, the grabber is punished and made to return the toy, the watching child is unlikely to imitate his action.

Peer models can influence positive behavior as well as aggression and disobedience. For example, Willard Hartup and Brian Coates (1967) asked four- and five-year-old children to watch one of their classmates complete a series of ten maze-drawing problems. Between problems, the model received a number of tiny plastic trinkets, which he divided between himself and a mythical child from another class. The model was actually the experimenter's confederate and had been coached to give away most of his trinkets to the "other child." Thus, the model appeared to be highly altruistic. After the model had left the room, the experimenter asked the watching children to complete the same maze-drawing task. They also received trinkets and were given an opportunity to divide them with the "other child." A control group of children, who had not seen the model, were given the same task, trinkets, and instructions. As Figure 13.2 shows, the children who had watched the altruistic model gave away many more trinkets than children in the control group did. This study provides straightforward evidence that, by the time a child is four or five, peer models can influence a socially approved activity such as sharing.

Just as peer encouragement is not always effective, so the effectiveness of a peer model varies. The Hartup and Coates study of altruism shows that two factors seem to bear upon the effectiveness of a model. In that study, a child's tendency to copy a model was related to the nature of his previous experience with the model and the nature of his interactions with the entire peer group. For example, popular children more often imitated a child who had previously reinforced them than a child who had never given them attention or approval. On the other hand, unpopular children seemed readier to imitate a child who had never paid them any attention than a child who had

reinforced them. Recall that popular children are generous with praise and approval and get a good deal of it themselves, whereas unpopular children are rarely reinforced.

Using slightly older children, Hicks (1971) demonstrated that the kind of behavior modeled also affects the likelihood of imitation. Young girls watched a model and judged several kinds of behavior as either "awful" or "nice." Two months later the girls imitated behavior they had rated "nice" much more frequently than behavior they had rated "awful." Earlier, it was pointed out that modeling can act as a signal of the appropriateness of a response. Although it seems evident that modeling does establish the appropriateness of an action when a child is unsure about what others expect, Hicks's results indicate that children continue to regard some behavior as inappropriate despite seeing a peer model it and that they are unlikely to imitate such behavior. It also appears that imitation is most likely to occur when the modeled actions are so clearly considered "good" or "bad" by watching children that they are unlikely to confuse them with other behavior.

Thus far, we have seen that both adults and peers can serve as models, which might lead one to wonder which model a child is likely to follow when their examples conflict. Hartup (1964b) has noted that children who imitate models tend to do so whether the model is an adult or another child.

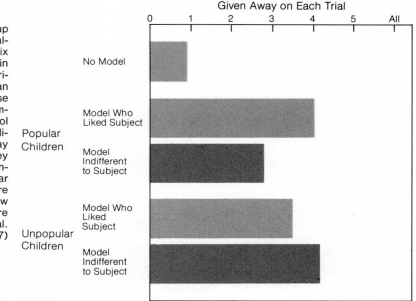

Figure 13.2   The results of Hartup and Coates' study of children's altruistic behavior. Children had six trinkets that they could give away in each trial. In all four of the experimental conditions, children saw an altruistic model, and in each case they shared more trinkets in comparison to the children in the control group, who saw no model. In addition, popular children gave away more trinkets when the model they saw was a child who usually reinforced them, whereas unpopular children tended to give away more trinkets when the model they saw was a child who had never before shown them attention or approval. (After Hartup and Coates, 1967)

Young children's play often includes elements of fantasy or role-taking. In this playground "space ship," children can easily imagine themselves to be astronauts or space travelers. (Ken Heyman)

But when it comes to learning new ways to express aggression, young children are more likely to imitate other children than adults (Hicks, 1965). In any case, models do exert a powerful effect on young children and can change their behavior in many ways.

FUNCTIONS OF PLAY

Children's play, in addition to being fun, serves a variety of functions: exploring the world, trying alternative roles, and testing new skills. When children enter the third year, their play takes on a more reciprocal quality (see Figure 13.3), in which the child is more attuned to the feelings and responses of others. Play also incorporates the child's increasing ability to symbolize and imagine, so

that it may include elements that are not present ("Pretend like we have horses") or material that is not factual ("You be the mommy").

Jean Piaget (1951) describes symbolic, imaginative play as essentially egocentric and as transforming the real into the desired. He writes:

> In most cases, indeed, the doll only serves as an opportunity for the child to re-live symbolically her own life in order to assimilate more easily its various aspects as well as to resolve daily conflicts and realize unsatisfied desires.

Using their increasing role-taking ability, young children engage in a great deal of fantasy play that intermingles elements from the roles they see enacted around them ("I'm Daddy getting the baby dressed for bed"), from television ("We're on a ship, and there are sharks all around us"), and from seemingly pure fantasy ("This is the time I learned how to fly"). Any available prop seems to generate a string of associations, which children weave into play that is sometimes infinitely flexible ("We can all walk on water") and sometimes extremely rigid ("You can't be a fireman because you don't have a hat on").

The play of young children builds on all the elements found in the toddler's play (Garvey, 1977). As children practice a variety of roles and deal with the inevitable conflicts that arise, their egocentrism decreases and their skill in role-taking increases. Children learn to understand the effects of their actions on others and to see their playmates as individuals, and less as objects of play. As they differentiate among people, children's specific attachments increase, and they form friendships that may be remarkably durable. At nursery school, children often seek out their preferred playmates as soon as they arrive and remain near them all day.

When Catherine Garvey and Robert Hogan (1973) looked at the play of young children, they found that the youngsters were mutually responsive and adapted their words and actions to those of their playmates. Such interaction is a clear indication of the young child's socialization.

The same influences in socialization—reinforcement, punishment, and modeling—that operate in relations with parents and peers affect the young child's play. But play differs in that here the child has the opportunity to create situations in which these socializing influences can operate. Through play, the child often tests different behavior without actually experiencing the dangers that the real action might hold, and directly or indirectly enjoys its positive results. The child can assume various roles and discover what happens to a person who behaves in these ways. For example, Matt can play the "bad guy" without being punished, or he can play the "good guy" and enjoy the pleasure of helping someone. A child can test skills in play that life might not allow him to test in reality. Thus, driving a car, riding a horse, and cooking a meal can all be practiced by a child of three or four.

During social play, a child also can try out various kinds of peer interactions by creating rules for games or by developing a way to cooperate or share (Bruner, Jolly, and Sylva, 1976). This interaction gives him the opportunity to experience the

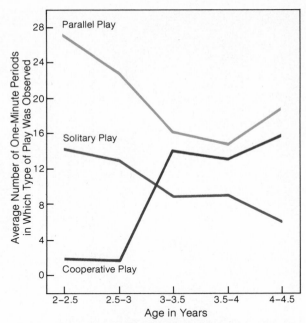

Figure 13.3   With increasing age and continued cognitive-social development, there are related changes in types of play. For example, solitary and parallel play decrease while cooperative play increases. (Adapted from Parten, 1932–1933)

results of certain social behavior within a limited setting. Finally, a child can find out how certain consequences "feel" by rewarding or punishing his own behavior. For example, a young child may slap his own hand and tell himself "no-no" when he spills his mud pie.

Modeling is incorporated into play in much the same way as reinforcement and punishment. An imaginary superhero can provide a model of generosity and helping. A child can learn new skills, such as building a self-supporting arch with blocks, by watching a more skillful playmate. Watching other children cooperate at play through sharing a set of cooking pots and pans may teach a child these positive skills. Play with dolls can provide self-generated modeling. As he plays, the child creates and then observes parent-child interactions. When he has the daddy doll spank the child doll for getting out of bed, a child provides himself with a form of modeling, even though he himself manipulated the doll's behavior.

Subcultural differences in socialization result in wide and enduring differences in most aspects of children's development. (Ken Heyman)

SUBCULTURES AND PERSONALITY

The values adhered to by a child's parents vary depending on the particular culture to which they belong. The United States is not a homogeneous population with one set of values and standards but rather a variety of subcultures, which often vary greatly in structure and values. These subcul-

tures may result from regional, religious, racial, ethnic, or economic differences. As we will also see in our discussion of adolescence, the way in which important personality and social behaviors such as aggression, sex-role development, dependence, and competitiveness are handled varies greatly within different groups (R. Hess, 1970).

The socialization of different values and personality characteristics may come about in two ways. First, different values are adhered to in separate cultures, so that the child is reinforced for different behavior. Thus, a black urban family may reinforce assertiveness more than a rural Chicano family does. Structural differences in the socializing unit may also influence socialization. Thus, a child whose father is absent learns different things from those learned by the child whose father is present. A variety of structural considerations may vary across subcultures: Lower-middle-class mothers are more likely to work than extremely wealthy mothers; families in low socioeconomic groups spend more time than families in high socioeconomic groups watching television; rural families are more likely than urban families to have grandparents, aunts, or uncles in the household; Catholic families are likely to have more children than Jewish families. Although subcultures may subscribe equally to independence or helpfulness, their structural differences may lead them to treat such behavior differently.

The values, child-rearing methods, and life styles of families in various subcultures differ as does their access to various resources and financial security. As Melvin Kohn (1963) puts it:

> Members of different social classes, by virtue of enjoying (or suffering) different conditions of life, come to see the world differently—to develop different conceptions of social reality, different aspirations and hopes and fears, different conceptions of the desirable.

What adults consider desirable, probable, and possible in life will determine the qualities that they instill in their children. Parents in one social class will emphasize one quality in their children while neglecting another, and the reverse may be true in a different social class. As we will see in more detail in discussing adolescence, lower socioeconomic class parents may value their child's overt conformity to the do's and don'ts of society, whereas middle-class parents may stress the development of self-direction in their child. In one social class, these lessons may be taught casually and with little pressure, but another social class may teach them intensely and under close guard (R. Hess, 1970).

Socioeconomic status has also been found to affect a great deal of social behavior. For example, most parents of lower socioeconomic status are more likely than parents of middle-class status to use physical punishment and ridicule with their children (Bayley and Schaefer, 1960). On the other hand, middle-class parents are more likely than lower-class parents to emphasize independence in early childhood, expect excellence in school performance, and believe in the possibility of success (Rosen, 1956).

Ethnic differences may also lead to the stressing of different values. Spencer Kagan and Millard Madsen (1971) studied children from Mexican, Mexican-American, and Anglo-American backgrounds to determine the extent to which each group socialized cooperation and competition. Pairs of children played a game that offered a choice of cooperation or competition. Kagan and Madsen found two important differences: Four- and five-year-olds were more cooperative than seven-, eight-, or nine-year-olds; and rural Mexican children were most likely of any group to cooperate in order to win a game, Mexican-Americans were next most cooperative, and urban Anglo-Americans, most competitive. Kagan and Madsen interpreted these results as showing that different subcultures have different norms of behavior and that the predominant Anglo-American orientation is competition.

Another important difference that has been found among subcultures regards locus of control. Mark Stephens and Pamela Delys (1973) found, for example, that by the time children entered nursery school, differences in locus of control appeared between socioeconomic classes. Middle-class children were more likely to feel internally controlled, whereas lower-class children were more likely to feel externally controlled.

Thus, differences in the behavior of children may be the result of both adherence to a subcultural norm and structural factors, such as access to various culturally enriching situations that make the likelihood of success higher. Whereas personality and social behavior are largely learned, the course of that learning and, therefore, the development of personality and behavior patterns may be radically different from family to family.

SUMMARY

1. The process of psychologically growing into a society is called socialization. A major mechanism in socialization and personality development is identification, through which children take on characteristics, values, and attitudes of people they admire.

2. Sex-role learning provides an excellent illustration of socialization and identification. Learning the behavior and qualities that society considers appropriate and desirable for a person of his or her gender is an important personality task. Sex-role stereotypes—simplified, fixed concepts about the behavior and traits typical of each sex—are established early, and, by the time they are five or six, children are strongly influenced by such sex-typed virtues as aggressiveness and independence for boys and attractiveness and dependence for girls.

3. Identification, sex-role learning, attractiveness, relations with peers, and the establishment of self-regulation all contribute to the development of young children's self-concepts. By the time they are six, most children understand their own assets and liabilities, and evaluate their efforts and characteristics in comparison with other children like themselves.

4. As the earliest and most durable source of socialization, parents remain the strongest influence in a child's personal and social development. Thus, the way that parents reward and punish their children's behavior has a potent effect on the development of such characteristics as aggressiveness and on sex roles in general.

5. The role of peers as agents of socialization usually becomes more intense and pervasive during early childhood. Children increasingly learn attitudes and behavior involved in various roles from other children. Within the peer group, they actively practice the learned roles they will perform in later years. As with their parents, much of what children learn to do from interacting with their peers depends on what they have observed the other children doing (modeling) and whether the actions were encouraged or discouraged (rewarded or punished).

6. Play may also involve such socialization influences as reward or punishment and modeling. Through play children can test different behavior by assuming various roles and discovering what happens to a person who behaves that way. As in infancy, play serves a variety of functions: it allows children to have fun, to explore the world, to test and strengthen new skills, and to learn how other children see and do things.

7. Because children are reared in different subcultures, they are likely to show different personalities and behavior patterns. Thus, from family to family, the development of different views, values, and behavior may be encouraged and strengthened.

Unit V Later Childhood: Growing Up

In later childhood, the developing boy or girl comes under further direct control of society in the form of school, which has the official task of presenting formal education. The child's cognitive structure evolves and stabilizes; he develops new and more realistic ways to categorize his world, to operate in it competently, and to perceive its parts and the logical and causal relationships among them. At the same time, through his games and social experiences, he develops social skills that help him to understand how others think and feel. During this period, the differences between appropriate male and female behavior sharpen, and each child tends to play primarily with peers of his or her own sex. Now he lays down friendships and patterns of social behavior that may last throughout his life. A sense of right and wrong continues to evolve; the child who began life as an amoral infant becomes a being with a sense of guilt that plagues him when he violates his own moral code. As a reminder that development is cumulative and continuous, this unit looks at the development of morality over the life span.

CHAPTER 14
Cognition: Advances in Thinking

SELECTIVE ATTENTION

ADVANCES IN CHILDREN'S THINKING
Concepts
Causal Reasoning
Problem Solving

CHANGES IN REPRESENTATIONAL SKILLS
Imitation
Language
Play
Memory

SOCIAL INTERACTION AND COGNITION

THE CONCEPT OF INTELLIGENCE
Changing Viewpoints About IQ
What IQ Does and Does Not Measure

SUMMARY

When David was four, he unwrapped his red and blue Superman costume with great excitement. He put on the suit, waited impatiently for his mother to tie the red cape around his neck, crouched down, tensed his muscles—and tried to fly. When his feet remained on the ground, he was surprised and disappointed. The innocence and gullibility of young children like David is a frequent theme in literature. Just as many children are sure that a man in a red suit drives a team of reindeer through the sky to bring them presents, many do not realize that the claims presented in television advertisements for breakfast cereals may not be true. The young child may think of truth as relevant only to statements that he makes and perhaps to those of a few immediate friends, his family, and neighbors.

Now that David is ten, he readily understands truth as also applying to the statements of people he meets and to the media, and he may use the concept to evaluate books that he reads. Most developmental psychologists would agree that the ten-year-old's understanding of concepts tends to be more general and inclusive than the young child's. However, the ten-year-old probably does not think of truth as a general concept that he can apply to any statement ever made about any subject by any person at any time in history. By the time he is fifteen, David's concept of truth will probably be in accord with the abstract and general definition "something that is the case," and he will be able to apply it to an infinite number of events or statements.

In this chapter, we will see that the growing child becomes more capable of abstract thought and less dependent on concrete, real-life examples in learning new concepts. The strategies that he uses to solve problems will become more systematic, more thorough, and more often based on deductions. We will find that, during the years from six to twelve, a child learns to attend more selectively. We will examine his understanding of natural phenomena and see him acquire the ability to comprehend and to deal more efficiently with relational concepts. It will become apparent that his increased sensitivity to language reflects this intellectual advance. As his word definitions become more abstract, he uses metaphor more effectively and appreciates the ambiguities of meaning. We will discover that the child gains increased ability to envision the viewpoint of another and that this appears in the language he uses when asked to teach a less competent child. We will also discuss recent insights into the cognitive roles that play serves during these years. Finally, we will look at the use and abuse of psychological tests that have been constructed to measure intelligence and intellectual development.

SELECTIVE ATTENTION

As a child grows, his attention becomes increasingly reliable and sustained, and he tends to focus on what he judges to be the important aspects of a situation.

Children, especially in school, are constantly presented with tasks that require them to pay sustained and formal attention to relevant parts of material to be learned and to ignore irrelevant parts. For example, in learning to read, children must pay close attention to the shapes of letters and to their sequential order. However, the shading of the print or the size of the letters is usually irrelevant. A **P** is a **p** is a *p,* but a "rose" is not a "sore" is not an "eros," nor is an *o* identical to a *q* or a *c.* It may be that developmental differences

exist in children's ability to determine which aspects of a situation are relevant to a learning task and which are not and to deploy their attention accordingly. Chapter 11 included evidence that four- to six-year-olds are more likely than eight-year-olds to respond to irrelevant cues that might distract them from a task.

John Hagen and Gordon Hale (1973) studied changes in selective attention among children between the ages of seven and thirteen by using a simple learning task. The children were told that they would have to remember the *location* of some pictures that they would see. Then each child was shown a row of picture cards. On each card were two pictures, one of a common household object, such as a television set or a lamp, and one of an animal, such as a camel or a cat. The experimenter then turned the cards face down and showed the child a "cue card" with one of the animals or one of the objects on it. The child was then asked to point to the one card in the set face down in front of him that pictured the same animal or object. The number of correct matches over a series of these trials was the measure of the child's *central learning.* After the child was tested on picture location, which was the task given to him, he was asked if he remembered which objects had been paired with which animals in the set of cards. His correct recall of the pairings measured his *incidental learning.*

Children who scored high on incidental learning must have paid attention to features that were irrelevant to the task described to them. Con-

In school, children must pay sustained, formal attention to relevant material while ignoring irrelevant parts. For example, shapes and order of letters are important, but style or size of script is not. (Ken Heyman)

Figure 14.1 In Hagen and Hale's study of children's attention and learning, there was an increase with age in the average number of pictures identified correctly on the basis of their location (central-learning task). The inset (*top left*) is a sample of the cards used in the study. The average number of pictured pairings of animals and objects remained relatively constant until age thirteen, when it dropped sharply (incidental learning). At about age twelve, a child's selective attention becomes so powerful that he seems to exclude extraneous material. (Adapted from Hagen, 1967)

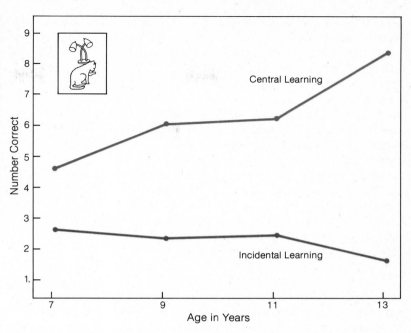

versely, children who scored low on incidental learning must have paid little attention to the irrelevant aspects. It is reasonable to infer, therefore, that children who scored high on central learning and low on incidental learning are more selective in their attention. As instructed, they concentrated exclusively on location and hence learned little or nothing about the pairings.

As Figure 14.1 shows, children's performances on the central-learning task improved with age in a very straightforward way (even though in this case the learning task also involved a possible distraction consisting of tape-recorded piano notes). The older the child, the higher his memory-for-position score. On the other hand, Figure 14.1 shows no significant change in incidental-learning scores for children from ages seven through eleven. All scored lower on incidental-learning than on central-learning tasks. However, the incidental-learning scores of twelve- and thirteen-year-olds dropped.

From these findings, it appears that even the youngest children are capable of directing their attention to the central aspect of a task and that this capacity continually improves with age. Because incidental learning does not increase with age, it seems that, as a child like Lauren grows older, she becomes more competent at selective attention, focusing on only the relevant features of a clearly defined task. In other words, the older child learns more about what she understands to be important.

However, at about the age of twelve, the child's selective attention seems to become so powerful that she appears to exclude irrelevant material from consciousness, learning less than she would have several years earlier about incidental features.

There are, of course, many situations in which a person does not know in advance which features are relevant and which are irrelevant, as the bitter experience of studying the "wrong" things for an examination testifies. In an ambiguous learning situation, therefore, it is often a wise policy to use broad and nonselective attention at first in order to find out by sampling from the range of possibilities and by searching memory which components are relevant and which are not. There is some evidence that eight-year-old children are superior to five-year-olds in using this sample-and-search strategy and are even as competent as twelve-year-olds (Hale and Morgan, 1973). Thus, as a person matures, his past experiences lead him to concentrate on what he expects will be the relevant aspects of a situation. As the rest of the chapter will show, attention, perception, and cognition become increasingly intertwined.

ADVANCES IN CHILDREN'S THINKING

As children grow, they continue to advance in their use of symbols. From about the age of seven, when what Jean Piaget (Inhelder and Piaget, 1958) calls the *concrete-operational* stage begins (see Chapter 2), children become more proficient in their use of logical operations to represent physical reality.

Concepts

Growing children show a continually increasing sophistication in their ability to deal with concepts and rules. A concept represents a characteristic common to a number of different events or objects. For example, a "fruit" is no single thing, but it is many more or less sweet, edible portions of plants that we generally group together for convenience. Like all human beings, children use concepts such as "fruit," "sweet," "friend," "star," "round," or "red" to organize the world about them. By applying these and a myriad of other concepts, children simplify their world, reducing the barrage of complex sensation to manageable proportions and, once they know that an object or event belongs in a certain category, using what they know about the category to tell them more about the object (Flavell, 1977).

Relational Concepts In Chapter 11 we saw that the young child may find it difficult to understand concepts that involve relations between two or more things or events. He may err when he reasons about the notion of conservation of quantity (rearranging a row of objects does not affect their number), about transitivity (if A is larger than B and B is larger than C, then A is larger than C), and about the relationship between the whole and its parts (if A = B + C, then A is more than B alone or C alone). During later childhood, the ability to handle some of these concepts appears to undergo developmental changes.

For example, Gerald Winer (1974) found measurable advances in reasoning about relational concepts among seven-, eight-, and nine-year-old children. He asked them six questions, such as "If I had four apples and three pears, would I have more apples or more things to eat?" and "If I had two butterflies and six birds, would I have more birds or more things that fly?" The nine-year-old children answered the questions correctly more often than the seven- or eight-year-olds did. When Winer showed a child a picture of, for example, two butterflies and six birds along with the question, the child's reasoning did not change. Apparently, the ability to comprehend the relationship between a class of objects and its

parts, like some other cognitive skills, develops gradually and at different times for different children. Thus, many children in primary school, faced with a traditional problem involving relational concepts, may still maintain that they have more lemon drops than candy. By the age of nine, however, nearly all children know they have more candy.

Conservation In the earlier discussion of relational concepts, we noted that young children seem to have difficulty understanding that transformations of perceptual features do not necessarily change other properties of physical substances. By the time a child is six or seven years old, he is more likely to understand the concept of the conservation of quantity. This means, for example, that his parents can no longer placate him when he begs for jelly beans (if they ever could) by simply spreading out the ones that he already has, nor does pouring orangeade from a squat glass into a tall, narrow one convince him that his amount of orangeade has doubled. He usually realizes that if he pours the orangeade back into the squat glass, the level will be just where it was before. Thus, he has acquired another of what Piaget classifies as concrete operations: **reversibility.** Having acquired reversibility, the child can prove to himself that the amount of orangeade has remained the same by mentally returning the liquid to its previous state, or by reversing the procedure in his mind.

In addition to number and quantity, other properties of physical substances remain constant, even though they appear to have undergone dramatic transformations. The Eiffel Tower would weigh the same as it does now if it were compressed into a solid square of metal. A short, thick chunk of clay stretched into a long, thin, spaghetti-like string would displace the same amount of water.

Piaget's experiments (Piaget and Inhelder, 1969) on children's notions of conservation reveal an interesting phenomenon. Although seven-year-olds realize that the mass of an object such as a piece of clay does not change when the clay is stretched or compressed, they may fail to realize that its weight and volume also remain unchanged. Piaget also found that children always acquire the various kinds of conservation in the same order. First the child understands conservation of quantity; then, at about the age of nine or ten, he grasps the notion of conservation of weight; and finally, at

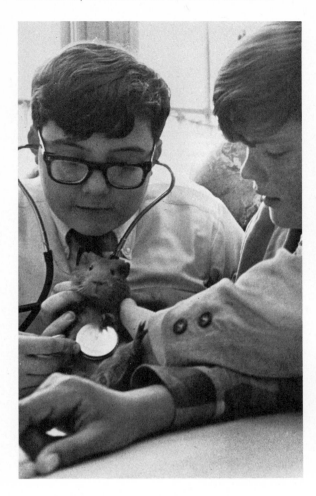

During later childhood, reasoning about objects, events, and concepts becomes more systematic. Children are less likely to let their reasoning be affected by perceptual changes that appear to alter physical relations. (*left:* Robin Forbes/Ford Foundation; *right:* Jane Bown)

about ten or eleven, he realizes that there is also conservation of volume, in the sense that the amount of water displaced by an object is not affected if its shape is changed (Piaget and Inhelder, 1941). Other researchers have confirmed Piaget's basic findings about the sequence of these acquisitions (Sigel and Mermelstein, 1966; Uzgiris, 1964).

Although a child of about nine realizes that changing the shape of an object does not affect its weight, he may not transfer this realization to other kinds of changes. For example, K. Lovell and E. Ogilvie (1961) found that children who "passed" the weight-conservation test when an object's shape was altered still thought that butter loses weight as it melts and that water becomes heavier as it freezes.

In a study with first-grade children, Gilbert Botvin and Frank Murray (1975) discovered that those who failed to conserve mass, weight, and number on standard tests could learn the concepts from other children. Botvin and Murray put the children in groups of fives, each made up of three nonconservers and two conservers. A researcher first asked each child to answer the same series of questions about weight and mass conservation, so they heard one another's answers. The group then talked over their explanations and agreed on an answer to the conservation problems. After they had reached an agreement, the researcher requestioned each child. In some cases, additional children who were nonconservers watched and listened as the group gave their answers both before and after the discussion, but did not observe the group discussion.

Most of the nonconservers, both those who participated in the discussions and those who simply heard the questioning, learned to conserve mass, weight, and number. An examination of their explanations showed they were not just parroting the reasons given by the original conservers. During the earlier group discussions, the original conservers tended to explain conservation by talking about the reversibility of the change, whereas the new conservers tended to give "identity" explanations, noting that nothing had been added or subtracted from the original amount, or that the change had been irrelevant. Botvin and Murray interpret the change as the result of modeling, suggesting that when the models gave correct answers, they produced mental conflicts, which prodded the children into reorganizing their thinking. According to Botvin and Murray, the first grasp of conservation appears to involve a different kind of understanding from that of later conservation, and a child moves from an understanding of identity to comprehending the concept of reversibility.

Developmental psychologists are still far from understanding exactly how a child acquires conservation concepts or why he seems to acquire them in a particular order. Conservation is an extremely complex cognitive skill, which Susan Carey (1974) sees as developing from two sources. First, the child's nervous system matures, increasing his ability to process information (that is, his memory becomes longer, he can handle more bits of knowledge at once, etc.). So all children get better at conservation simply by getting older. Second, the child acquires the pieces of knowledge that allow him to understand and solve problems of conservation. Once his information processing abilities have matured somewhat, the child can be taught by practice or by observation, as were the children in Botvin and Murray's study.

Even without formal schooling, children constantly experience the heaviness or lightness of objects they lift, push, or pull. They "know" from their handling of objects, although they may not realize that they know, that things do not get heavier or lighter if their shape or color changes. Many children may conserve weight in the sense of knowing to maintain constant muscular pressure in lifting a ball of clay that has just been elongated, even though, if asked, they would state that its

weight had changed. Thus, they may *know how* but not *know that* or *know about.*

Causal Reasoning

There are several kinds of precausal thinking, and the child does not shift from precausal to causal thought in all areas at the same time. By the time David is six or seven, he no longer believes that dreams are external to himself, and he realizes that others can neither see nor touch his dreams.

One kind of precausal thinking that continues to play a role in the beliefs of children is **artificialism,** which refers to explanations that involve either God or man as the artisan of all natural things. We should not confuse the child's belief in God as creator with the belief of the religious adult in a Creator. The child's God is more like a giant or a magician, as this discussion with a nine-year-old child on the origin of night makes clear:

Adult: Tell me, what is night?
Child: It's dark.
Adult: Why is it dark at night?
Child: The clouds make it dark.
Adult: Where does the dark come from at night?
Child: From the sky.
Adult: Where do these clouds come from?
Child: From the sky.
Adult: How does the sky make these clouds, with what does it make them?
Child: It's good Jesus. He makes them and hangs them in the sky. He makes them alone, with nothing. (Laurendeau and Pinard, 1962, page 174)

This child pictures Jesus as if He were cutting clouds out of cotton and then hanging them up in the sky to produce night. If the child had meant this as a poetic description, Monique Laurendeau and Adrien Pinard (1962) would not have considered it a precausal, artificialistic explanation. However, the child first tried to offer an explanation based on physical elements (the clouds), then shifted to the artificialistic one, presumably because he considered it to be more intellectually sound.

A twelve-year-old deals with these same questions about the origin of night in an entirely different manner. Consider the following discussion, which Laurendeau and Pinard classify as an example of causal thinking:

Adult: Tell me, what is the night?
Child: It's when the sun goes down. It's dark.
Adult: Why is it dark at night?

Figure 14.2 The way that children order and understand the physical world typically becomes less ego-centric, magical, and precausal during the later childhood years. These excerpts are from an illustrated children's book by Etienne Delessert, *How the Mouse Was Hit on the Head by a Stone and So Discovered the World,* produced with the assistance of Piaget, which describes the world through the eyes of five- and six-year-old children. The book tells of a mouse who never left his home beneath the ground until the day he discovered the world while digging a tunnel. (*top*) The mouse discovers the sky and clouds. (*bottom*) He talks to the moon.

Child: Because the sun is down and it's the sun which projects light during the day.
Adult: Where does the dark come from at night? What makes it night?
Child: It comes from nowhere, it's the color of the sky. In the daytime, it's the sun which makes it blue, and when the sun is gone it becomes dark.

. . .

Adult: Where does the sun go at night?
Child: Behind the clouds. (page 178)

Although this twelve-year-old's explanations are not at all scientifically "correct," he does base his reasons on concepts of physical causality. The sun does not really go behind the clouds, but the older child knows that, if a source of light is blocked by another object, then the light will not shine. Thus, it is not the correctness of the child's reasoning but its formal properties that determine whether it is causal or precausal.

Laurendeau and Pinard found that the transition in thinking from artificialism to notions of strict physical causality takes place gradually during the years from six to twelve. But, as was pointed out in Chapter 11, children tend to give physical explanations on matters with which they are experienced, resorting to artificial explanations in matters that are remote to them. Some children still offer artificialistic explanations for the origins of night when they are eleven or twelve, but older children use this kind of reasoning infrequently. Of the seven-year-olds that Laurendeau and Pinard studied, 74 percent attempted to explain the night by at least a partial appeal to either human or divine creation but, among the twelve-year-olds, only 10 percent resorted to this sort of reasoning. By the time they reach adolescence, many children have abandoned artificialism for other kinds of thinking.

Using easy problems that children solve early in life (in the sense of *knowing how*), Piaget (1976) explored the development of the child's growing awareness of causality (in the sense of *knowing about*). In one study, he placed two small balls (A and B) in line with an English ninepin (a much smaller version of an American bowling pin) and had children first knock the pin over using both balls, then hit ball B with ball A so that both balls missed the pin, and finally knock over the pin when it was about 45° out of line with the two balls. Four-year-olds could do the first two tasks but could give no general rule. Seven- and eight-year-olds knew that they must make ball A hit the side of B if they wanted B to change directions, but

they still failed at the third task. Nine- and ten-year-olds succeeded on all tasks and could generalize from the idea of hitting B at an angle to the rule that striking the ball at various points generates different directions, saying, "If you hit it more toward the edge of the ball, it goes more like that [correct direction]." Eleven-year-old children formulated a general relation between impact and direction, saying, "When you want it to go straight, you hit it in the middle; but if you can aim at the balls from another angle, they go off at another angle [the same angle]."

Problem Solving

As a child gets older, he more often tends to define common objects in terms of the abstract category to which they belong (an orange is a fruit) rather than in terms of their specific use (an orange is for eating) or their particular perceptual features (an orange is round). Thus, as David grows from the four-year-old who believed he could fly to the relatively sophisticated ten-year-old, his concepts become more general. But he is still a long way from the adolescent, who may easily manipulate hypothetical situations.

Children like David have many concepts that are less general or abstract than those of adolescents, but that does not mean children are incapable of learning and using abstract concepts in a meaningful way. Children between the ages of seven and eleven can learn new abstract concepts if they are provided with concrete examples, physical or verbal, of the new concept. They do find it extremely difficult, however, to learn an abstract concept simply from a general definition that mentions the abstracted attributes of the concept but fails to specify a concrete instance. For example, ten-year-old David would probably find the concept of "government" incomprehensible if he were told nothing more than "Government is the group of persons that makes and administers the policies of a political unit or organization." In general, it is not until he is twelve or so that the child is likely to think more abstractly and to need fewer specific examples to help his understanding.

Research in other countries among schooled and unschooled children and adults indicates that abstract categorization and reasoning may not be an inevitable outcome of growing up, but the direct result of formal education. Because nearly all children in the United States and Europe go to school, it has been difficult for developmental psychologists to separate the effects of human development from the effects of schooling. Based on numerous studies in Africa and Latin America, Michael Cole (1978) has concluded that formal education itself changes the mind in several ways: people group things into general classes according to formal rules (cow, horse, dog) instead of according to their function (cow, pasture, milk); they use these classes to solve problems and to organize their recall; and they treat problems in logic as hypothetical puzzles instead of as questions of fact or interpretation. Although literacy does not guarantee the development of formal thought, some children show these changes after as few as three years of schooling. Nine years of formal education, Cole discovered, will bring about the changes in most children.

The increasing capacity for abstract thinking that generally develops in early adolescence appears about the time that children have completed eight or nine years of schooling, and it is closely related to the strategies that are used in solving problems whose solution requires one to consider several factors. The adolescent in Piaget's formal-operational period (see Chapters 2 and 18) is more orderly, thorough, hypothetical, and logical than the younger child when called on to identify the factor or factors that are responsible for an event.

A look at the pendulum-problem experiment, which was conducted by Bärbel Inhelder and Jean Piaget (1958), illustrates differences that often appear among younger children, older children, and adolescents. These two Swiss psychologists presented elementary- and high-school students with strings of different lengths and objects of different weights, which the children could attach to a rod so that they swung like pendulums. Inhelder and Piaget pointed out to the children that each of the various possible pendulums would swing through its arc at a different speed. The problem before each child was to determine the factor or factors that account for the speed with which a pendulum

Using abstract categories and logical hypotheses to solve problems is probably the direct result of formal education, which appears to change the mind in several ways. (Ken Heyman)

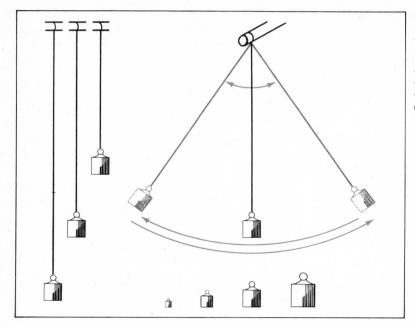

Figure 14.3 Illustration of a pendulum problem. The child is given a set of weights (pictured at bottom) and a string that can be shortened or lengthened (as pictured at left). His task is to determine which factor or factors account for the speed with which a pendulum traverses its arc. (After Inhelder and Piaget, 1958)

traverses its arc. The four intuitively plausible causes are (1) the weight of the object, (2) the length of the string, (3) the height from which the object is released, and (4) the force of the initial push.

Inhelder and Piaget were primarily interested in the thought processes of the children as they tried to solve the pendulum problem. Of the four possible factors, only the length of the string affects the speed of the pendulum. A child can discover this solution either by methodically trying all possible combinations of the four factors (varying a single factor with each trial) or by imagining trials of all possible combinations of factors.

The youngest children, six and seven, almost always concluded that the force of their own initial push determined the pendulum's speed. They did not approach the problem methodically; they failed to set up an experiment in which they varied each of the factors separately. It was hard for these children, who were judged to be in the preoperational stage, to imagine that the motion of the pendulum *may* be independent of their own thrusting.

Children between eight and thirteen were somewhat more systematic, but not enough so to solve the problem. At first they varied some but not all of the factors, having particular difficulty with weight. They also accurately judged the differences in the pendulum's movements. But not

until the experimenter showed the way could they isolate the effect of one factor from the effect of others. They did not generate on their own a set of procedures that specified all possible combinations of the four factors. As a result of these limitations, they concluded that length of the string is one determining factor but not that it is the only relevant one. They found it particularly difficult to exclude factors.

Only the fourteen- or fifteen-year-old anticipated all possible combinations, tested them experimentally, and deduced not only what affects a pendulum's speed but also what factors are irrelevant. On the basis of experiments like this, Inhelder and Piaget concluded that adolescent thought is characterized by the ability to hypothesize and to deduce.

Although Inhelder and Piaget found that eleven- and twelve-year-olds usually fail to solve the pendulum problem, Robert Siegler, Diane Liebert, and Robert Liebert (1973) have developed a training procedure that successfully taught even ten-year-olds the skills that enabled them to solve it. They conclude that Piaget is correct in stating that ten- and eleven-year-olds do not usually solve such problems on their own but that this does not mean that such problems are beyond children's intellectual grasp. As Chapter 11 indicated, a child's inability to solve a problem does not mean that he is unable to grasp the concept involved. Just as four-year-olds can be taught to understand conservation, a ten-year-old can learn to perform some of the mental activities that often do not develop until adolescence.

CHANGES IN REPRESENTATIONAL SKILLS

During the years from six to twelve, the growing human being becomes an even more skillful user of symbols. His cognitive advances in later childhood are characterized by more sophisticated representational skills that take several forms.

Imitation

Imitation takes various forms in the young child, as you will recall from Chapter 11. Imitation can be external action or internal image, and it can vary in the degree to which it corresponds with that which is imitated. During later childhood, imitation continues to contribute to cognitive acquisition.

For years, research on the relationship between imitation and intellectual development seldom went beyond the preschool years. Recently, however, psychologists have become interested in the connection between imitation and cognition during later development. It is common knowledge that, in learning to perform complex actions, it is often useful to watch another person and then try to imitate his behavior. Lynn McLaughlin and Joseph Brinley (1973) set up an experiment to find out if children could also learn to solve problems more efficiently by first observing a model solve them.

They devised two sorting tasks, one with fifteen blocks, the other with fifteen animal pictures. The blocks could be sorted into four separate groups according to either their *shape,* their *color,* or their *proportions.* The pictures could be sorted into groups according to either the *kind of animal,* the *number of animals* on each card, or the *presence or absence of faces and/or cage bars.* Children from seven through twelve were asked to sort the blocks into four groups. McLaughlin and Brinley told each child that, although there were several possible ways to sort, only one would be considered correct. The correct solution was to classify the material on the basis of multiple attributes.

McLaughlin and Brinley found that, regardless of age, children who watched the model and children who had a chance to practice sorted blocks better than children who neither saw the model nor practiced. However, only eleven- and twelve-year-olds were able to abstract the general principle that guided the solution and transfer it from blocks to animal pictures. Thus, it seems that children as young as seven can imitate the problem-solving performance of a model as long as the task is identical to the one that they watch. Even more promising, this study and others like it (Denney, Denney, and Ziobrowski, 1973; T. Rosenthal and Zimmerman, 1973) imply that using filmed, televised, and live models can be practical ways to teach children problem-solving and abstraction skills.

Language

By the time a child is four or five, as was stressed in Chapter 12, he has mastered a good part of the complex structure of his native language; his lin-

In learning to perform complex actions, such as playing the piano, children often find it useful to watch another person and then try to imitate his behavior. (Suzanne Szasz)

According to Piaget, a child learns new concepts and rules more readily by engaging in active play and exploration than by reading about them. (© Joel Gordon)

child's ability to understand how meaning changes as the order of identical words changes—as in the sentences "The boy was hit by the girl" and "The girl was hit by the boy"—is itself a cognitive feat of significance. Advanced language use and comprehension probably depend more on cognition than cognition depends on language, although language is undoubtedly important for certain kinds of intellectual skills and makes concept learning easier and concept use more flexible.

On the other hand, Piaget (1972) has argued that, during childhood, a child learns new concepts and rules best by working extensively with concrete materials. According to Piaget, concepts and rules can be derived more readily from active play, exploration, and investigation than from listening to or reading about them. He believes that verbal formulations tend to bore or frustrate the child. Although Piaget's emphasis on the fundamental importance of concrete over verbal experience is not universally accepted (Ausubel, 1968), he does focus on the role of language in formal concept learning, in everyday reasoning, and in a systematic approach to solving complex problems.

Words and Metaphors The growing child's increasing tendency to deal with abstractions shows clearly in developmental changes in his capacity to use metaphor, which depends on the ability to perceive relationships between different objects or qualities. In one study of metaphor, Howard Gardner (1974) asked children to match phrases like those shown in Column B in Figure 14.4 with the appropriate adjectives from Column A. Most adults would maintain that the first adjective of each pair in Column A is the most appropriate metaphor for the first phrase in each pair in Column B and that the second adjective is the most appropriate metaphor for the second phrase.

When Gardner presented students ranging in age from three and one-half to nineteen years with examples of phrases like those in Column B, he found that even the youngest children were able to make numerous metaphorical matches. However, seven-year-olds outperformed the younger children, and eleven-and-one-half-year-olds outperformed the seven-year-olds. But there the improvement stopped: Eleven-and-one-half-year-olds did as well as college students.

It is apparent, therefore, that children are intellectually capable of appreciating poetic meta-

guistic development will extend into adolescence. Much of this linguistic development seems intimately related to the child's cognitive development. Children cannot really understand the increasingly complex meanings of sentences that they hear if the concepts expressed in those sentences are beyond their intellectual grasp. After all, in order for a symbol to be meaningful, the symbol user must first comprehend the object, event, or relationship for which it stands. Furthermore, as our earlier discussion of language made clear, the

phor—they may even create poetry on their own (K. Koch, 1970)—and that this capability increases during the elementary-school years. Gardner's study indicates that a child's ability to perceive relationships between objects that differ in appearance improves steadily until about age eleven, when it reaches adult levels, and that this perception of relationships is expressed with language.

Jokes and Riddles   The appreciation of jokes and riddles is also tied to language and cognitive development. Many riddles and jokes are based on the fact that words and phrases have more than one meaning. In order to appreciate the humor, David and Lauren must be aware of the multiple meanings of the word or phrase and see how an unanticipated meaning resolves the incongruity.

Sigmund Freud (1960) suggested that there is a developmental sequence in the appreciation of humor. At first the child enjoys mere nonsense, which is a form of unresolvable incongruity. Later he is amused by jokes that have meaning—their incongruity can be resolved.

Thomas Shultz (1974), who has studied children's appreciation of both riddles and jokes, views a riddle as a misleading question followed by an incongruous answer. The listener must figure out how the incongruity makes sense; his pleasure comes when he succeeds in resolving the problem by explaining the incongruous answer. A similar analysis applies to jokes.

In his study of riddles, Shultz tested Freud's hypothesis by systematically studying children's appreciation of jokes and riddles at the ages of six, eight, ten, and twelve. The children heard a series of riddles, each having three possible answers. For example:

Why did the farmer name his hog Ink?
1. Because he kept running out of the pen.
2. Because he kept getting away.
3. Because he was black. (page 101)

As you can see, in Variation 3 the incongruity is removed: The hog was named Ink because he was black. In Variation 2 the incongruity remains but is not resolved: It is pure nonsense for a farmer to name his hog Ink because he keeps getting away. In Variation 1, however, the incongruity can be resolved. A clearly discernible change in the child's appreciation of humor appeared between the ages of six and eight. Six-year-olds did not appreciate jokes or riddles whose humor depended on resolving a linguistic ambiguity, whereas children of eight and older did. The six-year-olds found simple, unresolved incongruity humorous.

Figure 14.4 Adjective pairs (Column A) and related pairs of phrases (Column B) like those used by Gardner in his study of the development of the appreciation of metaphor, as discussed in the text. (After Gardner, 1974)

Column A	Column B
Sad—Happy	Hearing the phrase ''A cloudy afternoon''—Hearing the phrase ''A bright morning''
Warm—Cold	Seeing the color red—Seeing the color blue
Hard—Soft	Seeing a photograph of a frowning face—Seeing a photograph of a smiling face
Loud—Quiet	Seeing thick line drawings—Seeing thin line drawings
Dark—Light	Touching a piece of abrasive sandpaper—Touching a piece of mild sandpaper

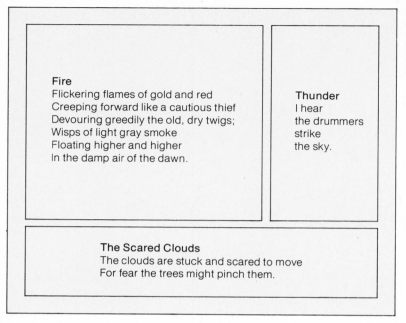

Fire
Flickering flames of gold and red
Creeping forward like a cautious thief
Devouring greedily the old, dry twigs;
Wisps of light gray smoke
Floating higher and higher
In the damp air of the dawn.

Thunder
I hear
the drummers
strike
the sky.

The Scared Clouds
The clouds are stuck and scared to move
For fear the trees might pinch them.

Figure 14.5 Poems written by nine- and eleven-year-old girls. Unconstrained by many adult preconceptions and rules, children often see and represent common phenomena in novel ways.

The eight-year-olds found both the incongruity and its resolution humorous. With age there was also an increase in comprehension of the dual meanings of key words and phrases in the jokes and riddles.

Daniel Yalisove (1978) extended Shultz's approach, testing riddle comprehension and liking among nearly 600 school children in grades one through ten. He discovered that first graders prefer reality riddles, that is, riddles that involve neither word play nor absurdity but that are based on a conceptual trick. For example, "How many balls of string would it take to reach the moon? One, but it would have to be a big one" tricks the listener, who at first assumes he is being asked to consider normal-sized balls of string. As in Shultz's study, riddles based on linguistic ambiguity were most popular in the fifth grade. But seventh, eighth, and ninth graders preferred absurd riddles, such as "How can you fit six elephants into a VW? Three in front and three in back."

Yalisove suggests three stages in the comprehension of riddles. In the first, strongest among first graders and lingering among a number of third graders, the child interprets the riddle as a test of his or her ability to tell the difference between the sensible and the silly. In the second stage, which is strongest among third graders, children focus on the reasonableness of the answer and attempt to explain away the incongruity of the riddle. They seem to be unable to tolerate the idea of the absurd, the illogical, or the implausible. In the third stage, which begins in the sixth grade and becomes increasingly prominent, children acknowledge the incongruity and then justify it on the basis of a special rule. Only the older children perceived the structural elements of each category of riddles.

Apparently, a six-year-old's mastery of language may not be developed enough for him to enjoy the linguistic subtleties involved. He may, as Freud suggested, be limited to the enjoyment of nonsense. As the child matures and his vocabulary expands, he becomes aware of multiple meanings and appreciates the resolution of incongruity.

Play

The function of children's play has been stressed many places in this book, and you will recall from the discussion in Chapter 13 that most investigators believe play helps the young child assimilate new information from the environment into his existing modes of understanding.

Jerome L. Singer (1973), who has studied fantasy and make-believe in children for many years, feels that children between the ages of nine and thirteen have a considerable interest in make-believe activities and fantasy games but that this interest is largely suppressed. Because our culture tends to discourage what it views as nonutilitarian thought, it may be that parents and teachers, without realizing it, signal disapproval of children's fantasy games (Pulaski, 1974).

Studies by Singer and a number of his students indicate that fantasy is associated with verbal fluency, increased concentration, originality, and imagination (Singer, 1973). Although there may be hereditary differences in the ability of individuals to fantasize spontaneously (Wallach, 1970), children can be taught to develop their imaginative capacities.

For example, Sybil Gottlieb (1973) has developed promising techniques with children under twelve. After classifying children as high or low on the ability to fantasize, she showed abstract films to groups of children and interpreted the films realistically to one group and imaginatively to the other. Then she showed another abstract film and asked the children for written interpretations. Those children in the group who had heard a fanciful interpretation of the first film showed a sharp increase in the amount of fantasy they used—even children who had originally been classified as low fantasizers. But her attempts to use the same techniques with children over twelve failed. One cannot conclude, on the basis of this study, that older children are unable to learn to use fantasy. But it appears that younger children are much more receptive to Gottlieb's techniques.

Memory

In the discussion of memory, it was pointed out that context helps a young child remember. Older children tend to group material that must be remembered into categories, which enhances their ability to recall it.

Some recent research supports Piaget's description of the way a child's memory for spatial relations develops. Children ranging in age from three and one-half to nine years were taken by an adult, one at a time, for a walk in locations that varied in their familiarity and distinctiveness (Acredolo, Pick, and Olsen, 1975). One place, for example, was a familiar playground, with many trees, swings, etc., that could be used as landmarks; another was an unfamiliar hallway lined with closed office doors. During the walk, the adult dropped a card or a key ring and asked the child to pick it up. After walking a little farther, the adult asked the child to return to the exact spot where the object had earlier been dropped. The child was next taken to a second location in the same setting

and asked to remember it so he could return; after walking a ways farther with the adult, the child was asked to return to the location.

The familiarity of the environment made little difference; children, regardless of age, did about as well in returning to a designated spot in both environments. All children were more accurate at finding a location when they had been instructed to remember it than when they had not. Seven years seemed to be a key age. Children younger than seven were significantly more accurate in returning to a location in an environment that contained landmarks than in one without them. Children older than seven were equally accurate with or without landmarks, and significantly more accurate than children younger than seven in finding a designated location without landmarks. Piaget has suggested that children younger than seven use topological relations in thinking about spatial relations, which does not require them to remember precise distances. The older, operational child uses Euclidean relations, which require children to code spatial locations in terms of distance so that adding landmarks makes little difference to them.

The child's developing cognitive skills can interact with his ability to code and retrieve information in a manner that has surprising results. If you, for example, were asked to recall an event that you had observed two weeks ago, you would expect to remember it reasonably well. But if you were asked to recall it after six months, you might expect the details to have faded. You certainly would not expect your memory of the event to improve with the passage of six months.

However, the interaction of the child's memory and cognition makes it appear that, in certain cases, his memory does improve with time. For example, Piaget and Inhelder (1968) showed children a group of ten sticks of various lengths and asked them to draw the arrangement from memory. After six months, the same children, asked to redraw the sticks, produced a copy that was closer to the original display than the first drawing they had produced. Apparently, the child's memory for objects is not simply an internal copy of his original perception. It appears that, as a child's comprehension of what he has once seen develops, his memory changes to conform to his new understanding.

In a similar study, Hans Furth, Bruce Ross, and James Youniss (1974) showed children ranging in age from five through nine years a picture of a glass tilted from the horizontal base to a 45° angle, as in Choice A of Figure 14.5. The children were told: "This is a glass with cola in it. It is tilted and on a table. Now draw this picture on your paper, just the way you see it here."

Many children in elementary school do not realize that the level of the liquid remains horizontal with respect to the table even though the glass is tilted. They have not yet acquired this particular understanding of spatial transformations, even though they have seen numerous tilted glasses of milk, water, orange juice, and so forth.

The same children again drew the tilted glass at varying intervals. Furth found that the oldest children reproduced the drawing more accurately on all these occasions. However, 20 out of the 116 children drew more accurate pictures in sessions that were held after six months than they had drawn earlier. Although this represents only 17 percent of the total sample, the finding is of interest because it goes against one's expectation that

Figure 14.6 A tilted-glass experiment like that carried out by Furth, Ross, and Youniss. (A) Depiction of the actual angle of the level of liquid in a tilted glass. (B and C) Depiction of the angle reproduced by two children. (Adapted from Furth, Ross, and Youniss, 1974)

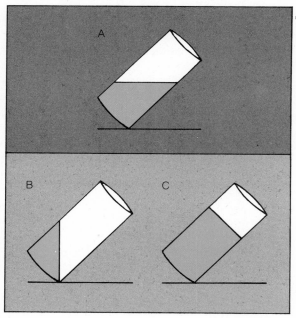

recollections will remain the same or deteriorate over time. Furth maintains that, during the six-month interval, these children had acquired a more sophisticated understanding of what happens to the level of contained liquids in general and that this knowledge affected the way that they remembered the picture. Thus, the child's memory of a perception is not a static photograph but the product of an active process in which advances in cognitive maturity modify the information that the child stored earlier.

By the time children are in kindergarten or the first grade, they know what it means to learn, remember, and forget. Mary Anne Kreutzer, Catherine Leonard, and John Flavell (1975) interviewed kindergarten, first-, third-, and fifth-grade children in order to discover their understanding of how memory works. Most of the youngest children were aware that events that happened a long time ago were hard to recall, that meaningless strings of items such as telephone numbers are quickly forgotten, and that once something is learned, it is easier to relearn the same material than to learn something new. Kindergartners and first graders also seemed to know that having to learn a lot of things is harder than having to learn only a few things. These young learners realized that they could plan their study time to help their memory and even proposed deliberate schemes, such as careful inspection of the items to be learned. They also proposed and understood the use of external memory aids such as other people, tape recordings, written notes, or even a string on the finger to help them remember.

Third and fifth graders were firmer than younger children about what they knew and had acquired additional information about memory. They not only recognized that time affects memory, but they also understood that more study time helps recall and having to learn more items will hinder it. They realized that these two factors interact, so that a short study of a short list leads to better recall than long study of a long list.

According to Flavell (1977), a main developmental difference between younger and older children lies in their ability to plan; older children are better at forming and maintaining a memory goal and can plan current activities that will maximize that goal. The older child is also more likely than the younger child to have developed effective and efficient ways of enhancing his ability to recall information.

Although children of six or seven can learn to play chess, they are unlikely to be able to plan their strategy several moves in advance, as this older boy will learn to do. (© Joel Gordon)

SOCIAL INTERACTION AND COGNITION

As earlier chapters noted, the young child may assume that other people see things just as he does, and be unaware that other perspectives exist. This apparent egocentrism may sometimes interfere with his attempts to communicate with language. When recounting an episode to a friend or a parent, for example, a young child may leave out essential details, making the story almost meaningless to the listener.

In an attempt to find out how long this tendency persists, John Flavell (1966) conducted a series of studies that examined role-taking and communication tasks. In one study, Flavell showed children from seven to sixteen a set of seven pictures that, like a comic strip, illustrated a story when "read" in the proper order.

For example, one set of pictures might tell the following story:

1. Boy is walking.
2. Boy sees dog.
3. Dog chases boy.
4. Boy sees apple tree.

5. Boy climbs apple tree to escape from dog.
6. Boy watches dog depart.
7. Boy eats apple.

The child narrates the story as he looks at the pictures. Afterward, the experimenter removes three of the pictures, leaving only four, which tell quite a different story:

1. Boy is walking.
4. Boy sees apple tree.
6. Boy sits in apple tree with dog in background.
7. Boy eats apple.

At this point, a second person enters the room, and the child is told that this person will see the four pictures for the first time. The child's task is to predict the story that the new person would tell after seeing the four pictures.

Flavell found that many of the seven- and eight-year-olds found it difficult to separate their predictions about the story that the newcomer would tell from their own prior narrations. Either they restated the seven-picture story or else they initially predicted a "pure" four-picture story but, upon questioning, reverted back to the information about the dog that only they had seen. One dialogue resulted in this exchange:

Child: He's singing, and then he runs—he sees a tree. He climbs up it and he's eating an apple.
Adult: Fine. Why does Mr. X think that the boy wanted to climb the tree?
Child: So the dog don't get him—bite him. (1966, page 170)

On the other hand, children who were nine or older had little difficulty in separating what they said from what the newcomer saw.

Other studies, however, have shown that even preschool children, in some circumstances, realize that others cannot see what they see and show, by their verbal descriptions, a high sensitivity to the plight of their listener (Maratsos, 1973).

THE CONCEPT OF INTELLIGENCE

The discussions in the chapters on intellectual and linguistic development have focused on the changing abilities of children as they progress toward biological and social maturity. These discussions have looked at the changing ways in which the typical child knows his world. In this final section, we will examine a related aspect of intellectual development: intelligence tests and the concept of IQ that grew out of attempts to assess a child's intellectual abilities.

Changing Viewpoints About IQ

Early developmentalists concerned themselves with plotting changes in mental age as chronological age increased. Put simply, the standard, or normal, mental age for a child would be that which was typical or usual for most other children of his age. In order to determine whether a given child deviated from the typical and if so, by how much, investigators used standard testing procedures to devise behavioral norms for each age. In order to assess intelligence, they developed the convention of IQ—a quotient that represents a child's performance relative to the performance of numerous other children who have previously been tested under the same conditions. Given the way that intelligence tests are constructed and standardized, the IQ score provides no more than a descriptive statistic relating a child's present performance to

that of other children of his chronological age.

Unfortunately, the early association of the psychological measurement of intellectual ability with a program of various physical measurements caused many people to suppose that tests of intelligence produced scores that are as accurate and immutable as physical measurements. People often assumed that IQ is largely determined by heredity and that experience has only minimal effects on the measure. Today psychologists know that environmental circumstances can produce considerable variability in IQ scores. They have also grown suspicious, on the basis of long-term repetitive measurements of intelligence, of the alleged stability of intelligence.

IQ scores often fluctuate; the scores of approximately 20 percent of American children change by at least fifteen IQ points between the ages of six and ten, and some children's scores, although not many, change by as many as fifty points. External influences at the time of the examination, including the manner of the examiner and the attitude of the child, can affect a child's performance. Thus, Lauren, who may have made average scores on standardized tests of intelligence at age six, could score considerably higher several years later. Many factors determine a child's intellectual performance, among them biological change, general education, life experience, motivation, and personality. Therefore, one should be wary of making important decisions about the future of an individual based on only one or even just a few assessments of his intellectual abilities (McCall, Appelbaum, and Hogarty, 1973).

For many years psychologists also thought that an IQ score measured practically everything of importance in cognitive development. Performance on an IQ test was taken as an index of creative abilities, productive thinking, and problem-solving abilities. Along with this faith in the IQ test went a belief that it was not possible to train mental capacities.

Evidence and experience have modified these ideas about IQ, and the concept of what IQ really measures is being redefined. Today psychologists know that a person's IQ score can be deceptive. They realize that intelligence is not a single, unitary entity. Rather, it refers to a wide range of abilities and skills, some of which are related to one another, and some of which are not; some of which are measured by IQ tests, and some of which are not measured by them.

What IQ Does and Does Not Measure

Most psychologists agree that intelligence is based on the ability to benefit from experience and the ease with which a child can learn a new idea or new behavior. It is generally assumed that each person has a ceiling, a point above which he will not be able to profit from experience in a particular activity, and that this ceiling is governed by environmental and hereditary factors. Chapter 3 discusses some of the data regarding hereditary influence on intellectual ability.

However, the debate about the genetic contribution to tested IQ performance continues to rage. Arthur Jensen (1969) fathered the modern contro-

versy by arguing that 80 percent of the differences among the IQ scores of individuals can be traced to differences in their genetic backgrounds, whereas others have suggested that a close examination of these data reveals so many problems in untangling genetic and environmental influences that there is little evidence for a genetic component to IQ (Kamin, 1973; M. Schwartz and Schwartz, 1974).

It is instructive to try to interpret Jensen's claim that the heritability for IQ is .80, in light of our previous discussion in Chapter 3. First, the statement implies that in a group of individuals, approximately 80 percent of the *difference* in their scores is associated with differences in their genetic make-up—not 80 percent of the entire scores. No one has claimed that 80 percent of an individual's entire IQ score is "determined" by genetics and 20 percent by environment, as if eighty of the one hundred points in an average child's IQ score were contributed by his genes. Most behavioral geneticists agree that it is impossible to put a number on the proportion of behavior that is inherited (Scarr and Weinberg, 1978). A complex and interdependent set of genetic and environmental circumstances that scientists are only beginning to understand causes the child's test performance.

Second, as we noted in Chapter 3, the heritability of .80 depends on the nature of the samples used to calculate it. Heritability may not be the same among blacks as among whites, among upper-middle-class individuals as among the poor, among individuals tested in the 1930s as among those tested in the 1970s or 1980s.

Third, because of the way genetic research must be done with human beings, often involving variation in both hereditary and environmental influences, the accuracy of that estimate of .80 heritability, even in the specific samples tested, is questionable.

Fourth, even if human heritability for IQ were .80, this finding does not suggest that all attempts to stimulate or improve intellectual functioning would be fruitless. It may be difficult to change intellectual ability or it may not, depending on

IQ tests measure what a child knows how to do and how deeply he has absorbed the dominant culture; they also predict his probable grades in school. (Photos by John Oldenkamp with permission of the Houghton Mifflin Company from Terman and Merrill Stanford Binet Intelligence Scale)

whether we can discover which experiences are most important for its development.

It is also particularly important to remember that an intelligence test includes few questions that require a child to learn anything. The majority of the questions measure a skill or a segment of knowledge that the child already possesses rather than his ability to learn something new. Thus, the IQ test does not measure the basic processes that most people acknowledge as contributing heavily to intelligence.

The intelligence test is a good measure of what a child knows how to do and what he has taken from his culture. It is also a reasonably good predictor of the child's grades in school. If the child has a strong motivation to improve the quality of his intellectual skills and has high standards for intellectual mastery, he is likely to have a higher IQ score than a child who is not highly motivated or who has low standards. Because middle-class children are more consistently encouraged than lower-class children to learn to read, spell, add, and write, a child's IQ, social class, and school grades all should be positively related to each other. This is generally the case. In addition, the personality attributes of children who do well in school (persistence, lack of aggression, and responsible behavior) are similar to the characteristics of children from middle-class homes.

The IQ score, when properly used, can be regarded, then, as an efficient and accurate way of summarizing the degree to which a child has learned the concepts and rules of middle-class Western society. The IQ score is useful because it predicts fairly well how easily a child of eleven like Lauren will master the elements of calculus or history when she enters college. However, the specific questions that are asked on an intelligence test have been chosen to make this prediction possible. The child is asked to define "shilling" rather than "peso." He is asked to state the similarity between a fly and a tree rather than the similarity between "fuzz" and "Uncle Tom." He is asked to copy a design rather than to defend himself against the neighborhood bully.

There is no reason to discard present IQ tests merely because they are biased toward measuring skills that upper- and middle-class white Americans value and teach. But the parent and teacher should appreciate the arbitrary content of the test. If one's primary objective is to predict the child's

success in school subjects, then the IQ test is the best instrument psychologists have devised so far. After the child is three or four years old, the test does a creditable job of predicting who will obtain good grades in elementary school, high school, and college. (For skills such as music or art, there are special tests that are more appropriate.)

Psychologists need more exact knowledge about the separate cognitive functions and how they are combined in thought, and everyone must come to realize that the behavior of a child in a test situation depends as much on his motives, fears, and expectations as it does on the richness and quality of his mental structures.

SUMMARY

1. During the years from six to twelve, children's attention continues to become more reliable, sustained, and selective. Thus children are likely to learn more about those aspects of a task that they and others understand to be important and meaningful and, in an ambiguous situation, to sample the range of possibilities in an attempt to decide which features are relevant.

2. Typically, children's attending and thinking also show advances in other ways. For example, children are likely to show a continually increasing sophistication in their ability to understand and use concepts such as those involved in a conservation task, and they may be able to imagine a reverse operation that proves they understand the physical relationships involved. Precausal thinking may also become less apparent during this period as children more often attempt to understand, examine, and explain things in causal terms. Similarly, problem solving is likely to become more complex and efficient as children develop a fuller understanding of how to solve problems involving several factors.

3. Advances in children's imitation, language, play, and memory reflect developmental changes in their ability to learn, reason, and acquire concepts. In addition, these representational skills interact to produce further conceptual development.

Thus, complementary changes in children's language skills and cognitive development are reflected in their understanding and use of words and metaphors and in their appreciation of the multiple meanings and linguistic subtleties of jokes and riddles.

4. Social interaction continues to have a strong influence on cognitive development. Through interactions with others, children are likely to show marked advances in both role taking and conceptual skills.

5. Although the concept of intelligence and the use of intelligence tests are often assumed to be adequate ways of measuring, describing, or explaining differences in cognitive development, there are serious limitations to such views. Basically, intelligence tests and IQ scores indicate a child's performance relative to the performance of other children. They do not measure or reflect many important cognitive skills or abilities, and they do not show or demonstrate that a child's performance is stable or that it cannot be changed by training or education.

CHAPTER 15

Personality: Expanding Social Interactions

ACQUISITION OF ROLES
Sex Roles
Peer Roles

PERSONAL-SOCIAL DEVELOPMENT
Positive Behavior
Negative Behavior

SELF-CONCEPT
Self-Appraisal
Self-Regulation

PARENT INFLUENCE

PEER INFLUENCE

FUNCTIONS OF PLAY
Rules and Practice
Social Cognition

TODAY'S CHILD AND TOMORROW'S
Television
Drugs
Education

SUMMARY

Eleven-year-old Matt watched the other boys jump off the end of the pier, bob to the top, and swim away. He took a hesitant step forward, then stopped and stared. His friends began calling to him: "Come on!" "Jump!" Matt could only dog paddle; the ten feet between him and the water seemed like a hundred. "What's the matter, sissie," yelled another boy, "are you scared?" The demands of his friends overcame his fear. Matt shut his eyes and jumped into the deep water.

During the years from six to twelve, the influence of a child's peer group can be extremely important in shaping his development. When the six-year-old first skips off to school, the process of role identification slips into high gear. During the later years of childhood, children learn what the adult society expects. They learn to meet a few of these expectations in the classroom itself, from books and pictures and teachers who tell them what is good and what is bad, what they must do and what they cannot do. However, most of what a child learns at school takes place on the playground. Thus, Matt may learn from playing basketball with his peers that cheating is not tolerated, or he may learn from playground intrigues that a person should stand up for his close friends.

In this chapter, we will examine some of the changes in the child's world as his personality develops throughout later childhood. We will focus on aspects of personality, such as sex roles, aggression, and self-concept, that were discussed in Chapter 13 and will broaden our discussion to consider other roles that the child plays as well as additional kinds of behavior. We will examine the development of generosity and helpfulness as examples of positive qualities and will look at the effects of popularity and leadership. We will also stress the relative decline in parental influence on the growing child, along with the relative increase of peer influence. We will see that play assumes additional functions in later childhood and that a child's ability to assume different roles also influences personality development. Finally, we will consider the growing impact of society on the child, particularly in the important areas of television, drug use, and education.

ACQUISITION OF ROLES

Children often learn more from their peers than they do from adults. But parents, peers, play, and society all have a major part in the socialization process (see Figure 15.1), and, as the child grows into his or her sex role, the interplay of these forces becomes clear.

Sex Roles

Around the age of five or six, children tend to segregate into same-sex friendship and play groups, and these segregated groups endure until the romantic interests of adolescence draw children out of them. Each sex professes a contempt for the other. Girls talk about "yukky boys," and boys refer freely to "dumb girls." Girls practice their girlness by playing house and rehearsing the romantic fantasy of being a bride, and boys assert their boyness by sports, rough-housing, and adventuring. The romantic chant used for years by girls to accompany jumping rope—

> Down in the valley where the green grass grows
> There sat Helen as sweet as a rose
> She sang and she sang and she sang so sweet,
> Along came her fellow and kissed her on the cheek

—is unlikely to be represented in boys' play. Boys and girls are aware of this division of interests, and Figure 15.2 shows the kinds of activities that children between the ages of eight and eleven see as being the domain of one sex or the other (Hartley and Hardesty, 1964). There is a good deal of continuity between girls' play activities and traditional adult female roles (home maintenance and child care) but much less continuity between boys' play and adult male roles. Boys seem to have a great need to assert their masculinity—perhaps to distinguish themselves from the primarily female influence at home. As Chapter 13 stated, calling a boy "sissy" is a strong weapon of behavioral con-

SIGMUND FREUD considers later childhood to be a period of sexual latency in contrast to early childhood when, in his view, the child's sexual fantasies resulted in a conflict between him and his parents. During later childhood, the repression (or exclusion from conscious thought) of the child's sexuality permits him to form relationships with children of the same sex and allows him to assume the role of either leader or follower. According to Freud, both the child's peers and the authority figures in his world, such as his parents and teachers, have a continuing influence, especially in strengthening the child's self-image or in causing him further to repress his sexual urges.

ERIK ERIKSON places great emphasis on the influence of others in role development during later childhood. The child's learning takes place in the context of school and society, and Erikson suggests that popularity and the potential for leadership are a function of the child's relative success in learning to exert control over his environment. Successful control enables him to make positive contributions to those around him. The child acquires a positive self-concept from his ability to be productive, self-directing, and accepted.

WALTER MISCHEL sees peer-group pressure and the impact of the school as two significant forces shaping the child's behavior. From observation and participation, the child learns to conform to the demands and expectations of peers as well as of parents and other adults; in the process he learns both positive and negative behavior. From observing what behavior meets with social approval and what is punished, the child learns to behave in ways that allow him to become popular or to assume a position of leadership. Through interacting with his expanded environment and through assessing his behavior in relation to its consequences, the child develops a clearer and more complete self-concept.

Figure 15.1 Some major theoretical viewpoints regarding personality development during later childhood.

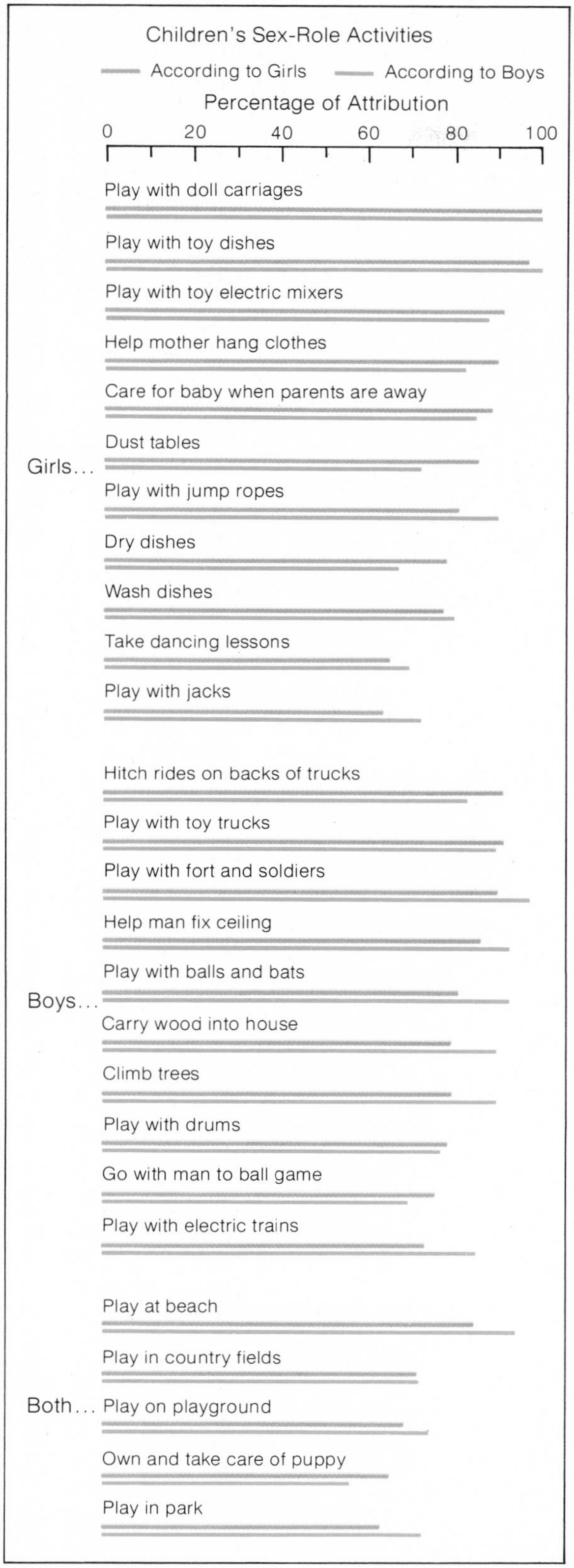

Children's Sex-Role Activities

——— According to Girls   ——— According to Boys

Percentage of Attribution

0   20   40   60   80   100

Girls...

Play with doll carriages

Play with toy dishes

Play with toy electric mixers

Help mother hang clothes

Care for baby when parents are away

Dust tables

Play with jump ropes

Dry dishes

Wash dishes

Take dancing lessons

Play with jacks

Boys...

Hitch rides on backs of trucks

Play with toy trucks

Play with fort and soldiers

Help man fix ceiling

Play with balls and bats

Carry wood into house

Climb trees

Play with drums

Go with man to ball game

Play with electric trains

Both...

Play at beach

Play in country fields

Play on playground

Own and take care of puppy

Play in park

trol. Girls are likely to engage in activities stereotyped for boys, whereas boys are reluctant to take part in girls' activities.

As the continuity between girls' play and female roles would suggest, the games that children play provide an important context for acquiring sex roles. Watch three seven-year-old girls playing house. The oldest (or the most dominant) will assign the roles at her pleasure, switching them around from time to time to add interest to the game. "Let's play like I'm the daddy," she may say. In almost every culture, children "play like" adults in their free time. Grownups may take this imitation as flattery, but the activity serves the same useful socialization process as more formal learning does. In playing house, a girl picks up some of the essentials of her adult role and, perhaps of greater importance, learns how to shift readily from one role to another.

If the little girl who is playing the mother wishes to go to the office and work and leave the father at home to care for the baby, the other children soon put her straight. In sex-role stereotypes, mothers just do not leave fathers at home to do dishes and wash diapers. Such cultural standards of appropriate sex roles exert far-reaching effects on children's personalities. Behavior that accords with traditional sex-role standards—aggressiveness and sexuality for boys, passivity and dependence for girls—tends to remain stable through adulthood (J. Kagan and Moss, 1962), whereas sex-inappropriate behavior is more likely to be modified.

This channeling of children's proclivities and capacities along lines defined by society as sex-appropriate can restrict a child's potential. Aletha Stein, Sheila Pohly, and Edward Mueller (1971) studied boys and girls in the sixth grade to see if labeling a neutral task as masculine or feminine or both led to a change in children's performance. They found that achievement on the tests was related to the label. Boys did best on "masculine" tasks, worst on "feminine" tasks, and in between

Figure 15.2 The effects of sex-role stereotypes on the way boys and girls classify childhood activities. As the chart shows, there is a high degree of agreement between boys and girls about the activities that are seen as the province of one sex or the other. For example, all boys and girls felt that playing with doll carriages is a girl's activity, and almost all saw playing with trucks as a boy's activity. (After Hartley and Hardesty, 1964)

Children's play channels them into sex roles approved by society; the Barbie doll inculcates the traditional feminine sex role and the boy who plays Little League baseball learns stereotypical male attitudes. (Karyn Meyer)

on tasks labeled as appropriate for both sexes. Girls did as well on "both" tasks as they did on "feminine" tasks but performed worst on tasks labeled "masculine."

The emotional components of sex-role identification become so strongly ingrained during childhood that many would reject as abnormal anyone who tried to reverse his or her sex-role behavior. The emotional conditioning associated with sex and gender roles so pervades the child's social environment that it is practically invisible to later, rational inspection. Because individuals cannot consciously recover the experiences that conditioned their attitudes toward sex roles, they often tend to believe that their own attitudes are genetic constants that accompany particular sex organs rather than an accumulation of years of learning.

Peer Roles

A child comes to have definite reactions to and expectations of other children (and of himself, depending on how other children respond to him). Organization creeps into children's relationships, and two kinds of patterns characteristically de-

velop during this period. The first is the elaboration of an ingroup-outgroup sense of belonging that is supported by special group activities and rituals and the exclusion of outsiders. A child learns to define his special qualities and ways of behaving in relation to how his group acts and, frequently, in contrast to how outsiders act. Fortunately, group organization is not rigid during these years, and many such cliques break up and re-form, so that temporarily and arbitrarily excluded children may later slip into the fold. A second pattern of group interaction that soon emerges is the development of hierarchies. Any child in a fifth-grade classroom can rattle off an ordered list of the smartest, the most athletic, and the most popular, and children show surprising agreement. The roles and positions that children take in peer-group play provide their training for later assuming adult social roles.

Chapters 9 and 13 emphasized that the developing personality of a child like Matt grows out of an interaction between what he brings to social situations and the ways that other people treat him. Perhaps nowhere is this so clear as in the child's popularity. The child who emerges from secure and rewarding relationships at home with his or her parents and siblings tends to be trusting, confident, and interested in and capable of both initiating rewarding interactions and receiving overtures from others. These characteristics correlate with a child's popularity as measured by **sociometric analysis,** a method that charts how often a child is chosen by peers as a preferred friend or companion (Campbell and Yarrow, 1961).

However, children's behavior, the responses of others to them, and their expectations form an interlacing web, each woven into the other, so that it is difficult to say which comes first. For example, research has shown that physique is likely to influence a child's popularity, indicating that the child's own behavior is not the only factor that determines his or her role in the group. J. Robert Staffieri (1967) investigated the relationship between the popularity and the physique of boys from six to ten years old and found that muscular boys are more popular than boys who are skinny or plump. Most of the boys he studied wished for a muscular build in accord with the masculine stereotype.

Although popular children tend to assume leadership roles in their peer group, children tend to be discriminating in their assignment of leader-

The child who leads in a group of peers is generally popular and also shows skills in the specific areas of activity demanded by the club, team, or gang. (Jane Bown)

ship roles. When children are organizing a baseball game, they generally listen to an athletically skilled child; when they are staging a play, they turn to an imaginative child. Thus, in a study of leadership among a large number of six- to eleven-year-old children, C. Wade Harrison, James Rawls, and Donna Rawls (1971) found that the leaders generally tended to be more intelligent, active, aggressive, achieving, and socially adept than children who rarely led; in addition, leaders tended to be more competent in a specific area of development.

The personal and social consequences of popularity show up in other ways. Herbert Harari and John McDavid (1969), for example, recruited both a popular and an unpopular child as collaborators and had them carry out certain prohibited acts in the classroom, such as stealing money from the teacher. The other children in the class, who had watched what took place, were later called into the principal's office and asked what had happened. Half the children were called in by themselves; the other half came to the principal's office accompanied by another child.

The principal questioned all the children, insisting that they tell on the culprit. When the children were interrogated alone, all complied with the principal's request and identified the guilty child. When the children were questioned in pairs, however, they refused to tell on the popular child but without hesitation told on the unpopular culprit. Children apparently realize that, when they are questioned along with another child, their actions are likely to get back to their peers. When they inform on a popular child, their betrayal could lead to their own rejection and unpopularity, whereas informing on an unpopular child is unlikely to have personal consequences.

It is apparent that children play many roles in these years before puberty and that the roles they assume can have major implications for their personality development. A look at some examples of positive and negative behavior will show more clearly how this happens.

PERSONAL-SOCIAL DEVELOPMENT

As growing children test themselves in a variety of roles, they discover much about themselves, about others, and about the world at large. The neonate who was unaware of the existence of other people becomes a child who must work with those people and allow for their needs as well as his or her own. Behavior that forwards such consideration is regarded as positive; behavior that interrupts such consideration of others is regarded as negative. This section will focus on generosity and assisting others as examples of positive behavior and on aggression as an example of negative behavior.

Positive Behavior

Although there is some evidence that helping others is an adaptive action that has been selected for in the course of evolution (Trivers, 1971), it does not spring forth fully developed at birth. Whether due to learning, to cognitive development, or to other factors, a child's readiness to help others definitely changes with age (F. Green and Schneider, 1974). The term "altruism" covers a great variety of specific helping actions, ranging from the simple sharing of candy or toys to springing to the aid of a child at the mercy of a bully.

Generosity is a form of positive behavior greatly valued by society and is a characteristic that is likely to increase with the child's age. Thus, older children usually are more willing than youngsters to share with others, whether they are sharing candy, toys, or money. This increased generosity appears to develop for several reasons. First, older children often find it easier to part with possessions simply because they do not seem especially valuable. For example, Susan, at the age of three, regarded a nickel as a huge sum that would bring her the pleasures of bubble gum, candy, or some trinket. Consequently, she would have been reluctant to part with it. In contrast, David, who is ten, sees a nickel as such an inconsequential amount that it can easily be given to help others.

Second, older children simply have had more opportunities to learn that people are supposed to help others. They may have seen their parents donate to charities or do volunteer work in hospitals. They may have rung doorbells on Halloween to collect money for UNICEF. They may have heard people say that "A friend in need is a friend indeed" and that "It is better to give than to receive." Such experiences generally make it clear to children that their society places a premium on helping other people.

Third, as Chapter 14 indicated, older children are also likely to be less egocentric than young children. Many have learned to take the perspective of others and to empathize with people who need help. Kenneth Rubin and Frank Schneider

(1973), for example, measured the egocentrism of their seven-year-old subjects and then gave them an opportunity to donate candy to poor children and to help a younger child complete a task. The children who were better able to see things from another's viewpoint were more likely both to donate candy and to assist the younger child.

In learning cultural norms of giving and sharing, children seem to develop a concern for justice early. In a series of experiments by Monroe Learner (1974), for example, five-year-olds worked together on a project and then were allowed to divide some rewards. In the first experiment, children who had worked as a team divided the rewards evenly among themselves. In the second experiment, the way the groups were defined affected the way the children distributed the rewards. When each work group was defined as a team, rewards were again distributed evenly. But when the children were told they were independent co-workers, they divided the spoils according to the relative contribution of each child. Such results indicate that even young children are not motivated solely by self-interest, but appear to follow learned norms of fairness.

Evidence that learning sex roles may affect the views children develop about fairness and rewards appeared when Edward Sampson (1975) had children ranging in age from three to twelve observe two dolls in play situations. In one situation, the dolls did an unequal amount of work. After watching the play, children were asked to allocate rewards to the dolls. Girls, regardless of age, tended to give each doll an equal reward. Boys, on the other hand, tended to give more rewards to the doll who had done more work, and the older the boys, the more rewards they gave to the hardworking doll. Apparently most boys learn early about male responsibilities in a competitive world, and become increasingly sensitive to the idea that people should be rewarded according to their efforts.

Sex differences in socialization may also help to explain why girls often are found to be more generous as well as more empathic than boys (M. Hoffman, 1977b). Although generosity and empathy may not be correlated in a given situation (Elmer and Rushton, 1974), the two may be associated more consistently in the case of girls than of boys. Girls are more likely than boys to be taught to express their emotions, to be sensitive to the feelings and needs of others, to be assigned respon-

Helping younger children gives both sexes an opportunity to try out new roles requiring cognitive and social skills, but girls generally learn to be more generous and empathic than boys. (Robert Isaacs)

sibility for caring for other children. Girls are also more likely than boys to experience nurturance and help from others.

Various sorts of experiences, of course, may lead children to become generous. Obviously, anything that causes children to become less egocentric will be likely to increase generosity, but seeing another act in a generous manner will have the same effect. For example, Joan Grusec and Sandra Skubiski (1970) found that children who watched an adult donate to charity were more generous in their own donations. However, when the adult simply said that the children should share their money with the charity, donations were markedly smaller than when the adult actually gave money. Verbal expressions had strong effects on children's giving only among girls who had previously had a warm relationship with the adult who urged generosity.

J. P. Rushton (1975) and other investigators have noted that, although exhortations do not affect children's behavior, they do increase children's statements that people should be altruistic. The lesson from these studies seems clear. If you want children to talk altruistically, just talk altruistically yourself. However, if you want them to behave altruistically, you should act in an altruistic manner (see Chapter 16). Children can learn hypocrisy just as they can learn altruism.

As indicated, a warm relationship did induce generosity in girls who heard exhortations to donate. Apparently, adult nurturance also increases the effectiveness of other methods. In one study of young children, Marian Yarrow, Phyllis Scott, and Carolyn Waxler (1973) found that, although any adult model could affect children's immediate behavior, children who saw a warm, nurturant model were still generous two weeks after they watched the generous adult. It seems that the models who have strong, lasting effects on children are likely to be those who have close, rewarding relationships with the children—such as parents. Without such a relationship, examples are likely to have only a fleeting effect.

Although giving aid is a second kind of altruism, it is quite a different form of positive behavior from generosity. While generosity is usually clearly defined, the circumstances in which aid may be appropriate are usually confusing and unclear. It may not be obvious to a child that an emergency exists, that responsibility for help rests on him or her, or even that the child is competent to help. As one might expect, this kind of altruistic behavior follows a different developmental course from that taken by generosity.

Ervin Staub (1970) has studied children's tendency to help in an emergency. He left children alone in a room for a few minutes, and, during this time, each child heard a crash and the sound of another child crying in an adjacent room. Staub noted whether the child either entered the room, presumably to give assistance, or offered unsolicited information to the experimenter about the sounds of distress that were heard. In contrast to the finding that older children are more likely to share, Staub found that children's tendency to assist a crying child first increased with age and then decreased. Staub suggests that the reason that few young children assist a child in distress is because they are less able to empathize with others in this sort of situation. As children get older, they are more capable of putting themselves in another's position, and so they are more likely to help in an emergency. In later childhood, however, children also become more sensitive to criticism and disapproval. Older children, therefore, are reluctant to help for fear of incurring an adult's disapproval.

In a subsequent investigation, Staub (1971) strengthened the case for believing that fear of disapproval affects a child's tendency to give aid when he studied the influence of modeling and nurturance on such helping. In a situation like that used in his earlier study, he found that children who had a warm relationship with the adult investigator were more likely to help than those who lacked this relationship. He suggests that, because children believe that a warm, nurturant adult is unlikely to criticize them, the principal barrier that keeps older children from giving aid is removed.

In this study, Staub also found that an adult example increases helping and speculated that this effect occurs because it demonstrates that the child will not be criticized if he or she leaves the room to help. In generosity, you will recall, other reasons appeared to account for the influence of an adult model. Presumably, the adult model showed the child that generous behavior was correct, but even young children are likely to know without adult guidance that they should help someone who is hurt.

If altruism is the kind of behavior that helps people, other behavior can be potentially destructive to human relationships. A further look at the way aggression can be increased or decreased, along the lines indicated in Chapter 13, will show how negative behavior often develops in the growing child.

Negative Behavior

Although theoretical debate over whether human beings have an inherent drive toward aggression continues to rage, there is no question that chil-dren do frequently respond to frustration or thwarting with aggression. One of the earliest forms of peer interaction is one child shoving another to obtain a desirable toy. Children are expected to learn to control the expression of aggression very early. As soon as they begin to throw tantrums, to hit, and to throw toys about, parents try to control these actions. On the other hand, as children continue to experience restraints at home, they also increasingly come to see that controlled aggression, such as that on the football field or in the fight ring, is highly valued. A child, therefore, must learn when, where, and how to express aggressiveness in order to maximize gain and minimize punishment.

As children get older, they appear to shift the way in which they express aggression. As they increasingly encounter punishment for aggressive acts, they become more discreet about when and where they commit them. Therefore, the development of aggression is not uniform. David, who gets away with aggression toward his siblings or his neighborhood playmates, may be a model of decorum in the classroom and a ferocious fighter on the playground. Matt, whose parents punish him severely for aggressive acts, may be docile at home and a terror at school.

Several studies have examined the manner in which aggressive expression changes as children grow older. Willard Hartup (1974), who has studied this development, distinguishes between **hostile aggression** and **instrumental aggression.** Hostile aggression aims at hurting another person, whereas instrumental aggression aims at retrieving or acquiring an object, territory, or privilege.

In two early studies (Dawe, 1934; Goodenough, 1931) it was found that young children were more likely to engage in instrumental than in hostile aggression and that the proportion of hostile acts increased with age. More specifically, Dawe found that 78 percent of the interpersonal conflicts among eighteen-month-old infants centered on possession of toys or other objects but that children about five or six years old quarreled over possessions only about 38 percent of the time.

As these results imply, the way that children express aggression appears to change with their cognitive development. Thus, as indicated in earlier discussions, in many situations children under six lack skill in imagining another viewpoint or in making inferences about other people (Flavell et al., 1968). If hostile aggression depends on the

Children often respond to frustration or thwarting with aggression. As they become older, their aggression is more likely to be verbal than physical. (Alex Webb/Magnum Photos)

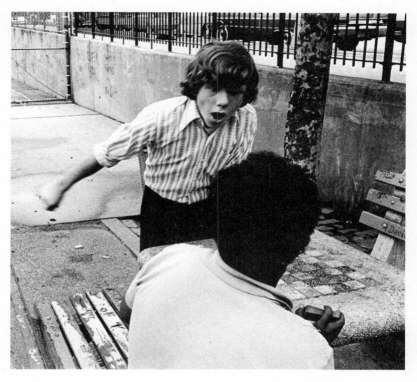

child's attributing negative intentions to the person who frustrates him, then younger children should be less likely than older children to show this kind of aggression.

Using this rationale, Hartup (1974) attempted to test and extend the earlier findings of Goodenough and Dawe. He observed children at play over a ten-week period and found that older children (from six to eight years) showed less total aggression than younger children (four to six years). This difference in total aggression was due primarily to the preponderance of instrumental aggression among younger children. As he had expected, older children showed a higher proportion of hostile aggression. Hartup also found, as had Goodenough, that children shifted from physical to verbal aggression as they got older, confirming a change in both the form and amount of aggression as children develop. Thus, as children get older and their acts of physical aggression are punished, they also become more subtle in the way that they express such behavior.

The same socializing influences that are important in teaching a child to behave in generous or helpful ways also operate in teaching a child to behave in aggressive ways. You will recall from Chapter 13 that watching someone behave in a violent or aggressive manner has a great deal of influence in eliciting aggressive behavior. And, as the section on television will show, witnessing a model may affect aggressive action in a variety of ways.

As noted before, watching others act aggressively does not always lead the observer to imitate the aggressor. For example, Marian Martin, Donna Gelfand, and Donald Hartmann (1971) allowed one hundred children to observe a model go through a unique sequence of aggressive behavior. The children then played either alone, in the presence of a male or female adult, or in the presence of a boy or girl of their own age. The investigators found that the children were most aggressive when a peer of the same sex was present. When an adult was present, a child initially showed little aggression. But if the adult showed no disapproval of the child's aggressive acts, the child became more and more aggressive. Apparently, the mere presence of an adult tends to inhibit aggression, but as children become aware that their aggressive acts are either acceptable or neutral in an adult's eyes, their inhibitions disappear.

Demands for obedience from adults can even overcome a child's inhibitions about aggression. Mitri Shanab and Khwala Yahya (1977) told Jordanian children, ranging in age from six to sixteen, that they were teachers in a learning experiment and that the learner (actually a confederate of the experimenter) must get a shock of increasing intensity each time he made a mistake. In this study, 73 percent of the children obeyed the experimenter and delivered what they thought were shocks until the highest level was reached—even though the children believed the shocks were harmful. Although neither age nor sex of the children made a difference in their behavior, girls were more likely than boys to report that they gave the shocks in order to obey the experimenter. Before condemning the children for obediently following the un-ethical demands of the experimenter, consider that Stanley Milgram (1974) surprised the psychological community in 1964 when he demonstrated that as many as 65 percent of the adults he studied would administer what they thought were severe, even lethal, shocks to an innocent person simply because an authority ordered them to do so in the course of an experiment. Clearly, under special conditions, people will behave in ways they ordinarily would reject.

Such conditions are rare. Under ordinary conditions, children do not respond to the demands of others without considering the consequences. Their past experiences and their developing self-concepts affect their decisions.

SELF-CONCEPT

During later childhood, children often become acutely sensitive as to whether they have reached other people's standards of ability, attractiveness, poise, and masculinity or femininity. If they decide they measure up, they feel reasonably secure and satisfied with themselves. If they decide they fail to measure up in important ways, they are likely to feel insecure and dissatisfied with themselves.

In an individualistic and competitive society like our own, children are almost inescapably drawn into comparing themselves with their friends and peers in school, on the playground, and elsewhere. Consequently, by comparing themselves to others like them, children continue to deepen and sometimes alter their self-concepts, as they decide how big, smart, attractive, strong, friendly, or talented they are and want to become.

Self-Appraisal

Like younger children, they remain primarily present-oriented in their views of themselves, but they

also begin to include the past and future. They see themselves in terms of what they have done and were like, and what they might do and be like later. Asked to describe themselves, they are likely to reply in terms of where they live ("I'm an American," "I live on Date Street in Aberdeen, Ohio"), body image ("I'm fat"), memberships ("I'm a Scout"), or even abstract terms ("I'm a person"). They may also begin to use terms more descriptive of their personal qualities, such as "I'm shy" or "I'm a hard worker."

Just as their physical appearances create expectations in others, so do their names. In a real sense, a child's name is not just a label but an attribute like age, sex, or race. Like other attributes, it is likely to influence both how others perceive him and how he perceives himself. As innocuous as a child's first name may seem, it is likely to be associated with several important personal and social outcomes.

An attractive first name is likely to be an asset

In a competitive society, children are inescapably drawn into comparing themselves with their peers; when they do, their own self-concepts are likely to deepen or change. (Burk Uzzle/Magnum Photos)

whereas an unattractive first name is likely to be a liability (McDavid and Harari, 1966). Children with attractive first names, like John or Karen, are more likely to be popular with their peers than children with unattractive names like Horace or Adelle. Herbert Harari and John McDavid (1973) found that children's names can bias teachers' judgments. In this study, they randomly assigned attractive names (e.g., David or Lisa) or unattractive names (e.g., Herbert or Bertha) to a group of fifth-grade essays of similar quality. When teachers then graded the essays, those with attractive names attached received marks that were a full letter grade higher than those that carried unattractive names.

In view of the expectations that names can carry, it is understandable that children's self-concepts may reflect similar effects. Among sixth-grade boys, for example, those with desirable names had a more positive view of themselves, their abilities, and their interpersonal relations than boys with undesirable names (Garwood, 1976). Boys with desirable names also believed they could do better work and get along better with others in more situations, and they also made significantly higher scores on a standardized achievement test.

Self-Regulation

The way parents behave toward their children during later childhood may further encourage either an internal or external sense of control. When fourth- and fifth-grade boys worked on a task after the researchers had told parents they could help their sons as much or as little as they liked, parents of sons with an external sense of control were more likely to intrude in the task and to be highly directive, whereas parents of sons with an internal sense of control were more likely to be supportive and give less direction (Loeb, 1975).

During later childhood, children's beliefs about locus of control are likely to become increasingly related to personal and social behavior and attitudes (Weiner, 1974). This seems particularly true in regard to school achievement. Research consistently shows that children who believe in internal control perform better in school than children who believe in external control (Lefcourt, 1976). Children who do well in school generally attribute their success to ability ("I succeed because I'm smart") and their failures to effort ("I didn't work hard enough"). Because effort is a matter of

personal control and can be changed, they perceive themselves as being able to overcome failure.

Children who do poorly in school are likely to develop a different pattern of perceiving causation, attributing their successes to external events such as difficulty ("It was an easy test") or chance ("I was just lucky"). They also are likely to attribute their failures to ability ("I failed 'cause I'm dumb"). Since ability is a stable, internal characteristic, they are likely to see no reason to try harder on future occasions.

These different attribution patterns, of course, are likely to be linked with other differences in children's self-concepts (Coopersmith, 1967). Children who are successful and perceive themselves that way are likely to have a positive self-concept; they feel confident about themselves and their abilities. Children who are unsuccessful and perceive themselves that way are likely to have a negative self-concept; they lack confidence in themselves and their abilities, and feel unworthy.

Once children start school, they may find it necessary to revise their expectations of themselves, depending upon their academic performance and how it is evaluated (Entwisle and Hayduk, 1978). Some children may experience repeated disappointments and frustrations that lower their expectations; others may encounter success that raises their expectations. The biggest change for some children may be that, for the first time, they are evaluated in terms of how well they do in comparison with other children instead of with their own previous performance.

Children who experience repeated frustration, failure, and punishment, and perceive them as due to external factors, are likely to believe that they can do little or nothing to change things. Because of this belief, they will fail to try even when situations are such that they can succeed. This inability to see any hope of success can easily lead to what has been called learned helplessness (Seligman, 1975). If this happens, children no longer try to deal with problems because they have learned from repeated experience that what happens to them is independent of what they do.

The school experiences of girls are especially likely to promote learned helplessness (Dweck and Bush, 1976). When boys fail, teachers often attribute their failure to lack of effort. In addition, when teachers criticize boys, much of their criticism is not related to ability but has to do with such things as the boys' failure to follow instructions or the

Because their teachers' criticism generally focuses on lack of ability, girls who do poorly in school, unlike boys, are likely to become victims of learned helplessness. (William Hubbell/Woodfin Camp & Assoc.)

messiness of their work. Because this criticism tends to attribute shortcomings to motivational factors rather than ability, boys are likely to attribute their failure to lack of effort. In contrast, when girls fail, teachers almost always attribute their failure to some lack of ability. Girls are also generally cooperative, and diligent and careful in their work, and teachers often praise them for their motivation and effort. Because the criticism girls receive tends to attribute their shortcomings primarily to lack of ability rather than lack of motivation or effort, girls are likely to attribute their failure to lack of ability. Although boys who experience frequent failure may continue to perceive themselves as capable and able to do better with increased effort, girls who experience frequent failure may develop a sense of helplessness.

PARENT INFLUENCE

In later childhood, parents continue to control many aspects of children's lives and to exert a strong influence on their socialization. Children still depend on their parents for their material wants: food, clothing, shelter, and other physical necessities. They also depend on them for attention, affection, physical contact, and play. Because the manner in which parents fulfill children's physical and psychological needs affects the children's behavior, parental control remains strong. As noted in Chapter 13, sex-role behavior continues to be heavily influenced by parents, and positive social behavior such as generosity or helpfulness is largely the result of parental responses to children's actions (Rosenhan, 1970).

On the other hand, parents' strong control over children's needs also gives them the power to withhold physical and psychological resources. Parents often punish infants or young children by withholding their affection or by spanking. Whether by withholding approval, affection, and rewards or by following a child's acts with unpleasant consequences, parents can and do continue to punish older children.

As the discussion of negative behavior has indicated, children may behave in a number of inappropriate or even antisocial ways. Their acquisition of roles comes about as much through their attempts to avoid unpleasant consequences as through their responses to praise or reward. These factors, together with children's increased sensitivity to harsh words, censure, and criticism, create innumerable situations in which parents are likely to resort to punishment.

But parents do more than punish. They may subtly teach their children both appropriate and inappropriate behavior, even when they are unaware of their effect. When Jeanne Block and her colleagues (1978) observed parents teaching their children a task, they found that mothers of boys and mothers of girls behaved similarly when instructing their children. Fathers, on the other hand, behaved differently toward sons and daughters. When teaching sons, fathers tended to emphasize achievement and performance on the task. When teaching daughters, fathers indicated that achievement was not the most important aspect of the task and seemed more interested in the interpersonal aspects of the situation.

Because they are such powerful models, the absence of one parent can be a potentially major force in a child's life. Single-parent homes may differ in many ways from homes in which both parents are present. As the discussion of sex roles noted, most psychological study of such homes has focused on the effects of father absence, especially on boys.

For example, E. Mavis Hetherington (1966) has found that boys without fathers tend to be less aggressive and more dependent on the peer group than boys whose fathers are present. Boys without fathers in the home also participate in fewer games

Sex-role behavior is learned from parents; this boy, whose father acts in unstereotypical ways, is likely to develop a less restrictive concept of masculinity than some of his peers. (James H. Karales/Peter Arnold)

that involve physical contact. Father absence seems to affect even academic skills; when boys without fathers enter college, they tend to show the typical feminine pattern of higher verbal than mathematical scores on entrance tests (Carlsmith, 1964).

Most developmental psychologists attribute these differences to the lack of a masculine model rather than to such factors as the disturbance of an attachment relationship, and there is substantial evidence to back up this belief. First, these differences are most common in males and seem to center on such sex-typed behavior as aggression and dependence. Second, children whose fathers are absent are much more active than children whose fathers are present in vying for the attention of older males, which suggests that the children feel a real need for a relationship with an adult male.

Finally, it appears that other male role models reduce the differences in behavior attributed to the absence of a father. As noted earlier, fatherless boys who have an older brother are more aggressive and less dependent than those without an older brother. Furthermore, the presence of an older sister does not reduce the influence of the older brother. Apparently, the mere presence of a male role model, rather than a balance between males and females in a family, is important. Of course, an older brother does not completely replace a father, even though he does seem to reduce the usual effects associated with the absence of a father.

A limited sort of father absence (and mother absence) may also be changing the way that American children are socialized. Urie Bronfenbrenner (1967) notes that the increasingly common white-collar job and community service of both parents means that they are likely to spend less time in the home interacting with their children than was true among earlier generations. The children are, in essence, pushed out of the family and into the peer group. Bronfenbrenner speculates that, as a result of such changes, American children may come more and more to look to the peer group as a model not only of peer relations but also of the values and ideals traditionally handed down from parents to children.

PEER INFLUENCE

With the beginning of the school years, the peer group increases in size and in importance. Chil-

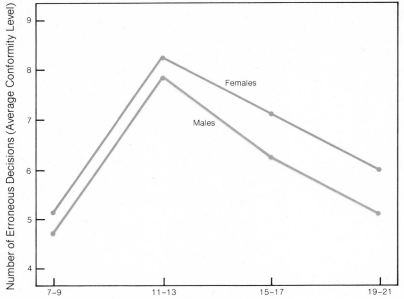

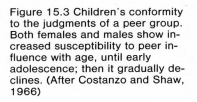

Figure 15.3 Children's conformity to the judgments of a peer group. Both females and males show increased susceptibility to peer influence with age, until early adolescence; then it gradually declines. (After Costanzo and Shaw, 1966)

dren find a large number of schoolmates of their own age as well as many others of slightly different ages. This new peer group includes children from different neighborhoods, children who would remain strangers without the school setting. A wider group of acquaintances, however, does not necessarily lead to an increase in the number of close friends. Whereas during early childhood the child became close to an increasing number of other children, during later childhood, friendships increase in intensity rather than in number. Older children spend more time with their friends. Occasionally they play after school at friends' houses or spend the night with friends. Along with this increased intensity comes stronger influence.

The strong influence that peers can have on a child's behavior was clearly demonstrated in a study by Philip Costanzo and Marvin Shaw (1966), who asked children to compare the lengths of a pair of lines. One line was obviously longer than the other, but all except one of the children were confederates of the investigators, and they chose the incorrect line. When the child who was not a confederate denied the evidence of his senses and agreed with the obviously incorrect judgment of the group, he had altered his own judgment to conform to that of his peers. As Figure 15.8 shows, a child's susceptibility to this form of peer influence increased with age, reached its peak during the preadolescent years, and then gradually declined. Such results as these indicate that peers can

be especially important as guides to appropriate behavior during later childhood.

Hartup's (1970) descriptions of peer influence may help to explain this rise and subsequent decline of peer influence. As Hartup has suggested, peer influence may initially rise as the growing child's ability to see things from the perspective of another increases. He also speculates that the later decline can be explained by children's ability to reinforce themselves. By self-reinforcement, Hartup means that, as children interact with their peers, they begin to internalize the statements other children make about their behavior as well as the effects of peers' responses to them. Through this process of internalizing the judgments of others, children develop the ability to evaluate their own actions.

Self-evaluation can be either negative or positive. Social punishment by peers—in the form of ostracism, ridicule, or finding a scapegoat—and physical punishment, such as fighting, are tremendously powerful forms of control. As children learn to internalize these negative reactions, their behavior gradually comes under the control of their own self-criticism and punishment. Thus, in a variety of ways, peers can exert a good deal of influence during later childhood.

At this time the child also begins to encounter a unique form of peer influence: the *group*, a formal structured collection of peers. The tendency of children to form structured groups has been inspected in a number of studies by Muzafer and Carolyn Sherif (1953, 1964). They divided boys into two groups and closely observed the group functioning. Inevitably, a hierarchical structure formed among the boys in each group. As would be expected from the discussion of leadership, the most popular boys did not automatically become leaders, nor were leaders always the most talented or the toughest.

No matter what status children hold in a group, group solidarity exercises a great deal of influence on their behavior. Competition within a group may decrease solidarity (Stendler, Damrin, and Haines, 1951), but the Sherifs have found that evenly balanced competition between groups results in greater cohesiveness within each group. Although occasional rancor may appear just after a competitive defeat, group members generally become much closer to one another in competitive situations. Because competition between groups produces a cooperative atmosphere within an individual group, it is not surprising that it should promote group solidarity. However, in a study of unbalanced competition, when one group consistently lost, the losing group threatened to collapse in disharmony (Sherif and Sherif, 1953). Apparently, when the unpleasantness generated by defeat becomes constant, it simply overcomes any tendency within the group for members to cooperate.

Whether competition was balanced or unbalanced, it produced a considerable amount of friction between groups. The boys looked down on

members of the other group, and the situation eventually exploded into open hostility. This intergroup hostility further strengthened group cohesiveness and increased the influence of the group over the behavior of its members. Further, boys who were not normally hostile participated in

Whether children are leaders or followers, group solidarity exercises a great deal of influence on their behavior. (*top:* © Joel Gordon; *bottom:* © Costa Manos/ Magnum Photos)

intensely aggressive acts for the sake of the group. In such a case, it seems that the structured group has the ability to overpower any tendency children have developed toward self-judgment and to lead them to engage in behavior they would normally avoid.

FUNCTIONS OF PLAY

In early childhood, play is characterized by dramatic fantasy and the use of symbols and imagery. The older child, however, is more socialized, more attuned and accommodated to social reality. Play during later childhood, therefore, increasingly consists of games regulated by rules that everybody accepts. Although dramatic play continues in a formal, structured way (as in plays put on for parents and friends or in neighborhood games of cops and robbers), the spontaneous activity of playfully transforming reality in order to act out personal desires and conflicts seems increasingly to become interior dialogue, fantasy, and daydreams.

The socializing function of play shows clearly in a study of children's games by Iona and Peter Opie (1969). The Opies found two main functions in all child-organized play. First, games provide a structure for children's relationships. Second, games allow a child to experience adult life in easy bits and nonthreatening pieces.

Rules and Practice

Rules provide the structure of games. Children spend a great deal of time making rules for the games they play, and it is usually important to them that those rules, no matter how silly they may appear, be followed without deviation. Younger children consider their rules to be absolutely binding, but as they grow toward adolescence, children come to understand rules as conventions, agreed upon for specific purposes and therefore open to modification by common consent. As noted earlier, Jean Piaget (1932) considers this change in attitude to be part of the child's development of mutual respect and cooperation.

Although a leader may break a rule, children with low group status find themselves under tremendous pressure to conform to the established rules. If they fail to do so, they are often expelled from the group and not allowed to come back until they promise to keep the faith. This slavish attention to detail probably serves children in many ways. They learn that social commerce must be

regulated in order to sustain interactions for any length of time. (At a younger age, children merely drift away from their peers if they do not like the rules.) They learn that, once a more or less formal structure has been set up, they can relax and enjoy themselves within its confines without having to worry about being rejected. And rules provide a means by which new arrivals to the group may rapidly find their places.

Play also continues to serve the second function: as the training ground for personality characteristics and social behavior that will be important in adulthood. Brian Sutton-Smith and John Roberts (1964) have characterized the world of play as a sort of buffer zone where pressures for successful social behavior are managed on a miniature scale. Children's games allow them to succeed in various ways: by decision-making ability in games of strategy such as checkers and chess; by speed and power in games of physical skill such as relays and baseball; and by luck in games of chance such as cards. Children learn to compete, but within a safe world that minimizes the penalties associated with losing or failing. Children often attach little significance to who wins or loses; they do not worry about prizes and show little concern if a game is not finished. Even when competition is strong and the desire to win high, children like games that restart almost automatically so that everyone gets a new chance. In contrast to adults, they often get most of their enjoyment from experiencing, not from winning.

Although games allow less symbolic elaboration than the younger child's dramatic play does, many themes that run through children's games reflect experiences from the real world that are frightening or seem beyond the child's comprehension or control. For example, Fritz Redl (1959) cites such recurrent themes as racing, chasing, attacking, seducing, capturing, harassing, searching, and rescuing. Within the world of the game, children experience excitement and tension. Playing hide-and-seek in the dark, the child feels the terror of waiting to be pounced on. The fun of such scary games seems to depend on their safeness. They provide quick reversals of tension within a limited and structured time period.

During later childhood, children not only learn from games to relate to other children but also discover further their own capacities and worth, thereby elaborating their self-concepts. Many games of prowess allow children to test their physi-

The rules of their games provide a structure for children's relationships and allow them to experience adult life in easy bits and nonthreatening pieces. (*top:* © Joel Gordon; *bottom:* © Suzanne Szasz)

cal abilities both against their own standards and in comparison with the abilities of others. Such games seem designed to let children explore the capabilities of their own bodies for personal satis-

faction. Follow-the-leader, skating, riding bicycles, tag, and even hopscotch are as much self-competitive as they are peer-competitive. Children issue their own physical challenge just to see if they can make their bodies do what they want them to do. Older children who set out on an expedition to no-where-in-particular may climb a fence, walk along a narrow board over a ditch, swing on a rope, jump a gulley, crawl through a drainpipe, and jump off a high ledge—all simply to exercise their physical powers.

Social Cognition

Games also further the child's cognitive development. This shows plainly when the child learns to play a game with rules, such as checkers or tic-tac-toe. In competitive games that require strategy, a child must be able to take his opponent's point of view if he is to figure out his enemy's strategy and adapt his own moves to it. M. Papst (1966) compared the behavior of six- and seven-year-old children at strategic games and found that the youngest children were slow to learn the moves that would assure them of winning and also had more difficulty articulating the strategy of their opponent and its implications. The changes in social cognition that arise out of child's play require further discussion.

Suppose that Susan is a fairly egocentric seven-year-old and has just learned to play checkers. She is likely to have much more difficulty teaching the game to a friend than eleven-year-old

Matt would. She will probably have trouble explaining the rules of the game in a systematic way that takes into account the point of view of her naive pupil. She may start out talking about kings before telling about jumping and the goal of capturing the opponent's checkers. Both Susan and her friend may become confused and frustrated.

The problem, of course, is that Susan is still unskilled at imaginative role taking. As Chapter 13 states, the play of very young children is characterized by overtly taking the role of others, but one may also play another's role in imagination, as adults do all the time. Such imaginative role taking facilitates smooth social interaction.

Storytelling illustrates the kind of social and cognitive role-taking skills needed to understand a complex social situation (Feffer, 1959). In this method, the child makes up a story involving at least three figures in a picture and then retells the story from the point of view of each of the actors, taking a different role for each retelling. As the child shifts roles, he or she must take into account each new person's experience of the action and the knowledge brought to the situation by that person. This requires the child not only to take each character's point of view but also to make sure that each new perspective fits the others. Using this procedure, Melvin Feffer and Vivian Gourevitch (1960) found a significant increase in role-taking ability among children from six to thirteen years old, with the strongest gains occurring between the ages of eight and ten. This marked improvement in role-taking ability during childhood suggests that later childhood may be the time for developing basic role-taking skills.

TODAY'S CHILD AND TOMORROW'S

The child's subculture continues to be significant as an agent of socialization throughout childhood and, as the scope his contact with society broadens, becomes even more important. But cultures change with time. Thus, differences in the same culture at two different times may be as dramatic as differences between two subcultures at the same time. Consequently, in a rapidly changing society, the experiences of today's children may vary dramatically from those of yesterday's and tomorrow's children.

Until the last decade or so, children had little freedom or money, and only thirty years ago even eight- to ten-year-olds were expected to have some

kind of part-time job (delivering papers, cutting grass, helping clean house) to supplement their meager allowances. Household chores were commonplace, as were large homework assignments for even very young children. And lacking the instant entree into the adult world that television now offers so pervasively, yesterday's children knew considerably less about the world than today's children do.

Television

Parents are still the single most important determiner of the normal child's attitudes toward the world. Next in importance are siblings and peers during later childhood; then close relatives, schoolteachers, and religious leaders; and finally the heroes and heroines that the child reads about, hears about, or watches on television. For any given child, one may be able to find exceptions to this rank ordering, but it is a fairly accurate rating of influence. In past generations, parents blamed their offspring's misbehavior on radio, comic books, pulp magazines, and, at the turn of the century, dime novels. These days, television bears the brunt of the blame.

Recently there has been a great deal of concern about the possible effects of television violence. As the section on the development of aggression states, models may be powerful transmitters of new behavior and for many children may also reduce inhibitions on existing behavior. Television, then, with its vivid depiction of an amazing variety of aggressive acts, has increasingly become an object of concern.

A variety of studies have been conducted to assess the effects of television on children. Early studies by Albert Bandura and his associates (1973) showed that children could learn new ways to express aggression from television and similar media. D. Keith Osborn and Richard Endsley (1971) went further and investigated children's emotional reactions to various sorts of television programs. Children saw four films depicting either human violence, cartoon violence, human nonviolence, or cartoon nonviolence. Children told what they liked best and what was the scariest. The two violent films produced the most emotional reactions; the children remembered details of the violent films the best; they found the human violence the scariest; and they preferred the nonviolent cartoon. This study shows that watching television violence evokes emotional responses in children and influences them to remember the details of depicted violence.

Moving closer to the central question of whether television violence affects the way that children behave, the Office of the Surgeon General (1972) commissioned an exhaustive study of the effects of television violence but failed to reach any definitive conclusions. However, existing investigations give some clues as to how television may affect behavior.

For example, Robert Liebert and Robert Baron (1972) investigated whether watching television aggression would make children more willing to hurt another child. Liebert and Baron showed brief excerpts taken directly from regular television shows to boys and girls from five to nine years old. The excerpts were either violent and aggressive (a fist fight or a shooting) or exciting but nonaggressive (a tennis match). After they saw one of these programs, the children were given a series of opportunities either to hurt or to help another child by pushing a button. Each child was told that pushing one button would help another child (who was not actually present) to win a prize but that pushing the other button would hurt the child. They were also told that the longer they pressed either button, the more the other child would be helped or hurt.

Despite their brief exposure to these television shows, children who had observed the violent television sequence chose to hurt the other child for a significantly longer period of time than those who had watched the nonaggressive scenes. Obviously, this study uses a specialized definition of aggression, but it demonstrates that watching one kind of aggression may lead to aggression of a very different sort. It suggests that television programs depicting aggression may remove or reduce some children's inhibitions against committing violence—at least immediately after a child sees the program. Additional studies support this position (Leifer and Roberts, 1972).

Television violence showed up in the classroom in a study by Monroe Lefkowitz and his colleagues (1972). They found a significant relationship between the amount of television violence that third-grade boys watched and their classroom aggression as rated by their peers. Even more impressive is their finding of a relationship between the amount of television violence that boys watched in the third grade and their aggression at age nineteen. Moreover, they concluded that it was not merely that children who commit aggressive acts watch more television violence but that children first watch television violence and then are rated as aggressive.

The factors controlling expression of aggression are exceedingly complex, but these studies appear to indicate that television violence may both teach new forms of aggressive behavior (such as the recent growth of interest in kung-fu) and relax inhibitions against aggressive expression. Other studies, however, indicate that the long-term effect of heavy television watching may be less violence, not more. When George Gerbner and Larry Gross (1976) compared viewing habits with perceptions of the world, they found that people who watched four or more hours of television each day tended to be significantly more suspicious of others and afraid of being involved in violence themselves than people who watched television two hours or less each day. They also discovered that nearly half the twelve-year-olds they studied watched at least six hours of television each day. Gerbner and Gross believe that heavy television viewing may teach people to play the role of victim and to become passive in the face of aggression.

The effects of television on children range beyond the effects of violent programming. Children at play often enact social roles that they have taken from television. As many feminists have pointed out, television has served as a rigidly conventional socializing influence in portraying women's roles as essentially home- and children-centered. As one author has asked, "What sort of self-concept do you develop when the role models you see on television are primarily devoted to finding the optimal coffee blend for their husbands or vanquishing kitchen odors?"

Television opens children to vast worlds of experience that were previously unavailable. It educates and illustrates things that remained abstractions to preceding generations. It may also induce children to spend hours in front of a television set, as on Saturday mornings, that a previous generation would have spent interacting with their peers. The generation of children who have never lived without television is now entering adulthood, so it is impossible at present to assess the long-range effects of television. But the electronic miracle affects children's knowledge of the world, their activities, heroes, time spent with their peers, and a variety of other factors. Tomorrow's child is going to be a product of that experience.

Drugs

If television was the parental scapegoat of the 1960s, it seems likely that drugs will bear the blame for juvenile misbehavior in the 1970s. For years, drug use remained the province of the urban ghetto dweller or the musician, but today a wide variety of drugs are available in virtually every community. The marked and rapid change in availability and use of drugs has produced a new dimension of the so-called generation gap. Although many parents may disapprove of alcohol use by the young, at least they understand the practice from their own experience. However, many adults grew up believing that drugs produced either insanity or incurable addiction. Thus, many of today's children know more about drugs and their properties than their parents do.

Strictly speaking, it is not adequate to speak of "drugs" without specifying the kind, because the various available drugs differ dramatically in composition and effect. But among the young, the most commonly used drug is marijuana. Recent national surveys show that over half of the adults between the ages of eighteen and twenty-five have used marijuana at least once, whereas less than 10 percent of adults forty years of age and older report ever trying the drug. Although there are no reliable data on marijuana use among children from six to twelve, national data for high-school seniors indicate that more than 50 percent of them have tried marijuana at least once and that about 30 percent smoke it regularly (Johnston, Bachman, and O'Malley, 1977). A better example of a generation gap could hardly be found.

The long-term effects of the use of marijuana are as yet unknown (as are the long-term effects of viewing violence on television) and can only be guessed at; the social effects of the generation gap are probably more predictable. Parents with problem children will tend to blame the erratic and antisocial behavior of their sons and daughters on pot rather than realize that marijuana probably does little more than heighten already existing problems.

Education

After the age of six, the school becomes an increasingly major force in a child's socialization. Today's schools are strongly influenced by a movement toward broadening the definition of education. The new definition supplements the traditional emphasis on scholastic material with a concern for personal growth (Minuchin et al., 1969). The proponents of this movement believe that social and emotional development should be given as much attention as intellectual growth.

One manifestation of the changing role of the school is the rise of sex-education programs in elementary schools. The transfer of this sensitive area to the classroom indicates people's increased awareness of the school as a socializing agent.

Although Freud claimed that sexual development is latent during later childhood, his work was based on observations of the children of Victorian Europe. Today sexual information and misinformation are widely available, and every child meets a barrage of sexual stimuli that only adults would have encountered in other eras. In addition, as Chapter 17 indicates, children are now maturing several years earlier than Freud's young patients did. Sexual activity also is likely to begin earlier today than in the past, so that interest in sexuality is often quite high even among young children. And early experiences with sexual information may have important and lasting effects on sexual attitudes.

Even today, most children learn the facts of procreation from their peers (Hunt, 1974), from

Although children learn most of the facts of procreation from their peers, classes in sex education represent the school's influence on the personal-social development of children. (Harry Crosby)

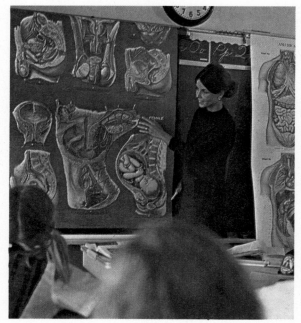

older siblings, from sex manuals thrust into their hands by blushing parents, from looking up "dirty" words in the dictionary, from searching the dusty recesses of public libraries, from pornography purloined from a parent's private collection, and from graffiti scrawled on restroom walls.

Although many middle-class American parents seem reluctant to discuss reproduction, they readily communicate their sexual attitudes to their children. The very fact that this subject is seldom discussed openly and factually in most family settings leads a child to a double understanding: sex is both evil and desirable.

With the advent of sex-education classes in the schools, some of the delicious wickedness associated with the topic may disappear. In some schools, instruction in human reproduction begins in the first grade, to be repeated at regular intervals throughout the rest of the child's schooling. Most instructional materials emphasize the biological aspects of conception and birth; more delicate questions, involving moral and social aspects of sexuality, are generally left to the teacher's discretion. This latter aspect of sex education disturbs some parents, who insist that a teacher may instill a too liberal or immoral sexual attitude in their children. Although critics of sex education in the schools have been successful in having programs removed from some schools, it seems that these critics constitute a minority. As matters now stand, the critics may have little to worry about, since sex-education classes seem to offer too little too late.

Although parents are likely to continue to be the primary instillers of attitudes and standards of behavior, the importance of television and the school as socializing agents is likely to increase. In addition, as children come to acquire many of their values and attitudes outside the family, it seems likely that the socializing influence of child on parent will also increase. In the future, children are more likely, then, to acquire more ideas and values outside their family and to transmit these to their parents, even if such ideas and values are not always accepted.

SUMMARY

1. During later childhood, the interplay of parents, peers, play, and society in socialization continues to be reflected in the personality development of children and in the different roles they assume. Peer roles involving popularity and leadership become more important as more organization enters peer relationships.

2. As children develop and test themselves in a variety of roles, they learn that behavior such as generosity and assisting others is likely to be regarded as positive, whereas behavior such as aggression is likely to be regarded as negative. However, whether children regularly engage in positive or negative behavior depends on social and situational effects, on modeling influence, and on other factors.

3. Among the attributes that affect a child's self-concept is the attractiveness of his or her name. Children's beliefs about locus of control are strongly influenced by their academic performance and by their personal and social behavior and attitudes.

4. Parents continue to exert a strong influence on the developing child. They selectively guide the continuing development of their child's behavior by giving or withholding their attention, affection, and material resources and by providing models of sex-role behavior, generosity, aggression, and other behavior.

5. During later childhood, the peer group usually increases in size and relative influence. Contacts with friends and acquaintances and participation in structured peer groups are likely to become more frequent and intense. These peer influences provide various models of behavior and selectively reward and punish prescribed behavior.

6. Through child-organized play and games, increasingly regulated by rules that all accept, children experience a structure for relationships with their peers and acquire behavior that will be important in adulthood. In addition, they learn more about their own abilities and worth and develop social-cognitive skills required in role taking.

7. Just as different subcultures result in different views, values, and behavior among people, time can bring changes within the subcultures. Consideration of the impact of television, drug use, and sex education on children suggests that such changes in experience may result in drastically different views, values, and behavior from one generation to the next.

CHAPTER 16
Morality: From Rules to Conduct

THE COURSE OF MORAL DEVELOPMENT

INCONSISTENCY IN MORAL CONDUCT

MORAL REASONING
Moral Judgment
Variation in Moral Reasoning
Developmental Changes

ROLE TAKING AND SOCIAL INTERACTION

GUILT AND SELF-REGULATION
Establishing Guilt and Self-regulation
Reasoning and Guilt
Reactions to Guilt

MORAL CONDUCT AND MODELING
Changes in Consequences
Verbal and Nonverbal Modeling

CONSISTENCY IN MORAL DEVELOPMENT

SUMMARY

On August 9, 1974, Richard M. Nixon resigned as President of the United States. His resignation, made when it had become virtually certain that he would be impeached and probably removed from office, was the culmination of a striking example of public immorality, the loosely connected events gathered together under the label of Watergate. When the transcripts of presidential conversations had been made public, philosophers, ministers, journalists, judges, and average citizens asked how supposedly moral men could have participated in immoral acts.

Perhaps the most tempting, and certainly the easiest, explanation of people's moral conduct is simply that some people are scrupulously moral, whereas others are less so. Observers of the national scene have consistently applied this type of explanation to the men involved in the Watergate affair. Yet most of these men were described by their neighbors as warm and helpful human beings, pillars of their communities. Many had strong religious convictions. How could their daily behavior have appeared so impeccably moral to friends and neighbors while they were involved in political immorality and illegality of such astonishing magnitude? This question should arouse our suspicions of easy explanations of morality. Therefore, an examination of contemporary findings on the way that moral conduct develops should help to explain how apparently moral men can behave in immoral ways.

Previous chapters in this book have concentrated on a single aspect of behavior or development during a particular phase of life. But human behavior is complicated, and intellectual, social, and emotional factors generally combine to influence any act. In this chapter, we take a particular kind of conduct, moral conduct; we consider how it involves intellectual, social, and emotional factors; and we focus on its development from early childhood to adolescence.

We will look at the way moral thought, feeling, and action can vary from one situation to another. We will trace developmental changes in thinking about moral problems and see that opportunities to take the roles of others may change the way that a child perceives and thinks about moral issues. We will discover that the way an individual child or adolescent feels when he remembers or anticipates a transgression will affect the way that he regulates his own behavior. After discussing the effect of discipline, we will examine the influence of modeling on moral development and moral conduct. Finally, we will discuss the complexities of judging the behavior of other persons.

THE COURSE OF MORAL DEVELOPMENT

For many generations, morality was the central category for defining social relationships and development, and the social sciences were called "the moral sciences." In the last few decades, morality has slipped in and out of focus as a central interest in developmental psychology. The important work of Hugh Hartshorne and Mark May in the late 1920s on children's moral conduct and that of Jean Piaget in the 1930s on moral judgment were followed by two decades of relative inactivity. In the 1930s and 1940s, thought about moral character concentrated on discussions of social adjustment, and specific concerns about moral development focused on discussions of socialization processes.

Recently, however, thoughtful psychologists and laymen have become acutely aware of the inadequacies of dealing with moral issues in terms of mental health or group adjustment. The mental-health labels are not scientific; they simply make value judgments about people in terms of social norms. And neither mental-health nor social-adjustment terms define the norms and values that represent basic ideals for people. The atrocities of the socially conforming members of the Nazi system and the crimes committed by politicians have made people acutely aware of the fact that adjustment to the group is no substitute for moral maturity.

In order to understand the moral conduct of groups, however, it is necessary to understand the development of moral conduct in the individual. Moral conduct, like any complex behavior, is determined by the interplay of many factors. When an adult such as ex-President Nixon or a preadolescent like Matt is faced with a problem that in-

volves morality, his conduct does not take place in a vacuum. His past experiences affect his present actions, and moral conduct changes greatly between infancy and adulthood. It is generally agreed that (1) babies come into the world as amoral beings; (2) they are active learners; (3) they acquire their first personal moral values and standards from their parents; (4) early moral edicts are tied to specific situations; (5) a child's early moral concepts and understandings differ from those of adults; and (6) a person's moral concepts and understanding change with increasing cognitive sophistication and social experience.

By the time they start school, most children still have literal conceptions of right and wrong. They are likely to show consistency between their thoughts, feelings, and actions to the degree that they have learned to do so at home. But soon they are also likely to show some discrepancy in the way that they think, act, and feel as they interact with new schoolmates. Some quickly learn by example and direct experience to be more devious in what they say and do. Others may become more consistent as they follow the precepts and ideas of peers, teachers, and others.

As children develop toward adolescence, they are likely to think and act in ways that are different from their earlier behavior. For example, the older child and the adolescent show more sophisticated ways of thinking, can move from a specific situation to a more general ethical rule, and are more likely to consider the needs and views of others. As we will see, these changes, along with increased self-regulation and wider learning experiences, usually result in a more complex form of moral conduct.

INCONSISTENCY IN MORAL CONDUCT

Although people continue to talk about moral conduct as a class of reactions that go together and that are governed by some central controlling process such as conscience, it is plain that most people display inconsistent moral conduct. After surveying the research, Douglas Graham (1972) concluded that a person is likely to show highly consistent moral conduct only when the range of situations that confront him is restricted or when a high level of abstract thinking allows him to apply general principles over many varied situations.

Children's sense of morality depends in part on the society in which they grow up. These North Vietnamese children have learned that fighting for their country's political ideals is highly moral. (Marc Riboud/Magnum Photos)

Over forty-five years ago, Hartshorne and May (1928) conducted a landmark study of consistency in moral conduct and disappointed all those who would like to divide the world into moral and immoral people. In the course of their research, Hartshorne and May tested literally thousands of children for many types of moral conduct (such as cheating, lying, and stealing) in different contexts (such as tests, games, and contests) in widely varied settings (such as home, church, and playground). They found that children's moral opinions and judgments as expressed on a questionnaire remained consistent, provided that the two questionnaires were administered in the same setting. When the setting was moved, for example, from a church to a clubhouse, the correlations between the scores on the two tests dropped drastically, making it appear that even the children's basic moral codes changed when the situation changed.

The children's moral behavior was even less consistent than their statements about morality. Hartshorne and May found that almost all children cheat some of the time and that knowing a child has cheated in one situation does not make it possible to predict that he will (or will not) cheat in another. Expediency appeared to determine a child's decision to cheat. When it seemed safe and easy to cheat or when it appeared that other children cheated or approved of cheating, a child was himself more likely to cheat. In some classrooms, for example, many children cheated, whereas in others, almost no one cheated. It also appeared that the child who cheats in the classroom is not necessarily the same child who tells lies there, nor is the child who lies to the teacher the same child who is likely to lie to his peers. Finally, the relationship between children's statements about morality and their actual behavior was virtually nonexistent. Their results convinced Hartshorne and May that it was foolish to try to categorize children or adults as moral or immoral. The crucial question was not whether an individual would behave morally or immorally but rather when he would do so.

Subsequent work has not challenged the basic conclusions reached by Hartshorne and May. For example, Robert Sears, Lucy Rau, and Richard Alpert (1965) compared six different tests of children's resistance to temptation in play settings. Almost all the resulting correlations were positive, but none indicated a very great degree of consistency, even though all were administered in the context of a play situation. A similar study of moral consistency led Wesley Allinsmith (1960) to conclude that a person with a truly generalized conscience is a statistical rarity.

Even when researchers have found a relationship between moral reasoning and moral behavior, it has generally been of the modest variety reported earlier by Hartshorne and May. Walter and Harriet Mischel (1976) surveyed the existing research and concluded that it is difficult to justify claims of strong links between moral reasoning and individual action. They suggest that knowing people's moral reasoning allows one to predict only 10 percent of the variation in their behavior in different situations. In such cases, it appears that it is often possible to predict moral behavior just as accurately from a person's need for achievement or his need for affiliation as from his level of moral reasoning.

Overall, inconsistency in moral conduct should not be surprising. Moral situations involve strong and conflicting pressures, and only a slight change in these pressures may shift the proposed situation from moral to immoral in a person's judgment. Different circumstances may also influence different people. For one person, the chances of getting caught may determine his behavior. For another, the magnitude of the payoff may be the determining factor, whereas a third person's behavior may depend on the amount of effort involved. Moral conduct also appears to be governed by a variety of factors that make adherence to social moral standards more or less likely. Although moral reasoning may become increasingly unified and consistent as a person develops, his behavior often depends on situational constraints. Moreover, resistance to temptation is a kind of behavior pattern different from the donation of money to a charity. Both may be examples of moral behavior, but they are not necessarily governed by the same processes nor do they necessarily manifest themselves in a consistent fashion across individuals.

MORAL REASONING

The various ways in which people come to think, act, and feel morally depend partly on developmental changes in their understanding, and the development of moral reasoning can be seen as a specific case of general cognitive development. Thus, we would expect the same factors that are

Circumstances influence a child's behavior. For some children, the chance of getting caught will determine whether they will steal. (© Sepp Seitz/Woodfin Camp & Assoc.)

important in general cognitive development to be important in moral development.

Moral Judgment

Jean Piaget (1932) proposed that children's moral judgments fall into two major and overlapping stages. In the first, sometimes called *objective morality*, judgments are marked by the belief that rules are given and unchangeable, and transgressions are defined in terms of what is punished or forbidden. In the second stage, sometimes called *subjective morality*, judgments are marked by the understanding that rules are agreed on, relative, and changeable; and transgressions are defined in terms of what is expected, fair, or just, considering the people or situation involved.

Although subsequent work has questioned Piaget's stages on empirical and theoretical grounds (Lickona, 1976), some of his findings have been supported by research. For example, when Piaget had children listen to a pair of stories—one in which a child accidentally broke fifteen cups while opening a door and one in which a child accidentally broke one cup while getting into a cookie jar—he found that young children were likely to consider the child who did the most damage naughtier and deserving of more punishment. Based on such results, Piaget concluded that although children as young as three or four might be able to distinguish between accidental and intended acts, they were unlikely to use such information in making a moral judgment, and instead were likely to use the consequences of an act as the basis of their decision. According to Piaget, young children believe that transgressions deserve punishment, and because their parents punish transgressions that do great wrong most severely, young children follow the same standards.

Recent research indicates that Piaget's results and interpretations are correct in only some respects (Karniol, 1978). The traditional pairs of stories used by Piaget are unlikely to provide a fair test of young children's understanding of a culprit's intent or their use of it in making a judgment. The stories require a child to remember and then compare two intents and two outcomes; the intentions of the actors are not stated clearly or explicitly; and the outcome is always stated last. When the stories are simplified so that only one intent and one outcome have to be considered at a time (e.g., Berg-Cross, 1975), and both intent and outcome are explicitly stated and systematically varied (e.g., Gottlieb, Taylor, and Ruderman, 1977), young children may show much more advanced moral reasoning than Piaget found. In such cases, young children not only can distinguish between accidental and intended actions, and between good and bad intentions, but they can also weigh both intention and consequence in making moral judgments (Surber, 1977). In addition, they are likely to distinguish between harm to human beings and other types of damage, and to judge the former more harshly (Elkind and Dabek, 1977).

As Piaget found, however, young children—even when they are fully aware of the intentions behind an action—may base their moral judgments primarily on the result of an act. Rachel Karniol (1978) suggests that young children appear to learn, first, that acts based on bad intentions are naughty regardless of their outcome, and therefore deserve punishment. When young children must decide between a well-intentioned act that results in great harm and an act with bad intentions that results in little harm, they may say the well-intentioned act is naughtier because they focus on the harmful consequences and give them greater weight in making their decisions. This interpretation, according to Karniol, is consistent with common socialization experiences of young children. That is, parents are more likely to pay attention to bad behavior and punish it than to reward good behavior, so children are likely to learn earlier what others consider wrong; they learn to distinguish good behavior later and more slowly.

Variation in Moral Reasoning

One of the most provocative and appealing ways to study developmental changes in moral thinking has been proposed by Lawrence Kohlberg (1963, 1969). His views are in part an elaboration and a refinement of some of Piaget's ideas about the nature and development of moral reasoning. In Kohlberg's approach, a child or adult is asked to respond to a number of moral dilemmas such as the following:

> In Europe, a woman was near death from cancer. One drug might save her, a form of radium that a druggist in the same town had recently discovered. The druggist was charging $2,000, ten times what the drug cost him to make. The sick woman's husband, Heinz, went to everyone he knew to borrow the money, but he could only get together about half of what it cost. He told the druggist that his wife was dying and asked him to sell it cheaper or let him pay later. But the druggist said, "No." The

Principled	**Stage 6**	This is a stage of fully internalized principles that the person holds as universally valid. He believes them personally and has not adopted them just because they have been laid down by authority. For example, the only soldier who refused to obey orders at the My Lai massacre during the Vietnam War had reached this stage. A person at Stage 6 believes that an act is right if it follows from self-chosen principles, principles that may even demand deviating from rules. The universal ethical principles of Stage 6 are based on a deeply balanced sense of the relationship among human beings and emphasize mutual trust and respect. A person at the highest level might say, "Do unto others as you would have them do unto you."

Pro If you don't steal the drug and let your wife die, you'd always condemn yourself for it afterward. You wouldn't be blamed and you would have lived up to the outside rule of the law but you wouldn't have lived up to your own standards of conscience.

Con If you stole the drug, you wouldn't be blamed by other people but you'd condemn yourself because you wouldn't have lived up to your own conscience and standards of honesty.

Stage 5 The person at this stage recognizes that, for the sake of agreement, rules or expectations must contain an arbitrary element. Rules are social contracts made for a purpose, and specific social purposes can change. The essential obligation is the contract, not the content of a specific rule, and majority will and welfare are extremely important. This stage represents a loosening of commitment to the expectations of others and the conventional order and an emphasis on personal standards of social responsibility. The Stage 5 person recognizes these standards as valid even when special circumstances might justify deviation. A person at this stage might say, "The end doesn't justify the means."

Pro You'd lose other people's respect, not gain it, if you don't steal. If you let your wife die, it would be out of fear, not out of reasoning it out. So you'd just lose self-respect and probably the respect of others too.

Con You would lose your standing and respect in the community and violate the law. You'd lose respect for yourself if you're carried away by emotion and forget the long-range point of view.

Conventional | **Stage 4** Sometimes people call this the law-and-order stage because a person at this stage bases his thinking on the dictates of established authority. Examples of this stage are numerous, because many people never get beyond it. Confronted with moral choices, a person in Stage 4 is likely to say, "Because he is the President" or "Because the Bible says so" or "A rule is a rule." He sees value in rules and obligations because he sees them as necessary for a stable society ("What would happen if everybody . . . ?"). The Stage 4 person does his duty and shows respect for authority.

Pro If you have any sense of honor, you won't let your wife die because you're afraid to do the only thing that will save her. You'll always feel guilty that you caused her death if you don't do your duty to her.

Con You're desperate and you may not know you're doing wrong when you steal the drug. But you'll know you did wrong after you're punished and sent to jail. You'll always feel guilty for your dishonesty and law breaking.

Stage 3 A person at this stage internalizes the values of others. He makes up his mind about a moral dilemma on the basis of how he believes his parents or his peer group would behave or want him to behave in the situation. He wants to please and help others, thereby gaining their approval. He believes that behavior should conform to stereotypical images of appropriateness. A person at this stage might say, "It's better to give than to receive."

Pro No one will think you're bad if you steal the drug but your family will think you're an inhuman husband if you don't. If you let your wife die, you'll never be able to look anybody in the face again.

Con It isn't just the druggist who will think you're a criminal, everyone else will too. After you steal it, you'll feel bad thinking how you've brought dishonor on your family and yourself; you won't be able to face anyone again.

Premoral | **Stage 2** The overriding concern is satisfying a person's own needs, and he is keenly sensitive to the consequences of any action. The Stage 2 person thinks acts are good whose outcomes are to his own advantage. He is inclined to exchange favors—"I'll do this for you, if you'll do that for me"—but he is satisfying his own desires. He does not share the perspective of others.

Pro If you do happen to get caught you could give the drug back and you wouldn't get much of a sentence. It wouldn't bother you much to serve a little jail term, if you have your wife when you get out.

Con He may not get much of a jail term if he steals the drug, but his wife will probably die before he gets out so it won't do him much good. If his wife dies, he shouldn't blame himself, it wasn't his fault she has cancer.

Stage 1 Children or adults tend to decide on the basis of personal fear and the avoidance of punishment. The physical dimensions of an act or its consequences loom large as the basis for judging its degree of badness. The Stage 1 person avoids trouble by obeying powerful authorities. For him, "Might makes right."

Pro If you let your wife die, you will get in trouble. You'll be blamed for not spending the money to save her and there'll be an investigation of you and the druggist for your wife's death.

Con You shouldn't steal the drug because you'll be caught and sent to jail if you do. If you do get away, your conscience would bother you thinking how the police will catch up with you at any minute.

husband got desperate and broke into the man's store to steal the drug for his wife. Should the husband have done that? Why? (1969, page 379)

Using a person's responses to such dilemmas, as well as interviews that probe the thinking or reasoning behind them, investigators attempt to ascertain the nature and extent of his moral reasoning. This method assumes that moral judgments are largely the result of moral thought in contact with a moral dilemma like the one faced by Heinz—to do or not to do good or bad under certain circumstances. By definition, no moral dilemma is easy to resolve; none of the possible outcomes is ideal, and most people would prefer to avoid such dilemmas altogether. But in a moral dilemma, even doing nothing leads to a certain outcome. In a moral dilemma, no matter what action a person takes or fails to take, he must break at least one rule. In studying a person's proposed action in the face of Heinz's dilemma, the important thing is not whether the person would steal the drug but his reasons for choosing a particular course of action.

Drawing on studies that have used this method to examine the moral reasoning of children and adults, Kohlberg has suggested that there is a progressive series of six developmental stages of moral reasoning, as illustrated in Figure 16.1. Notice that the stages differ in the reasons that a person is likely to give for making a decision and in the type of concerns that he indicates for himself, authority, and/or society. The figure also illustrates how a person at each stage might reason in deciding whether Heinz should steal the drug. As can be seen, it is not the decision to steal or not to steal but the form of justification for his proposed actions that identifies a person's stage of reasoning. A person at any stage may decide either way in a given situation.

Each succeeding stage is assumed to consist of a more complex and balanced way of looking at the moral-social world. A child or adult presumably advances through the stages in sequence; he must understand the reasoning typical of one stage before he can learn to understand the greater complexities of the next. It is also assumed that, as an individual moves to a new stage of understanding, he must reorganize his thoughts and feelings and not just add new ones. Thus, as a child advances through the stages, old moral-social relationships between the child and other people, and between people in general, acquire a new look.

As Figure 16.1 shows, the proposed six stages form three basic developmental levels of moral reasoning, distinguished by what defines right or moral action. The first two stages form what is called the **premoral** level, because value is placed not in persons or social standards but in physical acts and needs. The next two stages form the **conventional** level, with value placed in maintaining the conventional social order and the expectations of others. The final two stages form the **principled** level, where value resides in self-chosen principles and standards that have a universal logical validity and that therefore can be shared. Because the distinctness of each stage remains uncertain (Kurtines and Greif, 1974), we will focus on levels of moral reasoning.

Developmental Changes

There is at least suggestive evidence that, as a developmental sequence, the levels do appear related to age. For example, Figure 16.2 shows that, among children from seven to sixteen, older children tend to be at more advanced levels. Moral statements that reflect the premoral level decrease with age. Those at the conventional level appear to increase until about age thirteen and then stabilize; statements that reflect the principled level appear to increase slowly after age thirteen, although they still constitute only a limited proportion of the judgments among sixteen-year-olds.

In general, the speed with which children move from one level to the next also appears to vary with their intellectual ability. Higher-level moral concepts and attitudes are acquired only in late childhood or in adolescence; apparently they require an extensive foundation of cognitive growth and social experience. On the other hand, although a certain level of intellectual ability seems to be necessary for a given level of moral reasoning, intellectual ability in itself does not guarantee the development of higher levels of moral reasoning. Thus, children who are above average in intellectual ability are as likely as other children to vary in their level of moral reasoning. However, a child's relative brightness and his level of moral reasoning do combine to affect what he does. In a study by

Figure 16.1   Kohlberg's proposed order of progression in the development of moral reasoning. The reasoning characterizing each stage and level is illustrated by examples showing possible responses to Heinz's dilemma. (After Kohlberg, 1963)

Richard Krebs (1968), for example, it was found that, among children who were at an opportunistic, premoral level of reasoning, those who were bright and attentive enough to see that they could cheat jumped at the chance. Among those children who were at a rule-oriented, conventional level of moral reasoning, however, the ones who cheated seemed to be those who were not bright or attentive enough to succeed by understanding and following the rules.

Although there are still too few studies using Kohlberg's moral dilemmas to tell just how valid or reliable different results are, there is at least tentative evidence concerning several other aspects of the development of moral reasoning. It appears, for example, that under natural conditions people do not skip a level when advancing to a higher level of reasoning (Kohlberg and Kramer, 1969). In addition, children and adolescents appear to rate moral reasoning that is below their own level as inferior and that above their own level as better. However, they recall moral reasoning that is below their own level more accurately than they recall reasoning above their level (Rest, 1973; Rest, Turiel, and Kohlberg, 1969). In terms of people's

verbal reasoning about moral dilemmas, it further appears, as Figure 16.3 suggests, that levels of moral reasoning may develop in a similar way in various cultures (Kohlberg, 1969).

In response to criticisms of his theory, Kohlberg (1976) has recently revised his scoring method to make it more objective and easier to use, and other researchers have used his dilemmas to develop a more objective and simpler test (e.g., Rest, 1976). Yet findings based on the use of moral dilemmas have been questioned. Elizabeth Simpson (1974), among others, has pointed out that Kohlberg's theory may be culturally biased and not universal, because it is based on a social organization and values that fit only Western culture. She argues that because Kohlberg's approach focuses on issues of equality, rights, and justice, moral reasoning at a principled level fits only a constitutional democracy, and, in addition, that the highly abstract thinking involved is likely to be beyond most of the people in the world. It may be that, like formal, abstract reasoning, principled moral reasoning requires formal education for its development.

Other evidence suggests that a sex-related bias is built into Kohlberg's proposed sequence of stages; females do not show the expected pattern of movement through the stages (Gilligan, 1977; Holstein, 1976)—a difference that may be the result of socialization. Values of compassion, responsibility, and obligation are more likely to be stressed in the socialization of females than with males, but because Kohlberg has assigned these values to the conventional level of moral reasoning, females who base their reasoning on these values are automatically classified at a lower level of moral development.

ROLE TAKING AND SOCIAL INTERACTION

The active social-cognitive process of role taking appears to play a critical part in moral development generally and in moral reasoning in particular. During childhood, for example, an individual actively participates in many social situations and practices taking the role of others. Thus, in the process of acquiring moral values, a child increasingly becomes able to take (that is, to internalize) the position or role of another person. This ability enables him to restructure the way that he perceives and thinks about moral-social issues.

Figure 16.2   Variations with age in the proportions of different levels of moral reasoning in a sample of American boys. (After Kohlberg, 1963)

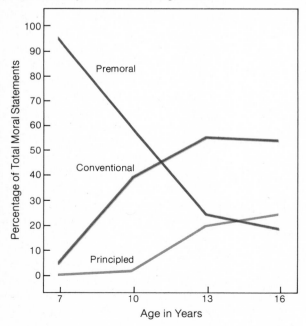

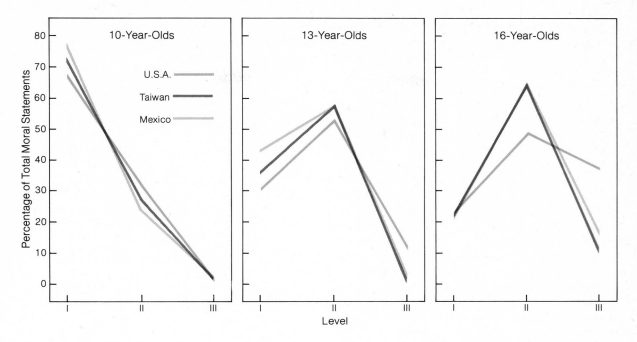

Figure 16.3   Variations with age in the proportions of different levels of moral reasoning in three cultures: the United States, Taiwan, and Mexico. The sample from each culture consists of middle-class urban boys. Levels I, II, and III indicate, respectively, premoral, conventional, and principled levels. (After Kohlberg, 1968)

This development means that young Lauren first sees standards of morality as something given and external to herself. At this level of reasoning, she is unlikely to adopt the viewpoint of others, and she may simply perceive moral matters in terms of personal consequences—whether her actions are rewarded or punished. If she reaches the conventional level of reasoning, her moral standards will begin to be more general and internal, and based on ideas of cooperation, respect, and conformity. She takes into consideration the views of others in order to do what is expected of her. Should Lauren reach the principled level, her moral standards will become even more general and largely internal, and based on more fully developed ideas of mutual respect, trust, fairness, and justice. Before acting, she will consider the viewpoints and needs of other people and of society in general.

As children develop their moral reasoning, social interactions with peers, which stimulate role-taking abilities, seem to be particularly important. For example, Charles Keasey (1971) studied fifth- and sixth-grade children and found that children who took an active part in social interaction were more likely than children who did not to show a conventional level of moral reasoning. Apparently, the ability to see that one's own actions can affect the way that another person reacts is also necessary if a child is to reach a conventional level of moral reasoning. This connection was illustrated in a study by Robert Selman (1971), who found a significant relationship between the ability to take the role of another and the attainment of conventional moral reasoning among eight-, nine-, and ten-year-olds. In addition, among the children who were deficient in role-taking skills, some later learned role-taking skills without developing conventional reasoning, but none developed conventional reasoning without also developing proficiency in role taking.

Families, of course, also influence the development of moral reasoning by providing opportunities to take another's role. For example, Robert Peck and Robert Havighurst (1960) found that a child's moral understanding was related to participation in family activities, sharing of confidences, sharing in family decisions, and being trusted with responsibility. More recently, Constance Holstein (1972) found that parents who take their child's opinions on moral issues seriously and discuss them (thereby providing a role-taking model as well as opportunities for the child to practice role taking) are more likely to have children who reason at a conventional than at a premoral level. In addition, she found that mothers who show a principled level of moral reasoning are more likely than those who show a conventional level of reasoning to have children who show a higher conventional level of moral reasoning. This finding suggests that mothers at the principled level are more likely to be skilled in role taking, to value opportunities for role taking, and to provide them for their children.

Given their superior role-taking skills, parents also are likely to adjust their own moral reasoning and action to fit their child's present level of moral understanding. For example, with small children they are likely to key their words to direct rewards or punishment, whereas with older children they are likely to talk about personal, interpersonal, or perhaps even abstract social consequences. Thus, parents are unlikely to speak to a three-year-old in terms of property rights or justice. Instead, they are likely to admonish the child in concrete terms: "Don't touch that, it'll break" or "Don't do that, or you'll get spanked." Parents of an older child, in contrast, are likely to emphasize social consequences and personal intentions and, as the child nears puberty, to begin to justify moral action in terms of more abstract principles. An eight-year-old is likely to be told, "The lady only broke the law to help somebody else," whereas a fifteen-year-old may be told, "Laws discriminating against women are unjust."

Socioeconomic status also appears to influence the development of moral reasoning (Kohlberg and Kramer, 1969). As Figure 16.4 indicates, mid-dle-class and working-class adolescents and young adults seem to go through the same levels of moral reasoning, but the middle-class subjects appear to advance faster and further. This finding suggests that middle-class adolescents and young adults experience a wider range of opportunities and stimulation for role taking and social participation and that they become able to see themselves and others from more general, organized, and flexible perspectives.

In a related way, differences in level of moral reasoning between a university professor and a preadolescent gang member, for example, can also be seen as stemming in part from differences in role-taking skills, social-learning factors, and cognitive ability. The professor's peer group is likely to approve and reward the use of abstract principles in reasoning, whereas the preadolescent's peer group is likely to approve and reward on a more concrete basis. Such differences in group orientation reflect the primary interests of each group and are likely to have a strong influence on the moral reasoning of the group's members.

GUILT AND SELF-REGULATION

The language of morality is full of terms that relate to feelings, and most people regard the emotions of guilt, shame, anxiety, and indignation as important influences on their behavior. In fact, without resorting to the notion that it would make them "feel bad," it is difficult to understand why people do not more often engage in immoral thoughts and actions. When a person speaks of conscience, he

Families influence the development of moral reasoning. The chances are that none of the Hatfields (shown here) or the McCoys saw anything wrong in the feud that nearly destroyed both families. (The Bettmann Archive)

Figure 16.4   Variations with age in the proportions of different levels of moral reasoning in samples of boys from two social classes. (Adapted from Kohlberg, 1968)

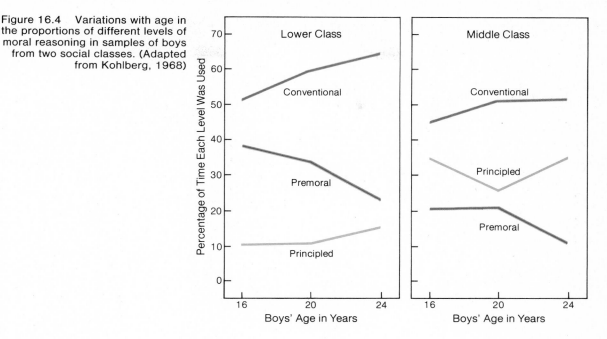

usually speaks not of a voice that quotes the Golden Rule or of the possible consequences of his actions. Instead, he thinks of his feelings when he remembers or anticipates some transgression. As this section makes clear, how one comes to feel about his actions can be a critical factor in the development of moral conduct.

When most people talk about the moral conduct of a child and its development, they refer to the child's ability to inhibit a desire (he does not take a toy from another child) or to his resistance to temptation (he does not cheat on a test or take a piece of pie that his sister was saving). Therefore, a good deal of the research on moral development has looked at the factors that affect the development of guilt and self-regulation.

Establishing Guilt and Self-regulation

Although there have been many different theories of how guilt and self-regulation are established, they generally converge on the idea that through conditioning a person gradually develops a sense of guilt and also comes to regulate his own conduct. Thus, the young child begins by trying to do and say things that his parents approve of and by trying not to do or say things that they consider wrong. He discovers that when he does or says things his parents approve of they generally give him affection, and through conditioning this affection becomes coupled with his feelings of self-ap-

The interests of the peer group are likely to have a strong influence on a person's level of moral reasoning, whether the group is made up of adolescent gang members, businessmen, or college professors. (© Joel Gordon)

proval. He also discovers, however, that when he does or says things his parents disapprove of they are likely to withdraw their affection or punish him in some other way, and through conditioning this punishment becomes coupled with his feelings of guilt and self-reproof. As a result of this kind of learning, the child eventually may behave morally even though his parents or other people are not present. Gradually, his own internal thoughts and feelings replace rewards and punishments administered by others, and he comes to regulate his own moral conduct. The child is also likely to keep learning various ways of reacting to his guilt over actual or contemplated transgressions.

Studies have shown that the nature of the parental relationship, the explanation of the reasons for discipline, and the timing of punishment are all important factors in the establishment of guilt and self-regulation in moral conduct.

Love and Reasoning   One of the clearest ways in which parents and others promote the development of guilt and self-regulation in moral conduct is by disciplining a child for disapproved acts. Discipline goes beyond spanking or hitting a child and includes the withdrawal of affection, verbal reprimands, and social isolation. Mild physical punishment, coupled with a mild withdrawal of love, appears to establish guilt and self-regulation much more efficiently than severe physical punishment does (M. Hoffman, 1977a). A child can always avoid the brief unpleasantness of physical punishment merely by avoiding the punisher, but if a normally loving parent also withdraws his or her love, the punishment lasts until the love is restored. Children disciplined by severe and unexplained punishment are unlikely to develop an effective sense of guilt or self-regulation and instead learn only to behave so that they will not get caught.

It was first thought that withdrawing love might be the most important factor in establishing guilt feelings and self-control. For example, Robert Sears, Eleanor Maccoby, and Harry Levin (1957) found that children who are disciplined by physical punishment develop less self-control and are less susceptible to feelings of guilt than children who are disciplined by the withdrawal of love and by reasoning. However, later studies by Martin Hoffman and Herbert Saltzstein (1967), Justin Aronfreed (1969), and others suggest that reasoning with the child and pointing out the effects of his wrongdoing are equally or more important.

One way to help a child internalize moral standards is to reason with him and point out the effects of his wrongdoings on others. (Suzanne Szasz)

Such verbal explanation and reasoning do two things: they encourage a child to take the role of others, and they help a child to internalize moral standards by providing him with thoughts to associate with his feelings and with reward or punishment. Thus, in terms of positive self-regulation, as Susan understands how her behavior affects others and how their behavior affects her, and as she comes to adopt the moral thoughts and attitudes of her parents, she soon responds with self-approval to what are now her own correct thoughts and actions. She learns to use self-instruction and self-praise. And when faced with a temptation, such as a dazzling display of dials and push buttons on a color television set, Susan may regulate her conduct by telling herself, "No. Don't touch it. That's a good girl. I'm a good girl for not touching it."

Timing of Discipline Whether physical punishment or other techniques are more effective in promoting self-adherence to moral standards is still a matter of debate (LaVoie, 1974). However, the timing of discipline appears to be especially important in the development of guilt and self-regulation. For example, in studies by Richard Walters, Ross Parke, and Valerie Cane (1965), a child was punished either just as he was about to play with a forbidden object or after he had begun to play with it. Afterward, the child was placed in a situation in which the same forbidden object tempted him. Generally, children who were punished early showed greater resistance than children who were punished later.

The explanation for such results is that, when children are punished early, the form of anxiety that we call guilt becomes associated with the anticipation of doing something wrong. However, when children are punished *after* they have disobeyed, doing something forbidden is followed by the fear that is generated when one is caught and punished. This distinction is often characterized as the difference between guilt and shame: **Guilt** stems from deviation from one's own internalized moral standards, but **shame** is a reaction to the disapproval of others. Thus some young children may regulate themselves by saying "No, No!" while looking at and not playing with a forbidden object; others may go ahead and play with the forbidden object and then get disciplined. Similarly, one five-year-old may feel guilt when she contemplates pulling her sister's hair and resists the act, whereas another five-year-old may pull her sister's hair and then feel afraid because her father may catch her.

It is often impossible to punish a child just before or just as he begins to do something that is forbidden. However, psychologists have also found, as have may parents before them, that delayed punishment can be effective if the situation that led to a transgression is re-created as fully as possible by talking with the child and describing the forbidden action at the time the child is disciplined. By using this sort of approach, Donald Meichenbaum and Joseph Goodman (1971) have been able to teach impulsive children with a history of getting into trouble to talk to themselves when they are tempted to do something forbidden. Using this kind of self-regulation, they end up modifying their own behavior.

Reasoning and Guilt

The importance of cognitive understanding and reasoning in the development of guilt and self-regulation is also shown in other ways. For example, the basic feelings that a person attaches to his moral actions may be the same throughout development, but his *interpretation* of these feelings appears to change with cognitive development (Kohlberg, 1969). Thus, anxiety over deviating from moral standards may register in the pit of the stomach for children and adults alike. But a young child is likely to perceive the physical sensation as a dread of external punishment. He resists the impulse to take a quarter from his mother's purse because he thinks that his parents are watching or

Because this child's punishment comes after her transgression, she will respond with shame (a reaction to disapproval) instead of guilt (a sense that she has deviated from personal standards). (© William Hubbell/Woodfin Camp & Assoc.)

that God will punish him. Older children and adults, on the other hand, are likely to perceive the same physical sensation as dread of their own self-judgment and to want to avoid feeling guilty or violating a principle.

Reasoning, feeling, and self-regulation are also interrelated in other ways in moral conduct; a violation of what a child or adult considers just or moral often elicits strong feelings, such as a sense of indignation or even moral outrage. For example, Kohlberg describes his son's first expression of moral reaction, which occurred at age four. At that time his son joined the pacifist and vegetarian movement and refused to eat meat because, as the child said, "It's bad to kill animals." In spite of lengthy parental arguments about the differences between justified and unjustified killing, the boy remained a vegetarian for six months. However, his principles recognized occasions of just or legitimate killing. Kohlberg recounts how, one night when he was reading aloud a book of Eskimo life that described a seal-killing expedition, his son got angry and said, "You know, there is one kind of meat I would eat, Eskimo meat. It's bad to kill animals so it's all right to eat *them*." It seems likely that the boy's attitude toward killing was not an internalization of the cultural rule "Thou shalt not kill" but a response based on his immediate empathy for other living beings and that his punitiveness was based on the primitive principle by which one bad act deserves another.

There is some evidence that girls may be more naturally empathic, and thus more susceptible to the development of guilt, than boys. Traditional socialization practices that emphasize emotional sensitivity and expressiveness for girls may reinforce this (M. Hoffman, 1977a). When involved in a transgression, boys are more likely to feel fear where girls would feel guilt; this disparity of feeling may also stem from socialization pressures on boys to achieve and to succeed—to the extent that concern with doing well may override any concern about being honest or doing what is right.

Reactions to Guilt

Because guilt is unpleasant, children generally learn how to avoid or reduce it, and this learning is likely to take many forms during the course of their socialization and the development of their moral conduct. As a child's ability to understand and to think increases and as he gains additional social experience, he learns new ways to manage

his guilt. And, although individual differences in this aspect of moral development are large, most children appear to develop somewhat similar ways of managing their guilt (McMichael and Grinder, 1966).

One of the most obvious ways to avoid guilt, as we have seen, is through self-control. For example, a child can resist temptation and refuse to do something that is forbidden. If, however, he believes that he will succumb to temptation, he may learn to avoid guilt by not even thinking about forbidden things, because the thoughts themselves provoke guilt feelings.

As their cognitive sophistication increases, however, most children learn even more elegant ways of avoiding the guilt produced by what they may do or think. For example, if Matt hurts another person, he may define his actions in benevolent terms, saying, "I just did it for his own good." Or he may learn to avoid guilt and self-condemnation by telling himself that the other person is a "tattletale" or a "cheater." Other learned ways of reducing the unpleasantness of guilt appear equally effective. Matt may instead learn to confess his transgressions or to apologize for what he says or does. Or he may learn to reduce his guilt by saying that his misbehavior was only half as bad as it could have been or as what others have done.

Some of these ways in which children and adults learn to handle their feelings of guilt and responsibility appear strikingly similar to what has been called the "just world hypothesis" (Fein, 1976). In general, people want to see the world as working in a consistent and just fashion, so that evil is punished and good is rewarded. Adopting this perspective allows people to see themselves as caring, helpful, and concerned human beings, no matter what happens to others. They have, therefore, a way to escape feelings of guilt or responsibility when someone else is the victim of an obvious wrong; if the world is just, the person must have deserved it.

MORAL CONDUCT AND MODELING

Like any complex human behavior, the development of moral conduct is determined by the interplay of many factors. Thus far, we have seen that role taking and empathy require experience and cognitive understanding, and we have considered some of the ways that reasoning and guilt and self-regulation develop and interact in moral conduct. But modeling also affects the development of moral conduct. As the child watches others, he learns new ways of behaving, gets information about the possible consequences of an action, and learns whether certain behavior is acceptable.

You will recall from our discussion of modeling in Chapter 15 that a child watching altruistic actions is likely to copy those actions and that what happens to the model affects the probability of the child's performing those same acts. By watching a model, the child learns how to do whatever the model is doing, whether the model is generous or selfish, aggressive or helpful, honest or hypocritical. However, once a child has learned to do or say something, he does not necessarily behave that way. As the discussion in Chapter 13 indicated, if the model is warm, powerful, and competent, the child may well copy his behavior, and especially in early childhood, that is just the way his parents are likely to seem to him. But, as we also saw in earlier discussions, the child's expectations of reward and punishment also affect the likelihood of his imitating a model. For example, if the model is rewarded, the child is likely to expect a reward for behaving in the same way. If the model is punished, however, the child is not likely to behave that way because he would expect to be punished himself.

Changes in Consequences

One of the most important findings to come out of research on the influence of observational learning on moral conduct is that an unpunished transgression appears to have the same effect on the watching child as a transgression followed by rewards. Thus, an early study found that children who see peers playing with forbidden toys are more likely to play with the toys than children who see no such transgressions (Grosser, Polansky, and Lippitt, 1951). This finding suggests that, when a child sees other children breaking a prohibition and getting away with it, the consequences anticipated by the child for violating that prohibition change.

A later experiment by Richard Walters and Ross Parke (1964) indeed indicated that, when punishment is expected, its very absence may act as a reward. They showed films of a model playing with forbidden toys to several groups of children. Some of the children saw the model rewarded, some saw him punished, others saw that nothing—either good or bad—happened to the model.

These children, along with another group who saw no film, were later tested in a situation like that depicted in the film. Both the children who had seen the transgression rewarded and those who had seen it go unpunished were more likely to play with forbidden toys than children who saw the model's actions punished or those who saw no film.

However, when the experimenter indicated that no one would be punished for playing with the forbidden toys, children who saw any of the films were more likely to play with the toys than children who did not see the films. Apparently all the children who saw the films learned the model's behavior; those who did not copy it were trying to avoid expected punishment.

Subsequently, Walters, Parke, and Cane (1965) also found that, in certain conditions, only the prospect of punishment may keep a child from transgressing. Once again, they showed children films of a model playing with forbidden toys, but this time the toys were so enticing that even many of the control children who saw no film at all succumbed to temptation and played with them. In a situation of great temptation, punishing the model was the only consequence that affected children's transgressions; children who saw the model rewarded, those who saw nothing happen to the model, and those who saw no film at all failed to resist the tempting toys.

When children watch a model go unpunished, two things happen. First, the punishment-free transgression suggests to them that for some reason the usual negative sanction does not apply in this situation, and they modify their own thinking accordingly. Second, the children then copy the model's violations because it is apparently all right to transgress and because playing with the forbidden toys is rewarding. Another research result helps to complete the picture of how consequences to a model can affect the observational learning of moral conduct. When children see a model go unrewarded for moral behavior, such as altruism, they will also fail to copy him (Staub, 1975). Thus, in a paradoxical sort of way, seeing moral behavior go unrewarded may decrease the rate at which it occurs, just as if it were immoral behavior and punished.

Verbal and Nonverbal Modeling

As we saw in our earlier discussion, other people, notably parents and peers, strongly influence the development of a child's moral reasoning. Parents promote the development of moral reasoning by providing a child with role-taking models. Although there are many gaps in our knowledge about the way moral reasoning and conduct develop, it seems clear that the verbal modeling of parents and others does have a strong instructional influence during the course of a child's moral development.

There is at least suggestive evidence that one of the ways parents and others influence a child's moral reasoning is by changing the factors that the child takes into consideration in arriving at moral judgments. For example, Albert Bandura and Frederick McDonald (1963) found that, by having an adult consider personal intentions or fail to consider them in making moral judgments about stories in the presence of a child, they could get children to shift their reasoning in either direction.

Using a method similar to those parents use in reasoning with their offspring, Moshe Blatt and Lawrence Kohlberg (1975) found it possible to change children's moral reasoning. As children discussed moral dilemmas in the classroom, teachers supported and clarified arguments that indicated a conventional level of moral reasoning but challenged those based on premoral reasoning. This procedure not only eventually led to changes in the children's levels of reasoning, but the differences between these children and others who had not heard premoral arguments challenged appeared to exist a year later.

Although it seems clear that verbal modeling produces changes in children's moral reasoning, there is no evidence to indicate that these changes will automatically appear in their moral behavior. As many parents have found, children tend to model what is done rather than what is said. As we saw in Chapter 15, a parent who spanks a child for hitting his sister is modeling the use of physical aggression. The child learns not that it is wrong to hit but that hitting is proper under certain (unknown) conditions. A study by James Bryan and Nancy Walbek (1970) tested the idea that actions influence children more strongly than words. A model played a game and won gift certificates, which he either selfishly kept or generously donated to a charity. At the same time, the model either said that people should be generous or selfish or made neutral statements. Later, children who had watched the model played the game and had their own opportunity to donate winnings to charity. Those children who had watched a generous model made more donations than those children who had watched a selfish model. Most important, however, no matter what the model had said, his words had no significant effect on the children's generosity. Other research shows that the way children perceive their own behavior also makes a difference. After seeing a model donate, for example, children are more likely to be generous themselves if they believe they are donating because of their own altruistic motives than because they have been told to give (e.g., Grusec et al., 1978).

For many people, the course of moral development results in moral reasoning and behavior coming together with guilt and self-regulation in a relatively cohesive way. For example, children with nurturant parents, who have seen their parents react with helpfulness in situations of both love and distress, are themselves likely to be more helpful and consistently altruistic in later situations (M. Yarrow, Scott, and Waxler, 1973). Another demonstration of lasting parental influence was shown by David Rosenhan (1970), who points out that people who engage in dramatic social action, such as those who went to the South to work in the Civil Rights Movement, are more likely to have parents who do not merely advocate positive social action but who engage in it themselves.

CONSISTENCY IN MORAL DEVELOPMENT

Just thirty days after President Ford took office, he pardoned ex-President Nixon for any crimes he may have committed while President. After all the explanations are in, it seems likely that they will cover every imaginable argument at every conceivable level of moral reasoning. No matter what President Ford's reasons, it also seems likely that different people will continue to see his moral conduct as more or less consistent, in terms of his own life history as well as in terms of some particular standard of morality. From the developmental perspective taken in this chapter, however, it should be clear that there are no easy or certain answers to many of the questions that have been raised about the moral conduct of either President Ford or ex-President Nixon. When applied to an individual case, such questions become particularly problematical, because the kind of reliable

People who engage in dramatic social action are likely to have parents
who do not merely advocate social
action but engage in it themselves.
(Charles Gatewood)

and relevant developmental information needed to
help answer them usually is unobtainable.

As this chapter has indicated, a person's consistency in moral conduct depends on the way that
intellectual, social, and emotional factors combine
during the course of his moral development. At
present, there is no way to predict to what extent
any individual or group will show consistency in
moral thought, feelings, and action.

Among children, adolescents, or adults of a
given chronological age, there is likely to be large
variation in moral development and conduct from

one situation to another. Individual variations in
moral conduct stem from developmental changes
in moral reasoning, different experiences in role-
taking skill, differences in learning and modeling
influences, and so forth. Thus, the degree of consistency shown by a child or adolescent in thought,
speech, or action is the result of the complex interaction of many factors.

In general, it seems likely that children and adolescents who tend to show consistent moral conduct usually are less influenced by immediate
situational pressures, show greater internal guid-

Warm, powerful, and competent people whose actions reflect their words can serve as models for children. (© Bob Adelman/Magnum Photos)

ance in their moral reasoning, and demonstrate a more mature sense of guilt and self-regulation across more situations. Their consistency can probably be traced to cognitive sophistication, varied role-taking experiences, and learning influences that emphasize consistency in both word and deed.

SUMMARY

1. During the course of moral development, the thoughts, feelings, and actions that make up moral conduct usually become less specific and literal and more complex in form and relationship.

2. Although moral conduct is often viewed as a group of related reactions governed by some central process such as conscience, research indicates that people are inconsistent in what they say, do, and feel.

3. In making moral judgments, young children often stress outcome over intention when good intentions lead to harm. Developmental changes in moral reasoning have also been studied by assessing people's reactions to posed moral dilemmas. This approach has led to the proposition that there may be a progressive series of stages

forming three basic developmental levels of moral reasoning: premoral, conventional, and principled.

4. The active social-cognitive process of role taking seems to be crucial to facilitating moral development in general and to moral reasoning in particular. In addition, research suggests that social interaction not only stimulates the development of role-taking skills but also influences the level of moral understanding that is reached.

5. Guilt and self-regulation in moral conduct are likely to develop gradually and to become more general in their effects. However, studies indicate that their establishment and development depend on such considerations as the nature of the parental relationship, the explanation of the reasons for discipline, and the timing of punishment. As a result of cognitive development, a child also may come to experience strong moral feelings produced by his own reasoning and may learn increasingly sophisticated ways of avoiding guilt.

6. What parents, peers, and other people who serve as models think, feel, and do has a strong influence on moral development. For example, as the child watches others, he learns new ways of behaving, finds out what is acceptable, and learns about consequences. Although verbal modeling by others is likely to influence the development of a child's moral reasoning, it does not necessarily lead to changes in moral behavior.

7. Although prediction of consistency in moral conduct is not possible, relatively greater consistency in moral development depends on an individual's cognitive sophistication, his role-taking experience, and the extent to which various learning influences emphasize consistency in word and deed.

Unit VI Adolescence: Building an Identity

The major physical changes of adolescence turn the child into the adult man or woman. Sexual development obviously has wide psychological and social consequences. When the adolescent attempts to find sexual gratification and to discover love and security outside the home, the personality that developed and established itself in late childhood faces an inevitable test: biological maturation forces sexual opportunities; the disappearance of the childhood home requires the construction of another. Life's joys as well as its pains arise from this confrontation between a still-developing personality and the rigor of biological and psychological development. Out of the confrontation comes the adolescent's sense of identity and self-esteem. This unit shows how boys and girls react to the transformations of adolescence and how cultural changes affect the range of choices that society presents to them.

CHAPTER 17
Physical and Sexual Maturation

GROWTH CHARACTERISTICS
Body Growth
Sexual Maturation in Girls
Sexual Maturation in Boys
Brain Maturation

PREDICTING PHYSICAL DEVELOPMENT

SIZE AND MATURATIONAL TRENDS

REACTIONS TO PHYSICAL CHANGE
Breast Development
Male Genitals
Obesity

PHYSICAL-SEXUAL AND SOCIAL CHANGE
Early and Late Maturing
Sexual Behavior

SUMMARY

As Lauren and David go through the transition from childhood to adolescence, the changes and interactions that characterize their development will be more pronounced than at any time since infancy. There will be large qualitative and quantitative changes in their bodies, primarily involving their sex organs and the secondary sex characteristics that differentiate man from woman. It is during adolescence that the adult emerges from the child.

One of the reasons that adolescence is seen as such an important phase of development is that, for the first time, the individual is truly aware of the physical changes that occur. Neither Lauren nor David can remain oblivious to the significance of the many events taking place in their bodies. The teen-ager sees, feels, and experiences body changes that are quite different from the sensations of childhood. An adolescent may experience these changes, especially those involving sexual maturity, as exciting, gratifying, embarrassing, wonderful, or even frightening.

In this chapter we will discuss the physical and maturational changes that characterize adolescence and the impact of these changes on both Lauren's and David's psychological and social development. We will look first at the adolescent growth spurt, then at sexual maturity and its impact on other areas of development. We will examine the predictability of adolescent growth and the trends toward earlier maturation and larger people over the last century. We will discuss how the individual reacts to the physical developments of adolescence and will focus on those changes that arouse the most concern in each sex. Finally, we will consider sexual behavior among adolescents and how it has changed in this century.

GROWTH CHARACTERISTICS

In the beginning, adolescence is a biological phenomenon, and sexual maturation is its central theme. Long before emotional considerations and social conflicts become important in the course of adolescent growth, hormonal changes begin to work their effects on the body. The main biological event is **puberty,** which is characterized by the attainment of biological sexual maturity. During puberty the reproductive glands first release sperm and ova. These glands are the **testes** in boys and the **ovaries** in girls. With the release of sperm or ova, the individual is, for the first time, capable of reproduction.

In a girl, the first menstruation provides an obvious milestone in puberty. In a boy, the signs are less sharply defined: pubic hair appears, sex organs grow, and nocturnal emissions occur. Gradually, a girl takes on the figure of a mature woman, and a boy develops the physique of a man.

Both boys and girls produce male hormones **(androgens)** as well as female hormones **(estrogens)** in relatively equal amounts throughout their childhood. As Chapter 6 noted, hormones help to regulate growth at all ages, but it is only when a child reaches puberty that the hypothalamus of the brain signals the pituitary gland to begin the hormonal production found in adult men and women. The pituitary gland stimulates other endocrine glands, the adrenals, ovaries, and testes (shown in Figure 17.1) to secrete hormones directly into the bloodstream, creating a balance that includes more androgens in boys and more estrogens in girls. These hormonal changes lead directly to the physical developments that emerge during puberty (Tanner, 1962).

During puberty, the ovaries and testes produce enough hormones to cause accelerated growth of the genitals and the appearance of secondary sex characteristics. In girls, a cyclic excretion of estrogens anticipates the rhythm of the menstrual cycle well before **menarche,** or the first incidence of menstruation (Meredith, 1967).

Body Growth

Velocity growth curves, which were discussed in Chapter 10, take on great significance during adolescence. The plateau period of childhood growth ends, and the adolescent growth spurt begins. Adolescence is virtually the only time in a person's life that this curve accelerates. Once the adolescent reaches the maximum point of growth velocity (in the case of stature, "peak height velocity"), deceleration again occurs until the annual growth increment is zero and growth for that factor ceases (see Figure 17.2).

The dramatic character of an adolescent's physical growth curve immediately provokes the question of where the energy to maintain such intense growth comes from. The answer is, of course,

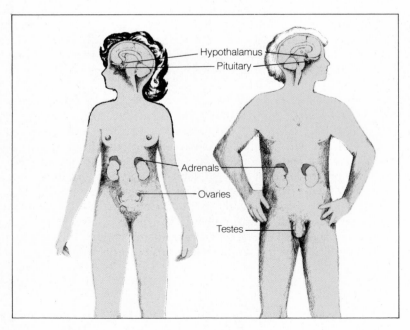

Figure 17.1   The endocrine system, showing only the major glands involved in pubertal changes. The hypothalamus (a part of the brain with neural and endocrine functions) signals the pituitary gland, which in turn stimulates hormonal secretions from other endocrine glands, resulting in many of the changes typifying adolescent physical and pubertal development.

Figure 17.2 Sample growth curves for adolescents eleven to twenty years of age (shaded area). (*top*) Notice that the early-maturing girl's rate of growth levels off by thirteen years of age, whereas the short boy continues to grow until approximately seventeen years of age. Individual variability is also reflected in the fact that the early-maturing girl reaches the average height for females, although the boy will be shorter than average. (*bottom*) Averaged and smoothed growth curves for boys and girls, showing inches gained in height per year. After the relatively stable period of gain in height during later childhood, the adolescent growth spurt starts, with its onset and end occurring earlier for girls than for boys. (Adapted from Bayley, 1956)

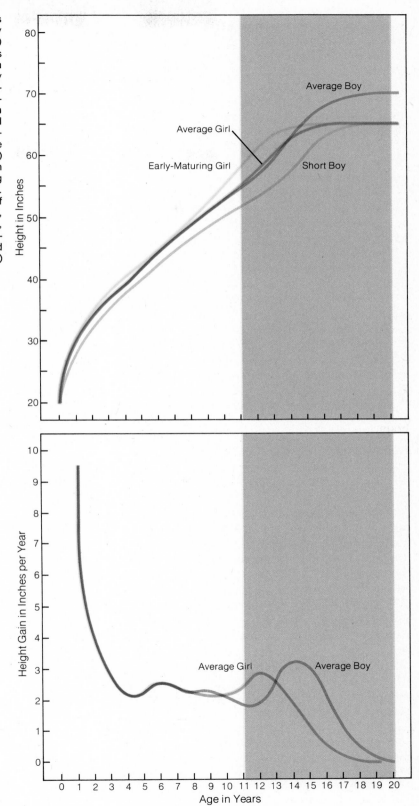

from calories. Some vigorous adolescent males at peak height velocity need a daily caloric intake comparable to that of a large adult doing heavy manual work, about 6,000 calories a day. (Little wonder that some adolescents always seem to be hungry and to spend time at the local hamburger stand indulging in carbohydrate orgies.) After an adolescent reaches peak height velocity, the extra energy needed for growth declines until the individual reaches the daily caloric intake that adult maintenance requires.

Although boys begin the pubertal growth spurt later than girls, their growth spurt lasts about three or four years longer than that of girls. For this reason, girls between the ages of twelve and fifteen tend to be taller than boys, but the boys catch up as they enter puberty and end their growth spurt significantly taller, on the average, than girls.

In general, bone and muscle tissue take part in the adolescent growth spurt, but the increase in muscle size is greater in boys than in girls; hence the adolescent male is stronger than the adolescent female. The average male also develops a larger heart and lungs, a greater capacity for absorbing oxygen in the blood and for eliminating the biochemical products of exercise, and wider shoulders, whereas the female develops a wider pelvis.

Only fat tissue develops oddly in adolescence. There is indeed an adolescent growth spurt in fat tissue, but it usually occurs before the main body begins its growth spurt. Thus, especially in some males, before the whole body spurts rapidly in size, "puppy fat" appears and often makes a healthy early pubescent male appear obese. As his body frame enlarges rapidly, this "puppy fat" is stretched and used up (presumably for the extra energy required by the growth spurt), and so the "string bean" phenomenon often replaces this early fat phase. The female adolescent does not lose fat (Faust, 1977); instead, she adds fat, and the average adult female has a good deal more fat than the male.

Both sexes experience a growth characteristic called **asynchrony.** Asynchrony refers to the fact that different body parts mature at different rates. This means that, at any given time during adolescent growth, certain body parts may be disproportionately large or small in relation to the rest of the body. This disproportion becomes most pronounced with puberty (Dwyer and Mayer, 1968–1969). For example, Lauren may complain that her hands and feet are too big, and David may

object that his nose seems large or that his jaw is too prominent. As growth progresses, body proportions usually become more harmonious.

Sexual Maturation in Girls

The female growth spurt typically begins at around age ten, peaks at twelve, and continues until about fifteen. A number of events signal the onset of puberty in girls. For example, the "breast bud" develops (Douvan and Gold, 1966), and pigmented pubic hair appears. Breast enlargement begins some time around the middle of the tenth year and continues for approximately three years until full size is reached. As the entire breast enlarges, other changes in its shape and appearance occur. The areas around the nipples grow larger, more conical in form, and darker in color. At the same time that her breasts develop, a girl's voice lowers somewhat, and her vagina and uterus also begin to mature.

Pubic hair usually appears when a girl is about eleven, but averages mean little in talking about an individual adolescent. Puberty varies so widely in its onset that such developments can occur at any time between the ages of eight and thirteen (Tanner, 1972).

Parents and adolescents often regard menarche as the true indicator of puberty, but this event occurs relatively late in the pubertal sequence. Nevertheless, because menarche is easily identified, it is often used as a basis for making normative comparisons of sexual maturity among girls. The norms for adolescent development suggest that the average American girl is likely to have her first menstrual period between the ages of ten and seventeen (Tanner, 1972). It is rare for a girl whose glands function normally to experience menarche before she is nine or after she is eighteen. Most girls have their first period when they are about twelve.

The relationship of menstruation to fertility is not well understood. One popular misconception is that menarche signals the attainment of full reproductive functioning. However, although menarche signals an advanced stage of uterine growth, the adolescent girl often, but not always, remains infertile for as long as twelve to eighteen months after menarche (Tanner, 1961). This period of infertility is shorter if a girl's first menstruation occurs later than average. Even four to six years after menarche, a girl is somewhat less likely to conceive than at a later time in life. Full sexual

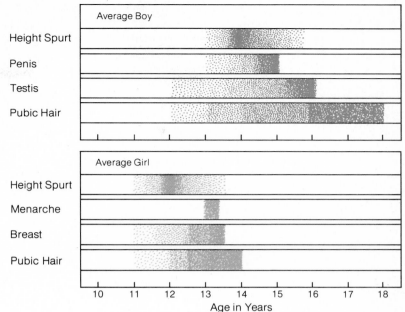

Figure 17.3 The pubertal development of an average boy and girl. Shaded areas represent the range of years during which such development usually occurs, with the darker shading indicating the period of most rapid growth or change. Although individual growth and change patterns may vary widely from these norms, girls generally start and end such development earlier than boys. (Adapted from Tanner, 1962)

maturity and fertility is generally reached sometime in the early or middle twenties.

Sexual Maturation in Boys

The adolescent growth spurt generally occurs about two years later in boys than in girls and peaks at about the age of fourteen. The onset of puberty typically occurs at about twelve among boys, and, as is the case for girls, puberty includes more than one event. The appearance of live spermatozoa in the urine marks the onset of puberty, but because this event can be detected only by clinical tests, more observable changes are often used. These include accelerated growth of the testes and scrotum and the pubertal height spurt. Pubic hair may also appear at the beginning of puberty or within the following year.

The penis and scrotum usually begin their accelerated growth when a boy is around twelve, but there are wide individual variations, and the growth may begin as early as ten and one-half or as late as fourteen and one-half. Maturation and development of the penis continue for about five years, and the scrotum reaches maturity in about seven years (Meredith, 1967). Although the external genitalia of girls change little, in boys the changes in the penis, testes, and scrotum are substantial. The shaft of the penis lengthens, and its head enlarges; the scrotum and testes grow larger and become pendulous. A boy is able to ejaculate

semen about one and one-half years after accelerated penis growth begins (Tanner, 1972).

During adolescence, the larynx enlarges, and the vocal cords lengthen. This change leads to the gradual deepening of the male voice and sometimes to the embarrassing cracking of the adolescent boy's voice into a squeaky falsetto.

The appearance of facial hair is a final and significant event for the adolescent male. The downy hair on his upper lip, especially at the corners, becomes longer, coarser, and darker. Next, long down appears at the sides of his face in front of the ears. Later, coarse hair appears on his chin and lower cheeks. However, the ultimate symbol of masculinity, a hairy chest, does not develop until a male reaches later adolescence or even his early twenties.

Brain Maturation

In the past it was generally believed that maturational changes in the brain were probably complete before adolescence. Today several lines of evidence suggest this is not the case. For one thing, continued myelination has been observed in the reticular system—the core of tissue that runs through the brain stem and filters incoming stimuli—and in some parts of the cortex as late as the third decade of life.

Based on recordings of brain waves (EEGs), it also appears that maturational changes in the structure and functioning of the brain may occur just before or around the time of puberty. For example, although characteristic wave patterns associated with drowsiness and arousal from sleep appear during infancy, they continue to change during childhood and apparently do not assume an adult form until a child is nine to ten years old (Gibbs and Gibbs, 1964). As noted in Chapter 6, the wave patterns recorded from the brain during sleep and wakefulness also change gradually during childhood, and it is not until a child is between eleven and fourteen that the typical adult patterns emerge (S. Rose, 1973). Alpha rhythm appears to follow a similar course of gradual change, assuming an adult form when a child is between ten and fifteen years old. In addition to these changes, Robert Dustman and Edward Beck (1966) found evidence of a further maturational change in the magnitude of the brain's electrical response to visual stimulation at about fifteen years of age.

Developmental research on possible hemisphere differences between boys and girls also suggests that there may be some relation between brain maturation rate and puberty. For example, in the study by Sandra Witelson (1976) described in Chapter 10, it was found that boys show a right-hemisphere dominance in processing spatial information by the time they are six. Since girls, however, continue to show a bilateral hemisphere involvement up to age thirteen—the most advanced age tested in the study—Witelson concluded that girls use both hemispheres to process spatial information until at least adolescence. A study by Deborah Waber (1976, 1977) is perhaps more instructive. She studied both early-maturing and late-maturing adolescent boys and girls. Waber found that, regardless of sex, early maturers performed better on verbal than on spatial tasks, whereas late maturers performed better on spatial than on verbal tasks. Although boys and girls who reached puberty late were better at spatial tasks than those who matured early, the reverse was not true. Early puberty did not give the early maturers an advantage over late maturers on tests of verbal ability. In discussing her results, Waber proposes that the differences she found are due to differences in the rate of maturation. Girls generally mature earlier than boys, and Waber suggests that the effects of sex hormones on the brain at puberty instead of biological differences at birth may account for general male superiority on spatial tasks. If she is right, it would mean that whatever neural structures are responsible for hemisphere dominance must be especially sensitive to sex hormones.

PREDICTING PHYSICAL DEVELOPMENT

The uncertain timing of the various stages of maturation perplexes most boys and girls and disturbs many. A late maturer may wonder when he will stop looking like a child in the midst of his (early) maturing peers. Similarly, an early maturer may feel somewhat embarrassed at her precocious sexual development. A physical growth specialist, using specialized equipment, can predict the timing of sexual maturity and ultimate stature with some degree of certainty, but such information is not available to most young people. These measures are usually taken only when significant deviance from the norm merits close medical scrutiny. The vast majority of teen-agers must simply wait and hope for the best.

The need for more precise measures of development and maturation than chronological age is obvious. Merely saying that Lauren is thirteen years old tells relatively little about her. We can predict only within a wide range how tall she might become or how physically mature she is. Individual variability in height is particularly large. For example, if Lauren is tall for her age, she may be maturing at an average rate and eventually become a tall woman. On the other hand, she may be growing at an accelerated rate, finish maturing at an early age, and become a medium-height woman.

The adolescent growth spurt in height is often spectacular and, to the boy or girl concerned, may seem completely erratic. Yet it occurs within certain boundaries, some of which are more stable than others. According to measurements of boys by Donald Broverman and his colleagues (1964), the beginning of pubertal growth is more variable than the end. Thus, the boy who has the earliest start in pubertal growth has a potentially longer period of growth than one with a late start.

Although individual height varies widely, one's size at the beginning of adolescence predicts a great deal about one's size at the end. Herbert and Lois Stolz (1951) found a correlation of more than + .80 between height at the onset and at the end of the pubertal period (not based on chronological age). Shifts in relative height do occur, but a boy who is taller than others at the beginning of his pubertal growth cycle is likely to be taller at the end.

SIZE AND MATURATIONAL TRENDS

Where records have been kept, they have indicated a trend toward earlier onset of puberty for more than a century. In 1840 the average girl's first menstruation occurred at the age of seventeen; each decade since, menarche has tended to occur about four months earlier. In 1960 the average age of menarche in the United States was about thirteen, and by 1970 the average age had dropped to slightly less than thirteen (Muuss, 1970).

Data about the onset of puberty in boys are not as complete as those for girls, but there has also been a trend toward earlier male maturation, at least since the beginning of this century. In addition to maturing earlier sexually, boys and girls today are also taller and heavier before, during, and at the end of adolescence than they were some generations ago. For example, Howard Meredith (1963) points out that in 1955 American boys were

Because boys and girls are heavier, taller, and mature earlier than their forebears, they often develop much higher levels of competence in athletic skills. (*top:* F.O.S., Inc.; *bottom:* © Joel Gordon)

five and one-quarter inches taller than boys of their same age in 1870. Over the same period, the average weight for fifteen-year-old boys increased by thirty-three pounds.

Both sexes now reach their final adult height at an earlier age than they did a century ago. The average boy now reaches his adult height at eighteen instead of at twenty-three, twenty-four, or twenty-five, as he would have in 1880. Similarly, the average girl now reaches her full height at about sixteen instead of at eighteen or nineteen.

Such changes are not unique to the United States; many countries around the world report similar trends. If the present trend continues, girls born this year can expect to be one-half inch to one inch taller and about two pounds heavier than their mothers and to reach menarche earlier. The trend toward taller adults also shows up in their feet; the size of the average American foot is increasing about one-half inch each generation (Muuss, 1970), which means that the average shoe size is increasing one size per generation.

Presumably these trends over the centuries depend on the interplay of environmental and genetic factors, in which better nutrition and other environmental factors presently allow human size to approach the maximum of the possible genetic range discussed in Chapter 3. If the trend were purely a linear progression, one would assume that in the Middle Ages females could not bear children before they were about twenty-five and that in a few centuries they would do so before they were eight. Further, a linear trend would mean that adults in the future would be giants. None of these assumptions, of course, is either likely or biologically sensible. First, size and maturation trends form an undulating curve over time. Second, although today adults are getting larger and larger, they are also maturing earlier and earlier, and hence their growth ends at an earlier age.

There are signs that the trend toward earlier menarche has stopped among the upper socioeconomic classes in Norway, the United States, and the United Kingdom. In the two latter countries, the trend toward greater height also seems to have stopped in the upper social classes.

It was emphasized in Chapters 6 and 10 that a person's diet plays a crucial role in development and maturation and that children from upper- and middle-class backgrounds become taller and heavier and reach puberty earlier than their lower-class peers do. Another factor is increased availability

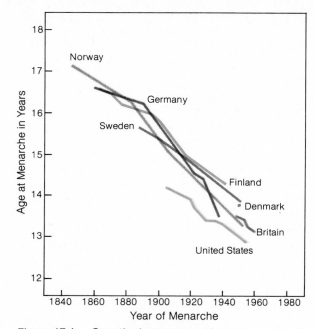

Figure 17.4   Over the last century, the average age of menarche (onset of menstruation) has declined in the United States and in various European countries. (After Tanner, 1962).

and sophistication of medical care. Today's children experience fewer of the severely debilitating diseases discussed in Chapter 10, and modern procedures prevent many diseases from exerting a negative influence. Finally, modern mobility affects the breeding patterns of the population. In earlier times, people lived in small towns or villages and lacked the transportation to move far from their homes. People tended to marry within their own communities. With the advent of better transportation, it became easier for people to marry outside the community, thus allowing genetic factors to operate more freely.

Other factors also influence the onset of puberty within any given generation. For example, geographic and climatic variations affect the average age of menarche. A girl living at sea level is likely to have her first menstrual period several months before a girl of the same age living at a much higher altitude. In spite of traditional beliefs and a few early studies, it also appears that girls who live in hot, humid climates are likely to reach menarche later than girls who live in cooler climates.

The three-year decrease in the average age of the onset of puberty represents a radical change in the timetable of development. Childhood is short-ened, and the social demands and urges associated with sexual maturity occur sooner. Unfortunately, the social and cultural climate has not adjusted to the trend toward earlier maturation. As Chapter 1 pointed out, today's adolescent is still treated in many respects as an overgrown child.

REACTIONS TO PHYSICAL CHANGE

Understandably, physical changes of the magni-tude experienced by adolescents have a significant effect on how they feel about themselves. As Chap-ter 15 noted, peer and social attitudes will influ-ence an individual's reactions to these changes. One important influence is that of the mythical **body ideal,** the body type defined by the culture as "attractive" and sex-appropriate. The individual learns these ideal characteristics from peer and family expectations and from the mass media. William Schonfeld (1963) has pointed out that movies, television, advertising, and the worship of sports heroes perpetuate the reverence for the ideal body and encourage the disparagement of those whose bodies do not conform to the ideal.

Cultural body standards may also influence a person's image of his or her own body. Stanley Schonbuch and Robert Schell (1967) asked male college students to select photographs that most nearly resembled themselves from a group of ten pictures. Males who were fifteen or more pounds overweight tended to overestimate their size, se-lecting photographs that portrayed fatter men. Schonbuch and Schell speculated that the negative comments and reactions of others may lead fat ad-olescents to regard their body differences as greater than they actually are.

Body image appears to determine to a large ex-tent how adolescents feel about themselves. For example, Boyd McCandless (1960) found a strong correlation between the way college-aged students view their bodies (body concept) and the way they judge themselves as people (self-concept). Accord-ing to McCandless, girls tend to be influenced by body image even more than boys are. This re-search suggests that a girl is more concerned about and places more personal emphasis on her physi-

An adolescent's self-esteem may depend in part on how far his or her own body image diverges from the ideal bodies held up by advertising, movies and television. (Sea & Ski advertisement prepared by Ogilvy & Mather, Inc.; photograph by The Image Bank)

cal appearance than a boy does. This is understandable when one considers the extent to which our society focuses on the beautiful woman with the perfect body, shiny hair, flawless complexion, gleaming teeth, and seductive eyes. The importance of a woman's appearance is reflected in the pervasive advertising of cosmetics, hair products, clothing, and fad diets. Although an athletic physique often is important for a boy, some alternatives exist, and boys are not as constantly confronted by the ideal physical stereotype as girls are. A man can look masculine by sporting a mustache or by flaunting chest hair. At present, men are probably less pressured by society to worry about their appearance than women are, although changing sex-role stereotypes may soon affect this difference in pressure.

Other investigators have also found that girls are more concerned than boys with the failure of their developing bodies to match the culture's body ideal. Girls perceive that boys prefer slender figures, long legs, and well-developed breasts, and they worry when their own bodies do not measure up to this ideal (Wiggins, Wiggins, and Conger, 1968). They worry about their social acceptability, and most girls tend to view their physical appearance as directly affecting their future prospects for courtship and marriage (Walster et al., 1966).

Adolescents of both sexes are especially sensitive to any body characteristic that might be interpreted as sex-inappropriate. From childhood, boys and girls learn which physical attributes are feminine and which are masculine, and they show deep concern over any deviations from those stereotypes (Schonfeld, 1964). Adolescent boys are particularly concerned about such characteristics as a circle of fat around the hips and thighs, underdeveloped external genitalia, or the development of subcutaneous tissue in the breast region. Although such developments as fatty hips and breast growth are normal and usually soon disappear, they are often a source of great embarrassment to a boy.

Herbert and Lois Stolz (1951) have identified certain physical characteristics that adolescent girls consider unfeminine. These include large hands and feet, a figure that is much too full or too thin, pigmented facial hair, and a large body. Thus, many of the normal temporary changes of adolescence may seem "unfeminine" to a girl. She grows body hair, her voice becomes lower, her hands and feet grow, and so forth. Eventually,

however, a girl may be comforted by the fact that her friends are experiencing the same changes.

Some cross-cultural data suggest that adolescents in other societies may not share the American adolescent's concern with body image. For example, David Friesen (1968) has shown that Canadian high-school students seem to place more value on academic performance and less on athletic prowess, popularity, and good looks than their American age-mates do.

Breast Development

Because breast development is an obvious indicator of sexual maturity in women, it is often the focus of attention from others and of concern to the individual. The development of a girl's breasts, including size and contour, plays an important role in her evaluation of herself as a female. The emphasis of the popular media (in advertisements for brassieres and the dimensions of the playmate of the month) and the behavior of many American men add to her concern.

Most adolescent girls are likely to have ambivalent feelings about their developing breasts. For example, Lauren may be proud of her new femininity yet be embarrassed by the sudden attention that she receives from boys. She may worry that tight blouses or sweaters are too revealing and may try to hide her new bustline by wearing loose-fitting clothes or by hunching slightly. Many girls complain that their breasts are too large or too small. Extremely large breasts can embarrass a girl because they draw attention to her and cause her to feel different from her peers. Extremely small breasts can make a girl worry whether she will ever reach sexual maturity or will be attractive to men. However, in most cases, as a girl reaches her adult body proportions, breasts that seemed too large or too small during adolescence begin to appear more appropriate to her stature.

Male Genitals

The size of his genital organs, especially the penis, can have profound significance for a boy. Boys' genitalia change in both size and contour more than girls' do. Because David can compare his genitals with those of his peers, they can become a primary source of concern. Men's rooms, showers, and gymnasiums provide ample opportunity for David to judge his development against that of other boys and men.

A boy with a small penis may feel particularly

distressed. He may be a victim of widely held beliefs that the size of a man's penis is related to his physical strength, his virility, and his ability to satisfy a woman sexually. Sometimes a boy may consider his penis to be particularly small because he is ignorant about the wide range of penis size among normal men. He can take comfort, however, from measurements that show a great variation in penis size at all ages.

The belief that a large penis is related to masculinity and virility showed up in a study by John Verinis and Samuel Roll (1970). They found that men and women aged eighteen to twenty rated such traits as a large penis and hairy arms and chest as indications of virility and masculinity. There is, however, no empirical support for the belief that the size of a man's genitals is related to his masculinity and strength. William Masters and Virginia Johnson (1966) found that penis size is less consistently related to general physical development than any other organ of the body is. They found that the largest penis (5.5 inches in the flaccid state) in a sampling of 312 men was displayed by a man who was 5 feet 7 inches tall, whereas the smallest (2.36 inches) belonged to a man 5 feet 11 inches tall. Masters and Johnson also noted that a small penis, when fully erect, shows a relatively greater increase in size than a large penis.

Masters and Johnson and others have also reported that the ability to provide sexual gratification for a female partner during intercourse does not seem to depend on the size of the erect penis.

The vagina is flexible and elastic. It accommodates to the insertion of small objects by contracting, and it distends sufficiently during the birth process to allow the passage of a baby. The vagina of a normally responsive woman therefore readily adjusts to a wide range of variation in penis size. Thus, penis size is usually a minor factor in sexual stimulation of the female; sexual technique makes the difference.

Obesity

About 10 percent of the children in the United States have been classified as obese (a judgment based on measures of weight relative to height), and in most samples the percentages become larger during the adolescent years. For example, Milicent Hathaway and Dorothy Sargent (1962) report that as many as 30 to 35 percent of adolescents are overweight.

Simply measuring the external dimensions of the body does not accurately determine obesity. Fat, muscle, bones, and skeletal shape all help determine body contours, and the contribution of each factor varies with individuals. For example, a girl with a wide bone structure may appear to have fat hips, although she may have a thinner layer of fat than a girl with narrow bone structure who looks slimmer.

Reactions to being overweight vary with sex. Girls are much more disturbed than boys by fatness, and girls are inclined to label excess weight as

Teenagers often choose poor diets, skipping breakfast and then eating too many high-calorie, low vitamin foods. As a result, about a third of all adolescents are overweight. (William Hubbell/Woodfin Camp & Assoc.

"fat," whereas boys are likely to view it as desirable bone and muscle.

Several factors can contribute to obesity in the adolescent. For instance, an increasing amount of evidence indicates that overfeeding babies (a common practice in the United States) causes a permanent increase in the number and size of fat cells (Mayer, 1968). Even if an overfed baby goes through childhood at a normal weight for his size, these extra fat cells remain in his body, leaving him susceptible to obesity during adolescence and adulthood. Glandular dysfunctions (for example, improper functioning of the hypothalamus or the thyroid gland) are rarely a cause of adolescent obesity. More often, teen-agers choose poor diets, eating too much starch and fat and not enough proteins, vitamins, and minerals. The young adolescent dashes off without breakfast, only to settle down later in the day to a lunch of hamburgers, French fries, a candy bar, and a malt, and then he tops off dinner with an extra piece of cake before going to bed. The tendency to eat high-calorie foods late in the day and evening can contribute significantly to obesity (Piscopo, 1970). Individuals who have such an eating pattern can be overweight and undernourished at the same time.

Whatever the reasons for obesity, the overweight adolescent is at a personal and social disadvantage. Because our culture associates obesity with such undesirable characteristics as gluttony, laziness, lack of will power, sloppiness, and general unattractiveness, the overweight adolescent often becomes the target of negative evaluations and cruel remarks. In addition, the obese adolescent may become biologically and sexually mature earlier than his age-mates and may find that his physical unattractiveness to the opposite sex only compounds his problems.

PHYSICAL-SEXUAL AND SOCIAL CHANGE

Sexual development obviously has wide psychological and social ramifications. The developing adolescent whose body conforms to the cultural ideal has a social advantage. But extremely tall, skinny adolescents and extremely short, fat ones are likely to evoke negative reactions from their peers. For example, J. Robert Staffieri (1967) found that classmates more often chose well-muscled and thin adolescents as friends than fat ones. Evaluations by others generally have a strong influence on an adolescent's social relations and behavior.

Early and Late Maturing

Developmental psychologists Mary Cover Jones and Nancy Bayley (1950) and their colleagues have followed groups of early- and late-maturing boys from early adolescence through the fourth decade of life. The boys differed markedly in social and physical characteristics during the years from thirteen to fifteen. At the same chronological age, the early maturers were taller, stronger, more attractive, and better coordinated than the later maturers, and they tended to have well-muscled bodies. The late maturers tended to be thin and were more talkative, active, busy, and uninhibited, yet they also tended to be tenser and bossier than the early maturers. These findings suggest that late maturers possess less social maturity and that they use negative behavior to get attention, thereby compensating for their physical disadvantages. Additional studies support this interpretation. Late maturers also show a greater need for social acceptance, greater anticipation of rejection, heightened dependence, and negative self-concepts (Mussen and Jones, 1957).

Schonfeld (1964) points out that many of the physical characteristics of late-maturing boys, which the boys themselves may regard as evidence of inadequate masculinity, fall within the normal range of development. When such is the case, a late-maturing boy need only wait until he catches up with his peers. But in the meantime, the values placed on athletic prowess and manly appearance (by boys and girls alike) may make him feel inferior to those who mature early.

The early maturer is more active in athletics and student government and has greater visibility in the school social system. The social advantages of early maturity also appear to continue into adulthood, when differences in physique no longer exist. In their thirties, early maturers tended to have higher occupational status, were more likely to work in supervisory or managerial positions, and reported more active social lives in clubs, organizations, and business (M. Jones, 1957). The differences that appeared when the groups were in their late thirties suggest that early maturers achieve in a conforming way, whereas later maturers' achievements are more likely to be idiosyncratic. Early maturers are likely to be conventional in both thought and attitude; they continue to have

social poise and to show responsibility. Late maturers appear to be more flexible and adaptive;
they tolerate ambiguity better than early maturers
(M. Jones, 1965). Thus, as Harvey Peskin (1967)
suggests, it appears that the greater social advantage of early maturers may lead them to fix on
their identity early in life, thereby producing
conventionality.

Studies of early- and late-maturing girls suggest that the early-maturing girl has less prestige in
early adolescence but that, as the growth process
continues, she comes to enjoy the social advantages of the early-maturing boy (Faust, 1960). At
first, the early-maturing girl is somewhat conspicuous and is likely to be far out of step developmentally with boys of her own age. However, early
maturity may be a source of satisfaction if a girl's
favorite companions are also early maturers. At
seventeen, girls who have matured early may have
a more favorable view of themselves and may rate
higher in popularity than they rated earlier in their
teens. However, studies that follow early- and
late-maturing girls into adulthood have not been
especially revealing, presumably because in the
past a woman's social life, status, and opportunities for achievement have depended on the status
of her husband (Eichorn, 1963).

Sexual Behavior

Because the higher brain centers also govern sex in
human beings, human sexual behavior is pliable
and shows great variation. Interest in sex is not so
tied to the reproductive cycle as it is in most mam-
mals. A wide variety of symbols, including pictures, movies, books, and even thoughts, can
arouse human beings. A woman continues to have
orgasm after menopause or after her ovaries are
removed, and a castrated man may be able to have
an orgasm even though he cannot ejaculate. As
this section makes clear, cultural changes in social
conditioning have led to great differences in sexual
attitudes and behavior.

The Kinsey Reports   Much of our knowledge
about the sexual behavior of Americans during the
first half of this century comes from the pioneering
work of Alfred Kinsey. The Kinsey reports (Kinsey, Pomeroy, and Martin, 1948; Kinsey et al.,
1953) on the incidence and variety of sexual outlets were milestones in the open exchange of information about sexuality. Kinsey's sample was far
from perfect; for example, there were too few rural

people and too little data on blacks to analyze sta-
tistically. Nonetheless, his studies yielded a great
deal of in-depth information.

One of Kinsey's major findings was that premarital virginity was much rarer than people
thought. Before 1915, three-fourths of all first-time
brides were virgins, but by the 1920s, the figure
had dropped to a little more than half. Among the
unmarried sixteen- to twenty-year-olds in the sample, 20 percent of the females and 71 percent of the
males were "sexually active"—that is, were having
sexual intercourse. Apparently a major shift in
American sexual values had occurred during the
"roaring twenties."

By the end of their teens, practically all boys
and girls had had some heterosexual contact,
ranging from holding hands to petting of the genitals. Furthermore, Kinsey's data indicated that by
age twenty, over half of all girls had experienced
orgasm, and nearly all boys. A majority of these
orgasms occurred during masturbation, which, like
premarital intercourse, was more common than
people realized. About two-thirds of all boys experienced their first orgasm through masturbation.
By the age of fifteen, 82 percent of all boys had
masturbated, and by age twenty, 92 percent had
done so.

For girls, the figures were lower: by age fifteen,
20 percent had masturbated, and by age twenty, 33
percent had done so. The figures continued to
climb, so that in the sample as a whole, 66 percent
of all females had masturbated. Masturbation was
also the most common source of first orgasm for
girls, accounting for 40 percent of the sample.

Social-class differences were related to the sexual behavior of men in Kinsey's study. For example, 98 percent of those with only a grade-school
education had experienced premarital intercourse.
For those with a high-school diploma, the figure
was 85 percent, and for men with some college
education, it was 68 percent. For women, however,
the link between social factors and premarital sex
was more apparent than real. Although it appeared at first that the more educated a woman
was the more likely she was eventually to have
premarital sex, this could be accounted for almost
entirely by the fact that less-educated women
tended to marry younger.

The Changing Sixties   Had this section been written ten or fifteen years ago, we could have said that
sexual behavior in the United States had changed

little since the 1920s. During the second half of the 1960s, however, a second major change in sexual behavior appeared, one that seems to be continuing to the present.

During the 1960s, there was a general liberalization of attitudes toward sex (Tavris and Offir, 1977). Behavior that once was considered unfit for public discussion began to appear in movies, television programs, books, magazines, and newspapers. At the same time, attitudes toward authority in general began to change—in part, perhaps, because of opposition to the Vietnam War. As a result, the social climate in which young people became sexually mature altered considerably.

Recent surveys show that Kinsey's figures are now out of date, especially for teen-agers and people in their twenties. For example, although the exact figures vary somewhat from study to study, nearly all studies find that premarital activity has become much more widespread since Kinsey's day. While Kinsey's figures showed that 17 to 19 percent of college women were sexually active, recent figures range from 37 to 56 percent (Cannon and Long, 1971). A national study in 1971 of 4,600 girls between fifteen and nineteen indicated that 46 percent of all female adolescents had intercourse by the age of nineteen (Zelnik and Kantner, 1972). A recent update of this study by the same researchers using the same methods shows that girls are now having intercourse at an earlier age than

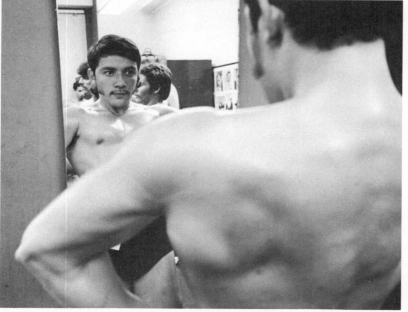

The marked physical changes of adolescence lead most boys and girls to become concerned with their own bodies and how they appear to the opposite sex. (*top*: Richard Kalvar/ Magnum Photos; *bottom*: Abigail Heyman/Magnum Photos)

With the general liberalization of cultural attitudes toward sex during the 1960s, premarital intercourse increased substantially among American teenagers. (© Marc Riboud/Magnum Photos)

have had premarital intercourse, more than double the figure in Kinsey's study. For those who did not plan to go to college, the figure was 75 percent, compared with a little over 66 percent in Kinsey's study (Hunt, 1974).

In sum, there have been substantial increases in premarital intercourse for both sexes. These increases have taken place in a relatively short period of time, and are dramatic when one considers the almost fifty-year plateau of unchanged behavior prior to the 1960s.

Although the incidence of premarital intercourse has risen sharply in the United States, American college students appear to be no more experienced than students in other countries and tend to look inhibited alongside English college students (Luckey and Nass, 1969). Tables 17.1 and 17.2 present the results of surveys among college men and women in five countries. However, this survey, which reports sexual intercourse among 58 percent of American college men, gives the lowest figure to come out of recent studies. One recent study indicates that 82 percent of American college men have engaged in intercourse. Whichever figure is accurate, there has been a sharp increase since Kinsey reported that 49 percent of college-educated males had had premarital intercourse before they were twenty-one.

Along with a rise in sexual experience has come a drop in the proportion of males who visit prostitutes. As Table 17.2 shows, only 4.2 percent of American college men have been involved with prostitutes, whereas earlier studies had reported that 20 to 25 percent had been so involved (Kinsey, Pomeroy, and Martin, 1948).

Sex Differences and Sex Roles   As all studies have shown, there are many differences in sexual behavior between males and females. Boys reach the peak of their sexual powers earlier than girls, even though girls reach menarche earlier than boys reach a corresponding level of development. Boys desire orgasm more often than girls; they resort more than girls to sexual fantasies; they are more responsive to sexual symbols; they reach a sexual climax in dreams more often; they require less constant physical stimulation to remain aroused; they more often have had sexual relations with more than one partner; they do not tend to insist, as many girls do, that there should be a feeling of affection between sexual partners; and they prefer to go steady less often than girls.

they used to, and the number who have had intercourse by age nineteen has climbed from 46 to 55 percent (Zelnik and Kantner, 1977). Girls are also beginning to masturbate at an earlier age, and with greater frequency (Hunt, 1974).

Changes have also taken place among young men, particularly among those headed for college. One recent survey found that by age seventeen, 50 percent of the males who are going on to college

Table 17.1   College Women's Sexual Experience

TYPE	UNITED STATES	CANADA	ENGLAND	GERMANY	NORWAY
Light embracing or fond holding of hands	97.5%	96.5%	91.9%	94.8%	89.3%
Casual goodnight kissing	96.8	91.8	93.0	74.0	75.0
Deep kissing	96.5	91.8	93.0	90.6	89.3
Horizontal embrace with some petting but not undressed	83.3	81.2	79.1	77.1	75.0
Petting of breast area from outside woman's clothing	78.3	78.8	82.6	76.0	64.3
Petting of breast area without clothes intervening	67.8	64.7	70.9	66.7	58.9
Petting below the waist under woman's clothing	61.2	64.7	70.9	63.5	53.6
Petting below the waist of both man and woman, under clothing	57.8	50.6	61.6	56.3	42.9
Nude embrace	49.6	47.6	64.0	62.1	51.8
Coitus	43.2	35.3	62.8	59.4	53.6
One-night affair involving coitus; did not date person again	7.2	5.9	33.7	4.2	12.5
Whipping or spanking before petting or other intimacy	4.5	5.9	17.4	1.0	7.1

Source: Adapted from Eleanore Luckey and Gilbert Nass, "A Comparison of Sexual Attitudes and Behavior in an International Sample," *Journal of Marriage and the Family,* 31 (1969), p. 375.

Kinsey and his colleagues tended to explain differences in male and female sexual behavior in biological terms, by assuming, for example, a more urgent male sex drive. A more balanced view suggests that these differences are the result of a complex interaction among neurological, hormonal, psychological, and cultural factors. It seems clear that male and female sexual behaviors are influenced by sex-role stereotypes and expectations, just as much other behavior is. According to traditional American standards, the girl should play a passive role in her sexual relations. The boy should take the initiative in petting, and he usually does. The girl accedes, and, if the approach threatens to go beyond the limits she allows, she is expected to serve as a calming conscience for both. In courtship, it is the man who is supposed to propose. Although our culture's sex-role stereotypes are gradually changing, few adolescents have escaped the social pressures that dictate appropriate sexual behavior for each gender. In the next chapter, we will look at the psychological aspects of sexual intercourse and examine adolescents' attitudes toward sexuality and appropriate sexual conduct.

SUMMARY

1. Adolescence begins as a biological phenomenon, and sexual maturation is its central theme. The first incidence of menstruation in girls and the appearance of pubic hair, nocturnal emissions, and enlarging sex organs in boys are among the signs most often used to mark the attainment of physical-sexual maturity. With the later release of sperm and ova during puberty, adolescents achieve the capability of biological reproduction. The physical and maturational changes that indicate increased hormone production are dramatically reflected in the adolescent growth spurt, and are apparently accompanied by changes in the structure and functioning of the brain.

Table 17.2 College Men's Sexual Experience

TYPE	UNITED STATES	CANADA	ENGLAND	GERMANY	NORWAY
Light embracing or fond holding of hands	98.6%	98.9%	93.5%	93.8%	93.7%
Casual goodnight kissing	96.7	97.7	93.5	78.6	86.1
Deep kissing	96.0	97.7	91.9	91.1	96.2
Horizontal embrace with some petting but not undressed	89.9	92.0	85.4	68.8	93.6
Petting of woman's breast area from outside her clothing	89.9	93.2	87.0	80.4	83.5
Petting of woman's breast area without clothes intervening	83.4	92.0	82.8	69.6	83.5
Petting below the waist of the woman under her clothing	81.1	85.2	84.6	70.5	83.5
Petting below the waist of both man and woman, under clothing	62.9	64.8	68.3	52.7	55.1
Nude embrace	65.6	69.3	70.5	50.0	69.6
Coitus	58.2	56.8	74.8	54.5	66.7
One-night affair involving coitus; did not date person again	29.9	21.6	43.1	17.0	32.9
Whipping or spanking before petting or other intimacy	8.2	5.7	17.1	0.9	5.1
Sex on pay-as-you-go-basis	4.2	4.5	13.8	9.8	2.5

Source: Adapted from Eleanore Luckey and Gilbert Nass, "A Comparison of Sexual Attitudes and Behavior in an International Sample," *Journal of Marriage and the Family*, 31 (1969), p. 374.

2. To the dismay of many adolescents, growth during this period is often asynchronous, with different body parts maturing at different times and rates. Because of this, and because the extent of growth varies widely, predictions of physical development often remain uncertain. Despite individual variability, maturation usually can be expected to occur within certain more or less stable boundaries.

3. Size and maturational trends over the decades indicate an earlier onset of puberty, increases in size and weight, and the earlier attainment of final adult height. Improved nutrition, more sophisticated medical care, and climatic variations are among the environmental factors that appear to explain these changes within and across generations.

4. In this age of mass media, individuals are constantly exposed to, and quickly learn, the mythical standards that make up the culture's ideal body type. Deviations from this body ideal—whether in height or weight, the timing of maturation, or the size and contour of body parts—are likely to have profound influences on the developing adolescent's self-concept and peer relationships.

5. Physical-sexual development typically has wide psychological and social ramifications. For example, early-maturing boys are likely to be taller, stronger, more attractive and poised, and better coordinated than later-maturing boys. However, apart from variations in rates at which they mature physically or sexually, it is also clear that more adolescents today engage in a greater variety of sexual behavior at an earlier age. Although sexual attitudes and behavior have generally become more open and some changes in sex-role stereotypes have occurred, few adolescents escape the social pressures that dictate appropriate sexual attitudes and behavior for each gender.

CHAPTER 18
Identity and Experience

IDENTITY: SELF AND SOCIETY
Defining the Self
Self-esteem

COGNITIVE CHANGE
Formal Thought
Concepts of Self and Others

MORAL REASONING

SEXUALITY AND INTIMACY
Personal Choice
Promiscuity
Gender and Equalitarianism

VOCATIONAL IDENTITY
Cognition and Vocational Choice
Gender Differences

SUMMARY

Matt is sixteen years old, six feet tall, shaves three times a week, is second-string tackle on the football team, and tries to be independent and self-sufficient. But he is not sure what he wants to do with his life, is afraid his girl friend doesn't truly love him, finds his parents are unreasonable, and—after behaving like an adult in a difficult situation—suddenly acts younger than his twelve-year-old sister Susan. In short, Matt is an adolescent.

As Chapter 1 pointed out, adolescence is a relatively new invention in Western societies. Many other societies recognize a change in status around the age of puberty. This sometimes overnight change drastically redefines the individual's rights and responsibilities. At the same time, it constitutes an important force for behavioral development and change. The longer transition period of adolescence in the West is no less important in influencing the development of the individual. The view that adolescence is only a recapitulation and working out of the themes of childhood does scant justice to its possibilities. To be sure, the preadolescent years are important in defining where Susan and Matt begin, how much they have to work with, and what they must work on. Human development is cumulative and layered. Adolescence is built on the early phases of life but at the same time has its own tasks. Whether the adolescent accomplishes these tasks depends not only on his past but on his present as well, on what he is offered and on what he can make of it.

It is impossible to discuss adolescent behavior and development without taking note of the wide variety of life styles and commitments that exist in our society, and the discussions in this and the following chapter will emphasize this point. In a pluralistic society, adolescence takes many forms. In contrast to the common stereotype, adolescents share the diverse values, beliefs, and attitudes characteristic of their elders.

In this chapter we will discuss the adolescent's search for a sense of identity. We will look at self-esteem and the role it plays in developing a secure sense of identity. We will see how the cognitive changes of adolescence and the development of formal thought affect a person's self-concept and moral reasoning. We will discover that the changes in sexual behavior discussed in the last chapter have been accompanied by large changes in sexual attitudes and by a trend toward mutually satisfying, equalitarian sexual relationships. Finally, we will look at the adolescent's choice of a career, and we will explore the ways that socialization can shape that important choice.

IDENTITY: SELF AND SOCIETY

Although matters of self-definition and self-esteem are important throughout the life cycle, it is during adolescence that these matters become paramount. Developmental change often brings about a developmental crisis, a disruption of the concept of self. As Erik Erikson (1968) has pointed out, at this time of life the adolescent's body goes through marked physical changes and is flooded with sexual impulses; the young person confronts both imminent intimacy with the other sex and an immediate future filled with conflicting possibilities and choices.

Before adolescents can regain a sense of unity with themselves and with the world about them, they must incorporate their new physical and sexual attributes and the opportunities they present into a new self-concept. A society that universally recognizes these changes and attaches meaning to them makes reworking self-concepts a relatively uncomplicated task. However, in a pluralistic society like our own, the prolongation of adolescence and its bewildering variety of choices can mean great difficulty. In either case, Erikson has postulated a "developmental crisis," a moment when development must move one way or the other.

Erikson's concept of identity has two facets. It refers to a person's feeling about himself, or self-esteem, and to the relationship between his self-concept and descriptions of him by significant others in his life. The most important descriptions involve the sort of behavior that society considers basic to a person's functioning, and these descriptions are organized into subgroupings that are

Figure 18.1 Some major theoretical viewpoints regarding personality development during adolescence.

SIGMUND FREUD considers adolescence as the time of the last identifiable stage of psychosexual development: the genital stage. During this stage, the individual's identity takes its final form and, in place of narcissistic self-love, love for others and altruistic behavior develop. Although the influence of peers and parents is as strong as it was during earlier stages, peers and parents still play an important role in providing love and realistic direction for the individual.

ERIK ERIKSON holds self-definition and self-esteem as central concerns for the individual during adolescence. As a result of physical changes, powerful sexual impulses, conflicting choices and possibilities, and confusion in the roles expected of him by parents and peers, the adolescent is confronted with an identity crisis. He must incorporate his new physical and sexual attributes into a new self-concept. He also must generate an orientation and a goal that will give him a sense of unity and purpose so that he can make a vocational choice that will best match his view of himself. Finally, he must integrate into his self-understanding the expectations and perceptions that others have of him.

WALTER MISCHEL takes the view that as the adolescent moves out of childhood, he encounters a multiplicity of adult roles and expectations and that each of these requires him to learn new discriminations and to make new responses to his environment. Physical and hormonal changes require the adolescent to learn patterns of socially appropriate sexual behavior. Social expectations and consequences also change during this time, forcing the adolescent to confront the responsibility of choosing a career. As agents of socialization, parents and peers continue to exert a strong influence on the adolescent's behavior.

usually called roles. Being a male or a female is one such fundamental role. As we have seen in earlier chapters, roles provide significant connections between self and society; a person's roles both link him meaningfully to the social order and define him as an individual.

The child enters adolescence with experience in three kinds of social groups: the family, the peer group, and larger organizations such as the school. He plays at least one role in each of these groups, and for each of his roles there is a set of role-definers—people with whom he interacts and who define his role by indicating appropriate behavior and by supporting and rewarding him when he displays it. In a similar manner, the teen-ager comes to judge himself—his appearance, his academic achievement, his social capacities—by the standards of those who define the roles in his social groups. Among these role-definers, parents, peers, and teachers continue to be a dominant influence.

Defining the Self

The childhood self is largely defined by parents and a few other key persons, including family members, certain peers, ministers, and teachers. It

reflects in a relatively uncomplicated way the immediate world of persons crucial to the child and is based on relatively simple identification with these people. The adolescent must often reexamine and reintegrate this self-concept so that it is consistent with his increased capacity for rationality, his moral values, and his possibilities for work, love, and play in modern society. This process requires him to integrate emerging cognitive and behavioral abilities and his new values and purposes.

Some adolescents are susceptible to groups that require strict conformity but allow them to develop synthetic identities. (*top:* Rogier Gregoire; *bottom:* Tim Eagan/Woodfin Camp & Assoc.)

Above all, an adolescent's sense of self involves a movement away from a simple mirrorlike view of himself—in which he sees himself as a reflection of parents, peers, and teachers—to a more autonomous and more individual sense of identity, integrating independence and uniqueness with interdependence and solidarity with other people.

There are wide individual differences in the methods that adolescents may use to attain new self-concepts. One youthful solution involves a determined attempt to change the society so as to bring it into line with the adolescent's principles and needs. Another solution is a systematic attempt to change one's self so as to fit into the existing system with less anxiety or discomfort. A third approach is the effort to carve out some special niche within society where the qualities of one's self can be preserved, enhanced, or acted on.

Some developmental changes, however, can threaten the adolescent's integration of his childhood self-concept and lead to what Erikson (1968) called **totalism,** an organization of one's self-concept that has rigid, absolute, and arbitrary boundaries. Totalism makes adolescents particularly susceptible to totalitarian movements and to ideologies of the left and the right. According to Erikson, if adolescents feel their emerging identities severely threatened by historical or technological development, they become ready to support doctrines that allow them to immerse themselves in a synthetic identity, such as extreme nationalism, racism, or class consciousness, and to condemn the stereotyped enemy of their new identities. This tendency toward total immersion in a synthetic identity can take other forms, and it characterized the participation of many American adolescents in the Civil Rights Movement of the 1960s, the 1968 crusade to nominate Eugene McCarthy for President, and the campaign to end the war in Vietnam.

A similar immersion into the peer group can play a major role in regulating feelings and in emancipating the adolescent from childhood dependence. What Peter Blos (1962) has called **uniformism,** or immersion into the peer group and acceptance of its norms as infallible and regulatory, may assist an adolescent in moving away from dependence on his family at a time when he still needs some external source of control. However, sometimes an adolescent clings to this source of control long after the need for it has passed, and conformity to peer-group norms merely replaces conformity to parental norms. When this happens, development is foreclosed before the adolescent can achieve real self-regulation and independence.

Self-esteem

Erikson (1968) has suggested that, at its best, identity is experienced as a sense of well-being. A person with a secure identity feels at home in his body, knows where he is going, and feels assured of recognition from people who count.

In general, people with low self-esteem have a relatively unstable self-concept, which means that they lack a consistent frame of reference within which to assimilate their experiences of self and others. Such a situation provokes anxiety, a state intensified by the strain of putting on a front. Persons with low self-esteem are more likely than others to be lonely. They are also more vulnerable. They are likely to be sensitive to criticism; they are bothered if others have a poor opinion of them, are deeply disturbed if they do poorly at some task, and are upset when they become aware of a personal fault or inadequacy. Others may describe them as touchy or easily hurt.

This internal distress is matched by the dismal picture of the adolescent with low self-esteem. He is awkward with others, assumes that they do not like him, has little faith in human nature, is submissive and nonassertive, and gets little respect. He infrequently participates in extracurricular activities and is rarely selected for leadership positions. He tends to be unpopular and avoids participating in class discussions and informal conversations. Caught up in this pattern, the adolescent with extremely low self-esteem becomes caught in a trap in which his very real isolation from others keeps him from developing a positive view of himself. His anxiety and vulnerability often keep him from entering into any social situations that might raise his self-esteem, thereby opening the trap.

The interdependence of attitudes toward self and others, which is a feature of most personality theories, showed up clearly in a survey that Morris Rosenberg (1965) made of 5,000 adolescents in New York State. He found that adolescents from upper socioeconomic groups were more likely than other adolescents to accept themselves, the difference being greater for boys than for girls. Adolescents from some sociocultural groups also showed greater self-esteem than others. However, Rosenberg found that the general prestige of an adoles-

The anxiety and vulnerability of adolescents with low self-esteem may so trap them that they cannot enter situations that would help them develop a positive view of themselves. (Alex Webb/Magnum Photos)

cent's social group was not the major influence on self-esteem. Instead, self-esteem had more to do with the adolescent's experiences in both family and peer groups. The social-class effect seems linked to the fact that many fathers in upper socioeconomic groups tend to support their sons strongly.

Rosenberg found the lowest self-esteem among minorities within a single neighborhood. That is, being a Catholic in a predominantly Catholic neighborhood leads to higher self-esteem than being a Catholic in a predominantly Protestant neighborhood. This result helps to explain the self-esteem of black adolescents from predominantly black neighborhoods, who generally do not have the low self-esteem that one might anticipate on the basis of their group's prestige in society (Rosenberg, 1975). Cases of low self-esteem among black adolescents appear to relate more to their experiences in family, peer, and neighborhood groups than to their group's general level of prestige.

COGNITIVE CHANGE

It is not accidental that adolescence is the first phase of life in which a person begins to think carefully about himself, his role in life, his plans, and the validity and integrity of his beliefs. Unlike the younger child, who deals largely with the present, the adolescent often is concerned with the hypothetical, the future, the remote. An adolescent remarked, "I found myself thinking about my future and then I began to think about why I was thinking about my future, and then I began to think about why I was thinking about why I was thinking about my future." This preoccupation with thinking is characteristic of formal thought.

Formal Thought

The adolescent like Susan who develops formal thought can achieve a new range and flexibility of mental processes. If encouraged and supported by her environment, Susan can develop her cognitive abilities in constructive and rational ways, developing an increased capacity for planning, for the mental rehearsal of alternate plans of action, and for guiding her behavior according to long-range purposes.

Formal thought is a generalized orientation toward problem solving that involves isolating elements of a problem and systematically exploring all the possible solutions. You will recall that Jean Piaget (1952b) calls this ability to deal with logical

possibilities the stage of *formal operations* (see Chapter 2). When Bärbel Inhelder and Piaget (1958) studied a group of Swiss college-preparatory students, they found that elements of formal thought first appeared among eleven- and twelve-year-olds and that fourteen- and fifteen-year-olds were consistently reasoning from hypotheses. As was noted in Chapter 14, when children are asked to determine what factors account for the speed with which a pendulum travels, only fourteen- and fifteen-year-olds usually can solve the problem successfully. These adolescents can anticipate all possible combinations of the four plausible factors involved, test them systematically, and then deduce which factors affect the pendulum's swing and which are irrelevant.

As this example indicates, the central feature of formal thought is the conception of possibilities that lie outside the immediate environment. However, some studies suggest that formal thought is neither as inevitable nor as universal a step in development as is the concrete thought of childhood (Niemark, 1975). Cross-cultural studies have shown that in some societies apparently few people develop this ability to reason from hypotheses. For example, in Turkey formal thought appears in city dwellers but not in residents of primitive villages (Kohlberg and Gilligan, 1971).

Patricia Greenfield and Jerome Bruner (1966) have stressed the association between the prevalence of formal schools and the typical level of cognitive operations in a society. They attribute the greater evidence of formal thought in societies with schools to the fact that schooling provides training in written language, a view that is similar to Michael Cole's conclusions, which were discussed in Chapter 14. Writing forces a child to separate thought from objects and thus may encourage the child to let his symbolic processes run ahead of concrete fact, allowing him to develop the capacity to think in terms of possibility rather than actuality. In modern societies with widespread school systems, more middle- and upper-middle-class adolescents show formal

Adolescents who develop formal thought are able to plan logically for the future and consider possibilities that lie outside the immediate environment. (both photos © Joel Gordon)

thought than adolescents from working- and lower-class backgrounds, and adolescents in the upper socioeconomic classes develop this thought earlier (Dulit, 1972; Peel, 1971).

Although formal thought is by no means a universal characteristic of adolescence, its development constitutes a change of primary importance for the individual. Because adolescents may see the world and the people in it, including themselves, in such a different way, speculating about what might be instead of accepting what is, it naturally follows that profound changes can occur in their identities and in their social relations.

Concepts of Self and Others

Erikson identifies formal thought as instrumental in the development of the identity crisis discussed earlier. Presumably, formal thought can predispose a person to the crisis as well as help him or her to resolve it. There is evidence that adolescents can take a far less simplistic view of themselves than they did before (Livesley and Bromley, 1973; Montemayor and Eisen, 1977) and that the ability to consider possibilities enables them to consider themselves more in terms of what might be. Indeed, Inhelder and Piaget (1958) point out that formal thought makes it possible for people to appreciate abstract ideals (such as honesty, courage, and love) and consequently to attach value to them. Thus, as they proceed to form an identity, adolescents must consider their own impressions of self and the impressions of others about them, and they must use formal thought in order to integrate their self-concepts.

To do this effectively, adolescents must monitor their own mental activity; they must think about their thought. Such reflective thought appeared among adolescents in the study by W. J. Livesley and D. B. Bromley (1973) of developmental changes in the descriptions that children and adolescents give of other persons. They provided 320 children ranging in age from seven to fifteen with the opportunity to write free descriptions of themselves and of liked and disliked persons of both sexes. Their findings suggest a qualitative change around the age of thirteen or fourteen.

Adolescents used descriptive terms more flexibly and precisely than younger children did, often adding subtle qualifying and connecting terms. They showed a greater ability to analyze and interpret another's behavior and an increased concern with making their descriptions convincing. That is, in describing another person, only adolescents would report an impression of the person and hastily add a qualifier to dissuade a listener from drawing an inaccurate conclusion. For example, fifteen-year-old Susan might say of a friend, "He is shy—but not anxious." In order to make such a statement, she had to consider other people's possible misinterpretations of her descriptions, thereby engaging in reflective thought.

Most impressive in the descriptions written by adolescents is the change in organization. Adolescents selected and organized their ideas in a coherent and complex fashion, whereas younger children's impressions were like beads on a string. A nine-year-old boy describes himself:

> I have dark brown hair, brown eyes and a fair face. I am a quick worker but am often lazy. I am good but often cheeky and naughty. My character is sometimes funny and sometimes serious. My behavior is sometimes silly and stupid and often good, it is often funny my daddy thinks. (Livesley and Bromley, 1973, page 338)

The adolescent no longer strings the elements of his impressions together but integrates them through the use of qualifying terms, distinctions between real and apparent qualities, and the verification and amplification of internal consistency. He tends to refer more often to ambitions, aspirations, wants, needs, expectations, fears, wishes, self-reproaches, beliefs, attitudes, values, and comparisons with others. Adolescents also use these categories far more in describing the self than in describing others. This change reflects both adolescents' greater competence at formal thought and the privileged information people have about themselves but not about others. Some of these attributes clearly appear in a fourteen-year-old girl's self-description:

> I am a very temperamental person, sometimes, well *most* of the time, I am happy. Then now and again I just go moody for no reason at all. I enjoy being different from everybody else, and like to think of myself as being fairly modern. Up till I was about 11, I was a pretty regular churchgoer (R.C.) but since then I have been thinking about religion and sometimes I do not believe in God. When I am nervous I talk a lot, and this gives some important new acquaintances a bad impression, when I am

trying to make a good one. I worry a lot about getting married and having a family, because I am frightened that I will make a mess of it. (pages 239–240)

MORAL REASONING

The intensity with which some adolescents espouse moral attitudes and values may not bear much relation to what they feel or do in the specific situations that they face. After all, adolescents are subject to the same kinds of powerful social influences as other people; they are also often aware of the radical discrepancies between what others tell them to do and what others actually do. Like the rest of us, they are likely to model their conduct on others' deeds and not on their words. These modeling influences can bring about changes in the moral reasoning of adolescents (Prentice, 1972) as well as in their self-regulation and actual moral conduct (Thoresen and Mahoney, 1974).

You will recall from Chapter 16 that an individual's moral development does not necessarily follow a consistent, age-graded pattern. Adolescents can range from the lowest to the highest levels of moral reasoning. Research suggests that only 10 percent of middle-class American adolescents and adults—and even fewer of lower socioeconomic status—are likely to develop the kind of moral autonomy that indicates a high level of moral reasoning.

Some evidence suggests that the failure to develop a high level of moral reasoning is in part the result of a failure to develop formal thought. Lawrence Kohlberg and Carol Gilligan (1971) found that a majority (60 percent) of the people above sixteen showed advanced formal thought but that only a small proportion (10 percent) of them also showed a principled level of moral reasoning. On the other hand, every individual who showed principled reasoning was also capable of formal thought. Such results suggest that the development of formal thought is a necessary condition for principled moral reasoning, but that formal thought does not ensure the development of such reasoning.

Among adolescents who do reach a principled level of moral reasoning, a major shift in thinking apparently takes place. The adolescent who appears to be preoccupied with exposing the clay feet of his former idols may also be using his capacity for reflective thought to reexamine his own internal values and codes of conduct. His attempt to establish moral autonomy in his conduct may be the natural accompaniment to his struggle for independence in other areas of his life.

In general, research indicates that adolescents who have developed both formal thought and a principled level of moral reasoning are most likely to show a high degree of both morality and consistency in what they think and do. For example, significantly fewer college students at a principled level of moral reasoning cheated in situations that required them to resist temptation than did those at a conventional or premoral level (Kohlberg, 1969). The adolescents at a principled level seemed

Political activism may express either a concern for basic liberties (principled reasoning) or an individual's personal conflict with power (premoral reasoning). (Charles Harbutt/Magnum Photos)

to define the tempting situations as ones that involved an implicit contract based on trust, whereas those at lower levels seemed to respond to the looseness and permissiveness of unsupervised situations.

College students at a principled level of moral reasoning also appear to have shown a higher, more consistent level of moral conduct than other students in an experiment conducted by Stanley Milgram (1963). In this study, undergraduates were ordered to administer what they thought were increasingly severe electric shocks to a "victim," who was supposed to be a subject in a learning experiment but who was actually a stooge. Only thinking characteristic of a principled level of reasoning clearly defines the situation as one in which the experimenter has no moral right to insist that pain be inflicted on another person. Accordingly, 75 percent of the students who had been judged to be at a principled level refused to shock the victim, but only 13 percent of those judged to be at lower levels refused to administer the shock (Kohlberg, 1965).

Finally, a study by Norma Haan, M. Brewster Smith, and Jeanne Block (1968) examined the possible relationship between moral reasoning and civil disobedience. They studied University of California students who did and did not participate in the original Free Speech Movement sit-in. Of the students studied, 80 percent of those who were at a principled level sat in as compared to only 10 percent of those who were at a conventional level. A clear majority of those students who were at a premoral level also sat in. However, the premoral students reported different reasons for their actions from those given by the principled students. Consistent with their level of moral reasoning, the principled students reported concern with the basic issues of civil liberties and rights and of the relationship of students as citizens within the university community, whereas the premoral students focused on the issue of their individual rights in a conflict with power. As the actions of both premoral and principled students show, similar conduct can result from widely varied moral reasoning.

SEXUALITY AND INTIMACY

The twentieth-century evolution of sexual beliefs and attitudes has included a new openness about sexual matters, a tendency to see sexual behavior

Few adolescents can talk freely with their parents about sex, and most such conversation is general and not directed toward the boy's or girl's own behavior or problems. (Thomas Hopker/Woodfin Camp & Assoc.)

as a matter of personal choice rather than of law or morality, and an emphasis on interpersonal norms and values. As noted in Chapter 17, the mass media reflect society's increasing openness about sexuality. For example, music and films directed at young people frequently center on frankly sexual themes:

> . . . lower-class youth assimilated by middle-class culture joined with middle-class rebels against middle-class culture to alter the tone of American popular music. To the lower class, sex was nothing to moan over or sing pretty little sad poems about. To the crusading middle-class student rebels it was something which must be handled robustly, erotically, honestly, rather than emphasized or sublimated out of all recognition as their parents had frequently done. Middle-class rebel and lower-class swinger, hippy and minority groups had a common distaste for pretty songs. (Mooney, 1972, page 183)

This new openness also shows in the proliferation of sex-education programs in the public schools. However, as was noted in Chapter 15, most such programs tend to concentrate on the physiology of sex. A survey of 1,500 girls, ages thirteen to twenty, showed that the programs they participated in provided instruction about the reproductive system, menstruation, and venereal disease but were less informative about the psychological and value aspects of sexuality (Hunt, 1970). Of the girls in this study, 98 percent believed the schools should provide sex education.

Personal Choice

At a more personal level, Robert Sorensen (1973) found that 72 percent of the boys and 70 percent of the girls between thirteen and nineteen reported that they and their parents still do not talk freely about sex. Many adolescents said that conversation about sex was general and not specifically directed toward the boy's or girl's own behavior or problems. Only 18 percent reported talking with parents about masturbation or birth control; 24 percent had talked about venereal disease. Many of the thirteen- to nineteen-year-olds suggested that parents delude themselves about their children's sexual behavior by refusing to acknowledge their adolescents' sexual nature or by simply ignoring blatant violations of their own sexual standards. Sorensen found that 51 percent of the boys and 44 percent of the girls agreed with the statement "I wish my parents could overcome their own early training so that they could realize that sex is natural and beautiful." Traditional parental evasiveness in the face of new public openness about sex no doubt contributes to adolescent charges of parental hypocrisy. Only 28 percent of the boys and 44 percent of the girls believed that their own sexual attitudes are the same as those of their parents.

Among adolescent girls, 60 percent claimed that they do not talk with parents about their sex lives because they consider sex to be a personal subject that is nobody's business but their own.

Sorensen found that 39 percent of all adolescents agreed that sexual intercourse is immoral unless it is between two people who like each other and who have something in common, and 69 percent agreed with the assertion that "Anything two people want to do sexually is moral, as long as they both want to do it and it doesn't hurt either one of them." There is no difference between younger and older adolescents on this point.

It appears that even young adolescents are aware of alternatives and value personal choice in sexual matters. For example, both high-school and college students see kissing, petting, and coitus as most acceptable when a couple is engaged and least acceptable outside an affectionate relationship (Reiss, 1967). Like most adults, most adolescents do not condone promiscuity. Unlike the average adult, however, the average adolescent evaluates a specific sexual behavior within the framework of the relationship of which it is a part. Whereas adolescents believe that premarital intercourse between loving partners is more acceptable than petting without affection, adults are more likely to condemn premarital intercourse and accept petting without affection.

In general, studies give evidence of an apparent difference between the generations concerning both premarital sexuality and the affectionate relationship in which behavior occurs. However, this apparent generational difference regarding sexual permissiveness is not as great as it may seem. Adults also are becoming more permissive, and single adults are likely to approve of premarital intercourse. Ira Reiss (1973) reports that, in 1963, 44 percent of single adults were highly permissive of premarital intercourse but that only 18 percent of married adults were permissive. By 1973 the figures had risen to 74 percent and 50 percent. Thus, differences in marital status are at least as important as generational differences in attitudes toward premarital sexuality.

It also appears that assuming the role of a parent affects a person's attitudes toward sexual behavior, generally leading to a decrease in permissiveness. For example, childless couples are more permissive than couples with adolescent children. Sexual stereotypes, or the fear of a daughter's pregnancy, also appear to affect a parent's attitudes. The more sons a parent has, the more likely he or she is to be permissive, but the more daughters a parent has, the more likely he or she is to condemn premarital intercourse (Reiss,

1970). It also appears that the number of adults who approve of premarital intercourse is considerably smaller than the number who themselves have engaged in premarital intercourse (Conger, 1973).

Promiscuity

It would be a mistake to interpret the data reported in Chapter 17 on sexual activity or the data reported in this chapter on changing sexual attitudes as evidence of widespread promiscuity. In one national survey of female sexual behavior among college students, 60 percent of the girls who reported premarital intercourse had had only one partner, and half indicated that they planned to marry him (Zelnik and Kantner, 1972). In the Sorensen (1973) study of thirteen- to nineteen-year-olds, 84 percent of the girls' first experiences with intercourse were with boys whom they knew well, liked a lot, went steady with, or were "engaged to be engaged to." Among boys, 56 percent of the first coital experiences were with partners whom they described in the same way. Among these adolescents, whereas 24 percent of those who had coital experience had had more than six partners before they were nineteen, 47 percent had had only one partner.

From the evidence gathered in the last decade, we can conclude that, particularly among females, there has been a change in the direction of earlier premarital sexuality but that the frequency has not increased much. It also appears that attitudes have changed so that more people judge sexual behavior as acceptable or unacceptable on the basis of the affection in the relationship. And, as we will see, this person-centered sexuality has traditionally been emphasized for females.

Gender and Equalitarianism

Traditional childhood and early adolescent socialization generally provides girls with a greater degree of competence than boys in interpersonal relationships. For most girls, sexual behavior involves incorporating sexuality into a social role and an identity that already included capacities for tenderness and sensitivity. For most boys, on the other hand, the pathway to mature heterosexual behavior involves sexuality first, and only secondarily does the capacity for concerned, tender, and loving sexual relationships develop. Thus, cultural stereotypes and parental and peer socialization emphasize, to use Reiss's (1973) terms, "body-cen-

Most adolescents do not condone promiscuity, but evaluate sexual behavior in terms of the relationship between two people, believing that loving intercourse is more acceptable than petting without affection. (*top:* © Joel Gordon; *bottom:* Leonard Freed/Magnum Photos)

tered" sexuality for the male and "person-centered" sexuality for the female.

The connection between this formulation and the pattern of sex differences cataloged in Chapter 17 should not go unnoticed. A girl's first intense sexual experience usually occurs in a heterosexual context; a boy's first experience is likely to occur when he is alone. Among their peers, groups of girls are likely to support and encourage one another for interpersonal competence and romantic interests, whereas groups of boys are likely to support and encourage one another for erotic interests, responsiveness to erotic stimuli, and proclaimed erotic activity. Adolescent peer groups also are likely to reward popularity with the opposite sex with status (G. Schwartz and Merten, 1967). Thus, during adolescence, both boys and girls learn to incorporate sexual behavior into their gender roles, but the experiences each brings to his or her relationships are likely to be quite different. Further, as William Simon and John Gagnon (1969) suggest, adolescent dating and courtship can be seen as a training process in which boys train girls and girls train boys in the meaning and context of each sex's commitment to the heterosexual relationship.

The evolutionary changes in American sexual behavior and attitudes can be seen as part of a more general movement toward equalitarianism and, therefore, may affect traditional gender roles. For example, after surveying these changes, Reiss (1973) concludes that the human sexual relationship is changing from an occasion for male satisfaction of body-centered sexuality to an equalitarian relationship that involves more than physical attraction. He notes that, although people will continue to pursue sexuality for pleasure, the pleasure is more likely to be mutual and equalitarian.

Much of the increase in premarital sexuality seems to have occurred among students (particularly females) from the most affluent, elite, and liberal schools (Conger, 1973). It is, of course, precisely the same kinds of schools that gave birth to the activist movements of the 1960s and that may have created the conditions that sparked the Women's Liberation Movement. In the liberal, questioning environment of these schools, young people apparently consolidated many of the attitudinal changes of the preceding fifty years, setting in motion this century's second major change in sexual behavior.

A similar equalitarian movement appears to be taking place in other aspects of behavior related to gender roles. For example, Sandra Bem (1974) has looked at sex roles in a different way and has discovered that adolescents and adults may see themselves as either masculine or feminine or as embracing both qualities. Bem calls the latter people **androgynous** in their sex-role self-concept because they are capable of being both masculine and feminine, both assertive and yielding, depending on the appropriateness of that behavior to the particular situation. Because healthy interpersonal relationships depend on both competent assertiveness and secure sensitivity to other people, it would seem that incorporating both traditionally masculine and feminine positive attributes might lead to fuller human functioning. Thus, the finding that highly creative males and females tend to incorporate attributes of the other sex as well as those of their own (Hammer, 1964; Helson, 1966) can be seen as support for both the possibility and value of androgynous sex-role development.

VOCATIONAL IDENTITY

During adolescence, gender-role concepts, self-concepts, and the concept of future occupational possibilities combine to narrow a person's vocational alternatives and orientations. For the male in our society, competence in a vocational role is as fundamental a dimension of his identity as is his masculinity in the sex role. For the majority of females, at least at present, it is marriage that continues to play a dominant role in identity formation and achievement, with career or other plans viewed as optional or secondary (Tavris and Offir, 1977).

Society holds the male to a sharply defined criterion. The position of the late-adolescent middle-class boy, in particular, is more complex and drastic than most people realize. Like most middle-class boys, Matt is in transition from the supporting influences of family, high school, and peer groups to the still distant adult world. He clings to an unrealistic, childhood-determined vocational goal, and the college curriculum is unlikely to tell him whether he will like his projected field of work or do well in it. Yet by the end of his sophomore year, the registrar will demand that Matt commit himself to a department and to an implied career, a commitment that he has neither the experience nor the facts to make. He can only guess.

Matt's ultimate vocational choice will be a compromise between his interests, aptitudes, and values and economic considerations. Theoretically and developmentally, such a choice involves the integration of internal and external factors. First, Matt will explore possible occupations through courses, summer work, and part-time jobs; next, he will crystallize his explorations into a tentative choice of vocations; and finally, he will specify his chosen career, overtly committing himself to an occupation (D. Super, 1976).

Cognition and Vocational Choice

Adolescents' capacity to generate possibilities and to reason from them means that their vocational thinking need not be restricted by their personal exposure to the world of work and the people in it and that they can do a good job of matching their personal attributes to future vocational possibili-

Although one's vocation is in good part determined by economic realities and personal opportunities, the interests developed in courses, part-time jobs, and hobbies can also play a major role. (Paul Fusco/Magnum Photos)

ties. One factor that affects adolescents' choice of an occupation is the prestige that they attribute to it.

Developmental studies of occupations and preferences provide an excellent example of the effects of cognitive organizational ability on career choice. Before children are eleven, their thinking about a vocation appears to be primarily subjective. Their preferences are based on occupational stereotypes and are unrelated to any assessment of aptitude or other personal characteristics. They also seem unaware of the opportunities they have or the barriers that may stand in the way of their goals (Jordaan and Heyde, 1978).

However, as adolescents confront vocational choices, their ability to use formal thought, com-

bined with their increased experiences, appears to enable them to assess various career possibilities more realistically. Thus, in a twelve-year longitudinal study of occupational preference, Leona Tyler (1964) reported that most adolescents begin to crystallize their occupational choices when they are about thirteen or fourteen. But even fourteen-year-olds know little about the choices that they soon must face, about the decision pathways any alternative might lead to, or about the irreversibility of some choices.

By the time they are sixteen, however, adolescents show a more realistic appraisal of the preparation required for their chosen occupations (Douvan and Adelson, 1966). The sixteen-year-old can offer more explanations for his or her choices than the fourteen-year-old, and the explanations are better organized. By sixteen, when adolescents are asked to specify an occupational choice, they are more precise. Matt will say that he wants to be an ornithologist instead of saying that he wants to be a scientist. An individual's appreciation of the role played by his or her personal opportunities and by harsh economic realities in vocational choice may continue to grow throughout adolescence. High-school seniors, for example, are more likely than younger adolescents to describe themselves as understanding the necessity for choosing an occupation, and they are also more able to consider relevant factors when making that choice (Jordaan and Heyde, 1978).

There is little doubt that increasing stability of occupational choice is also a characteristic of adolescence. Among adolescents in the ninth grade, the occupation named by a student one day or week or month is likely to change the next time he is asked about his chosen career. More stable career choices emerge later. In one study only 17 percent of the boys and 26 percent of the girls had the same vocational plans one year after graduation that they had had in the ninth grade (Project Talent, 1966). Among boys, science careers appear to be an exception; future scientists begin to crystallize their choices between the ages of ten and fourteen (Tyler, 1964). There is also little question that there are great individual differences in stability of occupational choice; as many as half of college students change their career choices (D. Super, 1976). However, many of these changes remain within the same general family of occupations, because the process of career choice soon becomes nearly irreversible. As adolescents make choices, they increasingly limit their range of remaining choices and absolutely preclude some careers.

Gender Differences

The developmental picture of occupational choice just presented is more characteristic of males and of middle- and upper-middle-class young people than of females and working-class youth. This reflects the ways in which gender identity tends to limit occupational choice and the fact that choice itself is granted more often to the advantaged than to members of the working class.

Careers are still presented to most girls as way stations on the road to marriage and motherhood.

This means that the continued development of interpersonal skills, of a capacity for intimacy, remains the major task of adolescence for many girls. Because the ultimate self-definition of a traditionally socialized girl like Susan depends on the marital role, her identity is likely to remain diffuse and misty. Her adolescent fantasies and prior gender-role learning usually have pointed her directly toward marriage. Her dependence on the marital role may also have taught Susan to derive her sense of esteem from her relationship to loved ones and from their achievements rather than from her own. It is this kind of socialization that has led Judith Bardwick (1971) to suggest that fear of the loss of love is a major motive for most women in our society and that such fear tends to result in emotional dependence among women who fail to develop any sense of vocational identity beyond that of wife and mother. Among males, on the other hand, identity is a far more active issue in adolescence and tends to center around the interrelated themes of autonomy, achievement, and vocational choice.

These kinds of gender differences appeared when Elizabeth Douvan and Joseph Adelson (1966) asked fourteen- to eighteen-year-olds a number of open-ended questions about their plans and daydreams for the future. The boys were oriented toward the future primarily in terms of an occupational identity. Their plans were concrete even if subject to change in detail. Boys were actively concerned with the future implications of their present strivings. Their aspirations for achievement were matched by their realistic assessment of the world of work and their own assets and limitations. The fantasy concerns of boys also focused on future occupational achievement and on preparation for it.

On the other hand, the future plans of most girls differed markedly. Although their direct plans also focused on work and schooling, few girls were committed to either. Their plans for implementing their avowed goals were often unrealistic. They stressed individual achievement and its rewards less than boys did. Of the girls' occupational choices, 95 percent fell into five categories, each representing an extension of traditional female roles. The girls tended to plan for jobs as nurses, social workers, teachers, secretaries, or stewardesses. When asked about their daydreams, girls shifted dramatically away from jobs and education, and the strong strivings for achievement that

Most girls are socialized to see careers as temporary stops on the way to marriage and motherhood, and fail to develop any other sense of vocational identity. (© Joel Gordon)

would support their vocational plans were entirely absent.

As yet, no data contradict the assertion that most girls continue to be socialized in the traditional feminine gender role and that many of them prefer it. However, some investigators (Bardwick, 1971) are beginning to see the emergence of a new feminine pattern in which the achievement ethic becomes as important as interpersonal success and traditional feminine behavior. At present, these girls come largely from upwardly mobile middle- and upper-middle-class families. Such a pattern supports the findings of Douvan and Adelson (1966), who discovered a small group of *personally mobile* girls. That is, their aspirations of social mo-

bility were directed toward their own achievements rather than dependent on the status of their future husbands. These personally mobile girls were more likely than traditional girls to be socially mature and active in leisure activities, in dating, and in seeking heterosexual friendships. They indicated a greater interest in assuming adult roles and responsibilities, and their time perspective extended further into the future. Girls in this group were also more self-confident and more self-accepting, and they appeared to think in a more organized fashion and to be more objective about themselves. They more often dreamed of individual achievement than traditional girls did, and they tended to judge prospective jobs by success criteria.

The number of girls who show this kind of feminine pattern will undoubtedly grow as society provides greater and more visible support for dual family and career roles and as girls who choose careers and reject motherhood less frequently become stigmatized. However, at present it appears that traditionally socialized girls are still in the majority.

SUMMARY

1. Although an individual's self-concept and self-esteem are important throughout life, a reexamination and reintegration of one's identity is often a major developmental task of adolescence. Given new physical and sexual status and redefined rights and responsibilities, the task is to formulate a satisfactory identity in which the adolescent experiences a sense of well-being and self-esteem.

2. Most often, adolescence is the first phase in which people begin to think carefully about themselves. Adolescents who develop formal thought are now able to imagine possibilities outside immediate reality, to plan, and to rehearse long-range purposes. As a result, and central to their self-concepts and identity, adolescents are also likely to reconsider, in less simplistic terms than before, their own impressions of themselves and others' impressions of them.

3. Adolescents are subject to the same kinds of powerful social influences that other people are.

Thus, there may or may not be much of a connection between their espoused moral values and attitudes and what they feel and do. Whereas higher levels of moral reasoning require formal thinking, such thinking does not always result in a higher level of moral reasoning.

4. In their sexuality and intimacy, adolescents reflect society's new openness about sexual matters. For example, adolescents are inclined to see sexual behavior as a matter of personal choice rather than of law or morality. Emphasis on interpersonal norms and values has resulted in a movement away from traditional sex-typed roles and toward more equalitarian and androgynous sex-role relationships.

5. During adolescence, concepts of self, gender role, and possible future occupations are likely to combine and to narrow an individual's vocational choices. In our society, vocational roles and sex roles interact, making different demands on males and females. For the adolescent male, competence in a vocational role is likely to be as fundamental a dimension of his identity as is his masculinity in the sex role. But for the majority of adolescent females, marriage is still likely to form a basic dimension of identity and achievement.

CHAPTER 19
Social Relations and Influence

SOCIAL-CLASS DIFFERENCES

FAMILY RELATIONS AND INFLUENCE
Jobs Versus Careers
Independence and Self-control
Adolescent Conformity

PEER RELATIONS AND INFLUENCE
Friendship
Cliques and Crowds
Gender and Achievement

THE GENERATION GAP

MOVING INTO ADULTHOOD
Commitment
Emergence of Youth

SUMMARY

Matt plays on the high-school football team. Given his choice, he would quit because he dislikes the violent body contact required in the sport. But athletic participation is valued among adolescents, and Matt lacks the self-confidence that would allow him to stop playing football. As a football player, Matt finds easy acceptance among his friends, whose dress, hair style, and speech patterns are nearly identical with his. To be popular in adolescence, one must conform to the codes of the informal peer group.

In the previous chapter we emphasized the wide variety of life styles in our society and the adolescent's effort to establish his or her identity. But most of us spend our social lives interacting with people who are like us in important ways. We grow up in neighborhoods, which are clusters of households headed by persons with jobs of roughly similar status, with similar educational histories, and, therefore, with similar ways of perceiving, thinking, and behaving. We usually go to neighborhood schools until we finish high school and so interact outside the family with people much like ourselves. And when the school is composed of several social classes, chances are that the informal peer groups that arise will also reflect social-class lines. Our parents and our friends' parents usually have about the same amount of money to spend on goods and services and often spend that money in the same way. Education, income, job prestige, social interaction, and patterns of consumption will correlate highly, and they constitute the criteria that psychologists, sociologists, and laymen use to define social status.

During our examination of social influences on the adolescent in this chapter, we will return to some of the topics discussed in Chapter 18, shifting our emphasis from identity to society. We will trace the social development of the adolescent and see how socioeconomic class affects attitudes toward life and work. We will examine the family's influences on the adolescent's choice of occupation and on the growth of autonomy. We will discuss the function of the peer group in adolescence and how the high-school social system affects social development. After a look at the generation gap, we will discuss the part that developmental commitments play in adolescence and early adulthood. Finally, we will turn to the concept of youth, testing it as a possible new phase of human development.

SOCIAL-CLASS DIFFERENCES

Patterns of values and beliefs stay alive as one generation transmits them to the next. Because patterns of values and beliefs and possessions constitute aspects of culture, we can say that each of us grows up in a particular subculture like those discussed in Chapters 13 and 15.

Social-class subcultures differ from one another in many ways (R. Coleman and Neugarten, 1971), and a major difference, as far as social development is concerned, is the subculture's attitude toward achievement. The values and beliefs that a subculture attaches to achievement can have an important influence on a person's future in our society. Bernard Rosen (1959) has identified three sets of beliefs that can affect motivation in achievement situations. One of them is locus of control, which Rosen calls *activism* (the belief that a person can manipulate the physical and social environment to his own advantage) versus *passivity;* the second is *individualism* (the belief that a person need not subordinate his own needs to the family group) versus *collectivism;* and the third is strongly related to self-regulation, called by Rosen *future orientation* (the belief that a person should forego short-term rewards in the interest of long-term gains) versus *present orientation.* Studies have repeatedly found a subcultural difference in these beliefs; activistic, individualistic, and future-oriented values are more likely to characterize higher socioeconomic groups in our society, whereas passivity, collectivism, and present orientation are more likely to be found in lower socioeconomic groups.

Adolescents from upper-middle-class families (professional and managerial occupations) and from lower-middle-class families (semiprofessional, semimanagerial, white-collar, and skilled-crafts occupations) are likely to have learned as children that their lives are under their own control and that they can achieve occupational status and other external symbols of success through

Middle-class adolescents generally learn as children that their own efforts can bring them status and success, hence many delay gratification in the interest of future rewards. (Charles Harbutt/Magnum Photos)

their personal efforts (Phares, 1976). Beginning in infancy and childhood, the experiences of upper-middle-class adolescents are likely to prepare them for careers, and they grow up believing in the importance of delaying gratification in the interest of future success (Mischel, 1976). By and large, upper-middle-class adolescents are likely to value their cognitive competencies, because the future roles they are being socialized for involve using the head more than the hands (R. Hess, 1970).

For the most part, lower-middle-class adolescents' experiences make them look forward to *jobs,* not careers (Kahl, 1961). They will value individualism and take an activistic stance toward the world and their future in it. However, lower-middle-class adolescents and their parents are likely to see that future in terms of the security, stability, and respectability that jobs bring rather than as opportunities for development, intrinsic satisfaction, or self-actualization. In addition, most middle-class young people, whether from professional or white-collar families, share attitudes and beliefs that correspond to those demanded by schools and colleges (Douvan, 1956). Thus, the idea of prolonged schooling also is more likely to make sense to upper- and lower-middle-class adolescents than it does to youths from other social strata.

If they do choose to go to college, they are likely to be wealthier and happier than their peers who do not. As part of the large-scale project TALENT, conducted by the American Institutes for Research, nearly 20,000 students were assessed on aptitude and personality during high school and then followed over the next fifteen years (Yen and McLaughlin, 1974). It is generally taken for granted that socioeconomic status and aptitude tests are good predictors of salaries and job satisfaction. However, when researchers controlled for the influence of both social class and test scores, they found that, eleven years after high school, college graduates were still happier in their jobs and earning more money than their high-school classmates who did not complete college. This pattern was particularly true among white students.

Students who began college and then dropped out earned no more money than students who never attended college. And among whites, those who dropped out were less satisfied than those who had never gone to college. A two-year community-college degree brought women but not men higher salaries than no college at all, and women who dropped out of college and then went back increased their incomes; men did not.

Asking a boy to go to college, thereby delaying immediate gratification in the interest of future success, is not likely to make much sense to the adolescent from a working-class family (semiskilled or unskilled blue-collar workers) or from a lower-class family that depends on irregular employment in marginal work roles or on welfare funds. Although fathers of working-class families take pride in their regular employment, they rarely move up; the tasks that they perform are simple, specialized, circumscribed, and repetitive. If they work in a factory, the pace and rhythm of work is imposed from above by supervisors and technicians. The worker on an assembly line is rewarded for following orders and coordinating his work with the rest of the line, not for showing self-direction, individuality, or innovative techniques (Blau, 1972). It is not difficult to see how conforming to authority becomes an important aspect of working-class life,

and this conformity is reflected in the socialization of working-class children and adolescents. Activism and a future orientation do not prevail in this kind of environment.

Among many working-class families, employment is valued primarily as a means of providing goods and services that lead to satisfaction in the extended family. A collectivistic orientation is likely to prevail, so that loyalty to the family may stand in the way of the decisions that would permit an adolescent to move out of the working class. Actions that are taken for granted by middle-class adolescents, such as moving away, going to school in another city or state, and taking advantage of opportunities that may weaken bonds with family members, are usually less possible for working-class youth.

The adolescent from a lower-class background is likely to have an external locus of control, characterized by a passive, even fatalistic attitude. "Luck" is a frequent explanation for accomplishments and setbacks. As Lee Rainwater (1966) put it:

> In the white and particularly in the Negro slum worlds little in the experience that individuals have as they grow up sustains a belief in a rewarding world. The strategies that seem appropriate are not those of a good, family-based life or of a career, but rather *strategies for survival*. (page 206)

In a survival-oriented economy, gratifications of the present are important. The child or adolescent has few opportunities to learn that active individual effort might pay off in the interest of some long-term goal, whether that effort means studying now for a good report card or earning money to save for a car.

FAMILY RELATIONS AND INFLUENCE

The chief interpersonal theme in early adolescence is the gradual move from childhood dependence toward ever greater involvement with the wider world. For some young people, this process is fraught with visible tension and conflict, but others move away from their families with only minor internal turmoil. In early adolescence most young people feel some ambivalence about their relative dependence or independence. The fact that Susan's parents increasingly permit her more freedom may bear little relation to her inner conflict between a desire for independence and her usually less conscious wishes to remain a child, to be cared

Conflict with parents can come both from the adolescent's ambivalence toward his independence and from his parents' tendency to project their own dreams and desires onto their child. (Jeffrey Foxx/Woodfin Camp & Assoc.)

for, and to avoid the potential problems and deprivations that she sees in adult life. The provocativeness of adolescents toward parents who may offer little occasion for rebellion can often be understood in the context of the adolescent's own profound ambivalence. Indeed, it is by alternating between provocative self-assertion and childlike requests for help that many adolescents gradually become able to emerge from their families.

But if the adolescent is capable of irrationality toward the adult world, adults often prove no less unreasonable. Parents may unwittingly project their unfulfilled dreams and suppressed desires onto their children, subtly encouraging them to live in a way that the parents cannot. Thus, in many cases, charges of youthful promiscuity, irresponsibility, drug abuse, violence, and hedonism may be as much the adults' expression of their own wishes as their ideas about the perversity of adolescents.

Jobs Versus Careers

Despite the ambivalent family relations that often characterize adolescence, parents and the home environment have lasting influences on such basic decisions as the adolescent's choice of occupation. For example, investigators have repeatedly discovered that adolescents from low-status families select high-status occupations less often than might be expected, whereas adolescents from high-status families select high-status occupations more often than chance would suggest (Elder, 1968). J. Ken-

neth Little (1967) found that the trend held good among all graduates of Wisconsin public and private high schools in the mid-1960s. Little examined both the aspirations of high-school students and their actual later attainments. Graduates from families in the upper third in socioeconomic status held 47 percent of the high-prestige occupations, whereas the lower third held only 20 percent of such positions. Some developmentalists have suggested that the difference comes about because higher- and lower-status families ascribe different levels of prestige to various occupations. However, other studies suggest that the difference more likely reflects the different perceptions of status groups as to the accessibility of occupations (Caro and Pihlblad, 1965).

When August Hollingshead (1949) earlier found social-class effects on young people's vocational choices, he suggested that lower-class adolescents tend to adjust their job desires to what they think they may hope to achieve. Lower-class black youths who look around them are unlikely to expect much from life. The unemployment rate among black youths runs about 40 percent, and some inner-city blacks may live their entire lives without ever securing a regular job. The only choices they may believe are open to them are welfare, odd jobs, or hustling.

A number of factors may influence their expectations—and those of other adolescents—most having to do with the way that parents in different social classes tend to influence their children's vocational development. Parents and other neighborhood and community adults model characteristics relevant to various vocations, and they also reinforce them when the characteristics show up in adolescents. As shown in Chapter 18, gender identity serves as a kind of filter for occupational choice, leading many adolescents to eliminate certain possible vocations. John Crites (1962) examined vocational interests among male college students in relation to how they perceived their similarity to their parents. He reported that males who identified strongly with their fathers had masculine interests, males who identified strongly with both parents showed a combination of masculine and feminine interests, and males who identified strongly with their mothers showed feminine interests, as did those who identified weakly with both parents. The common finding that working- and lower-class boys generally make higher masculinity scores than middle-class boys suggests an even finer gender-identity filtering of occupations at lower status levels.

Parents and neighborhood adults also influence the development of vocationally relevant attributes that bear no relation to gender role. Insofar as middle-class parents influence the development of fear of failure and hope of success, they have an impact not only on their children's success or failure in achievement situations but on their occupational choices as well. Young people with high hopes of success more often choose high-status occupations than their peers who have a high fear of failure (Elder, 1968).

Adolescents whose parents have fostered a high level of self-esteem look foward to the world of work with high aspirations and confidence; adolescents with low self-esteem place the same importance on occupational success but believe that they are unlikely to attain it (Rosenberg and Simmons, 1972). And, of course, parents model and reinforce attitudes and values about work in general and about particular kinds of jobs. They also may provide support when their children show high levels of educational and occupational aspiration.

Adolescents' vocational choices vary from class to class in part because parental resources also vary. A high income means more out-of-school lessons, more books at home, more travel, and residence in a neighborhood with an excellent school. Lower-class youngsters have seen, heard, read about, and experienced less, and so they have less

information about occupational alternatives. Should they discover some of the possibilities that exist, their parents can provide less money and other assistance to help them attain new goals.

Independence and Self-control

As earlier chapters on personality and moral development have shown, the typical middle-class parent uses love, approval, attention, and praise, and their withdrawal, to encourage independent action and personal responsibility in a growing child (Douvan and Adelson, 1966). When David misbehaves, he is likely to be asked why he did so and what consequences happen to other people who behave similarly; if he is to be punished, his parents are likely to explain why. By reasoning, David's parents teach him that he can and should control his own behavior on the basis of an internalized set of standards. The parents' object, often conscious, is the development of self-control.

Because job opportunities are few and the adults around them generally unsuccessful, many lower-class black youths believe they have no chance at high-status occupations. (Bob Adelman/Magnum Photos)

As the middle-class child grows into adolescence, he increasingly participates in decisions that affect him. By late adolescence, he will make decisions about peers, jobs, and money, either by himself or in consultation with his parents. Most of the time, when David indicates that he is learning to cope with his day-to-day problems, his parents will reward him, as they have always done. Middle-class parents train children for the sort of autonomy that most can later exercise in a job or career. If David's parents fail to train him for autonomy, they are likely to regret it. As Edward Devereux (1970) has shown, when parents are totally permissive or when they control all decisions and give their child no opportunity to make decisions, adolescence is likely to be a time of stormy parent-child relations and excessive peer conformity.

Working-class parents seem to begin later than middle-class parents to train their children for independence, and they are less likely to permit their offspring to help establish the rules for appropriate behavior (Douvan and Adelson, 1966). They are likely to value obedience instead of self-control and may often teach their children conformity to authority. On the other hand, working-class parents are less likely than middle-class parents to monitor an adolescent's activities outside the family circle (Blau, 1972). Although working-class adolescents are, therefore, freer than middle-class adolescents from parental supervision, when questions of obedience do arise, the working-class parent-child conflict is likely to be greater.

Adolescent Conformity

Two words often mentioned in discussions of adolescence are rebelliousness and conformity. Some accounts of adolescent development assume that, as a child reaches adolescence, conformity to parents' wishes decreases and conformity to peer wishes increases. Other discussions assume that conflict between peer and parental standards inevitably accompanies adolescence. However, no available evidence demonstrates that the onset of adolescence necessarily means any decrease in conformity to parental demands. Studies reviewed by Willard Hartup (1970) suggest only that conforming to peer wishes increases in childhood, reaches its maximum around puberty, and then decreases in later adolescence.

Studies of adolescent drug use illustrate this point. In most states, drinking is illegal for adolescents of high-school age. According to Margaret

Teen-age drinking is not a sign of drunken and uncontrolled behavior, but a reflection of community and parental patterns of alcohol use. (Jim Anderson/Woodfin Camp & Assoc.)

Bacon and Mary Brush Jones (1968), the number of adolescents who drink on at least some occasions varies from 86 percent in Nassau County, New York, to 44 percent in rural Kansas. However, in most communities widespread illegal drinking remains underground until an automobile accident or some other incident associated with drinking makes newspaper headlines. In the public rumblings that follow, worried parents often act on the implicit assumption that all teenage drinking involves drunkenness and uncontrolled behavior. They cite psychological disorder, rebelliousness, and the lack of "wholesome things to do" as possible causes of adolescent use of alcohol.

Actually, every study of alcohol use has found that the drinking patterns of teen-agers directly reflect those of their parents and the community in which they live. About two-thirds of all adults in the United States drink on occasion, and drinking is more prevalent among persons of higher social status than among those of lower status. Bacon and Jones found that most adolescents who drink tend to drink moderately, to begin drinking at home with their parents, and to follow the rules of alcohol consumption that their parents set. Other studies show that teen-age drinking patterns imitate adult drinking patterns: boys drink more than girls; city adolescents drink more than country adolescents; middle- and upper-middle-class adolescents drink more than working- or lower-class adolescents.

Because adolescents have learned from their parents and other adults to perceive drinking as an explicitly social affair, peer-group norms for acceptable drinking behavior tend to keep such behavior in line. Thus, when adolescents drink in the secrecy of the peer group, social control remains present. The use of alcohol has become common among adolescents. One recent study has shown that drinking of all kinds increases with age but that, except for beer drinking among boys, the number of adolescents who drink more than once a week remains low (Keller et al., 1974). Although boys tend to drink more than girls, alcohol use among girls is increasing.

Conformity also appears to affect the rate of smoking among adolescent boys. According to the U.S. Department of Health, Education, and Welfare (1976), 5 percent of the nation's children have smoked by the time they are eleven, and 20 percent have smoked by the time they are twelve. When they enter high school, 20 percent of the girls and 21 percent of the boys have established regular smoking patterns.

Adolescents know about the risks connected with cigarettes, but since the effects do not appear for decades, they are not gravely concerned about the personal consequences (Evans, 1976). Most psychologists believe that peer pressure is a primary cause of adolescent smoking. If such pressure is indeed an important factor, then self-confident individuals should be the most resistant and, therefore, the least likely to smoke. A study sponsored by the American Cancer Society showed that this was true among boys but not among girls. Boys who smoked were less self-confident than boys who did not smoke, but girls who smoked were more self-confident than girls who did not. The girl smokers were also heavier smokers and more socially outgoing than the boys, but the girls did not regard smoking as a social asset. Many girls and women, however, believe that, by keeping them from eating, smoking will help them control their weight.

Recently the press has reported that alcohol consumption by young people is increasing rapidly while marijuana usage has fallen off. A national study of high-school seniors fails to show any such trend within a two-year period (Johnston, Bachman, and O'Malley, 1977). High-school seniors were polled in 1975 and again in 1977, and daily use of alcohol remained constant (6 percent) while daily use of marijuana increased (from 6 percent in 1975 to 9 percent in 1977). When asked whether they had taken either drug within the past thirty days, 68 percent of the 1975 high-school seniors had drunk alcohol and 27 percent had used marijuana; in 1977, 71 percent of the seniors had drunk alcohol within the last thirty days and 35 percent of them had used marijuana. The study notes that heavy drug users tend to be male: 12 percent of male high-school seniors use marijuana daily as compared with 6 percent of the females; and 9 percent of males use alcohol daily as compared with 4 percent of the females.

Although marijuana is considered by some as "the first step" on the path to illicit drug usage, two longitudinal surveys by Denise Kandel (1975) among New York State high-school students indicate that it is better considered as a second or third step along the path. Legal drugs, such as beer, wine, distilled beverages, and cigarettes, nearly always precede use of marijuana. For example, 27 percent of high-school students who both smoke and drink hard liquor progress to marijuana, but only 2 percent of those who neither smoke nor drink do so. Among high-school marijuana users, 26 percent go on to LSD, amphetamines, or heroin; only 1 percent of students who use no drugs at all make the progression to hard drugs, and only 4 percent of those who use tobacco or alcohol make the jump. Using a particular drug does not mean that a student will invariably move on to the next drug in the path.

Adolescent drug use shows how behavior that poses problems for adults often is tied to the values and customs of the larger society. The adolescent has had more than a decade of exposure to adults

Despite press reports that marijuana use has dropped among adolescents, studies show that it remains a popular drug and that girls are unlikely to be heavy users. (A. De Andrade/ Magnum Photos)

whose behavior, legal and illegal, has been a model for his own experimentation and for the control of group behavior. But adults who smoke, drink alcohol, or take tranquilizers or barbiturates tend to ignore these connections; they generally consider any problem behavior as a purely adolescent problem and label the adolescents involved as problems.

PEER RELATIONS AND INFLUENCE

The peer group can be a major influence in resolving the identity crisis (Erikson, 1968). For instance, in assuming the badges of clique membership, the fads of dress and appearance, Matt is borrowing a stereotypic identity as a temporary defense against the loss of his own identity. This sort of behavior is an example of the adolescent uniformism discussed in Chapter 18. By his clannishness, intolerance, and cruelty toward outsiders or those who are different, the adolescent can temporarily clar-

ify who he is by affirming who he is not. But the peer group also offers positive opportunities and rewards that are crucial to identity formation. With his peers, Matt can try on new roles and use the reactions of others to judge how well the roles fit his self-concept. Identification with the heroes of the crowd may also give the adolescent a temporary sense of coherence. Even early instances of falling in love may have far less to do with sexuality than with a mutual opportunity to clarify one's self-concept through a close relationship with another person. As peer relationships are transformed during adolescence, friendship also changes, moving from the congenial sharing of activities to psychological sharing and intimacy.

Friendship

Assume that you are asked to list twelve persons who fit certain role descriptions (for example, mother, father, lover, best friend, favorite teacher, disliked male, self) and then to list for each possible combination of three people a characteristic that two of them share and that the third does not (G. Kelly, 1955). This method of eliciting the categories that individuals use to classify others can distinguish pairs of friends from random pairs of strangers. And, as Stephen Duck's (1973; 1977) studies of college students have shown, the nature of the similarity changes during the course of the friendship. In the beginning of the relationship, friends tend to apply such categories as physical characteristics or people's roles or activities to assess others. If the friendship lasts, they tend to use psychological categories such as "sly" or "tries hard"; that is, they share a way of perceiving and thinking about the unobvious attributes of self and others.

Investigators have found that similar personal characteristics are a major determinant of whether two people form a friendship (Byrne, 1971). These studies suggest that obvious similarities are more important in the early stages of friendship but that a friendship is not likely to last unless the persons involved go on to discover that they see the world of psychological intentions, motives, causes, and characteristics in the same way.

Intimate friendships are not likely to develop in the relative absence of compatible psychological constructs. For example, Duck (1973) found that only 5 percent of the twelve-year-olds he studied used psychological constructs to describe others and that the number rose to 25 percent among fourteen- and fifteen-year-olds. Among college students, 63 percent described others in terms of psychological characteristics.

The developmental course of friendship does not contradict such a view. Friendships among girls appear to progress from the activity-centered pairs of late childhood and preadolescence to the interdependent, emotional, and conflict-resolving relationships of middle adolescence, finally becoming relationships that are less emotional, less an instrument for reducing conflict, and more a sharing of personalities, talents, and interests (Douvan and Adelson, 1966). It is the emotional friendships that Harry Stack Sullivan (1953) had in mind when he described *chumship* and indicated that such a same-sex relationship was necessary to the later development of heterosexual intimacy and mature sexuality.

Although male friends in college use similar psychological constructs, junior-high and high-school boys appear to be less concerned with the personal relationship involved in friendship. Their friendships are more like those found among preadolescent girls and involve a congenial companion with whom one shares the same reality-oriented activities (Douvan and Adelson, 1966). As was shown in Chapter 18, this gender difference is part of a larger pattern of gender-role differences that make interpersonal relationships in this society a major factor in the formation of female identity. Males are also more likely than females to spend their adolescent social lives in cliques and gangs instead of in pairs.

Cliques and Crowds

Children who are popular with their peers are likely to be popular adolescents as well; indeed, popularity rankings from year to year throughout childhood and adolescence generally remain stable (Roff, Sells, and Golden, 1972). One factor that is likely to have an important impact upon popularity is physical attractiveness. Adolescents and

Friendships among adolescent girls tend to be intense, emotional, and reciprocal, with each friend meeting the other's needs. (© Joel Gordon)

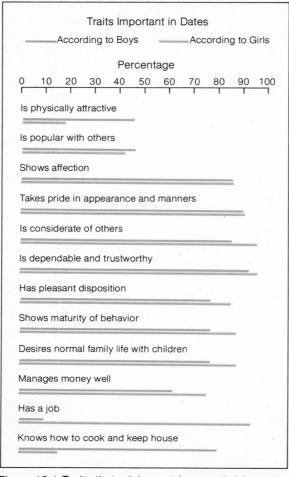

Traits Important in Dates

— According to Boys   — According to Girls

Percentage

0 10 20 30 40 50 60 70 80 90 100

Is physically attractive

Is popular with others

Shows affection

Takes pride in appearance and manners

Is considerate of others

Is dependable and trustworthy

Has pleasant disposition

Shows maturity of behavior

Desires normal family life with children

Manages money well

Has a job

Knows how to cook and keep house

Figure 19.1 Traits that adolescent boys and girls consider important in "dates" they might later marry. Sex-typing in behavior is reflected in the importance assigned to certain behavior for one sex or another by both boys and girls. (Adapted from Purdue Opinion Poll, 1961)

young adults often say that they are looking for honesty and sincerity in the opposite sex. However, when it comes to dating, they forget that they have said about personal characteristics and pursue the most attractive members of the opposite sex.

A different pattern may hold for peer relations within each gender, as Dennis Krebs and Allen Adinolfi (1975) discovered when they investigated friendship and dating choices of 60 male and 60 female residents of a student dormitory. Each resident chose the persons they liked and disliked most. The most liked persons were students who were attractive but not stunning. The most attrac-

tive students were rejected most frequently by members of their own sex, and the least attractive students were neither chosen as most or least liked—they were simply ignored.

Popularity is also highly related to conformity to peer-group norms, customs, and fads. During adolescence, as in childhood, the characteristics having most to do with peer acceptance are those that define appropriate sex-typed behavior in our society (Hartup, 1970). Athletic participation and skill, standing up for one's rights, sexual prowess, and sometimes drinking prowess are valued in the adolescent boy. The popular girl is one who is fun to be with and who has interpersonal skills. Because these characteristics bring with them the positive consequences of peer acceptance, they are in turn strengthened. Thus, participation in peer activities reinforces the childhood sex-role learning discussed in Chapters 13 and 15 This continuity in socialization may be largely responsible for the general stability of popularity rankings.

Special Dialects   Many individuals have observed that people who are close and who share a common history don't need a lot of words to get their meaning across. Similarly, adolescents often develop and use their own dialect to emphasize their group cohesiveness and sense of separateness from adult society. The exact forms of these adolescent dialects change from generation to generation (as they must if they are to fulfill their function). A striking feature of such dialects is the failure to make certain distinctions. For example, a generation ago, if a teen-ager wanted to say he understood, or liked, or was thrilled by something, he said, "I dig it." The exact meaning of the phrase depended on its context.

Two features that are likely to be part of the current adolescent dialect in some regions are the phrase "and stuff" after every sentence (it can mean absolutely anything) and the term "goes" instead of "says," "exclaims," "answers," "responds," "requests," "wonders," and so forth. Consider the following account by an adolescent of a conversation that took place between two others: "I saw them talking by her locker. He goes [whatever it was that "he" said] and then she goes [whatever it was that "she" said], then he goes . . . and then she goes . . . and then he goes. Then the teacher comes along and goes . . ." Notice also that the adolescent usually doesn't distinguish between tenses—present tense is used for all situations.

This usage is obviously not a matter of incompetence in Standard English. The adolescent recounting this conversation has a college-level vocabulary and scores high on all achievement tests of language skills, yet when she talks with her friends, her language loses its precision and takes on the characteristics of a dialogue that relies on imprecise references to shared feelings and experiences.

Structure Changes in Peer Groups As we saw in Chapter 15, social acceptance and its consequences generally occur in structured, role-related interactions among age-mates. However, adolescents bring a new element to peer relations: sexual maturation and heterosexual behavior. The structure of peer groups changes to accommodate these developments. At first the peer group is similar to the preadolescent gang; it is a clique of adolescents of the same sex. As Dexter Dunphy suggests (1963):

> In order to achieve and maintain membership in this group, the individual must show his readiness to conform to the group's authority. This is made easier through his identification with the clique leader who embodies many of the social skills and personality traits admired in the group. The clique establishes and reinforces the individual's drive to achieve heterosexuality, since it is, or becomes, a subsystem of the crowd; the crowd in its turn is only a subsystem of a hierarchy of crowds. . . .

About middle adolescence there is a major transformation of the clique system which has persisted in a relatively stable form. A new clique system evolves. . . . Groups become heterosexual, members having established a significant relationship with a member of the opposite sex. The crowd persists long enough to ensure that the basic role characteristics underlying this relationship are thoroughly acquired. It then breaks up into cliques of loosely associated couples as members move toward marriage. (pages 245–246)

Dunphy and other observers have also found that group members generally deny the existence of a hierarchy within the group. Nevertheless, status hierarchies do exist, and the formation of such hierarchies has been studied in detail, as the discussion of preadolescent groups in Chapter 15 indicated. The adolescent group leader gains high status through some combination of personal attributes and material resources that the group finds useful. In male cliques, high status generally goes to the assertive, actively sociable, and intellectually able boy (Hartup, 1970). In some groups, however, an adolescent may win status by virtue of his unique social or athletic skills or by the possession of a car or money or access to a suitable place for the group's activities. Changes in group goals are likely to lead to fluctuations in the hierarchy; as activities change, the resources of different members may become important (Sherif and

Adolescent boys generally have relatively impersonal, group-oriented friendships, regarding their clique or gang members as companions in social activities.

Sherif, 1964). Thus, status rankings over the months and years are less stable than popularity ratings.

The High-School Social System During high school, cliques become subsystems of crowds, and the crowds themselves may be ranked according to status. Members of the leading crowd generally embody the characteristics that bring young people to the forefront of their cliques or that made them popular with childhood classmates. The number of middle-class students in the leading crowds is likely to be out of proportion to their numbers in the student body as a whole. Because crowds are composed of cliques and because cliques are largely neighborhood affairs, crowd members tend to have the same social-class backgrounds (J. Coleman et al., 1966; Hartup, 1970).

Racial and ethnic backgrounds can also act as barriers to an individual's attempts to move up in the hierarchy of crowds. Social systems in large high schools, in which there is a mixture of racial or ethnic groups, are often almost totally segregated. Gifted athletes from minority groups frequently cross the line and are accepted into crowds composed of students in the majority, but few, if any, other accomplishments permit such changes (J. Coleman, 1961).

In addition to influencing the prestige of crowds, socioeconomic status affects aspirations. The average socioeconomic status of the student body tends to affect the social and vocational aspirations of individual students (Boyle, 1966). Thus, when students of lower social status attend high schools composed primarily of middle-class students, they tend to have higher aspirations than they do when they attend predominantly working-class schools. Similarly, when middle-class students are a minority, they have lower aspirations than when they are a majority. The greater aspirations of working-class boys who associate with middle-class boys showed clearly in a study by Richard Simpson (1962), who found that their patterns of participation in extracurricular activities resembled those of ambitious middle-class boys.

Gender and Achievement

Peers also affect the ways that adolescent girls like Lauren and boys like David approach situations involving achievement. In addition, factors that are unrelated to the task itself are more likely to af-

fect Lauren's motivations than David's. For example, James Coleman (1961) asked high-school students how they would prefer to be remembered when they left high school. Fewer girls than boys wanted to be remembered as brilliant students. Adolescents who were identified by their peers as "best scholars" were no more likely than average students to want to be remembered as brilliant. The differences that Coleman found between boys and girls appeared to develop during the high-school years. Roughly the same percentages of freshman boys and girls wanted to be remembered as brilliant scholars; then the sexes diverged dramatically, with fewer and fewer girls and more and more boys wanting to be remembered in this way.

This study tells us something about the images of self and others that adolescents find acceptable, and it also tells us about actual achievement. In every high school studied, the average achievement of the girls was greater than that of the boys. However, a girl's grades showed less variation than a typical boy's grades did, and, through the high-school years, such variations increased more among boys than among girls. The girls named as best scholars were not the brightest girls, whereas the boys named as best scholars were likely to be the brightest boys. Finally, in those schools where academic achievement brought social rewards, the brightest students were more likely to be the actual high achievers.

These findings illustrate the potentially powerful influence that the peer culture can have on adolescent achievement. Girls apparently become increasingly subject to the norm "Good girls get good grades—but not too good." Such a norm can account for the lower amount of variation in a girl's grades, the lower amount of increase in such variation through the high-school years, and the lower relationship between intellectual ability and achievement among girls. In relation to socioeconomic factors, these kinds of findings are strongest in predominantly middle-class high schools. Girls in working-class schools are more likely than those in middle-class schools to feel that grades are important in their popularity with boys. And boys in middle-class schools appear to prefer girls who are leaders in activities to girls who are academic achievers.

This class difference led Coleman (1961) to suggest that, as society becomes more predominantly white collar and as the working class shrinks, high-school girls will strive less for aca-

Although academic achievement has not been prized among middle-class girls, recent changes in feminine roles indicate that it may become increasingly desirable. (© Joel Gordon)

demic achievement than to succeed as an activities girl, the teen-age replica of the adult clubwoman. However, since Coleman examined adolescent society, the personally mobile girl discussed in Chapter 18 has begun to emerge. Should her numbers increase, academic achievement is likely to become more desirable for many girls.

Some of the ambivalence that girls may feel toward achievement has been captured by Matina Horner (1969) in her notion of "fear of success." She theorizes that, if we are to understand achievement in most women, we must understand the role played by a learned motive to fear success. When women discover that aversive social consequences follow when they expend effort, persist in the face of obstacles, or compete and actually succeed, they may learn to avoid and withdraw from achievement situations—or at least learn to play down their accomplishments. They withdraw, then, not because they are afraid of failing but because they are afraid of succeeding.

Because of the way that most adolescent girls are still socialized, adolescence can be a critical period in the development of a female fear of success. As Judith Bardwick and Elizabeth Douvan (1971) have suggested:

> Marriage and maternity are held out as wonderful goals, not necessarily as inhibiting dead ends. Although girls are rewarded for conformity, dependence, passivity, and competence, they are not clearly punished for the reverse. Until adolescence the idea of equal capacity, opportunity, and life style is held out to them. But sometime in adolescence the message becomes clear that one had better not do too well, that competition is aggressive and unfeminine, that deviating threatens the heterosexual relationship. (page 152)

THE GENERATION GAP

Stereotypes that ignore the pluralism of American society have been created about both adults ("the silent majority") and adolescents ("hippies"). The activism of a few students (who generally acted in accord with their parents' values) and of the sensationalized counterculture that developed in the country's elite colleges and universities have often been taken to represent the views and actions of all young people. Adult opposition to the counterculture is also taken for granted. As these chapters on adolescence have indicated, the generation gap has been both overstated and oversold by the mass media, by bewildered parents, and by the community.

Manifestations of rebelliousness are by no means universal among the young, and adolescence is frequently a more peaceful and less conflict-filled period than it is generally held to be. Most exaggerations of the generation gap go back to earlier studies, such as those that produced the findings discussed in the last section. After demonstrating that peer standards tended to have negative impacts on school achievement and on the self-esteem of high achievers, some of these studies concluded not only that an adolescent society existed, one that increasingly affected the aspirations and behavior of young people, but also that adolescents' families progressively lost any ability to influence them.

Since that time, many studies of adolescents have documented the existence of an adolescent society, yet they have always found its connections to adult society to be far more robust than earlier conclusions would lead one to believe. For example, Clay Brittain's (1963) results suggest that adolescents conform to peers in matters pertaining to choice of friends, language fads, and clothes but conform to parental values in matters pertaining to achievement, such as academic performance and job or career aspirations.

Studies by Denise Kandel and Gerald Lesser (1972) compared adolescents and their parents in the United States and in Denmark. They found that in both countries parental influence is much stronger than peer influence on an adolescent's life goals. Although they confirmed earlier findings that adolescents rarely reward intellectual achievement in their peers, they also found that peers have less influence than parents on adolescents' future educational goals. As Douvan and Adelson (1966) have reported, close and harmonious relationships with parents are the rule, even among young people who are full participants in the adolescent society. In neither society is there evidence for a generation gap.

Kandel and Lesser concluded that interactions with peers often support parental values and that the adolescent subculture is coordinated with the culture of the larger society. They suggest, as does the research on drinking patterns discussed earlier, that the specter of the generation gap may arise because the young openly express the divisions that exist within society. When they can attribute social problems to a generation gap, adults may find differences that come from race, class, or conflict of interest less threatening.

Of course, adolescent social behavior varies widely from situation to situation. As Chapters 13 and 15 indicated, children learn very early, from parental reinforcement of their behavior, how to behave at different times and places. By adolescence they have become expert discrimination learners and respond on the basis of the cues built into each situation. Thus, differences in the adolescent's behavior within the family and in the peer group should be expected.

As long as the adolescent lives at home, his

An adolescent's parents exert a major influence on his behavior; by giving or withdrawing attention, approval, affection, and money, they maintain both behavior they prize and that they detest. (© Joel Gordon)

parents continue to exert a major influence on his behavior. As they have done for years, parents grant, withdraw, and reinstate privileges; provide and withdraw attention, approval, affection, and money; and even use coercive techniques. Thus, much adolescent behavior that is either prized or detested by parents is maintained by the consequences that the parents themselves provide.

The primary changes of adolescence do, however, result in a radically changed organism, and parents who do not realize this may fail to appreciate greater autonomy in their son or daughter. It is tempting to speculate that what is so commonly reported as adolescent negativism may be the son's or daughter's reaction to the parents' failure to modify their expectations in relation to the adolescent's new capabilities and sexual maturity.

It is true, on the other hand, that parents and their adolescent children frequently disagree and that each often feels that the other simply doesn't understand. Friction over choices of friends, clothes, hair styles, use of the family car or telephone, family responsibilities, attitudes toward parents, grades, study habits, drugs, drinking, smoking, sex, and staying out of trouble may arise. Parents may try to give an adolescent the benefit of experience only to have the adolescent angrily reject it with a plea to "let me live my own life." In most cases, however, the problems are momentary and minor; the gap between generations appears to be, in most cases, a crack rather than a chasm.

MOVING INTO ADULTHOOD

Adolescence is a phase of life that encompasses profound transformations. A challenging, responsive, and confirming environment can enable Matt to move into a reasonable and satisfying maturity. He has the opportunity to become many things and, if he is properly encouraged, can emerge as an independent, self-directing, tolerant, humane, and ethical adult.

Commitment

From a developmental point of view, adolescence is a formative time of life. Adolescents who use these years to examine and test their values have a better chance to develop their possibilities in satisfying ways. One of the possibilities that develops during adolescence is the capacity for commitment—the capacity for loyalty to a set of imagined possibilities, to values and ideals, and to enduring relationships. The ability and willingness to make commitments is a characteristic of the psychological adult.

Underlying all other commitments is a *commitment to one's self,* not to the selfish pursuit of personal pleasure but to one's values, founded on a realistic understanding of one's capacities, potential usefulness, and real and possible achievements. Such commitment to one's self is made possible by the kinds of family and social experiences we have discussed and by opportunities that enable adolescents to test and define their strengths and weaknesses. Forces that convince individuals of their inadequacy or that deprive them of avenues for accomplishment and respect can undermine this commitment to self.

As adolescence ends, the discrepancy in many adolescents' thinking between grandiose fantasy and slight accomplishment narrows, and the young adult turns to the accomplishment of specific tasks. In an achievement-oriented society like modern America, a central aspect of commitment is *commitment to a task.* The meaning of the task will vary from man to man and from woman to woman—the maintenance of a home and the rearing of healthy children, the reform of society, competent performance of a job, the achievement of a life's work, the writing of a poem, or the manufacture of goods. Making this commitment requires adolescents to establish their vocational identity, a process discussed in Chapter 18. However the task is defined, young adults ideally will turn from wondering what to do with their lives to actually doing it. In this work they will strive for competence, whether they define competence in personal terms or in terms of the traditional roles and rewards of society.

Interpersonal commitment requires that the individual have a capacity for mutuality; that is, for an intimate reciprocal relationship in which the needs and characteristics of each person are important to the other. Because such relationships usually develop in a sexual context, most young people will realize this capacity in marriage, where each partner identifies with the other and with the creation of a new family. Others will realize this same capacity for mutuality in friendship, in work, or in shared play.

This concept of interpersonal commitment entails in addition a concern for the welfare of the community and for the care of the next generation. Young people first feel themselves part of the community in adolescence; in adulthood, they translate this feeling into activities that facilitate the development of others. Most will express commitment to the community and to those who embody its future through their willingness to bear and rear children.

Finally, in a striving society that rewards and praises work, it is important to stress that one of the attainments of adolescence should be the *capacity for invigorating play*. The American legacy of puritanism makes us tend to forget that one of the tasks of adolescence is the development of the capacity to live zestfully as well as purposefully, to be capable of free and spontaneous pleasure. Adults who fail to develop a commitment to play might be moral, virtuous, and responsible, but they are also likely to be driven, compulsive, and grim.

Emergence of Youth

In the past decade, a constellation of factors has created a concept of "youth" as a possible phase of life and has created a consciousness of it similar to that associated with the concept of adolescence more than a century ago (J. Coleman et al., 1974). The consciousness of youth has grown since it came to pass that at least two-thirds of all young people in this country finish high school and that over one-fourth of those between twenty-one and twenty-five are still in school. This means that substantial portions of young people are segregated into concentrated settlements with their peers, mostly in universities and colleges but also, as Richard Flacks (1971) has pointed out, in urban, often black, ghettos inhabited by those whom the educational system has not prepared for jobs. Such segregation no longer is restricted to members of the male upper-middle-class who are being educated for elite roles; today most young people live separately from their families. This means that conditions exist that encourage the transformation of an *age grade* into an *age group,* and the mass media and business have encouraged this growth of self-consciousness of youth.

Defining Characteristics Most commonly, youth is seen as beginning with the end of secondary education. There is general agreement that youth ends when the individual assumes an adult occupational role. Those who leave school at sixteen or when they finish high school are far more likely to work and to marry sooner than those who stay in

Adolescents who fail to develop the capacity for zestful and spontaneous pleasure are likely to become driven, compulsive, and grim adults. (Elihu Blotnick/BBM/Woodfin Camp & Assoc.)

school. Youth, then, appears to be primarily a creature of social definition.

Kenneth Keniston (1968), who has popularized the notion of a period of youth, defines the concept in restrictive social-psychological terms. He sees the defining characteristics of youth as the testing of the connection between self and society, a relative disengagement from that society, and the adoption of youth-specific identities that are not expected to outlast this period of life. The involvements of youth differ from the shallower, more fluctuating enthusiasms of adolescence in that they often last many years, inspire deep loyalty, and generally provide a vantage point outside the system. As soon as a young person makes a definitive engagement with society, youth is over, whether this engagement takes the form of commitment to revolution and social change, an acceptance of the existing society, or an intermediate position.

Those whom Keniston defined in his study as youth had accomplished the traditional tasks of adolescence. They were emancipated from the family; were relatively tranquil concerning sexuality; had formed a stable and relatively integrated self-concept; showed a capacity for commitment, intimacy, and play; displayed synthesis in the moral and ethical areas; and had passed through and beyond any adolescent rebellion. Despite their accomplishments, these young men and women continued to emphasize remaining open, fluid, and in motion, not foreclosing their development in any way, and not being prematurely integrated into the established society.

Social Change In the face of rapid social change, young people reexamine and redefine their personal relationships to the past, including the cultural past, before they are ready to move ahead in the task of creating their own future. This reexamination of the cultural tradition by perceptive young people frequently has had important and desirable consequences for society. It means that the obsolete is continually being winnowed from the enduring, that the problems and future directions of society are continually being scrutinized, and that society is assured a critical commentary on its own functioning.

Put more generally, the opening of a period of youth to larger numbers of young men and women may turn out to be part of the essential dynamic of social change and reform in modern societies. Within the past decade, youth have played a major role in social change in this country.

However, in view of the low incidence of principled morality, the foreclosure of identity, and the gender-related difficulties in integrating sexuality and intimacy among many adolescents, it must be apparent that Keniston's definition of youth probably applies to only a small and privileged minority. Indeed, it must be noted that interest in youth grew out of the study of youthful dissent of the 1960s, in itself a phenomenon of the upper-middle class.

It is not certain whether youth as a separate phase of life will find its way firmly into public consciousness or formal developmental theory. At present, when the word is defined in social-psychological terms, the incidence of youth is quite low. Given the decline in dissent, the social definition of the period may decrease in the future.

Finally, it is misleading to separate adolescence drastically from early adulthood, for in most men and women these two phases of life merge and blur. Adolescence does not end; it fades away, either into youth or into early adulthood. This fading away of adolescence marks not the end of psychological development but the beginning of a lifetime of future development, as we will see in the next chapters.

SUMMARY

1. The personality characteristics and social development of adolescents are determined by their prior socialization. Social-class differences in social relations and influences illustrate subcultural variations that affect almost all areas of development.

2. A chief interpersonal theme in early adolescence is the gradual move from childhood dependence, on which parents and the home environment have a lasting influence. Parents affect their adolescent son's or daughter's basic decisions about an occupation and the amount of independence and self-control that he or she is likely to show.

3. Peer relationships also change during adolescence, and their influence on an adolescent's identity formation may be crucial. Friendships often move from the sharing of activities to psychological intimacy. Early chumships often evolve into intimate, mature heterosexual companionships. Although popularity and peer acceptance may be stable from childhood to adolescence, sexual maturation and heterosexual behavior provide new influences that affect an adolescent's status within a group.

4. Despite the troubled interpersonal relationships that sometimes characterize adolescence, the "generation gap" between adolescents and adults is an exaggeration. In general, research indicates a high degree of adolescent peer support of parental values and views as well as a coordination of the adolescent subculture with that of the larger society.

5. A challenging, responsive, and confirming environment can enable an adolescent to move into a reasonable and satisfying adulthood. A major potential consequence of this formative period of life is the development of the capacity of commitment, first to one's self but also to a task, to interpersonal relationships, and to play. In recent years, a concept of youth has been proposed that draws on this theme of commitment.

Unit VII Adulthood: Functioning in Society

Our society has no rite or social ceremony to mark the passage from adolescence to adulthood. Although one may become a legal adult at eighteen or twenty-one, there is no one age at which a person becomes mature. We will, therefore, arbitrarily define adulthood as the years from twenty until death. To look more closely at this phase of development, we will further divide adulthood into three periods: (1) early adulthood, from twenty to forty; (2) middle adulthood, from forty to sixty; and (3) later adulthood, from sixty until death. Most people assume that growth and development halt once an individual reaches adulthood. However, as these chapters will show, adulthood is a time of change, of growth, and of development. Although the child does make the man, the experiences of a lifetime make the man of sixty the same and yet very different from the adult of twenty-five.

CHAPTER 20
Early Adulthood: Selecting the Options

THE CONCEPT OF MATURITY

PHYSICAL CHARACTERISTICS

IDENTITY AND INTERPERSONAL BEHAVIOR
Self-concept and Self-esteem
Sexuality
Intellectual Skills

MARRIAGE
The State of Being Married
Parenthood
Divorce and Remarriage

ALTERNATIVES TO MARRIAGE

SOCIAL LIFE AND CHANGE

SUMMARY

As she enters the adult world, Lauren has many more choices to make than her grandmother faced. Her grandmother knew that women married and became mothers, and her goals were simply and clearly set. Lauren, too, may choose a traditional marriage and devote the major part of her adult life to being a wife and mother. But, unlike her grandmother, she may also choose to marry and remain childless or to reject marriage altogether without feeling that she has failed as a human being. Lauren also has a third choice, one that more and more young women are selecting. She can marry and have both a family and a career, perhaps choosing a contract marriage, in which both she and her husband share in the obligations of making a home and rearing a family.

The choices that confront Lauren show that early adulthood is a time when individuals are confronted with the tasks of becoming adult. It is generally a time of becoming independent, a time to choose a vocation or career, and a time to choose a marriage partner and begin a family. Adolescents see an adult as someone who no longer plays and who is no longer playful; nevertheless, adolescents generally look forward to becoming adults themselves. Perhaps one reason that adolescents look forward to entering the adult world of commitments and responsibility is that they look forward, not to adulthood itself, but to the freedom and social respect associated with adulthood.

In this chapter we will describe the developmental and psychological characteristics that are typical of early adulthood. We will see that achieving independence and self-sufficiency is the central developmental task of these years. We will find that one's identity seems to remain fairly stable from adolescence into early adulthood and that younger adults are generally at their peak of physical ability and performance. We will look at marriage and parenthood, divorce and remarriage as transition points in development that challenge individuals to change and adjust. Throughout the chapter, we will emphasize that there are important differences in the ways individuals experience and cope with the tasks of early adulthood and that some of these differences depend on whether one is male or female, on one's concepts of appropriate sex-role behavior, on social class, on education, and on one's unique developmental history. Finally, we will see that there is no longer a single model for these early adult years and no one best road to maturity.

THE CONCEPT OF MATURITY

Almost all personality theories have described the development of maturity in early adulthood. Each of these views offers a unique perspective, yet there are some human characteristics that all these theories consider as mature. For example, all regard the ability to be intimate, to give and accept love, and to be affectionate and sexually responsive as necessary components of maturity. All stress the ability to be sociable, to have friends, to be devoted to and nurturant of other important people. They also agree that some clear, vivid sense of who one is, of what one's aims and powers are, and of what is best for oneself typifies a mature individual. One probable result of these characteristics is an interest in productive work and an ability to do it.

In each of these theories, the mature person constantly changes and adapts. He or she is a person who successfully and flexibly copes with the responsibilities and demands of adulthood. Maturity is not a final state, but a lifelong process of becoming.

One way to look at maturity, then, is to think of it in terms of being able to cope successfully with the typical events and decisions that most people face at characteristic times in their lives. Throughout this book we have considered life as divided into developmental phases. In this sense, a mature adult would be one who successfully deals with the demands to grow, develop, and change throughout adult life. In terms of Erik Erikson's (1963) concept of developmental stages, a mature individual is one who successfully resolves the crisis at each stage of development in the ideal direction. Thus, maturity in early adulthood, in Erikson's terms, means (1) having resolved the possible developmental crises of childhood and adolescence, (2) having ability for and interest in relating closely to another person (intimacy), and (3) having the ability and desire to be productive and to nurture and devote oneself to others, as to children and to productive work (generativity). But no matter how it is defined, maturity in adulthood is cumulative and changing. It involves a continuing adjustment to the constantly changing expectations and responsibilities of adulthood. A mature adult is able to cope successfully with the tasks, problems, and decisions that generally confront people of his or her age.

There is another, related way of looking at maturity. A mature person is likely to feel good about himself. In this view, maturity is determined more by a person's subjective assessment of how things are going than by society's judgment that he is doing things appropriate to his age. Adulthood is not only a time of doing things, it is also a time when an individual looks critically at himself, at the direction his life is taking, and at the ways other people see him. James Birren and Margaret Reedy (1978) have suggested that, in the mature person, there is often a fairly close fit between the way he sees himself, the way he would ideally like to be, and the way he believes other people see him. A young man like Matt, for example, may have unrealistic career goals for himself. He may also perceive himself to be much more aggressive with women than he actually is. In the process of maturing, he will bring his career expectations and ideals more in line with career goals that he could realistically hope to achieve. For Matt, maturing will also involve becoming more aware of his own shyness and caution in approaching women.

To be mature does not necessarily mean that one has to get married, work hard at a career, or have children. Maturity means being aware of who one is now, of where one wants to go in life, and it means working toward one's goals. In a real sense, the popular phrase "getting it all together" refers to young adults' struggle to become mature.

PHYSICAL CHARACTERISTICS

In these early years of adulthood, Matt and Lauren, Susan and David can enjoy being at the peak of their physical agility, speed, and strength. The healthy young adult stands erect and walks with a firm step. There are curves where there should be curves and firmness where one should be firm.

For most people, these are the years when

their bodies, inside and out, are at their best. Despite this sense of physical perfection, some of the physical hallmarks of aging begin, almost imperceptibly, in early adulthood. Around the age of twenty, slow, continuing changes affect the workings of the human body (Weg, 1975). Muscle tone and strength are generally at their peak between the ages of twenty and thirty and decrease after that. Height begins to decrease slowly but measurably around twenty-five. Visual acuity and hearing are at their best around twenty and decline after that. And, even if weight remains constant, the proportion of fatty tissue in a person's body begins to increase.

Considering society's overwhelming focus on youth and beauty, it might be expected that these small but noticeable changes in body appearance would have a negative effect on the way that young adults feel about themselves. However, this does not appear to be the case. A survey by Ellen Berscheid, Elaine Walster, and George Bohrnstedt (1973), which investigated Americans' attitudes toward their bodies, found that there was no difference between people under twenty-five years old and people twenty-five to forty-four years old in their overall liking for their bodies. Despite our focus on youth, today's young adults apparently are not bothered much by these small changes in their physical appearance.

One reason for the lack of concern over the physical changes of early adulthood may be that, aside from an occasional gray hair or a new wrin-

kle beside the eyes, the early adult years are typically the years of peak physical fitness and performance. Reaction times generally improve from childhood until the age of nineteen and then remain constant until around twenty-six. In any competitive situation or in any situation that demands a fast response, young adults usually come out ahead. Such factors may explain why only the young excel in some sports. In such competitive sports as basketball, boxing, skiing, and baseball, it takes early-adulthood strength and speed to stay on top. Other sports such as bowling or golf depend on concentration and experience and not at all on speed, so that adults can excel in these activities well into the later years.

NEW DEVELOPMENTAL TASKS

In adulthood as in childhood, each phase of life presents people with new tasks of development. Early adulthood is the first time in people's lives when they are truly on their own, when no one else makes their decisions for them. Younger adults are much more in control of their own lives and much more self-directing than adolescents.

If adolescence is a time for pulling up roots, young adulthood is a time for making commitments, taking on responsibilities, and making plans come true. During adolescence, concerns are on inner tasks: becoming independent, discovering a personal and sexual identity, and developing a set of values. For young adults in their twenties,

Although young adults are at the peak of their physical agility, speed, and strength, the almost imperceptible signs of physical aging have begun. (© Joel Gordon)

the tasks are more external and oriented to the world: deciding where to live, finding a job, discovering a sexual or marriage partner, or beginning a family. According to George Vaillant (1977), a main focus in these years among the well-educated, middle-class males he studied is achieving intimacy, both in romantic, sexual relationships and in platonic relationships with both sexes.

For many in their twenties, "shoulds" are important in determining the pattern of their lives. These "shoulds" may be defined by an individual's family, the surrounding culture, or the ideas of friends and acquaintances. If the culture David lives in insists that young men should get married and settle down with children, David is likely to do just that. If David's friends pressure him to "do his own thing," however, he may decide to buy a van, put together a house on wheels, and take off on an indefinite trip around the country. In this case, David is committed to having no commitments.

As young adults move into their thirties, the quality of life changes. Many will alter commitments they made earlier and expand and deepen other long-standing commitments. Whereas individuals in their twenties feel their course of life is set and try hard to fill the role established by themselves and their culture, the thirties are often a time when people begin to question themselves, their goals, and their values.

When Roger Gould (1972) studied the important life concerns of adults, he found that life in the thirties was more painful and difficult and less certain than it had been in the twenties. In their thirties, many question their earlier decisions concerning their personal lives. For some, the thirties are a time of tearing up what was put together in the twenties. If David is single, he may try to find a lifelong partner. If Matt married early, he may decide to get a divorce. If Susan has been happy as a mother, she may now want to go back to school or work. If Lauren and her husband have been childless, they may decide to start a family.

The thirties are also a time for settling down. According to Daniel Levinson and his associates (1978), there are three aspects to settling down. The first involves getting one's life in order and achieving stability, security, and control. Career consolidation becomes a major goal and adults concentrate on developing their skills and deepening their bases of experience. As an employee, Matt may find his growth in skill and experience

rewarded by promotions. Young scientists produce research papers, teachers teach effectively, mothers become competent at childrearing. A second aspect of settling down concerns the attempt to move onward and upward and reach major goals according to one's inner timetable. The executive has to get into the corporate structure by age forty. The truck driver must be a union official by thirty-five. The third aspect contrasts with the first two. People in their thirties also want to be free, unattached, and not tied down to any structure, no matter how satisfying it is. According to Levinson, the thirties are also a time for wanting to be "open to new possibilities, ready to soar, wander, quest in all directions as the spirit moves one." The thirties are a time of learning from mishaps, building on experiences and successes, and developing a sense of self-confidence and mastery.

Not all people get married and not all people settle into careers or have children at approximately the same age. What is considered appropriate behavior for a particular age group depends to some extent on who one is, the era one lives in, and one's social class. Each person has expectations regarding the kinds of behavior that are appropriate at various ages. Bernice Neugarten (1968) suggests that men and women have "social clocks" in their heads to help them judge other people's behavior, as well as their own, as being early, late, or on time. What constitutes the appropriate time for certain developmental events may change with the passing of generations. In 1940 the young woman who was not married by the age of twenty-five faced the threat of spinsterhood. By 1966 it was the twenty-one-year-old who faced such a fate. In the 1970s the appropriate age for marriage once again has become older, and young women who want to marry can postpone fears of spinsterhood.

According to Neugarten, early adulthood is both quantitatively and qualitatively different for people in different socioeconomic classes. Early adulthood lasts longer for a person in the upper middle class than for a member of the working class. The upper middle class regards forty as the end of early adulthood, whereas the working class believes that it ends at thirty-five. Further, the upper-middle-class person sees young adulthood as a time of exploration and groping, of "feeling one's way" and trying out jobs and careers, marriage and adulthood. To the working-class man, young adulthood is not a time of experimentation; it is a time when issues are settled. Sometimes this

Today women have a wide choice of careers; they may choose one of the occupations traditionally open to them, a career in a field formerly restricted to men, or the role of wife and mother. *(top and left:* © Joel Gordon; *right:* Suzanne Szasz)

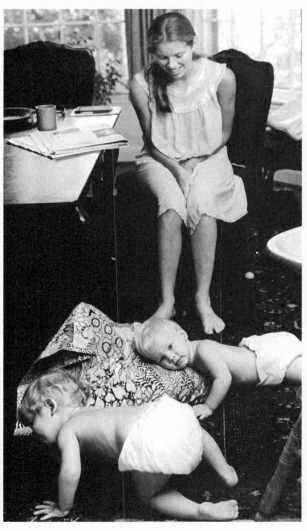

Whether they choose to become policemen or composers, men—and women—use early adulthood as a time for consolidating their careers and developing skills and experience. (*Left:* © Eric Kroll/Taurus Photo; *right:* Charles Gatewood)

IDENTITY AND INTERPERSONAL BEHAVIOR

The direction in which a young adult's personal and interpersonal skills grow and develop is primarily the result of experience and not simply the product of growing older. In general, gradual stabilization rather than radical change seems to be the rule, and many of the changes that occur are similar to those discussed in Chapter 19 with regard to the adolescent's capacity for commitment.

As Robert White (1966) has suggested, under reasonably favorable circumstances there is a stabilizing of one's identity. The individual's sense of who he or she is becomes sharper and clearer and also becomes more consistent and free of transient influences. Accumulated personal experience increasingly determines identity, and individuals progressively gain autonomy from the daily impact of social judgment and their successes and failures.

A second growth trend is toward a freeing of personal relationships. Whereas a small boy may treat a teacher as if she were his mother and other children as if they were brothers and sisters, the adult is able to be increasingly responsive to another person's nature. Adolescents are likely to

is explained as an obligation and there is some regret: "The responsibility is hung on you." Others in the working class see these decisions as necessary for independence; it is time to "be a man." The working man is likely to regard young adulthood as a time when youth is gone and when it is time to get down to the serious business of living, of job, marriage, children, and responsibility.

When people are asked, "When is the best time to marry?" or "When is the best time to finish school?" there is widespread agreement within social classes on the answers. As Neugarten reports, in the middle class, most say that the best age for a man to marry is between twenty-five and thirty-five. By contrast, working-class people believe that the best age for a man to marry is somewhat younger. The ages at which such major events as marriage actually occur also show a great deal of regularity within social classes. The higher the social class, the older people are likely to be when they leave school, get their first jobs, get married, and have children.

think primarily of themselves in social interactions; that is, they are generally concerned only with the impressions they make or with what they are trying to say. In early adulthood a person begins to be able to interact with others as people in their own right. Typically, a young adult becomes less defensive and anxious and more flexible, more sensitive to the verbal and nonverbal behavior of others, and more friendly, warm, and respectful.

A third area of change is in the direction of deepening interests. Lifelong interests can, and often do, develop early in life, but young adults tend to move toward a full engagement with those objects of interest. They feel an increased effectiveness and a growing command over their spheres of interest. At this time, an individual deepens existing interests or develops new interests as ends in themselves rather than as means to ends. As a person's interests and commitments become clearer and deeper, he or she is likely to have a heightened sense of self-confidence.

The humanizing of values is often a fourth area of development among young adults. During these years, a person may become increasingly aware of the human meaning of values as opposed to their absolute meaning. The young adult may use his own experiences and motives to affirm and promote a value system that seems best to him, and his value system becomes increasingly personal.

A final area of change involves the expansion of caring. Individuals typically outgrow the self-centeredness of their childhood and adolescent phases. An individual's self becomes "extended," and the welfare of another person, a group, or some valued object becomes as important as his own welfare. This caring becomes apparent only when there is involvement in and feeling for the welfare of others and not just a profession of interest.

Self-concept and Self-esteem

As Matt moves from adolescence to young adulthood, he will experience no sharp discontinuity between his adolescent self and his self as a young adult. But since an individual's self-concept is so closely related to his physical appearance and to his social roles and abilities, and since all these change in adulthood, it would seem likely that his self-concept would change as well. In fact, when Jack Block (1971) looked at changes in personality from adolescence to young adulthood, he found in young people a combination of both continuity and change. Both men and women tended to show less self-centered impulsiveness and an increased ability to cope with problems. When young adults are shown pictures and asked to tell stories about them, their sense of self-control, confidence, and mastery over the environment becomes evident. David Gutmann (1970) and Bernice Neugarten (1964) report that a majority of young adults tell stories that reflect feelings of being in control of their own lives and destinies and confidence that they can get what they want by their own actions.

An I-can-handle-it attitude is typical of many young adults, and it is reflected in their self-portraits. When people are asked to draw themselves, men's drawings get bigger and bigger until they are about thirty years old, and women's self-portraits increase in size until they are forty (Birren, 1964). Because this kind of drawing is presumed to reflect a person's self-concept, the inference is that young adults sense their increasing power and control over their own lives.

This sense of mastery and self-control may be stronger for Matt than for Susan or Lauren. As we have seen in earlier discussions of personality, learning what it means to think, act, and feel male or female is a critical part of adolescent and childhood development. The concepts men and women have about themselves clearly indicate that our social stereotypes about male and female roles have a profound impact on the kinds of adults that boys and girls are likely to become. Traditionally, girls are socialized to be dependent, passive, emotionally expressive, and warm, whereas little boys learn to be assertive, independent, and to think rationally. Brought up in this way, young women are less likely than men to have a sense of control over their lives, successes, and failures. Whereas young men believe in their power to control their fate, women are more likely to believe that outside powers are in control. Kay Deaux (1976) found, for example, that when a man and a woman perform equally well on some task, especially a traditionally masculine task such as playing darts, women tend to attribute their success to luck, whereas men tend to see skill as the reason for their fine performance.

Women may also find different ways to express their needs for self-control and mastery. For example, men who have high needs for achievement typically express their needs directly in their jobs, but women who are highly achievement-oriented may express themselves either directly or indirectly. If Susan expresses this need directly, she might pursue her career in art or become involved in community work, gourmet cooking, or decorating her home. However, she is more likely to meet her achievement needs indirectly, deriving satisfaction from the successes of her husband and children. Lauren, however, is likely to postpone marriage until she completes her education and establishes herself in her profession, expressing her need for achievement directly through her job.

Perhaps as a result of the women's movement in this country, young men and women are changing their concepts of masculinity and femininity; among young adults, sex-role stereotypes are breaking down. In a recent survey of more than 28,000 young adults, Carol Tavris (1977) found that neither sex saw the ideal man as being tough, strong, and aggressive, with many sexual conquests. Instead, he is seen as able to love, self-confident, ready to stand by his beliefs, and —especially by women—as warm and gentle. Among both the sexes, the ideal woman, like the ideal man, is seen as able to love, ready to stand by her beliefs, self-confident, intelligent, and warm. More women than men think the ideal woman should be successful at work, whereas more men than women value her physical attractiveness. Clearly, young men and women are now reaching toward less rigid definitions of masculinity and femininity.

Young adults are going beyond new concepts of maleness and femaleness and are behaving in less traditional ways. In a three-generation study, Lillian Troll (1975) found that less than a handful of grandmothers had had any higher education, but a quarter of their daughters were either planning to attend college, were in college, or had finished college. The young adult granddaughters, in contrast to the older two generations, wanted to be successful themselves instead of achieving vicariously through the successes of their husbands or children, and they believed more strongly than their mothers or grandmothers that they could control their own lives.

When Margaret Reedy (1977) looked at the personal needs of young, middle-aged, and older men and women, she also found that today young men and women define their roles and themselves less traditionally than earlier generations did. She found that in the middle-aged and older groups, men needed to be dominant and independent and women needed to be nurturing, friendly, and moral. These traditional sex differences did not characterize the young men and women; young men were comfortable with their "feminine" qualities, and young women were able to express their "masculine" side. Both young adult men and women would like to see themselves as self-confident, intelligent, independent, loving, and understanding.

People are human beings first and sexual beings second. Their self-esteem is rooted in self-confidence and a sense of control over their lives as well as in their sexual identities. As most young adults develop an increasing sense of control over their lives, their self-esteem generally becomes greater than it was when they were adolescents (Lowenthal and Chiraboga, 1973). Since one's sexual identity is a central part of one's self-concept, it is also important in determining how good one feels about oneself as an adult. Like adolescents, men and women typically derive their self-esteem from different sources. For example, men are prized and prize themselves for what they accomplish, whereas women tend to like themselves when they are esteemed and regarded highly by others (Bardwick, 1971). Because in most cases our society values accomplishment over interpersonal success and admiration, women whose self-esteem depends on being liked by others tend to have lower self-esteem than men do.

One recent survey of young adults (Shaver and Freedman, 1976) showed that the happiest individuals were those who felt in control of their lives and evaluated their progress by their own standards, not those of others. As one woman put it, "Happiness is driving your own truck." At this time of life, increasing self-satisfaction means either increasing one's successes or lowering one's goals and aspirations. Summarizing the feeling of personal control that brought him self-satisfaction, one man said: "Although my life is far from perfect, I now have a good understanding of myself, my limitations, abilities, weaknesses, and strong points. And I now have laid a good, strong, solid course ahead for the remainder of my life, which I know will be actualized (some of it already has been!). If I changed places with Johnny Bench, John Denver, or Jimmy Connors, I would have to start all over again. No thanks."

Sexuality

Sexual relationships and sexual performance continue to be important concerns during early adulthood. The data presented in the Kinsey reports indicated that the average American male establishes a pattern of orgasm and ejaculation that remains fairly consistent from adolescence through later adulthood and that is relatively independent of marital status. However, the relative frequency of various sexual behavior does change over the years. Whereas masturbation is the dominant type of male sexual behavior before puberty and in early adolescence, sexual intercourse is more prominent in early adulthood (Kinsey, Pomeroy, and Martin, 1948; Masters and Johnson, 1966).

Especially during the first years of marriage, a young couple is likely to have intercourse frequently. In addition to its physiological benefit and its value as one of life's great pleasures, sexuality can be an affirmation of closeness, caring, and affection.

A survey by Robert Bell and Norman Lobsenz (1974) of the sexual practices and attitudes of 2,372 moderately well-educated American wives revealed that most young adult wives enjoy a high level of sexual pleasure in marriage. Wives in their twenties tended to derive most pleasure from the physical aspects of love-making, whereas the thirty-year-olds tended to regard the emotional aspects as most important. The majority of wives reported that they had orgasms "most of the time" or at least "some of the time." Orgasmic satisfaction was related to a woman's feelings of contentment with her marriage: happier women reported a higher frequency of orgasms. Frequency of intercourse was also related to sexual satisfaction and marital happiness, as is true of men. Although both the quantity and quality of a sexual relationship are related to marital happiness, it is not clear whether good sexual relations make a good marriage or a good marriage leads to good sex. Undoubtedly both are true.

Most of the women in Bell and Lobsenz's survey were satisfied with the frequency of coitus. Of the women surveyed, those between twenty-six and thirty had coitus just over nine times a month, whereas women between thirty-one and forty reported that they had intercourse around seven times a month. Those who said that coitus was too infrequent explained that it was not due to their husbands' lack of interest but due to the pressures of jobs, childrearing, and housework, which left them with little time and energy. Wives who reported that intercourse was too infrequent also tended to talk less with their husbands about their sexual relationship.

Sexuality is an important concern during early adulthood, and can go beyond simple physical pleasure into expressions of closeness, caring, and affection. (Michael Alexander)

Young adult wives were more likely than teenage wives or wives in their forties to experiment with love-making techniques, and those women who reported such experiments tended to be more satisfied with their marriages. Wives in their twenties and thirties reported more experience with oral-genital sex and were somewhat more concerned with the "environment of sex"—what they looked like, where they engaged in it—than teenage or middle-aged wives. Generally, wives under thirty found it easy to talk to their husbands about their sexual desires and needs, and most said that their husband usually initiates the love-making.

Intellectual Skills

People's intellectual skills, or at least their own perception of them, are likely to affect both their self-concept and their self-esteem. The young adult finds that these years are a time of improved performance in all areas of intellectual ability. In the areas of verbal skills, stored facts, and information processing, young adults do better than they ever have before. Young adults also reach

Young adults are at the peak of many of their intellectual skills; they can learn, remember, shift from one
way of thinking to another, and process visual material
faster than they ever have. (© Joan Liftin/Woodfin
Camp & Assoc.)

their peak performance on tests involving psycho-
motor skills, especially speed and coordination.

According to Paul Baltes and K. Warner
Schaie (1974), young adults are better than they
ever have been, but not necessarily better than
they ever will be, in three major areas of intellectual functioning: (1) verbal comprehension and
number skills, which are acquired through education and socialization; (2) the ability to shift easily
from one way of thinking to another, as when a
person must provide an antonym or a synonym to
a given word, depending on whether the word is
printed in upper- or lower-case letters; and (3) the
ability to organize and process visual materials,
such as finding a simple figure in a complex one or
identifying a picture that is incomplete.

However, age is not the only factor that affects
intellectual skills during adulthood. For example,
our species is becoming smarter with each new
generation (Baltes and Schaie, 1974). We are also
better educated and healthier, and both education

and health are at least as important as age in determining an individual's intellectual ability (Botwinick, 1973).

Beyond measures of intellectual skill, there
also are matters of learning and memory, thinking,
problem solving, and creativity. In young adulthood, the ability to learn and remember is generally at its peak. Thus, on any kind of learning or
memory task, young adults usually perform better
than they ever have before. In addition, if success
at a task depends on how quickly they complete it,
they probably do the best that they will ever do.

In the case of thinking, early adulthood is
likely to be the time when people have the maximum flexibility to form new concepts and find it
easiest to shift the way they think in order to solve
problems. This ability to shift an approach to a
problem is most likely to be shown when the solution involves discovering the details of categories
and using the information at hand. But again, age
is not the only determinant; intelligence, educa-

tion, and memory also contribute heavily to thinking ability.

As for creativity, which involves finding original and unique solutions, the early adult years often provide the most fertile ground for creative thought. For example, maximum creativity in the arts and sciences may occur during the thirties (Lehman, 1953). The most influential books tend to be produced by writers in their late thirties, and many popular children's books and short stories are written by people in their early thirties. The twenties are the time when poetry usually flourishes, whereas drama seems to be a favorite mode of expression for people in their thirties. Inventions and discoveries tend to be made by people in their thirties. The production of novels, paintings, poetry, plays, and inventions reaches a peak during these years, but this does not mean that creativity ends with one's fortieth birthday. As we will see, creative individuals are likely to continue to produce works of high quality throughout their lives.

MARRIAGE

Nearly everyone gets married. In the United States, somewhere between 95 and 98 percent of the population choose to make this legal commitment to another person (Carter and Glick, 1970).

Generally, this major developmental decision takes place during the early adult years. Although people live, die, marry, and divorce in the name of love, a number of other factors are also important in determining who one marries and how well that marriage lasts.

Choosing a mate, or choosing not to choose one, is one of the most significant decisions a person will ever make. The person one chooses to marry will have a great influence on one's way of life, one's lifetime experiences, and even one's lifetime happiness. Despite the importance of marriage and its impact on one's life, the decision to marry often is made quickly, easily, and rather casually. Most decisions to marry, however, do consider social level, temperamental compatibility, and similarity of outlook on life.

People tend to marry people who are like themselves. Individuals look for mates who have a suitable background; that is, a background that matches their own ethnically, religiously, and socially (Murstein, 1971). Although interracial and interfaith marriages and some forms of interclass marriages are more likely to be accepted today, in the past society has condemned, if not outlawed, such marriages.

People also tend to choose marriage partners who share their interests, values, and ways of behaving. This kind of selectivity reflects a human

Nearly everyone in this society gets married, and most choose to make this legal commitment during early adulthood. (Inge Moratti/Magnum Photos)

tendency to seek out persons who validate one as a human being and who approve of the way that one lives. If engaged couples are questioned separately, a striking agreement between the two partners appears on such issues as smoking and drinking, as well as in their attitudes toward working women, the number of children they want, and where they should live (Burgess and Wallin, 1953). In general, residential proximity and similarity of background tend to be important in starting a relationship. Whether it stands the test of time and marriage is likely to depend in part on a similarity in the couple's values, attitudes, and interests (Z. Rubin, 1973). The course of choosing a mate appears to follow a pattern somewhat like the course of friendship discussed in Chapter 19.

When one looks at young adults' attitudes toward love and the person they would like to marry, interesting sex differences appear. A series of studies that followed nearly 200 Boston couples for two years found that men are likely to fall in love more quickly than women, to be more easily satisfied with the woman's qualities, to be more romantic, and to fall out of love less easily (Hill, Rubin, and Peplau, 1976). Women, in general, tend to be more practical about whom they marry. To put it succinctly, young adult women are picky. But in a traditional relationship, they may have more to gain in marriage, in terms of economic and emotional security and social status, than men. Willard Waller (1938) said it well, if bluntly, more than forty years ago: "A man, when he marries, chooses a companion and perhaps a helpmate, but a woman chooses a companion and at the same time a standard of living." However, with women's increasing equality on the job market, this is perhaps becoming less of a truism.

The State of Being Married

For couples who do not live together before marriage, and they remain in the majority, marriage means adjusting to all the social roles associated with marriage. To a considerable degree, people learn how to act as married people long before they become adult. In the process of socialization, they develop concepts of what it means to be a husband or a wife, and their ideas about the way husbands and wives are "supposed" to act (Ahammer, 1973). Parents, family, and early heroes and heroines provide models of married people and show growing children how wives and husbands

behave. Later, children and adolescents learn from friends, from experiences in intimate relationships, and from the mass media. The concepts of masculinity and femininity that are absorbed as children learn male and female roles also affect the characteristics of marriage relationships.

In addition to presenting new roles, marriage also requires couples to adjust to living with another person. The honeymoon may be over once the dirty dishes and laundry have to be washed and the bathroom scrubbed. The smallest things can have a profound impact on a marriage: Susan may roll the toothpaste tube from the bottom; her husband may just squish it out and leave the top uncapped. The romance and sexual attraction of dating and courtship are not enough to hold a relationship together through the realities of everyday living. If young adults have had good parental models to help them learn what a good relationship is like, they are at an advantage. If they also have the willingness and the patience to develop emotional intimacy and to communicate their feelings, the relationship will have more potential for enduring growth (C. Rogers, 1972).

New marriages can be described in terms of a few general characteristics (Cox, 1968). Newly married couples soon discover that their individual freedom is reduced, that they must make financial adjustments, and that they face problems involving the maturity or lack of maturity of their partners. By marrying in early adulthood, at a time when this freedom may still be critical to one's individual growth, people often find the restrictions of marriage difficult to handle. Adding children to the marriage generally exaggerates whatever problems already exist.

Many marriages remain happy, and happily married couples find different kinds of satisfaction in their relationships. When Margaret Reedy (1977) asked happily married couples of all ages about the characteristics of their relationship, women said that emotional security and intimacy were extremely important, whereas men emphasized loyalty and a sense of commitment to the future of the relationship. Young couples placed a high value on their ability to communicate openly and honestly with each other and to express sexual feelings freely.

A new marriage confronts a couple with the problem of power. In the traditional, male-dominated relationship, the husband holds the power, and the wife either accepts his superior decision-

Although people learn how to ''act'' married long before they are adult, living with another person requires patience and the willingness to adjust to another's habits. (Thomas Hopker/Woodfin Camp & Assoc.)

making abilities or attempts to assert her power in less direct, more subtle ways (Bernard, 1972). Another kind of relationship is becoming common today, one in which the power is divided more equally between the man and the woman. Susan Kaplan (1976) looked at power in intimate relationships and found that both men and women strongly supported an egalitarian relationship. Asked to describe an ideal relationship, 95 percent of the women and 87 percent of the men indicated that both the boyfriend and the girlfriend should have an equal say. In their own relationships, however, only 49 percent of the women and 42 percent of the men perceived their current relationships as equal in power. When the relationship was unequal, the male was generally more powerful than the female. Male-dominated relationships tended to be those in which males and females had traditional sex-role attitudes, the male was less involved in the relationship, and the woman's educational

plans were limited to high school or to a bachelor's degree.

It is common for the young wife to work during the early years of a marriage, at least until the couple decides to start a family. Today, the period between marriage and parenthood is becoming longer as couples devote more time to getting to know each other and to enjoying life together. In addition, a growing number of women are continuing to work even after they begin a family. Some work because their income is economically important; college-educated wives may feel that they have important careers to develop; some wives simply find work rewarding. Among couples with well-educated working wives, more and more are choosing not to have children at all or to divide the responsibilities of child care more evenly between the husband and wife. There no longer seems to be a single, rigid model for the right kind of marriage (C. Rogers, 1972). Instead, the trend is toward es-

Perfect Wife Quiz

1. Do you allow your husband an appropriate amount of the family income, to spend as he chooses, without accounting? 0 1 2 3 4

2. Do you still "court" him with an occasional gift of flowers; by remembrance of birthdays and anniversaries; by unexpected attentions?
0 1 2 3 4

3. Are you cooperative in handling the children, taking your full share of responsibility and also backing him up? 0 1 2 3 4

4. Do you make it a point never to criticize him before others? 0 1 2 3 4

5. Do you share at least half your recreation hours with him? 0 1 2 3 4

6. Do you show interest in and respect for his intellectual life? 0 1 2 3 4

7. Do you show as much consideration and courtesy to his relatives as you do to your own? 0 1 2 3 4

8. Do you enter sympathetically into his plans for social activities, trying to do your full share as a hostess in your own home and, when a guest in the homes of others, trying to make him appear to the best possible advantage?
0 1 2 3 4

Perfect Husband Quiz

1. Do you try to make the home interesting, attractive, cheerful, a place of rest and relaxation—devoting as much thought and study to that as you would to a job "downtown"?
0 1 2 3 4

2. Do you encourage your wife to go out frequently with her women friends, though it means leaving you home alone? 0 1 2 3 4

3. Do you serve meals that are enticing in variety and attractiveness? 0 1 2 3 4

4. Do you handle household finances in a businesslike way? 0 1 2 3 4

5. Do you keep yourself attractive (though not offensively so!) in appearance, in order that your wife may be proud to have everyone know you are her husband? 0 1 2 3 4

6. Are you a "good sport," cheerful and uncomplaining, punctual, not nagging, not insisting on having your own way or the last word, not making a fuss over the trifles or requiring her to solve minor problems that you should handle alone? 0 1 2 3 4

7. Do you bolster your wife's ego by not comparing her unfavorably with more successful women but making her feel that she is the most successful woman you ever met?
0 1 2 3 4

8. Do you prevent your mother and other relatives from intruding unduly, and show courtesy and consideration to her own relatives? 0 1 2 3 4

Figure 20.1 A spoof on quizzes from *Radical Therapist* (*left*) for a perfect wife, and (*right*) for a perfect husband. Scoring on each item is as follows: 0 = "never," 1 = "sometimes," 2 = "an average amount," 3 = "usually," and 4 = "regularly." The "perfect" score on the eight items is a total of 32.

tablishing a relationship that optimizes the personal satisfaction and growth of each individual.

Parenthood

Although young married couples today tend to postpone beginning a family, eventually most young adult couples do have children. Statistics tell us that over 90 percent of the women in the United States have at least one child (Lasswell and Lasswell, 1973). Today, however, fewer couples have children because their religion or their economic situation demands it. Increasingly, couples have children because they want to.

Just as becoming a husband or a wife requires an individual to change and adapt, becoming a mother or father requires learning new roles and making adjustments. Many women claim that the greatest change in their lives came about not as a result of their marriage but after the birth of their first child (Ahammer, 1973). The adjustments are even greater for women who are professionally trained and who have had working experience, because they must make more extensive changes in their way of life.

The demands and responsibilities of parenthood change the marriage relationship. Children can, and often do, detract from the happiness of marriage. Although only about 2 percent of married couples choose childlessness deliberately, the idea is gaining popularity. The decision not to have children does not doom a couple to unhappiness, misery, and loneliness. Young childless couples, especially husbands, report greater satisfaction with life than do couples with young children (Campbell, Converse, and Rogers, 1975).

Recent social changes are influencing the transition to parenthood and the resulting experience. For example, Alice Rossi (1968) notes that there is now less cultural pressure on women to assume the role of mother. As a result, motherhood can be a more voluntary and pleasurable experience than it used to be. In addition, the increased time between marriage and parenthood, when the wife generally works, and the tendency for more mothers to continue working gives an equalitarian marital relationship a chance to develop, so that decisions and household responsibilities are shared by the spouses. This sharing of responsibilities is likely to carry over into childrearing, giving the woman more autonomy and the man more responsibility. Not all men are ready to participate in childrearing, however; not even those who are experimenting with new forms of marriage. In a recent study of parents in communal and contract marriages, the mother was the primary caretaker of the child in 95 percent of the families (*Science News*, 1977). As Rossi points out, parenthood remains irrevers-

ible. It is possible to divorce a spouse, but not a child. Unwanted children may be neglected and their parents are unlikely to find gratification in their offspring.

Some women find that motherhood does not help them grow and mature; instead, they like themselves less than they did before their children were born (Bradburn and Caplovitz, 1965). This does not appear to be the case with working and nonworking mothers who are happy with their roles. Mothers who like their jobs and who like working, whether their job is that of homemaker or career woman, are apt to like their children and themselves more than are women who dislike what they are doing (Ferree, 1976).

Fathers are traditionally thought of as simply providing the paycheck so that the child has food to eat and clothes to wear. Although many fathers do see their children as an economic responsibility and many children see their fathers as the provider of the allowance, fathers play an important role in the child's emotional and social development. As earlier discussions have stressed, fathers can play a major role in caregiving. More and more fathers are becoming more active and involved in their children's growth and development. An increasing number of divorced or separated men feel they

The birth of a child not only requires both wife and husband to learn the roles of mother and father but also affects their own relationship. (© 1978 Joel Gordon)

Although not all men are ready to participate in child-rearing, more and more fathers are taking an active role in caring for their children. (Constantine Manos/Magnum Photos)

have a right to take care of their children. And while they often feel badly prepared for their new responsibilities, the evidence indicates that men can successfully rear their children alone. Many of their problems are similar to those faced by divorced mothers; among the major concerns of single fathers are juggling work with child care and providing their daughters with adequate sex education (Orthner, Brown, and Ferguson, 1977).

Divorce and Remarriage

When a marriage is unhappy, divorce offers a way out. Divorce has become less stigmatized in recent years. As a result, increasing numbers of young adults find themselves making decisions about divorce and remarriage. Such major changes in one's life place additional demands on one's ability to change and develop.

Failures in marriage might better be defined in terms of psychological unhappiness and dissatisfaction than in legal terms. A number of factors tend to make marriages unhappy but do not neces-

sarily lead to divorce. In general, unhappy marriages go along with low occupational status, low income, low educational level, and with differences in socioeconomic status, age, and religion between husband and wife. When a man and woman do not accurately see what the other is like, there is apt to be a great deal of marital discord and dissatisfaction. In addition, the less the husband and wife agree about their roles, the lower their marital satisfaction will be. The less emotional involvement in the relationship, and the less communication between the partners, the less likely couples will be satisfied with their marriages. Finally, an unwillingness to change and adapt to the changing demands, roles, and responsibilities of the marital relationship usually accompanies an unsatisfactory relationship (Murstein, 1971).

Some relationships seem to last in spite of it all; others do not. In the young adult years, marriages seem especially subject to failure. Beyond the fact that marriage tends to be less stable among poorly paid blue-collar workers and less stable in the nonwhite population, divorce is most likely to occur early in a marriage. More divorces occur in the third or fourth year of marriage than any other, and the divorce rate drops steadily after that (Hicks and Platt, 1971). Age at marriage is also related to the probability of divorce, and adolescent marriages are the most likely to fail. Men who marry before they are twenty-one and women who marry before they are nineteen are least likely to stay married, whereas men who marry after they are thirty tend to stay married (Troll, 1975).

Increasingly, and this is especially true for young adults, couples who are unhappy in marriage are less likely to persist in a dismal relationship. The United States has the highest divorce rate in the world; about 40 percent of all American marriages end in divorce. But in sunny, single California, the divorce rate in 1971 reached 70 percent. These statistics do not account for remarriages and divorces, so that the number of first marriages that end in divorce is about 25 percent nationwide.

Being divorced means changing one's role and status and reexamining one's identity. There are no norms or expectations for the "once-married," and divorced people are likely to feel cast adrift, rootless, and anxious. A survey of more than 2,000 people showed that those who were divorced were less satisfied with their lives than the married at any age, the never-married, or the widowed

(Campbell, Converse, and Rogers, 1975). Divorced people often regard the breakup of their marriages as evidence of personal failure; in addition, they are likely to find themselves in serious financial straits and to experience a loss of friends as people who related to them as part of a couple drift away.

When Mavis Hetherington, Martha Cox, and Roger Cox (1977) looked at the problems faced by newly divorced fathers, they found that both men and women had difficulty handling their affairs, at least at first. Men found the practical problems of daily life were particularly difficult, especially if their wives had not worked and they were used to having a full-time homemaker. Money problems often caused disagreements between divorced parents, who found it difficult to support two households on one salary.

The effects of divorce on self-concept were different for men and for women. Divorced mothers said they felt helpless and unattractive, and complained of a loss of identity because they were no longer linked to their husbands' status. Divorced fathers often said they no longer knew who they were and that they felt rootless and homeless. Both parents, but especially fathers, plunged into social activities; many tried self-improvement and took courses in photography, Eastern religions, or physical fitness. Men who had dressed conservatively often changed to flashy, fashionable clothing.

Divorced men and women generally tend to be less active socially than their married counterparts. Since American social life is centered around couples, divorced people tend to see less and less of their married friends, although they do begin to share time with divorced, separated, or never-married people. Divorced mothers who have primary custody of their children have less contact with adults than their ex-husbands do, and often report feeling "trapped" or "locked into a child's world."

Two years after divorce, couples in Hetherington's study were having sexual intercourse about as frequently as married couples, but the married people were happier with their lives. Some of the divorced men and women had a variety of sex partners, especially in the first year after divorce. Neither the men nor the women were satisfied with a series of superficial encounters, however, and both said they wanted sustained, meaningful relationships.

Most people do learn from failure, at least in marriage. Second marriages generally are as happy as those first marriages that endure. Statistics show that 75 percent of divorced people remarry within five years of their decrees (Kimmel, 1974). Chances for remarriage vary by sex and age. Divorced women under thirty are most likely to remarry; the tables turn after thirty, however, and after that divorced men have the advantage and are most likely to find another spouse. Apparently, people are not disillusioned with marriage but only with the relationship they were in. More and more, the trend in our society is toward serial or sequential marriages.

The reasons for remarrying are similar to the reasons for marrying in the first place. People remarry for love, and when they marry again seem to work hard at making the marriage work.

Remarrying, however, does not guarantee living happily ever after the second time around. A second marriage has problems that past experience does not necessarily prepare people to handle. When Lillian Messinger (1976) interviewed seventy remarried couples, she found that they, like divorced persons who had not remarried, ranked their previous spouses' immaturity, sexual problems, and personal lack of motivation and readiness for marriage as the biggest problems in their broken marriages. Problems in the second marriages were different; whereas children and money were at the bottom of the list in the first marriages, they were at the top of the list in the second marriages.

Remarried people with children often find it difficult to maintain a comfortable relationship with their former spouses and to develop new households. Some partners find themselves caught between loyalty to their own children and their desire to please their new mates, whereas others feel guilty for not loving their new children. Financial responsibilities remaining from the first marriages create problems for the second. Some women reported feeling guilty about the burden their children placed on their new husbands, and some men felt uncertain about revising their insurance policies and wills.

ALTERNATIVES TO MARRIAGE

In the view of some younger adults, traditional marriage has failed and must be replaced with other styles of intimacy. Such alternative life-styles as singlehood, cohabitation, mate sharing, contract marriage, communal living, and group marriage,

Singlehood has become a familiar way of life as more and more men and women postpone the time of marriage, and increasing numbers are not marrying at all. (© Joel Gordon)

all of which are being experimented with today, are not new forms of human relationships. What is new is the increasing openness to and awareness of these different styles of expressing human sexuality, intimacy, and affection.

Singlehood is becoming increasingly common in Western societies as women and men remain single longer than in past years. The number of young people between twenty-five and thirty-five who have never married increased by 50 percent between 1960 and 1975 (U.S. Bureau of the Census, 1964, 1974). The proportion of women from twenty to twenty-four who remained single increased from 29 percent to 40 percent during the same period. At any one time, about a third of all adult Americans are unmarried, separated, or in some way unattached (Libby, 1977). Although most divorced people remarry, the number of persons under thirty-five who have divorced but not remarried has doubled in the past ten years.

Increasing numbers of people are choosing singlehood as an alternative way of life. In interviews with young adults who had been involved in some type of exclusive sexual relationship before they chose a nonexclusive single life, Peter Stein (1975) found that both men and women agreed that, although marriage offered economic, emotional, and sexual security, singlehood was attractive because it offered personal freedom, career opportunities, sexual availability and diversity, and a chance for self-improvement. In addition, singlehood offers both sexes time to find themselves and enjoy themselves.

Cohabitation, or living together without a marriage contract, is not a new phenomenon. What is new are its present visibility, the frequency of these relationships among college-educated individuals, and their tendency to be emotionally rather than financially based. Approximately 11 percent of the adult population (U.S. Bureau of the Census, 1973) are cohabiting, as were from 10 to 33 percent of all young adults on college campuses (Macklin, 1974).

Most couples do not make a conscious decision to live together. Instead, it happens gradually as the couple spends increasing amounts of time together. Although only a minority of cohabitants are committed to marrying their partners (Cole, 1977), most see living together as a kind of trial marriage, a time for getting to know each other and for seeing whether the relationship can bear the closeness and realities of everyday life. The characteristics of cohabiting relationships are similar to those of marital relationships. Cohabitants, as do marrieds, frequently divide labor along sex-role lines and agree to be sexually monogamous (Bernard, 1977).

Sometimes partners become dissatisfied with this kind of arrangement because it lacks the apparent stability, security, and futurity of the married relationship. If the relationship does not work out, the partners are legally free, although generally not emotionally free, to leave. When cohabitation ends, the emotional, social, financial, and physical adjustments the partners must make are like those faced by divorcing couples.

A growing number of couples in this country have chosen not to confine their sexual activities to the marital relationship and generally adopt either of two approaches to extramarital sex: the sexually open marriage, or mate sharing. Most people who enter sexually open marriages seek complexity, novelty, excitement, and increased personal awareness. According to Jacquelyn Knapp and Robert Whitehurst (1977), this sort of marital arrangement attracts two kinds of couples: (1) those who have a strong, affectionate, and respectful marriage and agree on the importance of expanding their interpersonal experiences, and (2) those who have unhappy marriages and are searching for an alternative to divorce. For couples in a shaky relationship, the sexually open marriage is rarely an effective band-aid. According to Knapp and Whitehurst, couples with strong marriages who adopt the principle of sexual openness report improved personal awareness and fulfillment and increased self-esteem. They say that their sexual freedom strengthens their marital bond. According to these couples, the uncertainty, anxiety, and emotional pain of the open relationship generate high levels of communication, mutual problem solving, and continual excitement in their marital relationship.

Mate sharing, also called "swinging," refers to a mutual sexual exchange of partners between legally married couples. Few Americans are involved in mate sharing—only about 2 percent of all married couples, or 900,000 couples (Hunt, 1974). Couples who have tried mate sharing are likely to be well-educated and not particularly religious. Comparing swinging and nonswinging couples, Brian Gilmartin (1977) found that swingers had less emotionally satisfying relationships with their parents, saw their friends more often and depended on them more, and were less likely to become involved in conventional political or religious institutions. When he compared their sexual histories, he found swingers had very early strong romantic interests and that they married earlier and had had sex with more partners than had nonswingers.

Husbands usually introduce the idea of mate sharing to their wives, and most men report learning about mate sharing by reading about it in newspapers, magazines, and books. People who support this way of life say that it enriches their marriage, provides variety, and contributes to individual growth, which makes marriage mutually satisfying. People who disapprove of mate sharing say that it is immoral, that it makes sex too impersonal, or that it violates the marital vows. Because mate sharing requires the consent of both partners, advocates of swinging claim that it is not adultery.

Among young couples who try to keep their re-lationships open and flexible, contract marriages are becoming popular. In this form of marriage, the couple draws up a contract or statement that specifies their values and communicates their expectations for the relationship. Many of the contracts emphasize an egalitarian rather than a traditional, male-dominated relationship. Common provisions in the contracts concern division of household responsibilities, division of assets held before marriage and income after marriage, caring for and supporting children, and rules regarding career decisions and relationships with others—including sexual relationships. Many contracts also have clauses that cover changes, renewals, and termination of the agreement.

Communal living is generally associated with the young and unmarried. There are, however, a number of communes made up of married couples who feel that only this style of living can make marriage and families satisfying. One thing most communes seem to have in common is the desire to achieve intimacy within the context of an extended family unit (Kanter, 1973).

Communes are one alternative to traditional marriage. Some communes are made up of married couples who believe that only group living can provide a satisfying life. (Bob Fitch/Black Star)

Group marriage, which may involve any number of married couples, is a relatively rare alternative relationship in American society. Larry and Joan Constantine (1973, 1977) found that the average group consisted of four adult partners and three children and that personal growth was the most important reason for entering a group marriage. Other reasons for group marriage were similar to those given for entering a monogamous relationship: love, security, sex, childrearing, and companionship. As with sexually open marriages, couples who believed that multiple intimacy would solve their marital problems usually found that group marriages aggravated the problems.

Among the group marriages the Constantines studied, 80 percent of the participants regarded jealousy as a problem and, especially early in the history of most groups, the exchange of partners was fixed by a schedule of rotation in order to minimize the destructive emotion. By the conclusion of their research, the Constantines found that most group marriages had broken up and that monogamous marriages that predated the group's formation generally survived the dissolution.

SOCIAL LIFE AND CHANGE

As we have seen, young adults begin to focus their lives and to make lifetime decisions about career, marriage, and family. These years are also a time of experimentation and expansion, a time for making friends, and a time for developing new leisure interests, as well as for deepening old interests and friendships.

Many of the factors important to the development of love relationships that lead to marriage are also important in the development of friendships. People who live close together are more likely to be friends, and so are people who share similar interests, attitudes, and values. Not much is known, however, about the friendship patterns of adults. What little is known indicates that most married couples have two close friends who live nearby and that, at any age in adulthood, men are more likely than women to initiate friendships for the couple (Babchuk, 1965). In addition, it is especially characteristic of young-married friendships that all the friends tend to be of the same age.

Because opportunities for vocational advancement may require well-educated younger couples to be highly mobile, the friendships they make in this period of life are not likely to be lasting. In contrast, less well-educated couples are more likely to have permanent friendships that revolve around the husband's job and that involve old high-school or even elementary-school friends.

Married individuals are more likely to have same-sex friends than opposite-sex friends. One simple reason for this arrangement is that society generally regards opposite-sex friends as a threat to a marriage. Both married and unmarried people who work have opportunities to develop same-sex friendships with fellow employees. A married woman who does not work outside the home is likely to feel relatively friendless and isolated.

The fact that much of the young adult's life is bound up with his or her work is likely to have major implications for leisure activity. Ideally, work should be play. Unfortunately, the work most people do usually does not match their ideals, and so they must find other outlets for recreation and play. The importance of recreation and play for the developing child and adolescent has been discussed throughout this book. Time for recreation and play is also important to an adult like Lauren; it helps her use up her surplus energy and meet her needs for relaxation, creativity, and self-expression. Depending on their particular needs, adults may choose either physical or passive recreation. For example, if David has been lifting beams all day on a housing project, he may prefer to spend a leisurely evening relaxing with a beer in

Most young married couples have two close friends who live nearby, but among well-educated people, the friendships are rarely permanent. (© Joel Gordon)

front of the television. On the other hand, if Matt has been trying to develop a series of equations to solve a complex engineering problem, he may look forward to playing tennis with a friend or to jogging along the beach.

Although leisure interests and activities in young adulthood are influenced by childhood experiences within families, marriage and parenthood also have their impact on the use of leisure time. Among married adults, leisure time is likely to be spent in joint activities that encourage interaction between husband and wife and the development of shared commitments. As in later years, leisure activities are shaped by occupational choice, family roles, health, available time, financial resources, and personality (Kelly, 1974, 1975). During their thirties, when husbands and wives may be heading at full speed in different directions—men focusing on their careers and women on their families and perhaps on their own careers as well—leisure time spent together is important for sustaining marital and family closeness as well as for expressing personal interests and needs.

As Chad Gordon, Charles Gaitz, and Judith Scott (1976) point out, the most popular leisure activities in young adulthood are centered on home and family: visiting with family and friends, watching TV, gardening, pursuing hobbies, reading, and walking. Younger adults who read as a leisure activity are likely to prefer being amused rather than educated by what they read, and they generally read on diverse topics. The young adult years are often filled with physically strenuous and exhausting activities: fishing, hunting, camping, swimming, skiing, and tennis. At this time, as in later years, men often prefer physical activity and activities away from home, whereas women spend much of their leisure time reading, cooking, and improving their homes.

Young adults do not spend all their leisure in play. Some go back to school, some work in the garden, and others spend long hours practicing musical instruments or developing skills in some sport. What is work to one person, however, may be recreation or play to another. A leisure activity is anything an individual freely chooses to do. It has been estimated that adults today have twice as many free hours as they had in 1900. This extra time means that the kind of leisure activity an adult chooses is becoming more and more important in determining his self-concept and his satisfaction with life.

SUMMARY

1. Early adulthood is a time when individuals are confronted with the tasks of being adult, independent, and self-sufficient, and of becoming mature. Becoming mature in turn means becoming aware of who one is now, of where one wants to go in life, and it means working toward one's goals.

2. In these years an individual typically reaches the peak of physical agility, speed, and strength. Although physical aging begins during these years, its effects generally are not noticed, and are relatively inconsequential for most people.

3. During their twenties, many young adults make choices in such matters as a vocation or marriage, which give them social identity. During their thirties, they turn their attention to deepening and expanding their skills and bases of experience. For some, these years may involve questioning commitments made during the twenties. The way these early adult years are perceived and the kinds of choices that are considered possible are likely to vary depending on an individual's sex, socioeconomic level, and other considerations.

4. Stabilizing, clarifying, and deepening one's identity, self-concept, and self-esteem, rather than radical change, is likely to be the rule during early adulthood.

5. Marriage is a major developmental decision that is often made during early adulthood. Once married, adjustments must be made to new social roles and to living with another person. Once a couple has children, further adjustments must be made. For those who do not choose traditional marriage, other styles of marriage and living, such as singlehood or cohabitation, have become popular.

6. Young adulthood is usually a time of experimentation and expansion in making friends and developing new leisure interests, as well as a time for deepening old interests and friendships. People's friends are likely to live close by and to share similar interests, attitudes, and values, and married individuals' friends are likely to be of the same sex. Young adults may choose either physical or passive recreation and play, but, whatever its form, leisure activity usually remains important as a way to use up surplus energy and to meet one's needs for relaxation, creativity, and self-expression.

CHAPTER 21

Middle Adulthood: Making the Most of It

MATURITY IN MIDDLE ADULTHOOD

PHYSICAL CHANGES

NEW DEVELOPMENTAL TASKS

IDENTITY AND INTERPERSONAL BEHAVIOR
Self-concept and Self-esteem
Changes in Sexuality
Intellectual Skills

MARRIAGE AND FAMILY LIFE
Parental and Postparental Life
Divorce and Remarriage

ALTERNATIVES TO MARRIAGE

SOCIAL-LIFE CHANGES

SUMMARY

Our uncertainty about middle age is reflected in the jokes we tell. For example, the middle-aged woman is sometimes a common object of humor: "Middle age is when a woman's youth changes from present tense to pretense" and "Forty is when a man doesn't have to climb a mountain just because it's there." In our society youth is often regarded as the most promising time of life, and many young people seem to feel that, once they reach forty, they may as well find a rocking chair in which to spend their remaining days.

Although our society may be oriented toward youth, it is controlled by the middle-aged adult. In fact, the term "the Command Generation" has been coined to describe middle age and the position of the forty- to sixty-year-old in American society. Middle-aged adults like Lauren and Matt are now likely to be in charge of and responsible not only for themselves but also for the young and the old. The advantage of all this responsibility is that it brings rewards in terms of power, prestige, and money. If for everything there is a season, and if young adulthood is a time to plant, then middle adulthood is the time to harvest what has been planted. The middle adult years are likely to be a period of both maximum productivity and maximum rewards.

One change that marks the middle adult years is that chronological age no longer is the positive marker that it was at an earlier age, when growing older meant becoming bigger, smarter, and more powerful. Instead of marking change and progress with chronological age, middle-aged people typically use their positions within various life contexts: self, career, family, community. In this chapter we will examine what it means to be middle-aged and will focus on those characteristics of middle age that differentiate it from other periods of development. After discussing the meaning of maturity in middle adulthood, we will look at the physical changes that affect the middle-aged person and the new developmental tasks that must be confronted. We will note that, although people's self-concepts are likely to remain stable, they may think they have changed greatly. We will find that, as their children leave home, parents must make adjustments in their family life and many look forward to grandparenthood. Finally, we will examine social life in the middle years and see that friendship and leisure patterns also change.

MATURITY IN MIDDLE ADULTHOOD

Maturity was defined in Chapter 20 as the ability to deal successfully with the changing tasks and responsibilities of adulthood. Thus, a mature individual in the middle adult years is usually seen as one who accepts and adjusts to the new demands of these years. Having learned to handle demands to change in childhood, adolescence, and young adulthood, middle-aged people generally have a substantial and effective set of strategies for dealing successfully with the stresses and complexities that now confront them.

As noted in the last chapter, a mature individual also can be seen as one who achieves a fairly close fit between the way that he sees himself, the way that he would ideally like to be, and the way that he thinks others see him. In the middle years, then, maturity involves being aware of and realistic about the changes occurring inside and outside oneself and about one's ideals and goals in life.

Men and women generally become aware of middle age for different reasons. As Bernice Neugarten (1968) has suggested, women tend to define their place in the life cycle by events within the family. For a married woman, middle age is closely linked to the time that she sends her children out into the adult world. An unmarried woman is likely to become aware of middle age as she begins to reflect on the kind of family she might have had. Men, by contrast, are more likely to become aware of middle age because of cues outside the family setting. For example, a man may find himself deferred to or ceremoniously treated by others for the first time in his life. Because middle age is generally thought of as the time of achieving occupational goals, men who have not succeeded in line with their expectations are likely to have a heightened awareness of middle age (Kay, 1974).

An individual's social class also has an important influence on his or her awareness of middle age (Neugarten and Hagestad, 1976). Middle age typically occurs later for middle-class men and women than for working-class people. An upper-middle-class man, say a business executive, is "in the prime of life" at forty and considers middle age as beginning around fifty. By contrast, life goes more quickly for the blue-collar worker. To the working class, people are "in their prime" at thirty-five and middle-aged at forty (Neugarten and Peterson, 1957).

Middle age is also often marked by a change in life values and in the way that time is perceived. Instead of looking at life in terms of time-since-birth, as the young generally do, most individuals begin to look at life in terms of time-left-to-live. Generally, an awareness grows that time is finite, that there is only a certain amount of time left. Instead of taking the youthful view that anything is possible, middle-aged people generally begin to structure their lives, their ideals, and their aspirations in terms of priorities.

Maturity in the middle adult years also refers to the individual's ability to deal effectively with the complexities and competing demands typical of middle-aged life. The mature individual usually has developed strategies that allow him to respond effectively to stress and change and to make judgments and decisions (Birren, 1969; Neugarten, 1968). For example, adults often find that they have too much to do and not enough time to do it. A young adult in this situation, even a mature one, is likely to get bogged down intellectually and emotionally. The mature individual in the middle years, however, seems to know when to pull back. David is more likely to be aware of the signs that tell him he is doing too much: the headaches, the stomachaches, the quick temper, the fact that nothing looks good to eat. A mature person is likely to say, "I cool myself down by accepting the fact that other people around me have to do their own learning and make their own mistakes. I stand back and simply don't let my insides get as involved as they used to . . ." (Birren, 1975). Thus, one strategy that mature individuals use is to be less emotionally involved in a stressful situation.

Maturity in middle age also tends to be characterized by a sense of self-confidence and competence. This I-know-I-can-handle-it attitude helps individuals deal effectively with the demands and events in their lives. Because expectations are important in determining the outcome of events, the person who feels that he can respond successfully increases the chances that he will. Mature individuals are characteristically less self-conscious about the impression that they are making on others, more sensitive to their strengths as well as their limitations, and more confident about their ability to control and direct their lives than they were when they were younger.

PHYSICAL CHANGES

Adolescents look forward to the social strength and power that adulthood brings, but middle-aged adults begin to look backward, wishing they could recapture their youthful appearance and vigor (Nowak, 1977). The middle adult years are characterized by noticeable changes in the way the body looks and works. All those little changes that began in early adulthood progress steadily. Muscles do not work as strongly, as quickly, or as long as they used to. A less active life results in morning aches and pains and in middle-aged spread. The skin no longer stretches so tightly over the body, the face has a few wrinkles, and laugh lines lurk at the corners of the eyes. The hair does not grow as fast as it once did, and it may become thinner and begin to gray.

However, middle-aged declines in muscle strength and speed of reaction are likely to be of only marginal significance in a person's everyday life. Middle-aged people are not likely to be bothered much by these losses, because they have learned to compensate for them (Belbin, 1967). That is, a person learns to pay attention to the features of a task in order to determine what he must do to maintain or even improve his performance in view of his changing physical abilities. He begins to carry only two bags of groceries at a time instead of four, and at work he tries to avoid jobs where speed is an important factor and instead looks for jobs where he can go at his own speed.

Among women, menopause is the medical marker of middle age. During menopause, which typically occurs between the ages of forty-five and fifty-five, ovulation, menstruation, and reproductive capacity cease. With menopause, the body's production of the sex hormones estrogen and progesterone drops off to a negligible level. Until recently, estrogen, or hormone-replacement, therapy was being used by many women in an attempt to eliminate such menopausal symptoms as hot flashes, loss of hair, loss of skin elasticity, and changes in the breasts and genitals. Although estrogen therapy increases the physical comfort of

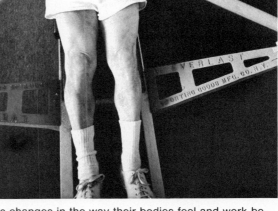

As changes in the way their bodies feel and work become noticeable to middle-aged adults, many turn to exercise in a conscious attempt to retard aging. (Ken Heyman)

menopausal and postmenopausal women, recent studies have shown that it also increases women's risk of developing uterine cancer (Finch and Flurkey, 1977). As a result, estrogen therapy is becoming less common. Among men there is no known similar abrupt cessation of reproductive ability. Instead, the level of the male hormone testosterone drops off gradually during the middle years in some men. In the later middle years, sperm are not produced as quickly and fewer sperm are viable.

During middle age, many people, especially men, tend to become concerned about their health. The most common major disorders in otherwise healthy middle-aged Americans are overweight (16 percent), hypertension (8 percent), and arthritis (4 percent) (Weg, 1975). The death rate also begins to accelerate in the middle adult years, especially among individuals in their late fifties. The most common cause of death in these years is cardiovascular disease; the second most common cause of death is cancer; and the third, hypertension (American Heart Association, 1977).

There are, however, great individual differences in the rates of aging and in the way that people age. One can easily say that a woman looks young for her age or old for her age. In addition, not all physical changes that people connect with middle age are either necessary or due to the normal processes of aging; some may be due to pathology, others, to disuse. There are, of course, a number of things that an individual can do to decrease his susceptibility to the common changes of middle age (Weg, 1975). For example, good nutrition, exercise, avoiding cigarettes and too much di-

rect sunlight, and minimizing emotional stress can retard or eliminate many of the expected changes in health and appearance.

Because American society stresses the importance of a youthful appearance, especially for women, making fading men and women feel, think, and look young again is big business. For those who can afford it, cosmetic surgery, health spas, gymnasiums, and weight-control centers offer youthful rejuvenation. Make-up techniques, hair creams and dyes, treatments for balding, wigs, ointments and creams, and vitamin therapies all promise to make the middle-aged look young again.

With all the emphasis on looking and feeling young, it would seem likely that middle-aged men and women, who no longer look or feel as young as they used to, would be less happy about themselves and their physical appearance than younger adults. Generally, however, people over forty-five report just as much overall happiness with their bodies as people under forty-five (Berscheid, Walster, and Bohrnstedt, 1973). Facial attractiveness does become a central concern for women. Carol Nowak (1977) found that middle-aged women are more concerned with their facial appearance than are older or younger women, and are more likely to see the traces of aging as affecting their general attractiveness. Physical appearance tends to be less important for men; both men and women report that age enhances a man's attractiveness.

NEW DEVELOPMENTAL TASKS

Being middle-aged means being part of the age group that runs society and therefore means being in power, in command, and responsible. The middle years are characterized by a concern with expanding and asserting one's adulthood and, perhaps, with developing a new way of life. The developmental tasks unique to these years include maintaining oneself as an effective worker, which may involve additional schooling or retraining; continuing to relate to one's spouse; assisting teenage children to become responsible adults; relating to aging parents and parents-in-law; establishing and maintaining an economic standard of living congruent with needs; achieving adult civic and social responsibility; maintaining friendships and social ties; and sustaining and developing leisure activities (Havighurst, 1972).

Whereas the twenties are a time for making

Paul Gauguin, who in 1883 switched from stockbroker to painter, is a famous example of a radical career change that may come when an adult realizes that life will end. (New York Public Library)

commitments and achieving intimacy, and the thirties a time for deepening commitments and furthering one's career, the forties and fifties are a time for reevaluating the past and for achieving Erikson's state of generativity. As we saw in Chapter 18, during adolescence a person engages in introspection and tries to find a sense of personal identity. During the middle years, there is a return to introspection in an attempt to reassess commitments and goals and to develop increased self-awareness. Daniel Levinson and his associates (1978) have called the early forties a period of "mid-life transition" and suggest that self-evaluation occurs whether or not one achieves one's life goals. The central issue in this period is discovering "what it is I really want."

Individuals now become aware that their future is finite. Roger Gould (1972) found that, beginning in the late thirties and clearly in the middle years, people develop an increasing sense of not having enough time to do most of the things they want to do. One task of the middle years, then, is to deal with the realization that life will end. The acceptance that one's remaining time is short leads many people to restructure their lives in terms of their priorities. For some, this may mean becoming more realistic about their goals. In his interviews with more than 500 white, middle-class people, Gould found that, beginning in the forties, men and women increasingly agree that "I try to be satisfied with what I have and not to think so much about the things I probably won't be able to get." Middle-aged people also increasingly feel that "It's too late to make any major change in my career," that "Life doesn't change much from year to year," and that "My personality is pretty well set."

Becoming more realistic about goals doesn't mean being resigned or giving up dreams. For some individuals, the realization that life will end leads them to make a radical change in the time they have left. Some may try to make old dreams come true. Others, realizing that old dreams no longer offer satisfaction, may develop new ones. A scientist may shift to a radically different area of research; a businessman may enter the priesthood; an executive may sell a thriving company or give up a successful career to go back to school, to get into another line of work, or to travel. A woman who has devoted herself to her family may develop a career, become active in a service organization, get a divorce, or go back to school.

The middle years are also the years when individuals become increasingly concerned for the growth and development of others. Erikson's stage of generativity, which characterizes the middle years, involves wanting to care for others and becoming more concerned for their productivity. For some, generativity may be achieved by helping children grow into independent, capable, competent, and loving adults. For others, it may mean helping younger workers become successful and competent in their jobs.

Additional tasks in the middle years include adjusting to new family roles. Adults are likely to assume the responsibility of being the child of aging parents and the task of establishing new boundaries of authority between themselves, their parents, and their children. Men and women face

In recent years, women have also realized that the middle years may be the last chance they have to realize their dreams. (Suzanne Szasz)

different tasks. Many women now begin to prepare themselves for the deaths of their husbands, and many men face illness and increasing problems with their health (Neugarten, 1977). Once the children have left home, men are concerned with work-related problems, whereas their wives tend to concern themselves with their adult children and their own personal growth.

Although there may be a personal turmoil in the middle years, they are a fairly stable period in terms of an individual's identity, coping capacities, influence, and productivity. If people can resolve their own uncertainties about their past and future, life is likely to become mellow. During the fifties, according to Roger Gould (1972), parents are no longer seen as the cause of one's problems, one's children become potential sources of warmth and satisfaction, one's spouse provides valued companionship, an increased desire for friendships develops, and one develops increasing self-acceptance.

Other tasks that generally have to be dealt with during the fifties are the accelerating changes in body appearance and health described earlier, as well as changes in feelings of sexual potency and in sexual relationships. As William Masters and Virginia Johnson (1974) note, this decade is characteristically a time of tenderness, contentment, and tranquility in sexual relationships, and some individuals find this change disturbing when compared with the sexual fires of youth.

As at any age, approaching developmental tasks successfully in middle adulthood can sometimes be quite different from handling them successfully. For example, an adult may achieve occupational success in the middle years but may be unable to deal with that success. Some people turn to alcohol just at the moment of success and ruin what they had worked so hard and long to achieve. Others who had been successful at finding a spouse find that their marriage falls apart once the children are gone.

IDENTITY AND INTERPERSONAL BEHAVIOR

Understandably, the way that an individual characteristically responds to life's changes and challenges and to success and failure affects his or her sense of identity. Successful middle-aged adults are likely to show both continuity and change in their sense of self. As new occupational and family roles are assumed, they incorporate these new aspects of themselves into their identities. For example, when David at last starts his own business after twenty years of working for others, he will have a new image of himself as an entrepreneur. On the other hand, people's sense of who they are guides their life choices and decisions, and most individuals behave in ways that maintain their sense of self. If Susan views herself as having an eye for color and design, she is more likely to look for a job as an interior decorator than as a plumber.

Self-concept and Self-esteem

As individuals move into middle adulthood, they are likely to feel that they have changed greatly over the years, but studies indicate that large changes are uncommon. For example, Diana Woodruff and James Birren (1972) asked a group of middle-aged people who had taken a personality test as young adults to fill out this same test again but to answer it twice: once to describe themselves now and once to duplicate the way that they thought they had answered it twenty-five years before. There was almost no real change between their scores as young adults and their scores in middle age. That is, they described themselves in young adulthood and in middle age in almost the same terms.

However, the second test, in which middle-aged adults gave retrospective pictures of their adolescent selves, tended to be relatively negative; they viewed their past selves as much less competent and as handling life less well than they actually had as adolescents. These adults generally experienced a subjective, but apparently nonexistent, discontinuity between their adolescent and adult views of themselves. These results suggest that, as they grew older, this group of adults may have manufactured a kind of identity gap.

The sense of self-control and confidence that grows in the twenties and thirties continues to increase during the forties. George Vaillant (1977) found that men in their forties tend to use more mature strategies in coping with personal problems and to assume greater responsibility for them than they did as adolescents and young adults. They also show a more realistic sense of their strengths and weaknesses. Instead of assuming the young adult's attitude of "I can handle anything" or "I want to do it all myself," middle-aged adults have

The middle years are a stable period for many; adults whose jobs give them control over people or machines are especially likely to have positive self-concepts. (*left:* Joel Gordon; *right:* Leo Choplin/Black Star)

a growing awareness that other people can be relied on for valuable advice and help.

In a study of over 300 middle-aged men and women in North Carolina, Vira Kivett, Allen Watson, and Christian Busch (1977) found that individuals who have positive self-concepts and who see themselves as active, optimistic, and autonomous feel that they are in control of their lives. This is especially true of men and women whose jobs give them control over people or machines or who find a personal meaning in religion. By contrast, people who are laborers or service workers, who have high ideal self-concepts, or who use religion for status or prestige are more likely to feel at the mercy of their environment.

Some time in the middle years, perhaps when one realizes that life is finite, one's sense of mastery over the environment often shifts. As was discussed in Chapter 20, young adults tend to feel confident that they can get what they want by their own actions, and they believe that boldness and risk taking bring rewards. At some point in midlife, according to David Gutmann (1975) and Bernice Neugarten (1964), people start to focus on thoughts and feelings instead of on actions and events and begin to be less confident that they can control their lives by their own actions.

As in young adulthood, men are more likely than women to have a sense of mastery over the direction their lives take (Palmore and Luikart, 1972). The sex roles people learn as children continue to influence their self-concepts and their concepts of the other sex. Although the historical period in which men and women live certainly influences their concepts of masculinity and femininity, David Gutmann (1975) has suggested that the experience of parenthood encourages the development of traditional sex differences. Feeling the weight of parenthood, middle-aged men are likely to take responsibility for protecting and providing for the family, whereas women are likely to be the social directors for their families, allowing their interpersonal skills to develop.

A person's self-esteem continues to increase into the middle years; middle-aged men and women, however, are likely to look to different sources for a sense of self-worth and self-esteem (Bardwick, 1971). Men are likely to continue to see themselves as being worthy or unworthy in terms of their careers or work achievements. By contrast, Florence Livson (1977) has identified two kinds of married women who function successfully during their fifties. Both had developed stable personality styles by adolescence, but each followed a different path of psychological development. At fifty, the "traditional" women are conventional, sociable, and nurturing; they are wives and mothers and move easily into middle age, finding satisfaction in interpersonal relationships even as their children grow up and away. The "independent" women at fifty are intellectual, achievement-oriented, and unconventional; they have been doers, not socializers, from adolescence. As forty-year-old wives and mothers, they are depressed and irritable, but by fifty, their crises are resolved. Their children leave home and relieve them of the mothering role, allowing them to revive their intellectual and career interests.

Changes in Sexuality

Until middle age, the relationship of a woman's youthful beauty or a man's strength and virility to sexual ability is taken for granted. Consequently, as youthful beauty and strength fade, many men and women begin to question their ability and adequacy in sexual performance (I. Rubin, 1968). Telling middle-aged people that youthful beauty and strength have little, if any, relationship to sexual ability or to the ability to give and receive sexual pleasure does not stop them from worrying about it.

Historically, menopause has always been thought of as the time when a woman loses not only her ability to reproduce but her sex drive and her femininity as well. Myths about the relationship of menopause to sexuality saturate our society. Old wives' tales warn: "After menopause a woman is no longer a woman," "Menopause makes women crazy," or "Menopause marks the end of a woman's sexual desires and sexual attractiveness." The reality of menopause is altogether different. One survey of 500 women (Boston Women's Health Book Collective, 1977) found that whereas younger women are likely to be fearful and negative about menopause, middle-aged women, who have actually experienced it, are more positive and matter-of-fact.

The best thing about menopause, as most middle-aged women see it, is that they no longer have to worry about getting pregnant or about menstruation. Many women also report that their relationships with their husbands improve. Most middle-aged women feel that menopause has no effect on sexual relations, and some report that sexual relations become more important and more enjoyable (Neugarten et al., 1963). Postmenopausal women typically feel better, more confident, calmer, and freer than before. Thus, from a developmental standpoint, menopause is far from being "the change of life." Most middle-aged women do not see menopause as creating a major discontinuity in their lives. Instead, they feel that "You get what you are looking for." Women who expect to have difficulty during menopause are likely to experience uncomfortable symptoms. But most middle-aged women tend to view menopause as a temporarily unpleasant period that is followed by a period of being happier and healthier.

Psychologically, a man's sexuality is more likely to be affected by age than a woman's. Changes in health, strength, appearance, and sexual responsiveness may threaten a man's sense of himself as "virile" or "manly." As we have seen, there are real changes in strength and appearance in the middle years. There are also real changes in sexual response. Men are slower to be aroused, slower to climax, and do not necessarily feel the urge to climax at every sexual encounter. Middle-aged men find that they need more direct stimulation to become aroused and that, after a climax, they require more time before they can become aroused again. These changes in sexual response in the middle years affect the nature of sexual experiences but do not make sexuality less pleasurable. According to Masters and Johnson (1970), how well a man copes with changes in his sexual responsiveness depends not only on his general ability to adapt to changes in his life but also on his past sexual relationships, his attitude toward aging, and his self-concept.

Thus, the loss of sexual responsiveness is likely to be due to psychological factors, not physiological ones. Nevertheless, the incidence of sexual inadequacy in the human male increases sharply

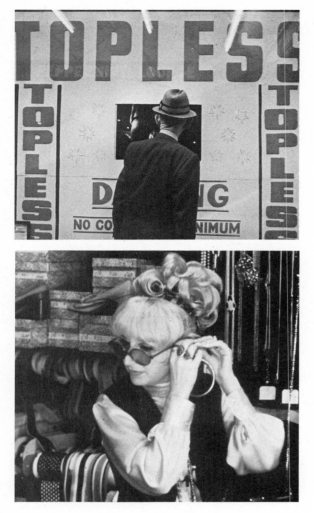

after the age of fifty. According to Masters and Johnson (1974) the single most important factor in reduced sexual responsiveness among middle-aged men appears to be the monotony of a repetitious sexual relationship. Other factors that may have a negative effect on a man's sexual responsiveness are preoccupation with his career or with economic pursuits, mental or physical fatigue, overindulgence in food or drink, or "fear of failure." In general, however, the richer and the more regular a man's sexual life has been, the more likely it is that his sexual interest and activity will be maintained throughout the middle years.

Intellectual Skills

Many middle-aged men and women fear the loss of their mental abilities. Often their memory for little things does not seem to be as good as it once was. It sometimes takes them longer to finish a task or solve a problem because they become distracted. As we will see, these common changes in intellectual skills are no reason for a person to believe that his mind is slipping.

Instead, if one is healthy, one's verbal and reasoning skills are likely to get even better. For example, individuals continue to store new information just as they always have. In fact, there may be considerable increases in a person's vocabulary during middle age (Birren, 1976). An individual's ability to organize and process visual information, as in finding a simple figure in a complex one, also improves in middle adulthood. In addition, the ability to think flexibly, to shift the set of one's mind to solve a particular problem, is likely to be as good as it was in early adulthood. Only when an individual is asked to do a task that involves coordinated eye-hand movements does he or she tend to do less well than before. Overall, this means that people are likely to show no change or even an improvement in their intellectual abilities and information skills into middle age, although some of their nonverbal skills may not be as good as they once were (Botwinick, 1977). If successful performance depends on speed, middle-aged David will probably do worse than a younger person. However, this poor performance is likely to be

Although middle-aged adults may at times doubt their sexual attractiveness or worry about fulfillment, sexual interest and expression remain stable and enjoyable. (*top:* Charles Gatewood; *center:* Steve McCarroll; *bottom:* Kirk Breedlove/Photophile)

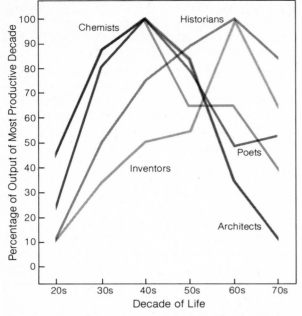

Figure 21.1   Productivity for certain professions, expressed as a percentage of the output of the most productive decade (designated as 100 percent). Poets, architects, and chemists usually achieve maximum professional productivity during their forties, whereas inventors and historians do so during their sixties. The data summarized here should be considered illustrative, because the subjects were not uniform in degree of eminence. Also, the units of productivity (for example, a sonnet versus a history of Rome) are not equivalent. (After Dennis, 1966)

do about as well as younger adults. Again, health, education, and individual differences make a difference. In addition, how motivated an individual is to learn or remember, how interesting or meaningful the information is, how supportive the environment is, and how much recent educational experience he or she has had are likely to be more important than age in affecting learning and memory abilities.

Many people presume that middle-aged adults are somehow more rigid than younger adults. They believe that a middle-aged person holds a particular point of view and resists change when the situation calls for it. This assumption appears to be strengthened by the finding that a person over fifty-five is more likely to agree with clichés than younger adults and adolescents are (Riegel and Riegel, 1960). However, what appears to be a rigid approach to problem solving is less likely to be due to a "rigid" or "cautious" attitude than to the way that the middle-aged adult's abilities have been affected by past experiences. For example, a middle-aged adult tends to solve problems and to think as well as a younger adult, but his or her greater number of past associations and experiences may interfere with how flexibly he or she solves problems. In addition, well-established ways of solving problems, which tend to look rigid in laboratory-test situations, may serve individuals well as they confront the problems of everyday life.

The ability to be creative also does not belong solely to youth. Adults in their middle years are often equally creative. In fact, when creativity is examined in terms of total productivity, rather than in terms of quality, creativity peaks in the middle and later years. For example, the decade of the forties is generally the most productive period of life in the humanities, sciences, and arts (Dennis, 1966). Although an individual's productivity in the arts declines somewhat during the middle years, the productivity of persons working in the sciences and humanities remains fairly stable. The earlier decline in productivity in the arts is likely to be due in part to the fact that scholarly or scientific creativity requires more time and a greater amount of study than artistic genius does.

due more to his relatively slower responses than to any changes in his intellectual abilities.

Differences in intellectual functioning among people also are likely to become even more marked throughout middle adulthood. Thus, individuals who were high in intellectual skills in their younger years are likely to become even more skilled. As in young adulthood, the amount of education that one has had, his social class, his health, how active he is, and how stimulating his current environment is are likely to be more important than age in determining just how well or how poorly he functions intellectually.

Despite the fact that many middle-aged people believe that their memory is not as good as it was and fear that they cannot learn new skills as easily as they used to, a person's ability to remember and to learn shows little decline in middle age. If middle-aged individuals are given as much time as they need to learn or remember, they are likely to

MARRIAGE AND FAMILY LIFE

The life cycle of the family began in the early adult years with marriage followed by a time of bearing and rearing children. Now, as Susan and her husband enter their middle years, they face the tasks of relating to adolescent children, encouraging them to become independent and responsible adults, and adjusting to being alone together once the children have left home. As Evelyn Duvall (1971) points out, in many ways the family cycle resembles the life cycle of individual development. In each phase of the family cycle, changes occur that require individuals to adjust to new roles and to develop new ways of seeing themselves in the context of changing interpersonal relationships.

Historically, the postparental period of family life is new. At the turn of the century it was rare for both parents to live to see their last child marry and leave home. Today, because people are living longer and having smaller families, marital partners can expect to have a life together for a decade or two after their children leave home. On the average, men are fifty-four and women are fifty-one when their last child is married for the first time (Norton, 1974). This postparental period is characterized by its own unique set of psychological and social challenges.

Parental and Postparental Life

The middle years of parental and married life are a time of both relative stability and considerable stress. Although couples are less likely to divorce after twenty years of marriage, their satisfaction with marriage often continues to decline until their children are grown. Adolescent children are likely to put a considerable emotional and financial strain on the marital relationship. In a study of over 800 married couples, Boyd Rollings and Harold Feldman (1970) found that marital satisfaction, especially for women, decreased during the early adult years of childbearing and child-rearing and reached its lowest point just before adolescent sons and daughters left home for good. Couples in midlife generally report less communication, companionship, and affection than in their early years of marriage.

Although many couples experience this disenchantment with love and marriage, not all do. Middle-aged couples who have never considered divorce fall into several kinds of relationships (Cuber and Harroff, 1965). On the negative side, some marriages are characterized by continual tension and others by unsatisfying relationships between people with happy memories of their early years together. A third group of couples expect little from their relationship and get their satisfaction from material possessions and children. But a considerable proportion of marriages are highly satisfying and are characterized by genuine sharing, companionship, and affection.

The majority of middle-aged couples find themselves entering a new era of freedom: freedom from financial responsibilities, freedom to be mobile, freedom from household responsibilities and chores, and freedom to be the people they want to be (Deutscher, 1968). Most couples also report that, once their children are gone, they laugh more together, they have more calm discussions, they have more stimulating discussions, and they work together more often on projects. Wives, especially, are likely to feel much more satisfied with their marriage once the children have left home. Apparently companionship in the relationship, which tends to be reduced when children are growing up, is critical to a woman's satisfaction with her marriage.

Although the newly childless home presents an important transition point in the lives of middle-aged men and women, it does not mark the end of family involvement; instead, involvement with sons and daughters enters a new phase.

Parenthood Family conflicts are inevitable between generations because each generation is at a different point in its developmental agenda and has different developmental tasks to face. Middle-aged parents and their almost-grown children often find themselves arguing over their changing roles and relationships, their various responsibilities, the children's striving for autonomy, and what the parents may see as a disintegration of family ties. The adolescent's search for identity and independence is not only a developmental issue for an adolescent, but is also a developmental issue for his middle-aged parents. Parents must deal with the task of letting their children go. This can be an especially difficult issue for a mother who has defined her own identity in terms of her parental role. Some women are reluctant to encourage their offspring to leave home and become autonomous because, once the grown children are gone, the women will have to redefine themselves. The transition to postparental life, however, is neither as abrupt nor as difficult as it generally is thought to be. Most parents gradually prepare for the day when their offspring get married or leave home to live by themselves. In fact, preparing for

Parents who prepare in advance for the time when their grown children leave find the transition to a childless home is eased. (Ken Heyman)

and anticipating postparental life is the most stressful point in the marriage relationship. By the time the event arrives, many parents have already handled the problem.

Parents prepare themselves in a number of ways. First, an important American value, the belief that change is both inevitable and good, lessens the impact of this transition. As one father put it: "Of course you hate to give up your daughter, but I think we all understand that it is the way of life. You can't stand still; you can't be the same forever. Life moves on and that is the more natural thing" (Deutscher, 1973). Second, middle-class parents often have a chance to "try on" the postparental role when their sons and daughters leave home for college. Other parents get an opportunity to try out what life alone together will be like when their son or daughter goes into military service. College and the military not only wean young adults away from their parents, but also wean par-

ents away from their offspring. Finally, in some families, young people spend so little time at home that the adjustment to postparental life is gradual.

The transition to the childless home is likely to be easier for women who perceive their sons and daughters as "on time" in such developmental events as college entrance and marriage. If a woman thinks that her offspring are well on the way to being educated, married, and fully developed as individuals, she is likely to feel free to pursue goals for herself. As Donald Spence and Thomas Lonner (1971) note, this means that the fewer long-range goals a mother has for her offspring, the sooner she will perceive herself as having completed the parental phase of her life. Fathers, especially those who work long hours, who are heavily involved in their careers, or who travel extensively, are likely to find the transition less difficult than mothers. Thus, parents who are aware of their periodic opportunities to experience what postparental life will be like and who take full advantage of them will find it easier to be alone with each other.

When the young adult leaves home, the parent-child bond does not end. In fact, young adults are likely to be in contact with their parents more often than with their siblings (Adams, 1970). Middle-aged parents also are likely to continue giving financial and emotional support to their grown children. If the two generations live near each other, parents often provide direct services to their children, shopping, baby-sitting, or caring for sick family members.

Relating to Aging Parents Middle-aged adults often find themselves responsible for two generations. They have their own children to care for, and they also may become responsible for their aging parents.

One of the major developmental tasks that is likely to confront middle-aged Matt and his sister Susan is becoming a parent to their own parents. Just as children and adolescents call on their middle-aged parents in time of need, aging parents are more likely to call on their middle-aged children than on anyone else. Marvin Sussman and Lee Burchinal (1968) note that the help middle-aged adult children give to their aging parents varies from economic support to personal care; from help with transportation to sharing of outings and holidays; from gifts of money and food to help with housekeeping and home chores. In general, research indicates that the relationship between a middle-aged adult and his or her aging parent is generally most satisfactory when it is characterized by independence and friendship rather than by dependence and authority (Adams, 1970).

When an aging parent faces disabling health problems, financial difficulties, or very old age, living alone may become difficult or impossible. The middle-aged child may be forced to choose between bringing a parent into his or her own home or putting the parent into a home for the aged. This decision involves both the child's and the parent's desires and the child's ability to provide adequate care for the parent. Although Susan may feel it is her "duty" to take care of her mother, who has suffered a disabling stroke, her mother may not wish to move in with her and Susan may not be able to provide the care her mother needs.

In this developmental task, as in all others, individuals have their own styles of meeting the problems that arise. For example, the ability of middle-aged adults to adjust to having an aging parent living in their home depends greatly on the middle-aged adult's expectations and feelings about whether this adjustment will be easy or difficult.

Grandparenthood Today, more parents are becoming grandparents during middle adulthood. The younger grandparent is likely to be working and married, and to have more money to spend as well as more leisure time. He or she may, therefore, find grandparenthood especially enjoyable. However, individuals differ in the amount of satisfaction that they derive from being grandparents. Also, depending on the individual, the meaning of being a grandparent will be different, as will his or her style of relating to grandchildren.

When Bernice Neugarten and Karol Weinstein (1968) asked a group of seventy grandparents how satisfied they were with that role, most expressed comfort, satisfaction, and pleasure. As few as one-third reported that the experience of being a

Most people find comfort, satisfaction, and pleasure in grandparenthood; the younger, working grandparent may find the experience especially enjoyable. (Ken Heyman)

grandparent brought them discomfort, disappointment, or lack of positive reward. When asked what being a grandparent meant to them, some said that they felt a sense of biological renewal ("It's through my grandchildren that I feel young again") or biological continuity with future generations. This aspect of grandparenthood tended to be more important for grandmothers than for grandfathers.

Some also found that grandparenthood provided emotional self-fulfillment in a way that being a parent did not. This aspect of grandparenthood is likely to be especially important for men, who feel that they are better grandfathers than they were fathers. Being a grandparent meant being a teacher or a resource person to some individuals. In this role grandparents were likely to see themselves as contributing to their grandchild's welfare by giving money or emotional support. Some people regarded grandparenthood as an extension of the self, so that the grandchild was expected to accomplish what the grandparent always dreamed of accomplishing.

Finally, there were some grandparents for whom the existence of grandchildren had little meaning or effect on their lives. These grandparents tended to feel a psychological distance from their grandchildren. Sometimes the distance developed because they were too busy themselves to cultivate the relationship; at other times it was because they disapproved of their own child's marriage or the younger couple's decision to have a child. Some grandparents who reported a psychological distance, however, said that it was physical distance that minimized the meaning of grandparenthood.

Neugarten and Weinstein further note that, beyond the meaning that individuals attribute to grandparenthood, grandparents find a variety of ways of relating to their grandchildren. There are three fairly traditional "styles" of being a grandparent. One is the formal kind of grandparent, who tends to leave the role of parent to the child's parent but who likes to offer special treats. The second type, the surrogate parent, typically a grandmother, takes care of the child at the parent's request and is most likely to be found in a home where the mother works. The third kind of traditional grandparent becomes the reservoir of family wisdom and sees himself or herself as being in authority and as teaching special skills. There are also two less traditional ways in which grandparents can relate to grandchildren. The fun-seeker is the grandparent who plays with the child simply to have fun. This style of grandparenthood is informal, and both the grandparent and the grandchild derive pleasure from the relationship. The distant-figure style characterizes the grandparent who relates to the child only on special occasions such as birthdays or religious holidays. These less traditional styles of grandparenthood occur more often today than in the past and are more commonly found among younger grandparents, whereas older grandparents are likely to adopt one of the three traditional styles.

Divorce and Remarriage

Some middle-aged couples wait until their children grow up and leave home and then end their marriage. Although the divorce rate is not quite so high in middle adulthood as it is in early adulthood, it remains substantial throughout the years just after the children are likely to have left home (U.S. Bureau of the Census, 1972a). As in the young adult years, the divorce rate is higher for blacks and for low-income individuals without college educations. Less wealthy people are more likely to separate instead of divorce, because separation is not so financially devastating as divorce. In middle age, the demands on the newly divorced individual to adjust and change, as well as the impact of divorce on individual development, are like those faced by the young adult.

Divorce can be especially difficult for middle-aged people. Neither women nor men may have had recent practice in developing new intimate relationships with the opposite sex, and the process is likely to be lengthier and more stressful for them than it is for young adults. A middle-aged woman who has depended on her husband's position for her own identity and for her financial security is likely to find divorce particularly stressful. The recent passage of no-fault divorce laws has led to a trend away from permanent alimony, placing an additional burden on the middle-aged woman who has no job skills or profession.

In middle age, as in the early adult years, most people who get a divorce remarry. The rate of marriage remains higher for divorced men and women than for single persons at any age. The major change in the middle years is that marriage rates among women drop below those for men. That is, whereas in the early adult years women are most likely to remarry, in the middle years it is the men who remarry. This situation comes about partly because death rates for men begin to increase and partly because women traditionally marry older men. The result is that middle-aged women have an increasingly limited pool of marriageable men, whereas men can choose from an expanding group of marriageable women.

ALTERNATIVES TO MARRIAGE

Middle-aged adults are less likely than young adults to adopt a nontraditional way of life as a conscious choice. Some may simply continue the nontraditional lives they adopted years before. A single adult becomes the "never-married" adult of the middle years. Although some would prefer to be married, death or divorce leaves a considerable number of people without partners. Finally, a few middle-aged people actively seek such alternatives to traditional marriage as extramarital relationships.

Most people who marry do so by the time they are forty. Those who stay single may be people who have rejected the idea of marriage or they may have been unable to find permanent partners. Among those who choose not to marry are a number of homosexual men and women. For whatever reason, about 4 to 5 percent of middle-aged men and women have never been married. The unmarried men tend to have lower incomes and occupations than their married counterparts, but never-married women are likely to have good incomes and to be well-educated. This adds to the problem of the single woman who wants to marry, because most people tend to marry people who are like themselves.

Living through the death of a spouse may be more stressful for the middle-aged than for the old, simply because the death occurs "too soon" and has not been anticipated (Neugarten, 1970). Older widows seem to have an easier time adjusting than younger widows because there are more companions available to them. A middle-aged woman who

The death of a spouse is always stressful, but when it occurs in middle age, women feel isolated and have a difficult time adjusting to their single status. (Charles Harbutt/ Magnum Photos)

loses her husband is likely to feel isolated, since most of her friends are occupied with their husbands. But at any age, the death of a spouse is stressful, and for a year or so after the spouse dies, death and suicide rates are substantially higher among the widowed than among married people.

The death of a wife or husband not only ends a man's role as a husband and a woman's role as a wife, but also changes relationships with in-laws, the spouse's friends, friends made as a couple, and even relationships with one's own family and co-workers. The more dependent an individual has been on a spouse, the more life is likely to be disrupted by the partner's death. Like the newly divorced person, the wife finds she is missing a handyman and the husband finds he is without a cook or a housekeeper. Beyond such practical matters is the loss of a friend, companion, or lover and, as we will see in Chapter 22, the sense of personal loss is acutely painful. As among the divorced, widowers have a higher chance of remarriage in middle age than do widows. People who have been widowed, however, are less likely to remarry than are their divorced counterparts.

Although extramarital relationships are becoming increasingly common among young adults (Libby, 1977), not much is known about sexual activity among adults in midlife. The most reliable information regarding middle-aged people comes from Alfred Kinsey (1948, 1953). He found that males in lower socioeconomic classes had the most extramarital intercourse as young adults, and that the frequency of their extramarital relationships dropped off steadily until they reached fifty. College-educated males, on the other hand, were more likely to increase their rate of extramarital response as they became older. Kinsey found no difference related to education among women. It may be that as women increasingly occupy the same kinds of positions in business and industry that were primarily filled by males in 1948, their added prestige, freedom, and money will lead them to adopt the sexual practices of college-educated males.

Extramarital relationships are not necessarily associated with marital unhappiness in midlife. In a study of middle-aged midwestern couples, Ralph Johnson (1970) found that 30 percent of the husbands with extramarital experience and 60 percent of the wives with such experience had high levels of marital adjustment. According to John Cuber

(1969), middle-aged people seek extramarital intimacy for three reasons: to compensate for a disappointing marriage; to cope with long separations from a spouse caused by the demands of one's occupation or by war; or because they believe in an open marriage in which extramarital intimacy is fully sanctioned.

SOCIAL-LIFE CHANGES

Social interaction tends to differ in both type and extent as adults move into their middle years. Adolescents generally use leisure activities to assert their autonomy from parents and to form closely knit groups with their peers. In young adulthood, peer-group involvement loses its intensity and leisure interests and social activities become family centered. Over the adult years of development, individuals tend to become more involved in organizational activities, and they also increase their civic and political participation. For example, middle-aged people are more interested in political issues, are more politically active, and are more likely to vote in national elections than are young adults (Hudson and Binstock, 1976). Throughout the middle adult years, individuals participate actively in politics by making contributions, circulating petitions, and occupying positions of political leadership.

Roger Gould (1972) found that people in their forties and fifties showed an increased interest in organizations and friends. Men and women were most likely to agree that they "like a very active social life" during their forties and that they would "feel lost without [their] friends" during their fifties.

While a married couple's children live at home, the social activities of both mother and father are likely to be determined by their children's activities and friends: Boy Scouts, Campfire Girls, Parent-Teacher Association, Sunday-school teaching, Little League. When their offspring marry, however, parents are free to develop their own circle of friends and leisure activities are likely to become less home centered. Couples are free to spend evenings out, to travel, and to develop their own personal interests. With fewer financial responsibilities, middle-aged individuals may find they have more money to spend on their leisure activities. Understandably, the transition from activities and attachments inside the home to activities

Although the concern for health has led to more joggers and tennis players, most leisure activities during the middle years require less physical activity. (Ken Heyman)

and friendships outside tends to be easier for a woman who develops outside interests and friendships before her offspring leave home (Deutscher, 1973).

In their middle years, adults are more likely to select friends who have similar interests and activities than friends who are their own age. Married couples are likely to have as friends couples who have children close in age to their own; plumbers are likely to have plumbers for friends; divorced people make friends with other divorced people; and newly married middle-aged couples are likely to find friendships with others like themselves. Friendships developed in earlier years are likely to be sustained despite physical separation. When Beth Hess (1972) talked to middle-aged people who had moved within the last five years, she found that they were most likely to name people who lived in their previous communities as their best friends.

A divorced person who remarries finds many new friendships, not only because the spouse has friends but also because married people just tend to have more friends than single people do. On the other hand, middle-aged adults who have never married find that their need for companionship, which a spouse would generally fill, must be met by one or more friends. Thus, most middle-aged women who have never married have a close friend or confidant whom they have traveled and partied with and whom they turn to for help and emotional support.

As a result of various life changes, individuals often have more time on their hands than ever before. David, who never had trouble finding some pleasurable activity to occupy his free time, now has more time to do what he wants to do. Matt, who had been too busy with job or career to develop interests outside of work, finds learning to use leisure a difficult adjustment. Yet Lauren looks at her new leisure as a freedom that challenges her to develop a different, more satisfying life-style.

When Chad Gordon, Charles Gaitz, and Judith Scott (1976) examined the leisure interests of nearly 1,500 men and women who ranged in age from twenty to ninety-four, they found that leisure and recreational activities in the middle adult years tended to require less physical activity. Middle-aged men and women were less likely to participate in activities, jobs, and hobbies that required quick adjustment, produced excitement, and might involve danger. These middle-aged people said they got the most pleasure out of watching sports, discussing important issues, participating in organizations, and improving their homes. Home-bound activities, such as entertaining friends, cooking, and watching television, were enjoyed as much in the middle years as in young adulthood. Men were more likely to use their leisure time for watching sports events and engaging in outdoor activities, whereas women were more likely to use their time for cooking, improving their homes, and going to plays, concerts, or museums.

Thus, a youthful mountain climber like David may become a backpacker in his middle years. A young adult who enjoys hang-gliding or motorcycling may prefer to watch others doing it once he becomes forty. Increasing numbers of middle-class men, however, have become concerned about the effect on their health of sedentary life, and have begun jogging, playing tennis, and engaging in other strenuous activities (De Vries, 1975). Such exercise can be relaxing in addition to increasing physical fitness. Middle-aged Matt may find that watching television or sipping a glass of wine relaxes him after a hard day's work, but he is also likely to note that he feels sleepy. By contrast, after jogging or swimming he is likely to feel more relaxed, but also more alert.

As John Kelly (1972) has pointed out, when one looks closely at various choices of leisure activity, it becomes clear that in most cases recreational activities also are related to work. For example, an auto mechanic may read a copy of *Car and Driver* magazine, a physician may read a medical journal, or an individual might go to school during the evenings to get a better job.

Americans apparently have trouble separating work from recreation and leisure.

This preference for work is deeply rooted in the history of our country and culture and is especially likely to be reflected in the values of middle-class middle-aged men and women. For example, when Eric Pfeiffer and Glenn Davis (1971) asked people if they would still work if they did not have to work for a living, 80 percent of the women and 90 percent of the men said that they would continue to work. Most reported that they got more satisfaction from work than from leisure and that they did not want more free time. The people who had been employed also said that they had had "more fun" lately than those who had not been working. It appears, then, that many middle-aged people have little interest in using their free time for purely recreational activities.

The preferences of middle-aged individuals for certain leisure or recreational activities and for particular ways of life also tend to be related more to social class and to personal adjustment than to age or to sex (Gordon, Gaitz, and Scott, 1976). People in low socioeconomic groups are likely to use their leisure time for relaxing diversions: watching television, visiting their families, pursuing their hobbies, hunting, or fishing. They are especially likely to spend their free time with friends or relatives of the same sex. People in high socioeconomic groups are likely to use their free time to engage in cultural and educational activities: going to plays and concerts, taking active roles in clubs and organizations, traveling, and going to parties. In terms of education and income, the more of each of these that an individual has, the more he tends to participate in activities that are unconnected with his work and the more positively he tends to view leisure. Presumably money frees a person to do what he wants to do where he wants to do it, and education tends to make him aware of more and varied ways of passing his leisure time.

SUMMARY

1. Most people enter middle adulthood with a set of strategies for dealing with the changes, responsibilities, and demands that confront them. A realistic self-awareness is often associated with self-confidence and a sense of competence.

2. Middle adulthood is characterized by noticeable changes in the appearance and functioning of

the body. Whereas menopause is the medical marker of middle age for women, there is no known comparable marker for men. Attention to one's physical appearance may increase in an attempt to maintain a youthful and attractive look; most middle-aged people learn to compensate for any declines or losses in physical abilities.

3. Typically, the developmental tasks of middle adulthood revolve around expanding and affirming one's skills, goals, productivity, and social relationships. For many, it may also require the development of a new way of life as their children grow up and leave home.

4. Many middle-aged people feel they have changed greatly over the years, but research indicates that large changes in one's self-concept or self-esteem are uncommon and that middle adulthood is generally a period of continuity and stability. Although there may be some decline in the frequency of sexual activity and the speed with which intellectual tasks are completed, such changes have little effect on psychological well-being.

5. During the middle adult years, many married couples must face such tasks as encouraging their adolescent children to become adults and caring for aging parents. The postparental years can bring new pleasure and fulfillment (as in becoming a grandparent) or dissatisfaction and disappointment (if there is friction with children or spouse). An increasing number of people are choosing to remain single or to divorce and remarry.

6. As adults move through the middle years, their social life tends to change in both type and extent. Friendship patterns often move from attachments inside the home to activities and friendships outside the family. Individuals tend to become more involved in organizational activities and to increase civic and political participation. Frequently there is also an increase in leisure time, allowing the individual to participate in new activities and to gain new satisfactions.

CHAPTER 22
Later Adulthood: Living Successfully

MATURITY IN LATER ADULTHOOD

PHYSICAL CHANGES

NEW DEVELOPMENTAL TASKS

IDENTITY AND INTERPERSONAL BEHAVIOR
Self-concept and Self-esteem
Sexuality
Intellectual Skills

FAMILY LIFE
Marital Life
Widowhood
Remarriage

ALTERNATIVES TO MARRIAGE

SOCIAL-LIFE CHANGES

SUMMARY

Human development continues into the last years of life. Just as change and development characterize the early and middle adult years, the years after sixty place their own unique demands on the individual to grow, develop, and change. Although Matt is different now from the child, the adolescent, and the adult we have followed throughout this book, he remains the same person, and he continues to develop and change. He has more memories and a longer history than he once did, but he still lives in the present. At seventy-three, Matt's physical abilities are somewhat diminished, but he retains the human capacity and desire to control his environment. He has lost some of those he loved, but he still needs to love and to be loved. His friends are fewer, but he still has the capacity for friendship. He may depend on other people more, but he values his independence.

Until recently, most people never had to worry about later adulthood or about growing old. They simply did not live that long. In the Middle Ages, to be forty was to be old. This new period of life is technology's gift to humankind. Continuous improvements in health care, diet, and the physical environment allow more people to reach their seventies, eighties, and even nineties than ever before. The twentieth century's gift of years is a welcome present to those who learn to manage and exploit them for what they can be. The later years of life can be fantastic or awful, depending on what a person makes of them. Although our society is youth-oriented, the hard facts and figures are that America is graying. Whereas in 1900 only 4 percent of the population of the United States was age sixty-five or older, today 23 million people, or nearly 11 percent of the total American population, are over the age of sixty-five. Although there are 2.5 times as many under sixty-five today as in 1900, there are over 7 times as many over sixty-five (Bouvier, Atlee, and McVeigh, 1977).

In this chapter, we will see that the major developmental tasks of later adulthood are to clarify, deepen, and accept one's own life and to use one's experiences to manage personal change. We will find that some older people are happiest if they keep active, whereas others are happiest if they take a more passive and disengaged approach. We will see that the later years tend to accentuate early- and middle-life characteristics and abilities rather than alter them. We will look at the changes of later life and discover that reasonably healthy older people continue to have a rich sexual life and that the more people use their minds and memories, the better and longer they will be able to think, learn, and remember. An examination of family life will show that the husband's retirement is a major transition point, that the major loss in this period is the death of a spouse, that older people who remarry are generally happy, and that alternative ways of life are not just for the young. We will see that whereas it is harder to remain especially active in later life, most older people are highly interested in world events and seek out relationships with others.

MATURITY IN LATER ADULTHOOD

What growing and being older means to a person in the later years is largely determined by the culture he or she lives in. In Asia, the older people are, the wiser they are thought to be and the more they are respected, esteemed, and listened to by those around them. According to Eastern philosophy, both life and death are part of the life cycle and within human experience. In Western societies, by contrast, death is regarded as being outside of life. Because this culture emphasizes individuality and control in life and because aging and death are outside their control, most people in Western societies are inclined to look at aging and death as an outrage to their existence. Far from believing that older means wiser, we too often think of older as having one foot in the grave.

Many popular stereotypes reinforce our fears about growing older. As Robert Butler and Myrna Lewis (1973) have pointed out, these stereotypes are more myth than reality. One myth is that chronological age determines physical age. However, the saying that one is only as old as one feels has a good deal of truth in it. People who say that they feel young at seventy tend to age more slowly and more gracefully than people who say that they are old at seventy. Another myth is that all older people become senile. In truth, senility has nothing to do with the normal process of development and

aging. Healthy older people still have active, inquiring minds. A third related myth is that older people are unproductive. The fact is that about one-third of older people have some income from employment, and a good number are still active in a variety of civic affairs. A final myth is that older people resist change. However, the ability and willingness to change in later years has more to do with life-long habits and behavior patterns than with age. People who challenged themselves to change and adapt earlier in life will continue to do so in their later years; those who never did still will not.

If we look at a mature person in his later years, we usually find that he is able to accept his own and only life cycle. He may have achieved maturity by achieving "ego integrity," the final stage of Erik Erikson's (1963) theory of development, which is described in Chapter 2. Because the mature individual has had a great deal of experience with change, he knows what to accept, what to oppose, when to sit quietly, and when to fight, and is able to accept his own limitations. As Erikson notes, the mature person is also likely to be one who can accept his or her own death. Failure to achieve integrity may leave the individual in a state of despair; he feels that he would like to live his life over again but that he does not have the time.

A person's expectations about growing older also seem to be important in how successfully one handles the stresses and changes of later life (Birren, 1975). Men who look forward to retirement adjust to it more easily and enjoy it more than men who find the idea distasteful. Those few who look forward to growing older also tend to grow old more gracefully than those who fear old age.

Maturity in later adulthood, as in the middle years, also means relying on others for help. Perhaps more than before, mature individuals are willing to be dependent on others when it is necessary. Hopefulness, as opposed to helplessness, characterizes the mature adult who is living successfully and aging happily. Hope helps mobilize a person's energies and increases the ability to cope with change. When a person feels that all hope is gone, he is likely to lose the will to live. In the later years, the death of a loved one, the sudden loss of power, status, or purpose in life, or the loss of physical abilities can result in death if an individual reacts to the stress with a sense of hopelessness and helplessness (Seligman, 1974). Because Matt

Passing 65 does not mean an end to activity; many people still have years of healthy, vigorous life ahead of them. (Ken Heyman)

continues to hope and to believe that he has some control over the direction of his life, he is not only likely to handle the events of later life successfully but also to live longer.

PHYSICAL CHANGES

To most people, getting older means continuing to lose beauty, strength, and vigor. Although physical changes characterize the entire phase of adulthood, these changes rarely have much effect on a person's everyday life in the early and middle adult years. It is only in later life that the cumulative changes tend to catch up with people and begin to interfere with their everyday effectiveness and their daily patterns and habits (Weg, 1975).

Although there are great individual differences in the rates of aging, most people can estimate an individual's age, give or take a few years, just by looking at him. During later adulthood, the hair turns white and becomes sparse. Whereas hair tends to get thinner on top of the head, it starts to grow for the first time on the chins of older women. The skin loses its natural moisture and elasticity, and it becomes more and more wrinkled. Changes in the structure of the jaw cause the lower part of the face to become shortened and bring the nose, which lengthens as the skin's elasticity decreases, nearer to the chin. Eyelids thicken, and

hollows develop beneath the eyes. As the skeletal structure changes, people in their sixties become shorter. The chests of men and women are no longer as full or as broad as they were thirty years before. Shoulders become narrower, and the pelvis broadens. If they are not exercised, muscles atrophy and joints become stiff, so that a person's strength and movement become impaired. The dense part of the bone becomes spongy and fragile, so that bones break more easily in the later years.

Other changes also take place inside the older adult's body. Although these changes have little or no effect on appearance, they have a profound effect on the older person's ability to function and to adapt to stress and change. Although the heart works as well as it ever did when people are resting, when they are exposed to stress, as during exercise or an emotional upset, their hearts will not react as fast or as well. It takes longer for the older heart to return to its normal level of beating and pumping (Shock, 1977). For example, older people often complain that they feel hot or cold in a room where younger people are perfectly comfortable.

Many other gradual changes begin to make a difference in later years. The circulatory system no longer carries the blood as well as it did. As circulation becomes slowed by thickening artery walls, blood pressure rises. In addition, by the time a person is eighty-five, the lungs can hold only about

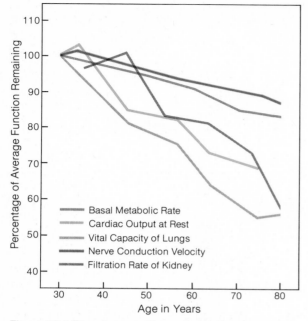

Figure 22.1 The change with age in cardiac output and certain other physiological functions, using 100 percent at age thirty as the standard. (Adapted from Nathan W. Shock, ''The Physiology of Aging,'' copyright © 1962 by Scientific American, Inc. All rights reserved)

three-fifths of the volume of oxygen that they held when the person was twenty-five. Because the lungs hold less oxygen, an older adult generally has less energy for activity and less reserve to deal with stresses. Because signals travel more slowly along the motor nerves, the individual's reactions also become slower. Digestion is no longer as good, and neither is the process of eliminating body waste.

All five senses are less acute. In the later years, vision, hearing, touch, taste, and smell are much less sensitive than they once were. Older people are more bothered by glare, see less well in the dark, require more light to see clearly, and have more trouble seeing than they did when they were younger. Although glasses help compensate for visual losses in acuity and in the ability of the eyes to accommodate to close objects, older people are also helped by increased and diffused light. Men tend to suffer a greater hearing loss than do women, and their loss is greatest for high tones. Older people hear better when people speak slowly and distinctly and when people speak directly to their faces, providing visual cues. Because older people get less sensory information from the environment, they are more isolated from the world around them than when they were younger. As a

As people age, their senses become less acute; hearing, vision, touch, taste, and smell deliver less information about the environment than they once did. (Abigail Heyman/Magnum Photos)

Although some older people slow down, others refuse to curtail their activities. Many switch from paid to volunteer work, like this foster grandmother. (© Timothy Eagan/Woodfin Camp & Assoc.)

result, some older people act irritable, moody, temperamental, or even paranoid because they can no longer perceive and interpret their surroundings as acutely and rapidly as they once did.

Older people frequently complain that they sleep badly. Typically, people in their later years awaken more often during the night and sleep less deeply. However, especially in very old age, it is normal for people to make up for their lost sleep at night by taking cat naps during the day (Pfeiffer, 1977).

As physical changes become noticeable, the alterations in body appearance during later years tend to be more disturbing for women than for men. Older women complain more than men about their bodies, and they also worry about their bodies more (Plutchik, Weiner, and Conte, 1971). Despite various physical changes, however, a person may retain robust health and a zest for living

into the eighties and beyond. Some of the distressing physical changes are unnecessary; many are the result of lack of exercise and lack of preventive health care, not inevitable changes that occur with advancing age. In the remaining sections of this chapter, we will consider in more detail some of the factors that contribute to health and vigor in late adulthood.

NEW DEVELOPMENTAL TASKS

The developmental tasks of the later years are much more personal than the tasks of earlier life phases. Childhood, adolescence, and early adulthood are years for gathering and increasing strength and experience, which can be put to productive social use during middle adulthood. By contrast, the major developmental task of the later years is to clarify, deepen, and accept one's own life and to use a lifetime of experiences to deal with personal changes or loss. During late adulthood, a person must also adjust to decreasing physical strength and health, adjust to retirement and to reduced income, perhaps adjust to the death of a spouse, and establish satisfactory but certainly less gracious physical living arrangements.

When people reach their sixties, they usually also have to decide whether they are going to continue to be as active as they were in their middle years. Robert Havighurst, Bernice Neugarten, and Sheldon Tobin (1968) found that not until individuals are in their sixties do many begin to change their social behavior and level of activity. Some people refuse to slow down. For example, a man who is confronted with retirement may find new jobs and activities. A woman who becomes a widow may refuse to withdraw from social events and instead seek out new friendships and a new life style with other widows. Some people find that the sixties are full of conflict: they want to stay active, but their bodies and their friends pressure them to slow down. Other people may be ready and willing to give up social activities and roles, but they are likely to be people who have never wanted to be socially active.

When people reach their seventies, the task is still to make the best out of life. Many people achieve a new and satisfying outlook on life during this decade. "Self-fulfillment," "integrity," and "self-actualization" are terms that various theories use to characterize the older individual who is dealing with developmental tasks in the best possible way. Although some people withdraw completely from social participation, most prefer to remain active even if their activities are curtailed (Havighurst, 1972). Thus, it does not appear to be activity or the lack of it that makes an older individual more or less able to handle change. Instead, success in handling the social aspects of aging usually depends on how an older adult feels about being active or inactive. Some older people are "active" and doing quite well; others are "disengaged" and also doing fine.

IDENTITY AND INTERPERSONAL BEHAVIOR

The Romans described the relationship between body and mind as "Sound mind, sound body." This relationship is especially true in the later

years of life. Older people who take no pleasure in life or in living typically have little desire to adjust to the changes in body functions. On the other hand, as long as people have their health, they are likely to maintain their emotional, interpersonal, and intellectual skill and curiosity. As we will see in this section, changes in views of oneself, in interpersonal relationships, and in intellectual skills are less likely to be related to age than to health and the amount of stress and social change that an individual experiences.

Self-concept and Self-esteem

Throughout the adult years, most people keep their personal style of relating to the world. The social aspects of one's identity continue to remain stable as one moves from middle age into later adulthood. As Bernice Neugarten (1977) points out, people stay themselves from middle age into their later years. If anything, people become more like the people they have always been. If Matt is quick-tempered in middle age, for example, he is likely to become even more quick-tempered in his later years. If middle-aged Susan is a person who leans heavily on others, she is likely to be even more dependent as she grows older. When major changes appear suddenly in a person's behavior, they are likely to be reactions to illness or to an experience of loss such as the death of a spouse (Alpaugh and Hickey, 1977).

Although the young often fail to realize it, there are as many similarities as differences in the way people of different ages see themselves. When Inge Ahammer and Paul Baltes (1972) asked adolescents, adults, and older people how desirable it is to be affiliative, achieving, nurturing, and autonomous at their own ages, both adolescents and older people felt that being affiliative was more desirable than middle-aged people did. Middle-aged adults were more concerned about achievement than were the other two generations. All three generations thought it was equally desirable to be nurturing and autonomous. When these different generations were asked to report what other generations are like, the misperceptions were consistent. Older adults were consistently misjudged by others on those aspects of self-concept that remain the same across generations. That is, both adolescents and middle-aged people saw older adults as wanting to be more nurturing and less autonomous than they themselves actually wanted to be. Clearly, the self-concept that an older person generally would like to have of himself as an autonomous and fairly independent person is quite different from the view that the younger and middle generations have of him.

In later adulthood both men's and women's ideas about appropriate sex-role behavior generally change. Bernice Neugarten and David Gutmann (1968) found that, regardless of their social class, older men and women, as compared to middle-aged individuals, see themselves as reversing their roles in family authority. Most people over sixty-five think of an older man as being submissive, whereas they think of the older woman as being dominant and an authority figure. The behavior of some older men and women also appears to undergo a change that is consistent with this reversed image of sex roles. Some older men become more accepting and open about their needs to nurture and to be nurtured. Older women sometimes become more tolerant of their own needs to be assertive and selfish.

As long as people refuse to see themselves as old and feel they are managing their own lives, they can maintain their middle-aged self-concepts. (*top:* Tim Eagan/Woodfin Camp & Assoc.; *bottom:* Constantine Manos/Magnum Photos)

In later life, both men and women often take a less active, less aggressive approach to life, and many view themselves as passive characters dominated by forces in the world. Seventy-year-old Matt is less likely to believe that he can actively control the direction of his own life than he did at fifty. He may be right. It is quite likely that Matt will experience changes that are beyond his control: forced retirement, loss of income, death of a loved one, a disabling stroke. When an older person has health problems, finds it difficult to move about freely, retires, faces a drop in income, or loses a spouse, he or she also loses many aspects of middle-aged identity. The person may begin to feel that the old self hardly exists.

As Robert Atchley (1972) points out, however, two factors make it possible for older individuals to continue to see themselves as they always have. For one thing, older people often depend less on feedback from others and more on their own judgment. They frequently pay no attention to the cues from other people that they are old or dependent, and some older people simply reject the image of being old. Also, despite all the changes in social roles that older individuals may have experienced, they generally continue to think of themselves in terms of former roles. A widow may still think of herself as Mrs. So-and-So, and a man may still think of himself as a carpenter or a lawyer after he retires.

Their own judgment and their persistence in thinking in terms of old roles make it possible for many older people to keep their middle-aged self-concepts. Being able to maintain an acceptable, consistent sense of self in the face of changes and loss is important. When Morton Lieberman (1975) studied older people who were moving from their homes into institutions, he found that individuals who maintained their self-images despite this radical change coped best with the move.

Because our society seldom regards the later years as desirable, it might be expected that older people would have lower self-esteem than they had in middle age. However, the same kinds of processes that help preserve an older individual's self-concept also help him maintain his sense of self-esteem. For example, as long as a person refuses to see himself as "old," he does not have to accept the negative status that many associate with age. Thus, many people over seventy tend to identify themselves as "middle-aged" rather than as "old" (Bengtson, Wellar, and Ragan, 1977). Some

self-deception in the later years, then, serves some purpose. It makes it possible for an individual to sense a continuity with the rest of his life that is not supported by either the reality of his body or others' view of him.

As in earlier life, older adults who feel they are managing their own lives are likely to have a greater sense of self-esteem than those who sense that others are in control and are making decisions for them. In a study of nursing-home residents, for example, Ellen Langer and Judith Rodin (1977) found that residents who could decide how they wanted their rooms arranged, how they wanted to spend their time, and who could suggest changes in the nursing-home routine were happier and more alert than residents who were given no choice. Clearly, a sense of self-control and competence is important to a person's sense of well-being and self-esteem at any age.

Sexuality

Older people are not supposed to be sexy, interested in sex, or sexually active. American humor reinforces the notion that the years past sixty are sexless: "Definition of old age: The time of life when a man flirts with girls but can't remember why"; "Description of the sexual life cycle of a man: Tri-weekly. Try weekly. Try weakly"; "Young men want to be faithful and are not. Old men want to be faithless and cannot" (Puner, 1974).

Because as we grow up our society teaches us that sexual interest and desire do not exist in later life, some older people do lose their interest in sex and give up sexual activity because they are "supposed to." For these people, the "sexless older years" are the result of a self-fulfilling prophecy. Other people look forward to growing older because age provides them with an acceptable excuse for ending sexual relations. Usually these people have always thought of sex as a duty or as being unpleasant.

However, people are sexual beings throughout their lives. A majority of older people are still interested in sex and many continue to be sexually active well into their later years, as long as they have an interested partner. Sexual intercourse continues to be important and pleasurable, and sexuality often has an added dimension. When asked to describe the changes in their love relationships, older people often say that tenderness, a gentle touch, an affectionate embrace, or just the physical presence of the person they love has become increasingly important (Reedy, 1978). Although the lack of a partner may lead many older people to turn to masturbation in their later years, the myth of the dirty old man who is an exhibitionist or a child molester is completely unsupported. Exhibitionism is rare among people over forty, and older people are the least likely of any to be involved in child molesting (I. Rubin, 1968).

Some changes do occur in the sexual organs and in sexual performance during later adulthood. William Masters and Virginia Johnson (1966) found that these changes lead to differences in the experience of sexuality and sex but need not lead to impotence. Among women, the vaginal tissues gradually atrophy, vaginal lubrication decreases, and the uterus and cervix get smaller. Among men, there is a steady decline in the production of testosterone. It may take an older man two or three times longer to achieve an erection, but he can preserve it without ejaculating much longer than he could in earlier years. Older men also usually experience less intense orgasms, and it takes longer for them to be restimulated after an ejaculation.

Thus, although the capacity for sexual response gradually slows down, reasonably healthy men and women have the desire and the capacity for sexual activity well into their later years. When Adriaan Verwoerdt, Eric Pfeiffer, and Hsioh-Shan Wang (1969) asked older men and women about their sexual activity and interest over a ten-year period, older men generally reported more sexual activity than older women. The reason for this may lie in the fact that an older woman is less likely than an older man to have a spouse; therefore a woman is less likely to have a sex partner. It also was not unusual for men in their eighties and nineties to report continued sexual activity. Although the amount of sexual interest declined with age, nearly one-half of the individuals in their eighties and nineties reported mild or moderate sexual interest. Both older men and women also said that their sexual interest was generally higher than their actual sexual activity.

Gender is not the only factor that may influence sexual activity. Studies indicate that the more sexually active men or women are during youth, the more likely they are to continue being sexually active into the later years (Kinsey, Pomeroy, and Martin, 1948). The rule "Use it or you'll lose it" describes the nature of sexuality across the life span. Active and satisfying sex can last as long as

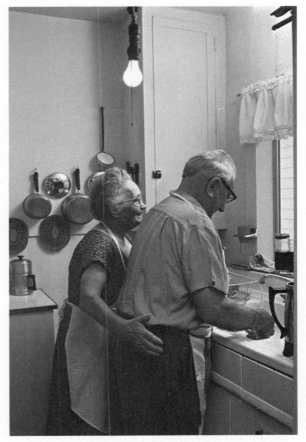

Contrary to popular belief, sexual interest and activity can continue as long as life itself; all that's required is an interested—and interesting—partner. (Wayne Miller/Magnum Photos)

life itself. According to Masters and Johnson (1968), several criteria appear to be necessary: an interesting and receptive partner, regular sexual activity, reasonably good physical health, and a healthy mental attitude toward aging. Thus, as in the middle years, the richer and happier a person's sexual life has been, the longer it continues.

Intellectual Skills

One common stereotype about old age is that intelligence invariably declines, but, as we noted earlier, the idea that all older adults are senile is purely myth. As we have seen throughout this book, individuals generally manage to become what they expect to become. People who assume that life after sixty is downhill all the way usually find their assumptions are correct. Along with ex-

Among healthy adults, intellectual skills do not decline; their minds and memories work as well as they ever did, but not as quickly. (both photos, Constantine Manos/Magnum Photos)

pectations, general health and how much people challenge themselves throughout life determine how well their minds work in later years. In general, the more often people put themselves in stimulating learning situations and the more they use their minds and memories, the better and longer they will be able to learn, think, and remember.

In some areas of intellectual functioning, individuals tend to improve well into their later years. A person's verbal skills, in terms of word use and comprehension, for example, will be better at sixty-five than they were at forty or at twenty-five. Visual skills, such as finding a simple figure in a complex one, also keep on getting better right into old age (Baltes and Schaie, 1974).

In later adulthood people also generally are about as flexible and as good at shifting from one way of thinking to another as they were in middle age. On tasks that involve eye-hand coordination, such as solving a puzzle or copying words, however, older people do progressively worse over the years. Older people also are quite likely to do worse on any task where speed is important. Being slower is perhaps the most characteristic thing about being older.

As noted earlier, the more stimulating an individual's life has been and continues to be, the more likely he or she is to make gains in intellectual skills during the later years. For example, in one study, men who had been bright as children showed considerable increases in intellectual ability during their adult years, whereas women who had been bright as children tended to make fewer gains in intellectual ability as they grew older. This difference seems to have come about because most of the men had stimulating jobs that forced them to think, whereas most of the women became housewives and had fewer opportunities for intellectual growth and stimulation (Correll, Rokosz, and Blanchard, 1966; Kangas and Bradway, 1971).

It also is not true that memory declines in the later years. For example, David's ability to learn and to remember is likely to be just as good as it ever was as long as he continues to stimulate himself to learn and to remember. And again, health, education, and motivation affect his ability. The meaningfulness of the material to be learned also affects how well older people learn and remember. Younger people, especially those who are well educated, are willing to learn almost anything, no matter how irrelevant it seems. Older people, by contrast, are more likely to be unwilling or unable to learn something that they judge to be meaningless, irrelevant, or trivial.

The amount of time that David has to learn something is also important in determining how well he learns it. Because older people generally tend to be slower, they tend to learn more slowly. Given enough time, older people generally learn and remember as well as the young (Monge and Hultsch, 1971).

Just as having more time increases an older person's ability to learn, so the opportunity to practice helps. Thus, as Harvey Taub and Margaret Long (1972) found, older people typically benefit as much from practice as younger people do. When older individuals are allowed to go at

their own speed and when they are given the opportunity to do a task rather than just watch it being done, they also learn better (Canestrari, 1963).

The capacity for creative thought and creative work also persists into the later years. People who are creative in youth are likely to be creative throughout their lives. Tolstoy, Voltaire, Marc Chagall, Pablo Casals, and Pablo Picasso are outstanding examples of older people who continue to produce literature, art, and music of high quality into their seventies, eighties, or beyond. Even more than in middle age, creativity and productivity are likely to be the result of accumulated experience and knowledge, as well as the result of a perspective that comes from having lived so many years. Wayne Dennis (1966) found that, in terms of their productivity, historians and philosophers, for example, tend to be most productive around the age

Creative people, like painter Georgia O'Keeffe, produce literature, art, and music of high quality into their eighties and beyond. (Dennis Brack/Black Star)

of sixty. Supreme Court justices and political leaders are also usually older.

Some people become creative for the first time in their later years. Grandma Moses is one outstanding example, but many older men and women use retirement as an opportunity to develop new talents. Some take up painting, some learn silvercrafting, and others start to knit or write for the first time in their lives. According to Alex Comfort (1976), curiosity, flexibility, and a certain joy for life are important characteristics of the creative person at any age. As long as individuals are healthy and as long as they challenge themselves to learn and to think, the myths of intellectual decline, fading memory, and worn-out genius are likely to remain just that.

In general, the most important measure of older people's abilities is how well they function in everyday life. As long as their abilities meet their needs, some decline in intellectual skills should make little difference. This point is exemplified by the eighty-two-year-old woman who operated a small business for her absent-minded and unreliable middle-aged boss. She opened and closed the shop, waited on customers, kept the accounts, took inventories, placed orders, and completed tax forms. In addition, she maintained her own apartment and never failed to remember the birthdays of her relatives and close friends. Everyone counted on her to help organize the scheduled events at her church. On the other hand, when asked as part of an adult intelligence test "How are north and west alike?" she received no credit for her reply: "Well, honey, I don't know how it is up your way, but around here the coldest winds come out of the north."

FAMILY LIFE

Each individual experiences his or her own life cycle of development, and participates in a family that also develops over time and has its own collective life cycle. As a person grows older, the family grows and contracts with births, deaths, and marriages of brothers, sisters, nieces, and nephews. The older person like Lauren who has never had children will experience a very different kind of family life and sense of family integrity and continuity from that known by Susan, who has watched her children grow up to have their own children. Grandparents may become great-grandparents; the death of a spouse may lead to remarriage or to

learning to live a single life. With retirement, Susan and her husband may sell a house that has grown too large and move into a retirement community.

As Frederick Brand and Richard Smith (1974) have noted, these communities, made up of houses, condominiums, or apartments inhabited exclusively by older people, require new adjustments. A couple may find themselves far from grown children and grandchildren and far from old friends. They must learn to live in a new town, in a new climate, and among new people. Some appear to thrive in these new communities, where planned activities may fill every minute of what might have been vacant hours. Others find that the lack of younger people cuts off an important source of intellectual stimulation. However, the fact that so many older people adjust so readily to such an abrupt change in life style makes it apparent that their intellectual and personal skills are in good working order.

Marital Life

Being married is a demanding and problematic state at any age, and the later years are no exception. Often, the most significant transition point in later marital life is the husband's retirement. The man finds himself suddenly without his job or career and without daily contacts with his fellow workers. If his wife has been working and retires at about the same time, she also loses both income and independence. On the other hand, if the wife continues to work for several years, the couple faces a role reversal that can create additional problems.

Women who do not work outside the home have a different problem. Alan Kerckhoff (1966) found that husbands typically look forward to retirement more than their wives do. After their husbands retire, wives who look upon "home maintenance" as their primary marital responsibility have a more difficult time adjusting to their husbands' retirement than do women who regard "affection and caring" as their primary marital responsibilities. Such women find it disconcerting to have their husbands home all day. A common reaction to a husband's retirement was former First Lady Betty Ford's comment, "I'm glad we will have more time to spend together, dear. But don't come home to lunch."

No matter what happens, the couple is faced with new problems and new demands to adjust.

Family life continues to change; some older people enjoy their grandchildren and greatgrandchildren; others move into retirement communities in distant towns where they live among new people. (Hella Hammid/Rapho/Photo Researchers)

There are likely to be complaints and worries about how fast the money is going, disagreements over relationships with children, disagreements about moving into a smaller house or apartment, and health problems (Stinnett, Carter, and Montgomery, 1972). However, a married couple who reaches the later adulthood years together has probably lived through enough stress to weather this period.

More older persons are married and living with their spouses than ever before. Because of sex differences in survival, men are more likely to be married than are women. Between the ages of sixty-five and seventy-four, more than 70 percent of men are still married, but only 48 percent of women aged sixty-five to sixty-nine and only 36 percent of women aged seventy to seventy-four have spouses (Riley and Foner, 1968). Most older people describe their relationships as happy or

very happy. The upswing in satisfaction that begins after the children leave home continues into the later years (Rollings and Feldman, 1970). The divorce rate among older couples is extremely low, partly because truly unhappy couples are likely to have divorced or separated years before and partly because being married is generally more desirable to an older person than living alone.

It appears that the more a marital relationship meets a person's needs for love, fulfillment, respect, and communication, as well as the need to find meaning in life and to sense a continuity with the past, the happier the marriage is in later life. Older couples who have happy marriages tend to have a more positive outlook on life and to be more active than those who are single or unhappily married. Apparently, once the couple adjusts to retirement and to having the children gone, the marriage relationship is better than ever. For some

it may even be the first time that they have been able to spend time together, to go at their own pace, and to enjoy each other's companionship.

On the other hand, an older adult is likely to remain in close contact with at least one child. Among American old people, 84 percent live an hour or less away from a child, and 30 percent are ten minutes or less from their nearest child. They see their children frequently, and, perhaps most characteristically in the middle classes, aged parents continue to help their children. As long as older parents are in relatively good health and financially secure, there is an equal exchange of services and money between parents and children (Troll, 1971).

Not all older parents, however, can support themselves adequately, and most generally get more from their children than they give (Hill,

In later life, marriage may be better than ever. For the first time, a couple can enjoy each other's companionship at their own pace. (*top:* Charles Harbutt/Magnum Photos; *bottom:* Guy Gillette/Photo Researchers)

1965). For example, about two-thirds report that they receive support from their families in the form of money or gifts. And nearly one-third depend on children or other relatives to help with housework, meals, or shopping. Also, the older a person is, the more likely he or she is to live with a child. Thus, about 28 percent of older people live with a middle-aged child, usually a daughter. This percentage increases with age and is higher for women than for men (Shanas et al., 1968).

Although most older people live close to their children and to other family members, about 10 to 20 percent of them have no relatives or family alive or living close to them (Riley and Foner, 1968). These people also tend to have inadequate financial resources. Thus, those older individuals who most need emotional and financial support are least likely to have them in times of need.

Widowhood

Three times as many women as men experience the trauma and grief of losing a spouse, which marks a transition to a new position in the human life cycle. More than half of women over sixty-five are widowed (U.S. Bureau of the Census, 1976). Among sixty-five-year-old widows, more than half can expect to live another fifteen years, whereas one-third have twenty or more years of life ahead of them. Widows are also much more likely to remain single than are widowers; widowers over sixty-five are eight times as likely to remarry as widows (Treas and Van Hilst, 1976).

The loss of a spouse is a major psychological and developmental issue, and dealing with it places heavy demands on the older individual to adjust. Paula Clayton and her associates (1971) interviewed more than one hundred recently widowed women and found that their physical symptoms included changed sleep patterns, lack of appetite or weight loss, headaches, blurred vision, and general body pains. Common psychological reactions included anger, guilt, depression and crying, restlessness, lack of zest, and preoccupation with the image of the deceased. Grieving over a spouse's death is a critical and necessary part of the process of handling the crisis.

As Marjorie Lowenthal and Clayton Haven (1968) have noted, the intensity and amount of grief that an older person feels when he or she loses a spouse and the amount of time required to complete the grief process can be somewhat reduced if there is at least one close friend who can help the person through the adjustment period. If the grieving person is supported by a warm and loving family, if he or she has been able to anticipate and prepare for the loss, and if there is something left to live for, the grieving process will be shorter and easier. In addition, if the individual can rationalize the loss or make it meaningful through some religious or philosophical belief, or if the bereaved person has a confidant he can talk openly to, the adjustment will be easier, and the loneliness will not be so profound.

Like the divorced person, the widowed person often must develop a new social identity. Most individuals learn to see themselves in a new way and learn to relate to other people differently, especially people of the opposite sex (Kimmel, 1974). Widowhood is often a time for learning to live alone, perhaps for the first time. Many find it a time of being socially marooned. Friends and even

Dealing with the loss of a spouse places heavy demands on the older person; once they manage their grief, many widows find themselves socially isolated. (© Elliott Erwitt/Magnum Photos)

relatives are likely to avoid the widowed person. They stay away because they do not know how to act or what to say or because it makes them feel pain over the loss or because they need to deny the reality that they are also getting old. Although this is a difficult period of adjustment, once the grieving is over and they learn to deal with their new status, many widows and widowers also find a new sense of freedom.

Remarriage

Older widows seek out other widows, whereas older widowers remarry. After the death of his wife, an older man generally finds many women his age to choose from, whereas the widowed woman has little choice. In addition, society approves when an older man marries a younger woman but frowns on the reverse. Although 20 percent of grooms who are more than sixty-five years old attract brides younger than forty-five, only 3 percent of older brides wed men who are younger than forty-five (Treas, 1975).

Remarriage makes it possible to avoid such unpleasant alternatives to widowhood as living alone, living with a friend or friends, or moving in with children. Equally important, most couples who do marry late in life have highly successful marriages. Widows who remarry generally say they are "very satisfied" or "satisfied" with their new lives. They give companionship as the most important reason for marrying, followed by the need to take care of someone. Most couples adopt traditional roles; the wives cook and clean, and the husbands do the heavy work around the house. Remarried widows tend to describe their marriages as calmer and more serene than their earlier marriages, and those who adapt easiest to married life are women who make no major changes in their way of life or their geographic location.

According to Walter McKain (1972), in many ways the courtship experiences of older adults resemble those of younger and middle-aged people. Older couples tend to have similar incomes and social and religious backgrounds. The older man is generally a little older than his bride. However, there is one major difference: over half of the older people who remarry have known their new spouses for a long time before being widowed, many for most of their lives. Some are already related by marriage, some are childhood sweethearts, others are neighbors or old friends. The courtship usually is short and sweet, and the mar-

riage, simple. Widowers rarely wait more than a year or two before remarrying. Widows are more likely to take their time, usually about seven years.

ALTERNATIVES TO MARRIAGE

Not all older couples who are in love and who get pleasure from one another's company marry. Like the young, increasing numbers of older people are seeking alternatives to marriage. Living together is becoming more common among older people who cannot afford to get married because the marriage could mean a reduction in social security benefits or in a widow's pension. According to census reports (U.S. Bureau of the Census, 1973), one in five unmarried men over sixty-five who shares his living quarters with an unrelated person has a female roommate. Beyond necessity, there is also the desire to be with each other that draws older men and women together outside of wedlock, although most who are cohabiting do not advertise their way of life.

Marvin Sussman (1976) found that an increasing number of older people are forming group marriages and are finding communes an attractive way of life. One such communal family is Share-A-Home group, which was formed by eleven persons from sixty-four to ninety-four years old who moved into a twenty-seven-room mansion in Winter Park, Florida, and hired a staff to run the household. Although neighbors contended that the group violated the single-dwelling zoning ordinance, the court ruled that the communal group was indeed a single family, noting that the residents were bound together for comfort, companionship, and ease of living, and generally applauded the idea.

Not all older people choose to live with members of the opposite sex. Some have never married and are quite content to stay that way. Others live alone because they cannot find a partner. About one-third of older women in the United States live alone, compared with only about half that many men. In this age group, women outnumber the men and more and more women are choosing to live together. On the basis of her own experience, Faith Conklin (1974) concluded that it is a good idea for older women to share living quarters, both because it guarantees them companionship and because it is cheaper than living alone. Even if all older men were to marry, the problem of older women would not be solved. Because society is not likely to accept polygamous marriages, many older women must live alone unless other ways to meet their needs for intimate companionship are developed.

SOCIAL-LIFE CHANGES

The major characteristic of the social interaction and social participation of older people is that they do less of it. However, most older people are not completely isolated. No more than 17 percent of the men and women between sixty and seventy-four have contact only with relatives who visit them or with people who live in their building (Lowenthal and Haven, 1968). Once people pass the age of seventy-five, they are more likely to be socially isolated, and older women are generally more isolated than men.

Despite decreasing opportunities for social participation, people over sixty continue to participate in the political process. Older people vote as often as the middle-aged and more often than other age groups. They actively discuss political issues and generally are well informed, because they watch the news on television and read newspapers (Glenn, 1969). The fact that there are more older people than ever before, combined with the fact that they are more likely to vote than any other age group, means that older adults, if they were organized, could wield a great deal of political power. Recently they have begun to organize, and groups like the Gray Panthers and the National Council of Senior Citizens have begun to exert political pressure.

In their personal lives, older people generally report having fewer friends than when they were younger; they also see them less often. When friends die or move away, many old people find it difficult to make new friends. According to Marjorie Lowenthal and her associates (1975), the same qualities that are important in sustaining friendships early in life play a major role in friendships between older adults—compatibility and companionship, shared experiences, and most of all, being able to depend on each other for help and support. There are some differences. Older adults are more likely than young and middle-aged adults to enjoy friendships with people who have different interests and backgrounds. They are also more likely to report having friends who are younger than themselves.

In recent years, retirement communities have

The fact that women are more likely than men to have a confidant in later life may be one reason they generally live longer. (© Joel Gordon)

become increasingly popular with older people in the middle class. Such communities provide physical security and, by providing recreation centers and various organized activities, make it easy for older people to find new friends. People who live in this kind of housing are more likely than those who live in areas where all ages reside to have neighbors who are also friends.

Some older people are more likely than others to have a close friend. For example, people just entering later adulthood (those between the ages of sixty and sixty-five) and people who are more than seventy-five are less apt to have a confidant than older adults between sixty-five and seventy-four (Lowenthal and Haven, 1968). The fact that women are more likely than men to have a close friend during the later years may help give them their advantage over men in survival and adaptability. And older married people who outlive the

People who have developed interesting ways to spend their time are likely to continue their activities as long as they remain healthy. (© Richard Kalvar/Magnum Photos)

widowed, separated, or divorced are also more likely to have a confidant.

In general, retirement ushers in major changes in people's social life. But money, more than retirement itself, determines what older people do with their time. Retirement makes it possible for older people like Matt or Lauren to spend more time in leisure activities, if he or she can afford them. Retirement generally cuts a couple's income in half; thus, a greater proportion of their income must go for food, housing, and medical expenses. Older people of higher socioeconomic status tend to be more active, to have more leisure activities outside the home, to participate more in community activities, to have more friends, and to be more concerned citizens than older people of low socioeconomic status (Havighurst and Feigenbaum, 1968). The reason that poorer older people

stay around their homes more is not because of lack of interest but because of lack of money.

The idea of retirement, which means that people can have as much free time as they choose, makes many people anxious. Thus, retirement makes some men feel useless and leads them to question who they are in a kind of identity crisis. This is more likely to happen to the man whose life has centered about his work (Vogel and Schell, 1968). However, well-educated professional women who have devoted themselves to work may be even more reluctant than men to retire.

Retirement has long been considered a crisis because work occupies so much time and provides many different kinds of rewards, including income, self-esteem, friendships, physical activity, outside interests, and for some, intellectual challenge. Most people, however, have identities other than their work roles, and only about 30 percent of older people report difficulty in adjusting to their own retirement. People who look forward to retirement, who choose to retire early, and who have many identities tend to be the ones who adjust most easily to retired life (Chown, 1977). Also, people with many friends who are actively involved in family, church, and other social organizations generally find the transition to retirement an easy one.

Despite the likelihood of reduced income, retired people are relatively free to decide what interests they will pursue and what leisure activities will occupy their time. What older adults find interesting and which leisure activities occupy their time are heavily influenced by the interests and activities of their middle age. If people have developed many ways to spend their free time during earlier adulthood, they will probably continue these leisure activities as long as their health remains good.

During later years, the tendency begun in middle age to participate less in active, physically demanding forms of activity outside the home increases. Chad Gordon, Charles Gaitz, and Judith Scott (1977) report that older people engage in solitary relaxing activities, such as thinking, planning, or daydreaming, more often than do young and middle-aged adults. They found that other forms of leisure are enjoyed equally from youth to later maturity. Home and family-centered forms of leisure, such as cooking and watching television, are a form of leisure activity equally popular throughout the adult years. In general, women are more likely than men to belong to community, social, and voluntary associations, whereas men are more likely than women to be active in politics.

Life after sixty-five, then, does not have to be a period of isolation and failing physical and intellectual powers. Some curtailment of activities is necessary—no eighty-year-old is likely to run a four-minute mile, although at eighty, King Gustav of Sweden often played a good game of tennis—but many older people live satisfying lives. Health, money, and their own expectations appear to be major determinants of the quality of most old people's lives.

SUMMARY

1. What growing and being older means to people in the later years is largely determined by the culture they live in. In America, many popular stereotypes reinforce our fears about growing older. In reality, productive living and functioning in later adulthood depend as much on life-long habits and behavior patterns as on anything else.

2. Although aging goes on throughout life, it is often only in later life that the cumulative effects of aging tend to catch up with people and begin to interfere with their everyday effectiveness.

3. The major developmental task of the later years is to clarify, deepen, and accept one's own life and to use a lifetime of experience to deal with personal changes or loss. This often includes adjusting to retirement and reduced income, the death of a spouse, and new social roles and living arrangements.

4. An individual's personal style of relating to the world is likely to be retained, if not accentuated, during later adulthood. When large changes do appear in an individual's self-concept, interpersonal relationships, or sexual or intellectual behavior, the shifts are likely to be due to changes in health or due to social or psychological losses.

5. In general, the more that family life meets an individual's needs for fulfillment, meaning in life, and a sense of continuity with the past, the more satisfying the later years are likely to be. The loss of one's spouse is a major developmental crisis and people who live long enough must face it. Following widowhood, many older people remarry, finding it a satisfying alternative.

6. Among the unmarried, some older people live alone, some live with friends of the same sex, and others share their living quarters with unrelated members of the opposite sex.

7. Although their social life may eventually decrease in type and extent, most older people do not become completely isolated; many, if not most, actively discuss politics and vote, most enjoy the company of other people, and most are likely to have a close friend or confidant with whom they can talk about their lives.

CHAPTER 23
The End of Life

LIFE EXPECTANCY
Historical Trends
Disease, Age, and Stress

LONGEVITY
Factors in Longevity
Increasing Longevity

MEANING OF DEATH
To Children
To Adults
Cross-Cultural Views

THE PROCESS OF DYING
How and Where
Experience of Dying
Phases in Dying
Easing the End

COPING WITH DEATH
Anticipatory Grief
Communication
Bereavement

SUMMARY

One of the things that gives life its urgency and meaning is the fact that it does not go on forever. For some, death comes too soon and interrupts plans and projects, learning and loving. For others, death comes too late or too slowly, making a dignified and appropriate end impossible. But no matter when the end comes, dealing with one's own death is life's last developmental task.

Just as it is difficult for people to see their own aging, so it is difficult for them to conceive of their own deaths. Our culture encourages us to avoid thinking about death: other people pass on, pass away, or depart—but they seldom die. As this reluctance to put death into words indicates, the fear and denial of death are common human experiences.

As far as we know, human beings are unique in their ability to contemplate their own deaths. Although death can occur at any age, today most people do not have to face their own dying until their later years. In this chapter, we will examine the factors that influence longevity and discover that people do have some control over how long they live, and that the meaning of death changes from youth to old age. Some of the psychological changes that occur in terminally ill patients will be discussed, as well as how people feel and react when they learn they are about to die. We will see that, at any age, death comes easiest when others continue to show that they care and when the person is allowed to die with dignity. Finally, we will look at the ways people face the death of others and learn that mourning is a normal way of coping with the grief that follows the death of a loved one.

LIFE EXPECTANCY

Death has only recently been associated primarily with advanced age. In times past, youth afforded little protection from death, and parents expected that some of their young children would die. Today, the best predictor of approaching death is advanced age.

Historical Trends

Life expectancy has increased considerably over the centuries. In ancient Greece, life expectancy was about twenty years, and by the Middle Ages, life expectancy had climbed to about thirty-three years. In the United States, the big leap in life expectancy occurred after 1900. At that time, life expectancy was only forty-seven years, but babies born today in the United States can expect to live until they are seventy-three (U.S. Public Health Service, 1974).

The recent dramatic increase in life expectancy does not mean that people are living longer, but that more people are reaching old age. The real increase in life expectancy has occurred in infancy and childhood. In the eighteenth century only three out of every ten newborns lived past the age of twenty-five. Today, at least nineteen out of every twenty live to become adults. Although medical science has almost eliminated deaths from smallpox and diphtheria, sanitation and improved nutrition have been responsible for the major decreases in infant and early childhood mortality (McKeown, 1977). The pasteurization of milk probably saved more babies than any other single advance.

Today, degenerative diseases such as heart disease, cancer, and strokes have replaced infectious diseases such as pneumonia, tuberculosis, and smallpox as the leading causes of death. Heart disease ranked fourth as the cause of death in 1900; today it is the most common cause of death. Cancer, which ranked eighth in 1900, is the second most common cause of death in the United States. And strokes, which ranked fifth in 1900, are now the third most common cause of death (U.S. Public Health Service, 1974). In addition to being associated with old age, the causes of death vary with sex and socioeconomic status. Men, for example, are more likely than women to die from heart disease and cancer, whereas women are more likely to die from a stroke. People who are poor are most likely of any to die from an infectious disease or when they are young, whereas white-collar, middle-class men are most likely to die at midlife and in old age from a degenerative disease (Lerner, 1976).

Disease, Age, and Stress

Age tends to make the older person more susceptible to disease, and disease tends to make people age faster. The circle is a vicious one: both proc-

esses work together and result in the loss of health and finally in death. Thus, the saying "Nobody ever dies of old age" has more than a glimmer of truth in it. In fact, when the causes of death were determined for some 12,000 individuals, the examiner found no cases of natural death and was always able to discover a pathological condition responsible for the death (Zur Aschoff, 1937). Half the people who die from heart disease and stroke are more than seventy-six, and half of those who die from cancer are more than sixty-eight (U.S. Public Health Service, 1974).

Even if disease does not kill them, old people are ill more frequently than the young. Because 80 percent have chronic health problems of one kind or another, they visit the doctor more frequently than the young do, go to the hospital more often and stay there longer, and spend more days each year sick at home (Weg, 1977). Older people chiefly complain of some ill-defined discomfort, rheumatism, arthritis, and digestive problems. Despite this ill health, 81 percent of older adults move around on their own, and only 5 percent live in institutions.

Older people are particularly affected by the close relationship between stress and disease. The more life changes that a person of any age undergoes in a short period of time, the more likely he or she is to experience a serious illness. Thomas Holmes and Richard Rahe (1967) have found that this relationship between stress and disease holds in spite of education, wealth, intellectual skills, or social class. They note that six of the thirteen most stressful life changes are characteristic of later life: death of a spouse, death of a close family member, personal injury or illness, retirement, change in the health of a family member, and sex difficulties. Because major life stresses and change tend to pile up in the later adult years, it is more likely that the older individual's abilities to handle change may be tested beyond his limits and that a serious and even terminal illness may result.

LONGEVITY

Some people appear to sail through their later years active, vigorous, and the picture of robust health. Others seem to spend those years in physicians' offices and in hospitals. To judge by the healthy, old age is merely a different period of life; to judge by the ill, it is a dismal period. Researchers interested in developmental changes over the life span are beginning to concentrate on

Although many old people have chronic health problems, only 5 percent are institutionalized. Many are active and independent throughout their later years, despite the changes that aging brings about in their bodies. (Burk Uzzle/Magnum Photos)

this final period and to advance a number of different ideas as to why some people seem to age faster and perhaps die sooner than others.

Aging refers to the increasing inability of a person's body to maintain itself and to perform its operations as it once did. The result is that, with the passing of time, there is a greater probability of dying by natural causes. Although this definition describes the biological process, it does not explain why people age.

At present, there are a number of theories that attempt to explain why aging occurs (Shock, 1977). As yet, none has been accepted as the primary cause of aging by the scientists who study these processes. The first is the "wear and tear" theory, which maintains that the human body simply wears out with constant use, as a complex machine would. The "waste product" theory proposes that damaging substances build up within the cells and interfere with their function. The "homeostatic imbalance theory" supposes that the mechanisms that maintain vital physiological balances in the body do not work as well in times of stress. The "auto-immune" theory maintains that, as an individual ages, his body's immune system, which is normally directed against foreign substances, begins to attack his own body cells. The body ages because it can no longer distinguish between its own cells and germs or viruses. According to the "free radical" theory, the aging process is related to the presence of fragments of molecules whose original bonds have become unstuck from other molecules. These fragments seek new substances to latch onto, thereby throwing body functions out of order.

The "cellular" or "error in copying" theory is based on the fact that during a person's life span, most cells in the body reproduce themselves again and again. According to this theory, errors build up during the repeated copying of the cells' genetic message, in the way that nicks build up on a frequently played phonograph record. As a result, the messages that control the orderly behavior of the cells gradually become so full of errors that the cells no longer function normally. The "genetic" theory supposes that the program spelled out at conception in the genetic material eventually runs out, simply ending cell function. The "pacemaker" theory proposes that aging is controlled by specific pacemakers in the body, probably located in the brain.

Although there is no consensus as to which, if any, of these theories is correct, other factors are generally agreed to play a role in determining how long a person can expect to live. As our earlier discussions would lead one to expect, the environment in which Matt lives, the food he eats, how active he is, the stability of his social roles and social environment, his marital status, his attitude toward aging, and how long he expects to live affect his chances of living a long life.

Factors in Longevity

In general, the more technologically advanced a society is, the longer the life expectancy at birth is. However, technology simply makes it possible for people to live longer and does not increase the life span appreciably. Thus, life expectancy for today's adults has not increased much since the turn of the century. An American who was sixty-five in 1900 could expect to live for thirteen more years. Today's life expectancy for sixty-five-year-olds is fifteen years, only an additional two years.

Heredity is another factor in determining how long an individual can expect to live. Longevity tends to run in families, and children of long-lived parents are more likely to live longer than children of short-lived parents. One of the best predictors of longevity is having four grandparents who lived long and healthy lives. People with such a heritage live longer because tendencies toward heart disease, hypertension, and some kinds of cancer appear to run in families. In other words, placed in the environmental conditions that encourage one

of these diseases, a person who has inherited a tendency to develop the ailment is likely to do so.

There is also a marked difference between life expectancies of men and women. Generally, women outlive men in societies where they no longer perform hard physical labor, where their chances of dying in childbirth are small, and where sanitation is adequate. In our society, although more boy babies are born than girl babies, girls begin to outnumber boys after age eighteen. In the later adulthood years, there are 135 women for every 100 men. The life expectancy of an American baby boy born in 1970 is 68.1 years, contrasted with 75.4 years for a baby girl (U.S. National Center for Health Statistics, 1974).

In this country, a person's ethnic background also affects the length of time that he or she can expect to live. Black men and women have a lower life expectancy than white men and women (U.S. National Center for Health Statistics, 1974). Black men generally live six years less than white men, or sixty-one years. However, black men who reach the age of sixty-five begin to show a greater survival rate than whites. Black women can expect to live almost five years less than white women.

In terms of life expectancy, Mexican-Americans fare even worse than blacks (R. Butler and Lewis, 1973). A Mexican-American has a typical life span of around 56.7 years. In comparison to American Indians, however, Mexican-Americans do well. The average American Indian can expect to live for forty-four years. Obviously, poverty, poor housing and sanitation, and lack of medical care and education have profound effects not only on the physical and intellectual development of blacks, Mexican-Americans, and American Indians, but also on their life expectancy.

Increasing Longevity

Extreme longevity is reported as customary in two communities in the world, and it is common to live beyond the age of one hundred in these places: Hunza in Kashmir and Abkhazia in the Soviet Republic of Georgia. By looking at these groups of long-lived people, one can see that environmental factors are closely related to their longevity. Their diets have much in common. Both areas are predominantly agrarian, and the people's diets contain a good deal of fiber and almost no saturated fats, which are generally found in meat and dairy products. The prevalence of fiber is believed to protect against cardiovascular diseases and some cancers (Burkitt, Walker, and Painter, 1974), and the absence of saturated fat is likely to delay the progress of arteriosclerosis and the incidence of cardiovascular disease. People in these communities also eat less than Americans do, and reduced caloric intake is known to be related to longevity.

Although all of these people may have uninteresting diets by some American standards, other aspects of their lives are far from bland. Alexander Leaf and John Launois (1973) observed that these older people continue to enjoy an occasional smoke or drink and that they continue to be interested in sex. One 110-year-old man from the Caucasus said that he thought that youth meant engaging in sexual activity and then admitted that he had considered himself a youth until he was 98.

The majority of these long-lived people were married, and those women who had borne many children tended to live longer. Several women had borne more than twenty children. A one-hundred-year-old who had been married to his seventh wife for only three years pointed out the importance of a happy marriage: "My first six wives were all wonderful women, but this present wife is an angry woman, and I have aged at least ten years since marrying her. If a man has a good and kind wife, he can easily live 100 years."

Another common element of life in these societies is that the people are used to prolonged physical labor, and they remain very active throughout life. People over one hundred continue to tend flocks, clean house, and care for grandchil-

People in Soviet Georgia often live to extreme old age. Their diets are high in fiber and low in saturated fats; they remain active; and they retain their social roles and responsibilities. (Eve Arnold/Magnum Photos)

dren. In these societies there is no such thing as retirement. In addition to being highly active, these long-lived people retain their social roles and responsibilities throughout life, thus facing few stressful transition points. In their societies there is little demand or need to be highly adaptive because there are few changes to adapt to. An additional factor that may contribute to their longevity is their joy for living and their emphasis on the importance of a worry-free and calm state of mind. Finally, as Leaf and Launois note, these people expect to live a long time, and, perhaps as a result, they generally do.

In our own country, a number of characteristics that appear to be common among people who live long and well recall the life style of these people from Kashmir and the Soviet Union. Findings from interviews with individuals between the ages of 87 and 103 indicate that these people have par-

ents who lived a long time, that they are happily married, and that they are sexually active. In fact, a good marriage appears to add five years to life.

Another characteristic of long-lived Americans is that their physical abilities and reaction times tend to remain above those considered normal for the later years, as do their intellectual skills and abilities. These people are physically and socially active. They refuse to give in to social or physical change. They remarry if they are widowed, they develop hobbies, and they take long walks and get plenty of exercise (Palmore and Jeffers, 1971). Long-lived Americans are also unlikely to be anxious, they generally have always been independent, and they have a joy for living. All are religious but not extremely orthodox. They tend to be moderate eaters of normal weight, and they have never slept long hours. Some drink, and some never have. Some smoke occasionally (C. Rose

In all parts of the world, long-lived people tend to be married. It appears that a happy marriage is an important factor in longevity. (Sepp Seitz/Woodfin Camp & Assoc.)

and Bell, 1971). Unlike the non-Americans who live to be centegenarians, long-lived Americans by necessity tend to be highly adaptable. Finally, all prefer to live in the present, with all its problems, rather than in the past (Jewett, 1973).

These examples of long-lived people demonstrate that living a healthy, long life is a matter over which people have some control. As other research shows, overweight people are predisposed to develop life-shortening diseases such as diabetes, hypertension, arteriosclerosis, or cardiovascular disease. Smoking is also a major factor in heart disease and lung cancer. It has been estimated that if all men in the United States stopped smoking, the sex difference in longevity would be cut in half.

Physiologists argue that many of the bodily changes associated with aging may be due more to lack of activity than to the aging process itself. They may be right. Bengt Saltin and his associates (1968) found that when young people are kept in bed for a number of weeks, their bodies undergo physiological changes that mimic those that occur with aging. In addition, it is generally agreed that a moderately vigorous program of exercise can reverse some of the physiological changes associated with aging. Regular exercise—that is, about ten to fifteen minutes, three times each week, and strenuous enough to raise the heart rate—can improve cardiovascular and respiratory functions, lower blood pressure, decrease the amount of body fat, and improve muscle tone (deVries, 1975).

Although the freedom and competition of modern life may be exciting and challenging, its chronic stress and unpredictability may not only be hard on the health of some people, but may also shorten their lives. The sort of person, for example, who is tension-ridden, time-pressured, angry, and competitive has been found to be particularly prone to coronary heart disease and early death from heart failure (Friedman and Rosenman, 1974).

Having a hopeful attitude toward life and the future, even in the face of stress, appears to contribute to a long life. When there is something to live for, people live longer. How long people live, however, may be a less important issue than how well people live. Perhaps a better and more reasonable goal than avoiding aging is stretching out the productive middle years of life into later adulthood.

MEANING OF DEATH

When we experience the death of someone we care about or when we contemplate our own deaths, we feel many different emotions—fear, anger, sadness, loneliness, helplessness, resentment, tranquility, peacefulness, inevitability, finality. Our attitudes toward death and the meaning it has for us will differ at different times in our lives. Death meant something quite different to Lauren when she was a young child from what it meant when she was a young adult just beginning a career or family. As she moved into her middle years and beyond, Lauren's concept of death continued changing as her friends began to die and she realized the years she had left were becoming fewer.

To Children

Children who are younger than two or three appear to have no understanding of death. When Maria Nagy (1948) studied 378 children in Budapest, Hungary, she found that their concepts of death fell into three phases. In the first phase, which characterized children between three and five, the child sees death as like a sleep or a journey; it is only a temporary separation. In the second phase, between the ages of five and nine, death is personified. For some children it may be an angel; for others, it may be an evil, frightening monster or a "death man." Although children now see death as final, they still believe their own deaths can be avoided—all they have to do is to outrun the death man. In the final phase, beginning around the age of nine or ten, children develop a realistic, adult view of mortality. They realize that death is final and inevitable; it is a permanent biological process that happens to everyone.

Since the concept of death changes as children grow, what fatally ill children fear most about death varies, depending on their age. The three- to five-year-old seems to fear separation most; death means not being able to be with Mommy or Daddy, Grandma or Grandpa. The five- to nine-year-old is likely to be anxious about death as the end of life and is especially concerned about any accompanying physical injury or mutilation. Among six- to ten-year-olds, there is likely to be an awareness that their illnesses are life-threatening, even if they have not been told they are likely to die. In a study of sixty-three children, Eugenia

The concept of death changes as children grow. Not until they are nine or ten years old do children develop a realistic view of mortality. (Constantine Manos/Magnum Photos)

Waechter (1971) found that when children with fatal illnesses were asked to make up stories about pictures, they were more likely to talk about death than were children with brief illnesses or healthy, nonhospitalized children. In a similar study, John Spinetta, David Rigler, and Myron Karon (1973) found that children who had leukemia were more anxious and more concerned with injury or interference with normal body functioning than were chronically but nonfatally ill children who had received the same number and duration of hospital-related treatments.

To Adults

Most young Americans have grown up in a culture where the topic of death was taboo. In a survey of more than 30,000 young adults, for example, Edwin Shneidman (1973) found that one-third of them never recalled any discussion of death during their childhoods; one-third said it was discussed, but in an uncomfortable atmosphere; and only the remaining third said it was talked about openly. The majority reported first being aware of death between the ages of five and ten, and nearly half reported that the death of a grandparent marked their first personal involvement with mortality. For these young adults, death had a number of meanings: the end and final process of life; the termination of this life with the survival of the spirit; or the beginning of a new life after death. When contemplating their own ends, about a third were fearful or depressed, and over half felt either resolved or pleased at being alive. The most distasteful aspect of death was that "one can no longer have any experiences" followed by the concern that "the process of dying might be painful."

Although young people are likely to have had few personal experiences with death, the middle years of life bring heightened awareness of it as a personal possibility. The middle-aged person is likely to have experienced the death of one or both parents and may have seen a friend die suddenly from a heart attack. As parents and friends begin to die with their goals and projects unfinished, men and women are likely to become apprehensive about death when they are least ready for it. Thus, in a national survey of more than 1,500 adults, John Riley (1970) found that middle-aged adults were most fearful of death and more likely than the young or old to believe that "death always comes too soon."

He also found that older people were least likely to believe that "death always comes too soon" and were more likely than any other group to have made plans for it. Death is generally less frightening to older people and, compared with young adults and the middle-aged, they tend to think more often of death and to talk about it more.

Among the reasons that have been suggested for the diminished fear of death among older persons are three put forth by Richard Kalish (1976). First, because older people have finished many of their life projects, may be facing ill health, or may be having financial problems, they may place less value on life. Second, although death at an early age seems unfair, people who survive beyond their allotted span may feel they are now on "borrowed" time. Third, as older people live through the deaths of friends and relatives, they may become used to the idea of their own deaths.

When people are close to death, a stable, caring environment is important. Dying persons need to be able to talk about dying and to come to terms with their own mortality. (Abigail Heyman/Magnum Photos)

Death also has special meanings for older people. For one thing, the fact that older people know themselves to be close to death alters their perception and use of time. Robert Kastenbaum (1966) found, for example, that when people were asked to tell about their plans for the future, older people did not plan as far ahead as did younger people. Many older people feel that they have completed what they set out to do with their lives, especially if they have achieved what Erik Erikson calls ego integrity. Thus, when Richard Kalish and David Reynolds (1976) asked people what they would do if they had only six months left to live, older people were less likely than younger people to say they would change the way they lived and were more likely to say they would spend their remaining time in quiet contemplation.

What death means to people and how they view it are also likely to depend in part on their education, the stability of their lives, and their religious beliefs. Individuals with little education, for example, are likely to think often of death and to have negative views of it. The less education people have had, the more likely they are to agree that "death always comes too soon" and that "to die is to suffer." Poorly educated people are also least likely to have made any plans for their deaths. The more education a person has, the more likely he or she is to have talked with others about death, to have made a will, and to have discussed funeral arrangements.

When people are close to death, a stable living situation may be particularly important. Morton Lieberman and Annie Coplan (1969) found that people who were near death, whether they lived in an institution or in the community, could talk easily about dying and had come to terms with their own mortality. In contrast, those who were near death but who were waiting to enter a nursing home or who had just been admitted, feared dying and had not come to terms with their own deaths.

Understandably, people's views of death are likely to be strongly influenced by their religious beliefs. Dealing with death and dying is likely to be easier for those who are religious and are regular churchgoers. But religion is not the only comfort. Being firm in one's beliefs, no matter what they are, is likely to ease the fear of death. People who are committed to religion or firm in their atheism are likely to fear death less than those who are less firmly religious and irregular churchgoers (Kalish, 1963).

Cross-Cultural Views

Different cultures offer different views on the nature and meaning of death. The culture in which an individual grows up will influence his attitudes toward dying and death, his experience of dying, and the way he deals with the deaths of others.

Most cultures offer philosophical or religious belief systems, traditions, or rituals that make it easier for individuals to deal with mortality. Death generally is not seen as the end of existence, and consciousness is believed to survive the death of the physical body; the dead person usually goes to a place where he is in the company of his ancestors, spirits, or gods. Most frequently the dead are seen as moving into two kinds of worlds: a heaven or a hell. Life may be viewed as a time of separation, a prison for the spirit, and death as a reunion, a liberation, or a return home (Grof and Halifax, 1977).

In simple societies, people react to death with fear, anger, anguish, calm, or joyful acceptance. Among the Murngin of Australia or the Gond of India, for example, where death is believed to be caused by magic or demons, anger and fear are the common reactions to death. In contrast, among the Tanala of Madagascar or the Tlingit of Alaska, where death is believed to be due to natural causes, calm or even joyful acceptance is the customary reaction. The Tanala believe that the afterlife is not much different from life. They believe that their ancestors wait for them in the afterlife and that at any time these ancestors can return to visit the living.

The idea of reincarnation is central to the meaning of death in a number of religions, including Hinduism and Buddhism. In both, death is an integral part of life, and existence is made up of a cycle of deaths and rebirths. Both religious traditions maintain that individuals can transcend the traumas of life and mortality by accepting death and by finding identity and unity with God. In these belief systems, the quality of an incarnation is influenced by a person's *karma*—his actions

from previous lives. In Hinduism, individuals learn that the body passes through childhood, youth, and old age, and that at death the soul will assume another body (Long, 1975). Death is a normal part of life, not something that must be resisted.

In some places, cultures have developed manuals to ease the encounter with death. The *Tibetan Book of the Dead,* for example, reflects the Buddhist teaching on how to die well; it teaches individuals how to attain a state of mind, characterized by alertness and a focus on the experience of dying, that will be conducive to a "good rebirth" or to a liberation from the death-rebirth cycle. Among Hindus, an individual's frame of mind at the moment of death will determine his later state of being.

In contrast to the Western view of death as sudden and unexpected, in some societies death involves personal choice. Murray Trelease (1975), a priest who worked with Indians in the interior of Alaska, noted that these people had considerable control over the time, place, and manner of their death. When asked to give the sacrament to a dying person, Trelease often found that the person had spent the past few days making plans, telling stories of his life, and praying for all members of his family. He generally died shortly after receiving the sacrament. Clearly, individuals have the power to take an active part in their own deaths.

Jewish traditions are directed toward easing the process of dying for the individual and for his loved ones. The dying person is encouraged to put his worldly and spiritual houses in order through repentance, confession, blessings, and ethical instructions for his survivors. In this way, the dying person can express his fears, find support, and communicate openly with loved ones. Jewish law also provides a structure that helps survivors mourn their loss and reaffirm their social ties. Customs like the bedside vigil, burial rituals, the tearing of clothes, the funeral eulogy, and the "meal of recuperation" encourage mourning and realism about death (Gordon, 1975). According to Jewish custom, the year of mourning is divided into three days of deep grief, seven days of mourning, thirty days of gradual readjustment, and eleven months of remembrance and healing. In this way, the mourners are gradually drawn back into community life.

In Western society, there are basically two views of death. From the scientific perspective, death means the end of existence: the death of the physical body ends life, awareness, consciousness. From a religious perspective, the soul continues to exist after the death of the body. The religious perspective is more widely held than the scientific view. Among the people they surveyed, Richard Kalish and David Reynolds (1976) found that well over half believed that they would live on in some form after their deaths. This belief in an existence after death was held most widely among the elderly. The majority of those who believed in a life after death expected to find some kind of paradise.

THE PROCESS OF DYING

Death can come in a number of different ways. Some people die quickly and unexpectedly, for example, from a heart attack or in an auto accident. For others, such as cancer patients, death comes more slowly and predictably. In addition, as Barney Glaser and Anselm Strauss (1968) have pointed out, the process of dying can often be charted in terms of ups and downs. The older woman who will eventually die of atherosclerosis or the older man with emphysema may find dying a slow, downhill process. For others—for example, the woman with multiple sclerosis—dying may be a kind of staircase with periods of remission during the course of a terminal illness.

How and Where

Given the choice, most young adults would prefer to die either a "sudden but not violent death" or a "quiet, dignified death," although one out of six believes there is "no appropriate kind of death" (Shneidman, 1973). Although one-third of the adults in Edwin Shneidman's survey were sure they would never commit suicide, one-half said that loneliness, illness, or physical pain might lead them to kill themselves. Men were more likely than women to say they might kill themselves because of failure or disgrace or to avoid pain and sickness. Loneliness, atomic war, or the loss of a loved one seemed more likely reasons for suicide

Religious rituals provide a structure that eases the encounter with death and allows survivors to mourn their loss. (Elliott Erwitt/Magnum Photos)

to women. Few of these adults wanted a formal funeral, and one-third wanted no services of any kind.

Most adults want a painless death, but older people are more likely than the young to think of slow and unexpected deaths as equally tragic (Kalish and Reynolds, 1976). Most older people also want death to come quickly in order to avoid suffering; they believe that dying in one's sleep is the best manner of death. Despite people's fears of a lingering and painful death, few spend many months being seriously ill before they die. Most people can expect only a few days or weeks of terminal illness that requires special care.

Even most terminally ill patients avoid a painful death, and older persons often die more easily than the young. In a sample of dying patients studied by John Hinton (1965), 45 percent of those under fifty had unrelieved physical distress or pain; among patients between fifty and seventy, those suffering unrelieved pain dropped to 32 percent, and only 10 percent of those over seventy experienced such discomfort. As death approaches, people are likely to feel increasingly drowsy and be quite unaware of what is going on around them. Drugs, the disease, and the psychological distancing of the dying patient from the world as death approaches all tend to contribute to this drowsiness. Only about 6 percent of dying patients are conscious shortly before death, and the moment of death is only rarely distressful (Hinton, 1965). There is even evidence that, as death approaches, the brain releases a chemical that makes the moment of death pleasant instead of painful (Thomas, 1976). For most, then, death comes as it is desired—quickly, painlessly, and peacefully.

Experience of Dying

Individuals who have narrowly escaped death say that the experience is not painful and may even be peaceful or blissful. Based on more than 35,000 deathbed observations reported by doctors and nurses, Karlis Osis (1961) concluded that fear was not common among dying patients who were conscious just before their deaths, and that a great many reported seeing visions of heaven, beautiful pastures, or lush vegetation.

Raymond Moody (1975) interviewed more than fifty people who had been resuscitated after having been pronounced dead or who had narrowly escaped death by accident. He found a considerable similarity in their reports, although no one had all the common experiences, and no single element was experienced by everyone. Many said it was difficult to talk about their experience because language was inadequate to describe it. The common elements of these brushes with death included overhearing a doctor pronounce one dead; pleasant sensations; noises; the feeling of being drawn quickly through a dark, enclosed space; the feeling of watching one's body from some point outside it; encounters with close relatives or friends who had died; visions of a radiant and benevolent being of light; a partial or total review of one's life; the feeling of approaching a border or limit.

In the process of dying, attitudes toward life changed. Although many first made desperate attempts to get back into their bodies and felt sad that death had come, they soon felt a sense of timelessness, peace, and tranquility, and were unwilling to return. Most had difficulty telling others about their experiences and reported that, as a result of their encounters with death, their attitudes toward life and death had changed. They were no longer afraid of death, they valued and enjoyed life more, and they were more philosophical about existence.

Russell Noyes (1974) reviewed the accounts of people who had faced death and found that such experiences have three phases: resistance, life review, and transcendence. In the first phase, the individual recognizes he is in extreme danger, reacts with fear, and struggles, but finally accepts the certainty of death with calmness. His mental activity and senses may become enhanced and quickened, and time may seem greatly expanded. In the phase of life review, the individual often has the sensation of being outside his physical body and watches himself approach death with detached interest. The past passes before him and this experience is typically pleasant. In the final phase, the individual experiences a cosmic consciousness, characterized by a sense of unity with other people, nature, and the universe; a feeling of being outside time and space; and extraordinary feelings of contentment or ecstasy.

Phases in Dying

As at every other period of life, individuals vary in the way they approach its end. Some welcome it, some simply accept it, some deny it, some disdain it, and some are filled with fear. When a person faces death, the developmental changes that occur are for the first time since birth timed more by the

As people approach death, they withdraw from the outer world; their detachment—a normal phase in the final coming to terms with mortality—often makes their families feel rejected. (James Motlow/Magnum Photos)

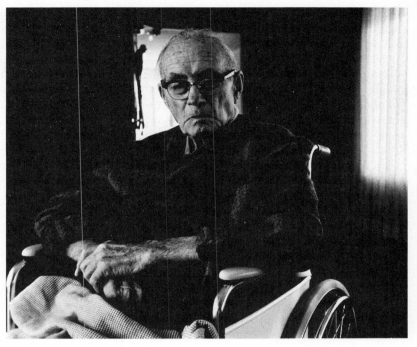

distance from life's end than by age. Shortly before they die, some people seem to act differently, although they may not be aware of subtle changes in their moods, their mental abilities, or the way their bodies function.

One change that may occur is a decline in intellectual abilities, which researchers have called "terminal drop" or "terminal decline" (Kleemeier, 1962; Riegel, Riegel, and Meyer, 1967). Robert Kleemeier did the first research on this decline. After he had tested older men on four occasions over a twelve-year period, he found that the men who died shortly after the last testing had declined more rapidly in their intellectual abilities than had the surviving men.

This decline may in part be connected with a tendency for the individual who is close to death to become less personally involved with the outer world, and to withdraw and become distant. When Morton Lieberman (1965) spent two and one-half years studying people in a home for the aged, he found that those who died shortly after they completed a series of psychological tests had less energy, were less able to organize information from their surroundings, and had less complex views of themselves and the world than did residents who were still alive a year afterward. According to Lieberman, people approaching death pull away from those around them, because they are struggling to

deal with the changes going on within their minds and bodies. This psychological withdrawal and reduced effectiveness in dealing with the world was not the result of physical illness, but of nearness to death. Residents in the same home who became seriously ill, but who recovered, showed none of these changes.

Children are also likely to become isolated from their parents and surroundings as they approach death. John Spinetta, David Rigler, and Myron Karon (1974) found, for example, that six-to ten-year-old children with leukemia placed figures of their mothers, nurses, and doctors farther from themselves in a dollhouselike hospital room than did chronically ill, hospitalized children. Like adults, children who are near death may feel a growing psychological distance from the people around them.

The reverse may also be true. It appears that one's surroundings can lead to psychological withdrawal from life. When Judith Rodin and Ellen Langer (1978) studied a home for the aged in which one group of old people was given some control over their lives and another group was not, they discovered psychological differences between the two groups. The group that had been given some control was happier, more active, and more alert than the other group. What is more, eighteen months later, 15 percent of the group that had control over their lives had died compared with 30 percent of the group that had no control. The normal death rate in the home was 25 percent.

Whether death comes quickly or slowly, according to Elisabeth Kübler-Ross (1969), most people pass through succeeding phases as they deal with it. At first the dying person denies the possibility of his or her death, saying "No, not me" and refusing to believe that the diagnosis is true. In the next phase, the person becomes filled with rage; the dominant reaction changes to "Why me?" and he or she feels anger at others who are healthy, envying their good fortune. In the third phase, the dying person attempts to bargain for life, trying to buy time from God, the doctor or nurse, or loved ones. At this time, the person believes that if one does the right thing, death can be postponed. The fourth phase is one of depression. Part of the depression may be a reaction to past losses, for example, the loss of physical health or of one's job because of illness. Another part is a prep-

aration so the dying person can give up things of the world and relationships with loved ones. The final phase is acceptance, characterized by quiet expectation, peacefulness, and a sense of distance from the world. Based on her experience, Kübler-Ross believes that acceptance is the healthiest way to face death. Once it is accepted, a person can await the end quietly and look back over the years, accepting life for what it has been.

Some dying people may experience only some of the phases described by Kübler-Ross; others may experience them in a different order, or may rapidly move back and forth between the phases in a period of hours or even minutes. In a matter of days, for example, a dying man may talk to a friend with complete honesty about his approaching death and then surprise that same friend with the declaration that he will leave the hospital the following week and begin a new job.

Some researchers believe that a more useful way to regard preparation for death is to see the

One way people prepare for death is by reviewing their past; this often takes the form of storytelling that helps them weave the past into a meaningful perspective. (Cornell Capa/Magnum Photos)

dying person's death as twofold. Edwin Shneidman (1976) argues that in facing death, which he calls "death work," the dying person first deals with his impending death at a psychological level, preparing himself to meet his end. Second, the dying person prepares himself for death in relation to those he loves, helping prepare his loved ones to be survivors. Shneidman suggests that the way people face death reflects their total personalities—their "philosophy of life." In this sense, people are likely to face death in much the same way they have faced life's other developmental tasks.

No matter how preparation for death is regarded, acceptance is one of its important features, and the tendency of the dying person to reminisce is one way to come to terms with his or her own life. At any age, a person enjoys looking back at his or her past and telling stories about it, but for people who are approaching death, this life review helps them integrate their lives as they have been lived in relation to how they might have been (Butler, 1963). In this sense, the storytelling and reminiscing not only enable older people to recall facts but also to weave the past into an acceptable and meaningful perspective.

Easing the End

At any age, people want to die at home. Over the past few decades, however, fewer people have been dying there. In New York City, for example, the proportion of deaths in institutions rose from 66 percent in 1955 to 73 percent in 1967 (Lerner, 1976). Most hospital deaths are due to stroke, heart disease, cancer, and chronic diseases like diabetes. By 1967, only 24 percent of the deaths in New York City occurred at home.

In the past few years, people with fatal illnesses—and those who are still healthy—have begun to emphasize their need to have some control over the time and place of their deaths. In one response to this demand, hospices have been established to provide a new option for the dying person. In hospices, individuals can die gracefully without the indignity of extraordinary measures to prolong life, such as intravenous feeding, transfusions, and respirators. The aim of the hospice is to provide a humane, dignified environment for the dying. St. Christopher's, the first hospice, was established in England by Cicely Saunders; others are now being established in England, Canada, and the United States. Medical treatment is available to ease discomfort and relieve pain, and

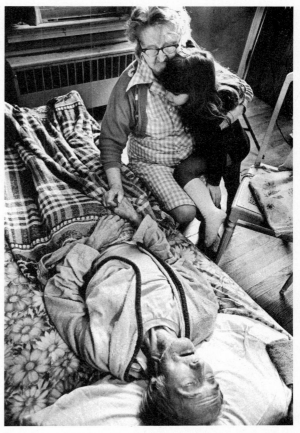

People want to die at home; 81-year-old Frank Tugend, who died at home after a three-year slide into senility, had the comfort of family life around him until the very end. (Mark and Dan Jury)

friends and family can visit at any hour. Hospices offer the dying person a warm, homelike atmosphere in which he can face death without placing the burden of care on his family.

In some places, physicians are releasing patients from the hospital so they can die at home. In Minneapolis, for example, children who are dying of cancer are allowed to go home. It has been reported that the parents of these children feel less guilty than parents of children who die in hospitals, and they are pleased that they can satisfy their children's wishes to be at home. Pain can be controlled as well at home as in the hospital, and when a family member dies at home, death can become less mysterious and frightening for the whole family. Among people who had experienced the death of a family member at home, most were glad that their loved ones had died among relatives (Cartwright, Hockey, and Anderson, 1973).

Whether a dying person has the right to choose death when the circumstances of his life are no longer acceptable continues to be debated. To some, the promise of a life filled with pain or considerable physical or mental damage makes death a preferred alternative. The practice of euthanasia, or encouraging a "good" or "easy" death, takes two forms, passive and active (Morison, 1971). In passive euthanasia, everything possible is done to ease pain and discomfort, but extraordinary life-prolonging measures are eliminated. One's life is not extended by the use of machines, drugs, transfusions, or intravenous feedings. In active euthanasia, death is hastened by the use of drugs or some other simple procedure.

Because many people would like to have some control over the manner of their deaths, an increasing number have begun to write "living wills," documents that give them an opportunity to decide how they will die by setting forth the circumstances at a time when they can make reasonable decisions. A living will specifies when the writer would choose death over life and expresses a preference for active or passive euthanasia. Although the will is not legally binding, it gives physicians and families some guidance at a time when their decisions can affect the quality of a loved one's death.

COPING WITH DEATH

Although it may be difficult for us to imagine our own deaths, we most certainly will experience the deaths of others. Coping with the death of a loved one, if death does not come quickly and unexpectedly, involves dealing with one's own feelings and reactions as well as maintaining a relationship with the dying person.

Anticipatory Grief

When people learn that a loved one is dying, they often begin to prepare themselves for the impending death. In this anticipatory grieving, people deal with their feelings about a death before the person dies. Thus, during a prolonged terminal illness, survivors may have completed much of their mourning before the death occurs. When this happens, mourning after the loved one dies may be shorter and easier.

According to Elisabeth Kübler-Ross (1976),

when family members anticipate the death of a loved one, their reactions go through a sequence similar to that felt by the dying person. The first response is denial, when family members cannot believe that the loved one will actually die. At this point, the family may shop around for a physician who will offer a more optimistic diagnosis. The second likely reaction is anger, commonly expressed toward the doctor, the hospital staff, or even toward the dying person. Family members also often feel guilty and want to make up for past mistakes and lost opportunities. As they anticipate the impending death, they become sad and depressed. Kübler-Ross believes that the most difficult time for the family is likely to be when the dying person is detaching himself from the world. Although this detachment is a normal way for a person to deal with his or her own death, it tends to make the family feel rejected.

Communication

Dealing with the death of another involves maintaining a warm and loving relationship with the dying person and communicating in a satisfying way with him. Since people find it hard to think about death, and even harder to talk about it, communicating with the dying can be difficult.

Dealing with death involves maintaining a warm and loving relationship with the dying person. When death can be talked about openly, the process is easier for both patient and family. (Leonard Freed/Magnum Photos)

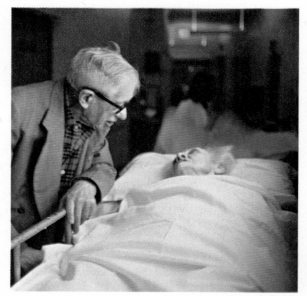

Grieving is a normal way of adjusting to the death of a loved one; survivors progress from numbness through yearning to despair, and at last are finally able to reorganize their lives. (Elliott Erwitt/Magnum Photos)

People frequently ask if a dying person should be told of his condition. The answer depends on the person's wishes. In one study 80 percent of cancer patients said they wanted to be told that their illness was fatal (Gilbertsen and Wangensteen, 1961). These patients felt that knowing they were going to die helped them understand their illness and gave them peace of mind. It also permitted them to plan for their deaths and to get their affairs in order. But not all people who say they want such information actually mean what they say (Cappon, 1962). Closeness to death may make some people less eager to know the truth. Even if people are not directly told they are dying, however, most people become aware that their illness is no ordinary ailment.

Many doctors prefer not to tell patients that they are dying, and when the patient, the physician, the hospital staff, and the family all know that a person is dying but are unwilling to discuss it, a problem exists. Barney Glaser and Anselm Strauss (1965) have called this situation "the ritual drama of mutual pretense." Although the pretense may offer dignity and privacy to the dying patient, it also keeps him from having warm and supportive relationships with his family and from being able to deal openly with his concerns about death. The dying person may wish to talk about death at some times and not at others, but when he needs to talk, it is important that a caring person is nearby and willing to listen.

When illness and death can be talked about openly, the patient finds it easier to face death and the family finds it easier to cope with the patient's condition. This is especially true in the case of dying children. When John Spinetta (1977) studied families with dying children, he found that children who belonged to families that talked openly were the most willing to express their anxiety and anger about their illnesses, the most willing to accept negative feelings expressed by their families, the most able to express their desires for more affection and love from their families, and had the most positive self-concepts.

Bereavement

The death of any person affects different survivors differently. When Susan's father died, she felt the loss acutely. However, the loss did not evoke the same kind of grief as would the death of her husband. The more closely the death affects the daily lives of the survivors, the more disruptive its impact is likely to be.

Grieving is a normal way of adjusting to the death of a loved one, and Colin Murray Parkes (1972) has identified four phases of the emotion: a period of numbness; a time of yearning, characterized by the desire to recover the lost loved one; a period of despair, when the reality of the loss sets in; and a period of reorganizing one's way of life to adjust to the loss. For many, this grief lasts a year or two. For some, however, the loss of a loved one can be overwhelmingly stressful. Death rates among widows, for example, are higher during the first year of widowhood than among married people of the same age. The suicide rate among the widowed, especially among older men, is also higher than among married people, as is the incidence of psychological and physiological disorders.

For parents, the death of a child is understandably painful and traumatic. At various points, we have emphasized the fact that developmental tasks are easier to handle when they occur on schedule. The death of a child is especially traumatic because it is untimely. Kübler-Ross (1976) points out that if parents are to cope with the death of a child, they need to be able to express their feelings of shock, grief, anger, and anguish; to be able to be with their dead child and to hold him; to be encouraged to go back to the hospital a few weeks after the child has died to ask questions and get the details that make their child's death real to them.

The death of a parent is equally difficult for children, and each year over three million American children under the age of nineteen lose one or both parents. The grief of children is made more difficult because they are rarely given any information about the death and are not helped to mourn by being encouraged to express their feelings. When children are not told how a parent died, they may feel that their own anger or resentment caused the death. But when children who have lost a parent are allowed and encouraged to express their feelings, later emotional difficulties may be prevented (Koch, 1977).

Unfortunately, the death of a parent often is hidden from a child. He may not be permitted to go to the funeral, to visit the cemetery, or to see the parent's body. This void can make it hard for a child to realize that the parent has died. When they compared children who had made good adjustments to the loss of their fathers with children who had developed psychological problems after the loss, Josephine Hilgard and Martha Newman (1959) found that children who adjusted successfully to the loss came from a home where there was a good relationship between the parents before the death and where family and community resources were used by the surviving parent; had a strong surviving parent who could cope with the demands and new roles after the death; and had an ability to tolerate separations, losses, and endings.

All of us are survivors, but all survivors must eventually die. Successful preparation for death is still a mystery and probably will always be one. By

The relationships of young and old, present and past, symbolize the continuity of human development. (Elliott Erwitt/Magnum Photos)

some objective standards, a person has success-fully prepared himself for a developmental task if he handles it well. The problem with death is that it is impossible to determine whether anyone has been successful. Dying is a personal and unique experience, and birth and death are the only two events in life that each individual must experience alone. Perhaps the most sensible preparation for the end of life, then, is a life well lived from its beginning.

SUMMARY

1. Life expectancy has increased dramatically in this century, primarily because more people survive infancy and childhood. Disease and aging tend to go together in older people, forming a vicious circle that is likely to result in faster aging, loss of health, and, finally, death.

2. A number of theories have been advanced to explain the precise mechanisms of aging, but re-searchers agree that longevity involves both environmental and genetic factors.

3. The meaning of death varies from youth to old age and from culture to culture.

4. Most people who are facing death pass through similar phases: denial, rage, bargaining for life, depression, and acceptance. At any age, death comes easiest when the person is allowed to die with dignity. For most people, the moment of death is quick, painless, and peaceful.

5. Grieving is a normal way of coping with the death of a loved one, and survivors go through a sequence of emotions like that passed through by the dying person.

6. Dying is a last and inevitable developmental task for everyone, and preparation for the end of life may begin at any age and may take many forms.

GLOSSARY

accommodation. According to Piaget, the modification of existing schemes to incorporate new knowledge that does not fit them.

action-instrument. In the two-word stage of language development, the indication of knowledge of the use of instruments, as in "Cut knife."

action-location. In the two-word stage of language development, the expression of the location of an action, as in "Sit chair."

action-recipient. In the two-word stage of language development, the indication of who is to benefit from an action, as in "Cookie me."

acuity. The ability to see objects clearly and to resolve detail.

adaptation. A key principle in ethological theories, referring to the way that behavior changes or develops to meet environmental demands and to insure survival and reproduction.

afterbirth. The placenta, its membranes, and the rest of the umbilical cord, all expelled in the final stage of labor.

agent, action, and object. In the two-word stage of language development, the expression of an agent's action on an object, using only two of the components of the thought, as in "Daddy ball" for "Daddy throw ball."

aggressiveness. Verbal or physical behavior that is inappropriate or harms someone.

alleles. The different forms that a gene can take at a given site on a chromosome.

amniocentesis. A means of detecting fetal abnormality by the insertion of a hollow needle through the maternal abdomen and the drawing out of a sample of amniotic fluid on which chro-mosomal analyses can be performed.

amnion. The inner membrane of the sac that surrounds and protects the developing fertilized ovum.

androgens. Male hormones.

androgynous. Capable of expressing both masculine and feminine behaviors and attitudes, depending on their appropriateness to the particular situation.

Apgar score. Developed by Apgar and James in 1962, a much-used and practical scoring system for assessing, on a scale from 0 to 2, appearance, heart rate, reflex irritability, activity, muscle tone, and respiratory effort in newborns. The totaled score may vary from 0 to 10 (10 being best).

artificialism. A kind of precausal thinking that refers to explanations involving either God or man as the artisan of all natural things.

assertiveness. Verbal or physical behavior that is appropriate and that injures no one.

assimilation. According to Piaget, the incorporation of new knowledge through the use of existing schemes.

asynchrony. The maturation of different body parts at different rates. This disproportion becomes most pronounced during puberty.

attachment. The primary social bond that develops between an infant and its caregiver.

attribution. In the two-word stage of language development, the modifying of nouns with attributes, as in "Red truck."

autonomy. A feeling of self-control and self-determination. According to Erikson's theory of psychosocial development, this feeling develops around the ages of two to four and manifests itself in the child's increasing demands to determine his own behavior.

babbling. The sound sequences of alternating vowels and consonants, such as "babababa." Produced by the infant, they may be a form of motor practice that facilitates later speech development.

basal metabolism. The rate of energy required to maintain the body's functioning while resting.

behavior. An observable act that can be described or measured reliably.

body ideal. The body type defined by one's culture as ideally attractive and sex appropriate.

canalization. The temporary deviation from and subsequent return to a child's normal growth curve.

cephalocaudal development. The progression of physical and motor development from head to foot. For example, a baby's head develops and grows before his torso, his arms, and his legs.

cerebral dominance. Refers to the fact that one cerebral hemisphere is dominant over the other in the control of body movements, as in handedness.

cervix. The pinhead-sized opening that separates the vagina from the uterus.

chorion. The outer membrane of the sac that surrounds and protects the developing fertilized ovum.

chromosomes. The beadlike strings of genes present in every cell of the body. Except in the gametes, they occur in pairs that reproduce and split during cell formation.

classical conditioning. A procedure in which conditioned reflexes are established by the association of one stimulus with another stimulus that is known to cause an unconditioned reflex. Also known as Pavlovian conditioning or respondent conditioning.

clinical study. A study consisting of in-depth interviews and observations. It can be controlled or can be varied for each subject.

cognition. The process of gaining knowledge about the world through sensing, perceiving, using symbols, and reasoning; the actual knowledge that an individual has about the world.

cognitive theorists. Theorists such as Jean Piaget and Jerome Bruner, who describe intellectual development, and Roger Brown, who describes early language behavior. They see children's thinking as different from but no less effective than that of adults.

cohorts. The members of a certain age group; a group of people of the same age.

conception. The uniting of the sperm and the egg, which signals the beginning of life.

concrete-operational stage. A subperiod of the representational stage, in Piaget's theory of cognitive development, which begins when children understand new kinds of logical operations involving reversible transformations of concrete objects and events.

conditioned reflex. In classical conditioning, a reflex that comes to be elicited by a previously neutral stimulus.

conjunctive concept. A concept in which all the attributes of a category must be present in order for the object to be included in the category.

conservation. The understanding that certain perceptual changes do not actually alter physical quantities. For example, rearranging a row of objects does not affect their number.

constructionist. A description of Piaget's theory that a child's actions on objects in his environment yield knowledge of the effects of his actions and the properties of the objects and that these actions thus construct his understanding of reality.

control. The intentional modification of any condition of an investigation. These modifications may include the selection of subjects for study, the experiences they have in the study, and the possible responses that they can give to that experience.

conventional level. The level of moral reasoning in which value is placed in maintaining the conventional social order and the expectations of others.

convergence. The mechanism by which the slightly different images of an object seen by each eye come together to form a single image.

correlation coefficient. The numerical expression of how closely two sets of measurements correspond. Correlation coefficients range from +1.00 (perfect positive correlation) to −1.00 (perfect negative correlation).

co-twin control. A method of studying the relative contributions of maturation and experience in which the experimenter gives one of a pair of twins some experiences believed to be important in learning a skill and withholds or delays those same experiences for the other twin.

cross-sectional studies. Studies that compare different age groups at some specific point in time.

deoxyribonucleic acid (DNA). The complex chemical containing the genetic code that guides development.

dependence. Reliance on others for comfort, nurturance, or assistance in accomplishing some task or activity.

detachment. The infant's desire to try out new experiences and to expand his competence. Developing in the second year, it coexists and interacts with the attachment system.

dichotic. Pertaining to a technique used in listening research in which two stimuli are presented at the same time, one to each ear.

differentiation. The developmental trend in which an infant's abilities become increasingly distinct and specific.

disjunctive concept. A concept in which a member of a category may possess some, but need not possess all, of several different attributes to be included in the category.

displacement. The ability to communicate information about objects, people, and events in another place or another time; one of three formal properties of language.

dominant gene. The gene whose corresponding trait appears in the individual when it is paired with a different gene for that trait.

Down's syndrome. A condition that can result from an extra chromosome in the fertilized egg, or when extra material from Chromosome 21 becomes attached to another chromosome. Formerly called mongolism, it produces various physical abnormalities and mental retardation in the affected child.

ecological. The approach to studying development which takes into account the limiting and determining effects of the physical and social environment.

ectoderm. The layer of cells in the embryo from which the skin, sense organs, and nervous system will develop.

ego. An aspect of personality, in Freud's theory, that guides a person's realistic coping behavior and mediates the eternal conflicts between what one wants to do (id) and what one must or must not do (superego).

egocentrism. In cognitive development, the tendency of an individual to think that others see things from the same point of view and that they also experience his own behavior, thought, and feelings in relation to these things.

embryonic period (embryo). The six weeks, following the two-week germinal period, during which the organism begins to take shape and its various organ systems begin to form.

emotional dependence. Dependence on others, which has as its aim the obtaining of their comfort and nurturance.

endoderm. The layer of cells in the embryo from which the visceral organs and digestive tract develop.

equilibration. The most general developmental principle in Piaget's theory, which states that an organism always tends toward biological and psychological balance and that development is a progressive approximation to an ideal state of equilibrium that it never fully achieves.

erythroblastosis. An abnormal condition that may develop in an Rh positive fetus if substances from the mother's Rh negative blood cross the placenta.

estrogens. Female hormones.

expectancy. Anticipation of a given stimulus determined by one's previous experiences with related stimuli. Deviation from expectancy is a factor in selective attention.

experimentation. A type of study designed to control the arrangement and manipulation of conditions in order to systematically observe particular phenomena.

extinguish. To gradually eliminate a response by withholding reinforcement.

Fallopian tube. The tube that connects the ovaries with the uterus.

fetal period (fetus). The developing organism from approximately eight weeks after conception to birth.

field study. A study of naturally occurring behavior in which the researcher controls only some aspects of the situation.

formal-operational period. The last of the major stages in Piaget's theory of intellectual development. It begins around age twelve when the individual starts to develop a formal logic that consists of "If . . . then" statements and to engage in thinking that is characterized by the ability to consider what is possible, as well as what is.

gametes. The mature reproductive cells; the sperm and the egg.

genes. The microscopic elements carried by the chromosomes. They contain the codes that produce inherited physical traits and behavior dispositions.

genetic epistemology. The developmental study of what is known and how it comes to be known; most closely associated with Piaget's theory.

genotype. The specific combination of alleles that characterize one's genetic make-up.

germinal period. The first two weeks after conception when the fertilized egg is primarily engaged in cell division.

gestation period. The total period of prenatal development calculated from the beginning of the mother's last menstruation (280 days, 40 weeks, or 9 calendar months).

gestational age. The age of the fetus calculated from the date of conception.

glial cells. Supporting and connecting cells in the brain that play an essential role in nourishing the neurons.

gonococcus. The bacterium that produces gonorrhea.

gonorrhea. A venereal disease.

grammar. The structural principles of a language; syntax.

grasping reflex. The tendency during the first few weeks of life for an infant to clutch any small object placed in his hand.

guilt. A negative feeling that stems from deviation from one's own internalized moral standards.

habituation. A decrement in responding associated with repeated stimulation; analogous to becoming bored with a stimulus.

heritability. An estimate, based on a sample of individuals, of the relative contribution of genetics to a given trait or behavior.

heterozygous. The condition in which cells contain different genes for the same trait. The dominant gene will determine the appearance of the trait.

homozygous. The condition in which cells have matching genes for a trait.

hostile aggression. Behavior that aims at hurting another person.

id. An aspect of personality, in Freud's theory, in which all unconscious impulses reside.

identification (language). In the two-word stage of language development, the verbal extension of a simple pointing response, as in "See doggy."

identification (socialization). A developmental process through which a child comes to be like specific people whom he has grown to respect, admire, or love.

imitation. The principle and the processes by which an individual copies or reproduces what has been observed.

implanted. Attached; after floating freely for several days, the fertilized ovum becomes implanted in the uterine wall.

imprinting. The phenomenon occurring during a sensitive period of an animal's infancy, in which the animal follows a certain type of moving object, usually its mother, and forms a strong, long-lasting social attachment to it.

induced abortion. The premature removal of the fetus by deliberate interference.

instrumental aggression. Behavior that aims at retrieving or acquiring an object, territory, or privilege.

instrumental conditioning. See *operant conditioning.*

instrumental dependence. Dependence that involves seeking assistance as a means of accomplishing some task or activity.

integration (hierarchic). The developmental trend of combining simple, differentiated skills into more complex skills.

kwashiorkor. The severe, often fatal, disease caused by prolonged protein deficiency.

lanugo. The fine hair appearing on parts of some newborns' bodies that may remain several weeks before disappearing.

lateralization. The developmental process in which one hemisphere of the brain becomes dominant.

location. In the two-word stage of language development, the signaling of the location of an object with such words as "here" and "there."

locus of control. The perceived location of the control over an individual's life. It can be internal, as when one believes he controls his own life, or it can be external, as when one believes his life is controlled by forces outside himself.

longitudinal studies. Studies that follow the same subjects over a specified period of time.

maternal deprivation. The loss or lack of mothering.

meiosis. The cell division that produces gametes, each containing twenty-three single rather than twenty-three pairs of chromosomes.

menarche. First menstruation.

menstrual age. The age of the fetus when calculated from the beginning of the mother's last menstruation.

menstrual cycle. The discharge of blood and tissue from the uterus, which occurs monthly from puberty to menopause, except during pregnancy.

mesoderm. The layer of cells in the embryo from which the muscular, circulatory, and skeletal systems will develop.

miscarriage. The spontaneous expulsion from the uterus of a fetus less than twenty-eight weeks old.

modeling. A principle and a process by which an individual learns by observing the behavior of others.

moral conduct. A form of complex behavior involving three aspects: reasoning, feeling, and action.

moral development. The nature and course of development of an individual's moral thoughts, feelings, and actions.

Moro reflex (response). A reflex which is most easily elicited during the infant's first three months of life and which consists of a thrusting out of the arms in an embracelike movement when the baby suddenly loses support for his neck and head.

mutagenic. Altering the genetic structure of cells, which results in the production of new forms.

myelin. A white, fatty substance that covers some nerve fibers.

naturalistic observation. A form of study in which there is observation of behavior without any interference from the investigator.

nature. The genetic-biological determinants used to explain developmental changes.

negation. In the two-word stage of language development, the use of a negative construction to contradict or to avoid a misunderstanding.

neonate. A technical term for a newborn baby.

neuron. One of the approximately 10 billion cells in the average adult brain.

nonexistence. In the two-word stage of language development, the expression of object disappearance or cessation of activity, as in "All-gone ball."

norm. An outline that describes the development of an important attribute or skill and the approximate ages at which it appears in the average child.

novelty. A possible factor in selective attention, involving a different or unique aspect of a stimulus.

nurture. The environmental determinants used to explain developmental changes.

object identity. In cognitive development, the understanding that an object remains the same even though it may undergo various transformations.

object permanence. In cognitive development, the understanding that an object continues to exist even though it disappears or is out of sight.

operant conditioning. A procedure by which the frequency of a response can be increased or decreased, depending on when, how, and to what extent it is reinforced. Associated with B.F. Skinner, it is also called *instrumental conditioning*.

ovaries. The female reproductive glands, which release ova.

overextension. A generalization in the apparent meaning of a word so that it includes a number of dissimilar objects or events.

overregularization. A kind of temporary error in language development in which the apparent attempt is to simplify or to make language more regular than it actually is. In English, this is likely to be shown when a child overregularizes the past tense of verbs ("breaked") and the plural forms of nouns ("foots").

ovum. A human egg cell; the largest cell in the human body.

perception. An important aspect of cognitive development, involving the transformation of sensations into information.

phase (in development). A concept that indicates that development is continuous across the life span; the divisions are culturally determined.

phenotype. The nature of a trait as it appears in the individual; it reflects the contributions of both genetic and environmental factors.

phenylketonuria (PKU). The inherited inability to metabolize phenylalinine, a component of some foods. It occurs when the two recessive genes for PKU are paired.

placenta. The organ that transmits nourishment and waste between the mother and the fetus.

placing. A reflex movement, which is most easily elicited during the first three months of an infant's life, consisting of a baby's lifting his foot onto a surface.

polygenic. Indicates that several genes have an equal and cumulative effect in producing a trait.

possession. In the two-word stage of language development, the expression of ownership, as in "Daddy coat."

precausal. A kind of thinking in which a child maintains that some events are either completely or partly caused by psychological, subjective factors. An example is a child's ideas about the origins of dreams.

premature delivery. The spontaneous termination of a pregnancy when the fetus is older than twenty weeks.

premoral level. The level of moral reasoning in which value is placed in physical acts and needs, not in persons or social standards.

preoperational stage. A subperiod of the representational period, in Piaget's theory of cognitive development, which begins when children start to record experiences symbolically, involves the use of language to record experiences, and involves the appearance of the ability to think in terms of classes, numbers, and relationships.

principled level. The level of moral reasoning in which value resides in self-chosen principles and standards that have a universal logical validity and can therefore be shared.

productivity. The ability to combine individual words into an unlimited number of sentences; one of the three formal properties of language.

proximodistal development. The progression of physical and motor development from the center of the body toward the periphery. For example, a baby learns to control the movements of his shoulders before he can direct his arms or fingers.

puberty. The main biological event of adolescence, characterized by the attainment of biological sexual maturity.

questions. In the two-word stage of language development, the transformation of all sentence types into questions by the use of rising intonation or question words, as in "Where ball?"

rapid eye movement (REM). A type of eye movement that occurs during a certain period of sleep and that is accompanied by changes in respiratory, muscle, and brain-wave activity.

reaction range. The limits set by genetic conditions on an individual's possible behavior.

reaction time. The interval of time that elapses between the instant a stimulus is presented and the individual's reaction to it.

recessive gene. The subordinate member of a pair of genes whose corresponding trait fails to appear.

recurrence. In the two-word stage of language development, the indication of the presence, absence, or repetition of things and actions, as in "Book again."

reductionism. A general point of view that holds that complex phenomena can be understood and explained by breaking them into simpler components.

reflex. An unlearned or naturally occurring reaction to a stimulus.

reinforcement. In operant conditioning, the presentation or withdrawal of an event following a response, which increases the likelihood of that response occurring again.

releasing stimuli. Those events that regularly evoke certain behavior in all members of a species; a key concept in ethological theories.

reliability. The dependability and consistency of a measure, observation, or finding.

replication. In studies, the attempt to repeat the essential features of an investigation and its findings.

representational skills. Those cognitive skills or ways in which an individual represents and constructs an understanding of his world and the people, objects, and events in it.

representational stage. A stage in Piaget's theory of cognitive development that begins with the preoperational and ends with the concrete-operational period.

respiratory distress syndrome. The lung condition (formerly called hyaline disease of the lungs) in which the fetus is unable to maintain necessary surfactin levels and dies.

respondent conditioning. See *classical conditioning*.

reversibility. The mental operation or understanding, according to Piaget's theory of cognitive development, in which one can think of a transformation that would reverse a sequence of events or restore the original condition.

rickets. The condition caused by a calcium deficiency during infancy and childhood and characterized by the softening and malformation of the bones.

role taking. The ability to take the role or point of view of another person; a requirement in cognitive and other forms of development.

rooting reflex. A reflex that is most easily elicited during the baby's first two weeks of life, consisting of the baby turning his head in the direction of any object that gently stimulates the corner of his mouth.

schedules of reinforcement. In operant conditioning, the timetables for reinforcing behavior; they have different effects on the rate of responding.

schemes. Piaget's term for action patterns that are built up and coordinated throughout the course of cognitive development. In the infant, they are like concepts without words. Throughout development, such schemes are presumed to be involved in the acquisition and structuring of knowledge.

self-actualizing. According to Maslow, the human tendency to realize one's full potential in work and love. It develops after the basic needs of food, security, and esteem are met.

self-concept. The sum of ideas one has about oneself.

self-demand feeding. A feeding schedule in which a baby is fed according to when he is hungry, not according to a schedule designed by others.

self-esteem. A concept or description involving the way that one evaluates himself.

self-regulation. The regulation of one's own conduct.

semanticity. The learning of the meaning of words, and the process of communicating meaning. One of the three formal properties of language.

sensation. A necessary aspect for cognitive development involving the reception, through the various sense organs, of stimulation from the external world.

sensitive periods. Periods of development during which an organism is most likely to be susceptible to a particular influence.

sensory-motor stage. The first major stage in Piaget's theory of cognitive development, which begins at birth and extends through the first two years of life. It is characterized by the development of sensory and motor functions and by the infant's coming to know the world as a result of interacting with and affecting it.

separation distress. The distinctly negative reaction of an infant to separation and his attempts to regain contact with his attachment figure.

sequence (in development). A concept used to explain the relationship among developmental changes in behavior, indicating that some behaviors precede others in a meaningfully related way.

sex role. The pattern of behavior

and attitudes considered to characterize each sex.

sex-role stereotypes. Simplified, fixed concepts about the behaviors and traits typical of each sex.

shame. A negative feeling response that is a reaction to the disapproval of others.

small-for-dates. The condition in which a baby is underweight for his gestational age.

social-learning theory. A set of concepts and principles from behavior-learning theory, frequently used in describing and explaining personality characteristics and social behavior.

socialization. The process of psychologically growing into a society, in which an individual acquires the behaviors, attitudes, values, and roles expected of him.

sociometric analysis. A method for charting how often a child is chosen by his peers as a preferred friend or companion.

spermatozoon. A single sperm cell.

spontaneous abortion. The expulsion from the uterus of a fetus older than twenty-eight weeks.

stage (in development). A concept used to explain the orderly relationship among developmental changes in behavior and indicating that the organization of behavior is qualitatively different from one stage to the next.

stepping. A reflex movement, which is most easily elicited during the infant's first two weeks of life, that consists of straightening the legs out at the knees and hip, as if to stand, when the infant is held with his feet touching a surface.

stranger fear. The negative response and withdrawal that occurs in reaction to strangers, usually developing a month or two after specific attachments begin.

sublimation. The altering, in socially acceptable ways, of forbidden impulses. According to Freud, it is one of the processes important in the development of rational behavior.

successive approximations. In operant conditioning, a procedure in which behaviors that resemble more and more closely the final desired response are reinforced.

superego. An aspect of personality, in Freud's theory, defined as the conscience; develops as the child internalizes parental and societal values and standards.

surfactin. The liquid that coats the air sacs of the lungs and permits them to transmit oxygen from the air to the blood.

symbolic play. Play that becomes more symbolic and complex as the ability to imagine and pretend develops.

syntax. See *grammar*.

syphilis. A venereal disease due to systemic infection with treponema pallidum.

term (prenatal development). The gestational age of 266 days from conception. Formerly, babies born before term were considered premature.

testes. The male reproductive glands, which release sperm.

theory (developmental). A set of logically related statements about the nature of development that help psychologists understand, predict, and explain human behavior.

totalism. Defined by Erikson as an organization of one's self-concept that has rigid, absolute, and arbitrary boundaries.

transfer. A process or phenomenon in which the learning of one task results in improvement of learning or performance in another related, but different, task.

transitivity. A concept that requires the joining together of two or more instances of an abstract relation; for example, if A is larger than B and B is larger than C, then A is larger than C.

trimester. A period of approximately three months; often used in discussing pregnancy.

Turner's syndrome. A condition resulting from a missing sex chromosome in the fertilized egg. It produces children with physical abnormalities and mental retardation.

unconditioned reflex. In classical conditioning, one of two kinds of reflexes; it is inborn and occurs naturally to a stimulus.

unconscious impulses. In Freud's theory, those irrational impulses that reside in the id and that the individual is unaware of.

uniformism. A concept indicating immersion into the peer group and the acceptance of its norms as infallible and regulatory.

variability. Variation due to individual differences as well as other sources of influence.

variables. Those factors in an investigation that can vary in quantity or magnitude, or in some qualitative aspect, and that may or may not affect the results of the investigation.

vernix. The white greasy material that covers and lubricates the newborn for passage through the birth canal.

visual accommodation. The ability to alternate focus for objects at different distances.

vital capacity. The air-holding capacity of the lungs.

Acheson, R. M. "Effects of Nutrition and Disease on Human Growth," in J. M. Tanner (ed.), *Human Growth*. New York: Pergamon Press, 1960, pp. 73–92.

———. "Maturation of the Skeleton," in F. Falkner (ed.), *Human Development*. Philadelphia: Saunders, 1966, pp. 465–502.

Acredolo, L. P., H. L. Pick, Jr., and M. G. Olsen. "Environmental Differentiation and Familiarity as Determinants of Children's Memory for Spatial Location," *Developmental Psychology*, 11 (1975), 495–501.

Adams, B. N. "Isolation, Function and Beyond. American Kinship in the 1960's," *Journal of Marriage and the Family,* 32 (1970), 575–597.

Adamsons, K., Jr. "The Role of Thermal Factors in Fetal and Neonatal Life," *Pediatric Clinics of North America*, 13 (1966), 599–619.

Ahammer, I. M. "Social Learning Theory as a Framework for the Study of Adult Personality Development," in P. B. Baltes and K. Warner Schaie (eds.), *Life Span Developmental Psychology: Personality and Socialization.* New York: Academic Press, 1973, pp. 253–284.

Ahammer, I. M., and P. B. Baltes. "Objective Versus Perceived Age Differences in Personality: How Do Adolescents, Adults, and Older People View Themselves and Each Other?" *Journal of Gerontology*, 27 (1972), 46–51.

Ahrens, R. "Beitrag zur Entwicklung des Physiognomie- und Mimikerkenens," *Zeitschrift für Experimentelle und Angewandte Psychologie,* 2 (1954), 412–454, 599–633.

Ainsworth, M. D. S. *Infancy in Uganda: Infant Care and the Growth of Love.* Baltimore: Johns Hopkins University, 1967.

Ainsworth, M. D. S., M. C. Blehar, E. Waters, and S. Wall. *Patterns of Attachment: Assessed in the Strange Situation and at Home.* Hillsdale, N.J.: Erlbaum, 1978.

Ainsworth, M. D. S., and B. A. Witting. "Attachment and Exploratory Behavior of One-year-olds in a Strange Situation," in B. M. Foss (ed.), *Determinants of Infant Behavior*. Vol. 4. London: Methuen, 1969, pp. 111–136.

Aldrich, C. A., and E. S. Hewitt. "A Self-Regulating Feeding Program for Infants," *Journal of the American Medical Association*, 135 (1947), 340–342.

Allinsmith, W. "The Learning of Moral Standards," in D. R. Miller and G. E. Swanson (eds.), *Inner Conflict and Defense.* New York: Holt, Rinehart and Winston, 1960, pp. 141-176.

Alpaugh, P., and M. Hickey. *Counseling the Older Adult: A Training Manual.* Los Angeles: University of Southern California Press, 1978.

Ambrose, A. (ed.). *Stimulation in Early Infancy.* New York: Academic Press, 1969.

American Psychological Association. "Ethical Standards for Research with Human Subjects," *APA Monitor*, May (1972) I-XIX.

Apgar, V., and L. S. James. "Further Observations on the Newborn Scoring System,"*American Journal of Diseases of Children*, 104 (1962), 419–428.

Ariès, P. *Centuries of Childhood: A Social History of Family Life.* R. Baldick (tr.). New York: Vintage Books, 1962.

Aronfreed, J. "The Concept of Internalization," in D. A. Goslin (ed.), *Handbook of Socialization Theory and Research*. Chicago: Rand McNally, 1969, pp. 263–323.

Aronson, E., and S. Rosenbloom. "Space Perception in Early Infancy: Perception within a Common Auditory-Visual Space," *Science.* 172 (1971), 1161–1163.

Asch, S. E., and H. Nerlove. "The Development of Double Function Terms in Children: An Exploratory Investigation," in B. Kaplan and S. Wapner (eds.), *Perspectives in Psychological Theory: Essays in Honor of Heinz Werner.* New York: International Universities Press, 1960, pp. 47–60.

Atchley, R. C. *The Social Forces in Later Life: An Introdution to Social Gerontology.* Belmont, Calif.: Wadsworth, 1972.

Ausubel, D. P. *Theory and Problems of Child Development.* New York: Grune & Stratton, 1958.

———. *Educational Psychology: A Cognitive View.* New York: Holt, Rinehart and Winston, 1968.

Babchuk, N. "Primary Friends and Kin: A Study of the Associations of Middle Class Couples," *Social Forces*, 43 (1965), 483–493.

Bacon, M., and M. B. Jones. *Teenage Drinking.* New York: T. Y. Crowell, 1968.

Baer, K. E. von. *De ovi mammalium et hominis genesi.* Lipsiae: Sumptibus Vossii, 1827.

Baltes, P. B., and K. W. Schaie. "Aging and IQ: The Myth of the Twilight Years," *Psychology Today,* 7 (March 1974), 35–40.

Bandura, A. "Social-Learning Theory of Identificatory Processes," in D. A. Goslin (ed.), *Handbook of Socialization Theory and Research*. Chicago: Rand McNally, 1969, pp. 213–262.

———. *Aggression: A Social Learning Analysis.* Englewood Cliffs, N. J.: Prentice-Hall, 1973.

———. *Social Learning Theory.*

Englewood Cliffs, N.J.: Prentice-Hall, 1977.

Bandura, A., and F. J. McDonald. "Influence of Social Reinforcement and the Behavior of Models in Shaping Children's Moral Judgments," *Journal of Abnormal and Social Psychology*, 67 (1963), 274–281.

Bandura, A., and R. H. Walters. *Social Learning and Personality Development.* New York: Holt, Rinehart and Winston, 1963.

Bandura, A., D. Ross, and S. A. Ross. "Imitation of Film-Mediated Aggressive Models," *Journal of Abnormal and Social Psychology,* 66 (1963), 3–11.

Bardwick, J. M. *Psychology of Women: A Study of Bio-Cultural Conflicts.* New York: Harper & Row, 1971.

Bardwick, J. M., and E. Douvan. "Ambivalence: The Socialization of Women," in V. Gornick and B. K. Moran (eds.), *Woman in Sexist Society: Studies in Power and Powerlessness.* New York: Basic Books, 1971, pp. 147–160.

Barker, R. G., H. F. Wright *et al.* *One Boy's Day: A Specimen Record of Behavior.* New York: Harper & Row, 1951.

Barry, H., III, M. K. Bacon, and I. L. Child. "A Cross-Cultural Survey of Some Sex Differences in Socialization," *Journal of Abnormal and Social Psychology*, 55 (1957), 327–332.

Baruch, D., with medical collaboration by H. Miller. *One Little Boy.* New York: Dell, 1964.

Bayley, N. "Consistency and Variability in the Growth of Intelligence from Birth to Eighteen Years," *Journal of Genetic Psychology*, 75 (1949), 165–196.

———. "Individual Patterns of Development," *Child Development*, 27 (1956), 45–74.

———. *Manual for the Bayley Scales of Infant Development.* New York: Psychological Corporation, 1969.

Bayley, N., and E. S. Schaefer. "Relationships between Socioeconomic Variables and the Behavior of Mothers toward Young Children," *Journal of Genetic Psychology*, 96 (1960), 61–77.

Beatty, R. A., and S. Gluecksohn-Waelsch. *Edinburgh Symposium on the Genetics of the Spermatozoan.* Edinburgh/New York, 1972.

Becker, J. M. "A Learning Analysis of the Development of Peer-Oriented Behavior in Nine-Month-Old Infants," *Developmental Psychology*, 13 (1977), 481–491.

Beit-Hallahmi, B., and A. I. Rabin. "The Kibbutz as a Social Experiment and a Child-rearing Laboratory," *American Psychologist*, 32 (1977), 532–541.

Belbin, R. M. "Middle-age: What Happens to Ability," in R. Owen (ed.), *Middle Age.* London: Cox and Wyman, 1967, pp. 98–106.

Bell, R. Q., and L. V. Harper. *Child Effects on Adults.* Hillsdale, New Jersey: Erlbaum, 1977.

Bell, R. R., and N. Lobsenz. "Married Sex: How Uninhibited Can a Woman Dare to Be?" *Redbook*, 143 (September 1974), 75+.

Bell, S. M. "The Development of the Concept of Object as Related to Infant-Mother Attachment," *Child Development*, 41 (1970), 291–311.

Bell, S. M., and M. D. S. Ainsworth. "Infant Crying and Maternal Responsiveness," *Child Development*, 43 (1972), 1171–1190.

Bellugi, U. "Linguistic Mechanisms Underlying Child Speech," in E. Zale (ed.), *Proceedings of the Conference on Language and Language Behavior, Ann Arbor, Michigan, 1966.* New York: Appleton-Century-Crofts, 1968.

———. "Learning the Language," *Psychology Today.* 4 (December 1970), 32–35+.

Belmont, L., and F. A. Marolla. "Birth Order, Family Size, and Intelligence," *Science*, 182 (1973), 1096–1101.

Bem, S. L. "The Measurement of Psychological Androgyny," *Journal of Consulting and Clinical Psychology*, 42 (1974), 155–162.

Bengtson, V. L., J. B. Cuellar, and P. K. Ragan. "Stratum Contrasts and Similarities in Attitudes Toward Death." *Journal of Gerontology*, 1977, 32(1), 76–88.

Bereiter, C., and S. Engelmann. *Teaching Disadvantaged Children in the Preschool.* Englewood Cliffs, N.J.: Prentice-Hall, 1966.

Berg-Cross, L. G. "Intentionality, Degree of Damage, and Moral Judgments," *Child Development*, 46 (1975), 970–974.

Berko, J. "The Child's Learning of English Morphology," *Word*, 14 (1958), 150–177.

Bernal, J. F. "Crying During the First Ten Days of Life and Maternal Response," *Developmental Medicine and Child Neurology*, 14 (1972), 367–372.

Bernard, J. *The Future of Marriage.* New York: World Publishing, 1972.

———. "Infidelity: Some Moral and Social Issues," in R. W. Libby and R. N. Whitehurst (eds.), *Marriage and Alternatives: Exploring Intimate Relationships.* Glenview, Ill.: Scott, Foresman, 1977, pp. 131–146.

Bernstein, B. "Linguistic Codes, Hesitation Phenomena and Intelligence," *Language and Speech*, 5 (1962), 31–47.

———. "Elaborated and Restricted Codes: Their Social Origins and Some Consequences," in A. G. Smith (ed.), *Communication and Culture.* New York: Holt, Rinehart and Winston, 1966, pp. 427–442.

Berscheid, E., E. Walster, and G. Bohrnstedt. "Body Image," *Psychology Today*, 7 (November 1973), 119–131.

Berzonsky, M. "The Role of Familiarity in Children's Explanations of Physical Causality," *Child Development*, 42 (1971), 705–715.

Bever, T. G. "The Cognitive Basis for Linguistic Structures," in J. R. Hayes (ed.), *Cognition and the Development of Language.* New York: Wiley, 1970, pp. 279–362.

Birren, J. E. *The Psychology of Aging.* Englewood Cliffs, N.J.: Prentice-Hall, 1964.

———. "Age and Decision Strategies," *Interdisciplinary Topics in Gerontology*, 4 (1969), 23–36.

———. *Coping with the Stresses of Aging: Blueprint for Health.* Chicago: Blue Cross Association, 1975.

———. "Aging: The Psychologist's Perspective," in R. H. Davis (ed.), *Aging: Prospects and Issues.* Los Angeles: University of Southern California Press, 1976, pp. 16–28.

Birren, J. E., and M. E.Reedy. *Physchology of the Adult Years.* Belmont, Calif.: Brooks-Cole, 1978.

Blank, M. "Cognitive Functions of Language in the Preschool Years," *Developmental Psychology.* 10 (1974), 229–246.

Blank, M., and W. H. Bridger. "Cross-Modal Transfer in Nursery-School Children," *Journal of Comparative and Physiological Psychology,* 58 (1964), 277–282.

Blatt, M., and L. Kohlberg. "Effects of Classroom Moral Discussions upon Children's Levels of Moral Judgment," *Journal of Moral Education,* 4 (1975), 129–162.

Blau, Z. S. "Maternal Aspirations, Socialization, and Achievement of Boys and Girls in the White Working Class," *Journal of Youth and Adolescence,* 1 (1972), 35–57.

Block, J. *Lives Through Time.* Berkeley: Bancroft Books, 1971.

Block, J. H. "Another Look at Sex Differences in Socialization Practices of Mothers and Fathers," in F. Denmark and J. Sherman (eds.), *Psychology of Women: Future Directions of Research.* New York: Psychological Dimensions, 1978.

Bloom, L. *Language Development: Form and Function in Emerging Grammars.* Cambridge, Mass.: M.I.T. Press, 1970.

———. *One Word at a Time: The Use of a Single Word Utterance Before Syntax.* Janua Linguarum, Series Minor, 154 (1973).

Bloom, L., P. Lightbown, and L. Hood. "Structure and Variation in Child Language," *Monographs of the Society for Research in Child Development,* 40 (1975), whole no. 160.

Blos, P. *On Adolescence, A Psychoanalytic Interpretation.* New York: Free Press, 1962.

Bornstein, M. H. "Qualities of Color Vision in Infancy," *Journal of Experimental Child Psychology,* 19 (1975), 401–419.

———. "Infants' Recognition Memory for Hue," *Developmental Psychology,* 12 (1976), 185–191.

Boston Women's Health Book

Collective. "Menopause," in S. H. Zarit (ed.), *Readings in Aging and Death: Contemporary Perspectives.* New York: Harper & Row, 1977, pp. 156–164.

Botvin, G. J., and F. B. Murray. "The Efficacy of Peer Modeling and Social Conflict in the Acquisition of Conservation," *Child Development,* 46 (1975), 796–799.

Botwinick, J. *Aging and Behavior.* New York: Springer, 1973.

———. "Intellectual Abilities," in J. E. Birren and K. W. Schaie (eds.), *Handbook of the Psychology of Aging.* New York: Van Nostrand Reinhold, 1977, pp. 580–605.

Bouvier, L., E. Atlee, and F. McVeigh. "The Elderly in America," in S. H. Zarit (ed.), *Readings in Aging and Death: Contemporary Perspectives.* New York: Harper & Row, 1977, pp. 28–36.

Bower, T. G. R. "The Visual World of Infants," *Scientific American,* 215 (December 1966), 80–92.

———. "The Object in the World of the Infant," *Scientific American,* 225 (October 1971), 30–38.

———. "Repetitive Processes in Child Development," *Scientific American,* 235 (November 1976), 38–47.

Bowlby, J. "Some Pathological Processes Set in Train by Early Mother-Child Separation," *Journal of Mental Science,* 99 (1953), 265–272.

Boyle, R. P. "The Effect of the High School on Students' Aspirations," *American Journal of Sociology,* 71 (1966), 628–639.

Brackbill, Y. "Cumulative Effects of Continuous Stimulation on Arousal Level in Infants," *Child Development,* 42 (1971), 17–26.

Bradburn, N. M., and D. Caplovitz. *Reports on Happiness: A Pilot Study of Behavior Related to Mental Health.* Chicago: Aldine, 1965.

Braine, M. D. S. "Children's First Word Combination," *Monographs of the Society for Research in Child Development,* 41 (1976), whole no. 164.

Brainerd, C. J. "Feedback, Rule Knowledge, and Conservation Learning," *Child Development,* 48 (1977), 404–411.

Brand, F., and R. Smith. "Life Ad-

justment and Relocation of the Elderly," *Journal of Gerontology,* 29 (1974), 336–340.

Bremner, J. G., and P. E. Bryant. "Place versus Response as the Basis of Spatial Errors Made by Young Infants," *Journal of Experimental Child Psychology,* 23 (1977), 162–171.

Bridger, W. H. "Sensory Habituation and Discrimination in the Human Neonate," *American Journal of Psychiatry,* 117 (1961), 991–996.

Bridges, K. B. "A Study of Social Development in Early Infancy," *Child Development,* 4 (1933), 36–49.

Brittain, C. V. "Adolescent Choices and Parent-Peer Cross Pressures," *American Sociological Review,* 28 (1963), 385–391.

Broen, P. "The Verbal Environment of the Language-Learning Child," *Monographs of the American Speech and Hearing Association,* 17 (1972).

Bronfenbrenner, U. "The Split-Level American Family," *Saturday Review,* 50 (October 7, 1967), 60–66.

———. *Two Worlds of Childhood: U.S. and U.S.S.R.* New York: Russell Sage Foundation, 1970.

———. "An Emerging Theoretical Perspective on Research and Social Policy." Paper presented at the biennial meeting of the Society for Research in Child Development, March 31, 1973.

Bronstein, I. P., S. Wexler, A. W. Brown, and L. J. Halpern. "Obesity in Childhood: Psychologic Studies," *American Journal of the Disturbed Child,* 63 (1942), 238–251.

Brooks, J., and M. Lewis. "Infant's Response to Strangers: Midget, Adult and Child," *Child Development,* 47 (1976), 323–332.

Broverman, D. M., I. K. Broverman, W. Vogel, R. D. Palmer, and E. L. Klaiber. "Physique and Growth in Adolescence," *Child Development,* 35 (1964), 857–870.

Brown, A. L. "The Construction of Temporal Succession by Preoperational Children," in A. D. Pick (ed.), *Minnesota Symposium on Child Psychology,* Vol. 10, 1976, pp. 28–83.

Brown, P., and R. Elliott. "Control of Aggression in a Nursery

School Class," *Journal of Experimental Child Psychology*, 2 (1965), 103–107.

Brown, R. *A First Language: The Early Stages*. Cambridge, Mass.: Harvard University Press, 1973.

———. "Introduction" in C. Snow and C. Ferguson (eds.), *Talking to Children: Language Input and Acquisition*. New York: Academic Press, 1977.

Brown, R., C. Cazden, and U. Bellugi-Klima. "The Child's Grammar from I to III," in J. P. Hill (ed.), *Minnesota Symplsia on Child Psychology*. Vol. 2. Minneapolis: University of Minnesota Press, 1968, pp. 28–73.

Bruch, H. *The Importance of Overweight*. New York: Norton, 1957.

Brück, K. "Temperature Regulation in the Newborn Infant," *Biologia neonatorum*, 3 (1961), 65–119.

Bruner, J. S. "Nature and Uses of Immaturity," *American Psychologist*, 27 (1972), 687–708.

———. "The Beginnings of Intellectual Skill: 2." *New Behaviour* (1975), October 9, pp. 58–61.

———. "Acquiring the Uses of Language." The Berlyne Memorial Lecture. Toronto, Canada, 1978. [unpublished]

Bruner, J., A. Jolly, and K. Sylva (eds.). *Play: Its Role in Development and Evolution*. Harmondsworth: Penguin, 1976.

Bryan, J. H., and N. H. Walbek. "Preaching and Practicing Generosity: Children's Actions and Reactions," *Child Development*, 41 (1970), 329–353.

Bryant, P. E. *Perception and Understanding in Young Children*. New York: Basic Books, 1974.

Bryant, P. E., P. Jones, V. C. Claxton, and G. M. Perkins. "Recognition of Shapes Across Modalities by Infants," *Nature*, 240 (1972), 303–304.

Bryant, P. E., and T. Trabasso. "Transitive Inferences and Memory in Young Children," *Nature*, 232 (1971), 456–458.

Buell, J., P. Stoddard, F. R. Harris, and D. M. Baer. "Collateral Social Development Accompanying Reinforcement of Outdoor Play in a Preschool Child," *Journal of Applied Behavior Analysis*, 1 (1968), 167–173.

Bullock, T. H., R. Orkand, and

A. Grinnell. *Introduction to Nervous Systems*. San Francisco: W. H. Freeman, 1977.

Burgess, E. W., and P. Wallin. *Engagement and Marriage*. Philadelphia: Lippincott, 1953.

Burkitt, D. P., A. R. P. Walker, and N. S. Painter. "Dietary Fiber and Disease," *Journal of the American Medical Association*, 229 (1974), 1068–1074

Butler, N. R., and H. Goldstein. "Smoking in Pregnancy and Subsequent Child Development," *British Medical Journal*, 4 (1973), 573–575.

Butler, R. N. "The Life Review: An Interpretation of Reminiscence in the Aged," *Psychiatry*, 26 (1963), 65–76.

Butler, R. N., and M. I. Lewis. *Aging and Mental Health: Positive Psychosocial Approaches*. St. Louis: Mosby, 1973.

Butterfield, E. C. "An Extended Version of Modification of Sucking with Auditory Feedback," Working paper No. 43, Bureau of Child Research Laboratory, Children's Rehabilitation Unit, University of Kansas Medical Center, October 1968.

Butterworth, G. "Object Disappearance and Error in Piaget's Stage IV Task," *Journal of Experimental Child Psychology*, 23 (1977), 391–401.

Byrne, D. *The Attraction Paradigm*. New York: Academic Press, 1971.

Callard, E. "Achievement Motive in the Four-Year-Old and Its Relationship to Achievement Expectations of the Mother." Doctoral dissertation, University of Michigan, 1964.

Campbell, A., P. E. Converse, and W. L. Rogers. *The Quality of American Life*. New York: The Russell Sage Foundation, 1975.

Campbell, J. D., and M. R. Yarrow. "Perceptual and Behavioral Correlates of Social Effectiveness," *Sociometry*, 24 (1961), 1–20.

Campos, J. "Heart Rate: A Sensitive Tool for the Study of Emotional Development," in L. Lipsitt (ed.), *Developmental Psychobiology: The Significance of Infancy*, Hillsdale, New Jersey: Erlbaum, 1976.

Canestrari, R. E. "Paced and Self-paced Learning in Young and Elderly Adults," *Journal of Gerontology*, 18 (1963), 165–168.

Cannon, K. L., and R. Long. "Premarital Sexual Behavior in the Sixties," *Journal of Marriage and the Family*, 33 (1971), 36–39.

Cappon, D. "Attitudes of and Toward the Dying," *Canadian Medical Association Journal*, 87 (1962), 693–700.

Carey, S. "Cognitive Competence," in K. Connolly and J. Bruner (eds.), *The Growth of Competence*. New York: Academic Press, 1974, pp. 169–193.

Carlsmith, L. "Effect of Early Father Absence on Scholastic Aptitude," *Harvard Educational Review*, 34 (1964), 3–21.

Caro, G., and C. T. Pihlblad. "Aspirations and Expectations: A Reexamination of the Bases for Social Class Differences in the Occupational Orientations of Male High School Students," *Sociology and Social Research*, 49 (1965), 465–475.

Carson, M. T., and A. Abrahamson. "Some Members Are More Equal than Others: The Effect of Semantial Typicality on Class-Inclusion Performance," *Child Development*, 47 (1976), 118–190.

Carter, H., and P. Glick. *Marriage and Divorce: A Social and Economic Study*. Cambridge, Mass.: Harvard University Press, 1970.

Cartwright, A., L. Hockey, and J. L. Anderson. *Life Before Death*. London: Routledge and Kegan Paul, 1973.

Cattell, P. *The Measurements of Intelligence of Infants and Young Children*. New York: Psychological Corporation, 1940.

Celotta, B. K. "Knowledge of the Human Figure as Measured by Two Tasks," *Developmental Psychology*, 8 (1973), 337–381.

Chabon, I. *Awake and Aware: Participating in Childbirth through Psychoprophylaxis*. New York: Delacorte Press, 1966.

Chall, J. S. *Learning to Read: The Great Debate*. New York: McGraw-Hill, 1967.

Charlesworth, R., and W. W. Hartup. "Positive Social Reinforcement in the Nursery School Peer Group," *Child Development*, 38 (1967), 993–1002.

Chernoff, G. "The Fetal Alcohol Syndrome in Mice: An Animal Model," *Teratology*, 15 (1977), 223–230.

Chodorow, N. "Being and Doing: A Cross-Cultural Examination of the Socialization of Males and Females," in V. Gornick and B. K. Moran (eds.), *Woman in Sexist Society: Studies in Power and Powerlessness.* New York: Basic Books, 1971, pp. 173–197.

Chomsky, N. *Language and Mind.* Enl. ed. New York: Harcourt Brace Jovanovich, 1972.

Chown, S. M. "Morale, Careers and Personal Potentials," in J. E. Birren and K. W. Schaie (eds.), *Handbook of the Psychology of Aging.* New York: Van Nostrand Reinhold, 1977, pp. 672–691.

Clark, E. V. "What's in a Word? On the Child's Acquisition of Semantics in His First Language," in T. E. Moore (ed.), *Cognitive Development and the Acquisition of Language.* New York: Academic Press, 1973, pp. 65–110.

Clark, H. H., and E. V. Clark. *Psychology and Language.* New York: Harcourt Brace Jovanovich, 1977.

Clayton, P. J., J. A. Halikes, and W. L. Maurice. "The Bereavement of the Widowed," *Diseases of the Nervous System*, 32 (1971), 597–604.

Cobb, W., and C. Mozociotti, (eds.). "The Evoked Potentials," *Electroencephalography and Clinical Neurophysiology* (Supplement No. 26). Amsterdam: Elsevier, 1967.

Cohen, L. B. "Attention-getting and Attention-holding Processes of Infant Visual Preferences," *Child Development*, 43 (1972), 869–879.

———. "Habituation of Infant Visual Attention," in T. J. Tighe and R. N. Leaton (eds.), *Habituation: Perspectives from Child Development, Animal Behavior, and Neurophysiology.* Hillsdale, N.J.: Erlbaum, 1976, pp. 207–238.

Cohen, S., D. C. Glass, and J. E. Singer. "Apartment Noise, Auditory Discrimination and Reading Ability," *Journal of Experimental Social Psychology*, 9 (1973), 407–422.

Cole, C. L. "Cohabitation in Social Context," in R. W. Libby and R. N. Whitehurst (eds.), *Marriage and Alternatives: Exploring Intimate Relationships.* Glenview, Ill.: Scott, Foresman, 1977, pp. 62–79.

Cole, Michael. "How Education Affects the Mind," *Human Nature* 1, no. 4 (1978), 50–58.

Coleman, J. S. *The Adolescent Society: The Social Life of the Teenager and Its Impact on Education.* New York: Free Press, 1961.

Coleman, J. S., et al. *Equality of Educational Opportunity.* Washington, D.C.: U.S. Department of Health, Education, and Welfare, Offffice of Education, 1966.

———. *Youth: Transition to Adulthood.* Chicago: University of Chicago Press, 1974.

Coleman, R. P. and B. L. Neugarten. *Social Status in the City.* San Francisco: Jossey-Bass,1971.

Comfort, A. *A Good Age.* New York: Crown, 1976.

Condon, W. "Speech Makes Babies Move," in R. Lewin (ed.), *Child Alive!* Garden City, New York: Anchor Books, 1975, pp. 75–85.

Condon, W. S., and L. W. Sander. "Synchrony Demonstrated between Movements of the Neonate and Adult Speech," *Child Development*, 45 (1974), 456–462.

Conel, J. L. R. *The Cortex of the Four-Year Child.* Vol. 7. *The Postnatal Development of the Human Cerebral Cortex.* 7 vols., 1939–1963. Cambridge, Mass.: Harvard University Press, 1963.

Conger, J. J. *Adolescence and Youth: Psychological Development in a Changing World.* New York: Harper & Row, 1973.

Conklin, F. "Should Retired Women Live Together?" *NRTA Journal*, 25 (November-December, 1974), 19–20.

Connor, J. M., L. A. Serbin, and M. Schackman. "Sex Differences in Children's Response to Training on a Visual-Spatial Test," *Developmental Psychology*, 13 (1977), 293–294.

Constantine, L., and J. M. Constantine. "The Group Marriage," in M. E. Lasswell and T. E. Lasswell (eds.), *Love, Marriage, Family: A Developmental*

Approach. Glenview, Ill.: Scott, Foresman, 1973, pp. 446–454.

———. "Sexual Aspects of Group Marriage, in R. W. Libby and R. N. Whitehurst (eds.), *Marriage and Alternatives: Exploring Intimate Relationships.* Glenview, Ill.: Scott, Foresman, 1977, pp. 186–194.

Coopersmith, S. *The Antecedents of Self-Esteem.* San Francisco: Freeman, 1967.

Coren, S. "Development of Ocular Dominance," *Developmental Psychology*, 10 (1974), 302.

Cornell, E. H. "Infants' Visual Attention to Pattern Arrangement and Orientation," *Child Development*, 46 (1975), 229–232.

Correll, R., S. Rokosz, and B. Blanchard. "Some Correlates of WAIS Performance in the Elderly," *Journal of Gerontology*, 21 (1966), 544–549.

Cosentino, F., and A. B. Heilbrun, Jr. "Anxiety Correlates of Sex-Role Identity in College Students," *Psychological Reports*, 14 (1964), 729–730.

Costanzo, P. R., and M. E. Shaw. "Conformity as a Function of Age Level," *Child Development*, 37 (1966), 967–975.

Cox, F. D. *Youth, Marriage, and the Seductive Society.* Rev. ed. Dubuque, Iowa: William C. Brown, 1968.

Crandall, V. "Differences in Parental Antecedents of Internal-External Control in Children and in Young Adulthood," paper presented at American Psychological Association meeting, Montreal, 1973.

Cratty, B. J. *Movement Behavior and Motor Learning.* 2nd ed. London: Kimpton, 1967.

Crites, J. O. "Parental Identification in Relation to Vocational Interest Development," *Journal of Educational Psychology*, 53 (1962), 262–270.

Crook, K. C., and L. P. Lipsitt. "Neonatal Nutritive Sucking: Effects of Taste Stimulation Upon Sucking Rhythm and Heart Rate," *Child Development*, 47 (1976), 518–522.

Cruise, M. O. "A Longitudinal Study of the Growth of Low Birth Weight Infants: 1. Velocity and Distance Growth, Birth to 3 Years," *Pediatrics.* 51 (1973), 620–628.

Cuber, J. F. "Adultery: Reality versus Sterotype," in G. Neubeck (ed.), *Extramarital Relations*. Englewood Cliffs, N.J.: Prentice-Hall, 1969, pp. 190–196.

Cuber, J. F., and P. B. Harroff. *The Significant Americans*. New York: Appleton-Century-Crofts, Inc., 1965.

Darwin, C. *The Origin of Species*. London: Murray, 1859.

Dawe, H. C. "An Analysis of Two Hundred Quarrels of Preschool Children," *Child Development*, 5 (1934), 139–157.

Dayton, G. O., Jr., M. H. Jones, P. Aiu, R. A. Rawson, B. Steele, and M. Rose. "Developmental Study of Coordinated Eye Movements in the Human Infant: I. Visual Acuity in the Newborn Human: A Study Based on Induced Optokinetic Nystagmus Recorded by Electro-Oculography," *Archives of Opthalmology*, 71 (1964), 865–870.

Deaux, K. *The Behavior of Men and Women*. Belmont, Calif.: Brooks-Cole, 1976.

Debakan, A. *Neurology of Infancy*. Baltimore: Williams & Wilkins, 1959.

Dement, W. "The Effect of Dream Deprivation," *Science*, 131 (1960), 1705–1707.

Denenberg, V. H. "Animal Studies on Developmental Determinants of Behavioral Adaptability," in O. J. Harvey (ed.), *Experience Structure and Adaptability*, New York: Springer, 1966.

Denenberg, V. H., and K. M. Rosenberg. "Nongenetic Transmission of Information," *Nature*, 216 (1967), 549–550.

Denney, D. R., N. W. Denney, and M. J. Ziobrowski. "Alterations in the Information-Processing Strategies of Young Children Following Observation of Adult Models," *Developmental Psychology*, 8 (1973), 202–208.

Dennis, W. "Infant Development Under Conditions of Restricted Practice and of Minimum Social Stimulation," *Genetic Psychology Monographs*, 23 (1941), 143–191.

———. "Causes of Retardation Among Institutional Children: Iran," *Journal of Genetic Psychology*, 96 (1960), 47–59.

———. "Creative Productivity between the Ages of 20 and 80 Years," *Journal of Gerontology*, 21 (1966), 1–8.

Dennis, W., and M. G. Dennis. "The Effect of Cradling Practices upon the Onset of Walking in Hopi Children," *Journal of Genetic Psychology*, 56 (1940), 77–86.

Dennis, W., and P. Najarian. "Infant Development Under Environmental Handicap," *Psychological Monographs*, 71 (1957), 436.

Dennis, W., and Y. Sayegh. "The Effect of Supplementary Experiences upon the Behavioral Development of Infants in Institutions," *Child Development*, 36 (1965), 81–90.

Deutscher, I. "The Quality of Postparental Life," in B. L. Neugarten (ed.), *Middle Age and Aging*. Chicago: University of Chicago Press, 1968, pp. 263–268.

———. "Socialization for Postparental Life," in M. E. Lasswell and T. E. Lasswell (eds.), *Love, Marriage, Family: A Developmental Approach*. Glenview, Ill.: Scott, Foresman, 1973, pp. 510–517.

Devereux, E. C. "The Role of Peer Group Experience in Moral Development," in J. P. Hill (ed.), *Minnesota Symposia on Child Psychology*. Vol. 4. Minneapolis: University of Minnesota Press, 1970, pp. 94–140.

DeVries, H. "Physiology of Exercise and Aging," in D. S. Woodruff and J. E. Birren (eds.), *Aging: Scientific Perspectives and Social Issues*. New York: Van Nostrand, 1975, pp. 257–276.

Dick-Read, G. *Childbirth without Fear: The Principles and Practice of Natural Childbirth*. New York: Harper & Bros., 1944.

Dion, K. K. "Young Children's Stereotyping of Facial Attractiveness," *Developmental Psychology*, 9 (1973), 183–188.

Dishotsky, N. I., W. D. Loughman, R. E. Mogar, and W. R. Lipscomb. "LSD and Genetic Damage," *Science*, 172 (1971), 431–440.

Dobbing, J. "Effects of Experimental Undernutrition on Development of the Nervous System," in N. S. Scrimshaw and J. E. Gordan (eds.), *Malnutrition, Learning, and Behavior*. Cambridge, Mass.: M.I.T. Press, 1968, pp. 181–202.

Dobbing, J., and J. L. Smart. "Vulnerability of the Developing Brain and Behavior," *British Medical Bulletin*, 30 (1974), 164–168.

Donaldson, M. *Children's Minds*. London: Fontana, 1978.

Douglas, J. W. B. "The Age at Which Premature Children Walk," *Medical Officer*, 95 (1956), 33–35.

Douvan, E. "Social Status and Success Strivings," *Journal of Abnormal and Social Psychology*, 52 (1956), 219–223.

Douvan, E., and J. Adelson. *The Adolescent Experience*. New York: Wiley, 1966.

Douvan, E., and M. Gold. "Modal Patterns in American Adolescence," in L. W. Hoffman and M. L. Hoffman (eds.), *Review of Child Development Research*. Vol. 2. New York: Russell Sage Foundation, 1966.

Dragastin, S. E., and G. H. Elder, Jr. (eds.). *Adolescence in the Life Cycle*. New York: Halstead Press, 1975.

Duck, S. W. *Personal Relationships and Personal Constructs: A Study of Friendship Formation*. New York: Wiley-Interscience, 1973.

———. *Theory and Practice in Interpersonal Attraction*. New York: Academic Press, 1977.

Dulit, E. "Adolescent Thinking *à la* Piaget: The Formal Stage," *Journal of Youth and Adolescence*, 1 (1972), 281–301.

Dunn, J. *Distress and Comfort*. Cambridge, Mass.: Harvard University Press, 1977.

Dunphy, D. C. "The Social Structure of Urban Adolescent Peer Groups," *Sociometry*, 26 (1963), 230–246.

Dustman, R. E., and E. C. Beck. "Visually Evoked Potentials: Amplitude Changes with Age," *Science*, 151 (1966), 1013–1015.

Duvall, E. M. *Family Development*. 4th ed. Philadelphia: Lippincott, 1971.

Dweck, C. S., and E. S. Bush. "Sex Differences in Learned Helplessness: I. Differential Debilitation with Peer and Adult

Evaluators." *Developmental Psychology*, 12 (1976), pp. 147–156.

Dwyer, J., and J. Mayer. "Psychological Effects of Variations in Physical Appearance During Adolescence," *Adolescence*, 3 (Winter 1968–1969), 353–380.

———. "Overfeeding and Obesity in Infants and Children," *Bibliotheca Nutritio et Dieta*, No. 18 (1973), pp. 123–152.

Dziadosz, G. M., and M. J. Schaller. "Acuity and Sighting Dominance in Children and Adults," *Developmental Psychology*, 13 (1977), 288.

Eckerman, C. O., and H. L. Rheingold. "Infants' Exploratory Responses to Toys and People," *Developmental Psychology*, 10 (1974), 255–259.

Eibl-Eibesfeldt, I. *Ethology: The Biology of Behavior*. E. Klinghammer (tr.). New York: Holt, Rinehart and Winston, 1970.

Eichenwald, H. F., and P. C. Fry. "Nutition and Learning," *Science*, 163 (1969), 644–648.

Eichorn, D. *Biological Correlates of Behavior*. Chicago: National Society for the Study of Education, 1963.

Eimas, P. D., E. R. Siqueland, P. Jusczyk, and J. Vigorito. "Speech Perception in Infants," *Science,* 171 (1971), 303–306.

Eisenberg, R. B. "The Development of Hearing in Man: An Assessment of Current Status," *Journal of the American Speech and Hearing Association*, 12 (1970), 119–123.

Eisenberg, R. B., E. J. Griffin, D. B. Coursin, and M. A. Hunter. "Auditory Behavior in the Human Neonate: A Preliminary Report," *Journal of Speech and Hearing Research*, 7 (1964), 245–269.

Elder, G. H., Jr. *Adolescent Socialization and Personality Development*. Chicago: Rand McNally, 1968.

Elkind, D. and R. F. Dabek. "Personal Injury and Property Damage in Moral Judgments of Children," *Child Development*, 48 (1977), 518–522.

Elmer, N. P., and J. P. Rushton. "Cognitive-Developmental Factors in Children'sGenerosity," *British Journal of Social and Clinical Psychology*, 13 (1974), 277–281.

Emde, R. N., T. J. Gaensbauer, and R. J Harmon. *Emotional Expression in Infancy: A Biobehavioral Study.* New York: International Universities Press, 1976.

Emmerich, W. "Continuity and Stability in Early Social Development: II. Teacher Ratings," *Child Development*, 37 (1966), 17–27.

Engen, T., and L. P. Lipsitt. "Decrement and Recovery of Responses to Olfactory Stimuli in the Human Neonate," *Journal of Comparative and Physiological Psychology*, 59 (1965), 312–316.

Entwisle, D. R., and L. A. Hayduk. *Too Great Expectations*. Baltimore: Johns Hopkins University Press, 1978.

Erikson, E. H. *Childhood and Society*. 2nd rev. ed. New York: Norton, 1963.

———. *Identity, Youth, and Crisis*. New York: Norton, 1968.

Ervin-Tripp, S. "Language Development," in *Master Lecture Series*, American Psychological Association, 1976.

Evans, R. I. "Smoking in Children: Developing a Social Psychological Strategy of Deterrence," *Journal of Preventive Medicine*, 5 (1976), 122–127.

Evans, W. F., and G. Gratch. "The Stage IV Error in Piaget's Theory of Object Concept Development: Difficulties in Object Conceptualization or Spatial Localization?" *Child Development*, 43 (1972), 682–688.

Fagan, J. F., III. "Infants' Recognition Memory for a Series of Visual Stimuli," *Journal of Experimental Child Psychology*, 11 (1971), 244–250.

Fagan, J. F., III, R. L. Fantz, and S. B. Miranda. "Infants' Attention to Novel Stimuli as a Function of Postnatal and Conceptual Age." Paper presented at the biennial meeting of Society for Research in Child Development, Minneapolis, Minnesota, 1971.

Fagot, B. I. "Sex Differences in Toddler's Behavior and Parental Reaction," *Developmental Psychology*, 10 (1974), 554–558.

Falbo, T. "Achievement Attributions of Kindergartners," *Devel-*

opmental Psychology, 11 (1975), 529–530.

Falkner, F. T. (ed.). *Human Development*. Philadelphia: Saunders, 1966.

Fantz, R. L. "The Origin of Form Perception," *Scientific American*, 204 (May 1961), 66–72.

———. "Visual Perception from Birth as Shown by Pattern Selectivity," *Annals of the New York Academy of Sciences*, 118 (1965), 793–814.

Farb, P. *Word Play: What Happens When People Talk*. New York: Knopf, 1974.

Faust, M. S. "Developmental Maturity as a Determinant in Prestige of Adolescent Girls," *Child Development*, 31 (1960), 173–184.

———. "Somatic Development of Adolescent Girls," *Monographs of the Society for Research in Child Development*, 42 (1977), Whole No. 169.

Feffer, M. H. "The Cognitive Implications of Role-taking Behavior," *Journal of Personality*, 27 (1959), 152–168.

Feffer, M. H., and V. Gourevitch. "Cognitive Aspects of Role-Taking in Children," *Journal of Personality*, 28 (1960), 383–396.

Fein, D. "Just World Responding in 6- and 9-Year-Old Children," *Developmental Psychology*, 12 (1976), 79–80.

Fein, G. G., and K. A. Clarke-Stewart. *Day Care in Context*. New York: Wiley, 1973.

Fenson, L., J. Kagan, R. B. Kearsley, and P. R. Zelazo. "The Developmental Progression of Manipulative Play in the Fist Two Years," *Child Development*, 47 (1976), 232–236.

Ferguson, C. A. "Baby Talk in Six Languages." J. Gumpertz and D. Hymes (eds.), *The Ethnography of Communication*, 66 (1964), 103–114.

Ferguson, C. A., and D. I. Slobin (eds.). *Studies of Child Language Development*. New York: Holt, Rinehart and Winston, 1973.

Ferree, M. M. "Working Class Jobs: Housework and Paid Work as Sources of Satisfaction," *Social Problems*, 23 (1976) 431–441.

Feshbach, S. "Agression," in P. H. Mussen (ed.), *Carmichael's Manual of Child Psychology*. Vol. 2. New York: Wiley, 1970, pp. 159–259.

Finch, C. E., and K. Flurkey. "The Molecular Biology of Estrogen Replacement," *Contemporary Obstetrics and Gynecology*, 9 (1977), 97–106.

Fitzgerald, H., and Y. Brackbill. "Classical Conditioning in Infancy: Development and Constraints," *Psychological Bulletin*, 83 (1976), 353–376.

Flacks, R. *Youth and Social Change.* Chicago: Markham, 1971.

Flavell, J. H. "Role-taking and Communication Skills in Children," *Young Children*, 21 (1966), 164–177.

———. "Concept Development," in P. H. Mussen (ed.), *Carmichael's Manual of Child Psychology.* Vol. 1, 3rd ed. New York: Wiley, 1970, pp. 983–1060.

———. *Cognitive Development.* Englewood Cliffs, N.J.: Prentice-Hall, 1977.

Flavell, J. H., et al. *The Development of Role-taking Communication Skills in Children.* New York: Wiley, 1968.

Flavell, J. H., D. R. Beach, and J. M. Chinsky. "Spontaneous Verbal Rehearsal in a Memory Task as a Function of Age," *Child Development*, 37 (1966), 283–299.

Floyd, J. M. "Effects of Amount of Reward and Friendship Status of the Other on the Frequency of Sharing in Children," *Dissertation Abstracts.* 25 (1965), 5396–5397.

Forgus, R. H. "The Effects of Early Perceptual Learning on the Behavioral Organization of Adult Rats," *Journal of Comparative Physiological Psychology*, 47 (1954), 331–336.

Fort, J. *The Pleasure Seekers: The Drug Crisis, Youth and Society.* New York: Grove Press, 1970.

Frank, L. K. *On the Importance of Infancy.* New York: Random House, 1966.

Fraser, C., U. Bellugi, and R. Brown. "Control of Grammar in Imitation, Comprehension, and Production," *Journal of Verbal Learning and Verbal Behavior*, 2 (1963), 121–135.

Freda, V. J., J. G. Gorman, W. Pollack, and E. Bowe. "Prevention of Rh Hemolytic Disease—Ten Years' Clinical Experience with Rh Immune Globulin," *New England Journal of Medicine*, 282 (1975) 19.

Freedman, D. G. "Constitutional and Environmental Interactions in Rearing of Four Breeds of Dogs," *Science*, 127 (1958), 585–586.

———. "Smiling in Blind Infants and the Issue of Innate vs. Acquired," *Journal of Child Psychology and Psychiatry*, 5 (1964), 171–184.

———. *Human Infancy, an Evolutionary Perspective.* Hillsdale, N.J.: Erlbaum, 1974.

Freud, S. *Psychopathology of Everyday Life.* New York: Macmillan, 1917.

———. "Three Essays on the Theory of Sexuality," in *The Standard Edition of the Complete Psychological Works of Sigmund Freud.* Vol. 7. London: Hogarth, 1953, pp. 125–245 (orig. pub. 1905).

———. *Jokes and Their Relation to the Unconscious.* J. Strachey (ed. and tr.). New York: Norton, 1960.

Frias, J. L. "Prenatal Diagnosis of Genetic Abnormalities," *Clinical Obstetrics and Gynecology*, 18 (1975), 221–236.

Friedl, E. "Society and Sex Roles," *Human Nature* 1 (1978) no. 4, pp. 68–75.

Friedman, M., and R. H. Rosenman. *Type A Behavior and Your Heart.* New York: Knopf, 1974.

Friedman, S. "Habituation and Recovery of Visual Response in the Alert Human Newborn." *Journal of Experimental Child Psychology*, 13 (1972), 339–349.

Friedman, S., L. A. Bruno, and P. Vietze. "Newborn Habituation to Visual Stimuli: A Sex Difference in Novelty Detection," *Journal of Experimental Child Psychology*, 18 (1974), 242–251.

Fries, M. E. "Some Hypotheses on the Role of the Congenital Activity Type in Personality Development," *International Journal of Psychoanalysis*, 35 (1954), 206–207.

Friesen, D. "Academic-Athletic-Popularity Syndrome in the Candian High School Society: 1967," *Adolescence*, 3 (1968), 39–52.

Frodi, A., J. Macaulay, and P. R. Thome. "Are Women Always Less Aggressive than Men? A Review of the Experimental Literature," *Psychological Bulletin*, 84 (1977), 634–660.

Fryer, J. G., and J. R. Ashford. "Trends in Perinatal and Neonatal Mortality in England and Wales 1960–69," *British Journal of Preventive and Social Medicine*, 26 (1972), 1–9.

Furth, H. G. "Research with the Deaf: Implications for Language and Cognition," *Psychological Bulletin*, 62 (1964), 145–164.

———. *Piaget and Knowledge.* Englewood Cliffs, N.J.: Prentice-Hall, 1969.

Furth, H. G., B. M. Ross, and J. Youniss. "Operative Understanding in Reproductions of Drawings." *Child Development*, 45 (1974), 63–70.

Galton, F. *Hereditary Genius.* London: Macmillan, 1869.

———. *Inquiries into Human Faculty and Its Development.* London: Macmillan, 1883.

Gardner, H. "Metaphors and Modalities: How Children Project Polar Adjectives Onto Diverse Domains," *Child Development*, 45 (1974), 84–91.

Garvey, C. *Play.* Cambridge, Mass.: Harvard University Press, 1977.

———. "Some Properties of Social Play," *Merrill-Palmer* Quarterly, 20 (1974), 163–180.

Garvey, C., and R. Hogan. "Social Speech and Social Interaction: Egocentrism Revisited," *Child Development*, 44 (1973), 562–568.

Garwood, S. G. "First-Name Stereotypes as a Factor in Self-Concept and School Achievement," *Journal of Educational Psychology*, 68 (1976), pp. 482–487.

Gelman, R. "The Nature and Development of Early Number Concepts," in H. W. Reese (ed.), *Advances in Child Development and Behavior.* Vol. 7. New York: Academic Press, 1972, pp. 115–167.

———. "How Young Children Reason about Small Numbers," in N. J. Castellan, D. P. Pisoni, G. R. Potts (eds.), *Cognitive Theory*, Hillsdale, N.J.: Erlbaum, 1977, pp. 219–238.

———. "Cognitive Development," *Annual Review of Psychology*, 29 (1978), 297–332.

Gelman, R., and M. Shatz. "Appropriate Speech Adjustments: The Operation of Conversational Constraints on Talk to Two-Year-Olds," in M. Lewis and L. A. Rosenblum (eds.), *Interaction, Conversation and the Development of Language*. New York: Wiley, 1977, 27–61.

Gerbner, G., and L. Gross. "Living with Television: The Violence Profile," *Journal of Communication*, 26 (1976), 173–199.

Gesell, A. L. *The Mental Growth of the Pre-School Child: A Psychological Outline of Normal Development from Birth to the Sixth Year, Including a System of Developmental Diagnosis*. New York: Macmillan, 1925.

———. *Infancy and Human Growth*. New York: Macmillan, 1928.

———. "Maturation and Infant Behavior Patterns," *Psychological Review*, 36 (1929), 307–319.

Gewirtz, J. L. "The Course of Infant Smiling in Four Child-rearing Environments in Israel," in B. M. Foss (ed.), *Determinants of Infant Behavior*. Vol. 3. London: Methuen, 1965, pp. 205–260.

Gibbs, F. A., and E. L. Gibbs. *Atlas of Electroencephalography*, Vol. III. Reading, Mass.: Addison-Wesley, 1964.

Gibson, E. J. *Principles of Perceptual Learning and Development*. New York: Appleton-Century-Crofts, 1969.

Gibson, E. J., and R. D. Walk. "The Visual Cliff," *Scientific American*, 202 (April 1960), 64–71.

Gilbertsen, V. A., and O. H. Wangensteen. "Should the Doctor Tell the Patient that the Disease Is Cancer?" in *The Physician and the Total Care of the Cancer Patient*. New York: American Cancer Society, 1961.

Gilligan, C. "In a Different Voice: Women's Conceptions of Self and of Morality," *Harvard Educational Review*, 47 (1977), no. 4, 481–517.

Gilmartin, B. G. "Swinging: Who Gets Involved and How?" in R. W. Libby and R. N. Whitehurst (eds.), *Marriage and Alternatives: Exploring Intimate Relationships*. Glenview, Ill.: Scott, Foresman, 1977, pp. 161–185.

Glaser, B. G., and A L. Strauss. *Awareness of Dying*. Chicago: Aldine, 1965.

———. *Time for Dying*. Chicago: Aldine, 1968.

Gleason, J. "Do Children Imitate?" *Proceedings of the International Conference on Oral Education of the Deaf*, 2 (1967), 1441–1448.

Glenn, N. "Aging, Disengagement, and Opinionation," *Public Opinion Quarterly*, 33 (1969), 17–33.

Gluck, L., and M. V. Kulovich. "Fetal Lung Development: Current Concepts," *Pediatric Clinics of North America*, 20 (1973), 367–379.

Goldberg, S. "Social Competence in Infancy: A Model of Parent-Infant Interaction," *Merrill-Palmer Quarterly*, 23 (1977), 163–177.

Goldberg, S., and M. Lewis. "Play Behavior in the Year-Old Infant: Early Sex Differences," *Child Development*, 40 (1969), 21–31.

Golomb, C. "Children's Representation of the Human Figure: The Effects of Models, Media, and Instruction," *Genetic Psychology Monographs*, 87 (1973), 197–251.

Goodenough, F. L. *Anger in Young Children* Minneapolis: University of Minnesota Press, 1931.

Goodnow, J. *Children Drawing*. Cambridge, Mass.: Harvard University Press, 1977.

Gordon, A. "The Jewish View of Death: Guidelines for Mourning," in E. Kübler-Ross (ed.), *Death: The Final Stage of Growth*. Englewood Cliffs, N.J.: Prentice-Hall, 1975, pp. 38–43.

Gordon, C., C. M. Gaitz, J. Scott. "Leisure and Lives: Personal Expressivity Across the Life Span," in R. H. Binstock and E. Shanas (eds.), *Handbook of Aging and the Social Sciences*. New York: Van Nostrand Reinhold, 1976, pp. 310–341.

Gottlieb, D. E., S. E. Taylor, and A. Ruderman. "Cognitive Bases of Children's Moral Judgments," *Developmental Psychology*, 13 (1977), 547–556.

Gottlieb, S. "Modeling Effects Upon Fantasy," in J. J. Singer (ed.), *The Child's World of Make-Believe: Experimental Studies of Imaginative Play*. New York: Academic Press, 1973, pp. 155–182.

Gouin-Décarie, T. *Intelligence and Affectivity in Early Childhood*. E. P. Brandt and L. W. Brandt (trs.), New York: International Universities Press, 1965.

Gould L. "X: A Fabulous Child's Story," *MS*, 1 (December 1972), 74–76+.

Gould, R. "The Phases of Adult Life: A Study in Developmental Psychology," *American Journal of Psychiatry*, 129 (1972), 521–531.

Govatos, L. A. "Relationships and Age Differences in Growth Measures and Motor Skills," *Child Development*, 30 (1959), 333–340.

Graham, D. *Moral Learning and Development: Theory and Research*. New York: Wiley, 1972.

Green, F. P., and F. W. Schneider. "Age Differences in the Behavior of Boys on Three Measures of Altruism," *Child Development*, 45 (1974), 248–251.

Greenfield, P. M., and J. Bruner. "Culture and Cognitive Growth," *International Journal of Psychology*, 1 (1966), 89–107.

Griffiths, R. *The Abilities of Babies*. New York: McGraw-Hill, 1954.

Grof, S., and J. Halifax. *The Human Encounter with Death*. New York: E. P. Dutton, 1977.

Grosser, D., N. Polansky, and R. Lippitt. "A Laboratory Study of Behavioral Contagion," *Human Relations*, 4 (1951), 115–142.

Grusec, J. E., L. Kuczynski, J. P. Rushton, and Z. M. Simutis. "Modeling, Direct Instruction, and Attributions: Effects on Altruism," *Developmental Psychology*, 14 (1978), 51–57.

Grusec, J. E., and S. L. Skubiski. "Model Nurturance, Demand Characteristics of the Modeling Experiment, and Altruism," *Journal of Personality and Social Psychology*, 14 (1970), 352–359.

Gusinow, J. F., and L. E. Price. "Modification of Form and Color Responding in Young Children as a Function of Differential Reinforcement and Verbalization," *Journal of Experimental Child Psychology*, 13 (1972), 145–153.

Gutmann, D. "Female Ego Styles and Generational Conflict," in J. Bardwick and associates, *Feminine Personality and Con-*

flict. Belmont, Calif.: Brooks-Cole, 1970.

———. "Parenthood: A Key to the Comparative Study of the Life Cycle," in N. Datan and L. H. Ginsberg (eds.), *Life Span Developmental Psychology: Normative Life Crises*. New York: Academic Press, 1975, pp. 167–184.

Gutteridge, M. V. "A Study of Motor Achievements of Young Children," *Archives of Psychology*, No. 244 (1939).

Haaf, R. A. "Visual Response to Complex Facelike Patterns by 15- and 20-Week-Old Infants," *Developmental Psychology*, 13 (1977), 77–78.

Haan, N., M. B. Smith, and J. Block. "Moral Reasoning of Young Adults: Political-Social Behavior, Family Background, and Personality Correlates," *Journal of Personality and Social Psychology*, 10 (1968), 183–201.

Haber, R. N., and M. Hershenson. *The Psychology of Visual Perception*. New York: Holt, Rinehart and Winston, 1973.

Hagen, J. W., and G. H. Hale. "The Development of Attention in Children," in A. D. Pick (ed.), *Minnesota Symposia on Child Psychology*. Vol. 7. Minneapolis: University of Minnesota Press, 1973, pp. 117–140.

Hainline, L. "Developmental Changes in Visual Scanning of Face and Nonface Patterns by Infants," *Journal of Experimental Child Psychology*, 25 (1978), 90–115.

Haith, M. M. "The Response of the Human Newborn to Visual Movement," *Journal of Experimental Child Psychology*, 3 (1966), 235–243.

Haith, M. M., T. Bergman, and M. J. Moore. "Eye Contact and Face Scanning in Early Infancy," *Science*, 198 (1977), 853–855.

Hale, G. A., and J. S. Morgan. "Developmental Trends in Children's Component Selection," *Journal of Experimental Child Psychology*, 15 (1973), 302–314.

Hall, G. S. "Notes on the Study of Infants," *The Pedagogical Seminary*, 1 (1891), 127–138.

———. *Adolescence: Its Psychology and Its Relations to Physiology, Anthropology, Sociology, Sex, Crime, Religion, and Education*. 2 vols. New York: Appleton, 1904.

Hammer, E. F. "Creativity and Feminine Ingredients in Young Male Artists," *Perceptual and Motor Skills*, 19 (1964), 414.

Harari, H., and J. W. McDavid. "Situational Influence on Moral Justice: A Study of 'Finking,'" *Journal of Personality and Social Psychology*, 3 (1969), 240–244.

———. "Teachers' Expectations and Name Stereotypes," *Journal of Educational Psychology*, 65 (1973), pp. 222–225.

Hardyck, C., and F. Petrinovich. "Left-Handedness," *Psychological Bulletin*, 84 (1977), 385–404.

Harlow, H. F., and M. K. Harlow. "Learning to Love," *American Scientist*, 54 (1966), 244–272.

———. "Effects of Various Mother-Infant Relationships on Rhesus Monkey Behaviors," in B. M. Foss (ed.), *Determinants of Infant Behavior*. Vol. 4. London: Methuen, 1969, pp. 15–36.

Harlow, H. F., and R. R. Zimmermann. "Affectional Responses in the Infant Monkey," *Science*, 130 (1959), 421–432.

Harper, L. V. "The Scope of Offspring Effects: From Caregiver to Culture," *Psychological Bulletin*, 82 (1975), 784–801

Harris, P. L. "Perseverative Search at a Visibly Empty Place by Young Infants," *Journal of Experimental Child Psychology*, 18 (1974), 535–542.

Harrison, C. W., J. R. Rawls, and D. J. Rawls. "Difference between Leaders and Nonleaders in Six- to Eleven-Year-Old Children," *Journal of Social Psychology*, 84 (1971), 269–272.

Hartley, R. E. "Children's Concepts of Male and Female Roles," *Merrill-Palmer Quarterly*, 6 (1960), 83–91.

Hartley, R. E., and F. P. Hardesty. "Children's Perceptions of Sex Roles in Childhood," *Journal of Genetic Psychology*, 105 (1964), 43–51.

Hartshorne, H., and M. A. May. *Studies in Deceit*. New York: Macmillan, 1928.

Hartup, W. W. "Friendship Status and the Effectiveness of Peers as Reinforcing Agents," *Journal of Experimental Child Psychology*, 1 (1964a), 154–162.

———. "Patterns of Imitative Behavior in Young Children," *Child Development*, 35 (1964b), 183–191.

———. "Peer Interaction and Social Organization," in P. H. Mussen (ed.), *Carmichael's Manual of Child Psychology*. Vol. 2. New York: Wiley, 1970, pp. 361–456.

———. "Aggression in Childhood: Developmental Perspectives," *American Psychologist*, 29 (1974), 336–341.

Hartup, W. W., and B. Coates. "Imitation of a Peer as a Function of Reinforcement from the Peer Group and Rewardingness of the Model," *Child Development*, 38 (1967), 1003–1016.

Hathaway, M. L., and D. W. Sargent. "Overweight in Children," *Journal of the American Dietetic Association*, 40 (1962), 511–515.

Havighurst, R. J. *Developmental Tasks and Education*. 3rd ed. New York: McKay, 1972.

Havighurst, R. J., and K. Feigenbaum. "Leisure and Life-Style," in B. L. Neugarten (ed.), *Middle Age and Aging: A Reader in Social Psychology*. Chicago: University of Chicago Press, 1968, pp. 347–353.

Havighurst, R. J., B. L. Neugarten, and S. S. Tobin. "Disengagement and Patterns of Aging," in B. L. Neugarten (ed.), *Middle Age and Aging: A Reader in Social Psychology*. Chicago: University of Chicago Press, 1968, pp. 58–71.

Haynes, H., B. L. White, and R. Held. "Visual Accommodation in Human Infants," *Science*, 148 (1965), 528–530.

Hebb, D., W. E. Lambert, and G. R. Tucker. "Language, Thought and Experience," *Modern Language Journal*, 55 (1971), 212–222.

Hécaen, H., and J. de Ajuriaguerra. *Left-Handedness*. New York: Grune & Stratton, 1964.

Heider, E. R. "Universals in Color Naming and Memory," *Journal of Experimental Child Psychology*, 93 (1972), 10–20.

Helson, R. "Personality of Women with Imaginative and Artistic Interests: The Role of Masculinity, Originality, and Other Characteristics in Their Creativity,"

Journal of Personality, 34 (1966), 1–25.

Hermelin, B., and N. O'Connor. "Functional Asymmetry in the Reading of Braille," *Neuropsychologia*, 9 (1971), 431–435.

Herron, R. E., and B. Sutton-Smith. *Child's Play.* New York: Wiley, 1971.

Hershenson, M. "Visual Discrimination in the Human Newborn," *Journal of Comparative and Physiological Psychology*, 58 (1964), 270–276.

Hess, B. "Friendship," in M. W. Riley, M. Johnson, and A. Foner (eds.), *Aging and Society*, Vol. 3, A Sociology of Age Stratification. New York: Russell Sage Foundation, 1972, pp. 357–396.

Hess, E. H. "Imprinting in Birds," *Science*, 146 (1964), 1128–1139.

Hess, R. D. "Social Class and Ethnic Influences on Socialization," in P. H. Mussen (ed.), *Carmichael's Manual of Child Psychology.* Vol. 2. 3rd ed. New York: Wiley, 1970, pp. 457–557.

Hetherington, E. M. "Effects of Paternal Absence on Sex-Typed Behaviors in Negro and White Preadolescent Males," *Journal of Personality and Social Psychology*, 4 (1966), 87–91.

———. "Effects of Father Absence on Personality Development in Adolescent Daughters," *Developmental Psychology*, 7 (1972), 313–326.

Hetherington, E. M., M. Cox, and R. Cox. "Beyond Father Absence: Conceptualizations of the Effects of Divorce," in E. M. Hetherington and R. D. Parke (eds.), *Readings in Child Psychology.* New York: McGraw-Hill, 1977.

Hetherington, E. M., and J. Deur. "The Effects of Father Absence on Child Development," in W. W. Hartup and N. L. Smothergill (eds.), *The Young Child: Reviews of Research.* Vol 2. Washington, D.C.: National Association for the Education of Young Children, 1972, pp. 303–319.

Hicks, D. J. "Imitation and Retention of Film-Mediated Aggressive Peer and Adult Models," *Journal of Personality and Social Psychology*, 2 (1965), 97–100.

———. "Girls' Attitudes Toward Modeled Behaviors and the Content of Imitative Private Play," *Child Development*, 42 (1971), 139–147.

Hicks, M. W., and M. Platt. "Marital Happiness and Stability: A Review of the Research in the 60s," *Journal of Marriage and the Family*, 32 (1971), 553–573.

Hicks, R. E. and M. Kinsbourne. "Human Handedness: A Partial Cross-Fostering Study," *Science*, 192 (1976), 908–910.

Higgins, E. T. "Social Class Differences in Verbal Communication Accuracy: A Question of 'Which Question?'" *Psychological Bulletin*, 83 (1976), 695–714.

Hilgard, J. R., and M. F. Newman. "Anniversaries in Mental Illness," *Psychiatry*, 22 (1959), 113–121.

Hill, C. T., Z. Rubin, and L. A. Peplau. "Breakups Before Marriage: The End of 103 Affairs," *Journal of Social Issues*, 32 (1976), 147–168.

Hill, R. "Decision-Making and the Family Life Cycle," in E. Shanas and G. Streib (eds.). *Social Structures and the Family: Generational Considerations.* Englewood Cliffs, N.J.: Prentice-Hall, 1965, pp. 113–139.

Hinton, J. M. "Distress in the Dying," in J. N. Agate (ed.), *Medicine in Old Age.* London: Pitman, 1965.

Hirsch, H. V. B., and M. Jacobson. "The Perfectible Brain: Principles of Neuronal Development," in M. S. Gazzaniga and C. Blakemore (eds.), *Handbook of Psychobiology.* New York: Academic Press, 1975.

Hiscock, M., and M. Kinsbourne. "Selective Listening Asymmetry in Preschool Children." *Developmental Psychology*, 13 (1977), 217–224.

Hoffman, M. L. "Moral Internalization: Current Theory and Research," in L. Berkowitz (ed.), *Advances in Experimental Social Psychology*, Vol. 10. New York: Academic Press, 1977a, pp. 85–133.

———. "Sex Differences in Empathy and Related Behaviors," *Psychological Bulletin*, 84 (1977b), 712–722.

Hoffman, M. L., and H. D. Saltzstein. "Parent Discipline and the Child's Moral Development," *Journal of Personality and Social Psychology*, 5 (1967), 45–57.

Hollingshead, A. *Elmtown's Youth: The Impact of Social Classes on Adolescents.* New York: Wiley, 1949.

Hollos, M. *Growing up in Flathill: Social Environment and Cognitive Development.* Oslo: Universitets-forlaget, 1974.

Hollos, M., and P. A. Cowan. "Social Isolation and Cognitive Development: Logical Operations and Role-Taking Abilities in Three Norweigian Social Settings," *Child Development*, 44 (1973), 630–641.

Holmes, T. H., and R. H. Rahe. "The Social Readjustment Rating Scale," *Journal of Psychosomatic Research*, 11 (1967), 213–218.

Holstein, C. "The Relation of Children's Moral Judgment Level to That of Their Parents and to Communication Patterns in the Family," in R. C. Smart and M. S. Smart (eds.), *Readings in Child Development and Relationship.* New York: Macmillan, 1972, pp 484–494.

Holstein, C. B. "Irreversible, Stepwise Sequence in the Development of Moral Judgment: A Longitudinal Study of Males and Females," *Child Development*, 47 (1976), 51–61.

Honzik, M. P. "Developmental Studies of Parent-Child Resemblance in Intelligence," *Child Development,* 28 (1957), 215–228.

Hooker, D. *The Prenatal Origin of Behavior.* Lawrence: University of Kansas Press, 1952.

Horner, M. "Fail: Bright Women," *Psychology Today*, 3 (November 1969), 36–38.

Horowitz, F. D. (ed.). "Visual Attention, Auditory Stimulation, and Language Discrimination in Young Infants," *Monographs of the Society for Research in Child Development*, 39 (1975), no. 158.

Hudson, R. B., and R. H. Binstock. "Political Systems and Aging," in R. H. Binstock and E. Shanas (eds.), *Handbook of Aging and the Social Sciences.* New York: Van Nostrand Reinhold, 1976, pp. 369–400.

Hunt, M. M. "Special Sex Education Survey," *Seventeen*, 29 (July 1970), 94–97+.

————. *Sexual Behavior in the 1970s*. Chicago: Playboy Press, 1974.

Hutt, C. J. *Males and Females*. Baltimore: Penguin, 1972.

Huttenlocher, J., K. Eisenberg, and S. Strauss. "Comprehension: Relation Between Perceived Actor and Logical Subject," *Journal of Verbal Learning and Verbal Behavior*, 7 (1968), 527–530.

Huxley, A. *Brave New World*. New York: Harper, 1932.

Ingram, D. "Motor Asymmetries in Young Children," *Neuropsychologia*, 13 (1975), 95–102. (a).

————. "Cerebral Speech Lateralization in Young Children," *Neuropsychologia*, 13 (1975), 103–105. (b).

Inhelder, B., and J. Piaget. *The Growth of Logical Thinking From Childhood to Adolescence: An Essay on the Construction of Formal Operational Structures*. A. Parsons and S. Milgram (trs.). New York: Basic Books, 1958.

Jack, L. M. "An Experimental Study of Ascendant Behavior in Preschool Children," *University of Iowa Studies: Study of Child Welfare*. 9 (1934), 7–65.

Jackson, E., J. J. Campos, and K. W. Fischer. "The Question of Decalage between Object Permananence and Person Permanence," *Developmental Psychology*, 14 (1978), 1–10.

Jakobson, R. *Child Language, Aphasia and Phonological Universals*. The Hague: Mouton, 1968.

James, W. *The Principles of Psychology*. Vol 1. New York: Dover, 1950 (orig. pub. 1890).

Jarvik, L. F., and D. Cohen. "A Biobehavioral Approach to Intellectual Changes with Aging," in C. Eisdorfer and M. P. Lawton (eds.), *The Psychology of Adult Development and Aging*. Washington, D.C.: American Psychological Association, 1973, pp. 220–280.

Jensen, A. R. "How Much Can We Boost IQ and Scholastic Achievement?" *Harvard Educational Review*, 39 (1969), 1–123.

Jensen, A. R., and W. D. Rohwer, Jr. "Syntactical Mediation of Serial and Paired-Associate Learning as a Function of Age," *Child Development*, 36 (1965), 601–608.

Jersild, A. *In Search of Self: An Exploration of the Role of the School in Promoting Self-Understanding*. New York: Columbia University Press, 1952.

Jersild, A., and F. B. Holmes. *Children's Fears*. New York: Columbia University Press, 1935.

Jewett, S. "Longevity and the Longevity Syndrome," *The Gerontologist*, 13 (1973), 91–99.

Joffe, J. M. "Genotype and Prenatal and Premating Stress Interact to Affect Adult Behavior in Rats," *Science*, 150 (1965), 1844–1845.

Johnson, P., and D. M. Salisbury. "Breathing and Sucking During Feeding in the Newborn," in *Parent-Infant Interaction*. Amsterdam: CIBA Foundation Symposium 33, new series, ASP, 1975.

Johnson, R. "Some Correlates of Extramarital Coitus," *Journal of Marriage and Family*, 32 (1970), 449–456.

Johnston, L. D., J. G. Bachman, and P. M. O'Malley. "Drug Use Among American High School Students, 1975–1977," National Institute on Drug Abuse, U.S. Department of Health, Education, and Welfare, 1977.

Jones, K. L. "The Fetal Alcohol Syndrome," *Teratology*, 12 (1975), 11–26.

Jones, M. C. "A Laboratory Study of Fear: The Case of Peter," *Pedagogical Seminary and Journal of Genetic Psychology*, (1924), 31, 308–315.

————. "The Later Careers of Boys Who Were Early- or Late-Maturing," *Child Development*, 28 (1957), 113–128

————. "Psychological Correlates of Somatic Development," *Child Development*, 36 (1965), 899–911.

Jones, M. C., and N. Bayley. "Physical Maturing among Boys as Related to Behavior," *Journal of Educational Psychology*, 41 (1950), 129–248.

Jones, N. B. (ed.). *Ethological Studies of Child Behavior*. London: Cambridge University Press, 1972.

Jordaan, J. P., and M. B. Heyde. *Vocational Development During the High School Years*. New York: Teachers College Press, 1978.

Kagan, J. "The Concept of Identification," *Psychological Review*, 65 (1958), 296–305.

————. "Acquisition and Significance of Sex Typing and Sex Role Identity," in M. Hoffman and L. Hoffman (eds.), *Review of Child Development Research*. Vol. 1. New York: Russell Sage Foundation, 1964, pp. 137–367.

————. "Do Infants Think?" *Scientific American*, 226 (March 1972), 74–83.

————. "Cognitive Development," in *Master Lecture Series*, American Psychological Association, 1976.

————. "The Baby's Elastic Mind," *Human Nature* 1 (January 1978), 66–78.

Kagan, J., et al. *Change and Continuity in Infancy*. New York: Wiley, 1971.

Kagan, J., and H. A. Moss. *Birth to Maturity, A Study in Psychological Development*. New York: Wiley, 1962.

Kagan, J., and S. R. Tulkin. "Social Class Differences in Child Rearing During the First Year," in H. R. Schaffer (ed.), *The Origins of Human Social Relations: Proceedings. Centre for Advanced Study in the Developmental Sciences Study Group*. New York: Academic Press, 1971, pp. 165–186.

Kagan, S., and M. C. Madsen. "Cooperation and Competition of Mexican, Mexican-American, and Anglo-American Children of Two Ages Under Four Instructional Sets," *Developmental Psychology*, 5 (1971), 32–39.

Kahl, J. A. *The American Class Structure*. New York: Holt, Rinehart and Winston, 1961.

Kalish, R. A. "An Approach to the Study of Death Attitudes," *American Behavioral Scientist*, 6 (1963), 68–70.

————. "Death and Dying in a Social Context," in R. H. Binstock and M. E. Shanas (eds.), *The Handbook of Aging and the*

Social Sciences. New York: Van Nostrand Reinhold, 1976, pp. 483–509.

Kalish, R. A., and D. K. Reynolds. *Death and Ethnicity: A Psychocultural Study.* Los Angeles: University of Southern California Press, 1976.

Kamin, L. J. "Heredity, Intelligence, Politics, and Psychology," Invited address, Eastern Psychological Association, Washington, D.C., March 1973.

Kandel, D. "Stages in Adolescent Involvement in Drug Use," *Science,* 190 (1975), 912–914.

Kandel, D. B., and G. S. Lesser. *Youth in Two Worlds.* San Francisco: Jossey-Bass, 1972.

Kangas, J., and K. Bradway. "Intelligence at Middle Age: A Thirty-eight Year Follow-Up," *Developmental Psychology,* 5 (1971), 333–337.

Kanter, R. M. *Communes: Creating and Managing the Collective Life.* New York: Harper & Row, 1973.

Kaplan, S. L. "The Assertion of Power: Ideals, Perceptions and Styles." Paper presented at American Psychological Association meeting, Washington, D.C., September 6, 1976.

Karniol, R. "Children's Use of Intention Cues in Evaluating Behavior," *Psychological Bulletin,* 85 (1978), 76–85.

Kastenbaum, R. "On the Meaning of Time in Later Life," *Journal of Genetic Psychology,* 109 (1966), 9–25.

Kay, E. "The World of Work: Its Promises, Conflicts and Reality," in American Medical Association, *The Quality of Life: The Middle Years.* Acton, Mass.: Publishing Sciences Group, 1974, pp. 63–69.

Kearsley, R. B., P. R. Zelazo, J. Kagan, and R. Hartmann. "Separation Protest in Day-Care and Home-Reared Infants, *Pediatrics,* 55 (1975), 171–175.

Keasey, C. B. "Social Participation as a Factor in the Moral Development of Preadolescents," *Developmental Psychology.* 5 (1971), 216–220.

Keller, M., *et al.* (eds.) *Second Special Report to the U.S. Congress on Alcohol and Health.* Secretary of Health, Education and Welfare. Washington, D.C.: U.S. Govt. Printing Office, 1974.

Keller, S. "The Social World of the Urban Slum Child: Some Early Findings," *American Journal of Orthopsychiatry,* 33 (1963), 823–831.

Kelly, G. A. *The Psychology of Personal Constructs.* New York: Norton, 1955.

Kelly, J. R. "Work and Leisure: A Simplified Paradigm," *Journal of Leisure Research,* 4 (1972), 50–62.

———. "Socialization Toward Leisure: A Developmental Approach," *Journal of Leisure Research,* 6 (1974), 181–193.

———. "Life Styles and Leisure Choices," *Family Coordinator,* 24 (1975), 195–190.

Kendler, T. S. "An Ontogeny of Mediational Deficiency," *Child Development,* 43 (1972), 1–19.

Keniston, K. *Young Radicals: Notes on Committed Youth.* New York: Harcourt Brace Jovanovich, 1968.

Kerckhoff, A. "Husband-Wife Expectations and Reactions to Retirement," in I. H. Simpson and J. C. McKinney (eds.), *Social Aspects of Aging.* Durham, N.C.: Duke University Press, 1966, pp. 160–172.

Kershner, J. R. "Ocular-Manual Laterality and Dual Hemisphere Specialization," *Cortex,* 10 (1974), 293–302.

Kessen, W., M. M. Haith, and P. H. Salapatek. "Human Infancy: A Bibliography and Guide," in P. H. Mussen (ed.), *Carmichael's Manual of Child Psychology.* Vol. 1. 3rd ed. New York: Wiley, 1970, pp. 287–445.

Kimmel, D. *Adulthood and Aging.* New York: Wiley, 1974.

Kinsey, A. C., W. B. Pomeroy, and C. E. Martin. *Sexual Behavior in the Human Male.* Philadelphia: Saunders, 1948.

Kinsey, A. C., W. B. Pomeroy, C. E. Martin, and P. H. Gebhard. *Sexual Behavior in the Human Female.* Philadelphia: Saunders, 1953.

Kivett, V. R., J. A. Watson, and J. C. Busch. "The Relative Importance of Physical, Psychological, and Social Variables of Locus of Control Orientation in Middle Age," *Journal of Gerontology,* 32 (1977), 203–210.

Kleemeier, R. W. "Intellectual Change in the Senium," *Proceedings of the Social Statistics

Section of the American Statistical Association, 1962 pp. 290–295.

Knapp, J. J., and R. N. Whitehourst. "Sexually Open Marriage and Relationships: Issues and Prospects," in R. W. Libby and R. N. Whitehurst (eds.), *Marriage and Alternatives: Exploring Intimate Relationships.* Glenview, Ill.: Scott, Foresman, 1977, pp. 147–160.

Koch, H. L. *Twins and Twin Relations.* Chicago: University of Chicago Press, 1966.

Koch, J. "When Children Meet Death," *Psychology Today* (August 1977), 64, 66, 79.

Koch, K. *Wishes, Lies and Dreams: Teaching Children to Write Poetry.* New York: Chelsea House, 1970.

Kohlberg, L. "The Development of Children's Orientations Toward a Moral Order: I. Sequence in the Development of Moral Thought," *Vita Humana,* 6 (1963), 11–33.

———. "A Cognitive-Developmental Analysis of Children's Sex-Role Concepts and Attitudes," in E. E. Maccoby (ed.), *The Development of Sex Differences.* Stanford, Calif.: Stanford University Press, 1966, pp. 82–173.

———. "The Child as a Moral Philosopher," *Psychology Today,* 2 (1968), 25–30.

———. "Stage and Sequence: The Cognitive-Developmental Approach to Socialization," in D. A. Goslin (ed.), *Handbook of Socialization Theory and Research.* Chicago: Rand McNally, 1969, pp. 347–480.

———. "Moral Stages and Moralization: The Cognitive-Developmental Approach," in T. Lickona (ed.), *Moral Development and Behavior,* New York: Holt, Rinehart and Winston, 1976, pp. 31–53.

Kohlberg, L., and C. Gilligan. "The Adolescent as a Philosopher: The Discovery of the Self in a Postconventional World," *Daedalus,* 100 (1971), 1051–1086.

Kohlberg, L., and R. B. Kramer. "Continuities and Discontinuities in Childhood and Adult Moral Development," *Human Development,* 12 (1969), 93–120.

Kohn, M. L. "Social Class and Parent-Child Relationships: An

Interpretation," *American Journal of Sociology*, 68 (1963), 471–480.

Krebs, D., and A. A. Adinolfi. "Physical Attractiveness, Social Relations, and Personality Style," *Journal of Personality and Social Psychology*, 31 (1975), 245–253.

Krebs, R. L. "Some Relationships Between Moral Judgment, Attention, and Resistance to Temptation," Unpublished doctoral dissertation, University of Chicago, 1968.

Kreutzer, M. A., C. Leonard, and J. H. Flavell. "An Interview Study of Children's Knowledge about Memory," *Monographs of the Society for Research in Child Development*, 40 (1975), no. 159.

Kübler-Ross, E. *On Death and Dying*. New York: Macmillan, 1969.

———. "Coping with the Reality of Terminal Illness in the Family," in E. S. Shneidman (ed.) *Death: Current Perspectives*. Palo Alto, Calif.: Mayfield, 1976, pp. 138–162.

Kumaresan, P., G. S. Han, P. B. Anandarangam, and A. Vasicka. "Oxytocin in Maternal and Fetal Blood," *Journal of Obstetrics and Gynecology*, 46, no. 3 (1975), 272–274.

Kurtines, W., and E. B. Greif. "The Development of Moral Thought: Review and Evaluation of Kohlberg's Approach," *Psychological Bulletin*, 8 (1974), 453–470.

Labov, W. "Contraction, Deletion, and Inherent Variability of the English Copula," *Language*, 45 (1969), 715–762.

———. *Language in the Inner City: Studies in the Black English Vernacular*. Philadelphia: University of Pennsylvania Press, 1973.

Lamb, M. E. "The Development of Mother-Infant and Father-Infant Attachments in the Second Year of Life," *Developmental Psychology*, 13 (1977a), 637–648.

———. "The Development of Mother-Infant and Father-Infant Interaction in the First Year of Life," *Child Development*, 48 (1977b), pp. 167–181.

Landers, W. F. "Effects of Differential Experience on Infants'

Performance in a Piagetian Stage IV Object-Concept Task," *Developmental Psychology*, 5 (1971), 48–54.

Langer, E. and J. Rodin. "The Effects of Choice and Enhanced Personal Responsibility for the Aged: A Field Experiment in an Institutionalized Setting," *Journal of Personality and Social Psychology*, 34 (1977), 191–198.

Langlois, J. H. and C. F. Stephan. "The Effects of Physical Attractiveness and Ethnicity on Children's Behavioral Attributions and Peer Preferences," *Child Development*, 48 (1977), 1694–1698.

Lasswell, M. E., and T. E. Lasswell (eds.). *Love, Marriage, Family: A Developmental Approach*. Glenview, Ill.: Scott, Foresman, 1973.

Laurendeau, M., and A. Pinard. *Casual Thinking in the Child: A Genetic and Experimental Approach*. New York: International Universities Press, 1962.

LaVoie, J. C. "Type of Punishment as a Determinant of Resistance to Deviation." *Developmental Psychology*, 10 (1974), 181–189.

Leaf, A., and J. Launois. "Every Day Is a Gift When You Are Over 100," *National Geographic*, 143 (1973), 93–119.

Learner, M. J. "The Justice Motive: 'Equity' and 'Parity' among Children," *Journal of Personality and Social Psychology*, 29 (1974), 539–550.

Leboyer, F. *Birth without Violence*. New York: Knopf, 1975.

Lefcourt, H. M. *Locus of Control: Current Trends in Theory and Research*. New Jersey: Halsted Press, 1976.

Lefkowitz, M. M., L. D. Eron, L. O. Walder, and L. R. Huesmann. "Television Violence and Child Aggression: A Follow-up Study," in G. A. Comstock and E. A. Rubinstein (eds.), *Television and Social Behavior, vol. 3: Television and Adolescent Aggressiveness*. Washington, D.C.: U.S. Government Printing Office, 1972, pp. 35–135.

Lehman, H. C. *Age and Achievement*. Princeton, N.J.: Princeton University Press, 1953.

Leiberman, M. A. "Psychological Correlates of Impending Death: Some Preliminary Observa-

tions," *Journal of Gerontology*, 20 (1965), 181–190.

Leiberman, M. A., and A. S. Coplan. "Distance From Death as a Variable in the Study of Aging," *Developmental Psychology*, 2 (1969), 71–84.

Leifer, A., and D. F. Roberts. "Children's Responses to Television Violence," in J. P. Murray, E. A. Rubenstein, and G. A. Comstock (eds.), *Television and Social Behavior, vol. 2: Television and Social Learning*. Washington, D.C.: U.S. Government Printing Office, 1972, pp. 43–180.

Lenneberg, E. "Understanding Language Without Ability to Speak: A Case Report," *Journal of Abnormal and Social Psychology*, 65 (1962), 419–425.

———. *Biological Foundations of Language*. New York: Wiley, 1967.

Leopold, W. F. *Grammar and General Problems in the First Two Years, Vol. 3: Speech Development of a Bilingual Child: A Linguist's Record*, 1939–1949, 4 vols. Evanston, Ill.: Northwestern University Press, 1949.

Lerner, M. "When, Why and Where People Die," in E. S. Shneidman (ed.), *Death: Current Perspectives*. Palo Alto, Calif.: Mayfield, 1976, pp. 138–162.

Lerner, M. J. "Desire for Justice and Reactions to Victims," in I. Macaulay and L. Berkowitz (eds.), *Altruism and Helping Behavior*. New York: Academic Press, 1970, pp. 205–229.

Lesser, G. S. *Children and Television: Lessons From Sesame Street*. New York: Random House, 1974.

Lester, B. M., M. Kotelchuck, E. Spelke, M. J. Sellers, and R. E. Klein. "Separation Protest in Guatemalan Infants: Cross Cultural and Cognitive Findings," *Developmental Psychology*, 10 (1974), 79–85.

Leventhal, A. S., and L. P. Lipsitt. "Adaptation, Pitch Discrimination, and Sound Localization in the Neonate," *Child Development*, 35 (1964), 759–767.

Levinson, D. J. *The Seasons of a Man's Life*. New York: Knopf, 1978.

Levinson, D. J., C. M. Darrow, E. B. Klein, M. H. Levinson, and B. McKee. "The Psychosocial

Development of Men in Early Adulthood and the Midlife Transition," in D. F. Ricks, A. Thomas, and M. Roff (eds.), *Life History Research in Psychopathology.* Minneapolis: University of Minnesota Press, 1974, pp. 243–258.

Levitin, T. E., and J. D. Chananie. "Responses of Female Primary School Teachers to Sex-Typed Behaviors in Male and Female Children," *Child Development,* 43 (1972), 1309–1316.

Levy, D. M. *Behavioral Analysis: Analysis of Clinical Observations of Behavior as Applied to Mother-Newborn Relationships.* Springfield, Ill.: Charles C Thomas, 1958.

Lewis, M. "Social Interaction in the First Days of Life: Discussion," in H. R. Schaffer (ed.), *The Origins of Human Social Relations.* New York: Academic Press, 1971.

Lewis, M. and J. Brooks. "Self, Other, and Fear: Infants' Reactions to People," in M. Lewis and L. Rosenblum (eds.), *The Origins of Fear: The Origins of Behavior,* Vol. II. New York: Wiley, 1974.

————. "Infants' Social Perception: A Constructionist View," in L. B. Cohen and P. Salapatek (eds.), *Infant Perception: From Sensation to Cognition,* Vol. II, New York: Academic Press, 1975, pp. 101–148.

Lewis, M., with the collaboration of S. Goldberg and H. Campbell. "A Developmental Study of Information Processing Within the First Three Years of Life: Response Decrement to a Redundant Signal," *Monographs of the Society for Research in Child Development,* 34 (1969), whole no. 133.

Libby, R. W. "Creative Singlehood as a Sexual Life-style: Beyond Marriage as a Rite of Passage," in R. W. Libby and R. N. Whitehurst (eds.), *Marriage and Alternatives: Exploring Intimate Relationships.* Glenview, Ill.: Scott, Foresman, 1977, pp. 37–61.

————. "Extramarital and Co-marital Sex: A Critique of the Literature," in R. W. Libby and R. W. Whitehurst (eds.), *Marriage and Alternatives: Exploring Intimate Relationships.* Glen-

view, Ill.: Scott, Foresman, 1977, pp. 80–111.

Lickona, T. "Research on Piaget's Theory of Moral Development," in T. Lickona (ed.), *Moral Development and Behavior.* New York: Holt, Rinehart and Winston, 1976, pp. 219–240.

Lieberman, M. "Adaptive Processes in Late Life," in N. Datan and L. H. Ginsberg (eds.), *Life Span Developmental Psychology: Normative Life Crises.* New York: Academic Press, 1975, pp. 135–160.

Liebert, R. M., and R. A. Baron. "Some Immediate Effects of Televised Violence on Children's Behavior," *Developmental Psychology,* 6 (1972), 469–475.

Lind, J. "The Infant Cry," *Proceedings of the Royal Society of Medicine,* 64 (1971), 468.

Lipsitt, L. P. "Learning in the Human Infant," in H. W. Stevenson, E. H. Hess, and H. L. Rheingold (eds.), *Early Behavior: Comparative and Developmental Approaches.* New York: Wiley, 1967, pp. 225–247.

Little, J. K. "The Occupations of Non-College Youth," *American Educational Research Journal,* 4 (1967), 147–153.

Livesley, W. J., and D. B. Bromley. *Person Perception in Childhood and Adolescence.* New York: Wiley, 1973.

Livson, F. B. "Coming Out of the Closet: Marriage and Other Crises of Middle Age," in L. E. Troll, J. Israel, and K. Israel (eds.), *Looking Ahead: A Woman's Guide to the Problems and Joys of Growing Older.* Englewood Cliffs, N.J.: Prentice-Hall, 1977, pp. 81–92.

Locke, J. *An Essay Concerning Human Understanding.* Collated and annotated by Alexander Campbell Fraser. Oxford: Clarendon Press, 1894 (orig. pub. 1690).

Loeb, R. C. "Concomitants of Boys' Locus of Control Examined in Parent-Child Interactions," *Developmental Psychology,* 11 (1975), pp. 353–358.

Loehlin, J. C., G. Lindzey, and J. N. Spuhler. *Race Differences in Intelligence.* San Francisco: W. H. Freeman, 1975.

Lomas, J., and D. Kimura. "Intrahemispheric Interaction Between Speaking and Sequential

Manual Activity," *Neuropsychologia,* 14, (1976), 23–33.

Long, J. B. "The Death that Ends Death in Hinduism and Buddhism," in E. Kübler-Ross (ed.), *Death: The Final Stage of Growth.* Englewood Cliffs, N.J.: Prentice-Hall, 1975, pp. 52–72.

Lorenz, K. "Die Angeborenen Formen Möglicher Erfahrung," *Zeitschrift Für Tierpsychologie,* 5 (1942–1943), 235–409.

Lovell, K., and E. Ogilvie. "A Study of the Conservation of Weight in the Junior School Child," *British Journal of Educational Psychology,* 31 (1961), 138–144.

Lowenthal, M. and D. Chiriboga. "Social Stress and Adaptation: Toward a Life Course Perspective," in C. Eisdorfer and M. P. Lawton (eds.), *The Psychology of Adult Developing and Aging.* Washington, D.C.: American Psychological Association, 1973, pp. 281–310.

Lowenthal, M. F., and C. Haven. "Interaction and Adaptation: Intimacy as a Critical Variable," *American Sociological Review,* 33 (1968), 20–30.

Lowenthal, M. F., M. Thurnher, and D. Chiriboga. *Four Stages of Life.* San Francisco: Jossey-Bass, 1975.

Luckey, E. B., and G. D. Nass. "A Comparison of Sexual Attitudes and Behavior in an International Sample," *Journal of Marriage and the Family,* 31 (1969), 364–379.

Lyle, J. "Television in Daily Life: Patterns of Use," in E. A. Rubinstein, G. A. Comstock, and J. P. Murray (eds.), *Television and Social Behavior, vol. 4: Television in Day-to-Day Life: Patterns of Use.* Washington, D.C.: U.S. Government Printing Office, 1972.

Maccoby, E. E. "Sex Differentiation during Childhood Development," in *Master Lecture Series,* American Psychological Association, 1976.

Maccoby, E., and C. Jacklin. *The Psychology of Sex Differences.* Stanford, Calif.: Stanford University Press, 1974.

Macfarlane, A. *The Psychology of Childbirth.* Cambridge, Mass.: Harvard University Press, 1977.

Macklin, E. D. "Heterosexual Cohabitation among Unmarried College Students," *Family Coordinator*, 21 1974, 463–472.

Maratsos, M. P. "Nonegocentric Communication Abilities in Preschool Children," *Child Development*, 44 (1973), 697–700.

Markman, E. M. *Factors Affecting the Young Child's Ability to Monitor His Memory.* Ph.D. Thesis, University of Pennsylvania, Philadelphia: 1973.

Martin, M. F., D. M. Gelfand, and D. P. Hartmann. "Effects of Adult and Peer Observers on Boys' and Girls' Responses to an Aggressive Model," *Child Development*, 42 (1971), 1271–1275.

Marvin, R. S., M. T. Greenberg, and D. G. Mossler. "The Early Development of Conceptual Perspective Taking: Distinguishing Among Multiple Perspectives," *Child Development*, 47 (1976), 511–514.

Maslow, A. H. *Motivation and Personality.* New York: Harper & Row, 1954.

———. *Toward a Psychology of Being.* 2nd ed. Princeton, N.J.: Van Nostrand, 1968.

Masters, W. H., and V. E. Johnson. *Human Sexual Response.* Boston: Little, Brown, 1966.

———. "Human Sexual Response: The Aging Female and the Aging Male," in B. L. Neugarten (ed.), *Middle Age and Aging.* Chicago: Chicago University Press, 1968, pp. 269–279.

———. *Human Sexual Inadequacy.* Boston: Little, Brown, 1970.

———. "Emotional Poverty, A Marriage Crisis of the Middle Years," in American Medical Association, *The Quality of Life: The Middle Years.* Acton, Mass.: Publishing Sciences Group, 1974, pp. 101–108.

Matas, L., R. Arend, and L. A. Sroufe. "Continuity of Adaptation in the Second Year of Life: Quality of Infant-Caregiver Attachment and Later Competence," *Child Development* (1978), in press.

Maudry, M., and M. Nekula. "Social Relations Between Children of the Same Age During the First Two Years of Life," *Journal of Genetic Psychology*, 54 (1939), 193–215.

Maurer, D. "Infant Visual Perception: Methods of Study," in L. B. Cohen and P. Salapatek (eds.), *Infant Perception: From Sensation to Cognition.* Vol. 2. New York: Academic Press, 1975, 3–31.

Maurer, D., and P. Salapatek. "Developmental Changes in the Scanning of Faces by Infants," *Child Development*, 47 (1976), 523–527.

Mayer, J. *Overweight: Causes, Cost, and Control.* Englewood Cliffs, N.J.: Prentice-Hall, 1968.

McCall, R. B. "Attention in the Infant: Avenue to the Study of Cognitive Development," in D. N. Walcher and D. L. Peters (eds.), *Early Childhood: The Development of Self-Regulatory Mechanism.* New York: Academic Press, 1971, pp. 107–140.

McCall, R. B., M. I. Appelbaum, and P. S. Hogarty. "Developmental Changes in Mental Performance," *Monographs of the Society for Research in Child Development*, 38 (1973), whole no. 150.

McCallum, C. "The Contingent Negative Variation as a Cortical Sign of Attention in Man," in C. R. Evans and T. B. Mulholland (eds.), *Attention in Neurophysiology.* London: Butterworths, 1969, pp. 40–54.

McCandless, B. R. "Rate of Development, Body Build, and Personality," *Psychiatric Research Reports*, 13 (December 1960), 42–57.

McCarthy, D. "Language Development in Children," in L. Carmichael (ed.), *Manual of Child Psychology.* 2nd ed. New York: Wiley, 1954, pp. 492–630.

McClearn, G. E. "Genetic Influences on Behavior and Development," in P. H. Mussen (ed.), *Carmichael's Manual of Child Psychology.* Vol. 1. 3rd ed. New York: Wiley, 1970, pp. 39–76.

McDavid, J. W., and H. Harari. "Stereotyping of Names and Popularity in Grade School Children," *Child Development*, 37 (1966), pp. 453–459.

McGraw, M. B. *Growth, A Study of Johnny and Jimmy.* New York: Appleton-Century-Crofts, 1935.

———. "Later Development of Children Specially Trained During Infancy: Johnny and Jimmy at School Age," *Child Development*, 10 (1939), 1–19.

McKain, W. "A New Look at Older Marriages," *The Family Coordinator*, 21 (1972), 61–69.

McKeown, T. *The Modern Rise of Population.* New York: Academic Press, 1977.

McLaughlin, L. J., and J. F. Brinley. "Age and Observational Learning of a Multiple-Classification Task," *Developmental Psychology*, 9 (1973), 9–15.

McMichael, R. E., and R. E. Grinder. "Children's Guilt After Transgression: Combined Effect of Exposure to American Culture and Ethnic Background," *Child Development*, 37 (1966), 425–431.

McNeill, D. "Developmental Psycholinguistics," in F. Smith and G. A. Miller (eds.), *The Genesis of Language: A Psycholinguistic Approach.* Cambridge, Mass.: M.I.T. Press, 1966, pp. 15–84.

———. *The Acquisition of Language: The Study of Developmental Psycholinguistics.* New York: Harper & Row, 1970a.

———. "The Development of Language," in P. H. Mussen (ed.), *Carmichael's Manual of Child Psychology.* Vol. 1. 3rd ed. New York: Wiley, 1970b, pp. 1061–1161.

Mead, M. *Coming of Age in Samoa: A Psychological Study in Primitive Youth for Western Civilisation.* New York: Dell, 1968.

Mead, M., and N. Newton. "Cultural Patterning of Perinatal Behavior," in S. A. Richardson and A. F. Guttmacher (eds.), *Childbearing: Its Social and Psychological Factors.* Baltimore: William & Wilkins, 1967.

Mehrabian, A. *Silent Messages.* Belmont, Calif.: Wadsworth, 1971.

Meichenbaum, D. H., and J. Goodman. "Training Impulsive Children to Talk to Themselves: A Means of Developing Self-Control," *Journal of Abnormal Psychology*, 77 (1971), 115–126.

Meltzov, A. N., and M. Keith Moore. "Imitation of Facial and Manual Gestures by Human Neonates," *Science,* 198 (1977), pp. 75–78.

Mendelson, M. J., and M. M. Haith. "The Relation Between Audition and Vision in the

Human Newborn," *Monographs of the Society for Research in Child Development*, 41 (1976), no. 167.

Menyuk, P. *The Acquisition and Development of Language.* Englewood Cliffs, N.J.: Prentice-Hall, 1971.

Menyuk, P., and N. Bernholtz. "Prosodic Features and Children's Language Production," *M.I.T. Research Laboratory of Electronics Quarterly Progress Reports*, no. 93 (1969), 216–219.

Menzel, E. W., Jr., R. K. Davenport, Jr., and C. M. Rogers. "The Effects of Environmental Restriction upon the Chimpanzee's Responsiveness to Objects," *Journal of Comparative and Physiological Psychology*, 56 (1963), 78–85.

Meredith, H. V. "Change in the Stature and Body Weight of North American Boys During the Last 80 Years," in L. P. Lipsitt and C. C. Spiker (eds.), *Advances in Child Development and Behavior.* Vol. 1. New York: Academic Press, 1963, pp. 69–114.

———. "A Synopsis of Pubertal Changes in Youth," *Journal of School Health*, 37 (1967), 171–176.

Messinger, L. "Remarriage Between Divorced People with Children from Previous Marriages: A Proposal for Preparation for Remarriage," *Journal of Marriage and Family Counseling*, 2 (1976), 193–200.

Michaels, R. H., and G. W. Mellin. "Prospective Experience with Maternal Rubella and the Associationed Congenital Malformations," *Pediatrics*, 26 (1960), 200–209.

Milgram, S. "Behavioral Study of Obedience," *Journal of Abnormal and Social Psychology*, 67 (1963), 371–378.

———. *Obedience to Authority.* New York: Harper & Row, 1974.

Millar, W. S. "A Study of Operant Conditioning Under Delayed Reinforcement in Early Infancy," *Monographs of the Society for Research in Child Development*, 37 (1972), whole no. 147.

Miller, D. R., and G. E. Swanson. *Inner Conflict and Defense.* New York: Holt, Rinehart and Winston, 1966.

Miller, N. E., and J. Dollard. *Social Learning and Imitation.* New Haven, Conn.: Yale University Press, 1941.

Miller, W., and S. Ervin. "The Development of Grammar in Child Language," in *Cognitive Development in Children.* Chicago: University of Chicago Press, 1970, pp. 309–334.

Milner, E. "A Study of the Relationship Between Reading Readiness in Grade One School Children and Patterns of Parent-child Interaction," *Child Development*, 22 (1951), 95–112.

Minkowski, A. *Regional Development of the Brain in Early Life.* Oxford: Blackwell, 1967.

Minuchin, P., *et al. The Psychological Impact of School Esperience.* New York: Basic Books, 1969.

Mischel, W. *Personality and Assessment.* New York: Wiley, 1968.

———. "Sex-Typing and Socialization," in P. H. Mussen (ed.), *Carmichael's Manual of Child Psychology.* Vol. 2. New York: Wiley, 1970, pp. 3–72.

Mischel, W., and N. Baker. "Cognitive Appraisals and Transformations in Delay Behavior," *Journal of Personality and Social Psychology*, 31 (1975), 254–261.

Mischel, W., and H. Mischel. "A Cognitive Social-Learning Approach to Morality and Self-Regulation," in T. Lickona (ed.), *Moral Development and Behavior.* New York: Holt, Rinehart and Winston, 1976, pp. 84–107.

Molfese, D. L., R. B. Freeman, Jr., and D. S. Palermo. "The Ontogeny of Brain Lateralization for Speech and Nonspeech Stimuli," *Brain and Language*, 2 (1975), 356–368.

Money, J., and A. A. Ehrhardt. *Man and Woman, Boy and Girl: The Differentiation and Dimorphism of Gender Identity from Conception to Maturity.* Baltimore: Johns Hopkins University Press, 1972.

Monge, R. H., and D. Hultsch. "Paired-Associate Learning as a Function of Adult Age and the Length of the Anticipation and Inspection Intervals," *Journal of Gerontology*, 26 (1971), 157–162.

Montemayor, R., and M. Eisen. "The Development of Self-Conceptions from Childhood to

Adolescence," *Developmental Psychology*, 13 (1977), 314–319.

Moody, R. *Life after Life.* Atlanta, Ga.: Mockingbird Books, 1975.

Mooney, H. F. "Popular Music Since the 1920s," in R. S. Denisoff and R. A. Peterson (eds.), *Sounds of Social Change: Studies in Popular Culture.* Chicago: Rand McNally, 1972, pp. 181–197.

Moore, B. S., A. Clyburn, and B. Underwood. "The Role of Affect in Delay of Gratification," *Child Development*, 47 (1976), 273–276.

Morgan, G. A., and H. N. Ricciuti. "Infants' Responses to Strangers During the First Year," in B. M. Foss (ed.), *Determinants of Infant Behavior.* Vol. 4. London: Methuen, 1969, pp. 253–272.

Morison, R. S. "Death: Process or Event?" *Science*, 173 (1971), 694–702.

Moro, E. *"Das Erste Trimenon,"* *Münchener Medizinische Wochenschrift*, 65 (1918), 1147–1150.

Moskowitz, A. I. "The Two-Year Old Stage in the Acquisition of English Phonology," *Language*, 46 (1970), 426–441.

Mossler, D. G., R. S. Marvin, and M. T. Greenberg. "Conceptual Perspective Taking in 2- to 6-year-old Children," *Developmental Psychology*, 12 (1976), 85–86.

Muller, E., H. Hollien, and T. Murry. "Perceptual Responses to Infant Crying: Identification of Cry Types," *Journal of Child Language*, 1 (1974), 89–95.

Mundy-Castle, A. C., and J. Anglin. "The Development of Looking in Infancy." Unpublished paper presented at Society for Research in Child Development, Santa Monica, Calif., 1969.

Murstein, B. I. "A Theory of Marital Choice," in B. I. Murstein (ed.), *Theories of Attraction and Love.* New York: Springer, 1971, pp. 100–151.

Mussen, P. H. "Early Sex-Role Development," in D. A. Goslin (ed.), *Handbook of Socialization Theory and Research*, Chicago: Rand McNally, 1969, pp. 707–731.

Mussen, P. H., and M. C. Jones. "Self-Conceptions, Motivations, and Interpersonal Attitudes of Late and Early-Maturing Boys," *Child Development*, 28 (1957), 243–256.

Muuss, R. E. "Adolescent Development and the Secular Trend," *Adolescence*, 5 (1970), 267–284.

Nagy, M. "The Child's View of Death," *Journal of Genetic Psychology*, 73 (1948), 3–27.

Needham, J. *A History of Embryology*, 2nd rev. ed., with the assistance of A. Hughes. Cambridge: Cambridge University Press, 1959.

Neimark, E. D. "Intellectual Development During Adolescence," in F. D. Horowitz (ed.), *Review of Child Development Research*, (Vol. 4), Chicago: University of Chicago Press, 1975, pp. 541–594.

Nelson, K. "Structure and Strategy in Learning to Talk," *Monographs of the Society for Research in Child Development*, vol. 38 (February, April 1973), whole nos. 1 and 2.

Neugarten, B. L. "Adult Personality: Toward a Psychology of the Life Cycle," in B. L. Neugarten (ed.), *Middle Age and Aging: A Reader in Social Psychology*. Chicago: University of Chicago Press, 1968, pp. 137–147.

———. "Adaptation and the Life Cycle," *Journal of Geriatric Psychiatry*, 4 (1970), 71–100.

———. "Personality and Aging," in J. E. Birren and K. W. Schaie (eds.), *Handbook of the Psychology of Aging*. New York: Van Nostrand, Reinhold, 1977, pp. 626–649.

Neugarten, B. L., and associates (eds.). *Personality in Middle and Late Life*. New York: Atherton, 1964.

Neugarten, B. L., and D. L., Gutmann. "Age-Sex Roles and Personality in Middle Age: A Thematic Apperception Study," in B. L. Neugarten (ed.), *Middle Age and Aging: A Reader in Social Psychology*. Chicago: University of Chicago Press, 1968, pp. 58–71.

Neugarten, B. L., and G. O. Hagestad. "Age and the Life Course," in R. H. Binstock and E. Shanas (eds.), *Handbook of Aging and the Social Sciences*.

New York: Van Nostrand Reinhold, 1976, pp. 35–55.

Neugarten, B. L., and W. A. Peterson. "A Study of the American Age-Grade System," *Proceedings of the Fourth Congress of the International Association of Gerontology*. 3 (1957), 497–502.

Neugarten, B. L., and K. K. Weinstein. "The Changing American Grandparent," in B. L. Neugarten (ed.), *Middle Age and Aging: A Reader in Social Psychology*. Chicago: University of Chicago Press, 1968, pp. 280–286.

Neugarten, B. L., W. J. Crotty, and S. S. Tobin. "Personality Types in an Aged Population," in B. L. Neugarten *et al.* (eds.), *Personality in Middle and Late Life: Empirical Studies*. New York: Atherton, 1964, pp. 158–187.

Neugarten, B. L., V. Wood, R. J. Kraines, and B. Loomis. "Women's Attitudes Toward the Menopause," *Vita Humana*, 6 (1963), 140–151.

Newman, O. *Defensible Space: Crime Prevention through Urban Design*. New York: Macmillan, 1973.

Norton, A. J. "The Family Life Cycle Updated: Components and Uses," in R. F. Winch and G. B. Spanier (eds.), *Selected Studies in Marriage and the Family*. New York: Holt, Rinehart and Winston, 1974, pp. 162–170.

Nowak, C. A. "Does Youthfulness Equal Attractiveness?" in L. E. Troll, J. Israel, and K. Israel (eds.), *Looking Ahead: A Woman's Guide to the Problems and Joys of Growing Older*. Englewood Cliffs, N.J.: Prentice-Hall, 1977, pp. 59–64.

Noyes, R. "The Experience of Dying," *Psychiatry*, 35 (1972), 1974.

Office of the Surgeon General. *Television and Growing Up: The Impact of Televised Violence*. Washington, D.C.: U.S. Government Printing Office, 1972.

Opie, I., and P. Opie. *Children's Games in Street and Playground: Chasing, Catching, Seeking, Hunting, Racing, Duelling, Exerting, Daring, Guessing, Acting, Pretending*. Oxford: Clarendon, 1969.

Orlando Sentinel, July 21 and August 20, 1971.

Orthner, D. K., T. Brown, and D. Ferguson. "Single-Parent Fatherhood: An Emerging Life Style," *Family Coordinator*, 24 (1977), 489–505.

Osborn, D. K., and R. C. Endsley. "Emotional Reactions of Young Children to TV Violence," *Child Development*, 41 (1971), 321–331.

Osis, K. *Deathbed Observations by Physicians and Nurses*. New York: Parapsychology Foundation, 1961.

Osler, S. F., and E. Kofsky. "Stimulus Uncertainty as a Variable in the Development of Conceptual Ability," *Journal of Experimental Child Psychology*, 2 (1965), 264–279.

Osofsky, J. D., and B. Danzger. "Relationships Between Neonatal Characteristics and Mother-Infant Interaction," *Developmental Psychology*, 10 (1974), 124–130.

Palermo, D. S., and D. L. Molfese. "Language Acquisition from Age Five Onward," *Psychological Bulletin*, 78 (1972), 409–428.

Palmore, E., and F. C. Jeffers (eds.). *Prediction of Life Span: Recent Findings*. Lexington, Mass.: Heath, 1971.

Palmore, E., and C. Luikart. "Health and Social Factors Related to Life Satisfaction," *Journal of Health and Social Behavior*, 13, (1972), 68–80.

Papoušek, H. "Conditioning During Early Postnatal Development," in Y. Brackbill and G. G. Thompson (eds.), *Behavior in Infancy and Early Childhood: A Book of Readings*. New York: Free Press, 1967, pp. 259–274.

Papst, M. "Das Verhalten von Kindern in einfachen strategischen Spielen," *Zeitschrift für Psychologie*, 172 (1966), 17–39.

Parke, R. D. "Punishment in Children: Effects, Side Effects, and Alternative Strategies," in H. L. Horn and P. A. Robinson (eds.), *Psychological Processes in Early Education*. New York: Academic Press, 1977, pp. 71–97.

Parke, R. D., and D. B. Sawin. "The Father's Role in Infancy: A Re-evaluation," *The Family Coordinator*, 25 (1976), 365–371.

Parkes, C. M. *Bereavement: Studies of Grief in Adult Life.* New York: International Universities Press, 1972.

Parry, M. H. "Infants' Responses to Novelty in Familiar and Unfamiliar Settings," *Child Development*, 43 (1972), 233–237.

Patterson, G. R. "Reprogramming the Families of Aggressive Boys," in C. E. Thoresen (ed.), *Behavior Modification in Education.* Chicago: University of Chicago Press, 1972, pp. 154–194.

Patterson, G. R., R. A. Littman, and W. Bricker. "Assertive Behavior in Children: A Step Toward a Theory of Aggression," *Monographs of the Society for Research in Child Development*, 32 (1967), whole no. 113.

Pavlov, I. P. *Conditioned Reflexes: An Investigation of the Physiological Activity of the Cerebral Cortex.* G. V. Anrep (ed. and tr.). London: Oxford University Press, 1927.

Peck, R. F., and R. J. Havighurst. *The Psychology of Character Development.* New York: Wiley, 1960.

Peel, E. A. *The Nature of Adolescent Judgment.* New York: Wiley-Interscience, 1971.

Peeples, D. R., and D. Y. Teller. "Color Vision and Brightness Discrimination in Two-Month-Old Infants," *Science*, 189 (1975), 1102–1103.

Peskin, H. "Pubertal Onset and Ego Functioning," *Journal of Abnormal Psychology,* 72 (1967), 1–15.

Pfeiffer, E. "Psychopathology and Socialpathology," in J. E. Birren and K. W. Schaie (eds.), *Handbook of the Psychology of Aging.* New York: Van Nostrand Reinhold, 1977, pp. 650–671.

Pfeiffer, E., and G. C. Davis. "The Use of Leisure Time in Middle Life," *Gerontologist*, 11 (1971), 187–195.

Phares, E. J. *Locus of Control in Personality.* Morristown, N.J.: General Learning Press, 1976.

Piaget, J. *The Language of the Child.* M. Warden (tr.). New York: Harcourt, 1926.

————. *Judgment and Reasoning in the Child.* M. Warden (tr.). New York: Harcourt, 1928.

————. *The Moral Judgment of the Child.* M. Gabain (tr.). Boston: Routledge & Kegan Paul, 1932.

————. *Play, Dreams and Imitation in Childhood.* C. Gattegno and F. M. Hodgson (trs.). New York: Norton, 1951.

————. *The Child's Conception of Number.* C. Gattegno and F. H. Hodgson (trs.). Boston: Routledge & Kegan Paul, 1952a.

————. *The Origins of Intelligence in Children.* M. Cook (tr.). New York: International Universities Press, 1952b.

————. *The Construction of Reality in the Child.* M. Cook (tr.). New York: Basic Books, 1954.

————. *Six Psychological Studies.* A. Tenzer and D. Elkind (trs.). New York: Random House, 1967.

————. "Piaget's Theory," in P. H. Mussen (ed.), *Carmichael's Manual of Child Psychology.* Vol. 1. 3rd ed. New York: Wiley, 1970, pp. 703–732.

————. *The Science of Education and the Psychology of the Child.* D. Coltman (tr.). New York: Viking, 1972.

————. "On Correspondences and Morphisms," paper presented at Jean Piaget Society. Philadelphia, 1975.

————. *The Grasp of Consciousness: Action and Concept in the Young Child.* Cambridge, Mass: Harvard University Press, 1976.

Piaget, J., and B. Inhelder. *Le Dévelopment des quantités chez l'Enfant; Conservation et Atomisme.* Neuchatel: Delachaux et Niestlé, 1941.

————. *Mémoire et intelligence.* Paris: Presses Universitaries de France, 1968.

————. *The Psychology of the Child.* Boston: Routledge & Kegan Paul, 1969.

Piazza, D. M. "Cerebral Lateralization in Young Children as Measured by Dichotic Listening and Finger Tapping Tasks," *Neuropsychologia*, 15 (1977), 417–425.

Piscopo, J. "Obesity: An Interdisciplinary Approach to a Major Health Problem," *The Physical Educator*, 27 (March 1970), 27–29.

Pitkin, R. M. "Nutritional Support in Obstetrics andGynecology," *Clinical Obstetrics and Gynecology* 19 (1976), no.3, 489.

Plutchik, R., M. B. Weiner, and H. Conte. "Studies of Body Image: I. Body Worries and Body Discomforts," *Journal of Gerontology*, 26 (1971), 344–350.

Powell, G. F., J. A. Brasel, and R. M. Blizzard. "Emotional Deprivation and Growth Retardation Simulating Idiopathic Hypopituitarism. I. Clinical Evaluation of the Syndrome," *New England Journal of Medicine*, 276 (1967), 1271–1278.

Pratt, K. C. "The Neonate," in L. Carmichael (ed.), *Manual of Child Psychology*, 2nd ed. New York: Wiley, 1954, pp. 215–291.

Prechtl, H. F. R. "Problems of Behavioral Studies in the Newborn Infant," in D. S. Lehrman, R. A. Hinde, and E. Shaw (eds.), *Advances in the Study of Behavior.* Vol. 1. New York: Academic Press, 1965, pp. 75–98.

Prentice, N. M. "The Influence of Live and Symbolic Modeling on Promoting Moral Judgment of Adolescent Delinquents," *Journal of Abnormal Psychology*, 80 (1972), 157–161.

Pritchard, J. A., and P. C. MacDonald. *Williams Obstetrics,* 15th edition. New York: Appelton-Century-Crofts,1976.

Pulaski, M. "The Rich Rewards of Make Believe," *Psychology Today*, 7 (January 1974), 68–74.

Puner, M. *To the Good Long Life: What We Know About Growing Old.* New York: Universe Books, 1974.

Rainwater, L. "Crucible of Identity: The Negro Lower-Class Family," *Daedalus*, 95 (1966), 172–216.

Ramey, C. T., and L. L. Ourth. "Delayed Reinforcement and Vocalization Rates of Infants," *Child Development*, 42 (1971), 291–298.

Ramsay, D. S. "Object Word Spurt, Handedness, and Object Permanence in the Infant," Unpublished manuscript, 1977, Department of Neurosciences, University of California at San Diego.

Redl, F. "The Impact of Game Ingredients on Children's Play Behavior," in B. Schaffner (ed.), *Group Processes: Transactions of the Fourth Conference.* New

York: Josiah Macy Jr. Foundation, 1959.

Reedy, M. N. "Age and Sex Differences in Personal Needs and the Nature of Love: A Study of Happily Married Young, Middle-aged and Older Couples," Unpublished doctoral dissertation, University of Southern California, 1977.

———. "Love, Sexuality, and Aging," in I. N. Burnside and R. Solnick (eds.), *Sexuality and Aging*. Los Angeles: University of Southern California Press, 1978.

Reiss, I. L. *The Social Context of Premarital Sexual Permissiveness*. New York: Holt, Rinehart and Winston, 1967.

———. "How and Why America's Sex Standards Are Changing," in H. Gagnon and W. Simon (eds.), *The Sexual Scene*. Chicago: Aldine, 1970, pp. 43–57.

———. *Heterosexual Relationships Inside and Outside Marriage*. Morristown, N.J.: General Learning Press, 1973.

Rest, J. "The Hierarchical Nature of Moral Judgment: A Study of Patterns of Comprehension and Preference of Moral Stages," *Journal of Personality*, 41 (1973), 86–109.

———. "New Approaches in the Assessment of Moral Judgment," in T. Lickona (ed.), *Moral Development and Behavior*. New York: Holt, Rinehart and Winston, 1976, pp. 198–218.

Rest, J., E. Turiel, and L. Kohlberg. "Level of Moral Development as a Determinant of Preference and Comprehension of Moral Judgments Made by Others," *Journal of Personality*, 37 (1969), 225–252.

Rheingold, H. L. "The Social and Socializing Agent," in D. A. Goslin (ed.), *Handbook of Socialization Theory and Research*. Chicago: Rand McNally, 1969, pp. 779–791.

Rheingold, H. L., and C. O. Eckerman. "The Infant Separates Himself from His Mother," *Science*, 168 (1970), 78–83.

Rheingold, H. L., J. L. Gewirtz, and H. W. Ross. "Social Conditioning of Vocalizations in the Infant," *Journal of Comparative and Physiological Psychology*, 52 (1959), 68–73.

Riegel, K. F., and R. M. Riegel. "A Study on Changes of Attitudes and Interests During Later Years of Life," *Vita Humana*, 3 (1960), 177–206.

Riegel, K. F., R. M. Riegel, and M. Meyer. "A Study of the Dropout Rate in the Longitudinal Research on Aging and the Prediction of Deaths," *Journal of Personality and Social Psychology*, 5 (1967), 342–348.

Riley, J. W., Jr. "What People Think About Death," in O. B. Brim, Jr., H. E. Freeman, S. Levine, and N. A. Scotch (eds.), *The Dying Patient*. New York: Russell Sage Foundation, 1970, pp. 30–41.

Riley, M. W., and A. Foner. *Aging and Society, Vol. 1: An Inventory of Research Findings*. New York: Russell Sage Foundation, 1968.

Robinson, H. B., and N. M. Robinson. *The Mentally Retarded Child: A Psychological Approach*. New York: McGraw-Hill, 1965.

Rodin, J., and E. J. Langer. "Long-Term Effects of a Control-Relevant Intervention with Institutionalized Aged," *Journal of Personality and Social Psychology*, (1978; in press).

Roff, N., S. B. Sells, and M. M. Golden. *Social Adjustment and Personality Development in Children*. Minneapolis: University of Minnesota Press, 1972.

Roffwarg, H. P., J. N. Muzio, and W. C. Dement. "Ontogenic Development of the Human Sleep-Dream Cycle," *Science*, 152 (1966), 604–619.

Rogers, C. R. *Becoming Partners: Marriage and Its Alternatives*. New York: Delacorte, 1972.

Rohwer, W. D., Jr. "Learning, Race, and School Success," *Review of Educational Research*, 41 (1971), 191–210.

Rollings, B. C., and H. Feldman. "Marital Satisfaction Over the Family Life Cycle," *Journal of Marriage and the Family*, 32 (1970), 20–28.

Rose, C. L., and B. Bell. *Predicting Longevity: Methodology and Critique*. Lexington, Mass.: Heath, 1971.

Rose, S. A. and M. Blank. "The Potency of Context in Children's Cognition: An Illustration through Conservation." *Child Development*, 45, 1974, 499–502.

Rose, S. P. R. *The Conscious Brain*. New York: Knopf, 1973.

Rosen, B. C. "The Achievement Syndrome: A Psychocultural Dimension of Social Stratification," *American Sociological Review*, 21 (1956), 203–211.

———. "Race, Ethnicity, and the Achievement Syndrome," *American Sociological Review*, 24 (1959), 47–60.

Rosenberg, M. *Society and the Adolescent Self-image*. Princeton, N.J.: Princeton University Press, 1965.

———. "The Dissonant Context and the Adolescent Self-Concept," in S. E. Dragastin and G. H. Elder, Jr., *Adolescence in the Life Cycle*, New York: Wiley, 1975, pp. 97–116.

Rosenberg, M., and R. Simmons. *Black and White Self-Esteem: The Urban School Child*. Washington, D.C.: American Sociological Association, 1972.

Rosenhan, D. L. "The Natural Socialization of Altruistic Autonomy," in J. R. Macaulay and L. Berkowitz (eds.), *Altruism and Helping Behavior: Social Psychological Studies of Some Antecedents and Consequences*. New York: Academic Press, 1970, pp. 251–268.

Rosenthal, R. "Self-Fulfilling Prophecy," *Psychology Today*, 2 (1968), 44–51.

Rosenthal, T. L., and B. J. Zimmerman. "Organization, Observation, and Guided Practice in Concept Attainment and Generalization," *Child Development*, 44 (1973), 606–613.

Rosenzweig, M. R., E. L. Bennett, and M. C. Diamond. "Brain Changes in Response to Experience." *Scientific American*, 226 (February 1972), 22–29.

Ross, H. S., H. L. Rheingold, and C. O. Eckerman. "Approach and Exploration of a Novel Alternative by 12-Month-Old Infants," *Journal of Experimental Child Psychology*, 13 (1972), 85–93.

Rossi, A. "Transition to Parenthood," *Journal of Marriage and the Family*, 30 (1968), 26–39.

Rousseau, J. J. *Emile*. New York: Dutton, 1911 (orig. pub. 1762).

Rubenstein, J., and C. Howes. "The Effects of Peers on Toddler Interaction with Mother and Toys," *Child Development*, 47 (1976), 597–605.

Rubin, I. "The 'Sexless Older Years'—A Socially Harmful Stereotype," *Annals of the American Academy of Political and Social Science*, 376 (1968), 86–95.

Rubin, K. H., and F. W. Schneider. "The Relationship between Moral Judgment, Egocentrism, and Altruistic Behavior," *Child Development*, 44 (1973), 661–665.

Rubin, Z. *Liking and Loving.* New York: Holt, Rinehart and Winston, 1973.

Rushton, J. P. "Generosity in Children: Immediate and Long Term Effects of Modeling, Preaching and Moral Judgments," *Journal of Personality and Social Psychology*, 31 (1975), 755–765.

Rutter, M. "Parent-Child Separation: Psychological Effects on the Children," *Journal of Child Psychology and Psychiatry and Allied Disciplines*, 12 (1971), 233–260.

Ryle, G. *The Concept of Mind.* New York: Barnes and Noble, 1949.

Sachs, J., and J. Devin. "Young Children's Use of Age-Appropriate Speech Styles in Social Interaction and Role Playing," *Journal of Child Language*, 3 (1976), 81–98.

Sachs, J. S., and M. Johnson. "Language Development in a Hearing Child of Deaf Parents," in W. von Raffler Engel and Y. Le Brun (eds.), *Baby Talk and Infant Speech.* Amsterdam: Swets and Zweitlinger, 1976, 246–252.

Saegert, S., and R. Hart. "The Development of Sex Differences in the Environmental Competence of Children," in P. Burnett (ed.), *Women in Society.* Chicago: Maaroufa Press, 1976.

Sagi, A., and M. L. Hoffman. "Empathic Distress in Newborns," *Developmental Psychology*, 12 (1976), 175–176.

Salapatek, P. H., and W. Kessen. "Visual Scanning of Triangles by the Human Newborn," *Journal of Experimental Child Psychology*, 3 (1966), 155–167.

Salk, L. "Mothers' Heartbeat as an Imprinting Stimulus," *Transactions of the New York Academy of Sciences*, 24 (1962), 753–763.

Saltin, B., G. Bloomquist, J. H. Mitchell, R. L. Johnson, K. Wildenthal, and C. B. Chapman. "Response to Exercise after Bed Rest and after Training," *American Heart Association Monograph*, 23 (1968).

Saltz, E. *The Cognitive Bases of Human Learning.* Homewood, Ill.: Dorsey Press, 1971.

Sameroff, A. J. "The Components of Sucking in the Human Newborn," *Journal of Experimental Child Psychology* 6 (1968), 607–623.

Sampson, E. E. "On Justice as Equality," *Journal of Social Issues*, 31 (1975), 21–43.

Sander, L. W. "The Regulation of Exchange in the Infant-Caretaker System and Some Aspects of the Context-Content Relationship," in M. Lewis and L. Rosenblum (eds.), *Interaction, Conversation, and the Development of Language.* New York: Wiley, 1977, pp. 133–156.

Scarr, S., and P. Salapatek. "Patterns of Fear Development During Infancy," *Merrill-Palmer Quarterly* 16 (1970), 53–90.

Scarr, S., and R. A. Weinberg. "IQ Test Performance of Black Children Adopted by White Families," *American Psychologist*, 31 (October 1976), 726–739.

———. "Attitudes, Interests, and IQ," *Human Nature*, 1, no. 4 (1978), 29–36.

Scarr-Salapatek, S. "Genetics and the Development of Intelligence," in F. D. Horowitz *et al.* (eds.), *Review of Child Development Research.* Vol. 4. Chicago: University of Chicago Press, 1975.

Schachtel, E. G. *Metamorphosis: On the Development of Affect, Perception, Attention, and Memory.* New York: Basic Books, 1959.

Schaffer, H. R. *The Growth of Sociability,* Baltimore: Penguin, 1971.

Schaffer, H. R. *Mothering.* Cambridge, Mass.: Harvard University Press, 1977.

Schaffer, H. R., and P. E. Emerson. "The Development of Social Attachments in Infancy," *Monographs of the Society for Research in Child Development,* 29 (1964a), whole no. 94.

———. "Patterns of Response to Physical Contact in Early Human Development," *Journal of Child Psychology and Psychiatry,* 5 (1964b), 1–13.

Schaie, K. W. "A General Model for the Study of Developmental Problems," *Psychological Bulletin,* 64 (1965), 92–107.

Schell, R. E., and J. W. Silber. "Sex-Role Discrimination Among Young Children," *Perceptual and Motor Skills,* 27 (1968), 379–389.

Schimmel, S. "Conditional Discrimination, Number Conception, and Response Inhibition in Two and Three-year-old Children." Unpublished doctoral dissertation, Wayne State University, 1971.

Schonbuch, S. S., and R. E. Schell. "Judgments of Body Appearance by Fat and Skinny Male College Students," *Perceptual and Motor Skills,* 24 (1967), 999–1002.

Schonfeld, W. A. "Body-Image in Adolescents: A Psychiatric Concept for the Pediatrician," *Pediatrics,* 31 (1963), 845–855.

———. "Body-Image Disturbances in Adolescents with Inappropriate Sexual Development," *American Journal of Orthopsychiatry,* 34 (1964), 493–502.

Schwartz, G., and D. Merten. "The Language of Adolescence: An Anthropological Approach to the Youth Culture," *American Journal of Sociology,* 72 (1967), 453–468.

Schwartz, M., and J. Schwartz. "Evidence Against a Genetical Component to Performance on IQ Tests," *Nature,* 248 (March 1974), 84–85.

Science News, "Avant Garde Parents: Traditional Infants," Vol. III., 1977, 262.

Scott, E. M., R. Illsby, and A. M. Thomson. "A Psychological Investigation of Primigravidae. II. Maternal Social Class, Age, Physique and Intelligence," *Journal of Obstetrics and Gynaecology of the British Empire,* 63 (1956), 338–343.

Scott, J. P. "The Development of Social Motivation," *Nebraska Symposium on Motivation,* 15 (1967), 111–132.

Scrimshaw, N. S. "Early Malnutrition and Central Nervous System Function," *Merrill-Palmer Quarterly*, 15 (1969), 375–388.

Scrimshaw, N. S., and J. E. Gordon (eds.). *Malnutrition, Learning, and Behavior*, Cambridge, Mass.: M.I.T. Press, 1968.

Searleman, A. "A Review of Right Hemisphere Linguistic Capabilities," *Psychological Bulletin*, 84 (1977), 503–528.

Sears, R. R. "Your Ancients Revisited: A History of Child Development," in E. Mavis Hetherington (ed.), *Review of Child Development Research*, Vol. 5. Chicago: University of Chicago Press, 1975, pp. 1–73.

———. "Sources of Life Satisfaction of the Terman Gifted Men," *American Psychologist*, 32, (1977), 119–128.

Sears, R. R., E. E. Maccoby, and H. Levin. *Patterns of Child Rearing.* Evanston, Ill.: Row, Peterson, 1957.

Sears, R. R., L. Rau, and R. Alpert. *Identification and Child-rearing.* Stanford, Calif.: Stanford University Press, 1965.

Seligman, M. E. P. *Helplessness: On Depression, Development, and Death.* San Francisco: Freeman, 1975.

———. Submissive Death: Giving Up on Life," *Psychology Today,* 7 (May 1974), 80–85.

Selman, R. L. "The Relation of Role Taking to the Development of Moral Judgment in Children," *Child Development*, 42 (1971), 79–91.

Semb, G. (ed.). *Behavior Analysis and Education.* Lawrence: University of Kansas Press, 1972.

Serbin, L. A., K. D. O'Leary, R. N. Kent, and I. J. Tonick. "A Comparison of Teacher Response to the Pre-academic and Problem Behavior of Boys and Girls," *Child Development*, 44 (1973), 796–804.

Shanab, M. E., and K. A. Yahya. "A Behavioral Study of Obedience," *Journal of Personality and Social Psychology*, 35 (1977), 550–586.

Shanas, E., P. Townsend, D. Wedderburn, H. Friis, P. Milhhoj, and J. Stehouwer. *Older People in Three Industrial Societies.* New York: Atherton Press, 1968.

Shatz, M. *Preschoolers' Ability to Take Account of Others in a Toy Selection Task.* M. A. Thesis, University of Pennsylvania, Philadelphia: 1973.

Shaver, P. and J. Freedman. "Your Pursuit of Happiness," *Psychology Today*, 10 (1976), pp. 26–32, 75.

Sheldon, W. H., *Atlas of Men: A Guide for Somatotyping the Adult Male at All Ages.* New York: Harper & Row, 1954.

Sherif, M., and C. W. S.Sherif. *Groups in Harmony and Tension: An Integration of Studies on Intergroup Relations.* New York: Harper & Row, 1953.

———. *Reference Groups: Explorations into Conformity and Deviation of Adolescents.* New York: Harper & Row, 1964.

Sherman, J. A. *On the Psychology of Women: A Survey of Empirical Studies.* Springfield, Ill.: Charles C Thomas, 1973.

Sherman, L. W. "An Ecological Study of Glee in Small Groups of Preschool Children," *Child Development*, 46 (1975), 53–61.

Shneidman, E. S. *Deaths of Man.* New York: Quadrangle, 1973.

———. "Death Work and Stages of Dying," in E. S. Shneidman (ed.), *Death: Current Perspectives.* Palo Alto, Calif.: Mayfield, 1976, pp. 443–451.

Shock, N. W. "The Physiology of Aging," *Scientific American*, 206 (January 1962), 100–110.

———. "Biological Theories of Aging," in J. E. Birren and K. W. Schaie (eds.), *Handbook of the Psychology of Aging.* New York: Van Nostrand Reinhold, 1977, pp. 103–115.

Shultz, T. R. "Development of the Appreciation of Riddles," *Child Development*, 45 (1974), 100–105.

Siegler, R. S., D. E. Liebert, and R. M. Liebert. "Inhelder and Piaget's Pendulum Problem: Teaching Preadolescents to Act as Scientists," *Developmental Psychology*, 9 (1973), 97–101.

Sigel, I. E., and E. Mermelstein. "Effects of Nonschooling on Piagetian Tasks of Conservation." Unpublished paper, 1966. (Cited in J. H. Flavell, "Concept Development," in P. H. Mussen (ed.), *Carmichael's Manual of Child Psychology*, 3rd ed. New York: Wiley, 1970.)

Simner, M. L. "Newborn's Response to the Cry of Another Infant," *Developmental Psychology,* 5 (1971), 136–150.

Simon, W., and J. H. Gagnon. "On Psychological Development," in D. A. Goslin (ed.), *Handbook of Socialization Theory and Research.* Chicago: Rand McNally, 1969, pp. 733–752.

Simpson, E. L. "Moral Development Research: A Case Study of Scientific Cultural Bias," *Human Development*, 17 (1974), no. 2, 81–106.

Simpson, R. L. "Parental Influence, Anticipatory Socialization, and Social Mobility," *American Sociological Review*, 27 (1962), 517–522.

Sinclair, C. B. *Movement of the Young Child: Ages Two to Six.* Columbus, Ohio: Merrill, 1973.

Singer, J. L. *The Child's World of Make-Believe: Experimental Studies of Imaginative Play.* New York: Academic Press, 1973.

Siqueland, E., and C. A. Delucia. "Visual Reinforcement of Non-Nutritive Sucking in Human Infants," *Science*, 165 (1969), 1144–1146.

Skinner, B. F. *The Behavior of Organisms: An Experimental Analysis.* New York: Appleton-Century-Crofts, 1938.

———. "Pigeons in a Pelican," *American Psychologist*, 15 (1960), 28–37.

Skodak, M., and H. M. Skeels. "A Final Follow-Up Study of One Hundred Adopted Children," *Journal of Genetic Psychology*, 75 (1949), 85–125.

Slobin, D. I. "Children and Language: They Learn the Same Way All Around the World," *Psychology Today*, 6 (July 1972), 71–74+.

———. "Cognitive Prerequisites for the Development of Grammar," in C. A. Ferguson and D. I. Slobin (eds.), *Studies of Child Language Development.* New York: Holt, Rinehart and Winston, 1973, pp. 175–208.

———. "On the Nature of Talk to Children," in E. H. Lenneberg and E. Lenneberg (eds.), *Foundations of Language Development: A Multidisciplinary Approach.* UNESCO-IBRO, 1975.

Smith, C. "Effects of Maternal Undernutrition upon the Newborn Infant in Holland (1944–45)," *Journal of Pediatrics,* 30 (1947), 229–243.

Smith, H. "A Comparison of Interview and Observation Measures of Mother Behavior," *Journal of Abnormal and Social Psychology*, 57 (1958), 278–282.

Smith, P. "Aspects of the Playgroup Environment," in D. Canter and T. Lee (eds.) *Psychology and the Built Environment*. London: Architectural Press, 1974, 56–64.

Snow, C. E. "The Development of Conversation Between Mothers and Babies," *Journal of Child Language*, 4 (1977), 1–22.

Snow, C. E., A. Arlman-Rupp, Y. Hassing, J. Jobse, J. Jootsen, and J. Vorster. "Mothers' Speech in Three Social Classes," *Journal of Psycholinguistic Research*, 5 (1976), 1–20.

Sontag, L. W. "Implications of Fetal Behavior and Environment for Adult Personalities," *Annals of the New York Academy of Sciences*, 134 (1966), 782.

Sontag, L. W., and H. Newbery. "Normal Variations of Fetal Heart Rate During Pregnancy," *American Journal of Obstetrics and Gynecology*, 40 (1940), 449–452.

Sorensen, R. C. *Adolescent Sexuality in Contemporary America: Personal Values and Sexual Behavior, Ages Thirteen to Nineteen*. New York: World Press, 1973.

Spelt, D. K. "The Conditioning of the Human Fetus *in utera*," *Journal of Experimental Psychology*, 38 (1948), 338–346.

Spence, D., and T. Lonner. "The 'Empty Nest': A Transition Within Motherhood," *Family Coordinator*, 20 (October 1971), 369–375.

Spinetta, J. J. "The Child with Cancer: Patterns of Communication," paper presented at the Western Psychological Association, 1977.

Spinetta, J. J., D. Rigler, and M. Karon. "Anxiety in the Dying Child," *Pediatrics*, 52 (1973), 841–845.

———. "Peronal Space as a Measure of a Dying Child's Sense of Isolation." *Journal of Consulting and Clinical Psychology*, 42 (1974), 751–756.

Sroufe, L. A., and J. P. Wunsch. "The Development of Laughter in the First Year of Life," *Child Development*, 43 (1972), 1326–1344.

Staats, A. "Linguistic-Mentalistic Theory Versus an Explanatory S-R Learning Theory of Language Development," in D. I. Slobin (ed.), *The Ontogenesis of Grammar: A Theoretical Symposium*. New York: Academic Press, 1971, pp. 103–150.

Staffieri, J. R. "A Study of Social Stereotype of Body Image in Children," *Journal of Personality and Social Psychology*, 7 (1967), 101–104.

Staub, E. "A Child in Distress: The Influence of Age and Number of Witnesses on Children's Attempts to Help," *Journal of Personality and Social Psychology*, 14 (1970), 130–140.

———. "A Child in Distress: The Influence of Nurturance and Modeling on Children's Attempts to Help," *Developmental Psychology*, 5 (1971), 124–132.

———. *The Development of Prosocial Behavior in Children*. New York: General Learning Press, 1975.

Stein, A. H., S. R. Pohly, and E. Mueller. "The Influence of Masculine, Feminine, and Neutral Tasks on Children's Achievement Behavior, Expectancies of Success, and Attainment Values," *Child Development*, 42 (1971), 195–207.

Stein, P. "Singlehood: An Alternative to Marriage," *Family Coordinator*, 24 (1975), 489–505.

Stendler, C., D. Damrin, and A. C. Haines. "Studies in Cooperation and Competion: I. The Effects of Working for Group and Individual Rewards on the Social Climate of Children's Groups," *Journal of Genetic Psychology*, 79 (1951), 173–197.

Stephens, M. W., and P. Delys. "External Control Expectancies Among Disadvantaged Children at Preschool Age," *Child Development*, 44 (1973), 670–674.

Stern, D. N. *The First Relationship: Infant and Mother*. Cambridge, Mass.: Harvard University Press, 1977.

Stevenson, H. W. *Children's Learning*. New York: Appleton-Century-Crofts, 1972.

Stewart, W. A. (ed.). *Non-standard Speech and the Teaching of English*. Washington, D.C.: Center for Applied Linguistics, 1964.

Stinnett, N., L. Carter, and J. Montgomery. "Older Persons' Perceptions of Their Marriages," *Journal of Marriage and the Family*, 34 (1972), 665–670.

Stirnimann, F. Über das Farbempfinden Neugeborener," *Annales Paediatrici*, 163 (1944), 1–25.

Stolz, H. R., and L. H. Stolz. *Somatic Development of Adolescent Boys: A Study of the Growth in Boys During the Second Decade of Life*. New York: Macmillan, 1951.

Sullivan, H. S. *The Interpersonal Theory of Psychiatry*. H. Perry and M. Gawel (eds.). New York: Norton, 1953.

Suomi, S. J., and H. F. Harlow. "The Role and Reason of Peer Relationships in Rhesus Monkeys," in M. Lewis and L. A. Rosenblum (eds.), *Friendship and Peer Relations*. New York: Wiley, 1975, pp. 153–185.

Super, C. M., J. Kagan, F. J. Morrison, M. M. Haith, and J. Weiffenbach. "Discrepancy and Attention in the Five-Month Infant," *Genetic Psychology Monographs*, 85 (1972), 305–331.

Super, D. E. *Career Education and the Meaning of Work*. Washington, D.C.: U.S. Office of Education, 1976.

Surber, C. F. "Developmental Processes in Social Inference: Averaging of Intentions and Consequences in Moral Judgment," *Developmental Psychology*, 13 (1977), 654–665.

Sussman, M. B. "The Family Life of Old People," in R. H. Binstock and E. Shanas (eds.), *The Handbook of Aging and the Social Sciences*. New York: Van Nostrand Reinhold, 1976, pp. 218–243.

Sussman, M., and L. Burchinal. "Kin Family Network: Unheralded Structure in Current Conceptualizations of Family Functioning." in M. Sussman (ed.), *Marriage and the Family*. 3rd ed. Boston: Houghton Mifflin, 1968, pp. 72–81.

Sutton-Smith, B. "Child's Play—Very Serious Business," *Psychology Today*, 5 (December 1971), 66–69.

Sutton-Smith, B., and J. M. Roberts. "Rubrics of Competitive

Behavior, *Journal of Genetic Psychology,* 105 (1964), 13–37.

Sutton-Smith, B., and B. G. Rosenberg. *The Sibling.* New York: Holt, Rinehart and Winston, 1970.

Tanner, J. M. *Education and Physical Growth: Implications of the Study of Children's Growth for Educational Theory and Practice.* London: University of London Press, 1961.

———. *Growth of Adolescence, with a General Consideration of the Effects of Hereditary and Environmental Factors upon Growth and Maturation from Birth to Maturity.* 2nd ed. Oxford: Blackwell, 1962.

———. "Physical Growth," in P. H. Mussen (ed.), *Carmichael's Manual of Child Psychology.* Vol. 1. 3rd ed. New York: Wiley, 1970, pp. 77–155.

———. "Sequence, Tempo and Individual Variation in Growth and Development of Boys and Girls Aged Twelve to Sixteen," in J. Kagan and R. Coles (eds.), *Twelve to Sixteen: Early Adolescence.* New York: Norton, 1972, pp. 1–24.

Tanner, J. M., R. H. Whitehouse, and M. J. R. Healy. *A New System for Estimating Skeletal Maturity from the Hand and Wrist, with Standards Derived from a Study of 2,600 Healthy British Children.* Parts I and II. Paris: Centre International de l'Enfance, 1962.

Taub, H. A., and M. K. Long. "The Effects of Practice on Short-Term Memory of Young and Old Subjects," *Journal of Gerontology,* 27 (1972), 494–499.

Tavris, C. "Men and Women Report Their Views on Masculinity," *Psychology Today,* 10 (January, 1977), 34–42, 82.

Tavris, C. and C. Offir. *The Longest War: Sex Differences in Perspective.* New York: Harcourt Brace Jovanovich, 1977.

Taylor, D. C. "Differential Rates of Cerebral Maturation Between Sexes and Between Hemispheres," *Lancet,* 2 (1969), 140–142.

Terman, L. M., and M. Oden. *The Gifted Group at Mid-Life.* (Genetic Studies of Genius, Vol. V.) Stanford, Calif.: Stanford University Press, 1959.

Thomas, A., S. Chess, and H. G. Birch. "The Origin of Personality," *Scientific American,* 223 (August 1970), 102–109.

Thomas, A., S. Chess, H. G. Birch, M. E. Hertzig, and S. Korn. *Behavioral Individuality in Early Childhood.* New York: New York University Press, 1963.

Thomas, L. "A Meliorist View of Disease and Dying," *Journal of Medicine and Philosophy,* 1 (1976), 212–221.

Thompson, W. R. "Influence of Prenatal Maternal Anxiety on Emotionality in Young Rats," *Science,* 125 (1957), 698–699.

Thoresen, C. E., and M. Mahoney. *Behavioral Self-Control.* New York: Holt, Rinehart and Winston, 1974.

Tinbergen, N. *The Study of Instinct.* Oxford: Clarendon Press, 1951.

———. *The Animal in Its World: Explorations of an Ethologist, 1932–1972.* Field Studies, vol. 1. Cambridge, Mass.: Harvard University Press, 1972.

Tonkova-Yampol'skaya, R. V. "Development of Speech Intonation in Infants During the First Two Years of Life," in C. A. Ferguson and D. I. Slobin (eds.), *Studies of Child Language Development.* New York: Holt, Rinehart and Winston, 1973, pp. 128–138.

Trabasso, T. "The Role of Memory as a System in Making Transitive Inferences," in R. V. Kail, Jr. and J. W. Hagen (eds.), *Perspectives on the Development of Memory and Cognition,* Hillsdale, N.J.: Erlbaum, 1977, pp. 333–366.

Tracy, R. L., M. E. Lamb, and M. D. Ainsworth. "Infant Approach Behavior as Related to Attachment," *Child Development,* 47 (1976), 571–578.

Trainham, G., and J. C. Montgomery. "Self-Demand Feeding for Babies," *The American Journal of Nursing,* 46 (1946), 767–770.

Treas, J. "Aging and the Family," in D. S. Woodruff and J. E. Birren (eds.), *Aging: Scientific Perspectives and Social Issues.* New York: Van Nostrand, 1975, pp. 92–108.

Treas, J., and A. Van Hilst. "Marriage and Remarriage Rates Among Older Americans," *Gerontologist,* 16 (1976), 132–136.

Trelease, M. L. "Dying Among Alaskan Indians: A Matter of Choice," in E. Kübler-Ross (ed.), *Death: The Final State of Growth.* Englewood Cliffs, N.J.: Prentice-Hall, 1975, pp. 33–37.

Trevarthen, C. "Early Attempts at Speech," in R. Lewin (ed.), *Child Alive!* Garden City, N.Y.: Anchor Books, 1975, pp. 57–74.

Trivers, R. L. "The Evolution of Reciprocal Altruism," *The Quarterly Review of Biology,* 46 (1971), 35–57.

Troll, L. E. "The Family of Later Life: A Decade Review," *Journal of Marriage and the Family,* 33 (1971), 263–290.

———. *Early and Middle Adulthood.* Belmont, Calif.: Wadsworth, 1975.

Tyler, L. E. "The Antecedents of Two Varieties of Vocational Interests," *Genetic Psychology Monographs,* 70 (1964), 177–227.

U.S. Bureau of the Census. *Census of Population, 1960: Persons by Family Characteristics.* Vol. II, 4B, U.S. Government Printing Office, 1964.

———. "Marital Status and Living Arrangements: March 1972," Current Popluation Reports, Series P-20, no. 242. Washington, D.C.: U.S. Government Printing Office, 1972a.

———. *Census of Population, 1970: Persons by Family Characteristics.* Vol. II, 4B, U.S. Government Printing Office, 1973.

———. *Marital Status and Living Arrangements: Current Population Reports,* Series P-20, no. 271, U.S. Government Printing Office, March 1974.

———. *Current Population Reports.* Series P-23, no. 59. "Demographic Aspects of Aging and the Older Population in the United States," Washington, D. C.: U.S. Government Printing Office, 1976.

U. S. National Center for Health Statistics. *Vital Statistics of the United States, 1970.* Vol. 2, Part A: Mortality. Washington, D.C.: U.S. Government Printing Office, 1974a.

———. *Vital Statistics of the United States, 1973.* Vol. 2, Part A: Mortality. Rockville, Md.: U.S. Department of Health, Education, and Welfare, 1974b.

──────. *Teenage smoking: National Patterns of Cigarette Smoking, Age 12 through 18, in 1972 and 1974.* Publication No. (NIH) 76–931. Rockville, Md.: U.S. Department of Health, Education, and Welfare, 1976.

Uzgiris, I. C. "Situational Generality of Conservation," *Child Development,* 35 (1964), 831–841.

──────. "Organization of Sensorimotor Intelligence," in M. Lewis (ed.), *Origins of Intelligence.* New York: Plenum, 1976, pp. 123–163.

Vaillant, G. E. *Adaptation to Life.* Boston: Little, Brown, 1977.

Van Leeuwenhoek, A., and J. Ham. "Observations de natis e semine genetali animalculis," *Philosophical Transactions of the Royal Society of London,* 12 (1677). No. 142, 1040. (Cited in J. Needham, *A History of Embryology.* 2nd rev. ed., with the assistance of A. Hughes. Cambridge: Cambridge University Press, 1959, p. 267.).

Verinis, J. S., and S. Roll. "Primary and Secondary Male Characteristics: The Hairiness and Large Penis Stereotypes," *Psychological Reports,* 26 (1970), 123–126.

Verwoerdt, A., E. Pfeiffer, and H. Wang. "Sexual Behavior in Senescence. II. Patterns of Sexaul Activitiy and Interest," *Geriatrics,* 24 (1969), 137–154.

Vlietstra, A. G., and J. C. Wright. "Sensory Modality and Transmodal Stimulus Properties in Children's Discrimination Learning and Trasfer," *Annual Report, Kansas Center for Research in Early Childhood Education.* Lawrence: University of Kansas, 1971.

Vogel, B. S., and R. E. Schell. "Vocational Interest Patterns in Late Maturity and Retirement," *Journal of Gerontology,* 23 (1968), 66–70.

Von Frisch, K. *The Dance Language and Orientation of Bees.* L. E. Chadwick (tr.). Cambrige, Mass.: Belknap Press of Harvard University Press, 1967.

Vygotsky, L. S. *Thought and Language.* E. Hanfmann and G. Vakar (trs.). Cambridge, Mass.: M.I.T. Press, 1962.

Waber, D. P. "Sex Differences in Cognition: A Function of Maturation Rate?" *Science,* 192 (1976), 572–573.

──────. "Sex Differences in Mental Abilities, Hemisphere Lateralization, and Rate of Physical Growth at Adolescence," *Developmental Psychology,* 13 (1977), 29–38.

Waechter, E. H. "Children's Awareness of Fatal Illness," *American Journal of Nursing,* 71 (1971), 1168–1172.

Wahler, R. G. "Child-Child Interactions in Free Field Settings: Some Experimental Analyses," *Journal of Experimental Child Psychology,* 5 (1967), 278–293.

Wallach, M. A. "Creativity," in P. H. Mussen (ed.), *Carmichael's Manual of Child Psychology.* Vol. 1. 3rd ed. New York: Wiley, 1970.

Waller, W. W. *The Family: A Dynamic Interpretation.* New York: Cordon, 1938.

Walster, E., V. Aronson, D. Abrahams, and L. Rottmann. "Importance of Physical Attractiveness in Dating Behavior," *Journal of Personality and Social Psychology,* 4 (1966), 508–516.

Walters, C. E. "Prediction of Postnatal Development from Fetal Activity." *Child Development,* 36 (1965), 801–808.

Walters, R. H., and R. D. Parke. "Influence of Response Consequences to a Social Model on Resistance to Deviation," *Journal of Experimental Child Psychology,* 1 (1964), 260–280.

Walters, R. H., R. D. Parke, and V. A. Cane. "Timing of Punishment and the Observation of Consequences to Others as Determinants of Response Inhibition," *Journal of Experimental Child Psychology,* 2 (1965), 10–30.

Waterlow, J. C. "Note on the Assessment and Classification of Protein-Energy Malnutrition in Children." *Lancet,* 2 (1973), 87–89.

Watson, J. B. "Psychology as the Behaviorist Views It," *Psychological Review,* 20 (1913), 158–177.

──────. *Behaviorism.* New York: People's Institute, 1924.

Watson, J. B., and R. Rayner. "Conditioned Emotional Reactions," *Journal of Experimental Psychology,* 3 (1920), 1–14.

Watson, J. S. "The Development and Generalization of 'Contingency Awareness' in Early Infancy: Some Hypotheses," *Merrill-Palmer Quarterly,* 12 (1966), 123–135.

──────. "Cognitive-Perceptual Development in Infancy: Setting for the Seventies," *Merrill-Palmer Quarterly,* 17 (1971), 139–152.

──────. "Smiling, Cooing and 'the Game'," *Merrill-Palmer Quarterly,* 18 (1972), 323–339.

Weg, R. B. "The Aged: Who, Where, How, Well (Education, Health, Income, Marital Status)." Unpublished manuscript, 1977. Gerontology Center, University of Southern California.

──────. "The Changing Physiology of Aging," *American Journal of Occupational Therapy,* 27 (1973b), 213–217.

──────. "Changing Physiology of Aging: Normal and Pathological," in D. S. Woodrull and J. E. Birren (eds.), *Aging: Scientific Perspectives and Social Issues.* New York: Van Nostrand, 1975, pp. 229–256.

Weiner, B. "Achievement Motivation as Conceptualized by an Attribution Theorist," in B. Weiner (ed.), *Achievement Motivation and Attribution Theory.* Morristown, N.J.: General Learning Corp., 1974.

Weir, R. H. *Language in the Crib.* The Hague: Mouton, 1962.

Werner, H. *Comparative Psychology of Mental Development.* E. B. Garside (tr.). New York: International Universities Press, 1948.

──────. "The Concept of Development from a Comparative and Organismic Point of View," in D. B. Harris (ed.), *The Concept of Development: An Issue in the Study of Human Behavior.* Minneapolis: University of Minnesota Press, 1957, pp. 125–148.

White, B. L. "An Experimental Approach to the Effects of Experience on Early Human Behavior," in J. P. Hill (ed.), *Minnesota Symposia on Child Psychology.* Vol 1. Minneapolis: University of Minnesota Press, 1967, pp. 201–226.

──────. *Human Infants: Experience and Psychological Development.* Englewood Cliffs, N.J.: Prentice-Hall, 1971.

White, B. L., and R. Held. "Plasticity of Sensorimotor Development in the Human Infant," in J. F. Rosenblith and W. Allinsmith (eds.), *The Causes of Behavior II: Readings in Child Development and Educational Psychology.* 2nd ed. Boston: Allyn & Bacon, 1966, pp. 60–70.

———. *Lives in Progress: A Study of the Natural Growth of Personality.* 2nd ed. New York: Holt, Rinehart and Winston, 1966.

White, S. "Age Differences in Reaction to Stimulus Variation," in O. J. Harvey (ed.), *Experience Structure and Adaptability.* New York: Springer, 1966, pp. 95–122.

Whiting, B. B. *Six Cultures: Studies of Child Rearing.* New York: Wiley, 1963.

Whiting, J. W. M. "Resource Meditation and Learning by Identification," in I. Iscoe and H. W. Stevenson (eds.), *Personality Development in Children.* Austin: University of Texas Press, 1960, pp. 112–126.

Wichern, F. and S. Nowicki, Jr. "Independent Training Practices and Locus of Control Orientation in Children and Adolescence," *Developmental Psychology,* 12 (1976), 77.

Wickelgren, L. W. "Convergence in the Human Newborn," *Journal of Experimental Child Psychology,* 5 (1967), 74–85.

Widdowson, E. M. "Mental Contentment and Physical Growth," *Lancet,* 260 (1951), 1316–1318.

Wiesel, T. N., and D. H. Hubel. "Effects of Visual Deprivation on Morphology and Physiology of Cells in the Cat's Lateral Geniculate Body," *Journal of Neurophysiology,* 26 (1963), 978–993.

Wiggins, J. S., N. Wiggins, and J. C. Conger. "Correlates of Heterosexual Somatic Preference," *Journal of Personality and Social Psychology,* 10 (1968), 82–90.

Wilkinson, A. "Counting Strategies and Semantic Analysis as Applied to Class Inclusion," *Cognitive Psychology,* 8 (1976), 64–85.

Winer, G. A. "An Analysis of Verbal Facilitation of Class-Inclusion Reasoning," *Child Development,* 45 (1974), 224–227.

Witelson, S. F. "Sex and the Single Hemisphere: Specialization of the Right Hemisphere for Spatial Processing," *Science,* 193 (1976), 425–427.

Wolf, T. M. "A Developmental Investigation of Televised Modeled Verbalizations on Resistance to Temptation," *Developmental Psychology,* 6 (1972), 537.

Wolff, G. "Increased Bodily Growth of School-Children Since the War," *Lancet,* 228 (1935), 1006–1011.

Wolff, K. F. *Theoria generationis.* Halle, German, 1759. (Cited in J. Needham, *A History of Embryology.* 2nd rev. ed., with the assistance of A. Hughes. Cambrige: Cambridge University Press, 1959, p. 291.)

Wolff, P. H. "The Role of Biological Rhythms in Early Psychological Development," *Bulletin of the Menninger Clinic,* 31 (1967), 197–218.

———. "The Natural History of Crying and Other Vocalizations in Early Infancy," in B. M. Foss (ed.), *Determinants of Infant Behavior.* Vol. 4. London: Methuen, 1969, pp. 81–109.

Wolff, P. H., and I. Hurwitz. "Sex Differences in Finger Tapping: A Developmental Study," *Neuropsychologia,* 14 (1976), 35–41.

Woodruff, D. S., and J. E. Birren. "Age Changes and Cohort Difference in Personality," *Developmental Psychology,* 6 (March 1972), 252–259.

Wright, J. C., and A. G. Vlietstra. "The Development of Selective Attention: From Perceptual Exploration to Logical Search," H. W. Reese (ed.), *Advances in Child Development and Behavior,* (Volume 10), New York: Academic Press, 1975, pp. 195–239.

Yakovlev, P. I., and A. R. Lecours. "The Mylogenetic Cycles of Regional Maturation of the Brain," in A. Minkowski (ed.), *Regional Development of the Brain in Early Life.* Oxford: Blackwell, 1967.

Yalisove, D. "The Effect of Riddle Structure on Children's Comprehension of Riddles," *Developmental Psychology,* 14 (1978), 173–180.

Yarrow, L. J. "Maternal Deprivation: Toward an Empirical and Conceptual Re-evaluation," *Psychological Bulletin,* 58 (1961), 459–490.

———. "Research in Dimensions of Early Maternal Care," *Merrill-Palmer Quarterly,* 9 (1963), 101–114.

Yarrow, M. R., P. M. Scott, and C. Z. Waxler. "Learning Concern for Others," *Developmental Psychology,* 8 (1973), 240–260.

Yen, W. M., and D. H. McLaughlin. *Post High School Education and Career Development.* Palo Alto, Calif.: American Institutes for Research, 1974.

Yonas, A., and H. L. Pick, Jr. "An Approach to the Study of Infant Space Perception," in L. B. Cohen and P. Salapatek (eds.), *Infant Perception: From Sensation to Cognition.* Vol. 2. New York: Academic Press, 1975, 3–31.

Zaporozhets, A. V. "The Development of Perception in the Preschool Child," in P. H. Mussen (ed.), "European Research in Cognitive Development," *Monographs of the Society for Research in Child Development,* 30 (1965), 82–101.

Zelazo, N. A., P. R. Zelazo, and S. Kolb. "Walking in the Newborn," *Science,* 176 (1972), 314–315.

Zelnik, M., and J. F. Kantner. *Sexuality, Contraception, and Pregnancy Among Young Unmarried Females in the U. S.* Unpublished manuscript, 1972. (Cited in I. L. Reiss, *Heterosexual Relationships Inside and Outside Marriage.* Morristown, N.J.: General Learning Press, 1973, p. 15.)

———. "Sexual and Contraceptive Experience of Young Unmarried Women in the United States, 1976 and 1971," *Family Planning Perspectives,* 9 (1977), 55–71.

Zimmerman, B. J. and T. L Rosenthal. "Observational Learning of Rule Governed Behavior by Children." *Psychological Bulletin.* 81 (1974), 29–42.

Zur Aschoff, L. "Normalen und Pathologischen Anatomie des Criesenalters," *Medisinische Klinik,* 33 (1937), 257–291.

INDEX

abortion, 86–87
Abrahamson, A., 223
Abravanel, E., 216
accommodation
  in Piaget's theory, 32
  infant, 148
Acheson, R., 201, 202, 208
achievement
  and gender, adolescence, 394–395
  and social class, 384–385
Acredolo, L. P., 295
activity, newborn, 104
Adams, B. N., 437
Adamsons, K. Jr., 92
adaptation
  of infant, 148
  of newborn, 102–104
adaptation theories
  of ethologists, 33–35
  organismic development, 29–30
  of Piaget, 30–33
Adelson, J., 378, 379, 380, 387, 388, 391,
  396
Adinolfi, A., 392
adolescence
  body growth, 348–350
  brain maturation, 351–352
  cliques and crowds in, 391–394
  cognition in, 369–372
  and concept of youth, 398–399
  conformity in, 388–390
  early and late maturing, 358–359
  emergence of concept, 7–9
  family relations and influence, 385–390
  formal thought in, 369–371
  friendship in, 390–391
  gender and achievement, 394–395
  and generation gap, 395–397
  identity in, 366–369
  moral reasoning in, 372–373
  obesity in, 357–358
  peer relations and influence in, 390–395
  physical–sexual and social change in,
    358–362
  promiscuity in, 375
  reactions to physical change, 355–358
  self-esteem in, 368–369
  sexual behavior, 359–362
  sexuality and intimacy in, 373–377
  sexual maturation in, 350–351
  size and maturational trends, 353–355
  social class differences in, 384–385
  vocational identity, 377–380
adulthood

development phase, 18
  see also early adulthood; later adulthood;
    middle adulthood
afterbirth, 80
age
  chronological vs. physical, 446
  gestational, 83
  and life expectancy, 466
aggression
  early childhood, 260–262
  hostile vs. instrumental, 310–311
  and peer reinforcement, 270
  and television, 57, 320–321
aging, theories, 467–468
Ahammer, I. M., 414, 416, 450
Ainsworth, M. S., 180, 183, 184
Ajuriaguerra, J. de, 123
alcohol
  and adolescent conformity, 388–389
  and birth complications, 86
Aldrich, C., 94
alleles, 73
Allinsmith, W., 326
Alpaugh, P., 450
Alpert, R., 326
alpha rhythm, 200
altruism, middle childhood, 308, 309–310
Ambrose, A., 107
amniocentesis, 83
amniotic fluid, 91
Anderson, J. L., 480
androgens, 348
androgyny, 377
Anglin, J., 141, 142
animals
  attachment in monkeys, 175–178
  genetic studies, 46–47
  peer influence in monkeys, 268–269
Apgar, V., 81
Apgar score, 81
Appelbaum, M. I., 298
Arend, R., 189
Ariès, P., 6, 7
Aronfreed, J., 334
Aronson, E., 137
artificialism, 286
Asch, S., 246
Aschoff, Z., 466
Ashford, J. R., 86
assertiveness, early childhood, 260–262
assimilation
  infant, 148
  in Piaget's theory, 32
asynchrony, 350

Atchley, R., 452
Atlee, E., 445
attachment
  vs. detachment in infant, 189
  in humans, 178–179
  in monkeys, 175–178
attention
  focused, early childhood, 218–219
  infant, 138–140
  and perception, newborn, 99–102
  preferences, early childhood, 217–218
  selective, middle childhood, 282–283
audition, newborn, 98–99
auditory attention, newborn, 101–102
Ausubel, D., 189, 222, 292
autonomy, 11
  in infant, 189–190
  in psychosocial development, 38

babbling, 156–157
Babchuk, N., 422
Bachman, J. G., 322, 389
Bacon, M., 259, 388, 389
Baer, K. von, 70
Baker, N., 265
Baltes, P. B., 62, 412, 450, 454
Bandura, A., 57, 271, 320, 338
  profile, 28
  social learning theory, 27–28
Bardwick, J., 379, 380, 395, 410, 432
Barker, R., 52
Baron, R., 321
Barry, H., 259
Baruch, D., 14
Bayley, N., 113, 114, 118, 124, 137, 276,
  358
Beach, D., 228
Beatty, R. A., 86
Beck, E., 200, 352
Becker, J., 190, 191
behavior-learning theories, 26–29
Beit-Hallahmi, B., 185
Belbin, R. M., 427
Bell, B., 471
Bell, Richard, 127
Bell, Robert, 411
Bell, S., 179
Bellugi, U., 239, 241, 242
  see also Bellugi-Klima, U.
Bellugi-Klima, U., 237, 244
  see also Bellugi, U.
Belmont, L., 54
Bem, S., 377

Bengtson, V. L., 452
Bennett, E. L., 122
bereavement, 482−483
Bereiter, C., 249
Berg-Cross, L. G., 327
Berko, J., 239
  see also Gleason, J. B.
Bernal, J., 106
Bernard, J., 415, 420
Bernholtz, N., 160
Bernstein, B., 248
Berscheid, E., 405, 428
Berzonsky, M., 226
Bever, T., 241, 242
Binstock, R. H., 440
biological determinants of development
  46−51
biology, and developmental psychology,
  12−13
Birch, H. G., 104
Birren, J., 404, 409, 426, 430, 433,
  446
birth, 90−91
  complications, and development, 82−87
  labor and delivery, 79−81
  methods, 81
  see also newborn
birth order
  and height, 202
  as social determinant of development,
    53−54
Black English, vs. Standard English,
  250−251
blacks
  divorce, middle adulthood, 438
  longevity, 468
  self-esteem of adolescents, 369
  unemployment and job aspirations, 386
Blanchard, B., 455
Blank, M., 216, 221, 228, 244
Blatt, M., 338
Blau, Z. S., 385, 388
Blizzard, R. M., 202
Block, Jack, 409
Block, Jeanne, 314, 373
Bloom, L., 165, 167, 168
Blos, P., 368
Blurton-Jones, N., 33
body
  in early adulthood, 405
  growth, adolescence, 348−350
  growth, early childhood, 198
  ideal, 355
body concept and self-concept,
  adolescence, 355−356
Bohrnstedt, G., 405, 428
Bornstein, M. H., 134
Botvin, G., 285, 286
Botwinick, J., 412, 433
Bouvier, L., 445
Bower, T. G. R., 97, 105, 116, 126, 134,
  142, 145, 148
Bowlby, J., 185
boys
  brain, 208−209
  friendship in adolescence, 392
  vs. girls, early childhood, 208−209
  masculinity and family relations,
    adolescents, 387
  sexual maturation, 351

see also peer(s); peer groups; sex-role
  development
Brackbill, Y., 104, 107
Bradburn, N. M., 417
Bradway, K., 455
brain
  cortical control, 121−123, 207−208
  development, 120−123
  girls vs. boys, 208−209
  growth, early childhood, 198, 200
  growth, infant, 120−121
  maturation, adolescence, 351−352
  prenatal development, 78
Braine, M., 168
Brainerd, C. J., 221
Brand, F., 456
Brasel, J. A., 202
breasts, development of, 350, 356−357
breech delivery, 80
Bremner, J. G., 144
Bricker, W., 270
Bridger, W. H., 216, 228
Bridges, K. B., 190
Brinley, J., 291
Brittain, C., 396
Broen, P., 245
Bromley, D. B., 371, 372
Bronfenbrenner, U., 51, 180, 315
Bronstein, I. P., 201
Brooks, J., 188
Broverman, D., 352
Brown, A. L., 417
Brown, Ann, 230
Brown, Paul, 267
Brown, Roger, 144, 152, 166, 168, 237,
  238, 241, 244, 245, 251, 252n
Bruch, H., 201
Brück, K., 91
Bruner, J., 34, 192, 245, 274, 371
Bruno, L. A., 102
Bryan, J., 338
Bryant, P., 138, 144, 223, 224
Buell, J., 210, 212
Bullock, T. H., 120
Burchinal, L., 437
Burgess, E. W., 414
Burkitt, D. P., 469
Busch, C., 431
Butler, N. R., 86
Butler, R., 446, 479
Butterfield, E., 154
Butterworth, G., 143
Byrne, D., 390

Campbell, J. D., 307, 418, 419
Campos, J., 134, 179
Cane, V., 335, 337
Canestrari, R. E., 455
Cannon, K. L., 360
Caplovitz, D., 417
Cappon, D., 481
careers vs. jobs, and family influence,
  adolescence, 386−387
caregiver, and attachment in humans,
  178−179
caregiving, multiple, in infancy, 185
Carey, S., 286
Carlsmith, L., 315
Caro, G., 386

Carson, M. T., 223
Carter, H., 413
Carter, L., 457
Cartwright, A., 480
Casals, P., 455
case histories, 14
catch-up growth
  early childhood, 201
  newborn, 83
Cattell, P., 114, 118
causal reasoning, middle childhood, 286,
  288
Cazden, C., 237, 244
Celotta, B., 216
central nervous system and brain growth,
  121
cephalocaudal development, 112−113
cerebral dominance, 123
cervix, 71
Chabon, I., 81
Chagall, M., 455
Chall, J. S., 16
Chananie, J. D., 262
Charlesworth, R., 270
Chernoff, G., 86
Chess, S., 104
Child, I., 259
childbirth methods, 81
childhood
  development phase, 18
  emergence of concept, 6−7
  see also adolescence; early childhood;
    infant; middle childhood; newborn
Chinsky, J., 228
Chiraboga, D., 410
Chodorow, N., 259
Chomsky, N., 152, 236
Chown, S. M., 462
chromosomes, 47, 71
chumship, 391
Clark, H. H., 162, 236, 246
Clark, E. V., 162, 163, 236, 246
Clark-Stewart, K. A., 16
classical conditioning, 26
Clayton, P., 459
clinical studies of determinants of
  development, 59, 60
cliques and crowds, adolescence, 391−394
Clyburn, A., 265
Coates, B., 271, 272
Cobb, W., 121
cognition
  in adolescence, 369−372
  and first words, 157−158
  infant, 132−133
  social, and play in middle childhood,
    319−320
  and social interaction, early childhood,
    232−233
  and social interaction, middle childhood,
    297−298
  and vocational choice, adolescence,
    377−379
cognitive development
  and language, 228, 244−248
  and play, 229−230
cohabitation, 420
Cohen, D., 47
Cohen, L., 139
Cohen, S., 52

cohorts, and cross-sectional studies, 62
Cole, M., 289, 371, 420
Coleman, J., 394, 395, 398
Coleman, R., 384
collectivism and achievement, 384
Comfort, A., 456
commitment
  adolescence, 397–398
  early adulthood, 406
communal living
  early adulthood, 421
  later adulthood, 460
communication
  of death, 480–481
  and semantics, early childhood,
    246–248
  and social relations, newborn, 105–107
competence, infant striving for, 188–190
competition
  ethnic differences, 276
  and group cohesion, middle childhood,
    317
concept(s)
  early childhood, 222–224
  language and formation of, 228
  middle childhood, 284–286
  and symbols, infant, 140–145
conception, 70–71
concrete-operational stage of intellectual
    development, 33, 284
conditioned reflex, 26
conditioning, 26–27
Condon, W. S., 107, 154
Conel, J. L., 121, 208
conformity, in adolescence, 388–390, 392
Conger, J. C., 356
Conger, J. J., 375, 377
conjunctive concept, 222
Conklin, F., 460
Connor, J. M., 209
conservation
  in middle childhood, 284–286
  of thought, early childhood, 219–222
Constantine, J., 422
Constantine, L., 422
Conte, H., 449
contradiction, in two-year-old's language,
    166
control
  and achievement, 384
  of behavior, 12
  cortical, 121–123
  locus of, 190
  and self-regulation, middle childhood,
    313–314
  in studying determinants of
    development, 59
  see also self-control
conventional level of moral reasoning, 329
convergence, in newborn, 98
Converse, P. E., 418, 419
cooperation, ethnic differences, 276
coordination
  early childhood, 203
  of movement, 123–126
  sensory and sensory-motor, infant,
    136–138
  sensory, early childhood, 216–217
Coplan, A., 473
Coren, S., 208

Cornell, E. H., 139
correlation coefficients, 48
Correll, R., 455
cortical control
  early childhood, 207–208
  infant, 121–123
Costanzo, P., 316
co-twin control, 126
Cowan, P., 250, 292
Cox, M., 419
Cox, R., 419
Crandall, V., 265
Cratty, B., 207
creativity
  early adulthood, 413
  later adulthood, 455–456
  middle adulthood, 434
Crites, J., 387
Crook, C., 99
cross-sectional studies of determinants,
    62–64
Cruise, M. O., 83
Cuber, J., 435, 440
cuddling, infant responsiveness to, 182
cultural anthropology, and developmental
    psychology, 13
culture
  and parent responsiveness, 180–182
  and sex-role development, 259–260
  as social determinant of development,
    57–58
  and views on death, 474–475

Dabek, R. F., 327
Damrin, D., 317
Danzger, B., 104
Darwin, C., evolution theory, 24
Davenport, R. K., 173
Davis, G., 442
Dawe, H. C., 310–311
daycare, and infant responsiveness, 185
Dayton, G. O. Jr., 98, 100
deafness, and intellectual development,
    228
death
  anticipatory grief, 480
  bereavement, 482–483
  communication of, 480–481
  cross-cultural views on, 474–475
  meaning to adults, 472–474
  meaning to children, 471–472
  and process of dying, 475–480
  rate, middle adulthood, 427–428
Deaux, K., 409
Debakan, A., 113
delivery, labor and, 79–81
Delucia, C., 146
Delys, P., 276
Dement, W., 93, 94
Denenberg, V. H., 173
Denney, D. R., 291
Denney, N. W., 291
Dennis, W., 126, 434, 455
deoxyribonucleic acid, 71
dependence, and sex-role development,
    262–263
deprivation, maternal, in infancy, 185, 202
depth perception, newborn, 98
detachment, in infant, 188–189

determinants of development
  biological, 46–51
  classes, 46
  environmental, 51–59
  studying, 59–64
  see also development
Deur, J., 53
Deutscher, I., 435, 436, 441
development
  birth complications, 82–87
  early adulthood, 405–408
  individual variation, 15–16
  later adulthood, 449–450
  middle adulthood, 428–430
  moral, 324, 338–340
  motor abilities, early childhood,
    202–208
  norms, 115–118
  organismic, 29–30
  phases, 17–19
  physical and social changes, 127–128
  prespeech, infant, 153–156
  sequences, 16–17
  types of knowledge, 14–15
  see also determinants of development
developmental crisis, adolescence,
    366–367
developmental psychology
  contributions of other disciplines to,
    12–13
  emergence of, 9–10
  studying, 10–11
  use of theory, 11–12
  uses, 19–20
Devereux, E., 388
Devin, J., 247
DeVries, H., 442, 471
dialects, 250–252; 392–393
Diamond, M. C., 122
dichotic listening technique, 207
Dick-Read, G., 81
diet
  and growth, 200–201
  and longevity, 468–469
differentiation, and integration, 113–114
Dion, K., 264
discipline, timing, and self-regulation, 335
disease
  and life expectancy, 466
  maternal, and birth complications, 84
Dishotsky, N. I., 85
disjunctive concept, 222
disobedience and peer modeling, 271
displacement, language, 152–153,
    236–237
divorce
  middle adulthood, 438–439
  and remarriage, early adulthood,
    418–419
Dobbing, J., 78, 120, 198
Dollard, J., 27
dominance hierarchies, children, 33
dominant gene, 73
Donaldson, M., 221, 223
Douglas, J. W. B., 123
Douvan, E., 350, 378, 379, 380, 385, 387,
    388, 391, 395, 396
Down's syndrome, 82–83
Dragastin, S. E., 7
drawing, as imitation, 226

drinking, adolescent, 388−389
drugs
  and adolescent conformity, 388, 389−390
  and birth complications, 85
  influence on children, 322
Duck, S., 390
Dulit, E., 371
Dunn, J., 183
Dunphy, D., 393
Dustman, R., 200, 352
Duvall, E., 435
Dwyer, J., 201, 350
dying
  experience of, 476
  phases of, 476−479
  process of, 475−483
Dziadosz, G. M., 208

ear dominance, 207−208
early adulthood
  alternatives to marriage, 419−422
  and concept of maturity, 404
  developmental tasks, 405−408
  divorce and remarriage, 418−419
  identity and interpersonal behavior, 408−413
  intellectual skills, 411−413
  and marriage, 413−419
  parenthood, 416−418
  physical characteristics, 404−405
  self-concept and self-esteem, 409−410
  sexuality, 410−411
  social life and change, 422−423
  see also adolescence; later adulthood; middle adulthood
early childhood
  aggression in, 260−262
  attention preferences, 217−218
  attention span, 219
  concepts, 222−224
  conservation, 219−222
  development of motor abilities, 202−208
  egocentrism, 224−226
  environmental influences on growth, 200−202
  focused attention, 218−219
  girls vs. boys, 208−209
  grammar, 237−244
  growth characteristics, 198−200
  imitation, 226
  language, 226−229, 244−248
  memory, 230
  parent-child relationships, 266−268
  peer influence, 268−273
  perceptual advances, 216−217
  physical and social changes, 209−212
  play, 229−230, 273−274
  representational skills, 226−232
  self-concept, 263−266
  sex-role development, 257−263
  social interaction and cognition, 232−233
  socialization, 256−257
  subcultures and personality, 275−276
  thinking in, 219−226
  using graphic symbols in, 230−232
  see also infant; middle childhood

Eckerman, C., 139, 184, 186, 187, 188
ecological approach to development, 51−52
ectoderm, 74
education
  of attention, early childhood, 217−219
  and income, 385
  influence on children, 322−323
  and reasoning, 288−289
ego, 35
egocentrism
  early childhood, 224−226
  infant, 144
  and positive behavior, middle childhood, 308
ego integrity, 38−40, 446
ego psychology, 40−41
Ehrhardt, A. A., 13, 258
Eibl-Eibesfeldt, I., 33, 178
Eichenwald, H., 120
Eichorn, D., 359
Eimas, P., 154
Eisen, M., 371
Eisenberg, K., 241
Eisenberg, R. B., 98, 102
Elder, G. H. Jr., 386, 387
elimination, in newborn, 94−95
Elkind, D., 327
Elliott, R., 267
Elmer, N. P., 308
embryonic period of prenatal growth, 75−76
Emde, R., 121
Emerson, P., 179, 182
Emmerich, W., 262, 268
emotion, and sex-role identification, 306
emotional condition, and birth complications, 86
emotional dependence, 262
emotional stress, and growth, early childhood, 202
endoderm, 74
Endsley, R., 320
Engelmann, S., 249
Engen, T., 99
environment
  and development, 51−58
  and growth, early childhood, 200−202
  infant interaction with, 145−148
  and language functioning, 248−252
  and maturation, 354
equalitarianism and gender, adolescence, 375−377
equilibration, in Piaget's theory, 32−33
Erikson, E., 54, 128, 184, 212, 390
  ego integrity concept, 446
  generativity concept, 429
  identity concept, 366−367
  maturity concept, 404
  profile, 37
  psychosocial development theory, 11, 36−40
  totalism concept, 368
Ervin, S., 237
  see also Ervin-Tripp, S.,
Ervin-Tripp, S., 248
  see also Ervin, S.
erythroblastosis, 84
estrogens, 348, 427

ethical considerations in studying determinants, 64
ethnic group and cooperation vs. competition, 276
ethologists, and adaptation theories, 33−35
euthanasia, 480
Evans, R. I., 143, 389
experience
  early, effects on infants, 173−175
  and maturation, motor abilities, 126−127
experimentation, in studying determinants of development, 59, 61
exploration
  early childhood, 219
  in infant, 147−148
extinguishing, in operant conditioning, 27
eye dominance, 207−208

facial hair and puberty, boys, 351
Fagan, J. F. III, 134, 140, 145
Fagot, B., 267
Falbo, T., 266
Falkner, F. T., 115, 116, 198
Fallopian tube, 71
family
  relations and influence, adolescence, 385−390
  as social determinant of development, 53−54
  see also parents
family life
  later adulthood, 456−460
  and marriage, middle adulthood, 434−439
fantasy and verbal fluency, 295
Fantz, R., 100, 134, 138
Farb, P., 152
fathers as caregivers, 180
  see also parents
Faust, M. S., 359
fear
  in infancy, 174−175
  of success, 395
feeding of newborn, 94
Feffer, M., 320
Feigenbaum, K., 462
Fein, G. G., 16
Feldman, H., 435, 457
femininity, changing concept of, 410
Fenson, L., 193
Ferguson, D., 417
Ferguson, C. A., 154, 238
Ferree, M. M., 417
fertility and menstruation, 350−351
Feshbach, S., 262
fetal alcohol syndrome, 86
fetal period of prenatal growth, 76−77
fetus, 74
field studies, 59, 60−61
Finch, C. E., 427
first sentences, 165−167
first words, 157−165
Fischer, K. W., 179
Fitzgerald, H., 104
Flacks, R., 398
Flavell, J. H., 133, 224, 228, 246, 247, 284, 296, 297, 310
Floyd, J., 270

Flurkey, K., 427
Foner, A., 457, 459
Ford, B., 456
Ford, G. R., 338
Forgus, R. H., 173
formal-operational stage of intellectual
  development, 33
formal thought
  in adolescence, 369–371
  and principled reasoning, 372–373
Freedman, D. G., 47, 178
Fort, J., 85
Frank, L. K., 94
Fraser, C., 241
Freda, V. J., 84
Freedman, M., 410
free-radical theory of aging, 467–468
Freud, S., 173, 256, 258, 293
  profile, 36
  psychodynamic theory, 35–36
Friedl, E., 259
Friedman, S., 102–103
friendship
  in adolescence, 390–391
  in early adulthood, 422–423
  in late adulthood, 461–462
  in middle adulthood, 440–441
Fries, M., 104
Friesen, D., 356
Frodi, A., 262
Fry, P. C., 120
Fryer, J. G., 86
Furth, H., 228, 295, 296
future orientation, and achievement, 384

Gagnon, J., 377
Gaitz, C., 423, 442, 462
Galton, F., maturation theory, 24–25
gametes, 71
Gardner, H., 292
Garvey, C., 248, 274
Gelfand, D., 311
Gelman, R., 42, 221, 226, 248
gender
  and achievement, adolescence,
    394–395
  and adolescent sexuality, 379–380
  and equalitarianism, 375–377
gender identity vs. sex role, 258
generation gap
  and adolescence, 395–397
  and drugs, 322
generativity
  in middle adulthood, 429
  in psychosocial development, 39–40
genes, 47, 71
genetic epistemology, 30
genetic factors, development, 46–50
genetic transmission, 73–74
genitals, male, reactions to physical
  changes in, 356–357
genotype, 73
Gerbner, G., 321
germinal period of prenatal growth,
  74–75
Gesell, A. L., 25, 114, 123
gestalts, 29
gestational age, 83
gestation period, 74

Gewirtz, J., 146, 156, 185
Gibbs, E. L., 352
Gibbs, F. A., 352
Gibson, E., 134
Gilbertsen, V. A., 481
Gilligan, C., 371, 372
Gilmartin, B., 421
girls
  brain, 208–209
  early childhood, 208–209
  fear of success, 395
  friendships in adolescence, 391
  sexual maturation, 350–351
  see also peer(s); peer groups; sex-role
    development
Glaser, B., 475, 481
Glass, D., 52
Gleason, J. B., 239
  see also Berko, J.
Glenn, N., 461
glial cells, 78
Glick, P., 413
Gluck, L., 77
Gluecksohn-Waelsch, S., 86
Gold, M., 350
Goldberg, S., 183, 186, 187
Golden, M. M., 391
Goldstein, H., 86
Golomb, C., 230
gonorrhea and birth complications, 84
Goodenough, F. L., 310, 311
Goodman, J., 335
Goodnow, J., 232
Gordon, C., 423, 442, 462, 474
Gordon, J., 120
Gottlieb, S., 295, 327
Gouin-Décarie, T., 144
Gould, L., 258
Gould, R., 406, 429, 430, 440
Gourevitch, V., 320
Govatos, L., 208
Graham, D., 324
grammar, 153
  awareness of, early childhood, 237–240
  overregularization, 238–240
  rules and performance limitations, early
    childhood, 242–244
  testing child's comprehension of,
    240–242
  from two words to, 167–168
grandparenthood, 437–438
grasping reflex in newborn, 95–96
Gratch, G., 143, 144
Gray Panthers, 461
Green, F., 308
Greenberg, M., 225
Greenfield, P., 371
Greif, E. B., 329
grief, anticipatory, 480
Griffiths, R., 114
Grinder, R. E., 336
Grinnell, A., 120
Grof, S., 474
Gross, L., 321
Grosser, D., 337
group
  age, 398
  and peer influence, middle childhood,
    316–317
  see also peer(s); peer groups

group marriage, 422, 460
growth
  body, in adolescence, 348–350
  body, in early childhood, 198
  brain, 120–121, 198, 200
  cephalocaudal, 112–113
  differentiation and integration, 113–114
  environmental influences, early
    childhood, 200–202
  proximodistal, 113
  rate, girls vs. boys, 208
Grusec, J., 309, 338
guilt
  reactions to, 336
  and reasoning, children, 335–336
  and self-regulation, children, 332–336
Gusinow, J., 217
Gutmann, D., 409, 431, 451
Gutteridge, M. V., 204

Haaf, R. A., 140
Haan, N., 373
Haber, R. N., 134
habituation
  and attention, infant, 139–140
  of newborn, 102
Hagen, J., 282
Hagestad, G. O., 426
Haines, A. C., 317
Haith, M. M., 95, 100, 101, 118, 133, 134,
  136, 140
Hale, G., 282, 283
Halifax, J., 474
Hall, G. S.
  maturation theory, 25
  on newborn, 90
Hammer, E. F., 377
handedness, 123, 207
Harari, H., 307, 313
Hardesty, F. P., 304
Hardyck, C., 123
Harlow, H., 15, 175, 177, 268, 269
Harlow, M., 175, 177, 268
Harper, L., 127
Harris, P. L., 143
Harrison, C. W., 307
Harroff, P. B., 435
Hartley, R., 259, 304
Hartmann, D., 311
Hartshorne, H., 324, 325
Hartup, W. W., 262, 270, 271, 272, 310,
  311, 316, 388, 392, 393, 394
Hathaway, M., 357
Haven, C., 459, 461
Havighurst, R., 331, 428, 450, 462
Haynes, H., 98
Head Start, 12
Healy, M. J. R., 208
hearing, infants, 136
Hebb, D., 244
Hécaen, H., 123
Held, R., 98, 126
Helson, R., 377
heredity
  and development, 46
  and intelligence, 25
heritability
  as determinant of development,
    50–51

and IQ, 299–300
Hermelin, B., 207
Herron, R. E., 209, 210, 229
Hershenson, M., 99, 134
Hess, B., 441
Hess, E., 174
Hess R., 58, 202, 248, 275, 276, 384
heterozygous, 73
Hetherington, E. M., 53, 315, 419
Hewitt, E., 94
Heyde, M. B., 378, 379
Hickey, M., 450
Hicks, D. J., 271, 272
Hicks, M. W., 418
Hicks, R. E., 123
hierarchies, middle childhood, 306
Higgins, E. T., 248
high school, social system, 394
Hilgard, J., 482
Hill, R., 414, 458
Hinton, J., 476
Hirsch, H. V. B., 78
Hiscock, M., 208
Hockey, L., 480
Hoffman, M., 106, 308, 334, 336
Hogan, R., 274
Hogarty, P. S., 298
Hollingshead, A., 386
Hollos, M., 250, 292
Holmes, F., 174
Holmes, T., 466
Holstein, C., 330, 331
homozygous, 73
Honzik, M. P., 49
Hood, L., 168
Hooker, D., 78
hormones, 348, 427
Horner, M., 395
Horowitz, F., 136
hostile aggression, 310–311
hostility, groups, middle childhood,
    317–318
Howes, C., 191
Hubel, D. H., 122
Hudson, R. B., 440
Hultsch, D., 455
Hunt, M. M., 322, 361, 374, 421
Hurwitz, I., 209
Hutt, C., 208, 209
Huttenlocher, J., 241
Huxley, A., 26

id, 35
identification
    sex role, and emotion, 306
    and socialization, 256–257
    in two-year-old's language, 166
identity
    in adolescence, 366–369
    crisis, 390
    to ego integrity, 38–40
    and interpersonal behavior, early
        adulthood, 408–413
    and interpersonal behavior, later
        adulthood, 450–456
    and interpersonal behavior, middle
        adulthood, 430–434
    adulthood, 430–434
illness and growth, early childhood,
    201–202

Illsby, R., 202
imitation
    early childhood, 226
    in middle childhood, 291
    and peer modeling, 272
    in social learning, 27
    imprinting in infants, 173–174
    incidental learning, middle childhood,
        282–283
independence
    and self-control, adolescence, 387–388
    and sex-role development, 262–263
individual
    time patterns, 118–119
    variability, 118–120
individualism and achievement, 384
induced abortions, 86
industry, from trust to, 36, 38
infancy, development phase, 18
infant
    adapting, 148
    attachment, 175–179
    attention, 138–140, 154–155
    cognition, 132–133
    concepts and symbols, 140–145
    effects of early experience, 173–175
    environmental interaction, 145–148
    exploring, 147–148
    first sentences, 165–167
    hearing, 136
    interaction with parents, 186–189
    interaction with peers, 190–192
    learning, 145–147, 148
    memory and thought, 144–145
    multiple caregiving, 185
    object identity, 141–142
    object permanence, 142–144
    and parent responsiveness, 179–182
    perceptual functioning, 133–138
    personality development, 172–173
    play, 192–193
    prespeech development, 153–165
    responsiveness, 182–185
    seeing, 134
    self-concept, 187–188
    sensory and sensorymotor coordination,
        136
    separation distress, 183–184
    sociability, 186–193
    speech sounds, 155–157
    striving for competence, 188–190
    wariness of strangers, 184
    see also early childhood; newborn
Ingram, Dianna, 207, 208
Inhelder, B., 219, 283, 284, 370
    test of memory, 295
    and pendulum problem, 289–290
initiative, in psychosocial development, 38
instruction and practice in motor skills,
    early childhood, 205–207
instrumental aggression, 310–311
instrumental dependence, 262
integration and differentiation, 113–114
intellectual development
    and deafness, 228
    and family, 54
    and imitation, 291
intellectual skills
    early adulthood, 411–413
    later adulthood, 453–456

middle adulthood, 433–434
intelligence
    concept of, 298–300
    as determinant of development, 48–50
    and heredity, 25
intercourse
    in adolescence, 361
    in early adulthood, 411
interpersonal commitment, 397–398
intimacy
    in psychosocial development, 39
    and sexuality, in adolescence, 373–377
intonation
    child, 167–168
    infant, 157
intelligence quotient (IQ)
    changing viewpoints about, 298–299
    what it measures, 299–300
irritability, newborn, 104
isolation and social relationships, 268–269

Jack, L. M., 210
Jacklin, C., 261
Jackson, E., 179
Jacobson, M., 78
Jakobson, R., 162
James, L. S., 81
James, W., on newborn, 89
Jarvik, L., 47
Jeffers, F. C., 470
Jensen, A., 49, 61, 299
Jersild, A., 174, 209
Jewett, S., 471
jobs
    adolescent perspective on, 384
    vs. careers, 386–387
    part-time, 377
Joffe, J. M., 86
Johnson, M., 246
Johnson, P., 99
Johnson, R., 440
Johnson, V., 357, 411, 430, 432, 433, 453
Johnston, L. D., 322, 389
Jolly, A., 274
Jones, K., 86
Jones, M. C., 26, 119, 358, 359, 388, 389
Jordaan, J. P., 378, 379

Kagan, J., 27, 136, 138, 139, 145, 180,
    259, 260, 261, 266, 305,
Kagan, S., 276
Kahl, J. A., 384
Kalish, R., 472, 473, 474, 475, 476
Kamin, L. J., 299
Kandel, D., 389, 396
Kangas, J., 455
Kanter, R. M., 421
Kantner, J. F., 360, 361, 375
Kaplan, S., 415
Karniol, R., 327
Karon, M., 472, 477
Kay, E., 426
Kearsley, R., 185
Keasey, C., 331
Keller, S., 249, 389
Kelly, G., 390
Kelly, J., 423, 442
Kendler, T. S., 228

Keniston, K., and concept of youth, 398, 399
Kenney, M. D., 174
Kerckhoff, A., 456
Kessen, W., 95, 100, 101, 118, 133, 134
Kimmel, D., 419, 459
Kimura, D., 207
Kinsbourne, M., 123, 208
Kinsey, A., 359, 360, 361, 411, 440, 453
Kivett, V., 431
Kleemeier, R., 477
Knapp, J., 421
Koch, J., 482
Koch, H., 53
Koch, K., 293
Kofsky, E., 218
Kohlberg, L., 185, 257, 259, 327, 329, 330, 332, 335, 336, 338, 371, 372, 373
Kolb, S., 126
Kohn, M., 275
Kramer, R. B., 330, 332
Krebs, D., 392
Krebs, R., 330
Kreutzer, M. A., 296
Kübler-Ross, E., 478, 480, 482
Kulovich, M. V., 77
Kumaresan, P., 79
Kurtines, W., 329
kwashiorkor, 120

labor and delivery, 79—81
Labov, W., 251, 252n
Lamaze method, childbirth, 81
Lamb, M. E., 180
Lambert, W., 244
Langer, E., 452, 477
Langlois, J., 264
language
    adolescent dialects, 392—393
    and autonomy, infant, 189—190
    Black English vs. Standard English, 250—251
    cataloging two-year-old mind, 166—167
    and cognitive development, early childhood, 244—248
    and dialect, middle childhood, 250—252
    early childhood, 226—229
    and environment, 248—252
    first sentences, 165—167
    first words, 157—165
    human, 152—153
    inflection, 168
    learning and parental teaching, 244—246
    meaning at two-word stage, 165—166
    middle childhood, 291—294
    prespeech development, infant, 153—165
    properties, 236—237
    semantics and communication, 246—248
    and socioeconomic class, 248—249
    and special schooling, 249—250
    verbal skills, later adulthood, 454
    vocabulary, middle adulthood, 433
    word order, 168
lanugo, 90
Lasswell, M. E., 416
Lasswell, T. E., 416
later adulthood

alternatives to marriage, 460—461
developmental tasks, 449—450
emergence of concept, 9
family life, 456—460
identity and interpersonal behavior, 450—456
intellectual skills, 453—456
marital life, 456—459
maturity in, 446—447
meaning of death in, 472—473
physical changes, 447—449
remarriage, 460
self-concept and self-esteem, 450—452
sexuality, 452—453
social life, 461—463
widowhood, 459
    see also early adulthood; middle adulthood
laughter, infant, 175
Launois, J., 469, 470
Laurendeau, M., 225, 286, 288
leadership and popularity, 307
Leaf, A., 469, 470
Learner, M., 308
learning
    central, middle childhood, 282—283
    conditions for newborn, 103—104
    infant, 145—147, 148
    and memory, early adulthood, 412
Leboyer, F., 81
Lecours, A. R., 198
Leeuwenhoek, A. van, 70
Lefcourt, H. M., 265, 313
Lefkowitz, M., 321
Lehman, H. C., 413
leisure activities
    early adulthood, 423
    later adulthood, 462
    middle adulthood, 442
Lenneberg, E., 13, 114, 116, 153, 157
Leonard, C., 296
Leopold, W., 160
Lerner, M., 466, 479
Lesser, G. S., 57, 396
Lester, B. M., 183
Leventhal, A. S., 98
Levin, H., 334
Levinson, D., 406, 429
Levitin, T. E., 262
Levy, D., 127
Lewis, Michael, 103, 127, 186—187, 188
Lewis, Myrna, 446
Libby, R. W., 420, 440
Lickona, T., 327
Lieberman, M., 452, 473, 477
Liebert, D., 290
Liebert, R., 290, 321
life expectancy, 465—471
life span, biological markers of, 9
Lightbown, P., 168
Lind, J., 106
Lindzey, G., 51
Lippitt, R., 337
Lipsitt, L., 14, 98, 99
Little, J. K., 386
Littman, R., 270
Livesley, W. J., 371, 372
living wills, 480
Livson, F., 432
Lobsenz, N., 411

Locke, J., 24, 89
locus of control, 190
Loehlin, J. C., 51
Lomas, J., 207
Long, M., 455, 474
Long, R., 360
longevity, 466—471
longitudinal studies of determinants of development, 62—64
Lorenz, K., 34
love, and self-regulation, 334
Lovell, K., 285
Lowenthal, M. F., 410, 459, 461
Luckey, E., 361, 362n, 363n
Luikart, C., 431
Lyle, J., 57

Macauly, J., 262
Maccoby, E., 261, 264, 268, 334
Macfarlane, A., 99
Macklin, E. D., 420
Madsen, M., 276
Mahoney, M., 372
make-believe play, early childhood, 229
malnutrition and development, 119—120, 200—201
Maratsos, M. P., 247, 298
marijuana, 322, 389
marital life, later adulthood, 456—459
Markman, E., 224
Marolla, F. A., 54
marriage
    alternatives, early adulthood, 419—422
    alternatives, later adulthood, 460—461
    alternatives, middle adulthood, 439—440
    early adulthood, 413—419
    and family life, middle adulthood, 434—439
Martin, C. E., 359, 361, 411, 453
Martin, M., 311
Marvin, R., 225
masculinity
    changing concept of, 410
    and family relations, adolescent boys, 387
Maslow, A. H., needs hierarchy, 40—41
Mason, W., 174
Masters, W., 357, 411, 430, 432, 433, 453
masturbation, adolescence, 359
Matas, L., 189
maternal care and growth, early childhood, 202
maternal deprivation in infancy, 185
maternal health and birth complications, 83—87
mate sharing, 420—421
maturation
    early and late, 358—359
    and experience, in motor abilities, 126—127
    sexual, 350—351
    and size, adolescence, 353—355
    theories of, 24—25
maturity
    concept of, 404
    in later adulthood, 446—447
    in middle adulthood, 426—427
Maudry, M., 190, 191

Maurer, D., 98, 140
May, M., 324, 325
Mayer, J., 201, 350, 358
McCall, R. B., 139, 298
McCallum, C., 200
McCandless, B., 355
McCarthy, D., 155, 162
McClearn, G. E., 46
McDavid, J., 307, 313
McDonald, F., 338
McGarrigle, J., 223
McGraw, M., 126, 205, 207
McKain, W., 460
McKeown, T., 466
McLaughlin, L. J., 291, 385
McMichael, R. E., 336
McNeill, D., 157, 160, 165, 244
McVeigh, F., 445
Mead, M., 9, 81
media, as social determinants of
    development, 57
Mehrabian, A., 161
Meichenbaum, D., 335
meiosis, 71, 73
Mellin, G., 84
Meltzov, A., 105
memory
    early childhood, 230
    later adulthood, 455
    middle adulthood, 434
    middle childhood, 295–296
    and perceptual analysis, newborn,
        102–103
    and thought, infant, 144–145
menarche, 348, 350, 353, 354
Mendelson, M., 136
menopause, 427, 432
menstrual age, 74
menstrual cycle, 71
menstruation and fertility, 350–351
Menyuk, P., 154, 160
Menzel, E. W. Jr., 173
Meredith, H., 118, 348, 353
Mermelstein, E., 285
mesoderm, 74
Messinger, L., 419
metaphors and words, middle childhood,
    292–293
Meyer, M., 477
Michaels, R., 84
middle adulthood
    alternatives to marriage, 439–440
    death rate, 427–428
    developmental tasks, 428–430
    divorce and remarriage, 438–439
    identity and interpersonal behavior,
        430–434
    intellectual skills, 433–434
    marriage and family life, 434–439
    maturity in, 426–427
    parental and postparental life, 435–438
    physical changes, 427–428
    self-concept and self-esteem, 430–432
    sexuality in, 432–433
    social life, 440–442
    see also early adulthood; later adulthood
middle childhood
    acquisition of roles in, 304–307
    causal reasoning, 286, 288
    concepts in, 284–286

imitation in, 291
language, 291–294
memory, 295–296
negative behavior, 310–312
parental influence, 314–315
peer influence, 315–318
peer roles, 306–307
personal-social development, 307–312
play in, 294–295, 318–320
positive behavior, 308–310
problem solving, 288–291
representational skills, 291–296
selective attention in, 282–283
self-appraisal, 312–313
self-concept, 312–314
self-regulation, 313–314
sex roles, 304–306
social interaction and cognition,
    297–298
thinking advances, 283–291
    see also adolescence; early childhood
Milgram, S., 312, 373
Millar, W. S., 103
Miller, D., 248
Miller, N., 27
Miller, W., 237
Milner, E., 249
Minkowski, A., 95, 121
Minuchin, P., 322
Miranda, S., 134
miscarriage, 86
Mischel, H., 326
Mischel, W., 257, 262, 265, 326, 384
Mitchell-Kernan, C., 251, 252n
modeling
    and moral conduct, children, 336–338
    peers, in early childhood, 270–273
    and play, early childhood, 274
    verbal and nonverbal, 337–338
Molfese, D. L., 123, 243, 246
Money, J., 13, 258
Monge, R. H., 455
Montemayor, R., 3
Montgomery, J., 457
Montgomery, J. C., 94
Moody, R., 476
Mooney, H. F., 374
Moore, B. S., 105, 265
moral conduct
    inconsistency of, 324–326
    and modeling, children, 336–338
moral development
    consistency in, 338–340
    course of, 324
moral judgment, children, 327
moral reasoning
    adolescence, 372–373
    children, 326–327
    developmental changes, 329–330
    and moral judgment, 327
    variation in, 327–329
Morgan, G., 184
Morgan, J. S., 283
Morison, R. S., 480
Moro, E., 95
Moro reflex in newborn, 95–96
Moses, Grandma, 456
Moskowitz, A., 162
Moss, H., 261, 266, 305
Mossler, D., 225

motor abilities
    coordination of movement, 123–126
    development, early childhood, 202–208
    handedness, 123, 207
    maturation and experience, 126–127
Mozociotti, C., 121
Mueller, E., 305
Muller, E., 155
Mundy-Castle, A., 141, 142
Murray, F., 285, 286
Murray, T., 156
Murstein, B. I., 413, 418
Mussen, P., 119, 259, 358
mutagenic drugs, 85
Muuss, R. E., 353
Muzio, J. N., 94
myelin, 78

Nagy, M., 471
Najarian, P., 126
Nass, G., 361, 362n, 363n
National Child Health Care Survey, 202
National Council of Senior Citizens, 461
natural childbirth, 81
naturalistic observation, 59–60
nature
    as determinant of development, 46
    vs. nurture, 24
Needham, J., 70
needs hierarchy, of Maslow, 40–41
negative behavior, middle childhood,
    310–312
neighborhoods, as social determinants of
    development, 55–56
Nekula, M., 190, 191
Nelson, K., 165
neonate, 90
Nerlove, H., 246
Neugarten, B., 10, 384, 406, 408, 409,
    426, 430, 431, 432, 437, 438, 439,
    450, 451
Newbery, H., 79
newborn, 90–91
    adapting to world, 102–104
    audition, 98–99
    auditory attention, 101–102
    basic functions and rhythms, 91–95
    conditions for learning, 103–104
    elimination in, 94–95
    feeding, 94
    memory and perceptual analysis,
        102–103
    perception and attention, 99–102
    personality and social relations,
        104–107
    reflexes, 95–97
    sensory capabilities, 97–99
    sleep, 92–94
    sucking, 95
    temperature, 91–92
    visual attention, 99–101
    see also birth; infant
Newman, M., 482
Newman, O., 56
Newton, O., 81
Nixon, R. M., 323, 338
norms, 114–118
Norton, A. J., 435
novelty and attention, infant, 139
Nowak, C., 427, 428

Noyes, R., 476
nurture
    as determinant of development, 46
    vs. nature, 24
nutrition
    and birth complications, 85
    and individual variability, 119–120

obesity
    in adolescence, 357–358
    and overfeeding, 201
object identity, infant, 141–142
objective morality, vs. subjective, 327
object permanence, infant, 142–144
    and exploring, 148
O'Connor, N., 207
Odem, M., 25
Offir, C., 258, 360, 377
Ogilvie, E., 285
old age, *see* later adulthood
O'Leary K. D., 267
Olsen, M. G., 295
O'Malley, P. M., 322, 389
operant conditioning, 26–27
Opie, I., 318
Opie, P., 318
organismic development, 29–30
orgasm
    in adolescence, 359
    in early adulthood, 411
    in later adulthood, 453
Orkand, R., 120
Orthner, D. K., 417
Osborn, D. K., 320
Osis, K., 476
Osler, S. F., 218
Osofsky, J., 104
Ourth, L. L., 145
ovaries, 348
overregularization, in child's awareness of
        grammar, 238–240
overweight, adolescent reactions to, 355,
        357–358
ovum, 70

Painter, N. S., 469
Palermo, D. S., 123, 243, 246
Palmore, E., 431, 470
Papoušek, H., 146, 148
Papst, M., 319
parenthood
    early adulthood, 416–418
    middle adulthood, 435–437
parents
    aging, relating to, 437
    and generation gap, 396–397
    infant interaction with, 186–187
    influence, middle childhood, 314–315
    relations with child, early childhood,
        266–268
    responsiveness, 179–182
    style, 179–180
Parke, R. D., 180, 268, 337
Parker, R., 335, 337
Parkes, C. M., 482
Parry, M., 139
pattern, newborn's response to, 100
Patterson, G. R., 266, 270
Pavlov, I., 26
Peck, R., 331

Peel, E. A., 371
Peeples, D. R., 98
peer groups
    adolescent and, 368
    and adolescent sexuality, 376
    structure change, adolescence, 393–394
peer roles, middle childhood, 306–307
peers
    and adolescent friendship and dating
        choice, 392
    infant interaction with, 190–192
    influence, early childhood, 268–273
    influence, middle childhood, 315–318
    and language functioning, 249
    modeling, 270–273
    reinforcement, 270
    relations and influence, adolescence,
        390–395
    as social determinants of development,
        54–55
penis, at puberty, 351
Peplau, L. A., 414
perception
    and attention, newborn, 99–102
    early childhood, 216–217
    infant, 132
    sensory coordination, early childhood,
        216
perceptual analysis and memory, newborn,
        102–103
perceptual functioning, infant, 133–138
personality
    development, infant, 172–173
    and social relations, newborn, 104–107
    and subcultures, early childhood,
        275–276
personal relationships, early adulthood,
        408–409
personal-social development, middle
        childhood, 307–312
Peskin, H., 359
Peterson, W. A., 426
Petrinovich, F., 123
Pfeiffer, E., 442, 449, 453
Phares, E. J., 384
phases of development, 17–19
phenotype, 73
phenylketonuria (PKU), 73
physical changes
    adolescent reactions to, 355–358
    early adulthood, 404–405
    early childhood, 209–212
    later adulthood, 447–449
    middle adulthood, 427–428
physical development, adolescence,
        predicting, 352–353
physical factors in development, 51–53
physical-sexual change, adolescence,
        358–362
Piaget, J., 14, 136, 137, 192, 228, 229,
        233, 257, 283, 318, 324
    adaptation theory, 30–33
    and childhood thinking about concepts,
        222–224
    and child's awareness of causality, 288
    clinical study of determinants of
        development, 60
    on cognitive precursors of first words,
        157–158
    and concrete vs. verbal experience, 292

    and conservation in middle childhood,
        284–285
    and formal operations, 369–371
    and pendulum problem 289–290
    on play, 273
    profile, 31
    study of egocentrism, 224
    study of object permanence in infant,
        143–144
    study of thought in childhood, 219–221
    tests of memory, 295
    view of child's moral judgments, 327
Piazza, D., 207
Picasso, P., 455
Pick, H. L. Jr., 98
Pihlblad, C. T., 386
Pinard, A., 225, 286, 288
Piscopo, J., 358
placenta, 74
placing response, newborn, 96–97
Platt, M., 418
play
    in early adulthood, 422–423
    in early childhood, 229–230, 273–274
    in infancy, 192–193
    in middle childhood, 294–295,
        318–320
Plutchik, R., 449
Pohly, S., 305
Polansky, N., 337
polygenic trait, 74
Pomeroy, W. B., 359, 361, 411, 453
popularity
    and attractiveness, adolescence,
        391–392
    middle childhood, 307
postparental life, 435–438
Powell, G., 202
practice, and instruction in motor skills,
        early childhood, 205–207
Pratt, K. C., 90
precausal reasoning, 225
Prechtl, H. F. R., 96
premature delivery, 86
prematurity, 83
premoral level of moral reasoning, 329
prenatal behavior, 78–79
prenatal development, brain, 78
prenatal growth
    embryonic period, 75–76
    fetal period, 76–77
    germinal period, 74–75
prenatal phase, development, 18
Prentice, N. M., 372
preoperational stage of intellectual
        development, 33
present orientation, and achievement, 384
prespeech development, 153–165
Price, L., 217
principled level of moral reasoning, 329
principled reasoning, and formal thought,
        372–373
problem solving
    adolescence, 369–370
    middle childhood, 288–291
productivity, language, 152, 236
promiscuity, in adolescence, 375
proximodistal development, 113
psychodynamic theory
    ego psychology, 40–41

of Erikson, 36—40
of Freud, 35—36
psychosocial development, Erikson's
    theory of, 11, 36—40
puberty, 348
    boys, 351
    early onset of, 354—355
    girls, 350
Pulaski, M., 295
Puner, M., 452
punishment
    and aggression, 268
    in middle childhood, 314
    and sex-role development, early
        childhood, 268

questions, in two-year-old's language, 167

Rabin, A. I., 185
Ragan, P. K., 452
Rahe, R., 466
Rainwater, L., 385
Ramey, C., 145
Ramsay, D. S., 123
rapid eye movement (REM) sleep, of
    newborn, 93–94
Rau, L., 266, 326
Rawls, D., 307
Rawls, J., 305
Rayner, R., 26
reaction range, 49—50
reaction time
    early adulthood, 405
    and speed, 203
reasoning
    causal, middle childhood, 286, 288
    and education, 288—289
    and guilt, children, 335—336
    and love, in promoting self-regulation,
        334
    precausal, 225
    principled, and formal thought,
        372—373
    see also moral reasoning
recessive gene, 73
Redl, F., 318
reductionist explanations of behavior, 13
Reedy, M., 404, 410, 414, 453
reflexes
    conditioned vs. unconditioned, 26
    and learning, 145—146
    in newborn, 95—97
reinforcement
    in operant conditioning, 26—27
    peers, in early childhood, 270
Reiss, I., 375, 377
relational concepts, middle childhood, 284
releasing stimuli, 33
reliability, 10
remarriage
    early adulthood, 418—419
    late adulthood, 460
    middle adulthood, 438—439
    and widowhood, 440
repetition and learning, newborn, 103
replication study, 16
representation, infant, 157—158
representational skills
    early childhood, 226—232

middle childhood, 291—296
representational stage of intellectual
    development, 33
research on nonhuman species, 15
respiratory distress syndrome, 77
respondent conditioning, 26
responsiveness
    infant, 182—185
    newborn, 104
    parent, 179—182
Rest, J., 330
retardation and emotional distress, 202
retirement, and marital life, 456—457
retirement community, 456, 461
reversibility, 284
Reynolds, D., 473, 475, 476
Rheingold, H., 139, 146, 156, 178, 184,
    186, 187, 188
Rh incompatibility, and birth
    complications, 84
Ricciuti, H., 184
rickets, 120
Riegel, K. F., 434, 477
Riegel, R. M., 434, 477
Rigler, D., 472, 477
Riley, J., 472
Riley, M. W., 457, 459
Roberts, J., 318
Robinson, H. B., 85
Robinson, N. M., 85
Rodin, J., 452, 477
Roff, M., 391
Roffwarg, H. P., 94
Rogers, C. M., 173, 414, 415, 418, 419
Rogers, W. L., 418, 419
Rohwer, W., 15, 61
Rokosz, S., 455
role acquisition, middle childhood,
    304—307
role-playing, early childhood, 273—274
role taking and social interaction, children,
    330—332
Roll, S., 357
Rollings, B., 435, 457
rooting reflex, newborn, 95
Rose, C., 470
Rose, S., 352
Rose, S. A., 121, 122
Rose, Susan, 221
Rosen, B., 276, 384
Rosenberg, B. G., 53
Rosenberg, M., 368, 369, 387
Rosenbloom, S., 137
Rosenhan, D. L., 314, 338
Rosenman, R. H., 471
Rosenthal, T., 221, 291
Rosenzweig, M. R., 122
Ross, B., 295
Ross, D., 271
Ross, Helen, 146, 156
Ross, Hildy, 139
Ross, S., 271
Rossi, A., 416, 417
Rousseau, J. J., 24
rubella, and birth complications, 84
Rubenstein, Judith, 191
Rubin, I., 432
Rubin, K., 308
Rubin, Z., 414
Ruderman, A., 327

rules and practice, play, middle childhood,
    318—319
Rushton, J. P., 308, 309
Rutter, M., 185
Ruzskaya, A. G., 216
Ryle, G., 132

Sachs, J. S., 246, 247
Sagi, A., 106
Salapatek, P., 95, 100, 101, 118, 133, 134,
    140, 174, 175
Salisbury, D. M., 99
Salk, L., 107
Saltin, B., 471
Saltz, E., 222
Saltzstein, H., 334
Sameroff, A., 14
Sampson, E., 308
Sander, L. W., 107, 187
Sargent, D., 357
Saunders, C., 479
Sawin, D. B., 180
Sayegh, Y., 126
Scarr, S., 49, 134, 174, 175, 299
    see also Scarr-Salapatek, S.
Scarr-Salapatek, S., 49, 50
    see also Scarr, S.
Schachtel, E. G., 230
Schackman, M., 209
Schaefer, E. S., 276
Schaffer, H. R., 104, 179, 182, 187
Schaie, K. W., 62, 63, 412, 454
Schaller, M. J., 208
schedules of reinforcement, 27
Schell, R., 259, 355, 462
Schimmel, S., 221
Schneider, F., 308
Schonbuch, S., 355
Schonfeld, W. A., 356, 358
school, as social determinant of
    development, 56—57
schooling
    and formal thought, 371
    special, and language functioning,
        249—250
Schwartz, M., 299
Scott, E. M., 202
Scott, J., 423, 442, 462
Scott, J. P., 173, 175
Scott, P., 309
Scott, P. M., 338
Scrimshaw, N., 120
scrotum, at puberty, 351
Searleman, A., 121
Sears, R. R., 10, 25, 326, 334
selective attention, in middle childhood,
    282—283
self
    commitment to, 397
    definition, in adolescence, 367—368
    infant's sense of, 188
    and others, concepts of, 371—372
    and society, in adolescence, 366—369
self-actualizing, 40
self-appraisal
    early childhood, 264—265
    middle childhood, 312—313
self-concept
    and body concept, adolescence,
        355—356

and divorce, 419
early childhood, 409—410
infant, 187—188
later adulthood, 450—452
middle adulthood, 430—432
middle childhood, 312—314
and play, middle childhood, 318—319
and sex-role development, early
childhood, 263—266
self-confidence, middle adulthood,
426—427
self-control
and confidence, middle adulthood,
430—431
and independence, adolescence,
387—388
and mastery, early adulthood, 409—410
self-demand feeding, newborn, 94
self-esteem
adolescence, 368—369
early adulthood, 409—410
later adulthood, 450—452
middle adulthood, 430—432
self-evaluation and peer influence,
middle childhood, 316
self-image, girls vs. boys, 209
self-regulation
and achievement, 384
early childhood, 265—266
and guilt, children, 332—335
middle childhood, 313—314
self-reinforcement and peer influence,
middle childhood, 316
Seligman, M. E. P., 313, 446
Sells, S. B., 391
Selman, R., 331
semanticity, language, 152
semantics and communication, early
childhood, 246—248
Semb, G., 27
sensation, infant, 132
sensitive periods, early experience,
173—174
sensory capabilities, newborn, 97—99
sensory coordination
early childhood, 216—217
infant, 136
sensory-motor coordination, infant, 136
sensory-motor stage of intellectual
development, 33
separation distress, infant, 183—184
sequences in development, 16—17
Serbin, L., 209, 267
sex cells, production of, 71, 73
sex education, in schools, 322—323, 374
sex role
later adulthood, 451
middle childhood, 304—306
and positive behavior, 308—309
and sex differences, adolescence,
361—362
sex-role development
assertion and aggression, 260—262
and culture, 259—260
and dependence vs. independence,
262—263
early childhood, 257—263
and family, 53—54
and self-concept, 263—266
sex-role stereotypes, 259—260, 410

sexual activity and longevity, 469
sexual behavior
adolescence, 359—362
personal choice, 374—375
sexual experience
college men, 363
college women, 362
sexuality
early adulthood, 410—411
and intimacy, in adolescence, 373—377
later adulthood, 452—453
middle adulthood, 432—433
and peer groups, adolescence, 393—394
sexual maturation
boys, 351
girls, 350—351
sexual relationships, in middle adulthood,
430
shame vs. guilt, 335
Shanab, M., 311
Shanas, E., 459
shape, in meaning of first words, 163
Share-a-Home, 460
Shatz, M., 224, 248
Shaw, M., 316
Sheldon, W., 212
Sherif, C., 317, 393—394
Sherif, M., 317, 393—394
Sherman, J. A., 208—209
Sherman, L., 54
Shneidman, E., 472, 475, 479
Shock, N. W., 447, 467
Shultz, T., 293
Siegler, R., 290
Sigel, I. E., 285
Silber, J. W., 259
Simmons, R., 387
Simner, M., 106
Simon, W., 377
Simpson, E., 330
Simpson, R., 394
Sinclair, C., 203, 205, 208
Singer, J. E., 52
Singer, J. L., 229, 230, 294, 295
singlehood, 420
single-parent homes, in middle childhood,
315
Siqueland, E., 146
Skeels, H. M., 49
Skinner, B. F., and operant conditioning,
26—27
Skodak, M., 49
Skubiski, S., 309
sleep, newborn, 92—94
Slobin, D. I., 166, 168, 238, 243, 251
small-for-dates, 83
Smart, J. L., 78
smell, newborn, 99
Smith, C., 85
Smith, H., 266
Smith, M. B., 373
Smith, P. K., 53
Smith, R., 456
smoking
and adolescent conformity, 389
and birth complications, 85
Snow, C. E., 159, 246
sociability, in infant, 186—193
social behavior, adolescence, 396—397
social changes

adolescence, 358—362
early childhood, 209—212
social clock, 406
social cognition and play, middle
childhood, 318—319
social determinants of development,
53—58
social interaction
and cognition, early childhood,
232—233
and cognition, middle childhood,
297—298
and role taking, children, 330—332
socialization
early childhood, 256—257
and parental absence, 315
social learning theory, 27—29
social life
early adulthood, 422—423
later adulthood, 461—463
middle adulthood, 440—442
social relations and personality, newborn,
104—107
socioeconomic class
and achievement, adolescence,
384—385
and awareness of middle age, 426
and development, early adulthood,
406—408
and divorce, middle adulthood, 438
and growth, early childhood, 202
and jobs vs. careers, 386—387
and language functioning, 248—249
and leisure activities, later adulthood,
462
and leisure activities, middle adulthood,
442
and parent responsiveness, 180
and puberty, 354
and self-esteem in adolescence,
368—369
and social behavior, 276
and vocational choice, 377
sociology, and developmental psychology,
13
sociometric analysis, 307
Sontag, L. W., 79, 86
Sorensen, R., 374, 375
speech
infant's attention to, 154—155
sounds, infant, 155—157
Spelt, D., 79
Spence, D., 436
spermatozoon, 70
Spinetta, J., 472, 477, 481
spontaneous abortion, 86
Spuhler, J. N., 51
Sroufe, L. A., 175, 189
Staats, A., 244
Staffieri, J. R., 307, 358
stages
concept of, 41—42
in Piaget's theory, 33
Staub, E., 309, 310, 337
Stein, A., 305
Stein, P., 420
Stendler, C., 317
Stephan, C., 264
Stephens, M., 276
stepping motion, newborn, 96—97

Stern, D., 154, 188, 192
Stevenson, H. W., 217
Stewart, W., 249
Stinnett, N., 457
Stirnimann, F., 100
Stolz, H. R., 208, 352, 356
Stolz, L. H., 208, 352, 356
strangers, infant's wariness of, 184
Strauss, A., 475, 481
Strauss, S., 241
strength, early childhood, 203
stress, and life expectancy, 466
style, parental, 179–180
subcultures and personality, early
    childhood, 275–276
subjective morality, vs. objective, 327
sublimated instincts, 35
success, fear of, 395
successive approximations, 27
sucking
    infant patterns, 14
    in newborn, 95
Sullivan, H. S., 391
Suomi, S. J., 269
Super, C., 138
Super, D., 377, 379
superego, 35
Surber, C. F., 327
surfactin, 77
Sussman, M., 437, 460
Sutton-Smith, B., 53, 192, 209, 210, 229,
    318
Swanson, G., 248
Sylva, K., 274
symbolic play, early childhood, 229
symbols and concepts, infants, 140–145
syntax, language, 153
syphilis, and birth complications, 84

tabula rasa, 24
Tanner, J. M., 118, 119, 120, 200, 208,
    348, 350, 351
taste
    in meaning of first words, 163
    in newborn, 99
Taub, H., 455
Tavris, C., 258, 360, 377, 410
Taylor, S. E., 327
teacher, and sex-role development, early
    childhood, 267–268
teaching, by parents, in middle childhood,
    314–315
television, influence on children, 57,
    320–321
Teller, D. Y., 98
temperature, newborn, 91–92
Terman, L., maturation theory, 25
terminal decline, 477
term, 83
testes, 348
theories
    adaptation, 29–35
    of aging, 467–468
    behavior-learning, 26–29
    defined, 11
    maturation, 24–25
    social learning, 27–29
    stage, 41–42
Thomas, A., 104
Thomas, L., 476

Thome, P., 262
Thompson, W. R., 86
Thomson, A. M., 202
Thoresen, C. E., 372
thought
    early adulthood, 412–413
    early childhood, 219–226
    formal, in adolescence, 369–371
    and memory, infant, 144–145
    middle childhood, 283–291
Tibetan Book of the Dead, 474
time patterns, individual, 118–119
Tinbergen, N., 47, 61
Tobin, S., 450
Tonkova-Yampol'skaya, R. V., 159
totalism, adolescence, 368
Trabasso, T., 223, 224
Tracy, R., 184
Trainham, G., 94
transitivity, 223
Treas, J., 459, 460
Trelease, M., 474
Trevarthen, C., 158
trimester, 83
Trivers, R. L., 308
Troll, L., 410, 418, 458
trust, 36, 38
tuberculosis, heritability, 51
Tucker, G. R., 244
Tulkin, S., 180
Turiel, J., 330
Turner's syndrome, 82
two-word stage, 165–168
Tyler, L., 378, 379

unconditioned reflex, 26
Underwood, B., 265
uniformism, 368
Uzgiris, I. C., 144, 285

Vaillant, G., 406, 430
values, humanizing, in early adulthood,
    409
Van Hilst, A., 459
variability, 50
variables, 59
    individual, 118–120
verbal modeling, 337–338
Verinis, J., 357
Verwoerdt, A., 453
Vietz, P., 102
violence, and television, 320–321
virginity, 359
vision, newborn, 97–98
visual accommodation, newborn, 97–98
visual acuity, newborn, 98
visual attention, newborn, 99–101
visual cliff, 134
vital capacity, girls vs. boys, 208
Vlietstra, A., 216, 219
vocational identity, adolescence, 377–380
Vogel, B. S., 462
Von Frisch, K., 152

Waber, D., 352
Waechter, E., 471–472
Wahler, R., 270
Walbek, N., 338
Walk, R., 134
Walker, A. R. P., 469

walking movements, newborn, 96–97
Wallach, M. A., 295
Waller, W., 414
Wallin, P., 414
Walster, E., 356, 405, 428
Walters, C. E., 104
Walters, R., 27, 335, 337
Wang Hsioh-shan, 453
Waterlow, J. C., 120
Watson, A., 431
Watson, J. B., and behaviorism, 26
Watson, J. S., 103, 146, 192
Waxler, C., 309, 338
Weg, R. B., 405, 427, 428, 447, 466
Weinberg, R. A., 49, 299
Weiner, B., 313
Weiner, M. B., 449
Weinstein, K., 437, 438
Weir, R., 244
Werner, H., 114
    adaptation theory, 29–30
White, B. L., 98, 126
White, R., 408
White, S., 218
Whitehouse, R. H., 208
Whitehurst, R., 421
Whiting, B., 262
Whiting, J., 27
Wickelgren, L. W., 98
widowhood
    in late adulthood, 459
    in middle adulthood, 439–440
Widowson, E. M., 202
Wiesel, T. N., 122
Wiggins, J. S., 356
Wiggins, N., 356
Wilkinson, A., 223
Winder, C. L., 266
Winer, G., 284
Witelson, S., 209, 352
Wittig, B., 183, 184
Wolf, T., 271
Wolff, G., 200
Wolff, K. 70
Wolff, P., 105, 155, 156, 209
Woodruff, D., 430
word order, child, 168
Wright, H., 52
Wright, J., 216, 219
Wunsch, J., 175

Yahya, K., 311
Yakovlev, P. I., 198
Yalisove, D., 294
Yarrow, L., 15, 180
Yarrow, M., 307, 309, 338
Yen, W. M., 385
Yonas, A., 98
Youniss, J., 295
youth, concept of, 398–399

Zaporozhets, A. V., 216
Zelazo, N. A., 126
Zelazo, P. R., 126
Zelnik, M., 360, 361, 375
Zimmerman, B. J., 221, 291
Zimmermann, R. R., 15
Zinshensko, V. P., 216
Ziobrowski, M. J., 291

About the Authors

Robert E. Schell received his Ph.D. from the University of Illinois and has held academic appointments at Michigan State University, Dartmouth College, and the Merrill-Palmer Institute. He has published articles in various journals, including *Child Development, Journal of Comparative and Physiological Psychology, Journal of Speech and Hearing Disorders,* and *Journal of Abnormal and Social Psychology.* He is the author of *Letters and Sounds* and has been a contributing author and consultant on several CRM/Random House texts, including *Abnormal Psychology: Current Perspectives, Readings in Developmental Psychology,* and *Educational Psychology: A Contemporary View.* He is currently Director of Research and Training for the Center for Research, Education, Applied Training, and Evaluation in San Diego, lecturer in the psychology department at San Diego State University, and a clinical and consulting psychologist in California.

Elizabeth Hall is Editor-in-Chief of *Human Nature* magazine, former Managing Editor of *Psychology Today* magazine, and the author of several popular psychology books, two of which were honored by the American Psychological Foundation's National Merit Award: *Why We Do What We Do: A Look at Psychology,* and *From Pigeons to People: A Look at Behavior Shaping.*

Credits and Acknowledgments

Units I, II, III, IV, and V: from R. Kellogg with S. O'Dell, *The Psychology of Children's Art,* © 1967 by CRM, Inc.

Unit VI: Aurilla Rivera; courtesy of Judy Earle.

Unit VII: Grandma Moses; gift of Mrs. Murray S. Danforth, Museum of Art, Rhode Island School of Design, Providence, R.I.

Page 48: Drawing after S. L. Washburn and R. Moore, *Ape Into Man,* Little, Brown & Co., 1974.

Page 50: Portions of graphs after M. Honzik, "Developmental Studies of Parent-Child Resemblance in Intelligence," *Child Development,* vol. 28, 1957, pp. 215–228. By permission of The Society for Research in Child Development, Inc.

Page 92: Chart after Roffwarg, Dement, and Fisher, *Behaviour in Infancy and Early Childhood,* Y. Brackbill and S. G. Thompson (eds.), Free Press, 1967.

Page 93: Graph after Roffwarg, Muzio, and Dement, "Ontogenetic Development of the Human Sleep-Dream Cycle," *Science,* vol. 152. Copyright © 1966 by The American Association for the advancement of Science.

Page 94: Chart after Gesell and Ilg, *The Feeding Behavior of Infants: A Pediatric Approach to the Mental Hygiene of Early Life,* J. B. Lippincott Co., 1937.

Page 101: Chart after Salapatek and Kessen, "Visual Scanning of Triangles by the Human Newborn," *Journal of Experimental Child Psychology,* vol. 3, pp. 156–167, © 1966 by Academic Press, Inc.

Page 103: Graph after Friedman, "Differential Dishabituation as a Function of Magnitude of Stimulus Discrepancy and Sex of the Newborn Infant" (unpublished paper).

Page 114: Drawing adapted from C. M. Jackson (ed.), *Morris' Human Anatomy,* 7th ed. Copyright © 1923 by P. Blakiston's Son & Co. Used by permission of McGraw-Hill Book Company.

Page 115: Chart adapted from E. H. Lenneberg, *Biological Foundations of Language,* 1967, John Wiley & Sons.

Page 119: Graph adapted from A. Prader, J. M. Tanner, and G. A. von Harnack, "Catch-up Growth Following Illness or Starvation: An Example of Developmental Canalization in Man," *Journal of Pediatrics,* vol. 62, 1963.

Page 125: Graph adapted from C. B. Hindley, A. M. Filliozat, G. Klackenberg, D. Nicolet-Meister, and E. A. Sand, "Differences in Walking in the European Longitudinal Samples," *Human Biology,* vol. 38, 1966. By permission of Wayne State University Press.

Page 140: Drawings adapted from R. Ahrens, *Zeitschrift für Experimentelle und Angewandte Psychologie,* 1954.

Page 159: Graph adapted from Tonkova-Yampol'skaya, *Phonology,* 1973.

Page 161: Graph adapted from P. Menyuk, *The acquisition and Development of Language,* © 1971. Reprinted with permission of Prentice-Hall, Inc., Englewood Cliffs, N.J.

Page 174: Graph adapted from A. T. Jersild and F. B. Holmes, *Children's Fears,* Child Development Monograph No. 20, New York, Columbia University, 1935.

Page 178: Graph adapted from H. R. Schaffer and P. E. Emerson, "The Development of Social Attachment in Infancy," *Monographs of the Society for Research in Child Development,* vol. 29, 1964. By permission of The Society for Research in Child Development, Inc.

Page 209: Graph adapted from R. C. Lewis, A. M. Duval, and A. Iliff, "Standards for the Basal Metabolism of Children from Two to Fifteen Years of Age," *Journal of Pediatrics,* vol. 23, 1943.

Page 218: Chart adapted from S. White, "Evidence for a Hierarchical Arrangement of Learning Processes," L. P. Lipsitt and C.

C. Spiker (eds.), *Advances in Child Development and Behaviour,* vol. 2, Academic Press, 1965; illustrations from *The Golden Book of Bird Stamps* by Sonia Bleeker, illustrated by James Gorden Irving and Janet Rumley. Copyright © 1949 by Western Publishing Co., Inc. Reprinted by permission of the publisher.

Page 231: Drawings after C. Golomb, *Genetic Psychology Monographs,* vol. 87, 1973.

Page 237: Graph after R. Brown, *A First Language: The Early Stages,* 1973, Harvard University Press.

Page 246: Graph adapted from E. H. Lenneberg, *Biological Foundations of Language,* New York, John Wiley & Sons, 1967.

Page 272: Graph after W. W. Hartup and B. Coates, *Child Development,* vol. 38, © 1967 by The Society for Research in Child Development, Inc. All rights reserved.

Page 274: Graph adapted from M. B. Parten, "Social Participation Among Preschool Children," *Journal of Abnormal and Social Psychology,* vol. 24, © 1932–1933 by American Psychological Association.

Page 283: Graph adapted from J. W. Hagen, "The Effect of Distraction on Selective Attention," *Child Development,* vol. 38, 1967. By permission of The Society for Research in Child Development, Inc.

Page 287: Illustrations from *How the Mouse Was Hit on the Head by a Stone and So Discovered the World.* Copyright © 1971 by Etienne Delessert. Reprinted by permission of Doubleday & Co., Inc.

Page 290: Drawing after B. Inhelder and J. Piaget, "The Oscillation of a Pendulum and the Operations of Exclusion," from *The Growth of Logical Thinking: From Childhood to Adolescence,* translated by A. Parsons and S. Milgram, © 1958 by Basic Books, Inc.

Page 293: Chart after H. Gardner, "Metaphors and Modalities: How Children Project Polar Adjectives Onto Diverse Domains," *Child Development,* vol. 45, 1974. By permission of The Society for Research in Child Development, Inc.

Page 294: From R. Lewis, *Miracles,* Simon & Schuster, © 1966 by R. Lewis. Reprinted with permission of the publisher.

Page 305: Graph after F. P. Hardesty and R. E. Hartley, "Children's Perceptions of Sex Roles in Childhood," *Journal of Genetic Psychology,* vol. 105, 1964.

Page 316: Graph adapted from P. R. Costanzo and M. E. Shaw, "Conformity as a Function of Age Level," *Child Development,* vol. 37, 1966. By permission of The Society for Research in Child Development.

Page 320: Chart after L. Kohlberg, "The Development of Children's Orientations Toward a Moral Order," *Vita Humana,* vol. 6, 1963. Reprinted by permission of S. Karger AG, Basel.

Pages 331, 333: Graphs after L. Kohlberg, "The Child as a Moral Philosopher," *Psychology Today,* September 1968.

Pages 351, 354: Graphs after J. M. Tanner, *Growth at Adolescence,* 2nd edition, Blackwell Scientific Publications, Oxford, 1962.

Page 392: Graph adapted from R. D. Franklin and H. H. Remmers, "Youth's Attitudes Towards Courtship and Marriage," Report of Poll 62 of the Purdue Opinion Panel. Purdue Research Foundation, 1961.

Page 416: Quiz reprinted by permission of *Rough Times* (formerly *Radical Therapist*), April 1972.

Page 434: Graph after W. Dennis, "Creative Productivity Between the Ages of 20 and 80 Years," *Journal of Gerontology,* vol. 21, 1966.